T0122618

Communications
in Computer and Information Science   1490

More information about this series at http://www.springer.com/series/7899

Hong-Ning Dai · Xuanzhe Liu ·
Daniel Xiapu Luo · Jiang Xiao ·
Xiangping Chen (Eds.)

Blockchain and Trustworthy Systems

Third International Conference, BlockSys 2021
Guangzhou, China, August 5–6, 2021
Revised Selected Papers

 Springer

Editors
Hong-Ning Dai ⓘ
Macau University of Science and Technology
Macao, China

Daniel Xiapu Luo ⓘ
Hong Kong Polytechnic University
Hong Kong, China

Xiangping Chen ⓘ
Sun Yat-sen University
Guangzhou, China

Xuanzhe Liu ⓘ
Peking University
Beijing, China

Jiang Xiao ⓘ
Huazhong University of Science
and Technology
Wuhan, Hubei, China

ISSN 1865-0929   ISSN 1865-0937 (electronic)
Communications in Computer and Information Science
ISBN 978-981-16-7992-6   ISBN 978-981-16-7993-3 (eBook)
https://doi.org/10.1007/978-981-16-7993-3

This Springer imprint is published by the registered company Springer Nature Singapore Pte Ltd.
The registered company address is: 152 Beach Road, #21-01/04 Gateway East, Singapore 189721, Singapore

Preface

Blockchain has become a prominent research area in academia and industry. The blockchain technology is transforming industries by enabling anonymous and trustful transactions in decentralized and trustless environments. As a result, blockchain technology and other technologies for developing trustworthy systems can be used to reduce system risks, mitigate financial fraud, and cut down operational costs. Blockchain and trustworthy systems can be applied to many fields, such as financial services, social management, and supply chain management.

This volume contains the papers presented at the International Conference on Blockchain and Trustworthy Systems (BlockSys 2021). This conference was held as the third in its series with an emphasis on the state-of-the-art advances in blockchain and trustworthy systems. The main conference received 98 paper submissions, out of which 38 papers were accepted as regular papers and 12 papers were accepted as short papers. All papers underwent a rigorous peer review process, in which each paper was reviewed by 2 to 3 experts. The accepted papers, together with our outstanding keynote and invited speeches, led to a vibrant technical program. We are looking forward to future events in this conference series.

The conference would not have been successful without help from so many people. We would like to thank the Organizing Committee for their hard work in putting together the conference. First, we would like to express our sincere thanks to the guidance from the honorary chairs: Song Guo, Xueming Si and Yan Zhang. We would like to express our deep gratitude to general chairs: Gang Huang, Jianwei Yin, Hong-Ning Dai and Wuhui Chen for their support and promotion of this event. We would also like to thank the program chairs: Xuanzhe Liu, Daniel Xiapu Luo, Jiang Xiao and Xiangping Chen supervised the review process of the technical papers and compiled a high-quality technical program. We also extend our deep gratitude to the Program Committee members whose diligent work in reviewing the papers lead to the high quality of the accepted papers. We greatly appreciate the excellent support and hard work of the publicity chairs: Chunpeng Ge, Yu Li, Bing Lin and Xiaohong Shi; publication chairs: Ao Zhou and Tianhui Meng; organizing chairs: Teng Teng and Mingdong Tang; and advisory board: Michael R. Lyu, Jiannong Cao, Kuan-Ching Li, Huaimin Wang and Zibin Zheng. Most importantly, we would like to thank the authors for submitting their papers to BlockSys 2021 conference.

We believe that the BlockSys conference provides a good forum for both academic researchers and industrial practitioners to discuss all technical advances in blockchain and trustworthy systems. We also expect that the future BlockSys conference will be as successful, as indicated by the contributions presented in this volume.

October 2021

Hong-Ning Dai
Xuanzhe Liu
Daniel Xiapu Luo
Jiang Xiao
Xiangping Chen

Organization

Honorary Chairs

Song Guo   The Hong Kong Polytechnic University, China
Xueming Si   Fudan University, China
Yan Zhang   University of Oslo, Norway

General Chairs

Gang Huang   Peking University, China
Jianwei Yin   Zhejiang University, China
Hong-Ning Dai   Macau University of Science and Technology, China
Wuhui Chen   Sun Yat-sen University, China

Program Chairs

Xuanzhe Liu   Peking University, China
Daniel Xiapu Luo   The Hong Kong Polytechnic University, China
Jiang Xiao   Huazhong University of Science and Technology, China
Xiangping Chen   Sun Yat-sen University, China

Organizing Chairs

Teng Teng   Peking University, China
Mingdong Tang   Guangdong University of Foreign Studies, China

Publicity Chairs

Chunpeng Ge   Nanjing University of Aeronautics and Astronautics, China
Yu Li   Hangzhou Dianzi University, China
Bing Lin   Fujian Normal University, China
Xiaohong Shi   Guangzhou University, China

Publication Chairs

Ao Zhou   Beijing University of Posts and Telecommunications, China
Tianhui Meng   Shenzhen Institute of Advanced Technology, Chinese Academy of Sciences, China

Advisory Board

Michael R. Lyu	The Chinese University of Hong Kong, Hong Kong, China
Jiannong Cao	The Hong Kong Polytechnic University, China
Kuan-Ching Li	Providence University, Taiwan, China
Huaimin Wang	National University of Defense Technology, China
Zibin Zheng	Sun Yat-sen University, China

Program Committee

Alexander Chepurnoy	IOHK Research, Russia
Ali Vatankhah	Kennesaw State University, USA
Andreas Veneris	University of Toronto, Canada
Ao Zhou	Beijing University of Posts and Telecommunications, China
Bahman Javadi	Western Sydney University, Australia
Bu-Qing Cao	Hunan University of Science and Technology, China
Chang-Ai Sun	University of Science and Technology Beijing, China
Claudio Schifanella	University of Turin, Italy
Debiao He	Wuhan University, China
Fangguo Zhang	Sun Yat-sen University, China
Gerhard Hancke	City University of Hong Kong, China
Guobing Zou	Shanghai University, China
Han Liu	Tsinghua University, China
Jan Henrik Ziegeldorf	RWTH Aachen University, Germany
Jiwei Huang	China University of Petroleum, China
Kai Lei	Peking University, China
Kenneth Fletcher	University of Massachusetts, USA
Laizhong Cui	Shenzhen University, China
Mario Larangeira	IOHK and Tokyo Institute of Technology, Japan
Pengcheng Zhang	Hohai University, China
Qianhong Wu	Beihang University, China
Qinghua Lu	CSIRO, Australia
Shangguang Wang	Beijing University of Posts and Telecommunications, China
Shizhan Chen	Tianjin University, China
Shuiguang Deng	Zhejiang University, China
Sude Qing	China Academy of Information and Communications Technology, China
Tao Xiang	Chongqing University, China
Ting Chen	University of Electronic Science and Technology of China, China
Tsuyoshi Ide	IBM, USA
Wei Luo	Zhejiang University, China
Wei Song	Nanjing University of Science and Technology, China
Weifeng Pan	Zhejiang Gongshang University, China
Xiaodong Fu	Kunming University of Science and Technology, China
Xiaoliang Fan	Xiamen University, China

Yucong Duan	Hainan University, China
Yutao Ma	Wuhan University, China
Zhihui Lu	Fudan University, China
Quanqing Xu	Alibaba, China
Yiming Zhang	National University of Defense Technology, China

Contents

Theories and Algorithms for Blockchain

Blockchain and Internet of Things

Blockchain and Smart Contracts

Blockchain Services and Applications

Trustworthy System Development

Blockchain and Data Mining

Identity Inference on Blockchain Using Graph Neural Network

Jie Shen[1,2], Jiajun Zhou[1,2], Yunyi Xie[1,2], Shanqing Yu[1,2(✉)], and Qi Xuan[1,2,3]

[1] Institute of Cyberspace Security, Zhejiang University of Technology,
Hangzhou 310023, China
yushanqing@zjut.edu.cn
[2] College of Information Engineering, Zhejiang University of Technology,
Hangzhou 310023, China
[3] PCL Research Center of Networks and Communications, Peng Cheng Laboratory,
Shenzhen 518000, China

Abstract. The anonymity of blockchain has accelerated the growth of illegal activities and criminal behaviors on cryptocurrency platforms. Although decentralization is one of the typical characteristics of blockchain, we urgently call for effective regulation to detect these illegal behaviors to ensure the safety and stability of user transactions. Identity inference, which aims to make a preliminary inference about account identity, plays a significant role in blockchain security. As a common tool, graph mining technique can effectively represent the interactive information between accounts and be used for identity inference. However, existing methods cannot balance scalability and end-to-end architecture, resulting high computational consumption and weak feature representation. In this paper, we present a novel approach to analyze user's behavior from the perspective of the transaction subgraph, which naturally transforms the identity inference task into a graph classification pattern and effectively avoids computation in large-scale graph. Furthermore, we propose a generic end-to-end graph neural network model, named I^2BGNN, which can accept subgraph as input and learn a function mapping the transaction subgraph pattern to account identity, achieving deanonymization. Extensive experiments on EOSG and ETHG datasets demonstrate that the proposed method achieve the state-of-the-art performance in identity inference.

Keywords: Blockchain · Identity inference · Graph classification · Graph neural network

1 Introduction

As a distributed database technology, blockchain achieves the function of decentralization, encryption, and tamper-proof. Benefiting from its anonymity, the past few years have witnessed the growing prevalence of cryptocurrencies. As of the first quarter of 2021, there are more than 8,700 kinds of cryptocurrencies

ⓒ Springer Nature Singapore Pte Ltd. 2021
H.-N. Dai et al. (Eds.): BlockSys 2021, CCIS 1490, pp. 3–17, 2021.
https://doi.org/10.1007/978-981-16-7993-3_1

with a total market cap of 1,721 billion dollars. People only need to create a pseudonymous account (synonymous with address in this paper), and they can implement transaction at almost no cost. However, as the volume of transactions surged, the blockchain system of cryptocurrencies has also become a hotbed of illegal and criminal behavior, such as various scams [1–3] (Ponzi schemes, mining scams, scam wallets, fraudulent exchanges, etc.), money laundering [4,5], abusing bot accounts [6] and vulnerability attack [7].

As an open technique, blockchain provides public and tamper-proof transaction records, which creates the condition for data mining and analysis. Recently, the emergence of related research has helped to analyze the transaction pattern and account behavior on the blockchain system, and most of them leverage graph modeling methods. Such as evolution analysis of market via the on-chain transaction graph [8–12], transaction patterns recognition via graph topology and motifs [13,14], detection of abnormal users or transactions via graph embedding or graph neural network [15,16], etc. Among them, identity inference, which can be regarded as a de-anonymization process, is particularly important in blockchain data mining. Generally, identity inference aims to make a preliminary inference about account identity by capturing the characteristics of the transaction pattern of the accounts. For this task, common researches mainly concentrate on manual feature engineering including transaction features [17], graph features [18] and external features [14]. These features are mainly intuitive information, and share the same drawback like weak representation ability for classification. Further, several methods based on random-walk [19] and graph motif [20] capture higher-order network features that are more representational. With the development of graph deep learning, graph convolution network (GCN) has attracted considerable attention and been applied in identity inference gradually, achieving outstanding results [21,22].

After reviewing the above various methods, we summarize two conflicting issues: scalability and end-to-end. On the one hand, real-world transaction data on blockchain systems are generally extremely huge. Although these methods based on feature engineering, especially manual features, show good scalability because of the independence of feature extraction, they cannot achieve end-to-end architecture. End-to-end can reduce the reliance on expertise which is the core of feature engineering, and optimize target task in a complete form rather than multi-flows. On the other hand, although the graph convolution network is commonly achieved via end-to-end, most of them have poor scalability. Because the training of graph convolution network is usually performed on the whole transaction graph, where the loading and computing are not realistic.

Motivated by the subgraph perspective [15], we propose a framework to reconcile the scalability and end-to-end solution for identity inference. Benefiting from previous work, we collect two kinds of on-chain transaction data including Ethereum and EOSIO, to infer the "phisher" and "bot" accounts, respectively. Firstly, we extract the transaction subgraph for each labeled accounts by a sampling mechanism. Through that, each account is transformed into an independent transaction subgraph. The sampling mechanism constrains the scale of transaction subgraph, which can effectively reduce the occupation of resources. Secondly, we propose an end-to-end model, to achieve **Identity Inference on Blockchain** using **Graph Neural Network** (named I^2BGNN).

The rest of paper is organized as follows. In Sect. 2, we introduce the related work about identity inference. In Sect. 3, we describe the details of our framework, including subgraph extraction and the architecture of I^2BGNN. Section 4 presents the experiment settings and the comparison of experimental results with discussion. Finally, we conclude the paper in Sect. 5.

2 Related Work

Identity inference, which aims to detect abnormal and illegal accounts, has become an effective means to monitor accounts for platform and measure transaction risks for users. For identity inference on blockchain, related works concentrate on manual feature, graph embedding, graph neural network, and the others.

Manual Feature. Manual feature is a kind of feature engineering that relies on the experience of experts relatively. Normally, the more expert experience involved, the more reliable the feature vectors are. Lin et al. [23] designed various features of transaction timestamps to express the transaction history about the accounts, and constructed a classifier against abnormal bitcoin addresses. Li et al. [17] considered three kinds of features: the basic account feature, the topological feature which is related to transaction patterns, and temporal feature which is captured from the distributions of transaction timestamp. In addition to transaction information, Huang et al. [6] also considered the calling information of smart contract to expand the feature space, and finally realized the identification of bot accounts in EOSIO.

Graph Embedding. Graph embedding aims to learn low-dimensional node representations that capture the graph structure and drive downstream graph mining task such as node classification to identify illicit accounts. Up to now, a series of methods based on DeepWalk (DW) [24] have been used to detect accounts. Yuan et al. [16] used the Node2Vec algorithm which is a variant of DW to extract the potential features of the accounts and classified the phishers by Support-Vector-Machine (SVM). Wu et al. [19] redesigned the walking strategy by using transaction volume, timestamps, and multi-edges features to make their embedding framework more suitable for this task. Subsequently, Yuan et al. [15] extracted the subgraphs for each target account and embedded their transaction topology into feature vector via an embedding method named Graph2Vec [25]. Besides, they introduced the line graph [26] to further enhance the network structure embedding. Chen et al. [27] also used subgraph mechanism and got the embeddings by a graph convolution layer combining graph auto-encoder in an unsupervised way, and achieved phisher classification by LightGBM [28].

Graph Neural Network. This part mainly about the graph neural networks with end-to-end architecture. In [22], the whole transaction graph was sliced into small graphs by timestamp. This operation reduced the computational complexity and memory consumption which alleviate the scalability problem. Subsequently, graph convolution network was used for inductive learning to realize account identity inference. Tam et al. [21] used the mechanism of sampling transaction neighbors which is similar to the subgraph extraction. They characterized edges by embedding the temporal features from the time-series of transactions and incorporating them into the graph convolution network.

Others. Besides the aforementioned methods, there are other frameworks to achieve this identity inference. Phetsouvanh [29] proposed a graph mining technology to detect the suspicious bitcoin flow and account by analyzing the path length and confluence account of the directed subgraph. Zhang [30] introduced the concept of meta-path from the heterogeneous network and constructed multi-constrained meta-path based on time, attribution and topology, which is an effective way to capture behavior pattern features in a complex network.

3   Method

In this section, we first define the identity inference problem on blockchain, then present the details of subgraph extraction for constructing graph classification dataset. Finally, we review the knowledge of using graph neural network (GNN) for learning node and graph representations, and represent the details of proposed I^{2}BGCN model for identity inference.

3.1   Problem Definition

From the perspective of graph mining, identity inference can be regarded as a node classification task. During node classification, the blockchain data will be modeled as a user network with million nodes, which results in unaffordable time and memory consumption for most practical algorithms. Inspired by the core of "neighborhood aggregation" in graph neural network, we transform the node classification problem into a graph classification pattern in return for less time and memory consumption.

Given a set of n_A labeled accounts $A = \{(a_i, y_i) \mid i = 1, 2, \cdots, n_A\}$, we can extract the transaction subgraph centered on each target account. Specifically, we extract the transaction subgraph of account a_i: $G_{a_i} = (V, E_v, E_t, X, y_i)$, where V represents the set of accounts in this subgraph, E_v and E_t represent the directed edge sets that contain information about transaction volume and transaction frequency respectively, X represents the calling information of smart contract, y_i is the label of subgraph G_{a_i}. Note that we assign the label of account a_i to the transaction subgraph centered on it, and transform the node classification problem into a graph classification task: $f_{nc}(a_i) \Rightarrow f_{gc}(G_{a_i})$. The final goal is to learn the transaction patterns of subgraphs and classify centered account into phishing or non-phishing via graph neural networks. The workflow of our framework is shown in Fig. 1, and the details of subgraph extraction and classifier design will be introduced in Subsects. 3.2 and 3.3, respectively.

3.2 Subgraph Extraction

For each account a_i in A, we check the number of its transaction partners (i.e. neighbor nodes) first. Here, an upper limit of neighbor size, denoted as n_u, will be set to control the scale of transaction subgraph. If the neighbor size of a_i is less than the threshold, all neighbors and all transactions between them will be extracted. Otherwise, we calculate and sort the total transaction volume between target account and its neighbors, and select the top-n_u neighbors. We assume that the larger the transaction volume, the higher the correlation between the two accounts. The above extraction mechanism can also be used to sample k-hop transaction neighbors from the $(k-1)$-hop neighbors. Therefore, the scale of one-order/two-order subgraph of target account will not exceed $n_u/(n_u)^2$ normally.

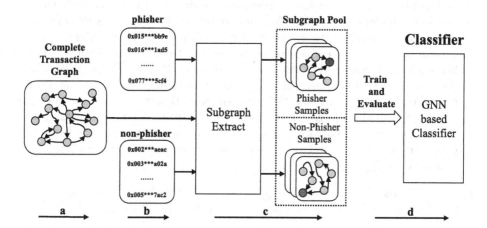

Fig. 1. The schematic depiction of our framework. The complete workflow proceeds as follows: a) modeling the transaction network; b) sampling the labeled accounts; c) extracting the subgraphs centered on target accounts; d) training and evaluating using GNNs.

The above process constructs the account (node) sets V, the transaction (edge) volume set E_v and the transaction (edge) frequency set E_t. Next, we briefly introduce two datasets which are named ETHG and EOSG and construct feature matrix X for them.

- **ETHG** It is from Xblock[1] which is a blockchain data platform for academic research. There is an account list that contains 1660 phisher accounts and

---

[1] http://xblock.pro/.

1700 non-phisher accounts with their 2-hop transaction records in Ethereum. Based on this, we filter the Contract-Account (CA) which will be considered as the contract calling feature of Externally-Owned-Accounts (EOA). And according to the span of the block where the transaction record is located, we collect all CAs from 0 to 10,000,000 blocks, filter them via the calling amount, and retain the top 14885 finally. After that, we construct the feature matrix of contract calling (cc) $X_{cc} \in \mathbb{R}^{n \times 14885}$, and each EOA has a 14885 dimension vector to represent their calling situation about those CAs.

- **EOSG** It is collected by [6]. They integrate and model the on-chain data of EOSIO: Enhanced Money Flow Graph (EMFG) which contains the transactions between accounts including timestamps and volume, Enhanced Account Creation Graph (EACG) which contains account creation tree data, Enhanced Contract Invocation Graph (ECIG) which contains smart contract calling data, and a list of labeled accounts which contains 229,907 normal accounts and 63863 bot-like accounts. Similarly, we extract the subgraph graph and contract calling features from EMFG and ECIG respectively, and construct the feature matrix of contract calling (cc) $X_{cc} \in \mathbb{R}^{n \times 1213}$. Further, we consider the account name restriction mechanism of EOSIO and add three kinds of node labels to expand features, since that the type of neighbors can also express the transaction pattern of the account. The three labels are the general account which consists of 12 characters, the auction account which is less than 12 characters but does not contain the character '.', and the sub-account of auction account which combines '.' with auction account name as the suffix. On the other hand, the neighbor extraction will stop at the system account whose name begins with 'EOSIO.'. Because the behavior pattern of the current center account has nothing to do with the transactions between other further accounts and system accounts. We construct the feature matrix of node label (nl) $X_{nl} \in \mathbb{R}^{n \times 3}$.

In summary, the feature matrix is $X = X_{cc} \in \mathbb{R}^{n \times 14885}$ for ETHG and $X = X_{cc} \oplus X_{nl} \in \mathbb{R}^{n \times 1216}$ for EOSG where $\oplus$ is concatenation operation.

3.3   Graph Neural Networks

By viewing the accounts interaction as graph data (i.e., transaction graph), recent deep learning methods for graph structural data, such as graph neural network (GNNs) [31–33], can be utilized to learn transaction pattern representation that can be fed to downstream machine learning models for phishing account detection. In this section, we will present the details of employing GNNs to obtain transaction pattern representation.

GNNs learn the representations of nodes by leveraging both the graph structure and node/edge features. This is done by a neighborhood aggregation function that iteratively takes the representation of all neighbors together with the graph structure as input, and outputs the aggregate representation of target node. The aggregation function can be defined using Graph Convolution layer

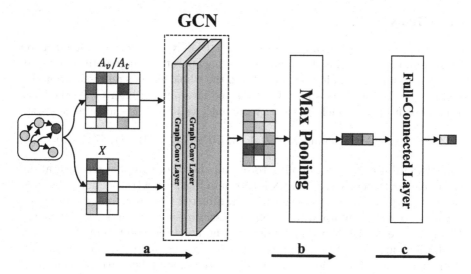

Fig. 2. The architecture of I²BGNN model. a) A_v (A_t) and X are captured from subgraph extraction and sent to graph convolution network; b) the max-pooling layer is used to compress the aggregated node representations to obtain the whole graph representation; c) the graph representation is used to predict the subgraph (account) label.

[31], Graph Attention layer [32], or any general message passing layer [33]. Formally, a graph convolution network (GCN) model follows the following rule to aggregate the feature of neighbors:

$$H^{(l)} = \sigma(\hat{A}H^{(l-1)}W^{(l-1)}), \tag{1}$$

where $H^{(l-1)} \in \mathbb{R}^{n \times k}$ is a matrix containing the k-dimensional representation of n nodes in the $(l-1)$-th layer, σ is the activation function (typically ReLU), $\hat{A}$ is a symmetric normalization of A and can be defined as:

$$\hat{A} = \tilde{D}^{-\frac{1}{2}}\tilde{A}\tilde{D}^{-\frac{1}{2}}, \quad \tilde{A} = A + I_n, \quad \tilde{D} = \text{diag}(\sum_{j=0}^{n} \tilde{A}_{ij}), \tag{2}$$

where $\tilde{A}$ is an $n \times n$ adjacency matrix of the graph with self connections added, $\tilde{D}$ is a degree diagonal matrix. After l layer of computation, the node representations $H^{(l)}$ is able to capture the information within their l-hop neighborhoods.

Generally, GCN model is used to learn the node representations in semi-supervised node classification. A 2-layer GCN model with softmax function can be formulated as:

$$Z = \text{softmax}(\hat{A} \cdot \text{ReLU}(\hat{A}XW^{(0)})W^{(1)}) \tag{3}$$

where $Z \in \mathbb{R}^{n \times y}$ is the prediction probability distribution and y is the dimension of node labels. $W^{(0)}$ and $W^{(1)}$ are the input-to-hidden and hidden-to-output weights, respectively.

3.4   I²BGNN

We now present the details of proposed I²BGNN for identity inference on blockchain. For graph classification, the pooling operations aggregate node representations from the final iteration to obtain the whole graph's representation. By stacking the pooling layer and fully-connected layer after 2-layer GCN, the basic graph classification model for identity inference can be constructed as follows:

$$Z = \text{softmax}(\text{MaxPooling}(ReLU(\hat{A} \cdot \text{ReLU}(\hat{A}XW^{(0)})W^{(1)}))W^{(2)} + b) \quad (4)$$

Note that we use the max pooling to obtain the whole graph's representation. The model architecture of I²BGNN is shown in Fig. 2. In a transaction subgraph, each node represents an account and each directed edge represents transaction flow that contains information about transaction volume and frequency. For the input layer of GCN, we first initialize the node representations using their attributions in transaction subgraph. Specifically, the node attributions include contract calling information (cc) and distinctive node-label (nl), as mentioned in Sect. 3.2, and we initialize node representation as $H^{(0)} = X$.

4   Experiment

4.1   Dataset

For EOSG dataset, we filter the labeled account list in term of subgraph size and obtain over 20,000 available accounts. Then, 1000 accounts per label are selected randomly for the follow-up experiments. The detailed dataset properties are given in Table 1. Finally, each dataset is split into training and testing sets with a proportion of 1:1, and they will be resplit 3 times using different random seeds. We report the average accuracy across all trials.

Table 1. Dataset properties. $|G|$ is the number of subgraphs in dataset, $Avg.|V|$ is the average number of nodes per graph, $Avg.|E_{di}|$ is the average number of edges per directed graph, $Avg.|E_{ud}|$ is the average number of edges per undirected graph which is transformed from corresponding directed graph, $|F|$ is the dimension of node features, $|Y|$ is the number of classes for labels.

Dataset	$|G|$	$Avg.|V|$	$Avg.|E_{di}|$	$Avg.|E_{ud}|$	$|F|$	$|Y|$	Label bias
ETHG	3266	80	239	222	14885	2	0.99
EOSG	2000	260	4250	3212	1216	2	1

4.2   Baseline

Since we implement identity inference with a graph classification pattern, we compare our framework with several SOTA graph classification algorithms including SF [34], Graph2vec [25], Netlsd [35] and FGSD [36]. The first two are graph embedding methods and the last two are graph kernel methods. Graph2vec extends the document embedding methods to graph classification and learns a distributed representation of the whole graph via document embedding neural networks. SF performs graph classification by spectral decomposition of the graph Laplacian, i.e., it relies on spectral features of the graph. Netlsd performs graph classification by extracting compact graph signatures that inherit the formal properties of the Laplacian spectrum. FGSD calculates the Moore-Penrose spectrum of the normalized laplacian and uses the histogram of the spectral features of this spectrum to represent the whole graph.

4.3   Experiment Setting

During subgraph extraction, the direction of edges in subgraph is determined by the transaction flow. However, during the experiments, we find that symmetric adjacency matrix of subgraph usually outperforms directed adjacency matrix. Therefore, we transform the directed adjacency matrix into a symmetric adjacency matrix by adding its transpose to itself. Other settings for models and datasets are as follows:

Method Settings. For all the four baseline methods, we set the embedding dimension to 128, and use default settings for other parameters. Further, we implement graph classification by using the following machine learning classifiers: Support Vector Machine (SVM) with radial basis kernel, k-Nearest Neighbors classifier (KNN) and Random Forest classifier (RF). As for I^2BGNN, we apply two layers of GCNs with output dimensions both equal to 128, and set the maximum number of eopchs to be 50, the batch size to be 30 and dropout to be 0.3.

Metric Settings. Both the datasets have two classes, so we evaluate the results of binary classification by precision, recall and F1-Score.

Table 2. Results of identity inference. The top-2 best results are highlighted in bold.

Method		Dataset					
		EOSG			ETHG		
		F1	Precision	Recall	F1	Precision	Recall
Graph2vec	SVM	0.8223	0.8132	0.8317	0.6487	0.7564	0.5678
	KNN	0.6171	0.9820	0.4499	0.5705	0.5709	0.5701
	RF	0.7637	0.8155	0.7180	0.6104	0.7355	0.5216
SF	SVM	0.9428	0.9222	0.9643	0.6287	0.6405	0.6173
	KNN	0.9089	0.9081	0.9098	0.6238	0.6401	0.6083
	RF	0.9333	0.9166	0.9507	0.6908	0.7056	0.6766
Netlsd	SVM	0.8730	0.8574	0.8891	0.7067	0.6869	0.7276
	KNN	0.8406	0.8417	0.8396	0.6774	0.6884	0.6667
	RF	0.8845	0.8625	0.9077	0.6702	0.6782	0.6623
FGSD	SVM	0.9617	0.9534	0.9701	0.7206	0.6810	0.7650
	KNN	0.9469	0.9404	0.9534	0.7161	0.6750	0.7625
	RF	0.9578	0.9579	0.9578	0.7372	0.7448	0.7297
I^2BGNN-v		**0.9940**	**0.9894**	**0.9986**	**0.8587**	**0.8190**	**0.9024**
I^2BGNN-t		**0.9950**	**0.9917**	**0.9983**	**0.8600**	**0.8697**	**0.8505**

4.4   Result and Discussion

Inference Performance. Table 2 reports the performance comparison between I^2BGNN and baselines, from which we can observe that I^2BGNN significantly outperforms other methods across the two datasets. Specifically, compared with baselines, our I^2BGNN achieves average improvement of 12%/19% in term of F1 on EOSG/ETHG. This may be due to the excellent expression ability of the graph convolution layer and the effectiveness of the features which are constructed by the contract calling information. In addition, these graph embedding and kernel methods which are based on spectral analysis are significantly better than Graph2vec. Their advantages are also reflected in the efficiency of model operation in experiments.

Furthermore, we investigate the influence of neighborhood depth and data division on the experimental results under various settings.

The Influence of Neighborhood Depth. Normally, the subgraph containing 3-hop neighbors will have a large scale, which leads to difficulties in feature learning. To further analyze the influence of different depth for subgraph extraction, we extract 1-hop and 2-hop neighbors to construct the subgraphs for each target account. Table 3 shows the properties of 1-order and 2-order subgraphs for two datasets. And Table 4 reports the performance comparison between 1-order and 2-order subgraphs using I^2BGNN. For EOSG, I^2BGNN with 1-order subgraph performs slightly better than that with 2-order subgraph. Actually, the 1-order transaction subgraph contains sufficient and effective characteristics of transaction behavior, while the larger scale of the 2-order subgraph leads to the redundancy of information. As for ETHG, the situation is just the opposite, I^2BGNN with 2-order subgraph outperforms that with 1-order subgraph. Obviously, the 1-order subgraph contains sparse transaction information, which is not conducive to inference, while the denser interactions in the 2-order subgraph facilitate behavior analysis and identity inference.

Table 3. The properties of 1-hop and 2-hop subgraphs.

Dataset	Subgraph	$Avg.|V|$	$Avg.|E_{di}|$	$Avg.|E_{ud}|$
EOSG	1-order	17	65	48
	2-order	260	4250	3212
ETHG	1-order	10	13	12
	2-order	80	239	222

Table 4. Results of I^2BGNN with different neighborhood depth.

Dataset	Method	1-order	2-order
EOSG	I^2BGNN-v	**0.9960**	0.9940
	I^2BGNN-t	**0.9980**	0.9950
ETHG	I^2BGNN-v	0.8356	**0.8587**
	I^2BGNN-t	0.8366	**0.8600**

The Influence of Data Split. Next, we analyze the sensitivity of models to different ratios of data split. Specifically, we vary the ratio of training set to testing set in {1:9, 1:7, 1:5, 1:3, 1:1, 3:1}. Figure 3 reports the inference results (F1) of different models with various proportion of training set. Obviously, for different ratios, our I^2BGNN holds the best performance compared with other graph classification models. In addition, with the increase of training data, the performances of all models are naturally improved.

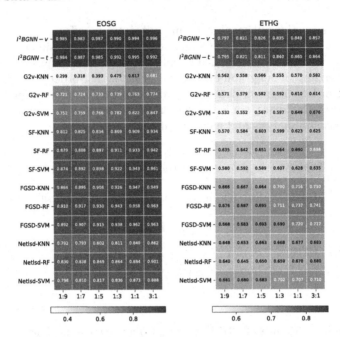

Fig. 3. Experimental results of different division ratios of the dataset on EOSG (left) and ETHG (right)

5 Conclusion

Traditional graph mining methods for identity inference are stuck in a dilemma where it is difficult to integrate scalability and end-to-end architecture into one model. In this work, we balance scalability and end-to-end architecture in model design. Specifically, we propose to learn the transaction subgraph centered on target account and transform the identity inference task on blockchain into graph classification pattern, resulting in a great reduction in resource consumption. Moreover, we design an end-to-end I^{2}BGNN model, which is capable of learning an effective graph representation. Finally, we conduct extensive experiments on two real blockchain datasets (EOSG and ETHG) to demonstrate the effectiveness of our proposed I^{2}BGNN. Experimental results show that the transaction pattern hidden in subgraph can actually reveal the account behavior, and our I^{2}BGNN achieves the outstanding performance in identity inference.

Acknowledgements. The authors would like to thank all the members in the IVSN Research Group, Zhejiang University of Technology for the valuable discussions about the ideas and technical details presented in this paper. This work was partially supported by the National Key R&D Program of China under Grant No. 2020YFB1006104, by the National Natural Science Foundation of China under Grant No. 61973273, by the Zhejiang Provincial Natural Science Foundation of China under Grant No. LR19F030001, by the Ministry of Public Security's Research Project "Research and Demonstration Application of Key Technologies of Criminal Social Network Model", and by the Special Scientific Research Fund of Basic Public Welfare Profession of Zhejiang Province under Grant LGF20F020016.

References

1. Vasek, M., Moore, T.: There's no free lunch, even using bitcoin: tracking the popularity and profits of virtual currency scams. In: Böhme, R., Okamoto, T. (eds.) FC 2015. LNCS, vol. 8975, pp. 44–61. Springer, Heidelberg (2015). https://doi.org/10.1007/978-3-662-47854-7_4
2. Wu, J., Lin, D., Zheng, Z., Yuan, Q.: T-edge: temporal weighted multidigraph embedding for ethereum transaction network analysis. arXiv preprint arXiv:1905.08038 (2019)
3. Chen, W., Zheng, Z., Cui, J., Ngai, E., Zheng, P., Zhou, Y.: Detecting ponzi schemes on ethereum: towards healthier blockchain technology. In: Proceedings of the 2018 World Wide Web Conference, pp. 1409–1418 (2018)
4. Bryans, D.: Bitcoin and money laundering: mining for an effective solution. Ind. LJ **89**, 441 (2014)
5. Fanusie, Y., Robinson, T.: Bitcoin laundering: an analysis of illicit flows into digital currency services. Center on Sanctions and Illicit Finance memorandum, January 2018
6. Huang, Y., et al.: Understanding (mis) behavior on the eosio blockchain. Proc. ACM Meas. Anal. Comput. Syst. **4**(2), 1–28 (2020)
7. Di Francesco, D., Maesa, A.M., Ricci, L.: Detecting artificial behaviours in the bitcoin users graph. Online Soc. Networks Media **3**, 63–74 (2017)
8. Kondor, D., Pósfai, M., Csabai, I., Vattay, G.: Do the rich get richer? an empirical analysis of the bitcoin transaction network. PloS One **9**(2), e86197 (2014)
9. Alqassem, I., Rahwan, I., Svetinovic, D.: The anti-social system properties: bitcoin network data analysis. IEEE Trans. Syst. Man Cybern. Syst. **50**(1), 21–31 (2018)
10. Tasca, P., Hayes, A., Liu, S.: The evolution of the bitcoin economy: extracting and analyzing the network of payment relationships. J. Risk Financ. (2018)
11. Bai, Q., Zhang, C., Xu, Y., Chen, X., Wang, X.: Evolution of ethereum: a temporal graph perspective. arXiv preprint arXiv:2001.05251 (2020)
12. Ferretti, S., D'Angelo, G.: On the ethereum blockchain structure: a complex networks theory perspective. Concurrency Comput. Practice Exp. **32**(12), e5493 (2020)
13. Huang, B., Liu, Z., Chen, J., Liu, A., Liu, Q., He, Q.: Behavior pattern clustering in blockchain networks. Multimed. Tools Appl. **76**(19), 20099–20110 (2017). https://doi.org/10.1007/s11042-017-4396-4
14. Ranshous, S., et al.: Exchange pattern mining in the bitcoin transaction directed hypergraph. In: Brenner, M. (ed.) FC 2017. LNCS, vol. 10323, pp. 248–263. Springer, Cham (2017). https://doi.org/10.1007/978-3-319-70278-0_16
15. Yuan, Z., Yuan, Q., Wu, J.: Phishing detection on ethereum via learning representation of transaction subgraphs. In: Zheng, Z., Dai, H.-N., Fu, X., Chen, B. (eds.) BlockSys 2020. CCIS, vol. 1267, pp. 178–191. Springer, Singapore (2020). https://doi.org/10.1007/978-981-15-9213-3_14
16. Yuan, Q., Huang, B., Zhang, J., Wu, J., Zhang, H., Zhang, X.: Detecting phishing scams on ethereum based on transaction records. In: 2020 IEEE International Symposium on Circuits and Systems (ISCAS), pp. 1–5. IEEE (2020)

17. Li, Y., Cai, Y., Tian, H., Xue, G., Zheng, Z.: Identifying illicit addresses in bitcoin network. In: Zheng, Z., Dai, H.-N., Fu, X., Chen, B. (eds.) BlockSys 2020. CCIS, vol. 1267, pp. 99–111. Springer, Singapore (2020). https://doi.org/10.1007/978-981-15-9213-3_8
18. Pham, T., Lee, S.: Anomaly detection in the bitcoin system-a network perspective. arXiv preprint arXiv:1611.03942 (2016)
19. Wu, J., et al.: Who are the phishers? phishing scam detection on ethereum via network embedding. IEEE Trans. Syst. Man Cybern. Syst. (2020)
20. Wu, J., Liu, J., Chen, W., Huang, H., Zheng, Z., Zhang, Y.: Detecting mixing services via mining bitcoin transaction network with hybrid motifs. IEEE Trans. Syst. Man Cybern. Syst. (2021)
21. Tam, D.S.H., Lau, W.C., Hu, B., Ying, Q.F., Chiu, D.M., Liu, H.: Identifying illicit accounts in large scale e-payment networks-a graph representation learning approach. arXiv preprint arXiv:1906.05546 (2019)
22. Weber, M., et al.: Anti-money laundering in bitcoin: experimenting with graph convolutional networks for financial forensics. arXiv preprint arXiv:1908.02591 (2019)
23. Lin, Y.-J., Wu, P.-W., Hsu, C.-H., Tu, I.-P., Liao, S.: An evaluation of bitcoin address classification based on transaction history summarization. In: 2019 IEEE International Conference on Blockchain and Cryptocurrency (ICBC), pp. 302–310. IEEE (2019)
24. Perozzi, B., Al-Rfou, R., Skiena, S.: Deepwalk: online learning of social representations. In: Proceedings of the 20th ACM SIGKDD International Conference on Knowledge Discovery and Data Mining, pp. 701–710 (2014)
25. Narayanan, A., Chandramohan, M., Venkatesan, R., Chen, L., Liu, Y., Jaiswal, S.: graph2vec: learning distributed representations of graphs. arXiv preprint arXiv:1707.05005 (2017)
26. Xuan, Q., et al.: Subgraph networks with application to structural feature space expansion. IEEE Trans. Knowl. Data Eng. (2019)
27. Chen, L., Peng, J., Liu, Y., Li, J., Xie, F., Zheng, Z.: Phishing scams detection in ethereum transaction network. ACM Trans. Internet Technol. (TOIT) 21(1), 1–16 (2020)
28. Ke, G., et al.: Lightgbm: a highly efficient gradient boosting decision tree. Adv. Neural Inf. Process. Syst. 30, 3146–3154 (2017)
29. Phetsouvanh, S., Oggier, F., Datta, A.: Egret: extortion graph exploration techniques in the bitcoin network. In: 2018 IEEE International Conference on Data Mining Workshops (ICDMW), pp. 244–251. IEEE (2018)
30. Zhang, R., Zhang, G., Liu, L., Wang, C., Wan, S.: Anomaly detection in bitcoin information networks with multi-constrained meta path. J. Syst. Archit. 110, 101829 (2020)
31. Kipf, T.N., Welling, M.: Semi-supervised classification with graph convolutional networks. arXiv preprint arXiv:1609.02907 (2016)
32. Veličković, P., Cucurull, G., Casanova, A., Romero, A., Liò, P., Bengio, Y.: Graph attention networks. In: International Conference on Learning Representations (2018). Accepted as poster
33. Gilmer, J., Schoenholz, S.S., Riley, P.F., Vinyals, O., Dahl, G.E.: Neural message passing for quantum chemistry. In: International Conference on Machine Learning, pp. 1263–1272. PMLR (2017)
34. de Lara, N., Pineau, E.: A simple baseline algorithm for graph classification. arXiv preprint arXiv:1810.09155 (2018)

35. Tsitsulin, A., Mottin, D., Karras, P., Bronstein, A., Müller, E.: Netlsd: hearing the shape of a graph. In: Proceedings of the 24th ACM SIGKDD International Conference on Knowledge Discovery & Data Mining, pp. 2347–2356 (2018)
36. Verma, S., Zhang, Z.-L.: Hunt for the unique, stable, sparse and fast feature learning on graphs. In: NIPS, pp. 88–98 (2017)

The Regional Clusting Effect of the Blockchain Industry Base on Unsupervised Learning Methods

Yuxi Zhang[1], Muran Su[2], Zhen Wu[2], Xiang Chen[3], Haifeng Guo[1(⊠)], Xinxin Chang[1], and Hongzhi Wang[3]

[1] School of Management, Harbin Institute of Technology, Harbin 150001, China
haifengguo@hit.edu.cn
[2] National Internet Emergency Center, CNCERT/CC, Beijing 100094, China
[3] Computer Faulty, Harbin Institute of Technology, Harbin 150001, China

Abstract. The blockchain industry has developed rapidly in China last years, but in an extremely uneven pattern, especially in different regions. This paper adopts unsupervised learning methods to delineate the uneven regional patterns in the blockchain industry. We conduct the analysis in five aspects, including blockchain company, blockchain projects, R&D ability, financing and talents allocation. We find that the blockchain industries cluster in four area, i.e., Guangdong, Beijing, Jiangsu, Zhejiang etc. However, since most of China's R&D activities are based on universities and research institutes, which tend to be concentrated in cities, the cluster of R&D capabilities is city-centric, other than area. Financing and talents allocations show similar clustering effect in different regions.

Keywords: Blockchain industry · Industry distribution · Regional clustering · K-means · Unsupervised learning method

1 Introduction

Blockchain technology, as the core technology that can maximize the utility of big data in the underlying technology of the Internet, has been bundled with bitcoin and other virtual currencies for a long time. Blockchain technology has been widely used in all walks of life with its characteristics of distributed accounting and decentralization in China. It is likely to achieve data consistency, anti-tampering and anti-breach of contract as an emerging technology, which has been gradually forming a blockchain industry nowadays.

On October 30, 2020, the National Internet Information Office issued the fourth batch of 285 domestic blockchain information service names and filing numbers. Since the formal implementation of the Regulations on the Management of Blockchain Information Services on February 15th, 2019, the Cyberspace Administration of China has announced 3 batches (730 in total) of the names and record numbers of domestic blockchain information services, Up to now, there are a total of 1,015 blockchain information service

© Springer Nature Singapore Pte Ltd. 2021
H.-N. Dai et al. (Eds.): BlockSys 2021, CCIS 1490, pp. 18–29, 2021.
https://doi.org/10.1007/978-981-16-7993-3_2

names and filling numbers in four batches, involving 814 companies. In terms of the distribution of regional divisions of information service filings, the number of filings in the five first-tier cities, including Beijing, Shenzhen, Shanghai, Hangzhou and Guangzhou, ranks among the top in China, accounting for more than 72% of the total.

Current researches barely focus on the blockchain industry pattern. On the contrary, most of them ignored the comparative study on the current regional development of blockchain industry in China from the macro perspective of government governance, but analyzed the development prospects of blockchain industry in one single city, the principles of blockchain technology, the meanings and characteristics of blockchain. By means of cluster analysis and principal component analysis, this paper explores the clustering and distribution of the blockchain industry and the factors affecting the distribution, so as to determine the weaknesses in the development process of the blockchain industry with different regions according to their own actual situations.

2 Data

All the data are collected from https://bc.cert.org.cn/.

3 Base on Unsupervised Learning Methods to Analysis of the National Blockchain Industry Pattern

3.1 Distribution Pattern of National Blockchain Companies

Judging from the regional distribution of company registration, as shown in Fig. 1, blockchain companies have spread to all parts of China, and have formed the Bohai Rim Gathering Circle with Beijing and Shandong as the main body, the Pearl River Delta Gathering Region represented by Guangdong, the Yangtze River Delta Gathering Region represented by Zhejiang and Jiangsu, the Central Gathering Area represented by Hunan and Hubei, and the Sichuan-Chongqing Gathering Area represented by Sichuan and Chongqing. Hainan is favored by blockchain companies and Internet giants because of the strong government support for blockchain.

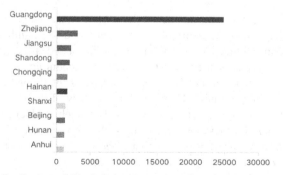

Fig. 1. Regional distribution of blockchain company registration Data source: The Home of Blockchain

In terms of the number of companies registered, Guangdong Province has the largest number of companies, which mainly distributed in Guangzhou and Shenzhen, with more than 24,000 companies, accounting for more than 50% of the total, far exceeding other regions in China. Followed by Zhejiang and Jiangsu, with 3,064 and 2,070 respectively.

Fig. 2. National clustering diagram of Chinese blockchain-related companies in 2020 Data source: The Home of Blockchain

From the perspective of the clustering of blockchain-related companies, as shown in Fig. 2, China's blockchain-related companies have formed into four major clusterings, namely, the Western Gathering Area represented by Shanxi, Sichuan and Chongqing, the Eastern Gathering Area represented by Shandong, Jiangsu, Zhejiang and Shanghai, the Southern Gathering Area represented by Guangdong, Hainan and Fujian, and the Central Gathering Area represented by Hunan and Hubei. According to incomplete statistics of The Home of Blockchain, as of November 2020, the blockchain-related companies registered in the top three clusterings accounted for 9.18%, 19.65% and 50.56% of China, and the total number of blockchain-related companies in the three major clusterings accounted for nearly 80% of the national total.

3.2   Distribution Pattern of Blockchain Projects in China

Different from the statistics on the number of global blockchain companies, the definition of blockchain company is the name of the company and the number of companies whose business scope includes blockchain. From the regional distribution of blockchain companies, Guangdong is at the top with 18,992 blockchain companies, accounting for more than 60% of the total in China, which surpasses the second-ranked Zhejiang with 1,826 blockchain companies. However, further study of these companies reveals that only about 1,000 companies that have actually launched blockchain business or focused on blockchain business, of which only 414 companies have been filed by the National Cyberspace Administration of China. Therefore, only about 4% of companies are actually engaged in blockchain-related businesses.

In order to explore the geographical distribution of all blockchain projects in China, this paper uses the data of all blockchain projects in 34 provinces, municipalities and autonomous regions in China published by the State Cyberspace Administration as samples, and the number of projects as the clustering reference. The final clustering results are shown in Fig. 3:

Fig. 3. National clustering diagram of the number of blockchain projects in China Data source: The Home of Blockchain

It can be clearly seen from Fig. 2 that the number of existing blockchain projects in Guangdong Province is the largest, Beijing and its surrounding radiation areas followed closely behind, next is southeast coastal economic belt. The long-standing strong economic strength of the Coastal Economic Belt has laid a foundation for the development of blockchain projects. Among the inland areas, Sichuan Province has become the province with the most rapid development of blockchain projects. In addition to the direct government policy support, there are also many universities in Sichuan Province that have trained a large number of excellent information technology talents. Expect as the inland areas other than Sichuan province, provinces along the Yangtze River Basin and provinces along the Yellow River Basin also gathered numerous blockchain projects. These provinces are contiguous and are the location of urban clustering vigorously developed by China. Additionally, as education provinces with many well-known universities, Hunan, Hubei and Shanxi have accumulated numbers of talents for the development of the blockchain industry.

3.3 Distribution Pattern of National Blockchain Research and Development Capabilities

Analysed from the level of each province, by 2020, among the enterprises that have actually carried out blockchain-related projects, the distribution of the number of patents ranks as follows: first in Guangdong, second in Beijing, third in Shanghai, fourth in Jiangsu and fifth in Sichuan. The first four of them, started early and have a certain degree of accumulation in the blockchain industry. The first-tier cities, Beijing, Shenzhen, Hangzhou, Shanghai and Guangzhou, rank in the forefront, mainly due to the strong foundations of the first-tier cities in economy, science and education. The multifactor aggregation has made them major cities of blockchain industry innovation, while the city has strong support and will further exert their industry synergy in the future. At the same time, Guangdong Province and Beijing Municipality are significantly higher in number than Zhejiang Province and Shanghai City, which reflects that Guangdong Province and Beijing Municipality are more active in blockchain technology innovation.

According to the assessment results of China Electronics Society on the research and development capabilities in the blockchain industry in various regions across the country, Beijing has accumulated the best domestic scientific research institutions in China, and has firmly established a leading edge in the field of research and development. Relying on Alibaba and many other blockchain innovative application research and development companies, Hangzhou ranks first in blockchain patent applications, and ranks second after Beijing in the overall ranking of research and development items (Fig. 4).

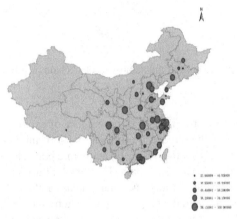

Fig. 4. Cluster distribution of China's blockchain research and development capabilities Data source: The Home of Blockchain

3.4 Comprehensive Analysis of the Distribution Pattern of the National Blockchain Industry

Mentioned by way of analyzing the different single measure block in all aspects of the chain industry clustering in our country. The distribution results presented by different measurement indexes are different. Among them, the distribution of all kinds of Guangdong Province is at the top. In other regions, due to different measurement indexes, the clustering distribution results presented by other regions also have certain differences.

In order to comprehensively observe the distribution of the national blockchain industry, the above indexes are integrated into the distribution index system of the blockchain industry. According to the degree of closeness, K-means method was used for cluster analysis. K-means clustering algorithm (K-means for short) is a classical algorithm in clustering analysis. After the first rough classification, it can be adjusted continuously until the satisfactory conditions are reached. The principle of k-means is to select K condensation points at random and calculate the Euclidean distance between other points and each condensation point.

$$d_q(x, y) = \left[\sum_{k=1}^{p} |x_k - y_k|^q \right]^{\frac{1}{q}}, \quad q > 0$$

When q = 2, is the Euclidean distance.

And then you distribute it to the condensation point closest to it. Each condensation center and the points assigned to it represent a cluster. When all the points are allocated, the center of gravity of each cluster will be recalculated to get new agglomerate points and then re-classified, and repeated until the termination condition is met. In this paper, values of K were assigned as 4, 5 and 6 respectively, and three clustering results were obtained, as shown in Fig. 5.

Euclidean distance (k=5)	Euclidean distance (k=6)	Euclidean distance (k=4)	
Beijing	3 Beijing	4 Beijing	4
Jiangsu	3 Jiangsu	4 Jiangsu	4
Guangdong	3 Guangdong	4 Guangdong	4
Tianjin	4 Tianjin	6 Tianjin	3
Liaoning	4 Liaoning	6 Liaoning	3
Fujian	4 Fujian	6 Fujian	3
Hubei	4 Hubei	6 Hubei	3
Chongqing	4 Chongqing	6 Chongqing	3
Sichuan	4 Sichuan	6 Sichuan	3
Shaanxi	4 Shaanxi	6 Shaanxi	3
Shanghai	5 Shanghai	5 Shanghai	2
Zhejiang	5 Zhejiang	5 Zhejiang	2
Shandong	5 Shandong	5 Shandong	2
Jilin	1 Anhui	1 Jilin	1
Anhui	1 Hunan	1 Anhui	1
Henan	1 Jilin	2 Henan	1
Hunan	1 Henan	2 Hunan	1
Guangxi	1 Guangxi	2 Guangxi	1
Hainan	1 Hainan	2 Hainan	1
Hebei	2 Guizhou	2 Hebei	2
Shanxi	2 Hebei	3 Shanxi	2
Inner Mongolia	2 Shanxi	3 Inner Mongolia	2
Heilongjiang	2 Inner Mongolia	3 Heilongjiang	2
Jiangxi	2 Heilongjiang	3 Jiangxi	2
Guizhou	2 Jiangxi	3 Guizhou	2
Yunnan	2 Yunnan	3 Yunnan	2
Tibet	2 Tibet	3 Tibet	2
Gansu	2 Gansu	3 Gansu	2
Qinghai	2 Qinghai	3 Qinghai	2
Ningxia	2 Ningxia	3 Ningxia	2
Xinjiang	2 Xinjiang	3 Xinjiang	2

Fig. 5. Results of K-means clustering algorithm

Among the three kinds of clustering results, the region with the largest clustering density, as shown in Figs. 6, 7 and 8, presents consistent distribution results. It can be seen that in addition to the capital Beijing, the development of the blockchain industry in the coastal areas is the best. In addition to Guangdong Province in the coastal areas with Jiangsu as the core of the Yangtze River Delta area followed. These regions not only have a profound economic foundation, but also gather China's top Internet enterprises, providing greater space for the development of the blockchain industry.

Fig. 6. Comprehensive distribution clustering results of six types of blockchain industries

Fig. 7. Comprehensive distribution clustering results of five types of blockchain industries

Fig. 8. Comprehensive distribution clustering results of four types of blockchain industries

4   Principal Component Analysis and Factor Analysis

Multi-index principal component analysis is generally used to find the comprehensive index of a certain thing and explain the information contained in the comprehensive index. This chapter wants to block multiple data normalization of chain industry, seeking to clustering index in each variable weighted composition, weight quantitatively reflects the various components for block importance of chain of industry clustering distribution form, again carries on the analysis, comparing two methods of analysis to determine the importance of block forming clustering distribution chain industry factors. By collating the data provided by Blockchain House and the website of the National Bureau of Statistics, The characteristic indicators for each province are set up from four perspectives: economy, infrastructure construction, talent construction and introduction, and supporting industry development.

"Number of blockchain projects" *NUM*
"Research and Experiment Grant " *R&D*
"Science and Technology Expenditure of Local Finance " V*ESTED*
"Electricity consumption (billion kilowatt-hours)"   *ELECT*
"Number of domain name"   *DOMAIN*
"Broadband Internet access port" *PORT*
"Information transmission, software and information technology service industries Employed persons in urban units" *PEOP*
"Enrollment Number of Regular Institutions of Higher Learning " *PRACT*
"Number of students in regular institutions of higher learning "   *STUDENT*
"Domestic number of patent grants" *PATENT*
"Value added of the tertiary industry" TERINDUS
"Software and information services business revenue" *INFORINCOME*
"GDP per capita" *PERGDP*

It can be seen from Fig. 9 that 2 principal components and 2 factor variables are reserved.

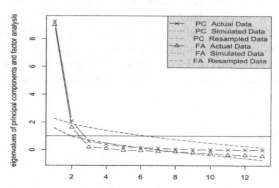

Fig. 9. Classification of principal components and factor analysis indicators of blockchain industry distribution

4.1 Principal Component Analysis

In order to make PCA more explanatory, this paper uses maximum variance rotation, which allows each component to be explained by only a finite set of variables.

Table 1. Principal component analysis results of the distribution of blockchain industry

	RC1	RC2	h2	u2	com
NUM	0.93	0.25	0.94	0.064	1.1
R.D	0.75	0.63	0.96	0.039	1.9
VESTED	0.69	0.64	0.88	0.12	2
ELECT	0.16	0.91	0.86	0.144	1.1
DOMAIN	0.58	0.47	0.56	0.439	1.9
PORT	0.25	0.95	0.96	0.039	1.1
PEOP	0.95	0.25	0.96	0.041	1.1
PRACT	0.86	0.31	0.84	0.164	1.3
STUDENT	0.05	0.9	0.82	0.184	1
PATENT	0.59	0.73	0.88	0.118	1.9
TERINDUS	0.58	0.8	0.98	0.023	1.8
INFORINCOME	0.87	0.43	0.93	0.067	1.5
PERGDP	0.88	−0.08	0.78	0.216	1

As shown in Table 1, RC1 and RC2 are component loadings, H2 is common factor variance, U2 represents component uniqueness, that is, the proportion of variance that cannot be explained by principal components.

Among them, RC1 is composed of the following components: NUM blockchain project number, PEOP information transmission, PRACT of urban units employed in software and information technology service industry, InforIncome of urban units employed in scientific research and technology service industry, PERGDP of software and information service business, and GDP per capita. RC2 is made up of the following components.RC2 is composed of: Elect electricity consumption PORT Internet broadband access PORT number of students regular colleges and universities added value of the tertiary industry.

4.2 Factor Analysis

As shown in Fig. 10, the results of factor analysis and principal component analysis were consistent.

This is shown in Tables 1 and 2, the results of the two analysis methods indicate that the foundation of the blockchain industry, including the early scale of the industry, the talent base and the economic base, has the greatest influence on the distribution of the

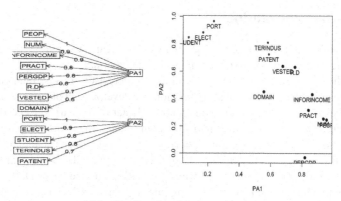

Fig. 10. Results of factor analysis

blockchain industry. The second most influential factors are infrastructure construction, the development of the tertiary industry and the talent pool, including the construction of power and communications facilities, the development of finance, logistics and service industries, and the development of research institutions such as regional universities and research institutes.

Table 2. Factor analysis results of blockchain industry distribution

	PA1	PA2	h2	u2	com
NUM	0.94	0.25	0.94	0.0588	1.1
R.D	0.75	0.63	0.97	0.0328	1.9
VESTED	0.68	0.64	0.87	0.1339	2
ELECT	0.17	0.88	0.81	0.1921	1.1
DOMAIN	0.55	0.45	0.51	0.4898	1.9
PORT	0.24	0.97	0.99	0.0108	1.1
PEOP	0.96	0.25	0.98	0.0223	1.1
PRACT	0.84	0.32	0.81	0.194	1.3
STUDENT	0.08	0.85	0.72	0.2765	1
PATENT	0.59	0.72	0.87	0.1316	1.9
TERINDUS	0.58	0.81	0.99	0.0078	1.8
INFORINCOME	0.86	0.43	0.93	0.0681	1.5
PERGDP	0.82	−0.03	0.67	0.3285	1

5 Conclusion and Outlook

Combined with the previous data and analysis, we can summarize the following characteristics of the development of China's blockchain industry.

First, whether it is in terms of the number of enterprise projects, financing conditions, R&D capabilities, and talent accumulation, the development of China's blockchain industry is basically consistent with the regional cluster of industries. According to the geographical location, regional culture of the country, and the national opinions on the development of urban clustering, the blockchain industrial clusterings can be divided into the following regions: the Beijing-Tianjin-Hebei region, the Bohai Sea Economic Zone centered on Shandong, the Pearl River Delta, the Yangtze River Delta, the Western Triangle of Shanxi, Sichuan and Chongqing, the Urban Clusterings in the Middle Reaches of the Yangtze River in Hubei, Hunan and the Central Plains Urban Clustering in Anhui, Henan.

Second, since the peak of development in 2018, the overall development speed of China's blockchain industry has gradually slowed down. According to China's national conditions, it can be inferred that after the initial explosive development of the blockchain industry, due to the fact that the blockchain industry involves more industries and has closer cooperation with the financial sector, the government has started to bring it into the scope of supervision. Various regions have also successively introduced regulations and policies for standardized development, the development of blockchain industry is becoming formal gradually.

Third, apart from the above-mentioned developed areas, among the inland regions, Henan, Anhui, Hunan and Hubei have developed transportation, high population density, and more rapid flow of people than other regions in the country, which raised the requirements for regional infrastructure construction. The infrastructure construction level of transportation and power in these regions is relatively more developed, with higher Internet penetration rate and stronger computing power, providing good hardware conditions for the development of the blockchain industry. Based on the available data, the author is using graph analysis techniques to try to prove the following findings.

First of all, there are different industries and project formats in different centers of blockchain industry aggregation and the scope of radiation. The differences of such clusters are caused by many factors, including but not limited to: the nature of the original enterprises in the region, the industrial and cultural characteristics of the region, the research scope of the regional colleges and universities, and the industry-university-research cooperation units, etc.

Secondly, although the number of blockchain policies issued in various regions is large, the implementation is not strong enough, so the strength of the enterprise is not strong. However, some regions have strong policies, although the number is not large, but the support for blockchain enterprises is strong, and the development of enterprises is relatively good. When the graph is analyzed, whether to choose quantity or strength for weight will eventually lead to different results. And whether the intensity is strong is related to the level of talents, learning ability and attitude towards talents within the government.

Thirdly, the author also found that investors and invests of blockchain companies also show a regular phenomenon (Fig. 11), which is also closely related to different

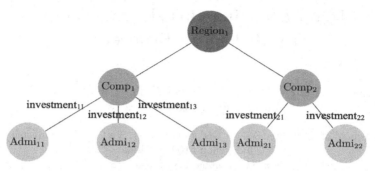

Fig. 11. Discover the investors and investees of blockchain companies through graph analysis

regions of China. Abstracting this problem into a graph theory problem, the vertex set V of the graph G(V,E) is: 1. Region; 2. Company; 3. Administrator. The edge set E is the relationship between the vertices.edge < Region,Comp) > is the regional relationship where the company is located; edge < Comp,Admi) > is the relationship between the company and its managers, and the weight of the edge is the amount of investment. Using graph analysis and graph mining technology, as well as the relevant knowledge of complex network analysis, clustering can be performed, the center point can be found, and the area can be divided.

Acknowledgments. This work was supported by The National Key Research and Development Program of China (2020YFB1006104), The National Natural Science Foundation of China (NSFC 71773025 and NSFC U1866602).

Deep Learning-Based Transaction Prediction in Ethereum

Zhuoming Gu[1,2], Dan Lin[1,2], Jiatao Zheng[1,2], Jiajing Wu[1,2(✉)], and Chaoxin Hu[3]

[1] School of Computer Science and Engineering, Sun Yat-Sen University, Guangzhou 510006, China
wujiajing@mail.sysu.edu.cn
[2] National Engineering Research Center of Digital Life, Sun Yat-sen University, Guangzhou 510006, China
[3] WeBank, Shenzhen 518055, China

Abstract. In recent years, deep learning has been applied to data analysis in the financial field. One of the important applications is time series prediction. Meanwhile, with the advent of blockchain technology, cryptocurrencies have attracted attention in the financial field and the public. Therefore, there has been a lot of researches done on the time series prediction of cryptocurrencies. However, most of these studies are about predicting the prices of various cryptocurrencies, lacking in predicting the transaction amount. As platforms for trading cryptocurrencies, cryptocurrency exchanges play an important role in the crypto market. In this paper, we collect the transaction data of 15 exchange addresses on Ethereum which is an open-source public blockchain platform with smart contract functions. By modeling the prediction of the transaction value as a time series prediction problem, we conduct experiments using deep learning-based methods to make predictions. Experimental results show that deep learning is more effective in predicting transaction value compared with traditional methods.

Keywords: Data analysis · Transaction prediction · Deep learnin · Blockchain · Ethereum

1 Introduction

Blockchain technology is characterized by decentralization and anonymity. Therefore, there are many blockchain-based applications such as cryptocurrencies, financial services, and public services [27]. In the last few years, cryptocurrencies have gained much attention in the financial field and the public since their price has increased incredibly. As the underlying technology of cryptocurrencies, blockchain provides a distributed, decentralized, and immutable ledger system for cryptocurrencies.

There are two popular applications of data analysis on cryptocurrencies. On the one hand, we can predict the future prices of cryptocurrencies based on historical prices with deep learning [21]. On the other hand, data analysis can help

ⓒ Springer Nature Singapore Pte Ltd. 2021
H.-N. Dai et al. (Eds.): BlockSys 2021, CCIS 1490, pp. 30–43, 2021.
https://doi.org/10.1007/978-981-16-7993-3_3

regulators identify illegal activities in cryptocurrencies since blockchain-based cryptocurrency has become the new target for criminals. Cryptocurrencies are attractive to criminals because trading partners are pseudonymous in cryptocurrency transactions. In recent years, illegal activities on various blockchain systems happen from time to time, such as scams [26], hacks [2], ransomware [1], and darknet markets [3]. However, all of the transactions between pseudonymous addresses are recorded in the blockchain, which is different from traditional scenarios. The open nature of blockchain helps identify illicit activities based on the traces left by illegal financial activities. For example, some studies have detected phishing scams on Ethereum via network embedding [25], and Ethereum transaction records are modeled as a complex network for analysis [16,17]. Ethereum is a decentralized blockchain framework with a smart contract function and also one of the main cryptocurrencies with the second-largest market assets and user base [10,24].

Besides the above-mentioned illegal behaviors in the cryptocurrency market, there are other illegal behaviors in the cryptocurrency exchanges. As a platform for custodial users' cryptocurrency assets, cryptocurrency exchanges play an important role in the entire cryptocurrency trading market. However, as an emerging market, the cryptocurrency market lacks effective laws to regulate market behaviors. Therefore, many unethical transactions have occurred in the cryptocurrency market, one of which is wash trading created by exchanges [6, 11,23]. In other words, exchanges will fake their trading volume. Trading volume is the number of cryptocurrencies that users trade on the exchange, reflecting the popularity of cryptocurrency exchanges. Due to commercial competition or commercial interests, exchanges tend to create falsely high transaction volumes to induce customers to make more investments or attract new customers.

The exchanges with wash trading will not only mislead users to invest impulsively but also affect the price of some cryptocurrencies and even manipulate the market. Therefore, it is important to analyse whether the exchanges are related to wash trading. In this work, we implement deep learning-based as well as traditional methods to predict the transaction value of some addresses owned by various exchanges. Predicting the transaction value of the addresses can help us identify that the exchanges are faking trading volume if their transaction volume suddenly rises.

With the emergence of deep learning, there have been many deep learning-based implementations for financial applications [19]. Financial time series prediction is a major application in financial field including stock price prediction [5], commodity price prediction [15], and forex price prediction [22], etc. Among them, cryptocurrency price prediction has been a hot topic in recent years [21]. In the existing research work, there are two main types of methods for predicting the price of cryptocurrencies. One includes classical methods like ARIMA [9], and the other is based on machine learning, such as Recurrent Neural Networks (RNNs) [8], Long-short term memory (LSTM) [12] and Gated Recurrent Unit (GRU) [7]. RNNs are the most commonly used in time series prediction while LSTM and GRU are two main variants of RNNs. LSTM is proposed to solve gradient vanishing and gradient exploding with some kind of forgetting and updating mechanisms. Research shows that LSTM achieves better performance in longer sequences than original RNNs [12]. Based on the mechanisms used in LSTM, GRU simplifies the network structure and reduces the time for training. However, LSTM has more parameters and is more suitable for situations with a large number of samples. Some studies have compared the above prediction methods on cryptocurrencies. For example, McNally, Roche, Caton, et al. compare RNN, LSTM, and ARIMA to predict Bitcoin price direction, where Bitcoin is another main cryptocurrency [18]. Their experimental results show that deep learning-based methods outperform traditional methods like ARIMA.

With the inspiration of predicting the price of a specific cryptocurrency, we aim to employ deep learning to predict the transaction value of a particular cryptocurrency based on the transaction records in the past.

Most transaction addresses in Ethereum only have a small number of transactions, and insufficient data cannot provide effective information for time series prediction, especially for models based on deep learning. Cryptocurrency exchanges are platforms for people to trade cryptocurrencies. Exchanges own many account addresses, and these addresses will have frequent transactions [13]. In this article, we collect transaction records of 15 addresses of 4 exchanges from the Ethereum browser etherscan.io[1], and we will dive into it in Sect. 2.

Currently, there is a lack of study on applying time series prediction techniques to Ethereum transaction value prediction. In this paper, we will employ these techniques to predict the transaction on Ethereum. Experiments on real Ethereum transaction records prove the effectiveness of deep learning in predicting the transaction value.

The remaining sections of this paper are arranged as follows: In Sect. 2, we make a definition of our problem and describe the process of data collection and features extraction. Then we describe the framework of our model in Sect. 3. In Sect. 4, we introduce the dataset, metric to evaluate different methods, baseline methods, and parameter settings. By comparing the experimental results, we discuss and analyze the performance of various methods and parameter sensitivity. Finally, in Sect. 5, we draw a conclusion of our work in this paper and point out the direction for future research.

2 Problem Definition

With the historical transactions of addresses, transaction prediction aims to predict the future status of the transaction (e.g. transaction number, transaction value, etc.). In this paper, we focus on predicting the total transaction value in the future.

We divide X, $(X = \{X_1, X_2, \ldots, X_T\})$ into two parts: the training set and the testing test. The training set consists of the data of the first P days, X_i $(i = 1, 2, \ldots, P)$, and the testing set consists of the data of the last Q days, X_j

---

[1] https://etherscan.io/.

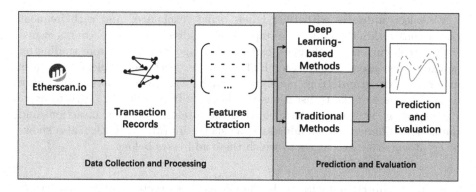

Fig. 1. The two-phase framework of predicting the transaction value in Ethereum: (1) Crawl the transaction records from Etherscan.io and extract features of address pairs in each period; (2) Using deep learning-based methods followed by a Dense layer and traditional methods to predict the transaction value in testing time steps and evaluate the difference between the actual value and the predicted value.

$(j = P+1, P+2, \ldots, P+Q)$. In other words, given the transaction data in the past P days, we aim to predict the transaction value in the coming Q days.

$$X_t = \begin{pmatrix} x_{1,1}^t & x_{1,2}^t & \cdots & x_{1,F}^t \\ x_{2,1}^t & x_{2,2}^t & \cdots & x_{1,F}^t \\ \vdots & \vdots & \ddots & \vdots \\ x_{N,1}^t & x_{N,2}^t & \cdots & x_{N,F}^t \end{pmatrix} \tag{1}$$

Let X_t $(t = 1, 2, \ldots, T)$ be the transaction data of the tth day and T is the number of the total time steps of the collected transaction data. X_t is composed of F features of N addresses as follows, where $x_{i,j}^t$ represents the jth feature of the ith address at the tth time step.

3   Framework of the Model

Our proposed model contains two processes as shown in Fig. 1. Firstly, we collect data in Ethereum, extract some features based on the transactions. Secondly, we employ LSTM and other traditional methods to make predictions and evaluate the performances.

3.1   Data Collection and Features Extraction

Data Collection. In Ethereum, a transaction happens if an amount of "Ether" or "ETH" is sent from an address to another, where "Ether" or "ETH" is the cryptocurrency transferred on Ethereum. Etherscan is an Ethereum explorer and we can get the transaction history of different addresses via APIs. Besides, Etherscan provides labels for some addresses like "exchange", "phishing", "gambling", etc.

We select addresses with their labels being "exchange" and with frequent transactions within the same time steps. These addresses are the accounts owned by the cryptocurrency exchanges, called "exchange wallets". Before trading on the exchanges, users will transfer ETH to these "exchange wallets", which is similar to users transferring money to a Stock Exchange before transferring stocks. The date of the transactions we choose is from June. 22, 2020 to Sept. 9, 2020, totally 80 days. We have counted the total number of transactions and transaction volume of these addresses, as shown in Table 1. Table 1 also shows the cryptocurrency exchanges to which these addresses belong.

Table 1. Descriptive statistics of the dataset and the cryptocurrency exchanges to which the addresses belong.

Address	Transactions	Transaction Volume (Ether)	Exchange
0x0681d8db095565fe8a346fa0277bffde9c0edbbf	493,913	6,365,462.04	Binance[a]
0x3f5ce5fbfe3e9af3971dd833d26ba9b5c936f0be	907,580	27,332,426.38	
0xd551234ae421e3bcba99a0da6d736074f22192ff	511,915	6,806,302.84	
0x0577a79cfc63bbc0df38833ff4c4a3bf2095b404	57,080	1,427,256.99	Huobi[b]
0x28ffe35688ffffd0659aee2e34778b0ae4e193ad	58,560	2,109,219.79	
0x3c979fb790c86e361738ed17588c1e8b4c4cc49a	31,429	1,273,052.26	
0x58c2cb4a6bee98c309215d0d2a38d7f8aa71211c	58,913	2,087,061.80	
0x73f8fc2e74302eb2efda125a326655acf0dc2d1b	60,980	1,529,177.52	
0x794d28ac31bcb136294761a556b68d2634094153	61,001	2,233,078.50	
0xc9610be2843f1618edfedd0860dc43551c727061	61,625	1,470,356.51	
0xf66852bc122fd40bfecc63cd48217e88bda12109	34,248	1,675,785.42	
0x2b5634c42055806a59e9107ed44d43c426e58258	319,334	1,683,430.43	KuCoin[c]
0x689c56aef474df92d44a1b70850f808488f9769c	125,529	1,671,387.56	
0x0211f3cedbef3143223d3acf0e589747933e8527	6,490	207,170.18	MXC[d]
0x75e89d5979e4f6fba9f97c104c2f0afb3f1dcb88	228,480	539,272.19	

[a] Binance (www.binance.com): As of January 2018, Binance was the largest cryptocurrency exchange in the world in terms of trading volume.
[b] Huobi (www.huobi.com): A cryptocurrency exchange founded in China.
[c] KuCoin (www.kucoin.com): One of the fastest growing cryptocurrency exchanges in the world.
[d] MXC (www.mxc.com): The world's first user-friendly digital asset service provider

Features Extraction. The transaction records of addresses include items like *From, To, Value, TimeStamp, TxHash, IsError*, etc. Firstly, we need to divide the dataset into 80 time steps according to the timestamp, with each period being 1 day. Secondly, we calculate the transaction information of all addresses in each time step, such as *tran_num, tran_sum, tran_mean* and *tran_var*. The specific meanings of these features are described in Table 2. The transaction information obtained above constitutes the features of our experiment.

To test the performance of different methods, we divide the dataset into two parts. The first part occupies features in the first 60 days and is used as the training dataset. The second part consists of features in the remaining 20 days and will be used as the test dataset.

Table 2. The notations of the extracted features.

Feature	Meaning
tran_num	the number of transactions
tran_sum	the total transaction value
tran_mean	the average transaction value
tran_var	the variance of the transaction value

3.2   Prediction and Evaluation

In this part, we will employ deep learning-based methods and traditional methods to make predictions and evaluate the performance of these methods.

Firstly, Standardization is an important step before training the model. Using the scaled data in the training set to fit the model, we will predict the transaction value with a de-standardization in the testing set with the trained model.

Then, we use a sliding window mechanism during training and testing as is shown in Fig. 2. The window length l is the number of time steps of each sequence that consists of the transaction data. We use the previous data of the transactions in l days to predict the transaction value in the $(l + 1)^{th}$ day and the window keeps moving backward.

At last, we will employ deep learning-based methods followed by a dense layer [20] to gain an output. We employ three kinds of RNN-based methods, which are general RNN, LSTM, and GRU.

RNN [21] is a deep learning network applied to time series or sequential data. The RNN model architecture consists of different numbers of layers and different types of units in each layer. The RNN unit accepts current and previous input data at the same time. The output depends on the previous data in the RNN model. RNNs process the input sequences one by one at any given time during operation. The units of the hidden layer use the "state vector" to store historical information. RNN structure has a backward dependence over time. Thus, RNN becomes increasingly complicated as the learning period increases. Studies have shown that when knowledge is stored for a long time, it is not easy to learn the long-term dependencies with RNN. To solve this problem, LSTM was proposed.

LSTM [21] is a type of RNN where the network is able to remember short-term as well as long-term values. LSTM models are mostly used for time-series data. The LSTM network is composed of different numbers of LSTM layers, and the LSTM layer is composed of LSTM units. An LSTM unit consists of a series of cells, and each cell regulates the information flow through three gates: input gate, output gate and forget gate. The gate mechanism allows these cells to memorize information over different periods. The form of the forward pass of the LSTM unit is shown in the following formula (x_t: the input vector, f_t: the activation vector of the forget gate, i_t: the activation vector of the input gate, o_t: the activation vector of the output gate, h_t: the LSTM unit's output vector, c_t: the state vector of the cell, σ_g, σ_h: sigmoid function, hyperbolic tangent function, $*$: Hadamard product, W, U and b: weight matrices and the bias vectors to be learned).

$$f_t = \sigma_g(W_f x_t + U_f h_{t-1} + b_f) \tag{2}$$

$$i_t = \sigma_g(W_i x_t + U_i h_{t-1} + b_i) \tag{3}$$

$$o_t = \sigma_g(W_o x_t + U_o h_{t-1} + b_o) \tag{4}$$

$$c_t = f_t * c_{t-1} + i_t * \sigma_h(W_c x_t + U_c h_{t-1} + b_c) \tag{5}$$

$$h_t = o_t * \sigma_h(c_t) \tag{6}$$

GRU [7] is another gating mechanism in RNNs. GRU is similar to LSTM but has fewer parameters as it lacks an output gate. GRU has two gates: the reset gate and the update gate. Intuitively speaking, the reset gate determines how to combine the new input information with the previous memory, and the update gate defines the amount of the previous memory stored to the current time step. The form of the forward pass of the GRU unit is shown in the following equations (x_t: the input vector, h_t: the output vector, $\hat{h}_t$: the candidate activation vector, z_t: the update gate vector, r_t: the reset gate vector, W, U and b: weight matrices and the bias vector to be learned, σ_g, σ_h: sigmoid function and hyperbolic tangent function).

$$z_t = \sigma_g(W_z x_t + U_z h_{t-1} + b_z) \tag{7}$$

$$r_t = \sigma_g(W_r x_t + U_r h_{t-1} + b_r) \tag{8}$$

$$\hat{h}_t = \sigma_h(W_h x_t + U_h(r_t * h_{t-1} + b_h)) \tag{9}$$

$$h_t = (1 - z_t) * h_{t-1} + z_t * \hat{h}_t \tag{10}$$

Besides deep learning-based methods, we will carry out experiments of other traditional prediction methods and evaluate the performances by comparing the predicted values and the real values of the testing data. The evaluation metrics will be covered in the following section.

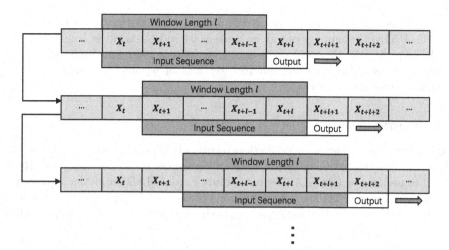

Fig. 2. Sliding window mechanism

4 Experiment

4.1 Methods and Experimental Setup

In this part, we compare deep learning-based methods with some traditional time series prediction methods from the fields of time series analysis and machine learning.

Historical Average (HA) uses the average value of training time series as the prediction results. HA should have a poor performance for simply averaging the historical transaction value for prediction, and it can be regarded as the lower bound of all methods. Autoregressive Integrated Moving Average (ARIMA) [9] is an advanced method for time series analysis and prediction which is widely applied in the financial field. Support Vector Regression (SVR) [4] is an important application of Support Vector Machine (SVM). By using kernel functions, SVR maps the data to high-dimension space and finds a hyperplane closest to the data. XGBoost Regression (XGBR) and Random Forest Regression (RF) uses decision trees for prediction.

We compare different methods based on deep learning: (1) Vanilla RNN [8], using the simplest RNN structure, lacking in the ability to remember long-term dependency; (2) Long-short Term Memory (LSTM) [12] neural network is specially developed to solve the long-term dependency of vanilla RNN by controlling the transmission rate through three gates. The gate mechanism helps LSTM remember the important features and forget the unimportant information; (3) Gated Recurrent Unit (GRU) [7] simplifies the structure of LSTM and achieves a close performance of LSTM.

The parameters of LSTM are set as follows: Training epochs is 10, learning rate $lr = 0.001$, and number of hidden units in LSTM is 64. We select Adam [14] as the optimizer and MSE as the loss function in the training process. For

GRU, the number of hidden units is 128 and the window length is 16. For RNN (vanilla RNN), the number of hidden units is 64 and the window length is 2. As for RF and XGBR, the total number of trees kept is 1000, and for SVR, we use a linear kernel. Also, we tried different settings of parameters and choose the optimal values for all methods.

4.2   Metric

To evaluate the transaction prediction results of different methods, we employ three metrics that are commonly used in regression problems. They are Root Mean Square Error (RMSE), Mean Absolute Error (MAE), and Mean Absolute Percentage Error (MAPE). The definitions of the metrics are shown as follows, where m is the size of the testing set, y_i is the real value, and $\hat{y}_i$ is the predicted value.

$$RMSE = \sqrt{\frac{1}{m}\sum_{i=1}^{m}(y_i - \hat{y}_i)^2} \tag{11}$$

$$MAE = \frac{1}{m}\sum_{i=1}^{m}|(y_i - \hat{y}_i)| \tag{12}$$

$$MAPE = \frac{1}{m}\sum_{i=1}^{m}|\frac{\hat{y}_i - y_i}{y_i}| \tag{13}$$

4.3   Results and Discussions

Predictive Performance. As Table 3 shows, the prediction models based on deep learning achieve better performance compared with all other methods in terms of RMSE. Among the rest methods, ARIMA outperforms the others in terms of the three metrics. ARIMA is more suitable for stationary series or stationary series after difference. The time series of transaction value does not have such stationarity, so this type of model may be unsuitable. SVR, XGBR, and RF achieve the worse performance. One of the reasons may be that they are developed from SVM, XGBoost, and Random Forest which are proposed to solve classification or clustering instead of regression.

The methods based on RNNs are superior to other methods because RNNs are designed for processing time-series data and able to better capture temporal information. Vanilla RNN achieves the worse performance compared with LSTM and GRU because it cannot solve the problem of long-term dependency. However, LSTM and GRU have a gated mechanism to deal with this problem and achieve better performance.

In Fig. 3, we select 4 addresses and plot the curve of the real transaction value in testing time steps (20 days) and the prediction of various methods. The blue solid line stands for the real transaction value, and the pink dashed one represents the predicted value of the method based on LSTM. The pink

Table 3. Performance comparison of various methods.

Categories	Method	Metric		
		RMSE	MAE	MAPE
Traditional	HA	65,159.78	26,004.54	0.49
	SVR	41,397.52	20,079.42	0.46
	ARIMA	*32,591.02*	*15,886.03*	*0.43*
	XGBR	46,947.51	22,290.52	0.53
	RF	39,062.45	18,429.13	0.47
Deep Learning-based	LSTM	15,762.72	**10,488.73**	**0.42**
	GRU	**15,591.35**	10,640.56	0.45
	RNN	17,538.17	12,590.90	0.50

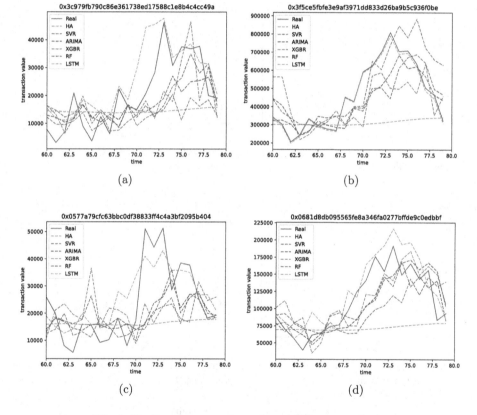

Fig. 3. Predicted transaction value of different methods.

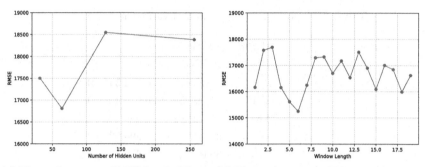

(a) The performance of LSTM with different (b) The performance of LSTM with different
number of hidden units   window lengths

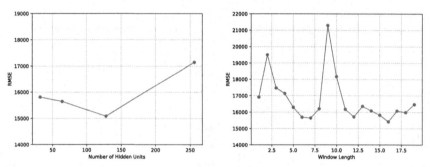

(c) The performance of GRU with different (d) The performance of GRU with different
number of hidden units   window lengths

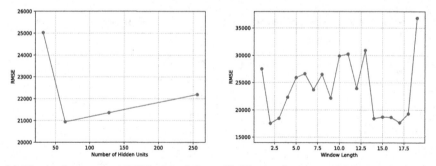

(e) The performance of RNN with different (f) The performance of RNN with different
number of hidden units   window lengths

Fig. 4. Parameter sensitivity

lines fit the blue lines better than any other lines as in scale and trend. Since
the predicted curves of GRU and RNN are similar to LSTM, we only show the
curve of LSTM among the RNN-based methods.

Parameter Sensitivity. For the method based on LSTM, there are some parameters that affect the results. In Fig. 4, considering RMSE as the performance metric, we evaluate the effects of the chosen parameters: the number of hidden units in LSTM, GRU as well as RNN, and the window length of the shifting window. To evaluate how the number of hidden units and the window length affect the performance, we gradually increase the number of hidden units from 32 to 256, and the window length from 1 to 20.

As is shown in Fig. 4(a), the optimal number of hidden units of LSTM is 64. In Fig. 4(b), the performance of the models with different window lengths is unstable. On the one hand, when the window length is too small, the sequence is too short to capture the temporal information of the historical transaction value. On the other hand, when the window length is too large, establishing memory for a long sequence may cause over-fitting. The optimal window length of LSTM is 6 in our proposed model. Figure 4(c), Fig. 4(d), Fig. 4(e) and Fig. 4(f) shows that the optimal number of hidden units of GRU and RNN are 128 and 64, respectively. The optimal window lengths of GRU and RNN are 16 and 2.

5 Conclusions and Future Work

In this paper, firstly we conduct a systematic study on financial time series prediction, specifically in cryptocurrencies. Then we present a new perspective to predict the transaction value in Ethereum and propose a two-phase framework. In the first phase, we collect transaction data of cryptocurrency exchanges from Etherscan and extract features from the original data. In the second phase, we employ deep learning methods, specifically RNNs to learn the temporal information of the historical transaction and make predictions. Besides, we conduct experiments of some traditional time series prediction techniques. Experimental results demonstrate that methods with deep learning can achieve better performance with lower RMSE, MAE, and MAPE compared with other traditional techniques. It proves that deep learning-based methods are suitable for prediction in scenarios of large-scale and long-term data, such as Ethereum.

In the future, we will apply the proposed method to other cryptocurrency systems and further evaluate the inductivity of the method.

Acknowledgments. The work described in this paper is supported by the National Key R&D Program of China (2020YFB1006005), the National Natural Science Foundation of China (61973325, U1811462).

References

1. Azmoodeh, A., Dehghantanha, A., Conti, M., Choo, K.K.R.: Detecting crypto-ransomware in IoT networks based on energy consumption footprint. J. Ambient. Intell. Humaniz. Comput. **9**(4), 1141–1152 (2018)
2. Boireau, O.: Securing the blockchain against hackers. Netw. Secur. **2018**(1), 8–11 (2018)

3. Broadhurst, R., et al.: Malware trends on 'darknet'crypto-markets: Research review. Available at SSRN 3226758 (2018)

4. Castro-Neto, M., Jeong, Y.S., Jeong, M.K., Han, L.D.: Online-SVR for short-term traffic flow prediction under typical and atypical traffic conditions. Expert Syst. Appl. **36**(3), 6164–6173 (2009)

5. Chen, K., Zhou, Y., Dai, F.: A LSTM-based method for stock returns prediction: a case study of china stock market. In: Proceedings of 2015 IEEE International Conference on Big Data, pp. 2823–2824. IEEE, Santa Clara (2015)

6. Chen, W., Zheng, Z., Cui, J., Ngai, E., Zheng, P., Zhou, Y.: Detecting ponzi schemes on ethereum: towards healthier blockchain technology. In: Proceedings of the 2018 World Wide Web Conference, pp. 1409–1418 (2018)

7. Cho, K., et al.: Learning phrase representations using RNN encoder-decoder for statistical machine translation. arXiv preprint arXiv:1406.1078 (2014)

8. Connor, J.T., Martin, R.D., Atlas, L.E.: Recurrent neural networks and robust time series prediction. IEEE Trans. Neural Networks **5**(2), 240–254 (1994)

9. Contreras, J., Espinola, R., Nogales, F.J., Conejo, A.J.: Arima models to predict next-day electricity prices. IEEE Trans. Power Syst. **18**(3), 1014–1020 (2003)

10. Crosby, M., Pattanayak, P., Verma, S., Kalyanaraman, V., et al.: Blockchain technology: beyond bitcoin. Appl. Innov. **2**(6–10), 71 (2016)

11. Gandal, N., Halaburda, H.: Can we predict the winner in a market with network effects? competition in cryptocurrency market. Games **7**(3), 16 (2016)

12. Gers, F.A., Schmidhuber, J., Cummins, F.: Learning to forget: continual prediction with LSTM. In: Proceedings of International Conference on Artificial Neural Networks, pp. 850–855 (1999)

13. Hileman, G., Rauchs, M.: Global cryptocurrency benchmarking study. Cambridge Centre Altern. Finance **33**, 33–113 (2017)

14. Kingma, D.P., Ba, J.: Adam: a method for stochastic optimization. arXiv preprint arXiv:1412.6980 (2014)

15. Lasheras, F.S., de Cos Juez, F.J., Sánchez, A.S., Krzemień, A., Fernández, P.R.: Forecasting the comex copper spot price by means of neural networks and arima models. Resour. Policy **45**, 37–43 (2015)

16. Lin, D., Wu, J., Yuan, Q., Zheng, Z.: Modeling and understanding ethereum transaction records via a complex network approach. IEEE Trans. Circuits Syst. II Express Briefs **67**(11), 2737–2741 (2020)

17. Lin, D., Wu, J., Yuan, Q., Zheng, Z.: T-edge: Temporal weighted multidigraph embedding for ethereum transaction network analysis. Front. Phys. **8**, 204 (2020)

18. McNally, S., Roche, J., Caton, S.: Predicting the price of bitcoin using machine learning. In: Proceedings of Euromicro International Conference on Parallel, Distributed and Network-based Processing, pp. 339–343. IEEE, Cambridge (2018)

19. Ozbayoglu, A.M., Gudelek, M.U., Sezer, O.B.: Deep learning for financial applications: a survey. Appl. Soft Comput. **93**, 106384 (2020)

20. Sainath, T.N., Vinyals, O., Senior, A., Sak, H.: Convolutional, long short-term memory, fully connected deep neural networks. In: Proceedings of IEEE International Conference on Acoustics, Speech and Signal Processing, Brisbane, QLD, Australia, pp. 4580–4584 (2015)

21. Sezer, O.B., Gudelek, M.U., Ozbayoglu, A.M.: Financial time series forecasting with deep learning: a systematic literature review: 2005–2019. Appl. Soft Comput. **90**, 106181 (2020)

22. Shen, H., Liang, X.: A time series forecasting model based on deep learning integrated algorithm with stacked autoencoders and SVR for FX prediction. In: Villa, A.E.P., Masulli, P., Pons Rivero, A.J. (eds.) A time series forecasting model based on deep learning integrated algorithm with stacked autoencoders and SVR for FX prediction. LNCS, vol. 9887, pp. 326–335. Springer, Cham (2016). https://doi.org/10.1007/978-3-319-44781-0_39

23. Sood, A.K., Bansal, R., Enbody, R.J.: Cybercrime: dissecting the state of underground enterprise. IEEE Internet Comput. **17**(1), 60–68 (2012)

24. Wood, G.: Ethereum: a secure decentralised generalised transaction ledger. Ethereum Project Yellow Paper **151**(2014), 1–32 (2014)

25. Wu, J., et al.: Who are the phishers? phishing scam detection on ethereum via network embedding. IEEE Trans. Syst. Man Cybern. Syst. To be published, https://doi.org/10.1109/TSMC.2020.3016821

26. Zetzsche, D.A., Buckley, R.P., Arner, D.W., Föhr, L.: The ICO gold rush: It's a scam, it's a bubble, it's a super challenge for regulators. University of Luxembourg Law Working Paper (11), pp. 17–83 (2017)

27. Zheng, Z., Xie, S., Dai, H., Chen, X., Wang, H.: Blockchain challenges and opportunities: a survey. Int. J. Web Grid Serv. **14**(4), 352–375 (2018)

Portraits of Typical Accounts
in Ethereum Transaction Network

Yijun Xia[1,2], Jieli Liu[1,2], Jiatao Zheng[1,2], Jiajing Wu[1,2(✉)], and Xiaokang Su[3]

[1] School of Computer Science and Engineering, Sun Yat-sen University,
Guangzhou 510006, China
`wujiajing@mail.sysu.edu.cn`
[2] National Engineering Research Center of Digital Life, Sun Yat-sen University,
Guangzhou 510006, China
[3] WeBank, Shenzhen 518055, China

Abstract. Ethereum is the largest blockchain system supporting Turing-complete smart contracts. In recent years, we have witnessed its boom and popularity in various applications. However, since users use pseudonyms in Ethereum, it is hard to know the true identity behind an account. Meanwhile, a large number of cyber-crimes in Ethereum emerged and have been reported. Therefore, it is an important task to analyze the transaction behavior of accounts in Ethereum and conduct account portraits based on the honest and public information which is transaction records. Although facing the anonymity challenge of blockchain, it makes this task possible that some Ethereum analysis platforms provide ground truth by classifying accounts into specific types. However, prior work tried to dig out features of one certain account type but lack of a comparative analysis of multi-class account types. In this paper, we model the partial Ethereum transaction data as a transaction network, then portray the characteristics of six types of accounts in Ethereum according to the obtained labels from both transaction statistics perspective and network structure perspective. Moreover, we adopt a Graph Convolutional Network (GCN)-based model to distinguish different kinds of accounts to verify the effectiveness of the properties we choose. The experimental results show that our model performs well in classifying various types of accounts in Ethereum.

Keywords: Blockchain · Ethereum · Network analysis · Account portrait

1 Introduction

Blockchain, originated from the foundational technique of Bitcoin proposed by "Satoshi Nakamoto" in 2008 [11], is a new type of distributed ledger database based on peer-to-peer (P2P) network, cryptography, and consensus mechanism. With a blockchain system, transactions between two peers can be efficient, verifiable, and permanently recorded without a trusted third party. Besides,

H.-N. Dai et al. (Eds.): BlockSys 2021, CCIS 1490, pp. 44–56, 2021.
https://doi.org/10.1007/978-981-16-7993-3_4

blockchain solves some problems widely existing in centralized organizations, such as high maintenance costs, low operation efficiency in cross-border trading, etc.

Ethereum [16] is the first open-source blockchain platform enabling smart contracts [13], which are self-executed contract programs running inside the Ethereum Virtual Machine (EVM). Due to the support of smart contracts, decentralized applications (DApps) can be deployed in Ethereum. And it is for this reason that Ethereum is well known as the foundation of blockchain 2.0. Since the launch of Ethereum in 2015, Ethereum has attracted a lot of attention. The main currency in Ethereum, namely Ether (abbreviation ETH), is the second-largest cryptocurrency with a market cap of more than 50 billion dollars[1].

Up to now, Ethereum has been widely used in commercial applications, and now there are more than 3,000 DApps in Ethereum based on the statistics of DappOnline[2], including DApps belonging to the types of exchanges, games, finance, etc.

User behaviors are widely different from each other in Ethereum due to the existence of rich types of applications. That is to say, accounts in Ethereum essentially belong to specific and diverse types.

Thus, characterizing the transaction behaviors and painting portraits for Ethereum accounts is a meaningful task in Ethereum ecology understanding, personalized DApp recommendation, and service analysis. However, since users use pseudonyms to transact with each other in Ethereum, which is a significant property of blockchain systems, it is difficult for us to directly know the ownership behind the accounts. In particular, various and considerable cyber-crimes in Ethereum emerged and have been reported for the last few years, such as Ponzi schemes [1,5], honeypot scams [15], phishing scams [19], etc. In 2018, scammers in Etheruem illegally obtain over $36 million, double the $17 million in 2017 according to a report from Chainalysis [2], a company tracking information of cryptocurrency ecosystem, indicating that it has been a critical issue to recognize tricksters and hackers behind malicious accounts. Hence depicting account portraits plays a positive and significant role in promoting the healthy development of the Ethereum ecosystem, since it assists us in understanding the transaction behaviors of accounts, even though the pseudonymous nature of Ethereum makes it a more challenging task.

Fortunately, all the data of transaction records between any two accounts in Ethereum are publicly accessible. Not only that, some Ethereum analysis platforms have collected label information of partial accounts or labeled accounts by themselves, setting forth an opportunity to characterize the transaction behaviors for certain types of accounts and mine the entity categories behind pseudo-anonymous accounts.

Prior studies [6,7,12,19,20] showed their work focusing on one certain account type in Ethereum and conducting detailed analysis. Through a comprehensive comparison of them, we can get to know that different types of accounts

---

[1] https://coinmarketcap.com/.
[2] https://dapponline.io/big-data.

indeed tend to have completely different purposes as well as transaction behaviors as a result. Among them, apart from the phishing accounts detection framework proposed by [19], no detection methods on the specific account types were put forward by the other three works. To this end, a study which unifies analysis about diverse Ethereum account types and classification method on these accounts is necessary, valuable, and can help us to compare different types of accounts more intuitively.

In this paper, we conduct account portraits on six typical Ethereum account types based on transaction records, namely ICO wallet account, converter account, exchange account, mining account, gambling account, and phish account. As shown in Fig. 1, the overall framework in this paper contains three steps. Firstly, we crawl the label information and the corresponding transaction records belonging to the labels in Ethereum from a famous blockchain explorer named Etherscan[3]. After constructing an Ethereum transaction network, we extract features for each account from a transaction perspective and a network perspective, then perform statistical analysis to characterize the features of each account type. Finally, we train a Graph Convolutional Network (GCN)-based model to execute the classification task on the multi-class account types. Details of the six types of accounts are as below:

1. **ICO wallet:** Accounts belong to ICO (Initial Coin Offering) wallets are used to receive the raised fund for an ICO project.
2. **Converter:** Accounts of wallets that provide users with automatic token conversion services.
3. **Exchange:** Accounts belonging to exchanges such as Binance, Huobi, usually include hot wallets, cold wallets, and temporary wallets.
4. **Mining:** Accounts of mining pools that users can join in to contribute computing power.
5. **Gambling:** Accounts belonging to gambling services like crypto-games in Ethereum.
6. **Phish:** Fraudulent accounts detected by platform or reported by users.

The remainder of this paper is organized as follows. We first summarize related past work in Sect. 2. Then we provide an account characteristic measurement on the mentioned six account types in Sect. 3. From the analytic results, we build a classification model according to the recognized features. Section 4 presents the account classification experiment and its results. Finally, we briefly conclude this paper in Sect. 5.

2   Related Work

Recently many studies have been devoted into the transaction data analysis in Ethereum.

---

[3] http://etherscan.io/.

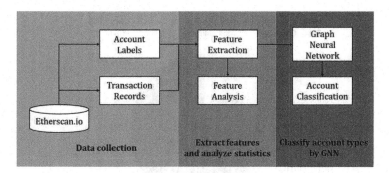

Fig. 1. The overall framework of multi-class accounts analysis and classification.

For data analysis from various angles, Hu et al. [8] analyzed the transaction data of over 10,000 smart contracts collected from Ethereum and found out four behavior patterns, then constructed features from them to distinguish different types of contracts. Although differ in research objectives, our work is similar to theirs on analyzing behaviors based on transactions followed by classifying objectives using the features. Wu et al. [18] summarized existing research on cryptocurrency transaction analysis from a network perspective which contains three aspects, i.e. network modeling, network profiling, and network-based detection. Chen et al. [4] modeled the smart contract creation, smart contract invocation, and money transfer activities as three independent networks and conducted an analysis on them from the perspective of complex network. Lin et al. [9] constructed a temporal weighted multidigraph to model the Ethereum transaction data. Wu et al. [17] provided a feature-based network analysis framework considered attributed temporal heterogeneous motifs to identify statistical properties of mixing services in Bitcoin.

In particular, for certain account type analysis, Fenu et al. [7] gathered information of 1837 ICO tokens in Ethereum and performed a multivariate analysis to find the factors that most likely influence the success of an ICO. To analyze the selfish mining in Ethereum, Niu et al. [6] model the behavior of a selfish mining strategy by applying a 2-dimensional Markov process and compute its long-term average mining rewards. Scholten et al. [12] found that top-ranked crypto-games in Ethereum satisfy the definition of gambling from a legal and psychological perspective after analyzing their typical technical features and gameplay. Wu et al. [10,19] proposed two embedding methods incorporating the temporal and financial properties of the Ethereum transaction network to detect phishing accounts. Chen et al. [5] characterized the illicit accounts involving in Ponzi scams with features extracted from the ether flow graph and opcodes. Tasca et al. [14] analyzed the transaction behaviors of four types of Bitcoin addresses, including exchange, miner, gambling, and black market.

However, very few researches provides a full feature portrait on different kinds of accounts in Ethereum, which is important in some downstream tasks like account de-anonymity and service recommendation.

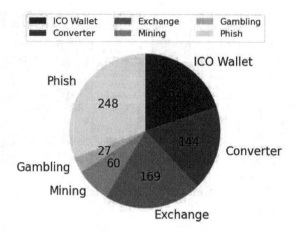

Fig. 2. The number of six types of typical Ethereum accounts we collected.

3   Account Characteristic Measurement

In this section, we conduct the first and the second steps of the framework. In detail, we present the data collection process firstly. Secondly, we describe the extracted features from two different perspectives. Finally, we perform the statistical results and summarize the characteristics of these six types of Ethereum accounts.

3.1   Data Collection

We collect 810 accounts with ground-truth labels from Etherscan, which are comprised of 162 ICO wallet accounts, 144 converter accounts, 169 exchange accounts, 60 mining accounts, 27 gambling accounts, and 248 phish accounts as shown in Fig. 2. To construct the Ethereum transaction network, we treat each labeled account as a central account, then we obtain transaction records of all its one-hop neighbor accounts (accounts trading with the central accounts) and randomly selected partial two-hop neighbor accounts (accounts trading with the one-hop neighbor accounts but not trading with the central accounts) since the volume of the transaction records is massive. In spite of this, while the number of central accounts is only 810, the number of neighbor accounts we collected has reached 635,271.

For each transaction record, it has a sender, a receiver, and other extra properties including the height of the block containing this transaction, timestamp, transferring amount, whether successful, etc. Furthermore, all neighbor accounts of the labeled central accounts are treated as unlabeled accounts regardless of whether they are labeled actually in Etherscan. After collecting all the data we need, a directed multi-edges Ethereum transaction network can be formed, and it contains 636,081 nodes and 3,691,579 edges totally.

3.2   Feature Characterization

We characterize the behaviors of different types of accounts based on the features we extracted from two perspectives.

1) Transaction Statistics Features. Aiming to characterize the transaction preference of accounts, for one account, we extract some basic statistics of it considering all of its successful transactions. The final statistics include 6 types of information: total transaction amount, total transaction number, average transaction amount, transaction frequency, number of one-hop neighbor accounts, and balance. Excluding balance information, the first five types will be formed into respective features based on two opposite transaction directions. By doing so, each of them corresponds to the 3 feature types, namely in-transactions, out-transactions, and the ratio of the first two. In order to explain clearly, we name the features as *Type_Direction*. For example, *Amount_In* represents the total in-transaction amount of an account. Then we apply the mean or median method on values of all accounts of a certain type to compare the different account types. It should be noted that the time span involved in calculating frequency refers to the difference between the timestamp of the earliest transaction record and the latest transaction record. In addition, we use the final balance (named *Balance*) and the peak balance (named *BalancePeak*) during all transactions as features while the initial balance of an account is treated as 0. At last, we extract 17 transaction features (i.e., $5 \times 3 + 2$).

2) Network Structure Features. The network structure features aim to not simply calculate values of transactions by adding up while ignoring relations among multiple transactions like transaction statistics features do, but treat each transaction and its one next transaction (or its one previous transaction) as a simple topological structure, then count the respective appearance frequencies of different kinds of structures to dig out the interaction behavior characteristic of accounts. As shown in Fig. 3, there are six types of transaction-based network structure, where the red node represents the central node, the green and the blue node represent the neighbor nodes, the weights of edges represent the order in which transaction occur. For example, in structure *c*, the central account transfers money to the account represented by the green node firstly, then receives money from the account represented by the blue node secondly.

3.3   Analysis Results

From the transaction statistics perspective, we summarize the statistics of some significant features and show them in Table 1. From the network structure perspective, we illustrate the distinct distribution of all transaction-based structures through Fig. 4. from which we can characterize the Ethereum accounts in different types. In order to make it clear, we bold the maximum and minimum values of each metric for each feature among six accounts.

ICO Wallet: The ICO wallet accounts have maximal values of *BalancePeak* while they have relatively large values of *Number_In* and *Number_Out*, which

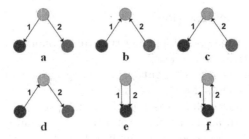

Fig. 3. The six types of transaction-based network structure.

Table 1. Partial transaction features statistics of labeled ethereum accounts.

Feature	Method	Account type					
		ICO wallet	Converter	Exchange	Mining	Gambling	Phish
Amount_In	Mean	7.6e+04	3912.36	**6.8e+05**	3.5e+03	4938.03	**84.82**
	Median	2.2e+04	15.92	**3.0e+04**	17.98	1249.75	**11.55**
Amount_Out	Mean	6.2e+04	2197.52	**6.3e+05**	3.3e+04	4179.48	**54.17**
	Median	2.0e+04	15.75	**2.4e+04**	9.5e+03	139.21	**11.00**
Number_In	Mean	2342.56	1962.88	3677.89	27.00	**6047.52**	**22.73**
	Median	3454.50	1193.00	1742.00	4.00	**8914.00**	10.00
Number_Out	Mean	224.26	172.30	5689.38	**7129.22**	4753.44	**11.86**
	Median	100.75	6.00	6231.00	**9987.00**	1927.00	**2.00**
Balance	Mean	1.4e+04	1714.84	**4.8e+04**	−2.9e+04[1]	758.55	30.65
	Median	10.02	0.00	**557.51**	−8303.89[2]	2.97	2.0e-03
BalancePeak	Mean	**6.3e+04**	3097.35	3.0e+05	1455.98	2.5e+03	**71.63**
	Median	**1.8e+04**	2.73	4738.12	**0.00**	247.96	9.48

[1,2]The values are negative because Etherscan can only display the latest 100,000 transactions of an account, so the older transactions are ignored

corresponds with its role of receiving money transferred from users to support ICO projects.

Converter: The structure a is mostly rare while the structure b is mostly large in transactions of the converter accounts as shown in Fig. 4, indicating that they always receive multiple transfers from different accounts in succession but hardly transfer out twice or more in a row. In addition, it's obvious that the type of account whose average value of the proportion of structure b is the converter account.

Exchange: As a service that enables clients to trade cryptocurrencies for other resources, an exchange always has connections with a large group of users and a massive money flow. It is distinctive that the $Amount_In$ and $Amount_Out$ of the exchange accounts are significantly large among these kinds of accounts as well as its balance.

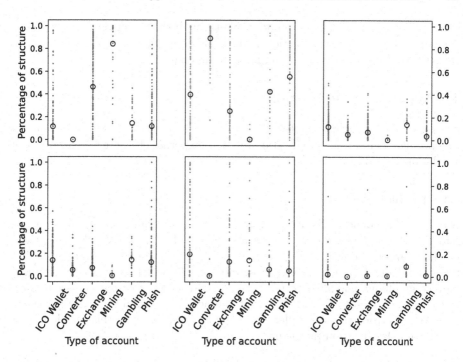

Fig. 4. Network structure proportions of labeled Ethereum accounts. Six subgraphs correspond to structure a (blue), b (orange), c (green), d (red), e (purple) and f (brown) in sequence. For each subgraph, each dot represents a labeled account (totally 810 dots in the subgraph), the x-axis is the type of account, the y-axis is the percentage of the corresponding structure among all structures counted based on transactions of an account. The black circle represents the average of all percentage values in its column. In this way, we can see the distribution of a certain structure of a certain type of Ethereum account. (Color figure online)

Mining: In the scenario of mining pools, a mining account transfers money to the accounts of participants as a reward. From the statistics, we can observe that its *Number_Out* is obviously large, and the main transaction-based structure of it is almost either a or e, indicating its continuous out-transactions. Moreover, the mining account exceeds other account types too much on their average value of the proportion of structure a.

Gambling: The *Number_In* of gambling accounts are large compared to the other types of accounts, while their transaction amount features are inconspicuous. From this, we can infer that the users who want to participate in gambling services like crypto-games have formed a large group.

Phish: The phish accounts are noticeable through the extremely small value of amount and number of transactions, which indicates victims in Ethereum often fall into fraud or phish scam losing a small amount.

4   Account Classification

In this section, we utilize the features to distinguish different kinds of accounts. The problem definition, classification method, experimental settings, and results are detailed as follows.

4.1   Problem Definition

Let $G = (V, E)$ denotes the Ethereum transaction network, where V is the node set, E is the edge set. Let V_L represents the set of all labeled nodes, and their labels compose the set Y. $Y \in \mathbb{R}^{|V| \times |\mathcal{L}|}$, where L represents the set of label types, i.e. 0, 1, 2, 3, 4, and 5 for accounts of ICO wallet, converter, exchange, mining, gambling, and phish respectively. After discussing the features we extract from transaction records, we construct the account portraits for the six types of accounts. To distinguish different account types, we treat this problem as a multi-class classification problem.

4.2   Method

We construct the Ethereum transaction network as an undirected single-edge network where each node represents an account and each edge represents the transaction relationship between a pair of accounts. In this task, we apply a Graph Convolutional Network (GCN)-based model to classify different types of accounts. With the GCN-based model, central nodes can learn the neighborhood information by aggregating their features while their labels are not needed. Here we apply FastGCN [3], which is a fast learning GCN method with importance sampling. Moreover, we compare its performance with traditional machine learning methods including Decision Tree, Logistic Regression, and KNN which only utilize the features of accounts while ignoring the network topology.

Table 2. Performance comparisons of different methods.

Method	Precision	Recall	F1
FastGCN	**0.8209**	**0.8450**	**0.8270**
Decision Tree	0.8164	0.8080	0.8079
SVM	0.6944	0.6579	0.6420
Logistic Regression	0.6005	0.6496	0.5779
KNN	0.8217	0.7284	0.7442

4.3   Experimental Settings

We set the training epoch as 200, the learning rate lr as 0.01, and set the number of hidden units in the first layer of FastGCN as 128. Besides, because there exists an extreme unbalance between labeled accounts and unlabeled accounts, we set a sampling rate to randomly sample the unlabeled accounts and merge them with the labeled accounts to build the sub-networks. As the sampling rate changing from 1.0, 0.9, 0.8, and 0.7, we get four sub-networks namely G1, G2, G3, and G4 corresponding to 636,081, 571,744, 508,217, and 444,690 nodes in total. We divide all labeled nodes into training set, validation set, and test set according to the ratio of 7:1:2. We repeat the experiment 5 times for each sub-network and record the average of the results.

Table 3. Performance comparisons of different sampling ratio.

Data	Sampling Ratio	Precision	Recall	F1
G1	1.0	0.8209	0.8450	0.8270
G2	0.9	0.8033	0.8328	0.8101
G3	0.8	0.8861	0.8248	0.8386
G4	0.7	0.8373	0.8379	0.8168

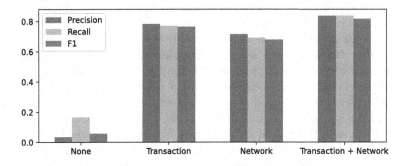

Fig. 5. Performance comparisons of different features.

To evaluate the multi-class classification results of this task, we choose the following metrics: precision, recall, and F1. Their computation formulas are as follows:

$$\text{Precision} = \frac{\text{true positive}}{\text{true positive } + \text{ false positive}},$$

$$\text{Recall} = \frac{\text{true positive}}{\text{true positive } + \text{ false negative}},$$

$$\text{F1} = \frac{2 \cdot \text{Precision} \cdot \text{Recall}}{\text{Precision} + \text{Recall}}.$$

4.4   Experimental Results

We first compare the performance among different kinds of classification models as shown in Table 2. We can observe that FastGCN achieves better performance compared to other traditional machine learning methods since it not only utilizes the feature information but also makes use of the network topology information.

We then adjust the sampling ratio of unlabeled accounts to test the changes in the performance while keeping other settings the same. According to Table 3, the experimental results show that our framework achieves a good performance among various sampling ratios. Besides, it is not absolute that the more complete the network is, the better performance will be.

Finally, we compare the performance among different features on G4, which has a corresponding sampling ratio of 0.7. With only the adjacency matrix, or the transaction statistics features, or the network structure features, or both of them as the input of FastGCN, we obtain the classification results and show them in Fig. 5. From the results, we can see that our features play an important role in effective classification. In addition, the combination of transaction statistics features and network structure features lead to the best performance since they learn neighborhood information from the different view.

5   Conclusion and Future Work

With the development of blockchain technology, a growing number of users have participated in studying and using blockchains. As the first open-source blockchain system enabling smart contracts, Ethereum occupies a huge market cap only after Bitcoin. Since users use pseudonyms in their transaction process, it is hard to know the true identity behind an account, which hinders the personalized service recommendation and regulation in Ethereum.

In this paper, we conducted account portraits on Ethereum accounts based on the real transaction data, aiming to provide a brief overview of the transaction characterises of the typical account types. We mainly focused on six types of accounts, including ICO wallet accounts, converter accounts, exchange accounts, mining accounts, gambling accounts, and phish accounts. After extracting various kinds of features from a transaction statistics perspective and a network structure perspective then perform statistical analysis to characterize these accounts, we constructed a transaction network based on their transaction records. Furthermore, we trained a GCN-based model to distinguish these accounts into various types. Experimental results showed us our model has good performance in characterizing and classifying these six kinds of accounts. In the future, we consider modeling the transaction network into a time-involving network to preserve richer information and characterize Ethereum accounts more accurately.

Acknowledgments. The work described in this paper is supported by the Guangdong Applied R&D Program (2015B010131006), the National Natural Science Foundation of China (61973325, U1811462).

References

1. Bartoletti, M., Carta, S., Cimoli, T., Saia, R.: Dissecting ponzi schemes on ethereum: identification, analysis, and impact. Futur. Gener. Comput. Syst. **102**, 259–277 (2020)
2. Brewster, T.: Ether cryptocurrency scammers made $36 million in 2018 - double their 2017 winnings. https://www.forbes.com/sites/thomasbrewster/2019/01/23/ether-scammers-made-36-million-in-2018double-their-2017-winnings
3. Chen, J., Ma, T., Xiao, C.: FastGCN: fast learning with graph convolutional networks via importance sampling. In: International Conference on Learning Representations (2018)
4. Chen, T., et al.: Understanding Ethereum via graph analysis. In: Proceedings of the 2018 IEEE Conference on Computer Communications, pp. 1484–1492. IEEE, Honolulu (2018)
5. Chen, W., Zheng, Z., Cui, J., Ngai, E.C.H., Zheng, P., Zhou, Y.: Detecting ponzi schemes on ethereum: towards healthier blockchain technology. In: Proceedings of the 2018 World Wide Web Conference, WWW 2018, pp. 1409–1418. ACM, Lyon (2018)
6. Feng, C., Niu, J.: Selfish mining in ethereum. In: 2019 IEEE 39th International Conference on Distributed Computing Systems (ICDCS), pp. 1306–1316 (2019). https://doi.org/10.1109/ICDCS.2019.00131
7. Fenu, G., Marchesi, L., Marchesi, M., Tonelli, R.: The ico phenomenon and its relationships with ethereum smart contract environment. In: 2018 International Workshop on Blockchain Oriented Software Engineering (IWBOSE), pp. 26–32. IEEE (2018)
8. Hu, T., et al.: Transaction-based classification and detection approach for ethereum smart contract. Inf. Process. Manage. **58**(2), 102462 (2021)
9. Lin, D., Wu, J., Yuan, Q., Zheng, Z.: Modeling and understanding Ethereum transaction records via a complex network approach. IEEE Trans. Circuits Syst. II Express Briefs **67**(11), 2737–2741 (2020)
10. Lin, D., Wu, J., Yuan, Q., Zheng, Z.: T-edge: temporal weighted multidigraph embedding for ethereum transaction network analysis. Front. Phys. **8**, 204 (2020)
11. Nakamoto, S.: Bitcoin: a peer-to-peer electronic cash system (2008). https://bitcoin.org/bitcoin.pdf
12. Scholten, O.J., Hughes, N.G.J., Deterding, S., Drachen, A., Walker, J.A., Zendle, D.: Ethereum crypto-games: mechanics, prevalence, and gambling similarities. In: Proceedings of the Annual Symposium on Computer-Human Interaction in Play, pp. 379–389. Association for Computing Machinery (2019). https://doi.org/10.1145/3311350.3347178
13. Szabo, N.: Smart contracts: building blocks for digital markets. EXTROPY: J. Transhumanist Thought, (16) 18(2) (1996)
14. Tasca, P., Hayes, A., Liu, S.: The evolution of the Bitcoin economy: extracting and analyzing the network of payment relationships. J. Risk Financ. **19**(2), 94–126 (2018)
15. Torres, C.F., Steichen, M., State, R.: The art of the scam: demystifying honeypots in ethereum smart contracts. In: 28th USENIX Security Symposium (USENIX Security 19), pp. 1591–1607. USENIX Association, Santa Clara, August 2019. https://www.usenix.org/conference/usenixsecurity19/presentation/ferreira
16. Wood, G.: Ethereum: A secure decentralised generalised transaction ledger (2014). http://gavwood.com/Paper.pdf

17. Wu, J., Liu, J., Chen, W., Huang, H., Zheng, Z., Zhang, Y.: Detecting mixing services via mining bitcoin transaction network with hybrid motifs. IEEE Trans. Syst. Man Cybern. Syst., 1–13 (2021). https://doi.org/10.1109/TSMC.2021.3049278

18. Wu, J., Liu, J., Zhao, Y., Zheng, Z.: Analysis of cryptocurrency transactions from a network perspective: an overview. arXiv preprint arXiv:2011.09318 (2020)

19. Wu, J., et al.: Who are the phishers? Phishing scam detection on Ethereum via network embedding. IEEE Trans. Syst. Man Cybern. Syst. (2020), to be published, 10.1109/TSMC.2020.3016821

20. Zetzsche, D., Buckley, R., Arner, D., Föhr, L.: The ico gold rush: It's a scam, it's a bubble, it's a super challenge for regulators. SSRN Electron. J., January 2017. https://doi.org/10.2139/ssrn.3072298

Blockchain Abnormal Transaction Behavior Analysis: A Survey

HuaLong Han, YuPeng Chen, ChenYing Guo, and Yin Zhang[✉]

University of Electronic Science and Technology of China, Chengdu, China
yin.zhang.cn@ieee.org

Abstract. Blockchain technology has been known to the public since cryptocurrencies such as Bitcoin were introduced. While blockchain technology is being developed and used by researchers, the technology is also used to conduct abnormal transaction behaviors, such as money laundering and fraud. After understanding a large amount of research data, this paper summarizes and analyzes the abnormal trading behaviors in blockchains from the basic characteristics of smart contracts and the topology of blockchain networks. These works provide a reference direction for future researchers.

Keywords: Blockchain · Smart contract · Characteristics · Topology · Classification

1 Introduction

As increasingly more money flows into blockchains, the impact of blockchain-based financial crimes is becoming increasingly more significant [1]. In 2018 alone, profits from Ethereum fraud rose from 17 million dollars in 2017 to 36 million dollars, a fraction of the 1.1 billion dollars in cryptocurrency stolen in 2018. Therefore, research on blockchain fraud is being rapidly conducted. At present, the main research methods include feature-based classification methods such as the Recurrent Neural Network (RNN), Decision Tree (DT) and Random Forest (RF), as well as the extraction of useful information from the transaction topology using subgraph matching and aggregate classification. In this paper, the classification methods, behavioral characteristics and topological structure commonly used in anomaly detection are summarized by referring to relevant work so as to provide ideas for subsequent research.

2 Related Work

In [2], it analyzes smart contracts and user behavior in Ethereum and the contract transaction behavior is divided into four categories. Fourteen basic characteristics are proposed to describe the transaction behavior, and a good classification of smart contracts is achieved through the training of an Long Short-Term Memory (LSTM) network. In [4], it proposes a method based on the Bidirectional Long Short-Term Memory (Bi-LSTM) model. According to smart

© Springer Nature Singapore Pte Ltd. 2021
H.-N. Dai et al. (Eds.): BlockSys 2021, CCIS 1490, pp. 57–69, 2021.
https://doi.org/10.1007/978-981-16-7993-3_5

contracts and the stability of programming language, the work solved sparse semantic problems of annotation in contracts. In addition, the combination of account and content information can effectively improve the classification effect. The approach in [3] used clustering based on bytecode hash similarity, cluster tagging, the manual analysis of name words and high transactions to determine the purpose of contracts. In [5], the method is improved for Ponzi Fraud contract decisions. The new behavior features are difficult to hide for criminals. The classification accuracy of the original method works better. In [11], it proposed two trading modes of abnormal behavior, air-dropping candy and greedy capital injection, through analyzing trading motivation. In addition, the article proposed a model for the recognition of abnormal Bitcoin trading behavior. In [7], it proposed a regression tree model built based on the extracted account characteristics and code characteristics. An unsupervised learning approach [8] is adopted to detect abnormal trading behavior through the topology of a transaction graph, using users and transactions as data characteristics. G. Di Battista et al. designed a system for visualizing Bitcoin blockchain traffic, BitConeView, allowing researchers to immediately learn when and how Bitcoins were mixed into an unusual transaction [20]. In [21], it designed and developed a tool for visualizing Bitcoin transactions that combines transaction diagrams and address diagrams into an associated high-fidelity visualization. The authors found many unusual trading patterns, such as money laundering. In [22], it applied three unsupervised learning methods, including K-means clustering, the Mahalanobis distance and Support Vector Machines (SVM), to the user graph and transaction graph generated according to the Bitcoin network to detect abnormal transactions in a blockchain.

3   Analysis of Abnormal Trading Behavior for Smart Contracts

3.1   Motivation-Based Classification of Smart Contracts

The purpose of this paper is to select characteristics from contract motivation. Based on the original three categories [2], we further refined types of recognition in order to ensure that motivation-based features are more pertinent.

Ponzi scheme: A Ponzi scheme is investment fraud that involves the payment of purported returns to existing investors from funds contributed by new investors [9], while the other types are shown in Table 1.

3.2   Feature-Based Analysis of Trading Behavior

Smart contracts expand the functions of the blockchain system, which leads to crime. In order to detect illegal contracts, much research in [5] and [6] has focused on finding features and models to analyze transaction behavior. Common methods for smart contract analysis are shown in Table 2.

Table 1. Types of smart contracts

Types of smart contracts	Definition
Game	Cryptographic games on a blockchain refer to games that store tokens on a distributed ledger [10]
Gambling	Restricted by the blockchain, the gambling type in this article considers singleround games, where the investment and return occur in one round [14]
Social Networks	Social networks mainly require user management, friends, posting, commenting and other functions [12]

Table 2. Anomaly detection approaches

Source	Main objective	Methods/algorithm
W. Chen et al. [2018] [7]	A classification model based on XGBoost for detecting smart Ponzi schemes	XGBoost
Hu T. et al. [2021] [2]	Training an LSTM network to distinguish different types of contracts	RNN
E. Jung et al. [2018] [6]	Providing 0-day and full-feature model to detect Ponzi behavior	J48/Random Forest/ Stochastic Gradient Descent (SGD)
Sheng M et al. [2021] [11]	The graph matchingtechnique is used to find abnormal behavior patterns in the blockchain network	Subgraph Matching Technology
R. Norvill et al. [2017] [3]	Automatic labeling of unknown contracts with clustering	K-medoids

3.3   Code Feature Analysis

The logic of smart contracts is embodied from the perspective of virtual machines, so the features extracted from OPCODE (Ethereum Virtual Machine Opcode) can be helpful in detecting the type of contract. However, the method to select them in the current work is mainly judged by the frequency. Like [5], it studies Rubixi Ponzi scheme contracts, and the 10 OPCODES selected were different from previous work because the data set and distribution of them were quite different. In fact, OPCODE is sample dependent.

3.4   Trading Behavior Feature Analysis

As transactions of smart contracts are stored on a blockchain, transaction content is public and not modifiable. Different smart contracts are a mapping of application, which results in different contracts corresponding to different transaction behaviors. Blockchain can help us rewind the contents of smart contracts. In [2], it provides three classifications of transactions.

- Balance of trade: The balance is amount of Ether left in the account at the time, and balance is the contract without externally owned accounts. Changes in balance can reflect differences between different types of contracts.
- Correlation between inflow ether and outflow Ether: The global income distribution can be obtained by analyzing the inflow and outflow of Ether for multiple users.
- The statistical features of transactions: The purpose of deployment of different smart contracts determines that transactions will also have unique statistical characteristics.
- Transaction-based features: In [2], it proposes four behavioral patterns of smart contracts and derives 14 basic characteristics to distinguish smart contracts. These characteristics are constructed according to the chronological sequence of contract transactions, which are the basic data description of the balance of the contract, the inbound and outbound transaction flows, and the transaction objects. Based on the summary of other work, we derived data features with more directivity to smart contract classification from the 14 features shown in Table 3. Through our investigation, we found that 14 characteristics can be used as basic characteristics to describe behavioral characteristics. A behavioral feature can be quantitatively analyzed using a combination of several basic features.

3.5   Derived from the Basic Feature of Trading Behavior

The trading behavioral includes the following features:

- Balance: The balance of the smart contract.
- Difference counts standard deviation (Dcsd): The standard deviation of the difference between the investment and payment times on different accounts.
- Difference amounts standard deviation (Dasd): The standard deviation of the profits on different accounts.
- Paid rate (Pr): The quotient of the payment to the contract divided by investment(Calculated by out_ex_Tran,in_in_Tran).
- Gini amt in (GNI)(resp. Gini amt out): The Gini coefficient computed over the number of Ether transactions to (resp. from) the smart contract.
- Overladdr: The number of addresses that paid to and were paid by the contract (Calculated by in_ex_addr and out_ex_addr).
- Known rate (Kr): The proportion of receivers who have invested before payment.
- Tot_in: The amount of in_ex_Ether and in_in_Ether.
- Tot_out: The amount of out_ex_Ether and out_in_Ether.
- N_minpay: The standard of the minimum number of payments to all participants.

Table 3. Basic feature of trading behavior

Feature	Definition
Balance	The number of a contract's balance;
in_ex_Ether	The number of inflow Ether from an external transaction;
in_in_Ether	The number of inflow Ether from an internal transaction;
out_ex_Ether	The number of outflow Ether from an external transaction;
out_in_Ether	The number of outflow Ether from an internal transaction;
Total_Tran	A contract's total number of transactions;
in_ex_Tran	The number of incoming transactions of external transactions;
out_ex_Tran	The number of outgoing transactions of external transactions;
in_in_Tran	The number of incoming transactions of internal transactions;
out_in_Tran	The number of outgoing transactions of internal transactions;
in_ex_addr	The number of unique incoming addresses of external transactions;
out_ex_addr	The number of unique outgoing addresses of external transactions;
in_in_addr	The number of unique incoming addresses of internal transactions;
out_in_addr	The number of unique outgoing addresses of internal transactions

- Rate of Return: The proportion of the remaining balance of the contract to the total amount of out_ex_Ether in each period.
- Number of operating trades: The number of transactions using a fixed Ether (Calculated by out_ex_Tran).
- Participation dividend ratio: In a period of time, the ratio of the contract's out_ex_addr to in_ex_addr.
- Income-to-investment ratio: The ratio of this round of investments to the previous round of returns.
- Recognition rate: The ratio of in_ex_addr and out_ex_addr.
- Nbr_tx_in: The amount of in_ex_Tran and in_in_Tran.
- Nbr_tx_out: The amount of out_ex_Tran and out_in_Tran.

There are following motivational analysis for different contract types, and corresponding classification characteristics.

- Ponzi scheme type: Based on fraud pattern of a Ponzi scheme, we can summarize characteristics of a Ponzi scheme that are different from other contracts.
  1. Few investors obtain the majority of the returns in the entire trading network while others do not, resulting in a large income gap among users participating in the contract.
  2. To create an image of fast and high returns, Ponzi contracts will reward participants quickly if there is sufficient capital.
  3. Ponzi contracts regularly make transfers to investment accounts.
  The features extracted from the motivation are as follows: Kr, Dcsd, Dasd, Pr, GNI, and overlap addr.

The characteristics above are designed to describe the unequal distribution caused by the spoil pattern of a Ponzi scheme. Kr, Dcsd, Dasd, Pr and overlap addr describe the distribution of the users' revenues and expenditures for the entire contract compared to overall and individual users, respectively. Analyzing the number of revenue and expenditure transactions and Ether reduces the possibility of smart Ponzi contracts covering up the true situation through a large number of small transactions.

The features extracted from the motivation are as follows: balance, nbr_tx_in, nbr_tx_out, Tot_out, and Tot_in.

Table 4. Statistics of behavioral-based feature frequency

Feature	Ponzi		Non-Ponzi	
	Avg	Stdev	Avg	Stdev
Known rate	0.89	0.29	0.49	0.43
Paid rate	0.62	0.3	0.43	0.41
Gini amt in	0.53	0.34	0.6	0.43
Overlap addr	6.98	16.39	13.83	220.48
Balance	4.65	15.51	22319.6	187549.23
nbr_tx_in	107.6	186.42	9594.61	40253.79

These characteristics are designed to describe the trading behavior of Ponzi contracts to maintain the illusion of high returns. A Ponzi contract quickly sends funds to the participants, which will cause 1) the contract balance to be maintained at a very low level; 2) the user needs to invest only once and obtains multiple returns, which is very abnormal; and 3) the contract does not charge a handling fee, which leads to a balance between tot in and tot out. Table 4 shows the statistics of the behavior-based feature frequency [5–7].

– Games and Gambling Types: In [10], we find the profit methods of game contracts deployed on Ethereum are same as those of gambling-type contracts.We summarized Cryptokitties, Crypto Energy, and Satoshi Dice to reach the following conclusions:

1. When an account participates in a game or gambling, it must pay the contract maintenance cost. Generally, the fee for each gamble is 10% of the current investment.
2. In both games and gambling, the probability of creating a rarer, more valuable virtual good is lower than the probability of creating a common good, giving players an incentive to try more.
3. No user can participate in every bonus.

The features extracted from the motivation are as follows: N_minpay standard deviation, balance, rate of return, number of operating trades, Kr, GNI, out_ex_addr, participation dividend ratio and income-to-investment ratio. With [14], we find the group can avoid risk is only a small part. The balance, number of operating trades and rate of return are used to track the behavior of gambling contracts, such as charging fees and underlying maintenance behavior. A completely random gambling contract will be more balanced in the GNI and participation dividend ratio. The income-to-investment ratio is used to find the psychological behavior of gamblers because winners tend to reduce investment, but others are the opposite.

– Social Type: In [12,13], the social type generally includes the blockchain, user, cache, interaction, and storage. Regarding the registration and post in the core functions of social networks, we can propose the following differences in social networks:

1. To ensure the uniqueness of accounts, registration contracts are designed in the user manager. Because registered accounts only need to complete transactions with sufficient gas, the contract balance is usually 0.

2. When a user registers an account, the returned key and contract address are not chained for safekeeping. Therefore, the registered contract only has input transactions, and there is no object of output transactions.

3. For post, multiple pseudoidentities are restricted in social networks. Therefore, the comments of participants must be generated between users who have confirmed their identities.

The features extracted from the motivation are as follows: balance, rate of return, out_ex_addr, and recognition rate.

4 Analysis of Abnormal Transaction Behaviors for a Blockchain Network

4.1 Pseudospam Transaction Behavior

Pseudospam transactions were first described in [23]. The author performed a considerable amount of analysis on the outliers in the entry distribution of the Bitcoin user graph and the high diameter of the user graph. The results show that these transactions are generated by the artificial transaction chain, and these special transactions are named pseudospam transactions. In article [24], the author further analyzes such transactions and describes the user graph of such transactions. The specific structure is shown in Fig. 1.

Figure 1 shows that a pseudospam transaction begins with a node. The node is an arbitrary amount of input. Then, the hearing of this node will be a payment to an address. The amount remaining after deducting transaction fees paid to a new generation of addresses forms a chain until the coins left are insufficient to pay the transaction fees to the address. The rest of the money is transferred to the link address, which receives a large amount of Bitcoin from another address and then proceeds with the next pseudospam transaction.

Figure 1, which has specially connected nodes, is mainly responsible for the connected nodes to collect the small coins because the chain of connected nodes

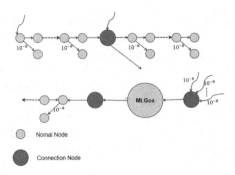

Fig. 1. Pseudospam transaction graph

opens a new transaction. The first payment will be transferred to specially connected nodes, and the connected nodes gather them together. Mt. Gox transfers
to new connected nodes and opens a pseudospam transaction chain.

As seen from the user graph, the pseudorefresh transaction has a large diameter and a small output amount. There are two reasons behind this particular
finding. One reason is that part of the attacks on users are anonymous attacks.
Because the transaction outputs are very small, usually if the recipient spends
this amount, it must be combined with other address amounts, which forms multiple inputs Then, the attacker can go through multiple input clustering heuristic
rules to determine multiple addresses that belong to an entity. Another reason
is that these transactions are used for advertising.

4.2   Money Laundering Transaction Behavior

Dorit Ron et al. [25] downloaded a large number of transaction addresses and
transaction records from the Bitcoin trading network. By running the union-find
algorithm, mapping addresses into entities, the authors constructed a network of
large Bitcoin transactions. Further analysis of this network revealed some special
types of transactions. Among them, bifurcation and self-cycling are considered to
be related to early money laundering behavior. Figure 2 is a transaction subgraph
of bifurcation and self-cycling.

As seen from Fig. 2, in early money laundering, in order conduct money
laundering, criminals usually divide a sum of Bitcoins into several small sums
and transfer them to different addresses which may or may not belong to the
same entities at different times so as to achieve the target of the diversion of black
money. Money laundering usually uses the same address for small amounts and
different address for large amounts. Furthermore, after receiving the currency,
the recipient transfers the money several times in the same way. Although this
type of transaction involves many entities and the time chain and transaction
chain are long, the money still flows back to the original transfer entity in the end.
It is through this seemingly "legal" transaction that criminals conduct money
laundering.

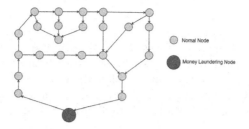

Fig. 2. Money laundering transaction graph

As another example, in [26], the author reconfigures the transaction diagram by exporting the transaction input and visualizing it by using the open source software Gephi. Examining the transaction diagram can allow one to understand how the money laundering service works and identify the money laundering pattern and its characteristics.

4.3   Blackmail Transactions

In [28], Huang et al. created a measurement framework for large-scale end-to-end measurements of ransomware payments, victims, and attackers. By combining a range of data sources, including large databases such as ransomware binaries, seed ransom payments, and Bitcoin address repositories, the authors outline the ecosystem and third-party facilities where ransomware is evolving.

In [29], Liao et al. measured and analyzed CryptoLocker ransomware. The author designed a framework to collect Bitcoin addresses belonging to CryptoLocker from the blockchain and built CryptoLocker's address topology network. Through the topological network system, the author studied CryptoLocker's financial infrastructure and money laundering strategy. In addition, the article found a link between CryptoLocker and BTC Fog and BTC-E. Figure 3 shows the visualized CryptoLocker address cluster.

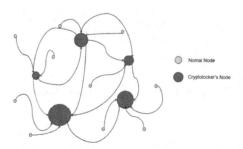

Fig. 3. CryptoLocker's topology network

As shown in Fig. 3, the large black node represents a community, which contains many addresses; and the ransom balance of all addresses within a community is transferred to a single aggregate address in the center. Therefore, we represent it with a single node.

In [30], Raquet-Clouton et al. used the GraphSense open source platform to extract transaction data from the Bitcoin blockchain and constructed two types of network representations of the blockchain: an address diagram and a cluster diagram. By analyzing these two graphs, the authors analyzed the down payment information of 35 ransomware families to track where the money went.

4.4   Ponzi Scheme and Other Abnormal Transaction Behaviors

In [7], it proposed a feature-based approach to detect Ponzi scheme smart contracts. The author extracted account characteristics and code characteristics from historical transaction information and smart contract opcodes to build a regression tree model to detect Ponzi scheme smart contracts.

The above methods detect a Ponzi scheme when the Ponzi scheme has been deployed on the blockchain and has caused damage. Sun et al. [31] proposed a Ponzi scheme detection method that does not rely on transaction data. The author directly analyzes the opcodes of smart contracts to infer the semantics of the smart contracts and develops the Ponzi detector to detect the scheme smart contract.

In fact, the blockchain is littered with all sorts of other unusual transactions in addition to the above. For example, Chen et al. found a large number of market manipulation patterns in [32]. The authors analyze the history of Mt. Gox Bitcoin transactions and construct them into three different account charts. Then, these charts are reconstructed as matrices, and the base networks with large price fluctuations are identified by singular value decomposition.

In [33], Lee et al. described the transaction behavior of the dark net in the blockchain. The authors collected a large number of dark web sites, extracted useful cryptocurrency information from them, and created a Bitcoin trading map for each illegal Bitcoin address to track the flow of black money on the dark web. This is shown in Fig. 4.

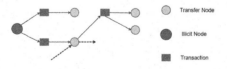

Fig. 4. Dark web transaction graph

5   Open Issues

From the perspective of smart contract classification, CODE and behavioral characteristics are considered. There are some problems. First, the selected feature leakage may cover up the criminal behavior by artificially creating meaningless transactions due to the knowledge of the existing detection methods of malicious contracts. Second, with constant update of smart contracts, the table of the contract implementation mode leads to the misjudgment that the corresponding features are no longer applicable to the newly deployed smart contracts. The third, it is difficult to choose the feature, and the standard of judging the quality of the feature is very vague.

From the perspective of the blockchain abnormal trading network topology, the abnormal trading behaviors considered by the researchers are all illegal behaviors, and there is no clear distinction between "abnormal trading" and "normal trading". Moreover, the existing studies on the topology of abnormal trading are all on specific abnormal behaviors, and there is no generalized study. Finally, regarding the topological structure of abnormal trading behavior, different researchers may construct different topologies, and the characteristic information contained in them is also different, which needs to be unified.

6 Conclusion

This paper classifies the existing smart contracts on Ethereum by searching for relevant work and analyzes, concludes and summarizes the identification and feature selection of hot smart contracts. The 14 basic features are used to construct the behavioral characteristics of the Ponzi scheme, game gambling contract and social network contract in smart contracts and improve the recognition rate of smart contract classification. Furthermore, this paper also analyzes the abnormal transaction behaviors, such as money laundering, extortion, Ponzi schemes and fake refreshes, in blockchains using the topological structure of typical abnormal behaviors. Constructing the user diagram and transaction diagram of blockchains clearly displays the abnormal transaction behavior in a blockchain, which provides another method for the supervision of blockchains.

Acknowledgement. This work is supported by the National Key R&D Program of China (No. 2020YFB1006002)

References

1. Nakamoto, S.: Bitcoin: a peer-to-peer electronic cash system (2009). http://bitcoin.org/bitcoin.pdf
2. Hu, T., Liu, X., Chen, T., Zhang, X., Huang, X., Niu, W., et al.: Transaction-based classification and detection approach for Ethereum smart contract. Inf. Process. Manage. 58(2)(2021), Article 102462
3. Norvill, R., Pontiveros, B.B.F., State, R., Awan, I., Cullen, A.: Automated labeling of unknown contracts in ethereum. In: Proceedings of the 26th International Conference on Computer Communications and Networks (ICCCN), pp. 1–6 (2017)
4. Tian, G., Wang, Q., Zhao, Y., Guo, L., Sun, Z., Lv, L.: Smart contract classification with a bi-LSTM based approach. IEEE Access **8**, 43806–43816 (2020)
5. Bartoletti, M., Pes, B., Serusi, S.: Data mining for detecting bitcoin Ponzi schemes. In: Proceedings of Crypto Valley Conference Blockchain Technology (CVCBT), pp. 75–84, June 2018

6. Jung, E., Le Tilly, M., Gehani, A., Ge, Y.: Data mining-based Ethereum fraud detection. In: Proceeding of the IEEE International Conference Blockchain (Blockchain), pp. 266–273, July 2019
7. Chen, W., Zheng, Z., Cui, J., Ngai, E., Zheng, P., Zhou, Y.: Detecting Ponzi schemes on Ethereum: towards healthier blockchain technology. In: Proceedings of World Wide Web Conference (WWW), pp. 1409–1418 (2018)
8. Pham, T., Lee, S.: Anomaly detection in Bitcoin network using unsupervised learning methods. CoRR, vol. abs/1611.03941 (2016)
9. Bartoletti, M., Carta, S., Cimoli, T., Saia, R.: Dissecting Ponzi schemes on Ethereum: identification, analysis, and impact (2017). CoRR abs/1703.03779
10. Scholten, O.J., Hughes, N.G.J., Deterding, S., Drachen, A., Walker, J.A., Zendle, D.I.: Ethereum crypto-games: mechanics, prevalence and gambling similarities. In: Proceedings of the Annual Symposium on Computer-Human Interaction in Play CHI PLAY, Barcelona, Spain, 22–25 October 2019, pp. 379–389 (2019). http://delivery.acm.org/10.1145/3350000/3347178/p379-scholten.pdf
11. Sheng, M., Sang, A., Zhu, L., et al.: Abnormal transaction behavior recognition based on motivation analysis in blockchain digital currency. J. Comput. Sci. **44**(01), 193–208 (2021)
12. Jiang, L., Zhang, X.: BCOSN: a blockchain-based decentralized online social network. IEEE Trans. Comput. Soc. Syst. **6**(6), 1454–1466 (2019)
13. Xu, Q., Song, Z., Goh, R.S.M., Li, Y.: Building an ethereum and ipfs-based decentralized social network system. In: 2018 IEEE 24th International Conference on Parallel and Distributed Systems (ICPADS) (2018)
14. Meng, J., Fu, F.: Understanding gambling behaviour and risk attitudes using cryptocurrency-based casino blockchain data. R. Soc. Open Sci. **7**, 201446 (2020). http://dx.doi.org/10.1098/rsos.201446
15. Liu, S., Liao, G., Ding, Y.: Stock transaction prediction modelling and analysis based on LSTM. In: 2018 13th IEEE Conference on Industrial Electronics and Applications (ICIEA), pp. 2787–2790 (2018)
16. Duhart, B.M.A., Hernndez-Gress, N.: Review of the principal indicators and data science techniques used for the detection of financial fraud and money laundering. In: 2016 International Conference on Computational Science and Computational Intelligence (CSCI), pp. 1397–1398 (2016)
17. Staderini, M., Palli, C., Bondavalli, A.: Classification of Ethereum Vulnerabilities and their Propagations. In. Second International Conference on Blockchain Computing and Applications (BCCA) 2020, pp. 44–51 (2020)
18. Bogner, A.: Seeing is understanding: anomaly detection in blockchains with visualized features. In: Proceedings of the International Joint Conference Pervasive Ubiquitous Computing International Symposium on Wearable Computers, pp. 5–8 (2017)
19. Wang, X., He, J., Xie, Z., Zhao, G., Cheung, S.-C.: ContractGuard: defend ethereum smart contracts with embedded intrusion detection. IEEE Trans. Services Comput. **13**(2), 314–328 (2020)
20. Di Battista, G., Di Donato, V., Patrignani, M., Pizzonia, M., Roselli, V., Tamassia, R.: Bitconeview: visualization of flows in the bitcoin transaction graph. In: 2015 IEEE Symposium on Visualization for Cyber Security (VizSec), Chicago, IL, USA, 2015, pp. 1–8 (2015). https://doi.org/10.1109/VIZSEC.2015.7312773
21. McGinn, D., Birch, D., Akroyd, D., et al.: Visualizing dynamic bitcoin transaction patterns. Big Data **4**(2), 109–119 (2016)
22. Pham, T., Lee, S.: Anomaly detection in bitcoin network using unsupervised learning methods. arXiv preprint arXiv:1611.03941 (2016)

23. Di Francesco Maesa, D., Marino, A., Ricci, L.: An analysis of the Bitcoin users graph: inferring unusual behaviours. In: COMPLEX NETWORKS 2016 2016. SCI, vol. 693, pp. 749–760. Springer, Cham (2017). https://doi.org/10.1007/978-3-319-50901-3_59

24. Maesa, D.D.F., Marino, A., Ricci, L.: Detecting artificial behaviours in the bitcoin users graph. Online Soc. Networks Media **3**, 63–74 (2017)

25. Ron, D., Shamir, A.: Quantitative analysis of the full bitcoin transaction graph. In: Sadeghi, A.-R. (ed.) FC 2013. LNCS, vol. 7859, pp. 6–24. Springer, Heidelberg (2013). https://doi.org/10.1007/978-3-642-39884-1_2

26. Mser, M., Bhme, R., Breuker, D.: An inquiry into money laundering tools in the Bitcoin ecosystem. In: 2013 APWG eCrime Researchers Summit, pp. 1–14. IEEE (2013)

27. Maksutov, A.A., Alexeev, M.S., Fedorova, N.O., Andreev, D.A.: Detection of blockchain transactions used in blockchain mixer of coin join type. In: 2019 IEEE Conference of Russian Young Researchers in Electrical and Electronic Engineering (EIConRus), Saint Petersburg and Moscow, Russia, 2019, pp. 274–277 (2019). https://doi.org/10.1109/EIConRus.2019.8656687

28. Huang, D.Y., et al.: Tracking ransomware end-to-end. In: 2018 IEEE Symposium on Security and Privacy (SP), San Francisco, CA, USA, 2018, pp. 618–631 (2018). https://doi.org/10.1109/SP.2018.00047

29. Liao, K., Zhao, Z., Doupe, A., Ahn, G.: Behind closed doors: measurement and analysis of CryptoLocker ransoms in Bitcoin. In: 2016 APWG Symposium on Electronic Crime Research (eCrime). Toronto, ON, Canada, 2016, pp. 1–13 (2016). https://doi.org/10.1109/ECRIME.2016.7487938

30. Paquet-Clouston, M., Haslhofer, B., Dupont, B.: Ransomware payments in the bitcoin ecosystem. J. Cybersecurity **5**(1), tyz003 (2019)

31. Sun, W., Xu, G., Yang, Z., et al.: Early detection of smart ponzi scheme contracts based on behavior forest similarity. In: 2020 IEEE 20th International Conference on Software Quality, Reliability and Security (QRS), pp. 297–309. IEEE (2020)

32. Chen, W., Wu, J., Zheng, Z., et al.: Market manipulation of bitcoin: evidence from mining the Mt. Gox transaction network. In: IEEE INFOCOM 2019-IEEE Conference on Computer Communications, pp. 964–972. IEEE (2019)

33. Lee, S., Yoon, C., Kang, H., et al.: Cybercriminal minds: an investigative study of cryptocurrency abuses in the Dark Web. In: NDSS (2019)

EthSniffer: A Global Passive Perspective on Ethereum

Wei Xia[1,2], Zhenzhen Li[1(✉)], Zhen Li[1], Gang Xiong[1], and Gaopeng Gou[1]

[1] Institute of Information Engineering, Chinese Academy of Sciences,
Beijing 100093, China
`lizhenzhen@iie.ac.cn`
[2] School of Cyber Security, University of Chinese Academy of Sciences,
Beijing 100049, China

Abstract. Ethereum is an open source public blockchain platform with smart contract functions and a model of blockchain 2.0. Its market value ranks second in the world of encrypted electronic currencies, second only to Bitcoin. Ethereum uses the underlying blockchain network to implement decentralized distributed data computing and storage. This decentralized mechanism can effectively protect the security and privacy of data. We combed through the existing work on Ethereum, launched an ISP-level passive measurement against Ethereum's underlying network, and collected the largest Ethereum connection data to date. In this article, we collect a 40GB data set containing tens of millions of nodes, provide the latest statistics of the four types of node discovery protocols as of May 2020, and reveal the basic connection properties of the underlying P2P network. And the node activity degree and corresponding relationship of the entire network are described and analyzed.

Keywords: Blockchain system · Ethereum · P2P network · Passive measurement · Basic connection properties

1 Introduction

The blockchain is based on a P2P network, scattering thousands of nodes around the world to reach a consensus on the creation of a block based on agreements and consensus mechanisms. Blockchain technology has received widespread attention for its excellent features such as decentralization, anonymity, tamper resistance, and traceability. In the blockchain system, Bitcoin and Ethereum are typical applications based on blockchain technology. Bitcoin was proposed by Satoshi Nakamoto in 2008 [15] and is currently the most widely used cryptocurrency in the world. It can also be called the blockchain 1.0 system. Ethereum is an open source public blockchain platform with smart contract functions, which is a model of blockchain 2.0. Its market value ranks second in the world of encrypted electronic currencies, second only to Bitcoin.

Researches on Ethereum are not as comprehensive as those on Bitcoin, relatively concentrating on limited facets. Ethereum uses an underlying blockchain

H.-N. Dai et al. (Eds.): BlockSys 2021, CCIS 1490, pp. 70–84, 2021.
https://doi.org/10.1007/978-981-16-7993-3_6

network to implement decentralized, distributed data computing and storage. This mechanism can effectively protect the security and proprietary nature of data. Therefore, some researches are driven by the security and empirical analysis of Ethereum's smart contracts [1,2,6,7,14], and some researches use active probe placement to simulate or trigger Ethereum interaction [9–11] to achieve data acquisition and mechanism analysis. Among the few works on passive measurement against Ethereum, [12] uses Netflow data to mine new counters using machine learning methods, and [13] mainly conducts in-depth analysis of the topological relationship. By far in literature, there has not been any global perspective to quantitatively analyze the basic statistical attributes of the underlying network of Ethereum, such as the amount of IP, port distribution, daily active IP, active period, and the correspondence between IP and NodeID. We cooperate with ISP-level backbones and thus have the basis for large-scale real-time passive measurement, so we are able to give a comprehensive analysis at the ISP level.

In this paper, we mainly make the following contributions:

- We perform by far the largest ISP-level passive measurement to date against Ethereum traffic on a major academic network of China.
- We propose and deploy a high-performance traffic processing framework and collect a 40GB data set containing millions of nodes.
- We present up-to-date statistics on the four types of node discovery protocol as of May 2020, and reveal the basic attributes of the underlying P2P network.
- We analyze and illustrate the IP and port attributes distribution of the Ethereum traffic carrying node discovery messages.
- We characterize and analyze node activity and the corresponding relationship between IP and ID.

We structure our work as follows: We start from Sect. 2 to give the background related to the ethereum network protocol. Section 3 reviews the work in the field of Bitcoin and Ethereum. Section 4 introduces the data acquisition device and the scale of the data set. We analyze the statistics of the ethereum dataset in Sect. 5. Then we conclude our work in Sect. 6.

2   Background

Ethereum is a decentralized blockchain platform built on a P2P network. This platform relies on a huge distributed hash table to maintain the logical address of each node in the network. This logical address is the basis for dividing the location of nodes in the network. Each node participating in the network obtains and maintains a part of the global hash table based on its logical address. When there is a resource that falls into its hash table for query, the node needs to provide query services. Similarly, it can be found by other nodes by accurately querying its location ID.

Ethereum uses a distributed hash algorithm similar to Kad to discover nodes and build the underlying P2P network topology. Each node uses K buckets to store nodes adjacent to itself. The nodes in Ethereum use the 512-bit public key of the ECDSA algorithm as their unique identifier in the network, which is the NodeID. This unique identifier is generated when the client is started for the first time and will not change. In the process of node discovery, it is calculated as LocalID.

2.1   Node Discovery Protocol

The node discovery mechanism of the Ethereum P2P network currently mainly relies on Discovery v4 (Discv4 protocol). Discv4 protocol is an application layer protocol based on UDP protocol. In the process of node discovery, four message types are used, mainly including Ping message, Pong message, FindNode message and Neighbors message. This node discovery protocol is prepared for a new node that is about to join a certain network.

Ping/Pong Message. When a new node joins the network and discovers other nodes, it reads the seed node information and sends Ping/Pong message handshake to each other. The local node puts the seed node that completed the handshake into the K bucket as the initial node list during the handshake.

FindNode/Neighbors Message. The local node randomly generates a TargetID, calculates those nodes whose TargetID and NodeID in the K bucket are less than the distance between TargetID and LocalID, and sends FindNode messages to those nodes. These messages carry TargetID information. After receiving the FindNode message, those nodes similarly finds nodes closer to the TargetID in the K bucket, and responds with the Neighbors message.

In this paper, we provide a passive global perspective by measuring and recording the key information of the four types of messages, thereby revealing the communication characteristics of the Ethereum network.

3   Related Work

At present, research on Ethereum focuses on the blockchain technology itself, such as quantitative analysis of the application of smart contracts, security analysis, vulnerability exploitation, prevention methods, and empirical analysis of the evolution strategy of Ethereum. [2] studied how Bitcoin and Ethereum interpret smart contracts, and quantified the use of smart contracts in their application areas. In addition, give the analysis of the most common programming patterns in Ethereum, in which the source code of smart contracts can be used. [1] analyzes the security vulnerabilities of Ethereum smart contracts and provides a taxonomy of common programming traps that may lead to vulnerabilities. [14] proposes methods to enhance the operational semantics of Ethereum to keep smart contracts from attacks. For Ethereum smart contract developers, build a symbolic execution tool called *Oyente* to discover potential vulnerabilities. [7] defined the EVM (Ethereum Virtual Machine) in Lem officially for the first time for executing the Ethereum smart contract verification of all instructions. Using this definition, the security features of Ethereum smart contracts are proved in Isabelle/HOL. [6] uses the K framework to build an executable formal specification *KEVM* based on a bytecode stack language, aiming at further formal analysis. The research above paid little attention to the overall situation of the underlying network responsible for information dissemination on Ethereum.

There are also some studies that establish a connection or complete an operation by inserting probes, modifying client programs, and actively simulating, and use this as a precondition for subsequent monitoring to construct a data set for measurement. A representative work on Ethereum is [11], which analyzes the Ethereum protocol used for P2P network construction and creates an active measurement machine. This machine can generate data to simulate the interaction of nodes in the Ethereum network [10]. Modified the Ethereum Geth client so that it measures and records all smart contract operations (deployment, invocation, destruction). By comparing the number of contracts created by users and contracts, we found malicious contracts that abnormally invoke self-destruct operations multiple times [9]. By inserting controllable nodes on the Ethereum hard fork network and Ethereum Classic, all blocks and transaction information synchronized and verified on them are retained and the mining revenue and intensity are analyzed. Similarly, [4,16] conducted a series of monitoring and analysis activities on Bitcoin using similar methods. However, due to the isolation of the network environment, the misunderstanding of the protocol and the implementation error of the application program, the active measurement method may be restricted as a result. On the contrary, we have a purely passive observation perspective that flows through the observation point to monitor the communication status of the underlying network of Ethereum.

There are not many representative research for passive measurement, except for [12,13]. Li et al. [12] uses the nodes obtained in an active way as prior knowledge, and uses machine learning methods on Netflow data which is a kind of flow sampling data to discover the work of new nodes. Netflow is a kind of flow sampling data. Another research by Li [13] combines complex network theory to probe the topology of the Ethereum network.

In addition, there are also some work on side channel attacks and man-in-the-middle attacks on Ethereum [5,17], which will not be discussed in our article.

4   Data Collection and Explanation

4.1   Experimental Setup and Methodology

In order to illustrate the global perspective on the Ethereum network, we designed a parallel structure *EthSniffer* deployed at the entrance and exit of the network we observed, to facilitate the collection and analysis of Ethereum nodes. We monitor the two-way link on the Internet of CSTNET, and the target network will connect a total of approximately 25,000,000 users to this place. The solution includes wired and WLAN scenarios. This *EthSniffer* connects Ethereum nodes from multiple universities, research institutes, and companies.

EthSniffer is a network analysis method based on the principle of passive listening. Using this framework, we can monitor the status of the network, the data flow, and the information transmitted on the network. Our solution does not attempt to change the original form of the network, so that *EthSniffer* is a bypass and duplicate device. We designed a high-concurrency, high-performance node discovery protocol traffic processing device to identify the traffic of the Ethereum communication on the boundary of the backbone network to obtain the Ethereum nodes. All traffic flowing through the two backbones will be captured and processed, and unidirectional 5-tuple traffic can be processed without the need to aggregate traffic. The design of the framework is shown in Fig. 1.

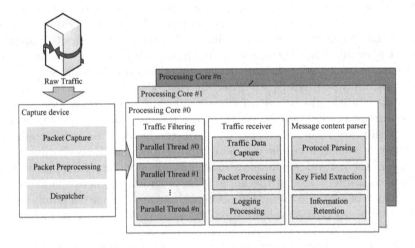

Fig. 1. Data collection framework EthSniffer

The processing device mainly includes four parts of instruments: i) Capture device. The module bypasses capturing and preprocessing data packets, and dispatching the preprocessed data packets to a parallel multithreaded queue for processing. ii) Traffic filter. All traffic conforming to the structure of the node discovery protocol will be quickly identified. Then the filter also combines the concise features of the handshake or find-neighbor protocol to quickly filter the traffic that contains the complete content of the message block. iii) Traffic receiver. We record the traffic of the node discovery protocol filtered out in ii) in a distributed manner, and retain the traffic data according to a set of internal log formats. It mainly includes meta-information and packet load information containing the main content. iv) Message content parser. According to the protocol format of the four types of messages, we analyzed the content of the traffic application layer payload screened in iii). Different types of messages extract relevant and meaningful information according to their communication purposes. We have completed the collection and storage of the data sets the following four protocol types. The contents of each message are as follows.

Ping. The IP and port of both ends of P2P communication, log time, protocol version number, Ping message source IP, TCP port, UDP port, Ping message destination IP, TCP port, UDP port, time stamp.

Pong. IP and port of both ends of P2P communication, log time, protocol version number, Ping message source IP, TCP port, UDP port, hash value, time stamp.

FindNode. IP and port at both ends of P2P communication, log time, TargetID, timestamp.

Neighbors. IP and port of both ends of P2P communication, log time, timestamp, number of nodes, node IP in K bucket, TCP port, UDP port, NodeID.

4.2   Ethical Considerations

We focused on the ethical considerations of Partridge and Allman [3] in the network measurement process. Before any measurement activities, we will conduct an internal approval process. The approval process is to assess whether the data collection can harm individuals or the collected data will reveal user privacy. Since the experimental infrastructure is deployed on an additional parallel system and belongs to the passive measurement range, we do not need anyone or cooperation, and will not directly (beneficial or harmful) change the operation of the network.

The measurements for this work were performed on an isolated measurement infrastructure that cannot be accessed from the Internet. The data we obtain in the measurement must be kept on this infrastructure. Before the measurement, the method of the experiment was thoroughly documented. The method of the experiment fully complies with the strict code of conduct required by our internal ethics review process, and our measurement in this process has been recognized. Therefore, we concluded that it is ethical to conduct experiments, but contrary to our usual policy, we will not share the raw data of this work with the public.

4.3   Data Set Size and Basic Statistics

We started to observe in Feburary 2020. As of May 2020, in nearly three months, we have collected tens of million connections ery month, of which millions of peer-to-peer addresses can be extracted.

5   Analysis

The basic characteristics of the Ethereum network refer to the network connection properties that do not focus on the analysis of specific application layer content, including the request and response of the four types of messages whose Pong is the response of Ping and Neighbors is the response of FindNode, and the geographical distribution of IP addresses, usage of ports, distribution of active IP and relationship between the active IP and NodeID.

5.1   Comparison of the Request and the Response

The Ping messages of the detection node are compared with the Pong messages in response to the detection, and the number of Ping messages, the number of Pong messages, and the number of Pong reply Ping messages are counted on a daily basis, as shown in Fig. 2. We compare the FindNode message found by neighbor nodes with the response message Neighbors, and count the number of FindNode messages, the number of Neighbors messages, and the number of FindNode messages replies from Neighbors on a daily basis, as shown in Fig. 3. The proportion of pong's response to ping messages is about 10%, while the proportion of Neighbors' response to FindNode is about 25%.

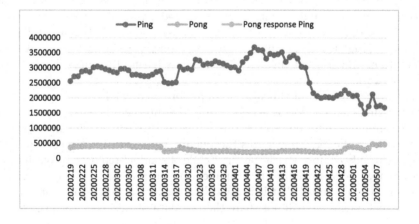

Fig. 2. Comparison of ping and pong messages

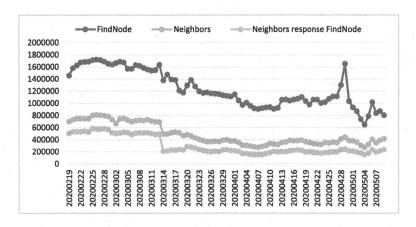

Fig. 3. Comparison of FindNode and neighbors messages

5.2 IP Attribute Analysis of Ethereum

IP Geographical Distribution. We measure the geographical distribution of IP addresses. The country distribution of IP addresses is shown in Fig. 4. The number of IP addresses in China is 66,007, accounting for 41.4%, ranking first. Other Top10 territories are the United States, Germany, LAN address, India, Japan, Russia, France, shared address and the United Kingdom.

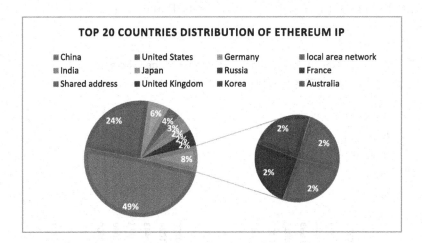

Fig. 4. Top 20 countries distribution of ethereum IP.

Draw the geographical distribution of IP addresses. As shown in Fig. 5, it can be found that active nodes are located in the eastern coastal areas of China, northern Shanghai, Guangzhou and Shenzhen, northeastern United States, western coastal areas, Tokyo, Japan, Germany, the Netherlands, and India.

Fig. 5. Geographical distribution of the ethereum active IP

Port Distribution. In the Neighbors message, the port distribution of TCP and UDP used by the nodes in the K bucket is measured. Among them, TCP uses 64790 ports and UDP uses 63034 ports, respectively using 98.86% and 96.20% of the 65535 ports randomly. The Top1000 ports used accounted for 94.95% and 98.5% respectively. Among them, TCP and UDP ports were mainly concentrated on the default port 30303, accounting for 53.56% and 56.48% of the total respectively. As shown in Fig. 6, based on the Top20 port used by TCP, the distribution of the Top20 port used by TCP and UDP is shown:

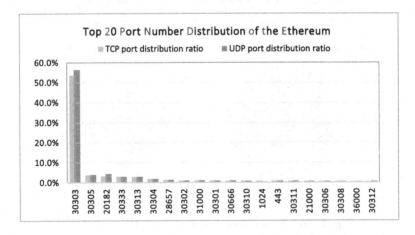

Fig. 6. Top 20 port number distribution of the ethereum

According to the TCP/UDP port registry, port numbers are assigned based on three ranges: System Ports (0-1023), User Ports (1024-49151), and the

Dynamic and/or Private Ports (49152-65535) [8]. We analyze the port type for TCP and UDP. Ports below 1024 are called system ports. Among them, TCP uses 278 system ports, accounting for 0.43% of the total, and UDP uses 121 system ports, accounting for 0.19% of the total. It is supposed that UDP uses a larger proportion of user or dynamic ports. The total amount of static/dynamic ports used is shown in Fig. 7: In the Neighbors message, the total number of K-bucket nodes measured is 254,395,396, and the number of logs with different TCP ports and UDP ports is 20,461,220, accounting for 8.04% of the total. It can be seen that the TCP and UDP protocols deployed on most nodes use the same port.

5.3   A Closer Look at Neighbors Message

When a node receives a FindNode message from another one, it will send back a Neighbours message, which carries nodes near it that is closer to the TargetID. Therefore, Neighbors messages often carry more fresh connectivity information in the current Ethereum network. So we pay special attention to the active node attributes and the relationship between NodeID and IP on the Neighbors message.

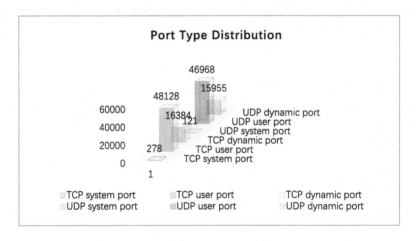

Fig. 7. Port type distribution

We conducted passive monitoring and measurement of Neighbors messages on Ethereum. The measurement time is from February 19, 2020 to May 10, 2020. A 82-day, 40G data set of Neighbors messages on science and technology networks has been constructed. The total number of passively measured IP is 159,438 nodes, the daily active amount fluctuates between 25,000 and 29,768, with an average daily active of 27,374 nodes. The total number of active IPs in Ethereum is shown in Fig. 8:

Fig. 8. Total number of ethereum active IP

We measure the distribution of the number of active days of nodes. Among the collected 159,438 nodes, the number of nodes that only appeared for one day was 32,909, accounting for 20.6% of all nodes. The number of nodes that were active for only one day accounted for the most, and the number of nodes that were active for 82 d is 10,632, accounting for 6.67%, which is relatively high. The distribution of active days of nodes is shown in Fig. 9.

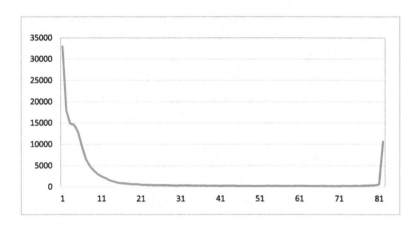

Fig. 9. Distribution of node active days

The cumulative distribution function curve of the amount of IP to the number of active days is shown in Fig. 10. It can be seen that the nodes with active days of 1–13 days account for about 80% of the total. The active 13–81 days have a relatively flat growth, and the active 82 days The proportion of IP in China has increased significantly.

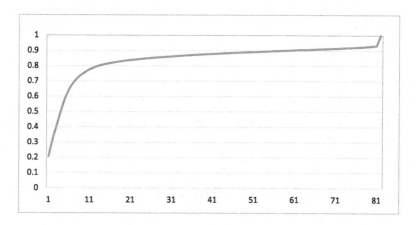

Fig. 10. Active Days-IP cumulative distribution function curve

We measure the NodeID carried on IP. Among the collected 159,438 nodes, the number of IPs with only one-to-one correspondence between IP and NodeID is 129,394, accounting for 81.2%. There are 66,832 NodeIDs corresponding to these IPs. As the number of NodeIDs carried on IP increases, the proportion basically presents a decreasing trend, close to a long-tailed distribution. The distribution curve of the IP number corresponding to the number of NodeIDs is shown in Fig. 11:

The cumulative distribution function curve of the corresponding IP amount to the number of NodeID is shown in Fig. 12, and it can be seen that the probability that the corresponding IP amount of NodeID is between 1–17 ID which has reached 99%.

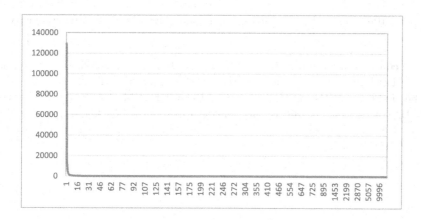

Fig. 11. Distribution of IP numbers corresponding to the number of NodeIDs

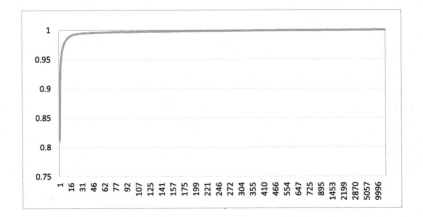

Fig. 12. NodeID-corresponding IP number cumulative distribution function curve

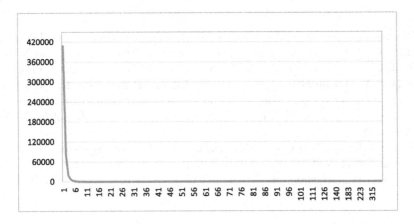

Fig. 13. IP-corresponding NodeID number cumulative distribution function curve

We collected a total of 530,019 different NodeIDs, and described the number of IPs distributed by the same NodeID and the cumulative distribution function of the number of IPs, as shown in Fig. 13 and Fig. 14. We can see that one NodeID corresponds to one IP, accounting for about 77%. There are a total of 60,170 IPs corresponding to these NodeIDs. One NodeID corresponds to 1–6 IPs, accounting for 99%.

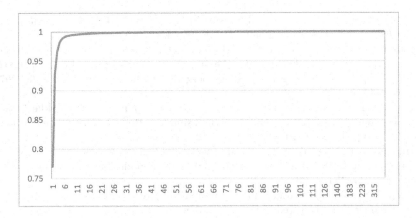

Fig. 14. IP-corresponding NodeID number cumulative distribution function curve

6   Conclusion

In this paper, we have conducted the largest ISP-level passive measurement to date on Ethereum traffic on major academic network in China. We propose and deploy a high-performance traffic processing framework *EthSniffer*, and collected four types of node discovery protocol connection information as of May 2020, including a 40GB data set of tens of millions of nodes. We analyz and explain the distribution of the IP and port attributes of the Ethereum traffic carrying the node discovery messages. We reveal the request-response ratio of different messages in the node discovery process. We find that from our perspective, China has more nodes, mainly in the southeast coast. The default port 30303 is obviously the most used, but some adjacent ports are also widely used. And we describe and analyze the relationship between node activity, IP and NodeID. By providing a global passive perspective, we reveal the basic connection properties of the underlying P2P network.

Acknowledgments. This work is supported by The National Key Research and Development Program of China (No. 2020YFB1006100, No. 2020YFE0200500 and No. 2018YFB1800200) and Key research and Development Program for Guangdong Province under grant No. 2019B010137003.

References

1. Atzei, N., Bartoletti, M., Cimoli, T.: A survey of attacks on ethereum smart contracts (SoK). In: Maffei, M., Ryan, M. (eds.) POST 2017. LNCS, vol. 10204, pp. 164–186. Springer, Heidelberg (2017). https://doi.org/10.1007/978-3-662-54455-6_8
2. Bartoletti, M., Pompianu, L., et al.: An empirical analysis of smart contracts: platforms, applications, and design patterns. In: Brenner, M. (ed.) FC 2017. LNCS, vol. 10323, pp. 494–509. Springer, Cham (2017). https://doi.org/10.1007/978-3-319-70278-0_31

3. Craig Partridge, M.A.: Ethical considerations in network measurement papers (2016). https://dl.acm.org/doi/fullHtml/10.1145/2896816

4. Donet Donet, J.A., Pérez-Solà, C., Herrera-Joancomartí, J.: The bitcoin P2P network. In: Böhme, R., Brenner, M., Moore, T., Smith, M. (eds.) FC 2014. LNCS, vol. 8438, pp. 87–102. Springer, Heidelberg (2014). https://doi.org/10.1007/978-3-662-44774-1_7

5. Ekparinya, P., Gramoli, V., Jourjon, G.: Impact of man-in-the-middle attacks on ethereum. In: 2018 IEEE 37th Symposium on Reliable Distributed Systems (SRDS), pp. 11–20. IEEE (2018)

6. Hildenbrandt, E., et al.: Kevm: a complete formal semantics of the ethereum virtual machine. In: 2018 IEEE 31st Computer Security Foundations Symposium (CSF). pp. 204–217. IEEE (2018)

7. Hirai, Y.: Defining the ethereum virtual machine for interactive theorem provers. In: Brenner, M., et al. (eds.) FC 2017. LNCS, vol. 10323, pp. 520–535. Springer, Cham (2017). https://doi.org/10.1007/978-3-319-70278-0_33

8. Touch, J., Lear, E., Mankin, A., et al.: Service Name and Transport Protocol Port Number Registry (2020). https://www.iana.org/assignments/service-names-port-numbers/service-names-port-numbers.xhtml

9. Kiffer, L., Levin, D., Mislove, A.: Stick a fork in it: Analyzing the ethereum network partition. In: Proceedings of the 16th ACM Workshop on Hot Topics in Networks, pp. 94–100 (2017)

10. Kiffer, L., Levin, D., Mislove, A.: Analyzing ethereum's contract topology. In: Proceedings of the Internet Measurement Conference 2018, pp. 494–499 (2018)

11. Kim, S.K., Ma, Z., Murali, S., Mason, J., Miller, A., Bailey, M.: Measuring ethereum network peers. In: Proceedings of the Internet Measurement Conference 2018, pp. 91–104 (2018)

12. Li, Z., Hou, J., Wang, H., Wang, C., Kang, C., Fu, P.: Ethereum behavior analysis with netflow data. In: 2019 20th Asia-Pacific Network Operations and Management Symposium (APNOMS), pp. 1–6. IEEE (2019)

13. Li, Z., Xia, W., Cui, M., Fu, P., Gou, G., Xiong, G.: Mining the characteristics of the ethereum p2p network. In: Proceedings of the 2nd ACM International Symposium on Blockchain and Secure Critical Infrastructure, pp. 20–30 (2020)

14. Luu, L., Chu, D.H., Olickel, H., Saxena, P., Hobor, A.: Making smart contracts smarter. In: Proceedings of the 2016 ACM SIGSAC Conference on Computer and Communications Security, pp. 254–269 (2016)

15. Nakamoto, S., Bitcoin, A.: A peer-to-peer electronic cash system. Bitcoin (2008). https://bitcoin.org/bitcoin.pdf 4

16. Pappalardo, G., Di Matteo, T., Caldarelli, G., Aste, T.: Blockchain inefficiency in the bitcoin peers network. EPJ Data Sci. 7, 1–13 (2018)

17. Shen, M., Zhang, J., Zhu, L., Xu, K., Du, X., Liu, Y.: Encrypted traffic classification of decentralized applications on ethereum using feature fusion. In: 2019 IEEE/ACM 27th International Symposium on Quality of Service (IWQoS), pp. 1–10. IEEE (2019)

Performance Optimization
of Blockchain

BDLedger: A Scalable Distributed Ledger for Large-Scale Data Recording

Gang Huang[1,2], Kaidong Wu[2], Chaoran Luo[2], Su Zhang[2], Huaqian Cai[2],
Xiang Jing[3], and Yun Ma[2,4(✉)]

[1] Peking University Shenzhen Graduate School, Shenzhen, Guangdong, China
hg@pku.edu.cn
[2] Key Laboratory of High Confidence Software Technologies (Peking University),
Ministry of Education, Beijing, China
{wukd94,blesser,samsuzhang,caihq,mayun}@pku.edu.cn
[3] School of Software and Microelectronics, Peking University, Beijing, China
jingxiang@pku.edu.cn
[4] Institute for Artificial Intelligence, Peking University, Beijing, China

Abstract. Nowadays, blockchain becomes a hot topic in academics and industry. Traditionally, due to the "Impossible Triangle", most existing blockchain systems prefer decentralization and security to scalability, which causes their limited throughput. However, it is undeniable that there exist scenarios that require extremely high scalability of blockchain, such as the on-chain record of vehicle driving data. In this paper, we propose a new blockchain-like distributed ledger called BDLedger that can realize an approximately linear increase of throughput to solve the above challenge. In BDLedger, we design a novel consensus mechanism called Random Witness Consensus and organize blocks as a DAG structure. To achieve the linear increase of throughput, we make sacrifices in two aspects: 1) abandoning the consensus on the order of transactions and keep only the consensus on the content of transactions, which means that there are no conflict transactions so that all transactions can be processed in parallel. 2) The content of each block only exists in a constant number of random nodes, which ensures that the overall storage and bandwidth costs will not increase rapidly as the number of nodes increase. We discuss the rationality of the above approach and introduce the design of BDLedger in detail. Experimental results show that BDLedger can achieve an approximately linear increase of throughput, from about 20000 TPS for 10 nodes to about 160000 TPS for 100 nodes.

Keywords: Distributed ledger · Blockchain · Scalability · Directed acyclic graph · Random witness consensus

1 Introduction

Nowadays, blockchain becomes a hot topic in academics and industry. In beginning, blockchain was used to manage cryptocurrencies [16]. Ethereum [22] introduces smart contract and make blockchain a decentralized computing platform

© Springer Nature Singapore Pte Ltd. 2021
H.-N. Dai et al. (Eds.): BlockSys 2021, CCIS 1490, pp. 87–100, 2021.
https://doi.org/10.1007/978-981-16-7993-3_7

[23]. In essence, blockchain is a distributed ledger that can record transactions with decentralized trust, and it has been used in many fields, such as healthcare, supply chain management and data recording [10].

There is a famous "Impossible Triangle" in blockchain technology which means that a blockchain system cannot meet the scalability, decentralization, and security at the same time [4]. Although the "Impossible Triangle" is no rigorous proof of blockchain architecture, it is indeed the summary of the key challenges of every blockchain system from the existing implementation and in the industry. No blockchain systems can perform well in all these three aspects.

Traditionally, most existing blockchain systems prefer decentralization and security to the scalability [25], which is the fundamental reason why the throughput of the existing blockchain is limited. Just like the fact that different distributed systems make different choices between consistency and availability due to the CAP theorems, blockchain should also trade-off among scalability, decentralization, and security in different scenarios. The scalability should not always be the "second-class citizen" and be sacrificed.

It is undeniable that there exist scenarios that require extremely high scalability of blockchain, such as the on-chain record of vehicle driving data. In 2021, Tesla fell into a credibility crisis in China: an owner of a Tesla car claimed that her car had caused a terrible accident due to brake failure. Later, Tesla released the collected driving data one minute before the accident to prove its innocence. Although the Tesla officials insisted that the data had not been tampered with, they still could not convince the public. Undoubtedly, to avoid such a situation from happening again, one of the best ways for Tesla is to store the driving data in the blockchain-based distributed ledger. However, due to the limited scalability, no blockchain systems can satisfy such a scenario with ultra high throughput and large-scale data recording requirements. In our opinion, when facing the above scenarios, the blockchain can take scalability as the priority and sacrifice part of the security. Of course, the sacrifice of security must be moderate and meet the basic requirements of business scenarios.

In this paper, we propose a new blockchain-like distributed ledger called BDLedger (aka, Big Data Ledger) that can realize the approximately linear increase of throughput. In BDLedger, we design a novel consensus mechanism called Random Witness Consensus and organize blocks as a DAG structure, to achieve the consensus on the contents of transactions. In our system, we sacrifice security in two aspects: 1) abandoning the consensus on the order of transactions and keep only the consensus on the content of transactions, which means that there are no conflict transactions so that all transactions can be processed in parallel. Therefore, BDLedger can be used only in data recording scenarios as mentioned above and not in scenarios such as ICO. 2) The content of each block only exists in a constant number of random nodes, which ensures that the overall storage and bandwidth costs will not increase rapidly as the number of nodes increase. Intuitively, this strategy seems to significantly reduce the tamper resistance, but it can be proved that the ability of tamper resistance of the system is of the same magnitude as that of systems adopting a network-wide storage strategy.

This paper makes the following contributions: 1) We discuss the key factors that limit the scalability of blockchain, and proposed a feasible solution to implement a scalable blockchain by sacrificing part of the security appropriately; 2) We propose a new blockchain-like distributed ledger called BDLedger that can realize the approximately linear increase of throughput, in which a novel consensus mechanism called Random Witness Consensus is specially designed and the blocks are organized as a DAG structure. 3) We implement BDLedger and verify its high scalability through experiments. Results show that BDLedger can process about 20,000 transactions per second in the cluster with 10 nodes, and it grows to approximately 160,000 in 100 nodes.

The remainder of this paper is organized as follows. At first, we introduce related work in Sect. 2 and give an overview of the whole system in Sect. 3. In Sect. 4, we give more details about the design. In Sect. 5, we verify the high scalability of BDLedger through experiments and discuss the results. Finally, Sect. 6 concludes this paper.

2   Related Work

In this section, we summarize the related work. There are two types of technologies related to BDLedger, distributed storage technology, and distributed ledger technology. Traditional distributed storage technologies mainly focus on providing crash fault tolerance, which is not enough to fit the decentralized environment. So, we just survey distributed ledger technologies.

Blockchain is representative of distributed ledger technologies. Existing work that optimizes the scalability of the blockchain can be divided into the following three categories: single-chain blockchain, sharding, and DAG-based blockchain.

2.1   Single-Chain Blockchain

Some single-chain blockchains optimize consensus algorithm based on Nakamoto PoW consensus. In these blockchains, blocks are organized as a tree of blocks and only one path from the root to leaf is agreed as the consensus by miners, namely the main chain. The time to produce a block is called an epoch.

Some researchers focus on the PoW consensus algorithm. They introduce a new type of blocks, improve the number of verified transactions in an epoch, namely make the blocks larger, to improve TPS. For example, Eyal et al. split transactions from blocks into micro blocks, use blocks to select the main chain and ensure epoch, and use micro blocks to commit transactions. [6] Bagria et al. use three types of blocks: proposer blocks, transaction blocks, and voter blocks. [3] These blockchains have higher TPS, but users also need to wait for transactions to be agreed upon. Forks (other paths in the block tree) will affect the consensus and take up storage space as well.

Other researchers choose new consensus algorithms, such as PoS. In these systems, other nonces are used to check whether a block is valid rather than the hash value of the block. Miners use their amounts of tokens (crypto-currencies maintained by the blockchain) to decide the right to generate blocks in the PoS algorithm, so they need verifiable random functions or another security technology to make sure that the probability a miner is selected to generate blocks in an epoch is just associated with the number of tokens the miner has, like Ouroboros [5,8,11]. These approaches have better throughput but are easily attacked by nothing-at-the-stake attackers.

In particular, Algorand [9] aims to generate just a chain of blocks. It uses a two-phase consensus, BA*, to make all nodes quickly agree on one block or empty block in each epoch. There are no forks in Algorand, but empty blocks are useless to the ledger. So, Algorand may not maintain the consensus in a bad network environment. PBFT and its optimizations are similar to Algorand, providing lightweight non-forked consensus. They are usually used in permissioned blockchains [7,14].

Single-chain blockchains try to increase the number of generated blocks per minute or the size of a block, pack more transactions, and optimize executions of them. But they are limited by the single-chain structure of blocks so that their throughput can not linearly increase as the scale expands. Besides, it makes huge pressure on the storage layer because each node has to save all blocks.

2.2 Sharding

Sharding is another idea, in which the whole network is partitioned into multiple smaller committees. Each committee collects a disjoint set of transactions and processes them, namely a shard. There are two types of sharding approaches: the computation-oriented and the storage-oriented.

ELASTICO [15], OmniLedger [12] DP-Hybrid [21] are three computation-oriented sharding approaches. They use a two-layer consensus. The top-layer consensus decides committees, and then these committees run the bottom-layer consensus to execute transactions. To support changing committees, nodes have to process all blocks generated. In theory, regular changing committees may resolve security problems, but the high cost prevents it.

Chainspace [1], RapidChain [24], Monoxide [20], etc. belong to the latter type. Committees execute transactions in their shards, and exchange information among shards to enable cross-shard transactions. These approaches work well, but each shard's computing power is less than that of the whole network, which makes shards more vulnerable. Because sharded blockchains usually use PoW consensus in committees, the problem is serious.

Sharded blockchains have higher TPS by paralleling transaction executions in multiple shards, but it grows with an increasing number of shards rather than nodes. Because of considering security, a shard can't be too small for defending attacks. So the throughput of the system just marginally benefits from the increase in the number of nodes.

2.3 DAG-Based Blockchain

DAG-based blockchains are high potential approaches. These consensus algorithms allow each block have more than one hash link to previous blocks, so blocks are organized as directed acyclic graph (DAG) structure. Because blocks in DAG can be just topologically ordered, it is hard to find the main chain. It means each generated block can be appended to any block, and blocks generated by any miners can be added into DAG.

IOTA is a famous DAG-based blockchain in the industry. Participants need to select two previous transactions for each transaction and then send them. The "main chain" is the largest sub-graph in which there are no conflicts. Every participant takes a pint of the risk.

SPECTRE [18] and PHANTOM [17] are naïve DAG-based blockchains. Miners generate blocks and append them into the DAG. In SPECTRE, two conflict blocks are voted by succeeding blocks, and just one block is selected in the final ledger, namely use GHOST protocol [19]. SPECTRE can straightly receive non-conflict transactions (whose result isn't related to the execution order) but will take much time when receiving conflict transactions (whose result varies when the order changes). And in PHANTOM, hash links among blocks are considered as references to decide relative orders among blocks, and finally, a robust total order on the block DAG is provided. But it takes time.

Conflux [13] is also a DAG-based blockchain. It organizes blocks as Tree-graph and combines advantages from single-chain and DAG. Each block has two hash links to previous blocks, parent edge, and reference edge. According to parent edges, Conflux builds a pivot chain (similar to the main chains in other blockchains) by GHOST protocol and then provides a total order by edges and epochs marked by blocks in pivot chain. Conflux optimizes TPS and confirmation delay, but they are limited as well.

In summary, DAG-based blockchains try to improve the throughput by process non-conflict transactions in parallel. They have the best throughput among the three categories, but it takes more time to build a consensus when faced with conflicts, which affects the throughput. And more generated blocks occupy more space on each node.

2.4 Summary

Some researchers optimize the throughput by increasing the number of transactions executed in some time. For sharded blockchains and DAG-based blockchains, they try to parallel transaction executions so that they have higher throughput. However, the throughput of all these blockchains does not linearly increase as the scale expands, and the growth of throughput leads to more pressure on the storage and bandwidth as well. Thus, none of them are suitable for scenarios with ultra high throughput and large-scale data recording requirements.

3   System Overview

In this section, we describe the key idea of our approach achieving an approximately linear increase in throughput.

3.1   Key Idea

In our opinion, the most critical limitation of the scalability of blockchain is the following two key factors: 1) the consensus requirement of the order of all transactions; 2) the full backup of all the transactions at all participants.

Specifically, if we satisfy the consensus requirement of the transaction order while ignoring the need for full backup, the storage and bandwidth resources of nodes can be reduced. However there will still be a large number of conflicts between blocks generated concurrently, and a large number of blocks will be discarded due to the consensus policy. Logically, the system still processes transactions in a serial mode, which is hard to achieve scalability. Instead, if we back up all the transactions at all participant nodes and ignore the consensus requirement, we can achieve scalability theoretically through concurrent processing, but the storage and bandwidth resources will soon become the bottleneck and restrict the throughput. As a result, the system is still not scalable. Therefore, to build a scalable blockchain system, we must break the above two restrictions.

In a data recording scenario, there is no conflict between transactions because the only operation for recording data is to append new data to the ledger, and there is no requirement of modifying the data which is already stored. Therefore, a consensus on the order of the transactions is no longer required. Furthermore, we do not need to back up all the transactions in all nodes, instead, we only store a constant number of data in the network. Intuitively, this will induce great data security to threaten the ledger. However, as we proved in Sect. 4, the anti-tampering ability of the system is the same order of magnitude as that of the whole network backup policy.

For these reasons, we design the BDLedger, in which: 1) we give up the consensus on the transaction order, but only on the transaction content (that is, the order between transactions is uncertain) so that all transactions can be processed concurrently; 2) The body of each block only exists in a constant number of random nodes, which ensures that the overall storage and bandwidth costs will not grow to fast as the number of nodes increases. Therefore, BDLedger can achieve an approximately linear increase of system throughput with the increase of the participant nodes.

3.2   System Architecture

As shown in Fig. 1, the architecture of a distributed ledger consists of 3 layers: network layer, storage layer, and consensus layer.

The top layer is the consensus layer. BDLedger uses a novel consensus algorithm called Random Witness Consensus. Nodes collect transactions to generate

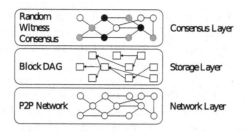

Fig. 1. System architecture of BDLedger.

blocks, send them to a constant number of random nodes called witnesses. And the witness node that receiving the block will send it to other random nodes whose number is constant again as backups. Because we break the order restriction, namely transactions don't need to be processed on each node to keep the order. Thus in BDLedger, only a constant number of the transactions copies are required to be stored, to significantly reduce storage and bandwidth resources.

The second layer is the storage layer. Unlike the chain structure in which all the transactions are ordered and processed serially, BDLedger uses DAG to organize the blocks of transactions. In chain structure, every new block has to choose the latest block as their father block to guarantee the transaction order. Thus only one block can be appended to the ledger at the same time. In BDLedger, each new block can choose arbitrary existing blocks as their father blocks so that nodes can process the transactions concurrently.

The network layer is the bottom, nodes are randomly connected and form an unstructured P2P network, to support the block propagation and consensus process.

4 System Design

In this section, we describe the details of BDLedger, including Random Witness Consensus in the consensus layer and DAG structure in the storage layer. In the network layer, a structured P2P network is used. At the end of this section, we discuss the security of BDLedger.

4.1 Random Witness Consensus

BDLedger keeps only the consensus of transaction contents, namely the content consensus. So transactions are just processed without executions. However, if each node processes all blocks, computing, and storage resources blocks need will be beyond what the system has. Considering that nodes don't need to do executions, a block can be persisted in some nodes to save occupied storage. These nodes will be randomly selected after the block generation.

There are two steps to run Random Witness Consensus: global knowledge consensus, and random witness and backup.

Global Knowledge Consensus. For random selection, nodes need some information about the network. The information is called global knowledge and consists of certificates of all nodes, a node list of the network, and a random seed to execute verifiable random functions. We use a committee to maintain global knowledge. The committee consists of some nodes and uses a non-forked consensus algorithm, like PBFT. They maintain global knowledge data in a single chain of blocks and share it with other nodes. Each node of the network has a backup of the global knowledge, to retrieve needed information in the consensus process. The process of Global Knowledge Consensus is shown in Fig. 2a.

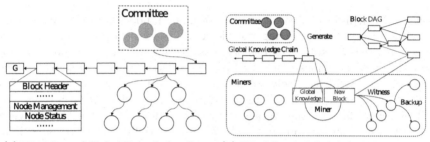

(a) Workflow of Global Knowledge Consensus.

(b) Workflow of Random Witness and Backup

Fig. 2. Workflow of random witness consensus.

A block of Global Knowledge Consensus also consists of block header and transactions. The transaction records the change of node list and status. When receiving a global knowledge block, each node verifies transactions and updates the local global knowledge data. So the block size is limited and meets the needs of periodic, lightweight, and non-forked Global Knowledge Consensus.

Random Witness and Backup. By global knowledge, Random Witness and Backup can be run. The process is shown in Fig. 2b. First, the miner uses the random seed in the latest global knowledge block and its private key to generate some random numbers and uses them and the node list of the network to generate a random node list. The random method is a verifiable random function so that other nodes can verify the result. Second, the miner sends collected transactions to these random nodes (witnesses). Witness nodes have to verify the data and return their signatures to the miner. If the miner determines that it receives enough signatures by checking responses and the list of witness nodes, it creates the block header and shares it in the network. Finally, all nodes will receive the block header. Witness nodes combine the block header and transactions into a whole block and save it as a backup. Other nodes just have to save it. So each node will finally get headers of all blocks and can use them as the previous blocks in the next block generation.

In each step of the random witness consensus, the number of selected nodes is a constant parameter. So a transaction just has constant backups and occupies finite storage. The consensus has low cost and high throughput, and TPS approximately linearly grows as the number of nodes increases.

4.2 Block DAG

Because of the distribution of blocks, there is another problem with the storage: it is hard to maintain the complete chain of blocks in each node. If we ask nodes to manage blocks as a single chain structure like the original, it has to take much time to find the latest block of the chain. So BDLedger allows each node to generate blocks based on only the blocks it has, namely forms a DAG structure.

When generating a block, the node selects some saved blocks as the previous. We don't need to order transactions and blocks, so there's no consensus problem in BDLedger. It means the number of previous blocks a block can select is unlimited in fact. The number can be customized to meet special requirements. To follow existing DAG-based blockchains, we allow a block to select at most 3 existing blocks as the previous.

Besides, if there is a block that no blocks select as one of the previous, it is easier to tamper with the block. We call these blocks to end blocks. To keep the security of the ledger, it is required to control the number of end blocks. So BDLedger asks each miner must try to select end blocks as the previous, and one of them must be generated by itself unless there are not eligible blocks in the local storage. It makes sure that the number of end blocks in the DAG is not more than the number of nodes of the network, and the DAG structure is not too divergent.

4.3 Security Analysis

BDLedger uses DAG structure and Random Witness Consensus to implement a scalable distributed ledger. Because of the safe environment of the permissioned blockchain, BDLedger has high security. We will give a brief proof.

We assume that there are n nodes in the network. For BDLedger just collects and processes transactions, attackers mainly want to prevent the sending or saving. When sending and saving transactions, BDLedger suggests all users or witnesses select some random nodes. If the number of random nodes is set to the same parameter m, the two executions can be modeled as the same question: m nodes are selected in n nodes, how many nodes the attackers have to control at least, to control all the m nodes?

Let x is the number of controlled nodes. When controlling k nodes, the precision that all m nodes are controlled is:

$$p(x = k) = \frac{C_{k-1}^{m-1} * C_1^1}{C_n^m} = \frac{C_{k-1}^{m-1}}{C_n^m} \triangleq p_k, k \in [m, n] \bigcap \mathbf{Z} \qquad (1)$$

We can find that $\sum_{k=m}^{n} p_k = 1$.
The expectation is

$$E(x) = \sum_{k=m}^{n} k * p_k = \frac{m(n+1)}{m+1} \tag{2}$$

So we can find

$$E(x) \in [m, n] \bigcap \mathbf{Z} \tag{3}$$

$$E(x) = \frac{m(n+1)}{m+1} = n + 1 - \frac{n+1}{m+1} \tag{4}$$

There is a positive correlation between $E(x)$ and m. When $m \in [1, n] \bigcap \mathbf{Z}$, $E(x) \in [\frac{n+1}{2}, n]$.

It means on average, selecting just one random node in saving transactions, attackers have to control half of all nodes to prevent the execution. Considering that BDLedger is a permissioned blockchain, it is hard to do attacking.

And how much value should m be? Considering $E(x) = n - k$, then there are

$$m = \lceil \frac{n-k}{k+1} \rceil \tag{5}$$

$$n = (k+1)m + k, k = \frac{n-m}{m+1} = \frac{n+1}{m+1} - 1 \tag{6}$$

So there is a negative correlation between m and k. And when m decreases, k slowly decreases. We can use a small m to keep the system highly secure.

Also, the variance of p_k should be taken into account:

$$D(x) = E(x^2) - E(x)^2 = \frac{m(n+1)(n-m)}{(m+2)(m+1)^2} \tag{7}$$

According to the estimate of m in Eq. 5, we get

$$D(x) = \frac{k(k+1)m}{m+1} \approx k^2 \tag{8}$$

It means, if we set m to an appropriate value, BDLedger can keep high TPS and security at the same time. When m is set to 3, we can get $E(x) = \frac{3}{4}(n+1)$, which means attackers have to control over $\frac{3}{4}(n+1)$ nodes to do attacking.

5   Evaluation

In this section, we briefly introduce the implementation of BDLedger, describe the setup of the performance test, and discuss the results.

5.1   Implementation

We implement BDLedger with Go, use the customized libp2p (common p2p network framework developed by the IPFS team) and Badger (open-source key-value database) to build the P2P network and manage local data. We select 3 nodes as the witnesses when generating a block because it is enough to build a robust CFT (crash fault tolerance) consensus according to the existing distributed storage systems and security analysis in Sect. 4.3.

Users can use the SDK of some programming languages (Go, Java, etc.) to connect to the BDLedger service and send and query transactions. We do the performance test by the SDK.

5.2   Experiment Setup

We use 200 nodes of Alibaba Cloud in the experiment. These nodes are in 10 cities of China. Each city has 20 nodes. 100 of them are used to deploy BDLedger, and other nodes are pressure nodes. The hard and software configure of each node are shown in Table 1.

Table 1. The hard and software configure of test node.

CPU	2 dual-core, 2.5 GHz
Memory & storage	4GB & 40 GB HDD
Network bandwidth	20 Mbps
Operating system	CentOS 7.8.2003, 64-bit

By SDK, the programs on the test nodes send transactions to these nodes BDLedger deploys, and count them. The size of each transaction is 100 Bytes. We change the size of the cluster by starting/stopping BDLedger services on nodes, to test how the TPS changes. In each case, we use pressure nodes whose number is the same as that of nodes in the cluster, and each pressure node sends requests in 4 threads. In each thread, the test program sends the next request 1ms after receiving the response of the previous one. Each test lasts one hour.

5.3   Result

There are five test cases in the performance test, in which the size of the cluster grows from 10 to 100. The result is shown in Fig. 3. The TPS increases approximately linearly with the number of nodes. In the cluster with 10 nodes, BDLedger can process about 20,000 transactions per second, and it grows to approximately 160,000 in 100 nodes.

The result proves that BDLedger has high scalability, namely, its throughput approximately linearly increases as the scale expands.

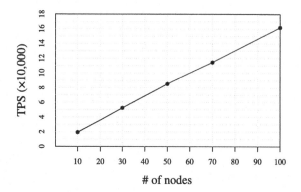

Fig. 3. The TPS of BDLedger in clusters with different sizes.

5.4 Discussion

BDLedger has a TPS of about 160,000 in 100 nodes. In contrast, HyperLedger Fabric has a TPS of only about 3,000 [2] when deployed in 100 nodes, and Conflux processes over 100,000 (10 Mbps/100 Bytes) [13] in the same scale. It shows that BDLedger has higher performance. And the high scalability comes from the fact that each transaction is only processed in a part of nodes.

However, each node needs to process headers of all the blocks. When the number of nodes is so large that block headers take a large amount of network bandwidth at the same time, the linear growth of TPS will be curbed. Assume the network bandwidth is W, TPS provided by a node is t, the size of a transaction is x, the size of the block header is h, the number of transactions in a block is s, there are n nodes in the network, and p and c are coefficients of broadcastings and transmissions, we can find:

$$W = (bx + \frac{nhp}{s})c * t \tag{9}$$

$$TPS = n * t = \frac{nsW}{(nhp + bxs) * c} = \frac{sW}{hcp} * (1 - \frac{bsx}{nhp + bxs}) \tag{10}$$

So, according to Eq. 10 and the current experiment setup, in a cluster with no more than 1,000 nodes, we can conclude that the TPS grows approximately linearly as the scale expands.

6 Conclusion

We present BDLedger, a scalable distributed ledger for data recording in which the throughput can grow approximately linearly as the participant nodes increasing. BDLedger achieves such a high throughput under two key assumption which is reasonable in data recording scenario: 1) the transactions order is insignificant so that we can process transactions and generate blocks concurrently; 2) compared with fully backup in all nodes, store a constant number of copies in random nodes can also protect the data from malicious tampering.

BDLedger consists of three layers: 1) consensus layer where a novel consensus algorithm called Random Witness Consensus is used to reduce the bandwidth and storage consumption while guaranteeing the data security at a certain extend; 2) storage layer where the blocks can choose a constant number (3 as default) of blocks as their previous blocks and formulate a block DAG; 3) network layer where nodes are organized as an unstructured peer-to-peer network, to manage nodes and communications among them.

We evaluate the scalability of BDLedger. In a cluster with 10 nodes, BDLedger can process about 20,000 transactions per second and 160,000 transactions per second when the nodes number increases to 100. These results show that the throughput of BDLedger increases approximately linearly as the scale expands.

Acknowledgements. This work was supported by the Key-Area Research and Development Program of Guangdong Province under the grant number 2020B010164002, the National Natural Science Foundation of China under the grant number 61725201, the Beijing Outstanding Young Scientist Program under the grant number BJJWZYJH01201910001004, and PKU-Baidu Fund Project under the grant number 2020BD007.

References

1. Al-Bassam, M., Sonnino, A., Bano, S., Hrycyszyn, D., Danezis, G.: Chainspace: a sharded smart contracts platform. In: NDSS (2018)
2. Androulaki, E., et al.: Hyperledger fabric: a distributed operating system for permissioned blockchains. In: Proceedings of the thirteenth EuroSys conference, pp. 1–15 (2018)
3. Bagaria, V., Kannan, S., Tse, D., Fanti, G., Viswanath, P.: Prism: deconstructing the blockchain to approach physical limits. In: Proceedings of the 2019 ACM SIGSAC Conference on Computer and Communications Security, pp. 585–602 (2019)
4. Chen, L., Cong, L.W., Xiao, Y.: A brief introduction to blockchain economics. In: Information for Efficient Decision Making: Big Data, Blockchain and Relevance, pp. 1–40. World Scientific (2021)
5. David, B., Gaži, P., Kiayias, A., Russell, A.: Ouroboros Praos: an adaptively-secure, semi-synchronous proof-of-stake blockchain. In: Nielsen, J.B., Rijmen, V. (eds.) EUROCRYPT 2018. LNCS, vol. 10821, pp. 66–98. Springer, Cham (2018). https://doi.org/10.1007/978-3-319-78375-8_3
6. Eyal, I., Gencer, A.E., Sirer, E.G., Van Renesse, R.: Bitcoin-NG: a scalable blockchain protocol. In: 13th USENIX Symposium on Networked Systems Design and Implementation (NSDI 2016), pp. 45–59 (2016)
7. Fang, Z., Wei, Z., Wang, X., Xie, W.: A blockchain consensus mechanism for marine data management system. In: Zheng, Z., Dai, H.-N., Fu, X., Chen, B. (eds.) BlockSys 2020. CCIS, vol. 1267, pp. 18–30. Springer, Singapore (2020). https://doi.org/10.1007/978-981-15-9213-3_2
8. Garay, J., Kiayias, A., Leonardos, N.: The bitcoin backbone protocol: analysis and applications. In: Oswald, E., Fischlin, M. (eds.) EUROCRYPT 2015. LNCS, vol. 9057, pp. 281–310. Springer, Heidelberg (2015). https://doi.org/10.1007/978-3-662-46803-6_10

9. Gilad, Y., Hemo, R., Micali, S., Vlachos, G., Zeldovich, N.: Algorand: scaling byzantine agreements for cryptocurrencies. In: Proceedings of the 26th Symposium on Operating Systems Principles, pp. 51–68 (2017)

10. Huang, G., Luo, C., Wu, K., Ma, Y., Zhang, Y., Liu, X.: Software-defined infrastructure for decentralized data lifecycle governance: principled design and open challenges. In: 2019 IEEE 39th International Conference on Distributed Computing Systems (ICDCS), pp. 1674–1683. IEEE (2019)

11. Kiayias, A., Russell, A., David, B., Oliynykov, R.: Ouroboros: a provably secure proof-of-stake blockchain protocol. In: Katz, J., Shacham, H. (eds.) CRYPTO 2017. LNCS, vol. 10401, pp. 357–388. Springer, Cham (2017). https://doi.org/10.1007/978-3-319-63688-7_12

12. Kokoris-Kogias, E., Jovanovic, P., Gasser, L., Gailly, N., Syta, E., Ford, B.: Omniledger: a secure, scale-out, decentralized ledger via sharding. In: 2018 IEEE Symposium on Security and Privacy (SP), pp. 583–598. IEEE (2018)

13. Li, C., et al.: A decentralized blockchain with high throughput and fast confirmation. In: 2020 USENIX Annual Technical Conference (USENIX ATC 2020), pp. 515–528 (2020)

14. Liang, Z., Huang, Y., Guo, Z., Liu, Q., Liu, T.: PBFT consensus performance optimization method for fusing C4.5 decision tree in blockchain. In: Zheng, Z., Dai, H.-N., Fu, X., Chen, B. (eds.) BlockSys 2020. CCIS, vol. 1267, pp. 87–96. Springer, Singapore (2020). https://doi.org/10.1007/978-981-15-9213-3_7

15. Luu, L., Narayanan, V., Zheng, C., Baweja, K., Gilbert, S., Saxena, P.: A secure sharding protocol for open blockchains. In: Proceedings of the 2016 ACM SIGSAC Conference on Computer and Communications Security, pp. 17–30 (2016)

16. Nakamoto, S.: Bitcoin: a peer-to-peer electronic cash system (2008)

17. Sompolinsky, Y., Zohar, A.: PHANTOM and GHOSTDAG: a scalable generalization of Nakamoto consensus. Technical report, IACR Cryptology ePrint Archive, Report 2018 (2018)

18. Sompolinsky, Y., Lewenberg, Y., Zohar, A.: SPECTRE: a fast and scalable cryptocurrency protocol. IACR Cryptol. ePrint Arch. **2016**, 1159 (2016)

19. Sompolinsky, Y., Zohar, A.: Secure high-rate transaction processing in bitcoin. In: Böhme, R., Okamoto, T. (eds.) FC 2015. LNCS, vol. 8975, pp. 507–527. Springer, Heidelberg (2015). https://doi.org/10.1007/978-3-662-47854-7_32

20. Wang, J., Wang, H.: Monoxide: scale out blockchains with asynchronous consensus zones. In: 16th USENIX Symposium on Networked Systems Design and Implementation (NSDI 2019), pp. 95–112 (2019)

21. Wen, F., Yang, L., Cai, W., Zhou, P.: DP-Hybrid: a two-layer consensus protocol for high scalability in permissioned blockchain. In: Zheng, Z., Dai, H.-N., Fu, X., Chen, B. (eds.) BlockSys 2020. CCIS, vol. 1267, pp. 57–71. Springer, Singapore (2020). https://doi.org/10.1007/978-981-15-9213-3_5

22. Wood, G., et al.: Ethereum: a secure decentralised generalised transaction ledger. Ethereum Project Yellow Paper **151**(2014), 1–32 (2014)

23. Wu, K., Ma, Y., Huang, G., Liu, X.: A first look at blockchain-based decentralized applications. Practice and Experience, Software (2019)

24. Zamani, M., Movahedi, M., Raykova, M.: Rapidchain: scaling blockchain via full sharding. In: Proceedings of the 2018 ACM SIGSAC Conference on Computer and Communications Security, pp. 931–948 (2018)

25. Zhang, K., Jacobsen, H.A.: Towards dependable, scalable, and pervasive distributed ledgers with blockchains. In: ICDCS, pp. 1337–1346 (2018)

xBCBench: A Benchmarking Tool for Analyzing the Performance of Blockchain Systems

Rui Wang[1,2], Kejiang Ye[1(✉)], Yang Wang[1], and Cheng-Zhong Xu[3]

[1] Shenzhen Institute of Advanced Technology, Chinese Academy of Sciences, Shenzhen 518055, China
{rui.wang2,kj.ye,yang.wang1}@siat.ac.cn
[2] University of Chinese Academy of Sciences, Beijing 100049, China
[3] State Key Lab of IoTSC, Faculty of Science and Technology, University of Macau, Taipa, Macau, China
czxu@um.edu.mo

Abstract. Blockchain is a technical solution to jointly maintain a reliable database in a decentralized and trustless way. Since the birth of blockchain technology, the performance of blockchain has always been a key issue that has attracted much attention and discussion. Therefore, a performance testing tool can help evaluate the performance of different blockchain systems and guide further optimization. This paper proposes xBCBench, a benchmarking tool for analyzing the performance of blockchain systems, which can be used to compare the performance of different blockchain systems. xBCBench evaluates the performance of blockchain systems based on the metrics like throughput, latency, and system resource utilization. We also use xBCBench to analyze four mainstream blockchain systems (i.e., Ethereum, Hyperledger Fabric, Hyperledger Sawtooth and FISCO-BCOS) and propose further optimization suggestions.

Keywords: Benchmark · Blockchain · Ethereum · Hyperledger fabric · Hyperledger sawtooth · FISCO-BCOS

1 Introduction

Blockchain technology is the fundamental technology for constructing the Bitcoin [1] blockchain network. It is based on the principle of cryptography rather than credit so that any parties who reach an agreement can pay directly without the participation of a third-party intermediary. Blockchain is a distributed ledger, which is a technical solution for jointly maintaining a reliable database in a decentralized and trustless manner. From the data point of view, blockchain is a distributed database that is almost impossible to be tampered with. The "distributed" here is embodied in the distributed storage of data and embodied

H.-N. Dai et al. (Eds.): BlockSys 2021, CCIS 1490, pp. 101–114, 2021.
https://doi.org/10.1007/978-981-16-7993-3_8

in the distributed record of data (that is, jointly maintained by system participants). From the technical point of view, blockchain is not a single technology, but the result of the integration of multiple technologies. These technologies are combined with a new structure to form a new way of data recording, storage, and expression. However, since the birth of blockchain technology, the performance of blockchain has always been a key issue that has attracted much attention and discussion in the industry and academia. It has become a barrier to the large-scale deployment of blockchain systems.

The performance of the blockchain is affected by many factors. For example, the factors such as the security issue, the degree of distribution, and the scalability of blockchain are mutually restricted. At the same time, the performance, resources consumption, and network scale of blockchain are also mutually restricted. If we optimize one metric, other metrics can be affected. Therefore, how to design a practical blockchain system has become the main challenge of current research. To meet this challenge, blockchain benchmarking has become particularly important. The benchmark is a unified testing specification that provides a standard platform for different blockchain systems to compare their performance.

This paper proposes a new blockchain performance benchmarking tool - xBCBench that uses predefined use cases to test different blockchain systems and obtains corresponding results. xBCBench is an extensible tool that provides a variety of workloads, and supports a variety of performance metrics such as transaction throughput, transaction latency and resource consumption.

By using xBCBench, we have performed performance analysis on four mainstream blockchain systems, i.e. Ethereum [2], Hyperledger Fabric [3], Hyperledger Sawtooth [4], and FISCO-BCOS [5]. At the same time, we have put forward some simple optimization schemes based on the test results. The main contributions of this paper are as follows:

1. We propose a general blockchain performance benchmarking tool - xBCBench.
2. We used xBCBench to analyze the performance of four mainstream blockchain systems and propose further optimization suggestions.

The rest of this paper is arranged as follows: Sect. 2 introduces the basic terms and key metrics about blockchain performance. Section 3 introduces the system design of xBCBench. Section 4 uses xBCBench to analyze the performance of Ethereum, Hyper ledger Fabric, and other systems. Section 5 introduces the related work, and the last section summarizes the whole paper and presents the future work.

2   Basic Terms and Key Metrics for Evaluating Blockchain Performance

2.1   Basic Terms

Consensus. Consensus refers to a community solution to a statement that is accepted by different parties. In the blockchain system, due to the decentralized design, nodes are scattered and parallel everywhere, so it is necessary to design a system to maintain the operating sequence and fairness of the system and unify the version of the blockchain. The consensus is that the node network provides a distributed process that guarantees a unique transaction sequence and verifies transaction blocks. Common consensus algorithms include PoW [6], PoS [7,8], PBFT [9], Paxos [10], RAFT [11], etc.

Network Size. Network size is the number of verification nodes participating in the consensus of SUT (System Under Test).

Query. Query is the ability to perform searches on the data sets contained in the blockchain.

Read. Read can be an internal mechanism of a blockchain node, such as extracting data during a verification transaction.

Transaction. A transaction is a state transition that changes data in the blockchain from one value to another. These data can represent asset volume, multiple IoT sensor readings, or any other type of data tracked using blockchain. The transaction is usually proposed by the client and then evaluated by the blockchain system according to a series of rules, sometimes called a smart contract. If it is valid, the system will make a transaction to change the status.

2.2   Key Metrics

We have defined several common metrics applicable to blockchains.

Read Latency. Read latency is the time between when the read request is submitted and when the reply is received. RL means Read Latency, TWRR means the time when the response is received, ST means submit time.

$$RL = TWRR - ST \tag{1}$$

Read Throughput. Read throughput is a measure of how many read operations are completed in a defined period, expressed as reads per second (RPS). RT means read throughput, TRO means total read operations, TTS means total time in seconds.

$$RT = TRO/TTS \tag{2}$$

Transaction Latency. A transaction is not completed instantaneously from issue to final confirmation on the chain, but it takes a short period, which may be ten minutes or even up to several hours. Transaction latency is the total amount of time the transaction spends in the entire network. TL means transaction latency, CT@NT means confirmation time at the network threshold.

$$TL = CT@NT - ST \tag{3}$$

Transaction Throughput. Throughput refers to the number of requests processed by the system in a unit of time, and transaction throughput is the rate at which the blockchain SUT conducts effective transactions within a specified period. TT means transaction throughput, TCT means total committed transactions, TTS means total time in seconds.

$$TT = TCT/TTS \tag{4}$$

3   XBCBench Design

3.1   Key Concepts

Before discussing the design of xBCBench, we introduce some concepts, including test environment, observation points, transaction characteristics, workload, and faultload.

Test Environment. The test results should be independent and repeatable. To support this goal, all environmental parameters and test software should be recorded and provided, including any workload, consensus protocol, network settings, hardware environment, number of nodes, etc.

Observation Points. The setting of the observation point is very important. It is a node that can receive notifications from SUT or query SUT about submitted transactions' status. When this goal cannot be achieved, the measurement points should be determined, and as many observation points as possible should be set for each node and summarized.

Workloads. Workload defines how to perform SUT. How to design an effective workload is very important, and the workload must match the actual production usage. For example, if the workload just creates new entries in the database, and the production use mainly modifies existing entries, then the workload is invalid and no valuable conclusions will be drawn. There are many ways to design a workload. Make the workload close to the actual work situation, or design a corresponding workload for the function that needs to be tested. The more workload a benchmark tests, the better it can evaluate the effectiveness of the system.

Faultloads. The design of the blockchain needs to fully consider fault tolerance. In the event of a disk failure, network overload, or intentional attack, whether the system can guarantee the immutability of the ledger, and whether it can operate normally without crashing is the core attribute of the blockchain. Since many blockchains are expected to operate in an environment with failures or attacks, performance benchmarks should also include errors or malicious attacks to simulate real-life situations.

3.2   xBCBench Architecture

xBCBench is a general framework for benchmarking different blockchain platforms. xBCBench is designed with scalability in mind, and can be easily integrated with the mainstream blockchain systems. xBCBench is divided into three layers, including the benchmark layer, the core layer, and the adaptation layer, as shown in Fig. 1. The three layers are connected to the SUT.

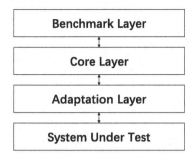

Fig. 1. xBCBench architecture

Benchamrk Layer. The benchmark layer is used to define the configuration of the blockchain network, the configuration of SUT and the configuration of the workloads. The network configuration determines what kind of blockchain network to choose, including the number of nodes, the number of organizations, and so on. The configuration of SUT will define the running round of the a benchmark. It also contains the setting of the observation point and the setting of the monitor. The observation point determines how the manager process collects progress information from the worker process, and the monitoring configuration determines what metrics can be collected by the manager process and where. Workload configuration is the core of the benchmark test. It determines when and how much workload is generated and handed it over to SUT.

Core Layer. The core layer includes a blockchain operation interface module, a resource monitoring module, a performance analyzer module, and a report generation module.

- Blockchain Operating Interfaces Module: Contains operations such as deploying smart contracts on the back-end blockchain, calling contracts, and querying status from the ledger.
- Resource Monitoring Module: Contains operations to start/stop the monitor and obtains the resource consumption status of the back-end blockchain system, including CPU, memory, network IO, etc. Two monitors are now provided, one is to monitor local/remote docker containers, and the other is to monitor local processes. More functions will be implemented in the future.
- Performance Analyzer Module: Contains operations to read predefined performance statistics (including TPS, latency, number of successful transactions, etc.) and print benchmark results. When the blockchain northbound interface is called, the key indicators of each transaction (such as the time of transaction creation, transaction submission time, transaction return result, etc.) will be recorded and used to generate the final predefined performance indicator statistics.
- Report Generator Module: Generate test reports.

Adaptation Layer. The adaptation layer is similar to the implementation part of the interface and implementation in the programming language, that is, various blockchain operations will eventually call the specific implementation of the Adaptation Layer user specified to operate the corresponding blockchain platform. At present, it has been adapted to Ethereum, Hyperledger Fabric, Hyperledger Sawtooth, FISCO-BCOS, and other platforms.

3.3 Implementation and Testing Process

We implement xBCBench in *Python* and *node.js*. It consists of two different processes: the main process and the helper process. The main process is responsible for initializing the SUT, coordinating the operation of the benchmark, and processing performance report generation based on the observed transaction statistics. The helper process performs the actual workload generation independently of each other. Even if the helper process reaches the limit of the host, using more helper processes can further increase the workload rate of xBCBench.

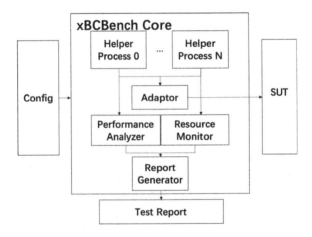

Fig. 2. xBCBench working process

The entire testing process mainly includes 3 phases: Preparation Phase, Testing Phase and Reporting Phase, as shown in Fig. 2.

Preparation Phase. The preparation phase is responsible for initializing the entire blockchain network, reading network configuration files, deploying smart contracts, and starting monitoring components. xBCBench executes the startup script from the configuration file. We will enter the relevant parameters as shown in Fig. 3. This step is mainly used for xBCBench and SUT deployment because it provides a convenient way to start the network and xBCBench in one step. Next, xBCBench deploys the smart contract to the SUT and starts the monitoring component.

Testing Phase. In the testing phase, xBCBench schedules and executes the round configured in the main process, and the specific workload is generated by the helper process. During the workload running cycle, the helper process sends progress updates to the main process.

Fig. 3. xBCBench parameter configuration interface

Reporting Phase. In the reporting phase, the system collects resource utilization data (including CPU utilization, memory utilization, network usage, etc.) and performance data (including TPS, delay, and a number of successful transactions), and summarizes the collected information to generate a visualization report, as shown in Fig. 4. After the report is generated, xBCBench will execute the cleanup script from the configuration file.

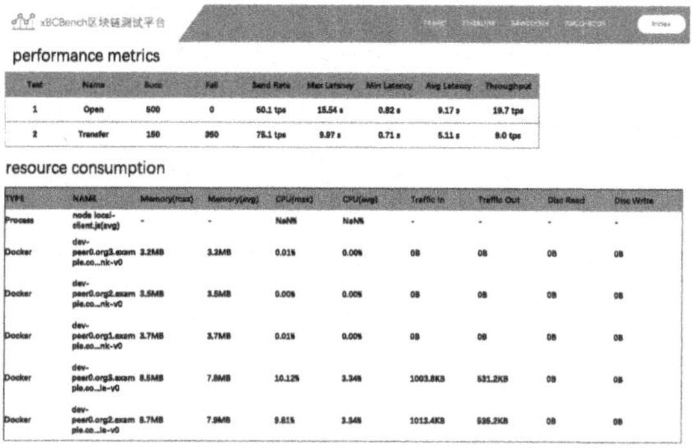

Fig. 4. xBCBench testing report

4 Blockchain Performance Evaluation by Using xBCBench

We use Ethereum, Hyperledger Fabric, Hyperledger Sawtooth, and FISCO-BCOS for case study because they are all mainstream blockchain systems. The test environment is as follows:

- Operating system: Ubuntu18.04 LTS
- CPU: Intel(R) Xeon(R) CPU E5-2630 v4 @ 2.20 GHz
- Memory: 64G DDR3 RAM
- Hard disk: mechanical hard disk 4T
- Number of Node: 16

We deployed SUT to the nodes for testing. The following results are the average of 5 independent runs.

4.1   Ethereum

We have prepared three workloads for Ethereum, i.e. account creation, account query, and transfer between accounts. We first configure Ethereum's network environment, and then, by setting different benchmark configs, we conduct many experiments on Ethereum and reach some conclusions. We first fix the number of nodes to 8. For account creation, as the number of requests gradually increases, TPS increases linearly, but when TPS reaches a bottleneck, even if the number of requests increases, TPS cannot continue to grow. For the transfer between accounts, when TPS reaches the bottleneck, it cannot continue to increase. Because the block production speed of Ethereum is fixed, the TPS value of Ethereum is determined by the number of transactions that can be packaged in a block. Although Ethereum does not limit the block size, it is subject to the network-wide broadcast speed limit and gasLimit limit. In terms of latency, transfer between accounts latency increases rapidly as the number of requests increases. When it reaches a peak, it decreases slightly, but still, maintains a high latency. The latency of account creation and account query is almost negligible, as shown in Fig. 5.

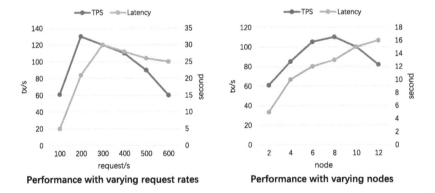

Fig. 5. Performance of Ethereum

Then we change the fixed number of requests to 200, and gradually increase the number of nodes. When the number of nodes exceeds 8, the TPS of Ethereum decreases linearly, and the delay increases linearly. This is because as the number of nodes increases, the network scale increases, so the delay increases.

Optimization Suggestion. Because of the current situation, Ethereum needs to modify the architecture to greatly improve the TPS. The Ethereum 2.0 currently under development will improve the performance of Ethereum through Casper [12], Sharding [13], eWASM [14], etc.

4.2 Hyperledger Fabric

For Fabric, we deploy fabric1.4.0 on 7 physical machines, each physical machine is used as an Organization. There are 2 peers in each Organization. We select GolevelDB as the database. The test results are shown in Fig. 6.

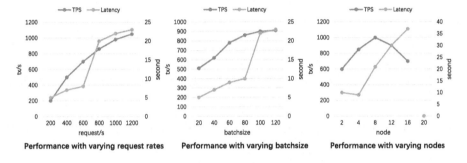

Fig. 6. Performance of hyperledger fabric

We first fix the batchsize and test the performance of the Fabric by adjusting the request rate. The results show that when we fix the batchsize to 100, by increasing the number of requests, the TPS of open workload and query workload increase linearly. When the number of requests reaches 500 request/s, the TPS of transfer workload will reach the bottleneck. In terms of latency, query workload has almost no delay. The delay of open workload will increase as the number of requests increases. The delay of transfer workload is relatively small before reaching the bottleneck. When the bottleneck is reached, the delay will increase significantly.

Next, we fix the number of request/s, and then adjust the batchsize to 20, 40, 60, 80, 100, 120, and the rest of the settings remain unchanged. The results show that as the batchsize increases, the TPS will increase linearly, but when the batchsize is greater than a threshold, the TPS will decrease. In terms of latency, when the batchsize is less than a threshold, the delay will slowly increase, and when the batchsize exceeds that threshold, the delay will increase significantly.

Finally, we fix the number of request/s and batchsize, and test the Fabric performance by adjusting the number of nodes. The results show that when the number of nodes is less than 8, the TPS increases rapidly with the increase of the number of nodes, and the delay will also increase rapidly. When the number of nodes exceeds 8, the TPS will be reduced and the delay will be reduced accordingly. When the number of nodes reaches 16, the system will stop working because it cannot reach a consensus.

Optimization Suggestion. Through the experimental results, we can find that to better improve TPS and reduce latency, we can reduce the size of batchsize when request/s has not reached a threshold. When the request exceeds the threshold, we need to choose a larger batchsize to increase the TPS and reduce the delay. To better improve the performance of the Fabric, Batchsize needs to match the request. At the same time, we need to limit the number of fabric nodes. If it exceeds a certain number, the system will not be able to reach a consensus, resulting in system failure.

4.3   Hyperledger Sawtooth

For Sawtooth, we selected the Sawtooth 1.0.5 version as the test benchmark. We have prepared query and smallbank workloads for sawtooth. Smallbank workloads include transaction savings, deposit checking, send payment, write a check, and amalgamate operations. We set the number of accounts in smallbank to 50, and the number of transactions in each block to 80. The results show that as the request/s increases, the TPS of the query workload also increases, and for the smallbank workload, the TPS will decrease after reaching the bottleneck. In terms of latency, the latency of query workload can be ignored. The latency of smallbank will continue to increase with the increase of request/s, and will show a linear growth trend in the early stage. When a threshold is reached, the latency will show an exponential growth trend.

Then we fixed the request/s and adjusted the number of transactions in each block. Through testing, we found that increasing the number of transactions in each block within a certain range can increase the TPS, and the peak value can reach about 2000. In terms of latency, latency will increase as the number of transactions per block increases. After reaching a threshold, latency will increase exponentially, as shown in Fig. 7.

With the increase in input transaction processing rate, CPU usage and memory usage have also increased exponentially to higher levels than before. This may become a potential bottleneck in transaction processing speed, because memory may continue to increase and cause problems in transaction success rate and latency.

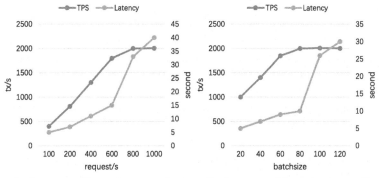

Fig. 7. Performance of hyperledger sawtooth

Optimization Suggestion. The Hyperledger Sawtooth blockchain network consists of verification program nodes, including a novel consensus algorithm PoET [15]. Compared with the proof-of-work algorithm, it supports large-scale networks with the least amount of calculation and more efficient resource consumption. Throughout the testing process, the throughput can reach up to about 2000 TPS. Besides, the development team is migrating the core components of Sawtooth from Python to Rust [16], which will further improve the performance of Sawtooth in the future.

4.4 FISCO-BCOS

For Fisco-Bcos, we first deployed the FISCO-BCOS network. We have prepared set and get workloads for Fisco-Bcos. Set is responsible for generating a hello world smart contract and deploying the smart contract, and get is responsible for calling the smart contract and outputting hello world. The test results are shown in Fig. 8.

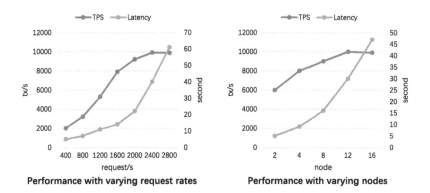

Fig. 8. Performance of FISCO-BCOS

We first fix the number of participating nodes to 4 and test FISCO-BCOS by adjusting request/s. The results show that with the continuous increase of request/s, the TPS of FISCO-BCOS increases linearly until it reaches 8000, the TPS starts to grow slowly and stops growing after reaching the peak of 10000. As for the delay, the initial delay increases slowly, and after the TPS reaches its peak, the delay increases substantially.

Next, we fix the request/s and adjust the number of participating nodes. As the number of nodes increases, the TPS will slowly increase. For delay, the delay will increase rapidly as the number of nodes increases.

Optimization Suggestion. FISCO-BCOS 2.0 adds support for distributed data storage. Nodes can store data in a remote distributed system, which overcomes many limitations of localized data storage. At the same time, FISCO-BCOS 2.0 will implement custom transaction mutually exclusive variables through a set of parallel transaction processing models. In the process of block execution, the system will automatically construct a transaction dependency graph - DAG based on transaction mutually exclusive variables, and execute transactions in parallel based on DAG. In the best case, the performance can be improved by several times (depending on the number of CPU cores).

5   Related Work

In 2017, the National University of Singapore and Zhejiang University jointly launched a private blockchain evaluation framework - BlockBench [17], currently supporting three platforms: Hyperledger Fabric, Ethereum, and Parity. Since the development time of blockbench is relatively early, its applicability and completion are relatively poor.

In 2018, Hyperledger and Huawei launched a blockchain testing tool - caliper [18]. As a large community open-source platform, the advantage of this product is that the degree of completion is very high. It currently supported performance indicators such as success rate, transaction Throughput, transaction latency (minimum, maximum, average, percentage), resource consumption (CPU, memory, network IO, etc.). Because it is prepared for Hyperledger series products, its universality is relatively poor. Although Ethereum is now supported, it is still inconvenient to use because there is no visual interface. Furthermore, Caliper's client has performance problems. After the request rate reaches a certain level, the CPU can run at full capacity and cannot continue to increase the request rate.

In 2019, TrustedBench is released by the China Academy of Information and Communications Technology [19]. As a general platform for blockchain performance testing, it supports cluster workload deployment, provides a graphical user configuration interface, and uses HTTP protocol. TrustedBench has better performance and more adaptation platforms, but the blockchain system under test needs to be actively adapted to TrustedBench. Due to the short development time, the current degree of completion is not good enough, and it does not support the monitoring of CPU load and utilization, disk IO, network bandwidth utilization, and memory utilization.

6 Conclusion

In this paper, we propose a benchmarking tool for evaluating different blockchain systems, called xBCBench. It allows users to use a set of predefined use cases to measure the performance of blockchain implementations, supports multiple blockchain systems, provides a visual interface, and is also easy to use. By using xBCBench, we have conducted a comprehensive analysis of the four mainstream blockchain systems, i.e. Ethereum, Hyperledger Fabric, Hyperledger Sawtooth, FISCO-BCOS. The results show that the performance of the public chain is far from comparable to that of the consortium chain. There is also a big difference in performance between different consortium chains. Different consortium chains have different focuses, and a suitable blockchain system should be designed for specific application scenarios. We will make xBCBench support more blockchain systems in our future work. At the same time, we will add more workloads to xBCBench to make the experimental results more convincing.

Acknowledgment. This work is supported by Key-Area Research and Development Program of Guangdong Province (NO.2020B010164003), National Natural Science Foundation of China (No. 62072451), Shenzhen Basic Research Program (No. JCYJ20200109115418592), Science and Technology Development Fund of Macao S.A.R (FDCT) under number 0015/2019/AKP, and Youth Innovation Promotion Association CAS (NO. 2019349).

References

1. Nakamoto, S.: Bitcoin-A-Peer-to-Peer-electronic-Cash-System (2008)
2. Wood, G.: Ethereum: a secure decentralised generalised transaction ledger. Ethereum Project Yellow Paper **151**(2014), 1–32 (2014)
3. Androulaki, E., et al.: Hyperledger fabric: a distributed operating system for permissioned blockchains. In: Proceedings of the Thirteenth EuroSys Conference (2018)
4. Ampel, B., Patton, M., Chen, H.: Performance modeling of hyperledger sawtooth blockchain. In: 2019 IEEE International Conference on Intelligence and Security Informatics (ISI), pp. 59–61 (2019)
5. Webank. Fisco-bcos. [EB/OL]. http://www.fisco-bcos.org/ Accessed 19 March 2021
6. Gervais, A., Karame, G., Wüst, K., Glykantzis, V., Ritzdorf, H., Capkun, S.: On the security and performance of proof of work blockchains. In: Proceedings of the 2016 ACM SIGSAC Conference on Computer and Communications Security (2016)
7. King, S., Nadal, S.: PPcoin: peer-to-peer crypto-currency with proof-of-stake (2012)
8. Kiayias, A., Russell, A., David, B., Oliynykov, R.: Ouroboros: a provably secure proof-of-stake blockchain protocol. IACR Cryptol. ePrint Arch. **2016**, 889 (2016)
9. Castro, M.: Practical byzantine fault tolerance. In: OSDI 1999 (1999)

10. Lamport, L.: The part-time parliament. ACM Trans. Comput. Syst. **16**, 133–169 (1998)
11. Ongaro, D., Ousterhout, J.: In search of an understandable consensus algorithm. In: USENIX Annual Technical Conference (2014)
12. Ethereum. Casper. [EB/OL]. https://ethereum.org/en/developers/docs/consensus-mechanisms/pos/#finality. Accessed 19 March 2021
13. Yu, G., Wang, X., Yu, K., Ni, W., Zhang, J., Liu, R.: Survey: sharding in blockchains. IEEE Access **8**, 14155–14181 (2020)
14. Ethereum. ewasm. [EB/OL]. https://ethereum.org/en/developers/docs/evm/. Accessed 19 March 2021
15. Chen, L., Xu, L., Shah, N., Gao, Z., Lu, Y., Shi, W.: On security analysis of proof-of-elapsed-time (poet). In: SSS (2017)
16. Rust. Rust. [EB/OL]. https://www.rust-lang.org/. Accessed 19 March 2021
17. Dinh, T., Wang, J., Chen, G., Liu, R., Ooi, B.C., Tan, K.: Blockbench: a framework for analyzing private blockchains. In: Proceedings of the 2017 ACM International Conference on Management of Data (2017)
18. Hyperledger. Hyperledger caliper. [EB/OL]. https://hyperledger.github.io/caliper/. Accessed 19 March 2021
19. CAICT. Trustedbench. [EB/OL]. http://www.trustedblockchain.cn/. Accessed 19 March 2021

Ladder: A Blockchain Model
of Low-Overhead Storage

Peng Chen, Xunhui Zhang, Hui Liu, Liangliang Xiang, and Peichang Shi[✉]

National Key Laboratory of Parallel and Distributed Processing, College of Computer
Science, National University of Defense Technology, Changsha 410073, China
{chenpeng15,zhangxunhui,liuhui,xiangliangliang19,pcshi}@nudt.edu.cn

Abstract. Emerging blockchain accounting mechanism allow mutually
distributed parties to transport trusted information and ensure the correctness of data. Every blockchain node stores the complete block locally.
Although this measure improves security, it causes huge storage overhead. We present *Ladder*, a multi-level low-overhead storage model for
blockchain, which can greatly reduce the storage overhead of nodes while
ensuring that the blockchain cannot be tampered easily and the block
information is complete. *Ladder* distinguishes the retrieved frequency
and importance of different blocks by value-density, dividing them into
Hot-Blocks, *Warm-Blocks* and *Cold-Blocks* adopting different storage
strategies respectively. Through experimental verification of time and
space cost of different storage strategies, *Ladder* can greatly reduce the
local storage overhead of nodes.

Keywords: Blockchain · Low-overhead · Storage · Block ·
Value-density

1 Introduction

Blockchain was proposed in 2008 by Nakamoto in "Bitcoin: A Peer-to-Peer Electronic Cash System" [11]. In recent years, Bitcoin-based digital currencies have
been gaining attention from all over the world. According to Pricewaterhouse
Coopers(PwC), there are more than 1.4 billion dollars invested to research about
blockchain [8] in the first of 9 months. Meanwhile, the blockchain has caused rev-
olutionary changes in finance and other fields [7,22]. Ethereum [17] provides an
open-source smart contract platform, and releases a special encrypted digital
currency, *ether*, to provide a decentralized Ethereum Virtual Machine (EVM)
processing peer-to-peer transaction contracts. Ethereum and blockchain are represented as *Public Blockchain* in which block can be read, sent and confirmed
by anyone. Relatively, *Private Blockchain* means that the counterpart operation
to the blockchain need to be authorized by the special node. In addition, the
consensus process of *Consortium Blockchain* is controlled by pre-selected nodes,
which is regarded as partially decentralized such as Hyperledger Fabric [2].

© Springer Nature Singapore Pte Ltd. 2021
H.-N. Dai et al. (Eds.): BlockSys 2021, CCIS 1490, pp. 115–129, 2021.
https://doi.org/10.1007/978-981-16-7993-3_9

Blockchain is firstly been applied to integrate with finance, but it also shows strategic prospects in *IoT*, insurance, medical, banking, government and so on. For example, the combination of the internet of things(IoT) and the blockchain can ensure the credibility of the data transmission process and ensure that the system will not be attacked by malicious participants [9]. In fact, the blockchain is a decentralized database. Each node stores the blockchain from the latest block to the genesis block. Data blocks are linked by time or other logical order to form an append-only chain. Miners verify transactions and package them to form a new block [3]. If spoilers want to tamper with the block, they must tamper with all the blocks from this block to the latest block [19]. As the number of nodes increase, the cost of tampering with blockchain will be higher.

While the storage mode of the blockchain improves the reliability of the blockchain, the storage overhead of nodes continues to increase. Take Bitcoin as an example, the block height has reached 666,840, and 607,924,131 transactions have been completed on Jan 20, 2021. The total block capacity is about 383.27GB, and the total number of nodes holding coins has reached 34,214,269 [6]. At the same time, the total number of registered addresses has been increasing continuously. *Public Blockchain, Consortium Blockchain* or *Private Blockchain* have proposed restrict to participants and differ their consensus [4,15], but the block storage method is the same. Each node that joins the system needs to simultaneously save all blocks, wasting storage space seriously. The storage overhead is an important factor that limits the scalability of blockchain technology in IoT, finance and other industries [13].

In this paper, we design and implement a secure low-overhead storage model, called *Ladder*. The use frequency of different blocks of the blockchain has obvious differences, the newly generated blocks have been retrieved frequently, and this frequency will decrease with time. We define the concept of blockchain *value-density (VD)* to distinguish the importance and retrieved frequency of different blocks. The details of *VD* will be clarified in 3.2. As shown in Fig. 1, we divide the blocks into three types, *Hot-Blocks*, *Warm-Blocks* and *Cold-Blocks*, adopting different storage strategies to lower the overhead of node.

Hot-Blocks: These blocks have been generated just before and it will be frequently retrieved in the next period of time. Therefore, They are stored locally on the node so that they can be accessed almost immediately.

Warm-Blocks: These blocks have been generated in the past period of time and will not be retrieved frequently in the next. We separate the block to several *caches* and each node stores one of *caches* to replace original complete block. When retrieving the block, it combines all *caches* to obtain a complete block.

Cold-Blocks: The using frequency of this type of block is particularly low or even will not be retrieved. To ensure the integrity of the blockchain, we store the block in the remote database. Once node wants to retrieve the block, we can get the complete block from the remote database sacrificing time efficiency.

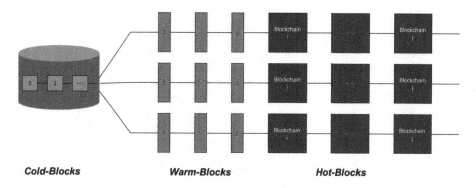

Cold-Blocks   **Warm-Blocks**   **Hot-Blocks**

Fig. 1. Basic *Ladder* storage architecture

In summary, we make the following contributions:

We systematically analyze reasons why blockchain consumes so much storage. Additionally, we introduce a system, called *Ladder*, a multi-layer storage model solving blockchain storage.

We formally define and complete calculation of *VD* to distinguish the importance of different blocks, dividing the blocks into *Hot-Blocks*, *Warm-Blocks* and *Cold-Blocks*. Meanwhile, we design the storage frame oriented different block types and expand the block structure to complete homologous operations.

We verify the efficiency of storing and retrieving to *Warm-Block* in terms of time and space. At the same time, the conclusions show *Ladder* can save storage space without affecting the completeness of blockchain.

The remainder of this paper is organized as follows. Section 2 provides background on blockchains and discusses related research. Section 3 describes our design for value density, and the detailed steps to different blocks. Section 4 presents our implementation, and reports the performance of Ladder. Section 5 concludes this work.

2 Background and Overview

In this section, we present relevant background and related work of blockchain storage systems, and analyze the reasons that increase consumption of blockchain.

2.1 Block Structure

The block is the basic structure of the blockchain, and the miners pack the unpackaged legal transactions to form block. The block structure is different, we select the most common block. As is shown in Table 1, a complete block is mainly composed by a block size, a block header, and a block body. The transaction information is stored in the block body with a form of a Merkle tree [14].

Table 2 summarizes the structure of block header, which contains the hash of the current block and the hash of the previous block. Through this hash value, every block is linked to form a blockchain. The *merkleRoot* indicates that hash of the *Merkle* tree organized by transactions of this block. The miner searches for a random number, *nonce*, to make the hash of the block meet certain conditions (such as hash value of first six digitalis equals 0) completing the block mining [3]. Meanwhile, blockchain system maintains the mining time about ten minutes by adjusting *difficulty*.

Table 1. The structure of block

Item	Size (bytes)	Description
magicNo	4	Magic number, a constant
blocksize	4	The size of this block
blockHeader	112	The block head constructure, see Table 2
counter	1–9	The number of transactions of block
transaction	Uncertain	The transaction data and information is packaged in this block

Table 2. The structure of block header

Item	Size (bytes)	Description
version	4	The version of block
preBlock	32	Hash value of previous block
hash	32	Hash value of present block
merkleRoot	32	Root hash value of transactions Merkle tree
time	4	The time of block generated
difficulty	4	Difficulty for mining
nonce	4	Random number

2.2   Related Researach

Tung from Northeastern University proposed a scalable model [12,16] for the storage capacity of the blockchain. The complete copy of the blockchain is separated, and the segment is stored in a certain proportion of nodes. At the same time, the reliability of the node is verified. While ensuring data security, reduce the storage space of the blockchain.

The mini-blockchain [5] proposed by Franca is an improvement on the basis of blockchain, which deletes the old blocks and shortens the length of blockchain. In another word, it allows discarding the blockchain that was generated before long, as long as the most recent blocks of the current block are saved.

The above two methods reduce the storage overhead to a certain degree, but the two solutions do not distinguish block. And the first solution stores the separated block with a static method, so it is not suitable for complex circumstances. The latter method deletes the old block, the security of the blockchain is affected, and the old data cannot be gained when it is retrieved.

Most relevant for our research is protocol *LS4BUCC* [18], which firstly proposes the concept of *VD* and the storage strategy of different blocks. However, the paper does not specify specific details. We extend the original *LS4BUCC* protocol by making details, implement and evaluation. We complete the formula and calculate of value density, design the operation detail to different block types, implement the process to *Warm-Blocks* and verify *Ladder* correctness.

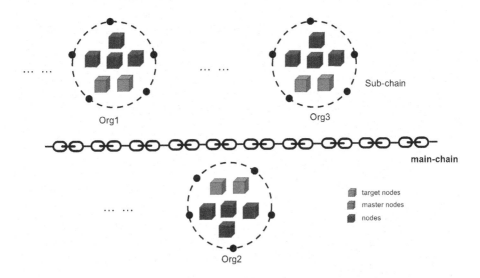

Fig. 2. Example of a Ladder blockchain Model

3 *Ladder* Protocols

3.1 Blockchain Model

In a broad sense, the *sub-chain* [20] of the blockchain refers to the blockchain with other functions derived from the *main-chain*. In this paper, the *sub-chain* specifically refers to the local blockchain constructed within each organization in *Consortium Blockchain*, which corresponds to the *main-chain* between each organization but independent of each other, like Fig. 2. The transactions and data exchange within the organization are stored on the local *sub-chain*, and the internal computing nodes of organization maintain consistency of the ledger. Each organization has several *target nodes* to communicate with other organizations. Meanwhile, all organizations elect *master* from *target nodes* by Raft [1], which responsible for block operation and *VD* calculation.

The data interaction and transaction information between organizations are packaged by *target node* to form a new block. The protocol for block creation is pluggable and supports main consensus protocols. The block becomes a *Hot-Block* just after being generated. The *target node* stores a backup locally, sends this to the *master* and other *target nodes*. The cross-organizational transactions and data are stored on the *main-chain* and maintained by the *target nodes* of every organization. *Ladder* oriented *Consortium Blockchain* and its methods are also suitable for *Public Blockchain* and *Private Blockchain*.

3.2   Value Desity

The value of a block indicates how important the block in the past and how often it will be used in the next stage. Different organizations elect *master* from *target nodes*, and *master* update the *VD* of the block with a time interval. In equation(1), N represents the number of times the block is retrieved, and T represents the time interval from the block is generated. The *VD* of a block is directly proportional to the block retrieve number, and inversely proportional to the generation time of the block.

$$VD(Block) \propto \frac{N}{T} \tag{1}$$

Equation (2) specifies the function of *VD*. Considering different occasions, we set parameters k_1 and k_2 ($k_1 \geq 1, 0 < k_2 \leq 1$). On the one hand, the failure rate of information is relatively fast in real-time system, so time interval in *VD* is more important. So we can increase k_2 and decrease k_1. On the other hand, there exist some systems where the information update frequency is relatively slow and the use number of blocks has influenced more seriously. To deal with this condition, we can increase the k_1 and decrease k_2. By setting different scale factors, the specific definition of value density in different application scenarios can be met.

$$VD(Block) = \frac{k_1 * log(N + e)}{log(k_2 * T + e)} \tag{2}$$

Meanwhile, *Ladder* distinguishes *Hot-Blocks*, *Warm-Blocks*, and *Cold-Blocks* based on the calculation results of value density. *Hot-Blocks* have the highest value density and are retrieved with the highest frequency. Correspondingly, *Cold-Blocks* have the lowest value density and are retrieved with the lowest frequency. The *VD* of the *Warm-Blocks* is in the middle, and the frequency of being accessed is not too high. In different IoT systems, the calculation method of *VD* is different, and the thresholds of *Hot-Blocks*, *Warm-Blocks* and *Cold-Blocks* will also change. Owing to complexity, diversity and continous evolution of all kinds of system, there is not a unified formula can solve such a huge system. To be specific, an adaptive mechanism needs to be found for setting parameters and thresholds.

3.3   Expanded Block Structure

In order to facilitate separation and combination to *Warm-Blocks* and *VD* calculation, we expand the structure of block header. The number of blocks used, *useNumber*, and the block separation structure are added into the block header. The expanded block header structure is shown in Table 3.

Table 3. The expanded structure of block header

Item	Size (bytes)	Description
...	...	... ...
useNumber	4	the number of this block is retrieved
separation	68	the structure of this block, see Table 4

In Table 4, we expand the structure of separation of block header. To be specific, *isSeperate* indicates whether the current block is fragmented, default false. Additionally, *presentHash* and *nextHash* are 32-bit byte codes, the former represents the hash value of current *cache*, and the latter represents the hash of next *cache*. Both of them are null by default.

Table 4. The separation structure of expanded block

Item	Size (bytes)	Description
isSeparation	4	Determine whether block is separated
presentHash	32	Hash value of present cache
nextHash	32	Hash value of next cache

3.4   *Ladder* Protocols

Ladder sorts the blocks into three types: *Hot-Blocks*, *Warm-Blocks* and *Cold-Blocks*. The newly produced block is *Hot-Blocks*, which will be stored locally in order to retrieve quickly. Then block value will reduce with time, and *Hot-Blocks* will become *Warm-Blocks*. *Ladder* will execute separation operation and store only one *cache* instead of complete block. When *cache* is retrieved, it can be combined with original block. Next, when *Warm-Blocks* become *Cold-Blocks*, the blocks value and use frequency drop further. *Ladder* will launch combination operation to get complete block. In order to lower storage size, the combined result is stored in remote database. These changes to the blockchain storage are invisible to client. The key operation will be illustrated below.

Block Separation. When the *VD* of *Hot-Blocks* reduce and become *Warm-Blocks*, which will be separated. *Target node* does not need to store the complete block, but only stores one *cache* of block.

The block separation process is described in Algorithm 1.When *master* updates the block *VD* and finds there exists *Hot-Blocks* becoming *Warm-Blocks*, it sends message $< separate, id_{block}, \phi >_\delta$ to *target nodes*, where ϕ indicates the separation strategy is going to perform, id_{block} is the block id to be operated and δ is signature confirmation of *master*. Each *target nodes* verify the signature after receiving the message and feedback the confirmation message $< ok, id_{block}, \phi >_{\mu_i}$,which indicates that it is in favor of separation to this block. After receiving more than half of confirmation, it executes the separation operation. The strategy is defined by formal function, including smart contracts [21] or other methods. This paper takes linear separation as an example and divides the block into n $caches(n \geq 1)$ .The specific steps are as follows:

a. Store this block in database remotely(details will be clarified below).
b. Set *isSeperate* to value of true.
c. Separate the block body into n equal parts, and the block header data remains unchanged.
d. Calculate the hash value of the current *cache* and fill it in the block header *presentHash*. Differently, the *presentHash* of *cache* head (the first *cache* of separated block) is the hash value of original block which is not separated.
e. Modify *nextHash* value of each *cache* to the *presentHash* of the next *cache* of same block. Specially, *nextHash* value of the last *cache* is null.

After the block is separated, the information of the block header remains unchanged except separation, and each *cache* is still a complete block, but the block body becomes 1/n of the original. Store the n *caches* and then delete the original complete block. The storage space occupied by the block is reduced to 1/n of the original (ignoring the block header space).

Algorithm 1. Block Separation

Input: Block block, num;
Output: List[Block] caches
  1: List [Transaction] TransLists = separation (block.transaction, ϕ, num)
  2: store(block, database)
  3: **for** k=0 →num **do**
  4:     new Block = Block (TransList[i])
  5:     Block.separation.presentHash = hash(TransList[i])
  6:     Block.separation.nextHash = hash(TansLists[i+1])
  7:     Block.separation.isSeparate = true
  8:     **if** i = 0 **then**
  9:         Block.separation.presentHash = this.block.hash
 10:     **if** i = num-1 **then**
 11:         Block.separation.nextHash = null

Caches Combination. There are two chances that *caches* must be combined to complete block. One is *Warm-Blocks* becoming *Cold-Blocks*. Another is *Warm-Blocks* are retrieved by *target nodes*. The difference is first situation will delete combination result, the whole block.

The *master* sends *caches* combination request messages $< combine, id_{block}, id_{top}, flag >_\delta$, to *target nodes*, where id_{block} indicates the hash value of the block, id_top represents the hash value of *cache* head which is stored in *master*, *flag* indicates two reasons why these *caches* need to be combined. Specifically, if flag is 1, it means the block becomes *Cold-Blocks*. Otherwise, this block is retrieved.

When *target nodes* have received combination messages and finished verification, send the *cache* stored by itself to *master*. Finally, *master* accept *caches* from *target nodes*, retain legal *caches*, and combine them to form a complete block. The specific steps are as follows:

a. The *master* gets *cache* head stored by itself.
b. Retrieve the hash value of next *cache* by *nextHash* and get the next *cache*.
c. Combine block body of two *caches* and update *nextHash*.
d. Repeat step b and c until the value of *nextHash* is null.
e. Set *isSeperate* to false.

After finishing combination operations, determine the flag value. If flag is 1, delete the whole block stored by all *target nodes*. Otherwise, send the whole block to retrieving node. The above steps are illustrated in Algorithm 2.

Algorithm 2. Caches Combination

Input: caches, flag
Output: block
1: block = null
2: **while** block.seperation.nextHash != null **do**
3:     block = block + cache
4:     cache = block.nextCache
5: block.separation.isSeparate =false
6: **if** flag = 1 **then**
7:     deletBlock(block)

Storage Locally. In case of storing a whole block, *target nodes* firstly need to send a storage request message $< storeRequest, id_{block} >_{\mu_i}$ to *master*. Then *master* verifies correctness of the transactions in block. Then it broadcasts the message $< store, id_{block} >_\delta$ to other all *target nodes*. After receiving message, it verifies the correctness of signature and transactions, then calculates hash value of the block and verify its integrity. Finishing the verification, *target nodes* store this newly generated block locally linking to the latest block. Finally, *target nodes* must give back to a confirmation message $< stored, id_{block} >_{\mu_i}$ to *master*.

In case of storing *caches*, *master* randomly matches *caches* and target nodes, satisfying two conditions: 1). Every node stores at least one *cache*; 2). Any

cache is stored by at least k *target nodes*. Then *master* sends a store request
$< storeRequest, id_{cache}, id_{node} >_\delta$, to special *target nodes*. *Target nodes* verify
signature, calculates the hash value of cache and verifies its integrity. Then they
delete the original complete block and store *cache*. Then *target nodes* send confirmation message $< stored, id_{cache}, id_{node} >_{\mu_i}$ to *master*. After all *caches* are
stored successfully, *master* stores *cache* head and deletes the complete block.

Algorithm 3. caches storage

Input: List[Block] caches
Output: successful or failure
1: **for all** cache in caches **do**
2:     assign(cache, nodes)
3:     **for all** node in nodes **do**
4:         store(cache, node)

***Cold-Blocks* Storage.** When Warm-Blocks become *Cold-Blocks*, which need to
be stored in remote database encrypted by ring-signature. Any *target nodes* can
read the block casually but write operations must be executed by multi-party
verification. Meanwhile, it is also an append-only database like blockchain. The
block is stored with a mode of chain in remote database and block can be added
only after verification by nodes with more than a certain amount.

Block Retrieve. When one node wants to use the block data, it firstly retrieves
the block locally and then checks whether this block is separated. If the block
is separated, it requests a *cache* combination from *master* to obtain a complete
block. If there are no result for searching block data locally, it will retrieve the
block in the remote database.

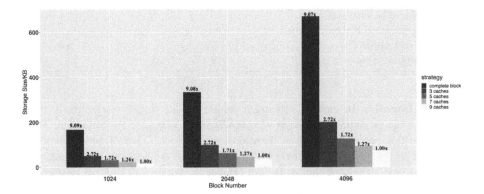

Fig. 3. The storage memory size of different strategy (of complete block, 3 caches, 5
caches, 7 caches, 9 caches) with 32 nodes.

4   Implement and Evaluation

In this section, we present our implement of *Ladder* based on Kademlia [10]. We mainly implement the operation to *Warm-Blocks*, including storage, retrieve, separation and combination. Kademlia is a distributed database. Every node and data has 32-bytes identifier, and distance can be calculated by XOR. Specially, it store data in k nodes that are closest. We completely replace the storage mechanism, storing data in all node. Meanwhile, data is structured as blocks and node can store and retrieve blocks. In particular, we added *separation* and *useNumber* to expand block. Based on expanded structure, we implement the separation to *Warm-Blocks* and combination to *caches*. We compare the storage overhead and time spent between the same block with different storage strategy and verify time spent of *caches* combination, further analyzing the effectiveness of *Ladder* reducing node storage overhead.

We evaluate *Ladder* with different *caches* number. In this paper, we set whole block as baseline, and separate block to several *caches*(with 3, 5, 7, 9) to test its performance in terms of storage and retrieve. Our experiment are conducted on a local computer and leverage thread to simulate node. The computer is equipped with Intel® Core™ i7-9700CPU @ 3.00 GHz, 8G RAM and 1TB disk.

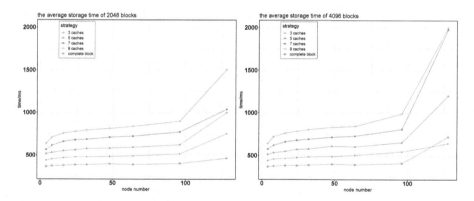

Fig. 4. The storage time of different strategy (of complete block, 3 caches, 5 caches, 7 caches, 9 caches) with nodes

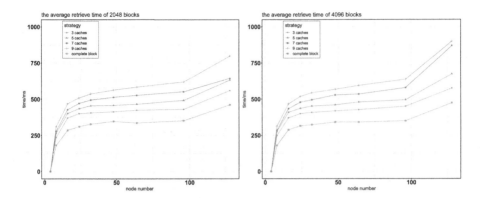

Fig. 5. The retrieve time of different strategies (of complete block, 3 caches, 5 caches, 7 caches, 9 caches) with nodes

Storage Size. We separate the whole block into certain caches and compare the memory size of different storage strategy. As show in Fig. 3, we leverage 32 nodes to store a number of blocks with the same size and examine memory size. It is obvious that *Ladder* decreases storage size to about $1/n$ after *Warm-Blocks* are separated and stored as *caches*. The result corresponds to our design.

Storage and Retrieve Time. After *Warm-Blocks* are separated, *cache* rather than whole block is stored in node. However, it will consume external time to complete block separation and storage position calculation, *caches* retrieve and combination. *Ladder* needs to examine whether time spend increases linearly with separation number. Similarly, we separate complete block into different number (3, 5, 7, 9) and measure storage time (Fig. 4) and retrieve time (Fig. 5) with node number. As shown in Fig. 4, the left shows the average time cost of different storage strategies with the number of nodes when storing 2048 blocks. Vertically, the time overhead increases when blocks separation number increases, but the time is much lower than the product of separation number and the complete block time. Horizontally, when the number of nodes increases, the average storage time increases slowly. Particularly, when the number of nodes is 128, the time overhead is greatly increased by the computer performance limit. The right of Fig. 4, the number of blocks is increased to twice of the left, showing similar results.

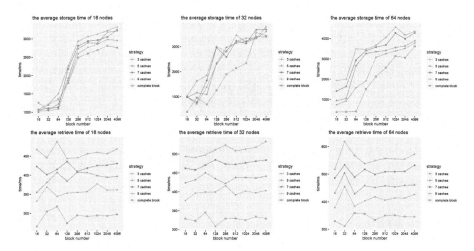

Fig. 6. The storage and retrieve time of different strategy (of complete block, 3 caches, 5 caches, 7 caches, 9 caches) with block number

As well, we record of average time of getting a *Warm-Blocks* in Fig. 5, including *caches* retrieve and combination. Similarly, average time increase with separation number and node number. Because complete block is stored locally, it only needs to read database with little time when it is retrieved. So *Warm-Blocks* retrieve time accelerate acutely. However, time increase slow quickly with node number. The value of time cost is not large.

Additionally, we analyze the average time of block storage and retrieve with block number. In Fig. 6, we set 16, 32 and 64 block node to store and retrieve data with different strategies. The conclusion shows the storage time increase with blocks number, but the time is controlled in a certain range which has a narrow gap. However, the separation number can not infinitely increase. When it exceed threshold, the storage size will increase and performance will decrease intensely. So another adaptive mechanism is needed to maintain appropriate separation number. Also, the retrieve time is steady with the same strategy, when the time grows with separation number. This means that when the system is running stably, the block storage time is less affected by the block strategy; at the same time, the block retrieve time will not increase significantly. *Ladder* can effectively resolve the problems raised in this paper.

Security and Integrity. As mentioned above, *Ladder* can lower storage size and its performance has been influenced weakly. Next, we would prove its security and integrity to blockchain. The way of blockchain connect has no change, just part of them are separated or stored remotely. First, *Hot-Blocks* are stored completely by every *target node*, it is the same with original blockchain. Every node has a backup of Hot-Blocks, so its security and integrity have no influence. Second, *Warm-Blocks* are separated into several *caches*, and every *cache* is stored by k nodes. Whole block can be accessed after *caches* combination. Block retrieve fails just when at least one *cache* lost, that means k nodes storing this *cache* all quit or mistake. In different system, stage or data, the value of k will change. Let there are n nodes, block is separated to m *caches*, and every *cache* is stored by k nodes. If node failure rate is $p(0 \leq p < 1)$, then failure probability of block combination is $m * p^k$. Although failure rate will decrease with *cache* storage number, *Ladder* cloud raise the block lost. To deal with this danger, we firstly store the block in database remotely before executing block separation. Third, *Cold-Blocks* are stored remotely, and security is protected by ring-signature. In conclusion, *Ladder* does not decrease security and integrity compared with blockchain.

5   Conclusion

In this paper, we present *Ladder*, a multi-level data storage system for blockchain. This system can distinguish the importance of different blocks by *VD*. It stores *Hot-Blocks* locally while storing the *caches* of *Warm-Blocks* and storing *Cold-Blocks* into remote database. Meanwhile, we expand the block structure on the basis of original block and complete the separation and combination operation to *caches*. The experimental results of block storage and retrieve show that the storage and retrieve time after block separation has improved. But the space overhead has been reduced to about 1/n(n is the number of block separated). The result of evaluation leveraging simulation experiment indicates that *Ladder* applicable in lowering storage from both the functional and performance perspectives.

Acknowledgment. This work was supported in part by the National Natural Science Foundation of China under Grant 61772030, in part by Major Scientific Research Project of Zhejiang Lab (2021PE0AC01) and in part by GF Innovative Research Program. Any opinions, findings, conclusions, or recommendations expressed in this material are those of the authors and do not necessarily reflect the views of the funding agencies.

References

1. Raft understandable distributed consensus. http://thesecretlivesofdata.com/raft/, Accessed 06 Mar 2021
2. Androulaki, E., et al.: Hyperledger fabric: a distributed operating system for permissioned blockchains. In: Proceedings of the Thirteenth EuroSys Conference, pp. 1–15 (2018)
3. Antonopoulos, A.M.: Mastering Bitcoin: Unlocking Digital Cryptocurrencies. O'Reilly Media Inc, Newton (2014)
4. Cachin, C., Vukolić, M.: Blockchain consensus protocols in the wild (2017). arXiv preprint arXiv:1707.01873
5. França, B.: Homomorphic mini-blockchain scheme (2015)

6. Hangzhou Time Stamp Information Technology Co., L.: Bitcoin block explorer. https://blockmeta.com/, Accessed 06 Mar 2021
7. Huh, S., Cho, S., Kim, S.: Managing IoT devices using blockchain platform. In: 2017 19th International Conference on Advanced Communication Technology (ICACT), pp. 464–467. IEEE (2017)
8. Kennedy, J.: $1.4 bn investment in blockchain start-ups in last 9 months, says pwc expert. Siliconerepublic. com 4 (2016)
9. Khan, M.A., Salah, K.: IoT security: review, blockchain solutions, and open challenges. Future Gener. Comput. Syst. **82**, 395–411 (2018)
10. Maymounkov, P., Mazières, D.: Kademlia: A Peer-to-Peer Information System Based on the XOR Metric. In: Druschel, P., Kaashoek, F., Rowstron, A. (eds.) IPTPS 2002. LNCS, vol. 2429, pp. 53–65. Springer, Heidelberg (2002). https://doi.org/10.1007/3-540-45748-8_5
11. Nakamoto, S.: Bitcoin: a peer-to-peer electronic cash system. Technical report, Manubot (2019)
12. Ng, W.S., Ooi, B.C., Tan, K.L., Zhou, A.: Peerdb: a p2p-based system for distributed data sharing. In: Proceedings 19th International Conference on Data Engineering (Cat. No. 03CH37405), pp. 633–644. IEEE (2003)
13. Reyna, A., Martín, C., Chen, J., Soler, E., Díaz, M.: On blockchain and its integration with IoT: challenges and opportunities. Future Gener. Comput. Syst. **88**, 173–190 (2018)
14. Szydlo, M.: Merkle Tree Traversal in Log Space and Time. In: Cachin, C., Camenisch, J.L. (eds.) EUROCRYPT 2004. LNCS, vol. 3027, pp. 541–554. Springer, Heidelberg (2004). https://doi.org/10.1007/978-3-540-24676-3_32
15. Tschorsch, F., Scheuermann, B.: Bitcoin and beyond: a technical survey on decentralized digital currencies. IEEE Commun. Surv. Tutor. **18**(3), 2084–2123 (2016)
16. Tung, Y.C., Lin, K.C.J., Chou, C.F.: Bandwidth-aware replica placement for peer-to-peer storage systems. In: 2011 IEEE Global Telecommunications Conference-GLOBECOM 2011, pp. 1–5. IEEE (2011)
17. Wood, G., et al.: Ethereum: a secure decentralised generalised transaction ledger. Ethereum Proj. Yellow Pap. **151**(2014), 1–32 (2014)
18. Zhang, X., Wang, H., Shi, P., Fu, X.: Ls4bucc: a low overhead storage architecture for blockchain based unmanned collaborative cognition system. In: 2019 IEEE International Conference on Service-Oriented System Engineering (SOSE), pp. 221–2215 (2019). doi: 10.1109/SOSE.2019.00038
19. Zheng, Z., Xie, S., Dai, H.N., Chen, X., Wang, H.: Blockchain challenges and opportunities: a survey. Int. J. Web Grid Serv. **14**(4), 352–375 (2018)
20. Zhou, Z., Cheng, Z., Ning, K., Li, W., Zhang, L.J.: A sub-chain ranking and recommendation mechanism for facilitating geospatial web service composition. Int. J. Web Serv. Res. (IJWSR) **11**(3), 52–75 (2014)
21. Zou, W., et al.: Smart contract development: challenges and opportunities. IEEE Trans. Softw. Eng. **47**, 2084–2106 (2019)
22. Wang, H., Shi, P., Zhang, Y.: Jointcloud: a cross-cloud cooperation architecture for integrated internet service customization. In: IEEE 37th International Conference on Distributed Computing Systems (ICDCS), pp. 1846–1855 (2017)

Blockchain Security and Privacy

Temporal-Amount Snapshot MultiGraph for Ethereum Transaction Tracking

Yunyi Xie[1,2], Jie Jin[1,2], Jian Zhang[1,2], Shanqing Yu[1,2], and Qi Xuan[1,2,3(✉)]

[1] Institute of Cyberspace Security, Zhejiang University of Technology,
Hangzhou 310023, China
xuanqi@zjut.edu.cn
[2] College of Information Engineering, Zhejiang University of Technology,
Hangzhou 310023, China
[3] PCL Research Center of Networks and Communications, Peng Cheng Laboratory,
Shenzhen 518000, China

Abstract. With the wide application of blockchain in the financial field, the rise of various types of cybercrimes has brought great challenges to the security of blockchain. In order to better understand this emerging market and explore more efficient countermeasures for effective supervision, it is imperative to track transactions on blockchain-based systems. Due to the openness of Ethereum, we can easily access the publicly available transaction records, model them as a complex network, and further study the problem of transaction tracking via link prediction, which provides a deeper understanding of Ethereum transactions from a network perspective. Specifically, we introduce an embedding based link prediction framework that is composed of temporal-amount snapshot multigraph (TASMG) and present temporal-amount walk (TAW). By taking the realistic rules and features of transaction networks into consideration, we propose TASMG to model Ethereum transaction records as a temporal-amount network and then present TAW to effectively embed accounts via their transaction records, which integrates temporal and amount information of the proposed network. Experimental results demonstrate the superiority of the proposed framework in learning more informative representations and could be an effective method for transaction tracking.

Keywords: Ethereum · Random walk · Network embedding · Temporal network · Link prediction

1 Introduction

Blockchain is a distributed ledger technology, which can record transactions among peers [1]. It could be described as a trusted database that has the characteristics of decentralized, anti-counterfeiting, as well as user tamper-ability and anonymity. With the support of the underlying blockchain technology, blockchain

© Springer Nature Singapore Pte Ltd. 2021
H.-N. Dai et al. (Eds.): BlockSys 2021, CCIS 1490, pp. 133–146, 2021.
https://doi.org/10.1007/978-981-16-7993-3_10

platforms such as Bitcoin and Ethereum also take this opportunity to flourish and become world-renowned new digital currency trading platforms. As the largest public blockchain-based platform enabling smart contracts, Ethereum [2] has become a widely used financial application platform and the corresponding cryptocurrency *Ether* is the second-largest cryptocurrency.

However, along with the rapid development of blockchain technology, various types of cybercrimes have arisen endlessly and thus Ethereum has become a hotbed of various cybercrimes [3–5]. Due to the anonymity of the blockchain, criminals attempt to evade supervision and engage in illegal activities by injecting funds into the blockchain system. It's reported that Ethereum has suffered from a variety of scams, such as hacks, phishing, and Ponzi schemes, showing that cybercrimes have become a critical issue in Ethereum. In order to create a favorable investment environment and preserve the sustainable development of blockchain-based systems, it's imperative to pay more attention to research in this field for formulating effective supervision.

This paper focuses on one of the solutions of Ethereum illegal activities, namely transaction tracking. The so-called transaction tracking is to maintain transaction security, identify fraud gangs, trace capital flows, retrieve stolen money, and improve the regulatory system. Furthermore, transaction tracking helps ordinary investors or cryptocurrency companies check whether certain funds or transactions are associated with illegal entities or contaminated by suspicious paths. In a summary, transaction tracking is an effective regulatory measure to prevent crime. The issues of transaction tracking have been widely discussed and many methods have been proposed. However, compared with traditional scenarios, illegal activities on Ethereum behave very differently. Traditional illegal activities generally rely on phishing emails and websites to obtain sensitive information from users. As a result, existing methods that aim to detect emails or websites that contain phishing and fraudulent information and thus cannot be directly applied to solve the transaction tracking problem on blockchain platforms like Ethereum.

Thanks to the openness of Ethereum, the available access transaction records that contain rich historical information can be used to study Ethereum matters. Here, we model Ethereum transaction records as a transaction network for further understanding and study transaction tracking on Ethereum from a network perspective, where a node represents an account and each edge represents a particular transaction (containing some unique information such as amount values and timestamps of the transactions). Network embedding [6] could be used to extract meaningful information as to representation features from transaction networks and thus can benefit lots of useful downstream tasks such as node classification [7], link prediction [8,9], graph classification [10,11], community detection [12], etc. The problem of tracking and predicting transactions on Ethereum transaction networks can be modeled as a link prediction task.

In this paper, we propose a transaction tracking framework on Ethereum from a network perspective. Firstly, we define a temporal-amount snapshot multigraph (TASMG) to model the Ethereum transaction records and make the successive snapshots connect to reduce temporal loss. Furthermore, we introduce temporal-amount walk (TAW) to learn representations of accounts. For each account, the searching strategy depends on the amount transition probability and the temporal transition probability. Various experiments conducted on real-world Ethereum datasets demonstrate that the proposed framework can efficiently learn informative account representation, and solve the problem of transaction tracking.

The main contributions of this paper are summarized as follows.

- We study the matter of transaction tracking in Ethereum from a network perspective, which provides a deeper understanding of Ethereum transaction records and may contribute to the long-term development of the blockchain.
- We construct temporal-amount snapshot multigraph (TASMG) to retain Ethereum transactions' temporal and amount properties. Moreover, we propose a temporal-amount walk (TAW) to effectively embed accounts based on their transactions, which integrates temporal information and amount information of the Ethereum transaction networks.
- We carry on transaction tracking experiments on realistic Ethereum datasets, which demonstrate that our proposed framework significantly outperforms the baselines in transaction tracking. More precisely, our method combined with Ethereum datasets' properties can be superior to general methods.

The remainder of this work is organized as follows. In Sect. 2, we give a review of related work on blockchain transaction data analysis and summarize the related work on network embedding and link prediction. In Sect. 3, we demonstrate the framework for Ethereum transaction tracking. In Sect. 4, we conduct extensive experiments on real-world Ethereum datasets and compare our method with several network embedding techniques and similarity-based link prediction methods. Finally, we conclude our work in Sect. 5.

2 Related Work

2.1 Blockchain Transaction Analysis and Mining

In the traditional financial scenario, transaction records are sensitive information, which is usually private for security. Thanks to the openness of blockchain with publicly accessible transaction records, researchers can independently access Ethereum transaction records, which brings unprecedented opportunities for blockchain analysis. The study of blockchain transaction records has recently attracted considerable attention from different applications like graph analysis, price prediction, and anti market manipulation.

Wu et al. [13] proposed the concept of *Attributed Temporal Heterogeneous Motifs* and further addressed the issue of mixing detection using a detection model. Recently, they presented a network embedding model named *trans2vec* for transaction networks, which incorporates the transaction amount values and timestamps. It is worth noting that the model makes contributes to phishing detection [4,5] and can be applied to other similar scenarios on transaction networks. Current researches on the blockchain mainly focus on cybercrimes, we argue that such preference may promote short-term security but may not conducive to the long-term development of the blockchain. In this paper, we consider the prediction of transactions and try to explore a deeper understanding of Ethereum transactions from a network perspective.

2.2 Network Embedding and Link Prediction

Network embedding has received extensive attention in the past decades [6]. Such embedding methods can transform each node into a low-dimensional vector, in which the structural information and topology properties of nodes are preserved as much as possible. Link prediction [14] aims at estimating the likelihood of the existence of links between nodes based on the current network information. Existing link prediction methods can be classified into several categories, e.g., similarity-based algorithms, maximum likelihood algorithms, and probabilistic models and most of the existing network embedding techniques can be applied to link prediction.

The earliest researches of network embedding are mainly based on random walk with Skip-Gram [15] model to learn node representation, where Deep-Walk [16] and Node2vec [17] are two classic examples using random walks on networks to obtain node representation. LINE [18] can optimize node's first-order and second-order proximity by designing specific objective function. Factorization based network embedding represents the connections between nodes in the form of a matrix and obtains the node embedding by factorizing this matrix. Graph Factorization (GF) [19] and HOPE [20] are two of the most notable factorization based methods. GCN based autoencoder [21], e.g., GAE and VGAE, has been widely used, which aims to minimize the reconstruction error of the output and input by its encoder and decoder.

Due to random walk based methods' high expressiveness and learning ability, and the diversity of Ethereum transactions, we model the general transaction network as a temporal-amount snapshot multigraph (TASMG), which combines transaction temporal and amount information. Furthermore, we propose several specific search strategies to perform random walk, namely temporal-amount walk (TAW), on the proposed TASMG. The random walk strategies reflect transaction amount and temporal properties simultaneously.

3 Methodology

3.1 Basic Definition

Network $G = (V, E)$ can be established by Ethereum transaction records, where V denotes the set of accounts (nodes) and E represents the transaction records (edges) with transaction temporal and amount information. According to the given time interval ϵ, the transaction network G can be divided into snapshots $\{G_1, G_2, G_3, \cdots\}$. In this paper, we define TASMG to both retain the current time and nearby time snapshot, which can capture the changing tendency of accounts' transaction behavior. Further, we propose TAW to capture the temporal and amount properties of each account in TASMG. Figure 1 demonstrates the main steps of the proposed framework, including network construction, network embedding, and transaction tracking.

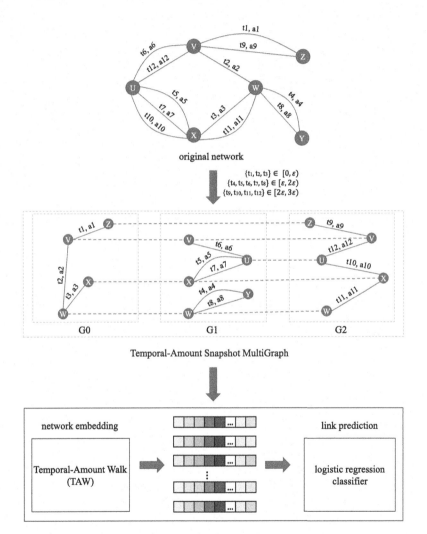

Fig. 1. The detailed framework for Ethereum transaction tracking.

Definition 1 (temporal-amount snapshot multigraph (TASMG)). *Divide $G = (V, E)$ into several snapshots according to time span ϵ, $G_t = (V_t, E_t)$*

be one of the snapshots. Nodes and edges in snapshot G_t are active between the timespan $[t\epsilon, (t+1)\epsilon)$, where time order $t \in \{0, 1, 2, \cdots\}$. Edge is represented as $e = (u, v, w, t)$, for $\forall e \in E$, $Src(e) = u$, $Dst(e) = v$, $W(e) = w$, $T(e) = t$, where u is the source node, v is the target node, w is the weight (transaction amount value) and t is the time accessibility. Self-connections are established when nodes exist in successive snapshots and on the premise that each snapshot is sorted in ascending order by time order t.

Self-connections in TASMG can make the random walk traverse across successive snapshots in non-decreasing order of edge's temporal information, which can capture the correlation between different snapshots and thus may result in more informative embeddings. For simplicity, we provide time accessibility for the edge between each pair-wise nodes and every two time slices linked nodes. Let $\eta_+ : \mathbb{R} \rightarrow \mathbb{Z}^+$ be a function that maps each node to an index based on the time order t, i.e., for a given node u in snapshot G_i, we have $\eta_+(u) = i$. In particular, we design a mapping function for each edge e in TASMG: $T(e) = \eta_+(v) - \eta_+(u) \in \{-1, 0, 1\}$, where v is the target node and u is the source node, to define the time accessibility of v from u, i.e., v is time accessible from u if and only if the corresponding $T(e) \geq 0$. Then, we define *successive edges* as shown below.

Definition 2 (Accessible Edge). *Given a TASMG $G = (V, E)$, the node v's accessible edges are defined as follows:*

$$L_t(v) = \{e \mid Src(e) = v, T(e) \geq 0\}$$

In the proposed network TASMG, a valid temporal walk is composed of accessible edges, i.e., a sequence of nodes connected by edges with non-decreasing $T(e)$. Next, we will present several sampling strategies by determining the selection probability for $e \in L_t(v)$.

3.2 Temporal Biased Walk

Based on the definitions in Sect. 3.1, we design a sampling strategy to choose accessible edges both in temporal and amount domains.

Temporal Transition Probability: The whole transaction network can be divided into different snapshots according to the time span, each snapshot represents a part of the network structure, and the gradual change of snapshot reflects the evolution process of the network. Ignoring the relevant information existing between two snapshots in successive time steps may result in the loss of temporal information. Therefore, we propose temporal transition probability to capture the behavior changes of nodes in different snapshots. In this case, the probability of selecting each edge $e \in L_t(c)$ can be given as follows:

$$P_T(e) = \frac{\psi_T(e)}{\sum_{e' \in L_t(c)} \psi_T(e')} \tag{1}$$

where $\psi_T(e)$ is expressed as

$$\psi_T(e) = \begin{cases} \alpha, & T(e) > 0 \\ 1 - \alpha, & T(e) = 0 \end{cases} \tag{2}$$

Here, the temporal bias α $(0.1 \le \alpha \le 0.9)$ determines that the temporal walk will stay on the current snapshot or transfer to the next.

Amount Transition Probability: Apart from transaction time, the transaction amount value of edges also plays an essential role in transaction networks. In the following, we present unbiased, biased, and linear strategies from the amount domain, respectively.

- **Amount Unbiased Sampling (AUS).** This is the default setting in the amount domain, which assumes that each successive edge $e \in L_t(c)$ of node c has the same probability to be selected:

$$P_A(e) = \frac{1}{L_t(c)} \tag{3}$$

- **Amount Biased Sampling (ABS).** The amount value of each transaction indicates the importance of the interaction between the two accounts involved. In most cases, a higher value of transaction amount implies that there is a greater connection between the two accounts. Thus each edge $e \in L_t(c)$ can be assigned the selection probability:

$$P_A(e) = \frac{W(e)}{\sum_{e' \in L_t(c)} W(e')} \tag{4}$$

where $W(e)$ is the transaction amount value between node c and its temporal neighbor x.

- **Amount Linear Sampling (ALS).** In order to avoid the extreme situation that the edge with a small amount value will never be sampled or the edge with a large amount value will always be sampled, we consider a linear mapping function to weaken the effects of the edge's transaction amount value. Thus we have:

$$P_A(e) = \frac{\omega_+(W(e))}{\sum_{e' \in L_t(c)} \omega_+(W(e'))} \tag{5}$$

with $\omega_+(v)$ mapping the amount value of edge to an ascending ranking. In other words, $\omega_+(v)$ maps each edge's transaction amount value to an index with $\omega_+(e) = 1$ for the smallest transaction amount value.

Joint Transition Probability: Furthermore, we normalize the aforementioned temporal transition probability and amount transition probability, and then combine them as one. We set the unnormalized transition probability to $P(e)$ and then normalize it to the final transition probability for each edge $e \in L_t(c)$, where

$$P(e) = P_T(e)\, P_A(e) \tag{6}$$

3.3 Learning Network Embeddings

This paper determines to obtain the d-dimensional representation of each node from a mapping function $f : V \to \mathbb{R}^d$. Let $N(v)$ and $f_t(v)$ denote the temporal neighbors generated according to the given sampling strategy and the representation of node v in the snapshot G_t, respectively. The following objective function aims to maximize the log-probability of observing $N(v)$ and historical embedding $f_t(v)$ conditioned on the node v's representation:

$$\max_f \sum_{v \in V} \log(Pr(N(v), f_t(v) \,|\, f(v))) \tag{7}$$

According to the conditional independence assumption in the Skip-Gram model, we factorize the formula:

$$
\begin{aligned}
&\log(Pr(N(v), f_t(v) \,|\, f(v))) \\
&= \log(\prod_{u_i \in N(v)} Pr(u_i \,|\, f(v))) + \log(Pr(f_t(v) \,|\, f(v)))
\end{aligned}
\tag{8}
$$

The definition of neighboring nodes is generally symmetric, i.e., the likelihood of a target node is independent of any other nodes. Therefore, we decompose the probability of the observation temporal neighborhood, and model the probability of each target neighborhood node pair as a softmax unit. Given the learning representation $f(v)$, the conditional probability of the observation node ui can be transformed as follows:

$$Pr(u_i \,|\, f(v)) = \frac{\exp(f(u_i)\, f(v))}{\sum_{n \in V} \exp(f(n)\, f(v))} \tag{9}$$

where $u_i \in N(v)$ is the ith near-neighbor of node v. With the above hypothesis, the objective function in Eq. (7) simplifies to:

$$
\begin{aligned}
\max_f \sum_{v \in V} \log(\prod_{u_i \in N(v)} \frac{\exp(f(u_i)\, f(v))}{\sum_{n \in V} \exp(f(n)\, f(v))}) \\
+ \log(Pr(f_t(v) \,|\, f(v)))
\end{aligned}
\tag{10}
$$

4 Experimental Results

4.1 Dataset

As the largest public blockchain-based platform, Ethereum's [22] transaction records are completely public and researchers can easily obtain the objective account's historical transaction data through the API of Etherscan (etherscan.io). Due to the size of the total transaction records is extremely large [23], we ascertain a number of target accounts and then obtain their transactions from Ethereum transaction records to make subgraphs for subsequent experiments. As shown in Fig. 2, we randomly sample a centered

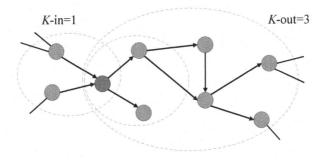

Fig. 2. Schematic illustration of K-order subgraph.

Table 1. Basic topological features of the three subgraphs. $|V|$ and $|E|$ are the numbers of nodes and edges, respectively, $\langle K \rangle$ is the average degree, and $\langle C \rangle$ is the average clustering coefficient.

	$|V|$	$|E|$	$\langle K \rangle$	$\langle C \rangle$
EthereumG1	2100	6995	6.662	0.211
EthereumG2	5762	9098	3.158	0.112
EthereumG3	10269	28431	5.537	0.147

account to obtain its local structure information and then extract K-order subgraph [24]. K-in and K-out are two parameters to control the depth of sampling inward and outward from the center, respectively.

In the following experiments, we collect three subgraphs for transaction tracking with different sizes from the whole Ethereum transaction records, i.e., randomly select different center accounts and collect three subgraphs with K-in = 1, K-out = 3. A summary of these networks is listed in Table 1.

4.2 Baselines and Experimental Setup

It is assumed that node pairs with higher similarity values are more likely to have interactions, and thus we calculate the similarity value for each node pair, e.g., Common Neighbors (CN), Adamic–Adar Index (AA), Resource Allocation Index (RA). Furthermore, we compare the performance of TAW with several baseline methods including GF, HOPE, GAE, VGAE, LINE, DeepWalk, and Node2vec. GF and HOPE are two of the most notable factorization based embedding methods, while GAE and VGAE are the GCN based autoencoder models. LINE preserves the first-order and second-order proximity between nodes and in this work, the final representation for each node is created by second-order representations. DeepWalk and Node2vec belong to the same category of Skip-Gram based methods. The parameters for both the node sampling and optimization steps of the two random walk based embedding methods, including ours, are set exactly the same: number of walks per node $w = 10$, the length of walk $l = 80$, and the size of context window $k = 5$. Since Node2vec requires the in-out and return hyperparameters, the ranges of its hyper parameters in this paper are set to $p, q \in \{0.5, 1, 2\}$. For our proposed method TAW, we take one month as the time span to construct TASMG for each dataset and temporal bias α varies in $[0.1, 0.9]$.

For all methods, the number of dimensions of output vector representations d is set to 128. After learning embedding for each node, we use hadamard[1] operation to calculate the vectors of the corresponding edges on the embedding vectors of the learned pairs of nodes. And we train a one-vs-rest logistic regression classifier to classify the links in the test set. Experiments are repeated for 5 random seed initializations and we report the average performance.

4.3   Metrics

- **AUC:** It can be interpreted as the probability that a randomly chosen missing link is given a higher score than a randomly chosen nonexistent link. If among n independent comparisons, there are n' times that the missing link gets a higher score and n'' times they get the same score, the AUC value is

$$\text{AUC} = \frac{n' + 0.5n''}{n}$$

  If all the scores are generated from an independent and identical distribution, the AUC value should be about 0.5. The degree to which the value exceeds 0.5 indicates how much better the algorithm performs than pure chance.
- **Precision:** Given the ranking of the non-observed links, the precision is defined as the ratio of relevant items selected to the number of items selected, which indicates how many predictions are accurate, from the perspective of prediction results. That is to say, if we take the top-L links as the predicted ones, among which L_r links are right, then the Precision equals L_r/L. Clearly, higher precision means higher prediction accuracy.

4.4   Results and Discussions

Transaction tracking can be modeled as a link prediction task in Ethereum, which goal is to predict the occurrence of links in a given network based on observed information. Before the experiments, we hide some account connections in the trading network. We aim to track these missing connections by using all the remaining information to predict the transaction records of the account. We first randomly hide 20% of links in the original network as positive samples of the training set and use the remaining to train all methods. Then we stochastically sample an equal number of node pairs with no link as negative samples of the training set. The test set consists of two parts, one of which contains all the hidden edges as the positive samples, and the other contains the unconnected pairwise nodes sampled randomly as the negative samples.

---

[1] $[f(u) \cdot f(v)]_i = f_i(u) * f_i(v)$.

Table 2. Performances of different methods for transaction tracking.

Metrics	EthereumG1		EthereumG2		EthereumG3	
	AP	AUC	AP	AUC	AP	AUC
CN	0.6907	0.6848	0.5134	0.4921	0.6826	0.6881
AA	0.7367	0.7002	0.5909	0.5099	0.6979	0.6912
RA	0.7378	0.7007	0.5909	0.5099	0.6986	0.6914
Jaccard	0.5088	0.6097	0.4523	0.4588	0.6234	0.6800
GF	0.7827	0.6821	0.7377	0.7050	0.7946	0.6662
HOPE	0.7698	0.6578	0.8300	0.7580	0.8714	0.8089
LINE	0.7761	0.7521	0.8627	0.8237	0.6371	0.6370
DeepWalk	0.6159	0.6637	0.6138	0.6307	0.7755	0.8024
Node2vec	0.6877	0.7149	0.6939	0.6990	0.8239	0.8501
GAE	0.7911	0.6752	0.5828	0.3729	0.8703	0.7885
VGAE	0.8179	0.7184	0.6683	0.4719	0.8934	0.8278
TAW	**0.8774**	**0.8819**	**0.9180**	**0.9134**	**0.9115**	**0.9108**

Transaction Tracking Performance. The experimental results of transaction tracking are given in Table 2. We find that similarity indices, i.e., CN, Jaccard, RA and AA, perform poorly among all methods. These similarity indices could only extract incomplete information, which is hard for mining deep structure information of transaction networks. We further observe that the sparser of network, the harder it for GCN-based methods to predict the appearance of links. GF, HOPE, and LINE achieve poor performance on most networks, indicating that preserving higher-order proximity is not conducive to predicting unobserved transactions. Here, the random walk based methods outperform other methods, indicating that random walks are especially useful when approximate node centrality and similarity in Ethereum transaction networks. However, it is still not as good as the results of TAW, for the reason that our proposed transaction tracking framework is more meticulous in the way of generating TASMG and extracting more precise features. Overall, the evaluation indicates that TAW achieves clear performance gains over the baselines for transaction tracking problem, which is reasonable since our method with flexible walking strategies is able to learn the similarity between nodes more effectively. Moreover, the outstanding performance of our proposed transaction tracking framework also suggests that TASMG, which better combines temporal and amount properties, can indeed uncover richer valuable information from the different dimensions of Ethereum transaction records.

Parameter Sensitivity. Table 3 shows the difference between different amount sampling strategies. Interestingly, using a biased strategy seems to improve slightly on the tested datasets, which implies that the probability of transaction occurrence is positively correlated with the amount value of the transaction between the two accounts. We thus can infer that the larger transaction amount value of the two accounts, the closer relationship between the two. In addition, since α is newly introduced in our method, we focus on the influence of temporal bias α on the proposed framework. In order to evaluate how temporal bias α could impact the transaction tracking performance, we gradually vary the temporal bias α in $[0.1, 0.9]$. The results are shown in Fig. 3, where we can observe that, overall, as the increasing of temporal bias α, our framework has achieved better performance for transaction tracking.

Table 3. Performances of different amount sampling strategies.

Metrics	EthereumG1		EthereumG2		EthereumG3	
	AP	AUC	AP	AUC	AP	AUC
AUS	0.8774	0.8819	0.9180	0.9134	0.9115	0.9108
ABS	**0.8852**	**0.8836**	**0.9287**	0.9184	**0.9189**	**0.9158**
ALS	0.8798	0.8811	0.9257	**0.9199**	0.9150	0.9137

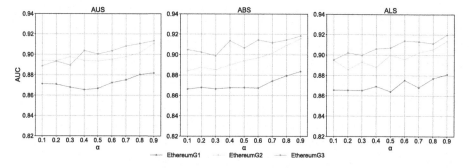

Fig. 3. Performance in terms of AUC under temporal bias α which change is in $[0.1, 0.9]$.

5   Conclusion

In this paper, we model a general transaction network as a temporal-amount snapshot multigraph (TASMG), which provides a novel network perspective for a deeper understanding of Ethereum transactions. Furthermore, we implement a random walk using specific search strategies to characterize accounts' behaviors on the proposed TASMG, namely temporal-amount walk (TAW). Experimental results demonstrate the effectiveness of our proposed transaction tracking framework, and indicate that TASMG has the potential to extract more information from Ethereum transaction records. Though Ethereum transaction records are publicly available, it's still relatively unexplored till now. For future work, we plan to apply deep learning methods to expand our methods and further extend the current framework to analyze more illegal activities on Ethereum and create a safe trading environment for Ethereum.

Acknowledgments. The authors would like to thank all the members in the IVSN Research Group, Zhejiang University of Technology for the valuable discussions about the ideas and technical details presented in this paper. This work was partially supported by the National Key R&D Program of China under Grant No. 2020YFB1006104, by the National Natural Science Foundation of China under Grant No. 61973273, by the Zhejiang Provincial Natural Science Foundation of China under Grant No. LR19F030001, by the Ministry of Public Security's Research Project "Research and Demonstration Application of Key Technologies of Criminal Social Network Model", and by the Special Scientific Research Fund of Basic Public Welfare Profession of Zhejiang Province under Grant LGF20F020016.

References

1. Swan, M.: Blockchain: Blueprint for a New Economy. O'Reilly Media, Inc. Sebastopol (2015)
2. Wang, S., Ouyang, L., Yuan, Y., Ni, X., Han, X., Wang, F.-Y.: Blockchain-enabled smart contracts: architecture, applications, and future trends. IEEE Trans. Syst. Man Cybern. Syst. **49**(11), 2266–2277 (2019)
3. Yuan, Z., Yuan, Q., Wu, J.: Phishing detection on Ethereum via learning representation of transaction subgraphs. In: Zheng, Z., Dai, H.-N., Fu, X., Chen, B. (eds.) BlockSys 2020. CCIS, vol. 1267, pp. 178–191. Springer, Singapore (2020). https://doi.org/10.1007/978-981-15-9213-3_14
4. Wu, J., Yuan, Q., Lin, D., You, W., Chen, W., Chen, C., Zheng, Z.: Who are the phishers? Phishing scam detection on Ethereum via network embedding. In: IEEE Transactions on Systems, Man, and Cybernetics: Systems (2020)
5. Yuan, Q., Huang, B., Zhang, J., Wu, J., Zhang, H., Zhang, X.: Detecting phishing scams on Ethereum based on transaction records. In: 2020 IEEE International Symposium on Circuits and Systems (ISCAS), pp. 1–5. IEEE (2020)
6. Cui, P., Wang, X., Pei, J., Zhu, W.: A survey on network embedding. IEEE Trans. Knowl. Data Eng. **31**(5), 833–852 (2018)
7. Rossi, R., Neville, J.: Time-evolving relational classification and ensemble methods. In: Tan, P.-N., Chawla, S., Ho, C.K., Bailey, J. (eds.) PAKDD 2012. LNCS (LNAI), vol. 7301, pp. 1–13. Springer, Heidelberg (2012). https://doi.org/10.1007/978-3-642-30217-6_1
8. Fu, C., et al.: Link weight prediction using supervised learning methods and its application to yelp layered network. IEEE Trans. Knowl. Data Eng. **30**(8), 1507–1518 (2018)
9. Zhang, J., Zheng, J., Chen, J., Xuan, Q.: Hyper-substructure enhanced link predictor. In: Proceedings of the 29th ACM International Conference on Information & Knowledge Management, pp. 2305–2308 (2020)
10. Xuan, Q., et al.: Subgraph networks with application to structural feature space expansion. IEEE Trans. Knowl. Data Eng. **33**(6), 2776–2789 (2021). https://doi.org/10.1109/TKDE.2019.2957755
11. Zhou, J., Shen, J., Yu, S., Chen, G., Xuan, Q.: M-Evolve: structural-mapping-based data augmentation for graph classification. IEEE Trans. Network Sci. Eng. **8**(1), 190–200 (2020)

12. Fortunato, S.: Community detection in graphs. Phys. Rep. **486**(3–5), 75–174 (2010)
13. Wu, J., et al.: Detecting mixing services via mining bitcoin transaction network with hybrid motifs. IEEE Trans. Syst. Man Cybern. Syst. (2021)
14. Lü, L., Zhou, T.: Link prediction in complex networks: a survey. Physica A: Stat. Mech. Appl. **390**(6), 1150–1170 (2011)
15. Mikolov, T., Chen, K., Corrado, G., Dean, J.: Efficient estimation of word representations in vector space. arXiv preprint arXiv:1301.3781 (2013)
16. Perozzi, B., Al-Rfou, R., Skiena, S.: Deepwalk: online learning of social representations. In: Proceedings of the 20th ACM SIGKDD International Conference on Knowledge Discovery and Data Mining, pp. 701–710 (2014)
17. Grover, A., Leskovec, J.: node2vec: scalable feature learning for networks. In: Proceedings of the 22nd ACM SIGKDD International Conference on Knowledge Discovery and Data Mining, pp. 855–864 (2016)
18. Tang, J., Qu, M., Wang, M., Zhang, M., Yan, J., Mei, Q.: LINE: large-scale information network embedding. In: Proceedings of the 24th International Conference on World Wide Web, pp. 1067–1077 (2015)
19. Ahmed, A., Shervashidze, N., Narayanamurthy, S., Josifovski, V., Smola, A.J.: Distributed large-scale natural graph factorization. In: Proceedings of the 22nd International Conference on World Wide Web, pp. 37–48 (2013)
20. Ou, M., Cui, P., Pei, J., Zhang, Z., Zhu, W.: Asymmetric transitivity preserving graph embedding. In: Proceedings of the 22nd ACM SIGKDD International Conference on Knowledge Discovery and Data Mining, pp. 1105–1114 (2016)
21. Kipf, T.N., Welling, M.: Variational graph auto-encoders. arXiv preprint arXiv:1611.07308 (2016)
22. Wood, G., et al.: Ethereum: a secure decentralised generalised transaction ledger. Ethereum Project Yellow Paper **151**(2014), 1–32 (2014)
23. Chen, T., et al.: Understanding Ethereum via graph analysis. ACM Trans. Internet Technol. (TOIT) **20**(2), 1–32 (2020)
24. Lin, D., Wu, J., Yuan, Q., Zheng, Z.: Modeling and understanding Ethereum transaction records via a complex network approach. IEEE Tran. Circ. Syst. II: Express Briefs **67**(11), 2737–2741 (2020)

Attention-Based Graph Neural Network for Identifying Illicit Bitcoin Addresses

Hao Tian[1,3], Yang Li[1,3], Yue Cai[1,3], Xiaohong Shi[2(✉)], and Zibin Zheng[1,3]

[1] School of Computer Science and Engineering, Sun Yat-sen University,
Guangzhou 510275, China
{tianh23,liyang99,caiy26}@mail2.sysu.edu.cn, zhzibin@mail.sysu.edu.cn
[2] School of Mathematics and Information Science, Guangzhou University,
Guangzhou 510006, China
[3] National Engineering Research Center of Digital Life, Sun Yat-sen University,
Guangzhou, China

Abstract. Soon after Bitcoin was proposed and became the most popular decentralized cryptocurrency, identification of illicit bitcoin addresses has become an important and popular study, which can help users avoid involvement in illicit activities. Most of the studies focus on digging the characteristic behavior of illicit addresses, or constructing features easier to distinguish illicit and licit addresses. The models used for identification in those studies include anomaly detection models and classification models. Although some of them have been proven effective, the following two insights are often neglected. First, the structure information of the Bitcoin transaction network, not only provides the direct transaction information but the indirect transaction information and trading preference group information based on the network graph. Second, the temporal information of transaction records, offers fine-grained and deep understanding of the address's trading behavior. These insights motivate us to propose the attention-based graph neural network in this paper. The Attention-based GNN(AT-GNN) part of the model recursively calculates the embeddings of address's neighbors with different distances based on the structure information of transaction network, and employs the convolution and attention mechanism to refine the address's embedding. The auto-encoder part of the model sufficiently capture the hidden temporal feature based on the temporal information of transaction records to enable more precise identification results. We conduct extensive experiments on the realistic dataset, demonstrating superiority over five state-of-the-art models. Further analysis verifies the importance of address's neighbor embeddings and hidden temporal feature for better identification, justifying the rationality and effectiveness of our model.

Keywords: Bitcoin address · Illicit identification · Graph neural network

© Springer Nature Singapore Pte Ltd. 2021
H.-N. Dai et al. (Eds.): BlockSys 2021, CCIS 1490, pp. 147–162, 2021.
https://doi.org/10.1007/978-981-16-7993-3_11

1 Introduction

Bitcoin is the first and widest spread cryptocurrency which was proposed in 2008 and released in 2009 as an open-source software [1]. All transactions are included in a public log available distributed ledger called blockchain [2,3], which is serving as a digital assets infrastructure and system. Up to now, Bitcoin has attracted significant attention and market cap surpasses $357 billion (coinmarketcap.com, 2020). Due to the decentralization and anonymity of Bitcoin, users can send and receive bitcoins without revealing their true identity. However, it is the pseudonyms (called addresses), which may even be generated fresh for each transaction, that increasingly makes Bitcoin a staple utility among cybercriminals [4]. Previous surveys in [5] have shown that at least 25% of Bitcoin users and around 44% of Bitcoin transactions are associated with illegal activities. Illicit bitcoin address identification has become an important and popular study, which can help users avoid involvement in illicit activities.

In order to identify illicit bitcoin addresses and avoid financial losses, many studies aimed at digging the characteristic behavior of illicit addresses [6,7], and appropriate models and features to improve the accuracy of identification results. There are two types of models in identifying illicit bitcoin addresses. One type is the anomaly detection model, which regards illicit addresses as abnormal. For example, [8] applies Trimmed k-means [9] (an improvement of k-means) on Bitcoin fraud detection, in which outliers are marked as illicit addresses related to fraud; the other type is the classification model, which divides addresses into two categories, licit and illicit. Traditional classification models like random forest, XGBoost and LightGBM used in [10], can be applied for identification of illicit addresses. Although these models have been proven effective, there still exist some issues as follows.

The first issue is the insufficient utilization of the structure information of the Bitcoin transaction network. Most of previous studies [6,7,11] build the Bitcoin transaction network diagram for analysis and feature extraction, but they only take the direct transaction information into account, without considering the indirect information or even further information. For example, [11] constructs features like in-degree, out-degree, unique in-degree, unique out-degree for identifying illicit addresses, which can only reflect the information of the adjacent address on the graph. However, the information of the addresses that are not directly adjacent can also be helpful for identification. In this paper, we present an algorithm to calculate neighbor embeddings with different distances, and employ the convolution and attention mechanism to refine the embeddings for better identification.

The second issue is the lack of exploiting the temporal information of transaction records. Although most of previous studies have constructed various features of addresses for identification, few of them consider the temporal information in transaction records. As in [8,12], more attention is paid to the information such as the amount of transactions. But the temporal information in transaction records is also helpful for identification. In [10], four types of temporal features are constructed. These features reflect the time interval between transactions, which have been proven helpful for identification, but the order of transaction sequence is not considered. If two transaction sequences have the same time interval but different order, the constructed features are the same.

To address the above issues, we propose the attention-based graph neural network in this paper, which incorporates sufficient structure information of the Bitcoin transaction network and temporal information of transaction records for identifying illicit Bitcoin addresses. In AT-GNN of the model, to make full use of the structure information of the transaction network, embeddings of address's neighbors with different distances, also called aggregate features, are recursively calculated; the convolution is employed to combine aggregate features to get convolved features; and the attention mechanism is employed to strengthen the effective part and weaken the invalid part of convolved features for better identification. In the auto-encoder part of the model, unlike previous studies calculating features based on statistics, we use an auto-encoder based on LSTM to extract temporal features of address's transaction records. The auto-encoder can learn efficient data codings in an unsupervised manner, and LSTM can exhibit sequences' temporal dynamic behavior and other details. What's more, among many different types of auto-encoders, we select the most suitable one according to their performance, which can maximize the use of the temporal information in transaction records. Our extensive experiments verify that the attention-based graph neural network is more effective than the five state-of-the-art models used in identifying illicit Bitcoin addresses, and also verify the importance of address's neighbor embeddings and hidden temporal feature for better identification, justifying the rationality and effectiveness of our model.

In summary, our contributions in this paper are as follows:

1. We highlight the importance of the structure information of the Bitcoin transaction network and the temporal information of transaction records in identifying illicit Bitcoin addresses.
2. We propose a new model—the attention-based graph neural network for identifying illicit Bitcoin addresses, which incorporates the structure information and the temporal information in the model, to enable more precise identification.
3. We provide deep insights on the rationales of our model's design mechanisms and extensive evaluation results over the realistic dataset in [13], to justify our model's superiority over the state-of-the-art models.

2   Related Work

There are three types of researches, one of which is the behavioral analysis of illicit Bitcoin addresses. As more and more illicit Bitcoin activities are exposed, which have caused great economic losses, most studies aimed at the behavioral analysis of illicit Bitcoin addresses, promoting the identification of illicit Bitcoin addresses. [6] performs a measurement analysis of a family of ransomware called CryptoLocker, which encrypts victim's files until ransom is paid. [7] analyzes illicit addresses by an inductive approach, parsing the illegal incidents and transaction data extracted from publicly available sources by BlockSci [14], and visualizing the transaction information of these addresses by Gephi [15]. These studies usually analyze illicit addresses qualitatively, which can find the characteristics and patterns of illicit groups, but cannot identify illicit addresses.

Another type is the anomaly detection for identification. Some studies that regard the identification as anomaly detection believe that illicit addresses will be very different from normal addresses in some extracted features, so they attempt to identify illicit addresses by applying some anomaly detection algorithms such as isolation forest [16] and k-means. [11] generates two graphs of transactions, using three unsupervised learning methods including k-means clustering, Mahalanobis distance [17], and unsupervised support vector machine (SVM) [18] to find abnormal nodes as illicit addresses on these graphs. [8] applies anomaly detection algorithms on Bitcoin fraud detection with Trimmed k-means [9], which is an improvement of k-means, to find anomalies. These abovementioned methods of using anomaly detection algorithms can only identify several scattered illicit addresses with extreme behavior, but difficult to classify illicit addresses with similar behavior as abnormal.

The other type is the classification for identification. Classification is the most used method to identify illicit Bitcoin addresses, and its results are more direct compared with the clustering method of anomaly detection. In general, there are two major classes of approaches to improve the result of classification, i.e., effective feature construction and suitable model construction. In the first class, [10] focuses on the construction of temporal features, proposing four types of transaction moments features, which are used to extract the temporal information contained in transaction records. [19] constructs a variety of distinctive features through the difference between illicit addresses in HYIP and normal addresses by the previous or its own statistics and surveys. But some differences are difficult to discover, so the effective feature construction alone are not enough. Inspired by the improvement of classification models, many classification models are applied to solve this problem, such as XGBoost [20] and random forest(RF) based on the tree model, artificial neural network(ANN) based on the neural network. [12] identifies illicit addresses of Ponzi schemes, using three classifiers, RIPPER, Bayes network and random forest for evaluation. [10] mentioned above uses linear regression, SVM, AdaBoost [21], random forest, XGBoost, LightGBM [22] and ANN in the experiments to prove the validity of their features. And [19] uses random forest, XGBoost, ANN, SVM, k-NN [23] and other classification models for training and prediction, and the results prove the effectiveness of the method. In order to get better results, we need to make improvement in both effective feature construction and model construction. More specifically, we need a model special for the Bitcoin transaction network, which can make full use of the information of the Bitcoin transaction network and integrate various features to construct new effective features. But most of the existing studies are only devoted to the feature construction, taking use of some general classification models, or making some minor adjustments to the existing models. There is no model special for the Bitcoin network.

3 Methodology

3.1 Overview

The attention-based graph neural network consists of three parts. Figure 1 shows the architecture of the model. The first part applies convolution and weighting on the features constructed by neighbor embedding. It includes two smaller parts, neighbor embedding and Attention-based GNN. Taking the structure of the Bitcoin transaction network into consideration, in the neighbor embedding part, we calculate the address's aggregate features from 1-hop to n-hop based on the features of each address; in the Attention-based GNN, we calculate multiple different convolutions of aggregate features, and add them together to form new features based on the attention weight. In the second part the auto-encoder is applied. We also consider the temporal information contained in the address transaction in this part. We calculate the transaction features' sequence of addresses, and based on the sequence, we use the auto-encoder based on LSTM to learn efficient temporal features of address transactions. In the last part, we concatenate the features obtained in the previous two parts to do the classification, and realize identification of the Bitcoin addresses.

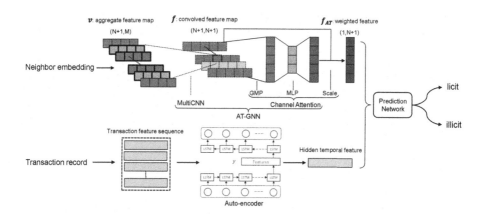

Fig. 1. The architecture of our model

3.2 Neighbor Embedding

Due to the traceability of the Bitcoin blockchain, for each address, we can obtain all its transaction information from the Bitcoin blockchain. Based on this information, we can construct various features of the address, which can be calculated from the Bitcoin blockchain. For an address, we think that those addresses that have transactions with it can reflect its features to a certain extent, therefore, its adjacent address features are also very important. In theory, we can construct the Bitcoin transaction network graph $G = (V, E)$. A node $v \in V$ is an

address in the transaction network and an edge $e \in E$ is a transaction. However, there have been more than 650,000 blocks so far, each block contains about
2,000 to 3,000 transactions, and each transaction can connect one or more pairs
of addresses. It is almost impossible to construct the entire Bitcoin transaction
network graph directly, and the increasing transactions makes this work more
difficult. Therefore, we choose to analyze the subgraph centered on the address.

First we choose the maximum number of hop n, and the subsequent calculations are based on the subgraph of the address within n-hop. For each address
to be identified, we calculate its 1-hop to n-hop set and the set's weights connected to the previous set, then calculate the aggregate features of each set.
Considering an address a in the transaction network, we use $S_0 = \{a\}$ to get
the 1-hop to n-hop set S_1, S_2 ... S_n. S_i is the set of addresses whose minimum
path length to the address a in the transaction network is equal to i. In order
to get $S_i(1 \leq i \leq n)$, traverse the transactions of each address in S_{i-1}, and add
addresses in these transactions that have not yet been added to S_i, the weight
of the added address to connect S_{i-1} is the transaction amount of this address
in the transaction. So we can get S_1, S_2 ... S_n in turn, and the weight of each
address in these sets connected to the previous set.

Figure 2 shows an example of a transaction network subgraph and the set
calculation results of an address. Figure 2(a) is a transaction network subgraph
of address a within 2-hop. First we get $S_0 = \{a\}$, traverse the transaction of a,
add the addresses b and c to S_1 based on $TX1$, add the address e to S_1 based
on $TX4$, then we get $S_1 = \{b, c, e\}$. The weight of b connected to S_0 is the
transaction amount w_{1_b} of b in $TX1$. Similarly, the weights w_{1_c} and w_{4_e} can
be obtained through $TX1$ and $TX4$. Then we traverse the transactions of the
addresses in S_1 to get S_2. By traversing the transactions $TX2$ of b and $TX3$ of
c, we get the address d and add it to S_2. The weight of d connected to S_1 is the
sum of its transaction amount in $TX2$ and $TX3$, i.e. $w_{2\_d} + w_{3\_d}$. Figure 2(b) is
the set calculation results.

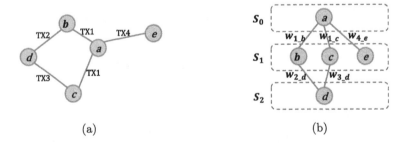

Fig. 2. An example of (a) a transaction network subgraph and (b) the set calculation
results of address a within 2-hop.

Then we calculate the aggregate features for each set based on the features of
each address in the set and the weight connected to the previous set. Assuming

that S_i has k addresses, their features are v_1, v_2 ... v_k, and their weights connected to S_{i-1} are w_1, w_2 ... w_k. The formula to calculate the aggregate feature v of S_i is: $v = \frac{\sum_{i=1}^{k} w_i v_i}{\sum_{i=1}^{k} w_i}$. We define the feature $v^{(0)}$ of the address a as the 0-hop feature. After calculating for each set, we can get the aggregate features $v^{(0)}$, $v^{(1)}$, $v^{(2)}$ ... $v^{(n)}$ of each set, which will be used as the input of our model.

3.3 Attention-Based GNN

In the following we will describe the overall architecture of the Attention-based GNN(AT-GNN), which is used to extract the significant part of the aggregate features obtained above. From Fig. 1, we can see that AT-GNN contains two parts. The first part is multiple convolution(MultiCNN), which combines aggregate features at different distances to get convolved features. The second part is the channel attention part, which learns the weight of the convolved features to strengthen the effective features and weaken the invalid features, and aggregates the features based on this weight.

For aggregate features calculated by neighbor embedding, MultiCNN uses $n + 1$ convolution kernels of different sizes, each of which is used to extract the features of aggregate features' sublist of a certain size. Suppose the feature of an address has shape $(1, M)$, then the aggregate feature map has shape $(N+1, M)$, the different convolution kernels have shapes $(1, M)$, $(2, M)$, ... $(N + 1, M)$. We define the shape of each convolution result as $(1, N + 1)$. In order to keep it consistent, we do padding for the aggregate feature map to get a suitable size for every different convolution.

Take the convolution with a kernel of shape (t, M) as an example. First, arrange the $n + 1$ aggregate features in the order of 0-hop to n-hop to form an aggregate feature map, then pad the feature map according to the shape of the convolution kernel. For this kernel we need to fill in $t - 1$ empty features. The shape of the feature map becomes $(N + t, M)$ after padding. Let $p = n + t$, the feature map $v_{padding} = [v^1, v^2 ... v^p]$, where $v^i = [v_1^i, v_2^i ... v_m^i](1 \le i \le p)$. The result of the convolution is $f^t = [f_1^t, f_2^t ... f_{n+1}^t]$. The formula of convolution is:

$$f_1^t = relu(\sum_{i=1}^{m} v_i^1 c_i^t + \sum_{i=1}^{m} v_i^2 c_{m+i}^t + ... + \sum_{i=1}^{m} v_i^t c_{m(t-1)+i}^t + bias_t)$$

$$= relu(\sum_{j=1}^{t}(\sum_{i=1}^{m} v_i^j c_{m(j-1)+i}^t) + bias_t)$$

$$f_2^t = relu(\sum_{j=2}^{t+1}(\sum_{i=1}^{m} v_i^j c_{m(j-1)+i}^t) + bias_t)$$

$$\cdots$$

$$f_{n+1}^t = relu(\sum_{j=n+1}^{p}(\sum_{i=1}^{m} v_i^j c_{m(j-1)+i}^t) + bias_t)$$

$relu$ is a commonly used non-linear activation function, $bias_t$ is the bias parameter of the convolution kernel, and these c^t are the weight parameters, which need to be trained later. After $n + 1$ different convolutions, there is a new feature map $\boldsymbol{f} = [\boldsymbol{f^1}, \boldsymbol{f^2} \dots \boldsymbol{f^{n+1}}]$ called convolved feature map with shape $(N+1, N+1)$ as the output of MultiCNN and the input of the channel attention part.

Since the effects of each convolution are inconsistent, it is not suitable to add convolved features with equal weights. The channel attention part uses attention to solve this problem. First there is a global max-pooling layer. It extracts the most significant part for each feature in the convolved feature map output by MultiCNN, then its output connects two fully connected layers. The first layer compresses $n + 1$ units into r and activates them with the $relu$ function. The second layer restores r units to $n + 1$ and activates them with the $sigmoid$ function. The final output is the attention weight that we need for adding the convolved features to get the most suitable feature for classification. The formulas of the channel attention part are as follows:

$$\boldsymbol{g} = GMP(\boldsymbol{f})$$
$$\boldsymbol{A} = MLP(\boldsymbol{g})$$
$$\boldsymbol{f_{AT}} = \boldsymbol{A} * \boldsymbol{f}$$

The GMP is a global max-pooling, MLP is two fully connected layers, $\boldsymbol{A}$ is the attention weight, and $\boldsymbol{f_{AT}}$ is the result of adding each feature of $\boldsymbol{f}$ according to the weight $\boldsymbol{A}$.

3.4   Auto-Encoder

Taking into account the temporal relationship of transactions of each address, we use an auto-encoder based on LSTM to extract temporal information in address's transaction records. The auto-encoder can learn efficient data codings in an unsupervised manner, and LSTM can exhibit sequences' temporal dynamic behavior. We need to construct the features of each transaction of an address to form a transaction feature sequence as the input of the auto-encoder. Since the input sequence length l of the auto-encoder needs to be the same, we set l to be greater than most of the number of addresses' transactions. Here is the method of constructing the feature sequence of length l. If the number of transactions of an address is less than l, first we form the sequence in the order of transaction time, then pad this sequence with empty features at the end of it until the length is equal to l; if the number of transactions of an address is greater than l, first we choose l transactions with the top l largest amount of these transactions, then use them to form the feature sequence in chronological order.

There may be noise in some addresses with many transactions. To avoid noise, we also adapt the denoising auto-encoder with LSTM. The main difference is that the denoising auto-encoder uses a denoising criterion, which can be described as each time a training example x is presented, a different corrupted version $\widetilde{x}$ of it is generated according to $q_D(\widetilde{x}|x)$, and $q_D(\widetilde{x}|x)$ is a stochastic mapping.

3.5 Prediction Network

This part completes the identification by the features calculated above. First concatenating the following three features, the results of $n+1$ different convolutions $f^1, f^2 \ldots f^{n+1}$ output by MultiCNN, the result f_{AT} of adding each feature of f according to the attention weight A output by the channel attention part, and the hidden feature y in the auto-encoder with LSTM. Then input the concatenated features into two fully connected layers to classify, use the *relu* function to activate nonlinear features, use the dropout layer [24] to prevent the model from overfitting in training, and finally use the *sigmoid* function to get the final prediction result. We choose Adam [25] as the optimization algorithm, which is a combination of RMSprop and Momentum [26], and makes the convergence of the model better.

4 Experiment

4.1 Dataset Description

We used the illicit Bitcoin addresses in the dataset released by [13] in our experiment. We de-duplicated all the addresses, and deleted the illicit addresses that have not been traded. These addresses may be related to ransomware or scam, but they didn't get the bitcoins. The final dataset used in our experiments contains various illicit groups. There are also some licit addresses. They are randomly sampled from the address data provided by `WalletExplorer.com`, which are common addresses in the Bitcoin transaction network. Besides, the data set is divided into train set (80% of the data set) and test set (20% of the data set) for experiment.

4.2 Experiment Detail

Feature Construction. We need two types of features as input of the model—the address feature and the transaction feature. Table 1 lists the calculated features. For the construction of the address feature, besides some simple features, we referred to the features proposed by other papers [10,12,27,28] related to Bitcoin. And for the construction of the transaction feature, we selected several simple features. In addition, for the time interval, if the transaction is the last transaction of the address, the time interval is set to 0.

Table 1. The list of calculated features

Type	Reference	Feature	Definition
Address feature		$S_{btc\_input}/S_{btc\_output}$	Sum of inputs/outputs transferred to/from the address
		$S_{balance}$	Final balance of the address
	[12]	$T_{lifetime}$	Lifetime of the address
		T_{active}	Activity days
		$N_{daily\_tx_{max}}$	Maximum number of daily transactions to/from the address
		G_{val}	Gini coefficient of the values transferred to/from the address
		$S_{val\_input}/S_{val\_output}$	Sum of values transferred to/from the address
		N_{input}/N_{output}	Number of incoming/outgoing transactions which transfer to/from the address
		R_{in_out}	Ratio between incoming and outgoing transactions to/from the address
		$A_{val\_input}/A_{val\_output}$	Average of the values transferred to/from the address
		$\sigma_{val\_input}/\sigma_{val\_output}$	Standard deviation of the values transferred to/from the address
		$T_{delay_{max}}/T_{delay_{min}}/T_{delay_{ave}}$	Maximum/Minimum/Average delay time between every transaction
	[27]	F_{tx}	Frequency of transactions
		$R_{payback}$	Payback ratio
		$A_{btc\_input}/A_{btc\_output}$	Average number of inputs and outputs in the transactions
	[10]	F_{tx_moment}	Four types of the transaction moment
	[28]	$N_{in\_exchange}/N_{out\_exchange}$	Number of input/output address comes from the exchange/service, etc.
Transaction feature		$N_{tx\_input}/N_{tx\_output}$	Number of input/output addresses of the transaction
		S_{tx_btc}	Amount of bitcoins in the transaction
		$T_{interval}$	Time interval to the next transaction

Baselines. To emphasize the superior performance of the attention-based graph neural network, we compared it with the following state-of-the-art illicit address identification models:

- AD-SVM [11], a well performed anomaly detection model based on Unsupervised Support Vector Machines (SVM), used to detect which addresses and transactions are the most suspicious.
- DPS-RF [12], a supervised method based on random forest, proven to be the most effective one in detecting Bitcoin Ponzi schemes.
- HYIP-XGB [19], a machine learning classifier, XGBoost (eXtreme Gradient Boosting) [20], used to identify addresses related to high yield investment programs (HYIP).
- THS-LGBM [10], a machine learning classifier, Light Gradient Boosting Machine (LightGBM) [22], used to compare features in Bitcoin address classification.
- THS-ANN [10], the Neural Network [29], also used in [10] to compare features in Bitcoin address classification.

Evaluation Metrics. In the experiments, the illicit addresses are labeled negative, the licit addresses are labeled positive. The following four terms are important for measurements. TP refers to the number of true positives, TN refers to the number of true negatives, etc. We use the following three metrics to evaluate all models' performance, *Precision*, *Recall* and $F1 - measure$, which have been widely used in previous identification evaluations.

Experiment Settings. We use Pytorch to build our model, which is an open source machine learning library. In the AT-GNN, the convolved feature map has shape $(N + 1, N + 1)$, and after max-pooling, its shape become $(1, N + 1)$. We set the units number r of the first layer in MLP to N. The second layer restores those N units to $N + 1$. In the auto-encoder part, a suitable value for the input sequence length l is needed. We counted the number of transactions for each illicit address in the data set, and found that more than 90% of the illicit addresses have less than 10 transactions, so 10 is a suitable value for l, and we also set the dimension of the hidden feature to 10. In the final prediction network, after concatenating calculated features, the two fully connected layers have 9 units and 4 units respectively, and finally use the *sigmoid* function to get the final result.

Our experiments applied different values of n, so that we can compare the experiment results with different values of n. The maximum number of hop n we used is 3, because if n is set to be larger, the calculation of aggregate features will be complicated and take a long time. And we did ablation experiments in the auto-encoder part. In the case of other settings being the same, we used the model within 3-hop to do experiments with no auto-encoder, with a normal auto-encoder and with a denoising auto-encoder respectively, and analyzed the effect of the auto-encoder part by comparing their results.

4.3   Results

The data and features used by these models are all the same. We use the 3-hop AT-GNN model with the auto-encoder for comparison. Table 2 shows the performance of five models and our model. We can see that our model performs better than AD-SVM, HYIP-XGB, THS-LGBM and THS-ANN in precision, recall and F1 score, and the performance of DPS-RF in precision is slightly better than that of our model, but the performance of it in recall and F1 score is very poor. The reason may be that DPS-RF marks most of the addresses as positive. On the whole, our model is better than these five models.

Table 2. Performance of other models and AT-GNN

Model	Precision	Recall	F1
AD-SVM	90.74%	73.95%	79.55%
DPS-RF	**93.55%**	72.93%	81.96%
HYIP-XGB	91.00%	85.40%	88.11%
THS-LGBM	91.04%	85.72%	88.30%
THS-ANN	86.62%	77.50%	81.81%
AT-GNN (3-hop)	93.44%	**89.79%**	**91.58%**

We use the AT-GNN model with the auto-encoder, and the value of n we use includes 1, 2, 3. Table 3 shows the performance of AT-GNN with different maximum number of hops. The results achieve the worst in precision, recall and F1 score when n is 1, because the convolution of the features within 1-hop leads to excessive compression of the features, which has a bad effect on the prediction of the model. Increasing n from 1 to 3 enhances the quality of the prediction as it digests more information from the Bitcoin transaction network, and the results achieve the best when n is 3. But it is not always true that the larger the n, the better the result. Our experiments on other small data sets have proved that when n is larger, the result will not be better, because too many adjacent address features will have a negative impact on the prediction.

Table 3. Performance of AT-GNN with different maximum number of hops

Model	Precision	Recall	F1
AT-GNN (1-hop)	87.13%	78.34%	82.50%
AT-GNN (2-hop)	91.97%	87.56%	89.71%
AT-GNN (3-hop)	**93.44%**	**89.79%**	**91.58%**

We did ablation experiments in the auto-encoder part to analyze the effects of the auto-encoder. Based on the 3-hop AT-GNN model, we compared the effects of the auto-encoder(AE) and the denoising auto-encoder(D-AE) on the results, and also compared the effects of the presence or absence of auto-encoders on the results. Table 4 shows the performance of AT-GNN with and without auto-encoders. We can see that the model without auto-encoders has the worst results, which proves that the hidden temporal features extracted by auto-encoders are helpful for prediction. And the result of the model with the auto-encoder is better than those with the denoising auto-encoder. The denoising auto-encoder theoretically prevents overfitting, but in this experiment it did not perform well.

Table 4. Performance of AT-GNN with and without auto-encoders

Model	Precision	Recall	F1
AT-GNN without AE	91.08%	86.53%	88.75%
AT-GNN with D-AE	92.26%	87.91%	90.03%
AT-GNN with AE	**93.44%**	**89.79%**	**91.58%**

In addition, we analyzed the effects of different ratios of illicit and licit addresses on the results of our model. We use the 3-hop AT-GNN model with the auto-encoder to classify data sets with ratios 1:200, 1:100, 1:50, 1:20, and 1:5 respectively, and these data sets are randomly sampled proportionally from the original data set. Figure 3 shows the performance of our model at the above different ratios of illicit and licit addresses. The result achieves the best at the ratio 1:20, and on the whole, the larger the proportion of illicit addresses, the better the result. In the experiment, we can solve the problem of the inappropriate ratio through sampling and cost-sensitive methods [30], to improve the prediction results.

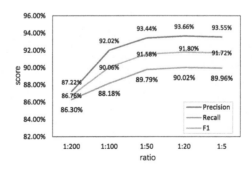

Fig. 3. Performance of AT-GNN at different ratios of illicit and licit addresses

5   Conclusions

In this paper, we present the attention-based graph neural network for identification of illicit bitcoin addresses, taking use of the structure information of the Bitcoin transaction network and the temporal information of the transaction records. Firstly, we calculate multiple aggregate features of the address to be identified based on the Bitcoin transaction network subgraph centered on this address, then the model combines aggregate features at different distances to get convolved features, and learns the weight of the convolved features to aggregate them based on this weight. Secondly, we construct a transaction feature sequence based on the transaction record of the address to be identified, then the model use the auto-encoder to extract the hidden temporal feature by this sequence for the subsequent classification. Lastly, we concatenate the above features to do the classification, and get the result of identification of the Bitcoin address.

The results from the above experiments show that our model can provide better predictive performance compared with other models of identifying illicit addresses. If the suitable ratio of the data set and the right parameters are available, the performance of our model will get better and better. One challenge is that the calculation of aggregate features is complicated and will take a long time when the maximum number of hop is large. In the future, we will propose a new algorithm to reduce the calculating complexity of aggregated features. Furthermore, we will improve our model to be more robust and convincing.

Acknowledgments. The research is supported by the Guangdong Applied R&D Program (2015B010131006) and the National Natural Science Foundation of China (62032025).

References

1. Nakamoto, Satoshi: Bitcoin: A peer-to-peer electronic cash system. Technical report, Manubot (2019)
2. Zheng, Z., Xie, S., Dai, H., Chen, X., Wang, H.: An overview of blockchain technology: Architecture, consensus, and future trends. In: 2017 IEEE International Congress on Big Data (BigData congress), pp. 557–564. IEEE (2017)
3. Zheng, Z., Xie, S., Dai, H.-N., Chen, X., Wang, H.: Blockchain challenges and opportunities: a survey. Int. J. Web Grid Serv. **14**(4), 352–375 (2018)
4. Ali, S.T.: Bitcoin: perils of an unregulated global P2P currency (Transcript of Discussion). In: Christianson, B., Švenda, P., Matyáš, V., Malcolm, J., Stajano, F., Anderson, J. (eds.) Security Protocols 2015. LNCS, vol. 9379, pp. 294–306. Springer, Cham (2015). https://doi.org/10.1007/978-3-319-26096-9_30
5. Bohr, J., Bashir, M.: Who uses bitcoin? an exploration of the bitcoin community. In: 2014 Twelfth Annual International Conference on Privacy, Security and Trust, pp. 94–101. IEEE (2014)
6. Liao, K., Zhao, Z., Doupé, A., Ahn, G.J.: Behind closed doors: measurement and analysis of cryptolocker ransoms in bitcoin. In: 2016 APWG Symposium on Electronic Crime Research (eCrime), pp. 1–13. IEEE (2016)

7. Samsudeen, Z., Perera, D., Fernando, M.: Behavioral analysis of bitcoin users on illegal transactions. Adv. Sci. Technol. Eng. Syst. J **4**, 402–412 (2019)
8. Monamo, P., Marivate, V., Twala, B.: Unsupervised learning for robust bitcoin fraud detection. In: 2016 Information Security for South Africa (ISSA), pp. 129–134. IEEE (2016)
9. García-Escudero, L.Á., Gordaliza, A.: Robustness properties of k means and trimmed k means. J. Am. Stat. Assoc. **94**(447), 956–969 (1999)
10. Lin, Y.J., Wu, P.W., Hsu, C.H., Tu, I.P., Liao, S.W.: An evaluation of bitcoin address classification based on transaction history summarization. In: 2019 IEEE International Conference on Blockchain and Cryptocurrency (ICBC), pp. 302–310. IEEE (2019)
11. Pham, T., Lee, S.: Anomaly detection in bitcoin network using unsupervised learning methods. arXiv preprint arXiv:1611.03941 (2016)
12. Bartoletti, M., Pes, B., Serusi, S.: Data mining for detecting bitcoin Ponzi schemes. In: 2018 Crypto Valley Conference on Blockchain Technology (CVCBT), pp. 75–84. IEEE (2018)
13. Li, Y., Cai, Y., Tian, H., Xue, G., Zheng, Z.: Identifying illicit addresses in bitcoin network. In: Zheng, Z., Dai, H.-N., Fu, X., Chen, B. (eds.) BlockSys 2020. CCIS, vol. 1267, pp. 99–111. Springer, Singapore (2020). https://doi.org/10.1007/978-981-15-9213-3_8
14. Kalodner, H., et al. Blocksci: design and applications of a blockchain analysis platform. In: 29th {USENIX} Security Symposium ({USENIX} Security 20), pp. 2721–2738 (2020)
15. Bastian, M., Heymann, S., Jacomy, M., et al.: Gephi: an open source software for exploring and manipulating networks. Icwsm **8**(2009), 361–362 (2009)
16. Liu, F.T., Ting, K.M., Zhou, Z.H.: Isolation forest. In: 2008 Eighth IEEE International Conference on Data Mining, pp. 413–422. IEEE (2008)
17. Maesschalck, R.D., Jouan-Rimbaud, D., Massart, D.L.: The mahalanobis distance. Chemometr. Intell. Lab. Syst. **50**(1), 1–18 (2000)
18. Schölkopf, B., Williamson, R.C., Smola, A., Shawe-Taylor, J., Platt, J.: Support vector method for novelty detection. Adv. Neural Inf. Process. Syst. **12**, 582–588 (1999)
19. Toyoda, K., Mathiopoulos, P.T., Ohtsuki, T.: A novel methodology for hyip operators' bitcoin addresses identification. IEEE Access **7**, 74835–74848 (2019)
20. Chen, T., Guestrin, C.: Xgboost: a scalable tree boosting system. In: Proceedings of the 22nd ACM SIGKDD International Conference on Knowledge Discovery and Data Mining, pp. 785–794 (2016)
21. Freund, Y., Schapire, R.E.: A decision-theoretic generalization of on-line learning and an application to boosting. J. Comput. Syst. Sci. **55**(1), 119–139 (1997)
22. Ke, G., et al.: Lightgbm: a highly efficient gradient boosting decision tree. In: Advances in Neural Information Processing Systems, pp. 3146–3154 (2017)
23. Abeywickrama, T., Cheema, M.A., Taniar, D.: K-nearest neighbors on road networks: a journey in experimentation and in-memory implementation. arXiv preprint arXiv:1601.01549 (2016)
24. Srivastava, N., Hinton, G., Krizhevsky, A., Sutskever, I., Salakhutdinov, R.: Dropout: a simple way to prevent neural networks from overfitting. J. Mach. Learn. Res. **15**(1), 1929–1958 (2014)
25. Kingma, D.P., Ba, J.: Adam: A method for stochastic optimization. arXiv preprint arXiv:1412.6980 (2014)
26. Qian, N.: On the momentum term in gradient descent learning algorithms. Neural Netw. **12**(1), 145–151 (1999)

27. Toyoda, K., Ohtsuki, T., Mathiopoulos, P.T.: Multi-class bitcoin-enabled service identification based on transaction history summarization. In: 2018 IEEE International Conference on Internet of Things (iThings) and IEEE Green Computing and Communications (GreenCom) and IEEE Cyber, Physical and Social Computing (CPSCom) and IEEE Smart Data (SmartData), pp. 1153–1160. IEEE (2018)
28. Jourdan, M., Blandin, S., Wynter, L., Deshpande, P.: Characterizing entities in the bitcoin blockchain. In: 2018 IEEE International Conference on Data Mining Workshops (ICDMW), pp. 55–62. IEEE (2018)
29. Haykin, S., Network, N.: A comprehensive foundation. Neural Netw. **2**(2004), 41 (2004)
30. Lin, T.Y., Goyal, P., Girshick, R., He, K., Dollár, P.: Focal loss for dense object detection. In Proceedings of the IEEE International Conference on Computer Vision, pp. 2980–2988 (2017)

Application and Challenges of Blockchain in Heterogeneous Identity Trust

Zhaolei Zhang[1](✉), Jian Xu[1], Guishan Dong[2], and Junyan Lin[1]

[1] Westone Information Industry Inc, Chengdu, Sichuan, China
[2] Southwest Computing Technology Research Institute, Chengdu, Sichuan, China

Abstract. Blockchain is an innovative technology with cryptography as the core, and network identity management is an important part of cyberspace security protection. In response to the needs of heterogeneous identity management and mutual trust services, this paper designs a heterogeneous identity mutual trust model based on the alliance chain, proposes the alliance chain system architecture which uses network identity management systems as of the nodes, and designs a heterogeneous network identity mutual trust protocol. This solution is useful to integrate the existed variety of heterogeneous identity management systems, and create a cross-domain mutual trust identity management system.

Keywords: Heterogeneous identity alliance · Unified identity · Alliance chain · Cross-domain access

1 Introduction

Trust is one of the important mechanisms of human society, and identity is the basis of trust. In the digital age, online identity is the key to achieving digital trust, promoting the integration of the real world and the cyberspace, and is the basis for implementing cyberspace governance.

Identity management systems of different organizations (trust domains) and different technical routes are difficult to communicate with each other, and network identities are difficult to recognize each other [2]. This creates trust "islands" and brings many challenges to the integration and development of cyberspace.

One of the research goals of heterogeneous identity management is to achieve safe, trustworthy and mutual recognition when identities are used across organizations and systems. The difficulty of this problem lies in how to establish trust between two systems with no trust relationship and obvious technological system differences, and then, construct an operable user identity credible evaluation and trust transfer mechanism.

"Alliance" is an effective way to achieve consensus and cooperation between different entities. This paper focuses on the issue of mutual trust and recognition of heterogeneous identities, proposes a technical model of building a heterogeneous identity alliance based on blockchain, expounds the key technical mechanisms, and designs a blockchain-based heterogeneous identity trust system architecture.

H.-N. Dai et al. (Eds.): BlockSys 2021, CCIS 1490, pp. 163–168, 2021.
https://doi.org/10.1007/978-981-16-7993-3_12

2   Blockchain Technology and Identity Management Applications

Blockchain technology ensures that records cannot be changed through the consensus mechanism of most participants. It has natural advantages in heterogeneous identity management. Identity management researchers can use its non-centralized architecture and the characteristics of establishing trust through distributed verification and consensus mechanisms to design identity alliance solutions. It mainly includes two categories.

- Integrate blockchain technology with PKI technology to enhance the ability of mutual trust between identities across CAs. The combination of blockchain and PKI is the main direction for researchers to explore. Muneeb Ali et al.proposed the Blockstack, which is based on the Namecoin blockchain [3], to ensure the integrity of identity data and the effective achievement of consensus mechanisms. The Authcoin [4], proposed by Benjamin Leading et al., realizes a distributed PKI. It uses a flexible challenge-response method to verify when the public key is released. The CertCoin [5], proposed by Conner From knecht and others at MIT, is a public and decentralized authentication scheme that uses blockchain and public key technology. It builds a distribution domain name book by maintaining a public ledger of web service domain names and public keys.

The blockchain-based identity management technology has made great progress in realizing decentralized identity information management and promoting the interaction of identity information between multiple identity service entities. However, there are still some shortcomings in the face of heterogeneous identity information management and cross-domain identity trust requirements.

3   Alliance-Chain Based Heterogeneous Identity Trust Model

3.1   Heterogeneous Identity Alliance Technology Model

The traditional method to solve the problem of entities' heterogeneous network identities being trusted is to develop multiple components in the identity authentication service

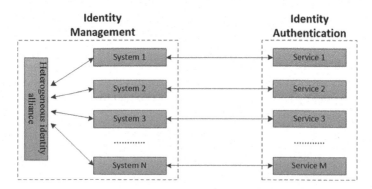

Fig. 1. Heterogeneous identity alliance technology model

to connect different identity management systems respectively, When multiple identity authentication services assist the application system in verifying the multiple identities of the entity, the problem of this method is obvious. It will bring N * M docking development complexity to identity management and identity authentication.

Through the heterogeneous identity alliance technology, the problems caused by the above methods will be effectively avoided, and the complexity of N * M connection will be transformed into the complexity of N + M. Its technical architecture is shown in Fig. 1.

In this model, the heterogeneous identity alliance serves as the backstage of identity management to provide identity trust support for each identity management system. The identity management system still serves as the provider of identity credentials, interacting entity identity information with other identity management systems through heterogeneous identity alliances, and provides support for the docked identity authentication service systems. The identity authentication service system only needs to connect to an identity management system to complete the verification of various heterogeneous identity tickets.

3.2 The System Architecture of Heterogeneous Identity Alliance Chain

Based on the above technical model, a heterogeneous identity alliance chain system can be built using blockchain.

The heterogeneous identity alliance chain system is a non-central distributed system. The alliance chain system consists of a limited number of node subsystems. The technical architecture of each node subsystem is unified, including the storage layer, the blockchain layer and the service interface layer, as Fig. 2.

The storage layer is mainly used to store heterogeneous identity alliance node information and block data. The block data records entity identification and verification data. The blockchain layer realizes the management of block generation, indexing, and query, and the registration, update, and verification smart contracts of user identity attributes. The service interface layer provides service interfaces for alliance nodes and entity

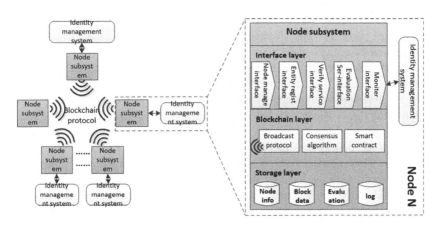

Fig. 2. Heterogeneous identity alliance chain system architecture

users, including alliance node management, entity registration, entity identity verification services, entity credibility evaluation services, and entity behavior supervision interfaces.

3.3   The Protocol of Heterogeneous Identity Management and Service

(1) Node Subsystem Management
The node subsystems are managed and coordinated according to the blockchain system.
The node subsystem is described as Eq. (1):

$$\{GID, \; SKey/PKey, \; Cert\} \tag{1}$$

where GID is the unique number of the node; SKey/PKey is the node's public and private key pair issued by the blockchain system for the node, and Cert is the node's certificate.

(2) Entity Identity Management
The identity management system performs entity identity information registration in the heterogeneous identity alliance chain system. The registration content will be stored in the next block after being checked and approved by each node, The entity identity information is defined as Eq. (2):

$$\{UID, \; ID, \; GID, \; [attNo, \; Hash\,(attNo, \; attVal)], \ldots \ldots\} \tag{2}$$

UID is the unique identity assigned to the entity by the blockchain system, and ID is the identity of the entity in the identity management system 'GID'. If there are multiple IDs for entity, the UID is used for associating them. [attNo, Hash (attNo, attVal)] is the summary of each attribute information of the entity, which is used for entity identity verification by other identity management systems.

(3) Cross-Domain Trust Protocol
The smart contract of the blockchain ensures the execution of trusted transactions without a trusted third party. For entities that cross-domain, firstly, the identity management system verifies the entity's identity through the heterogeneous identity alliance chain to ensure that the identity is legal; then verifies the entity's identity attribute information to ensure that it meets the requirements of trust verification.

The process of the smart contract for authentic verification of entity identity attributes is shown in the Fig. 3. Assuming that the domain A's entity needs to access the domain B's application, the domain B identity management system first queries the entity ID through the blockchain system, and then queries the summary information of the attribute number attNo which needs to be verified, and compare the attribute summary information in the blockchain with the locally calculated attribute summary to determine whether the entity's identity and attributes are credible, and return the result to the identity authentication service system.

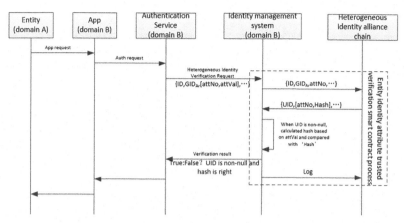

Fig. 3. Entity identity attribute trusted verification smart contract

4   Challenges and Countermeasures

4.1   Discovery of Unknown Network Identity of Entity

Generally, the different network identities of entity cannot be associated, it will bring risks to the results of heterogeneous cross-domain identity authentication. The heterogeneous identity alliance chain system needs to have the ability to automatically discover different network identities of the same entity.

A fuzzy association method based on attribute tags can be used. First, an attribute vector model is constructed by continuously collecting tags such as interest attributes, social attributes, and basic attributes of network identities. Then, the LDA model [6, 7] is used to calculate the similarity (probability) between the attribute vectors of different network identities, and the attribute similarity probability value matrix is obtained. The network identity correlation value is obtained through matrix calculate on to establishment the relation of network identities with similar attribute vectors.

4.2   Privacy Protection

In the process of entity identity verification, entity attribute information needs to be presented to the identity management system to facilitate attribute value comparison and verification, the presented attribute information needs to be effectively protected to avoid leakage of user privacy.

Privacy protection methods can be used, such as the secure sharing mechanism of identity privacy resources based on attribute-based encryption (including secure sharing and fine-grained access control mechanisms) and the secret state-based identity privacy data analysis and processing mechanism [8], Through the supervisable anonymous authentication model, the user's resource access rights and usage rights are determined by means of anonymous certificates.

5 Summary

This paper focuses on the cross-domain trust of entities in the context of heterogeneous identity management, and proposes the model and system to build a heterogeneous identity alliance based on blockchain technology to achieve heterogeneous identity trust. It also discusses the new challenges that the system faces in the application process based on the actual situation. In the follow-up, in-depth research will be conducted on issues such as unknown network identity discovery, identity privacy protection, identity credibility measurement, etc., to further improve the heterogeneous identity alliance system and model.

Acknowledgments. This work was supported by National Key Research and Development Program of China (No.2017YFB0802300) and Sichuan Science and Technology Program (2017GZDZX0002).

References

1. Oppliger, R.: Microsoft. Net passport: a security analysis. Computer **36**(7), 29–35 (2003)
2. Ellin, B.: About openID [EB/OL]. http://www.openidenabled.com/openid/about-openid. Accessed 20 June 2019
3. Hammi, B., et al.: A blockchain-based certificate revocation management and status verification system. Comput. Secur. **104**, 102209 (2021)
4. Leiding, B., et al.: Authcoin: validation and authentication in decentralized networks. arXiv preprint (2016). arXiv:1609.04955
5. Conner, F., Dragos, V., Sophia, Y.: CertCoin: A NameCoin Based Decentralized Authentication System. [EB/OL]. https://pdfkul.com/certcoin-mit_59b308131723dda273d97e76.html. Accessed 20 June 2019
6. Blei, D.M., Ng, A.Y., Jordan, M.I.: Latent dirichlet allocation. J. Mach. Learn. Res. **3**, 993–1022 (2012)
7. Ming, X., Zhang, S.: Multi-Dimensional Social Relationship Analysis Model Based onLDA[EB/OL]. Sciencepaper, Beijing. http://www.paper.edu.cn/releasepaper/content/202 103-274. Accessed 25 Mar 2021
8. Liu, F., Jie, Y.: A secure multi-party computation protocol for universal data privacy protection based on blockchain. J. Comput. Res. Dev. **58**(2), 281–290 (2021)

Exploiting the Medical Data Storage Implementation and Privacy Protection with Consortium Blockchain and IPFS

Shaojie Liu[1], Bin Wen[1,2,3]($\boxtimes$), and Zexu Wang[1]

[1] School of Information Science and Technology, Hainan Normal University, Haikou, China
[2] Cloud Computing and Big Data Research Center, Hainan Normal University, Haikou, China
[3] Key Laboratory of Data Science and Intelligence Education of Ministry of Education, Hainan Normal University, Haikou 571158, China
binwen@hainnu.edu.cn

Abstract. Due to the limitations of technologies, the traditional electronic medical record system has the risk of data being tampered with and attacked, which makes personal privacy easy to be leaked. Combined with the consortium blockchain development platform – FISCO BCOS, a new electronic medical record storage model is proposed. The model controls the access of medical records through blockchain and smart contract, strengthens the privacy protection of patients, improves the convenience of medical data sharing, and provides reliable data support for medical research. Finally, the proposed electronic medical record storage model is fully realized, and its effectiveness and practicability are proved.

Keywords: Medical data · Consortium blockchain · Medical service · Privacy protection · Smart contract

1 Introduction

With the continuous development of computer technology, electronic medical record storage has become a popular medical record storage scheme. However, due to the limitations of the technical structure, there is a data barrier between the electronic medical record system of medical units, which hinders the circulation of medical data. This makes it difficult for patients to control and share their own historical medical records, and medical record data are also difficult to be applied to scientific research and analysis. On the other hand, the traditional electronic medical record system contains more patient privacy information. When the database is leaked or attacked, personal privacy information faces a high risk. At the same time, medical record data also have the possibility of tampering and destruction.

© Springer Nature Singapore Pte Ltd. 2021
H.-N. Dai et al. (Eds.): BlockSys 2021, CCIS 1490, pp. 169–174, 2021.
https://doi.org/10.1007/978-981-16-7993-3_13

The input of scientific research makes the blockchain technology constantly improve and has been widely used in product traceability, financial supply chain and other scenarios. The untamperable and traceable characteristics of blockchain can also meet the technical requirements of application scenarios such as electronic medical record storage and medical data sharing. Using blockchain technology to construct electronic medical system has become an effective solution to improve the privacy of electronic medical records and strengthen the control of permissions.

2   Background

With the continuous development of Internet, cloud computing and network security technologies, the storage, review and transmission of electronic medical records have attracted more and more attention. Thomas F. Stafford [1] discussed the problems of centralized management and privacy disclosure in the existing electronic medical record system through interviews, and analyzed the applicability of blockchain technology in electronic medical record storage and medical information security.

Muhammad Usman et al. [2] firstly discussed how to solve the problems of privacy disclosure and internal tampering in existing medical records storage by blockchain technology. The system ensures the privacy, security and access of medical records through cryptography principle, and solves the problems existing in the existing electronic medical records system to a certain extent.

The characteristics of blockchain technology can provide support for many application scenarios of electronic medical records. Alevtina Dubovitskaya et al. [3] analyzed the shortcomings of the existing electronic medical record system from the perspectives of patient medical record sharing, medical research data collection and multi-agency participation, and introduced blockchain technology to propose an electronic medical record storage scheme to alleviate these problems. The scheme controls the access rights of medical records through smart contracts, encrypts the medical records data and stores them in the cloud database, so as to realize the sharing and privacy protection of patient medical records. The scheme proposed by Yi Chen [4] is similar to the scheme proposed in literature [3]. These strategies have solved some problems faced by the existing electronic medical record storage to a certain extent, but they are lack of thinking about the content storage of medical image medical records.

Medical cases are often accompanied by a large number of image information such as CT images. However, the data structure of blockchain determines that it has a congenital disadvantage in storing large text or image information, which makes it impossible to store these contents in blockchain. Through the thinking of this problem, Sanket Shevkar [5] introduced the InterPlanetary File System (IPFS) into the blockchain electronic medical records management. By storing image data and detailed medical records in IPFS, the occupancy of blockchain resources is reduced, so as to improve the speed of transaction transmission and effectively solve this problem. At the same time, through the way of permission control to improve the management ability of patients for medical records, not only can ensure the safety of user privacy, but also can achieve the purpose of medical records data sharing. Sihua Wu [6] also proposed a similar model structure, but its research lacks the design of permission control and the use of smart contracts.

This paper aims at study the architecture of medical data storage model with consortium blockchain and IPFS. We will mainly focus on privacy protection and data sharing mechanism in medical data storage process. The rest of the article is arranged as follows. Section 3 gives the related technologies involved in the study. Section 4 includes the system architecture and model optimization. Section 5 gives the implementation and empirical analysis of the model. Conclusions with main contributions of proposed approach are also touched upon in Sect. 6.

3 Related Techniques

3.1 Consortium Blockchain

With the continuous development of block chain technology, according to the different node access mechanisms, a variety of block chain structure systems such as public chain, consortium blockchain and private chain are formed and applied to different needs. FISCO BCOS as a typical open source consortium blockchain underlying platform, by combining with the actual needs, provides a visual middleware tool, can better and faster chain building and management maintenance, transaction delay can be shortened to second level, with high performance.

3.2 Smart Contract

The smart contract is the program code running on the block chain, which is triggered when the external call is detected and meets certain conditions. The execution results are packaged into the block as transactions, and then written into the block chain through consensus. In order to enable blockchain to be applied in a wider range of scenarios, Ethereum developed a fully fledged smart contract development language Solidity. FISCO BCOS also used Solidity as a contract programming language, and added a precompiler contract mechanism to enhance the efficiency of Solidity.

3.3 IPFS

IPFS is a file storage scheme designed by integrating distributed hash tables (DHTs), BitTorrent, version control system, self-certified file systems (SFS) and blockchain. It connects the data block by hash chain to ensure that the data cannot be tampered with. IPFS solves the problem of file loss by backup. At the same time, distributed data transmission effectively eliminates redundancy and saves bandwidth, reduces service cost and waste of idle resources, and alleviates single point failure and DDoS attack.

4   System Architecture and Optimization Design

The research of blockchain, IPFS and FISCO BCOS is of great significance to improve the electronic medical record system, which can strengthen the security and stability of medical record information storage. Based on the actual needs, this paper integrates and improves related technologies, and proposes a new electronic medical record storage model.

Based on the IPFS medical storage consortium chain, this paper takes the FISCO BCOS framework as the service core of the system, and controls the patient's ability to control medical records through smart contracts. The model structure is shown in Fig. 1.

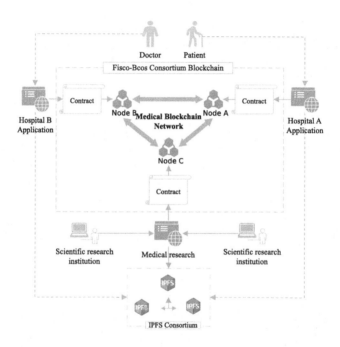

Fig. 1. Improved electronic medical record storage model

Each hospital deploys FISCO BCOS nodes to form the consortium blockchain. Through the deployment of smart contracts, hospitals, departments, doctors and patients accounts are created in the smart contract, and the IPFS address of medical records is stored in it. The smart contract not only stores data information, but also controls the patient's access to medical records.

5 System Implementation

In this paper, the proposed system model is developed and implemented. The front-end interface of the system is based on Vue and ElementUI framework, and the front-end and back-end are asynchronous data interaction through Axios. The back-end of the system uses the popular SpringBoot framework and applies FISCO BCOS's web3j SDK and IPFS's Java SDK to interact with blockchain and IPFS consortium chains, respectively. The smart contract is written in an efficient Solidity language. The main interface of the system is shown in Figs. 2 and 3.

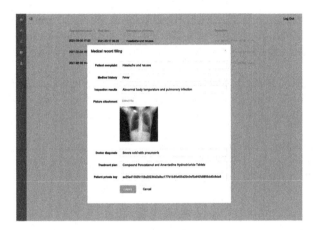

Fig. 2. Add medical records

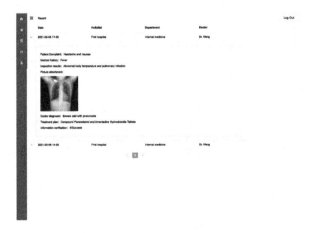

Fig. 3. View medical records

After testing, the developed medical system can well meet the needs of doctors and patients for the storage and sharing of electronic medical records, and can help patients to manage their own historical medical records more conveniently. At the same time, the online reservation function provided by the system also improves the efficiency of medical treatment. Secondly, the system can realize the storage of medical image information and ensure that the data cannot be tampered with through information verification. In summary, the effectiveness and practicability of the proposed model are proved by practice.

6   Conclusions and Future Works

A blockchain electronic medical record storage model based on FISCO-BCOS is proposed, which can break the data barriers between medical units, improve the flow of data, and enhance patient control of medical records by designing smart contracts.

In the future, we will continue to explore an efficient algorithm to improve the efficiency of IPFS medical storage chain, and combine cross-chain technology to expand and develop the comprehensive function of electronic medical system.

Acknowledgements. This research has been supported by the Natural Science Foundation of Hainan Province (No. 620RC605) and Postgraduates' Innovative Research Projects of Hainan Province (No. Hys2020-332).

References

1. Stafford, T.F., Treiblmaier, H.: Characteristics of a blockchain ecosystem for secure and sharable electronic medical records. IEEE Trans. Eng. Manage. **67**(4), 1340–1362 (2020)
2. Usman, M., Qamar, U.: Secure electronic medical records storage and sharing using blockchain technology. Procedia Comput. Sci. **174**(1), 321–327 (2020)
3. Dubovitskaya, A., Xu, Z., Ryu, S., Schumacher, M., Wang, F.: Secure and trustable electronic medical records sharing using blockchain. AMIA Ann. Symp. Proc. **2017**(1), 650–659 (2017)
4. Chen, Y., Ding, S., Xu, Z., Zheng, H., Yang, S.: Blockchain-based medical records secure storage and medical service framework. J. Med. Syst. **43**(1), 1–9 (2018). https://doi.org/10.1007/s10916-018-1121-4
5. Shevkar, S., Patel, P., Majumder, S., Singh, H., Jaglan, K., Shalu, H.: EMRs with blockchain: a distributed democratised electronic medical record sharing platform. arXiv preprint arXiv:2012.05141 (2020)
6. Wu, S., Du, J.: Electronic medical record security sharing model based on blockchain. In: Proceedings of the 3rd International Conference on Cryptography, Security and Privacy, Kuala Lumpur, Malaysia, pp. 13–17. Association for Computing Machinery (2019)

Ponzi Scheme Detection in Ethereum Transaction Network

Shanqing Yu[1,2], Jie Jin[1,2], Yunyi Xie[1,2], Jie Shen[1,2], and Qi Xuan[1,2,3(✉)]

[1] Institute of Cyberspace Security, Zhejiang University of Technology,
Hangzhou 310023, China
xuanqi@zjut.edu.cn
[2] College of Information Engineering, Zhejiang University of Technology,
Hangzhou 310023, China
[3] PCL Research Center of Networks and Communications, Peng Cheng Laboratory,
Shenzhen 518000, China

Abstract. With the rapid growth of blockchain, an increasing number of users have been attracted and many implementations have been refreshed in different fields. Especially in the cryptocurrency investment field, blockchain technology has shown vigorous vitality. However, along with the rise of online business, numerous fraudulent activities, e.g., money laundering, bribery, phishing, and others, emerge as the main threat to trading security. Due to the openness of Ethereum, researchers can easily access Ethereum transaction records and smart contracts, which brings unprecedented opportunities for Ethereum scams detection and analysis. This paper mainly focuses on the Ponzi scheme, a typical fraud, which has caused large property damage to the users in Ethereum. By verifying Ponzi contracts to maintain Ethereum's sustainable development, we model Ponzi scheme identification and detection as a node classification task. In this paper, we first collect target contracts' transactions to establish transaction networks and propose a detecting model based on graph convolutional network (GCN) to precisely distinguish Ponzi contracts. Experiments on different real-world Ethereum datasets demonstrate that our proposed model has promising results compared with general machine learning methods to detect Ponzi schemes.

Keywords: Ethereum · Ponzi scheme · Graph convolutional network · Node classification

1 Introduction

As the largest decentralized distributed electronic ledger, blockchain has the characteristics of decentralization, non-tampering, transparency, and traceability. Based on the above characteristics, blockchain not only lays the foundation for its trust but also creates a reliable cooperation mechanism for transactions. In a nutshell, blockchain achieves peer-to-peer trust [1] without an intermediate third party's credit endorsement, i.e., the transaction is supervised by the whole

© Springer Nature Singapore Pte Ltd. 2021
H.-N. Dai et al. (Eds.): BlockSys 2021, CCIS 1490, pp. 175–186, 2021.
https://doi.org/10.1007/978-981-16-7993-3_14

blockchain, and transaction records cannot misrepresent. There is no doubt that blockchain has broad application prospects.

Ethereum is an open-source public blockchain with smart contracts, which is called blockchain 2.0 [2,3]. Comparing with Bitcoin, Ethereum not only supports smart contracts but also allows to create and utilize decentralized applications [4]. With the development of blockchain technology, blockchain has evolved into two circles, i.e., "chain circle" and "coin circle". The "chain circle" focuses on the development and application of blockchain technology while the "coin circle" is related to digital cryptocurrency. Along with the flourishing of "coin circle" in digital cryptocurrency market, various fraudulent activities have been arisen, among which the most representative is Ponzi scheme. The traditional Ponzi scheme is that old investors get capital returns from new investors until the investment project is unsustainable, leading to the collapse of project [5]. Comparing with traditional scenarios, the combination of Ponzi scheme and blockchain technology in Ethereum has produced more fresh forms [6], implement fraud via deployment-and-execution smart contracts [7]. According to a report of *Cryptoanalysis*, a provider of investigation and risk analysis company for virtual currency, at least 725 million has been lost in frauds such as Ponzi scheme, ICO revocation and fraud ICO. Until now, cryptocurrencies such as Bitcoin are facing a new round of high value, attracting many inexperienced investors into the "coin circle", but most have been suffering from a variety of scams. In summary, it's indicated that financial security has become a critical issue in the blockchain ecosystem. Identifying Ponzi scheme in Ethereum can not only protect the interests of investors promptly and reduce the losses of investors but also strengthen the supervision of fraudulent activities in the "coin circle". Therefore, we mainly focus on Ponzi schemes, which has a very negative impact on Ethereum.

At present, many scholars have done relevant research on Ponzi scheme detection [8]. Most of them are based on machine learning methods which are nothing more than manually extracting contract transaction features, calculating contract code similarity, and counting the frequency of contract opcodes [9,10]. However, these methods are mostly based on feature engineering, but pay little attention to the topological structure of transaction networks, which may lose lots of details. In this paper, the problem of identifying Ponzi contracts in Ethereum transaction networks is modeled as a node classification task. Specifically, we propose a comprehensive identification model for the detection of Ponzi schemes in Ethereum. Due to the openness of Ethereum, we can easily obtain all the transaction records of the target smart contracts to establish transaction networks. The external accounts and smart contracts are regarded as nodes, the edges present the transaction between the two, and the node features are extracted from the transactions to facilitate the design of the following algorithm. Distinct from the traditional feature extraction method considering network topology, we apply the graph convolutional network (GCN) combined structural information with node features to solve an urgent but less studied security issue, i.e., Ponzi scheme in Ethereum.

The main contributions of this paper are summarized as follows.

- We study the matter of Ponzi scheme detection in Ethereum from a network perspective, which is crucial for Ethereum's sustainable development. In addition, the data used in this paper has been cleaned up and standardized, it will be available online for future study.
- We manually extract inherent characteristics of Ponzi smart contracts, and then incorporate these features with topological structure of transaction networks to design our Ponzi scheme detection method based on GCN.
- Extensive experiments on real-world Ethereum datasets validate the effectiveness of our proposed model on identifying Ponzi schemes, compared with a series of machine learning methods.

The rest of the paper is organized as follows. In Sect. 2, we review the related works of Ethereum, the detection of Ponzi scheme, and some network embedding methods. In Sect. 3, we present the data collection, contracts' features, and our proposed Ponzi scheme detection model. In Sect. 4, we conduct extensive experiments with discussions. In Sect. 5, we conclude the paper and highlight future work.

2 Related Work

2.1 Ponzi Schemes on Ethereum

Ethereum [2] that supports smart contracts is currently considered as the second-generation blockchain, and the corresponding cryptocurrency Ether (ETH) is the second-largest cryptocurrency. However, due to the high open-source nature of Ethereum and the convenience of using smart contracts, many fraudulent activities breed along with Ethereum's high-speed development. Initial coin offering (ICO) is the most classic application of smart contracts for the blockchain industry, which refers to financing through the issuance of tokens [11]. Some projects with practical significance can get project start-up funds quickly through ICO financing, but 10% of whole Ethereum smart contracts are Ponzi schemes and it's difficult for inexperienced investors to distinguish. In order to purify the investment environment of the cryptocurrency platform and reduce the investment loss of investors [12,13], many researchers have launched a lot of meaningful works to detect Ponzi scheme.

Ponzi scheme detection is to collect advertisements claiming high returns in various communities and forums, and capture their Bitcoin addresses for manual analysis of transactions to identify them [6]. Later, Bartoletti et al. [14] proposed to calculate the number of character edits that convert one byte-code to another byte-code based on the Normalized Levenshtein distance (NLD) as the contract similarity to identify Ponzi schemes. However, the amount of smart contract code limits the above methods, which need to rely on known codes to identify similar codes. And then, Chen et al. [9,10] proposed a method based on machine learning to identify schemes, mainly analyzing the characteristics of contract transactions and counting contract byte codes. Furthermore, Fan et al. [15] improved the method of combining feature engineering and machine learning, and used the idea of ordered enhancement to train the Ponzi detection model. Therefore, the ordered target statistics method can directly process category features and avoid the prediction offset caused by target leakage. The above identification of Ponzi schemes is mostly based on feature engineering, e.g., manually extracts the transaction features of the contract, counts the feature frequency of the contract byte-code, and combines the acquired features. In this paper, we propose a Ponzi scheme detection method that combined with manual contracts' features and topological structure of the transaction network by GCN, which can effectively detect Ponzi schemes.

2.2   Network Embedding Methods

Network embedding methods [16] have received much attention over the past decades, which convert each node into a low-dimensional vector and make each vector retain as much of the original structural information and topological structure as possible. There are many network embedding methods, which are mainly classified into the following categories, i.e., matrix factorization, deep learning, and other miscellaneous strategies.

Matrix factorization is based on global paired statistical information to learn the similarity of representations. However, matrix factorization methods have high time and space complexity, which is unsuitable for large networks. Deep learning (DL) can automatically recognize useful representations of complex network structures. Generally, DL can be divided into two categories, i.e., deep learning based on random walk and deep learning without random walk. Deep-Walk [17] and node2vec [18] are two classic examples using random walks on networks to learn node representation. Deepwalk is a random walk embedding algorithm that combines the Skip-Gram model to obtain node representations. While node2vec is an improved version of DeepWalk, which adjusts the super parameters of p, q, to make embedding balanced in structural equivalence and homophily. GCN [19] is a classic deep learning method that generates node representation by aggregating its own features and neighbors' features and stacking multiple graph convolutional layers to extract high-level node representations. Differ to the above methods, LINE [20] preserves both the local and global network structures modeling node co-occurrence probability and conditional probability. Considering the high expressiveness and learning ability of GCN, we propose a GCN-based model to well aggregate with the nodes features and topological structure of transaction networks to make Ponzi scheme detection.

3   Methodology

In this section, we first give a detailed description of data collection and data preprocessing, and then extract the following meta-features for the smart contracts, which can form more complex features. We also represent the details of our proposed model for Ponzi scheme detection. The framework of our proposed model is illustrated in Fig. 1.

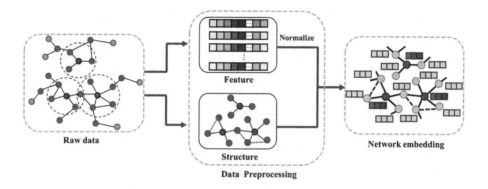

Fig. 1. Overall framework of our proposed model.

3.1 Data Collection and Preprocessing

Data collection is the basis of transaction network analysis. Thanks to the openness of Ethereum, we can easily access transaction records and smart contracts. In this work, we first collect 50 labeled Ponzi schemes from an authoritative website, *Ethercan*[1], which reports various illegal behaviors on Ethereum. However, only 50 contracts are labeled as Ponzi schemes, making it difficult to find the common characteristics of these smart contracts. We further explore more Ponzi schemes in *Xblock*[2], which collects datasets for researchers to autonomously access Ethereum meta-datasets.

Even though many fraudulent activities are very active on Ethereum, the fraudulent activities of Ponzi contracts still account for a small part, which shows that the number of Ponzi contracts and normal contracts are extremely imbalanced. Therefore, we take the number of Ponzi contracts as the guideline, selecting an equal number of normal contracts in all contract transactions, and then forming datasets for the following experiments. We collect transaction records from March 2015 to March 2020. It is worth noting that the transaction records are extremely large, and thus we ascertain a number of target smart contracts (Ponzi contracts and normal contracts) and then obtain their transactions from all Ethereum transaction records to make subgraphs for subsequent experiments. As shown in Fig. 2, we randomly sample centered contracts to obtain their 1st-order neighbors and the transaction records between all of them. In other words, we extract the transaction network into a sub-transaction network (the extracted subgraph is highly correlated with these target contracts), and then analyze and identify Ponzi schemes from a network perspective.

---

[1] Etherscan: `etherscan.io`.

[2] Xblock: http://xblock.pro/ethereum/.

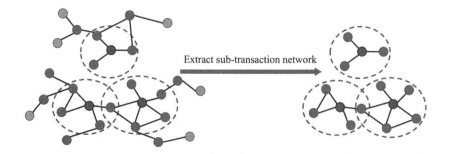

Fig. 2. Schematic illustration of the sub-transaction network.

For simplicity, the extracted sub-transaction network can be defined as $G = (V, E)$, where $V = \{v_1, \cdots, v_n\}$ refers to a set of nodes, and $(v_i, v_j) \in E$ represents the links among the nodes v_i and v_j. Considering the input of our deep model is a matrix, we denote the adjacency matrix as $A \in \mathbb{R}^{n \times n}$. The corresponding degree matrix and feature matrix refer to $D_{ii} = \sum_j A_{ij}$ and $X \in \mathbb{R}^{n \times d}$, respectively, where n is the number of nodes, d is the dimension of the feature vector, and each row $x_i \in \mathbb{R}^d$ is the feature vector of node v_i.

3.2 Contract Features

Due to the fraudulent essence, Ponzi contracts have distinct characteristics compared with normal contracts. The inherent characteristics of a smart Ponzi scheme determine its special behavior, which can be used to determine whether it is a Ponzi smart contract or not. Since the main behavior of contracts can be reflected through transactions with other accounts, we manually investigate the transaction history of the target smart contracts. After obtaining all the transaction records, we can directly obtain two types of information: transaction amount and transaction time. In order to distinguish the nature of the transactions, we use the transaction direction to measure the transaction-in and transaction-out. For each smart contract, we combine the direction of the transactions to count the in-degree and out-degree of the target contract, i.e., the number of contract in and out transactions. For the transaction amount, we calculate the total, maximum, minimum, average, and variance of the target contract's transaction amount from the inflow and outflow of contract transactions. For transaction time, we specifically count the contracts' lifetime and mainly calculate the time interval between the initial contract creation time and the latest contract run time. In summary, we obtain 14 features, which can be used as the basic features of our proposed model.

3.3 GCN

We first introduce the GCN model and then illustrate how to use it for Ponzi scheme detection. GCN is a semi-supervised convolutional neural network [19]

Table 1. Basic topological features of the sub-transaction networks. $|V|$ and $|E|$ are the numbers of nodes and edges, respectively, K is the average degree, and C is the clustering coefficient.

Dataset	$|V|$	$|E|$	K	C
DS1	34699	99745	7.562	0.386
DS2	17980	64299	6.914	0.383
DS3	23065	92200	7.222	0.418

that can work directly on the network and take advantage of their structural information. Graph convolution has a wide range of applicability, which is suitable for nodes and graphs of any topology. It can simultaneously learn node feature information and structure information end-to-end. After establishing sub-transaction networks and extracting contracts' features, we use a 3-layer GCN model with softmax function to learn node representations for Ponzi scheme detection as follows:

$$Z = \text{softmax}\left(\hat{A}\,\text{ReLU}\left(\hat{A}\,\text{ReLU}\left(\hat{A}XW^{(0)}\right)W^{(1)}\right)W^{(2)}\right) \tag{1}$$

where $Z \in \mathbb{R}^{n \times y}$ is the probability distribution of classification, n is the number of network nodes, and y is the dimension of node labels.

4 Experiments

In this section, we present our experimental results. We first introduce the datasets, followed by experimental settings and evaluation metrics. After that, we show the experimental results with discussion. Finally, we analyze the importance of features.

4.1 Dataset

We collect 250 labeled Ponzi smart contracts which are the target of our detection model, and randomly select 250 unlabeled smart contracts as the outliers. With these labeled and unlabeled smart contracts being the central nodes, we extract their 1st-order neighbors and the transaction records between all of them through the API of *Etherscan* and then splice them into a sub-transaction network. In our experiments, we repeat the random selection procedure of labeled and unlabeled nodes three times and thus obtain three sub-transaction networks. The basic statistics of these datasets are presented in Table 1.

4.2 Baselines and Experimental Setup

To validate the effectiveness of our proposed model, we compare it with LINE, as a widely used baseline network embedding method, as well as two popular network embedding approaches based on the random walk, i.e., DeepWalk and node2vec. Furthermore, we compare the results of the non-embedding methods which don't consider the structural information, but only the extracted features. In particular, the baselines are introduced as follows.

- **LINE** is suitable for large-scale networks, which preserves both the local and global network structures to model node co-occurrence probability and conditional probability, respectively. It defines the concept of 1st-order and 2nd-order similarity and enhances the expressive ability of embedding.
- **DeepWalk** is a proximity-based embedding method that obtains node context via random walk, which uses Skip-Gram model and uniform random walks to learn the neighborhood structure of the graph.
- **node2vec** further exploits a flexible neighborhood sampling strategy, i.e., Breadth-first Sampling (BFS) and Depth-first Sampling (DFS). It has two hyper-parameters to choose a proper balance between BFS and DFS to preserve community structure based on homophily as well as a structural equivalence between nodes.
- **Feature** only consider the extracted features as illustrated in Sect. 3.2.

To ensure a fair comparison, we implement DeepWalk and node2vec using OpenNE[3] (an open-source package for network embedding). For all embedding methods, we follow the literature by setting the dimension $d = 128$. For random walk embedding methods, we set hyper-parameters as follows: the size of window $k = 10$, the length of walk $l = 80$, and walks per node $r = 10$. For node2vec, we grid search over $p, q \in \{0.5, 1, 2\}$. For LINE, we use 2nd-order-proximity and set other parameters to the provided defaults. As for our proposed model, we closely follow the framework of Kipf[4] with 3-layer GCN, the dimensionality of output is fixed at 32, set the maximum number of epochs to be 1000, and dropout is set 0.5. We perform 5-fold cross-validation across all methods and datasets with Random Forest. To evaluate the performance of different methods in terms of Ponzi scheme detection, we consider three evaluation metrics, namely, Precision, Recall, and F1-score. Experiments are repeated for 5 random seed initializations and the average performance is reported.

4.3   Results and Discussions

Classifier Performance. Classifier selection of Ponzi scheme detection is an important factor affecting detection performance. Therefore, we consider several widely considered classifiers as baselines, namely, Logistic Regression (LR), Support Vector Machine (SVM), ADAM optimizer(ADAM), and Random Forest (RF). Here we compare the results of the non-embedding methods which only consider extracted features as illustrated in Sect. 3.2. The detection results of different classifiers are compared in Table 2. We can observe that the Random Forest classifier (RF) has the best performance among the above classifiers as it

---

[3] OpenNE: `github.com/thunlp/openne`.

[4] https://github.com/tkipf/gcn.

is more suitable for Ponzi scheme detection, and thus we select it as the classifier in this work.

Table 2. Performance of different classifiers using extracted features.

Metric	Classifier	DS1	DS2	DS3
Precision	LR	0.6779	0.6777	0.6644
	SVM	**0.8268**	0.7784	0.8205
	ADAM	0.7812	0.8222	0.8420
	RF	0.8042	**0.8364**	**0.8697**
Recall	LR	0.5389	0.5317	0.5408
	SVM	0.5890	0.5475	0.5947
	ADAM	0.7491	0.7088	0.7325
	RF	**0.7409**	**0.7421**	**0.7777**
F1-score	LR	0.5982	0.5900	0.5872
	SVM	0.6753	0.6410	0.6858
	ADAM	0.7633	0.7594	0.7785
	RF	**0.7700**	**0.7844**	**0.8183**

Performance Comparison. We compare our proposed model with the four baseline methods on the performance metrics Precision, Recall, and F1-score. Table 3 shows the performance of all the compared methods on the Ponzi scheme task. It is particularly necessary to be able to detect potential risks in time and remind users, even if these risks may not be a Ponzi scheme after passing specific tests. Such risk reminders are common in daily life, so we may be more inclined to recall accounts suspected of the Ponzi scheme. Therefore, we are most concerned about recalls among all indicators in this work. The performance of the feature-only method is the worst across all datasets. Compared with the model that only uses manual features, the precision of LINE, Deepwalk and node2vec are all significantly improved. A reasonable explanation is that the addition of structural information can indeed learn more informative representations and thus boost the classification. Moreover, we can observe that considering the combination of features and GCN leads to better classification performance than using only the extracting features. In particular, our proposed model consistently yields the generally best performance on all datasets. This result indicates that GCN can perceive the nearby information and well integrates node features into the topological structure, which achieves decent classification performance.

Feature Analysis. To further understand the discriminative power of the extracted features, we investigate the feature importance based on the Random Forest mean decreasing impurity as shown in Fig. 3. Next, we analyze why some of these features are important.

- *count_in/count_out* reflects the number of transactions between two accounts. These features are more important than others, and the reason is relatively

Table 3. Performance of different network embedding methods.

Metric	Method	DS1	DS2	DS3
Precision	Feature	0.8042	0.8364	0.8697
	LINE	0.9351	0.9015	0.8714
	Deepwalk	0.9397	**0.9450**	0.8729
	node2vec	**0.9444**	0.9351	**0.9313**
	GCN+Feature	0.8686	0.8766	0.8564
Recall	Feature	0.7409	0.7421	0.7777
	LINE	0.7307	0.5897	0.5823
	Deepwalk	0.5241	0.5235	0.5834
	node2vec	0.6961	0.6921	0.6699
	GCN+Feature	**0.9159**	**0.9159**	**0.9409**
F1-score	Feature	0.7700	0.7844	0.8183
	LINE	0.8111	0.7079	0.6874
	Deepwalk	0.6553	0.6634	0.6943
	node2vec	0.7986	0.7891	0.7780
	GCN+Feature	**0.8907**	**0.8940**	**0.8963**

easy to understand. For a Ponzi smart contract, a natural phenomenon is that the Ponzi scheme uses the funds of new investors to subsidize the old investors. However, with the exposure of the Ponzi scheme, the number of transactions will suddenly decrease or even disappear.

- *values_max_in/values_max_out* represents the largest transaction input (output) amount in the current contract. Ponzi scheme attracts investors to transfer money to it, which can accumulate a lot of wealth. Meanwhile, the Ponzi scheme will quickly transfer a lot of wealth to another account to avoid scam collapse. Due to the high cost of Ether currency, the transaction amount of most normal contracts is small. Therefore, the maximum value of the transaction can be used to distinguish Ponzi smart contract precisely.

- *lifetime_in/lifetime_out* represents the smart contracts' lifetime. The experimental results show that this feature can play a certain role but not the most critical feature. This is mainly because only a small number of smart contracts are frequently used and remain active, while most of them have a short lifetime in Ethereum. Ponzi scheme is often profitable in a short time, it will no longer be used by investors once reported or destroyed in time, resulting in a similar lifetime between normal contracts and Ponzi contracts.

These results reveal a noteworthy phenomenon that manually features can make different views of the smart contract from different angles. Therefore, our proposed model incorporates the extracted features that can facilitate Ponzi scheme detection.

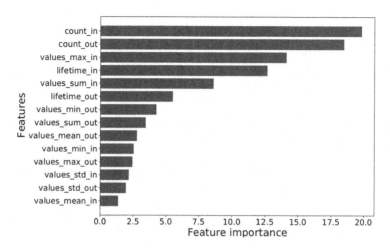

Fig. 3. The importance of the 14 extracted features.

5   Conclusion

In Ethereum, various scams are rampant and the Ponzi scheme is the most serious threat to the financial security of users involved. To deal with this issue, in this paper, we collect transaction records from Ethereum and detect Ponzi schemes from a network perspective. We propose a GCN model that incorporates extracted features to detect and identify Ponzi smart contracts. Compared with general machine learning methods, the experimental results indicate that our proposed model performs better than a series of baselines to identify the Ponzi schemes. In the future, we plan to further extend our proposed model to detect Ponzi schemes in time.

Acknowledgments. The authors would like to thank all the members in the IVSN Research Group, Zhejiang University of Technology for the valuable discussions about the ideas and technical details presented in this paper. This work was partially supported by the National Key R&D Program of China under Grant No. 2020YFB1006104, by the National Natural Science Foundation of China under Grant No. 61973273, by the Zhejiang Provincial Natural Science Foundation of China under Grant No. LR19F030001, by the Ministry of Public Security's Research Project "Research and Demonstration Application of Key Technologies of Criminal Social Network Model", and by the Special Scientific Research Fund of Basic Public Welfare Profession of Zhejiang Province under Grant LGF20F020016.

References

1. Swan, M.: Blockchain: Blueprint for a New Economy. O'Reilly Media, Inc. (2015)
2. Buterin, V., et al.: A next-generation smart contract and decentralized application platform, white paper, vol. 3, no. 37 (2014)

3. Wood, G., et al.: Ethereum: a secure decentralised generalised transaction ledger. Ethereum project yellow paper, vol. 151, no. 2014, pp. 1–32 (2014)
4. Wu, K.: An empirical study of blockchain-based decentralized applications. arXiv preprint arXiv:1902.04969 (2019)
5. Frankel, T.: The Ponzi Scheme Puzzle: A History and Analysis of Con Artists and Victims. Oxford University Press (2012)
6. Vasek, M., Moore, T.: There's no free lunch, even using bitcoin: tracking the popularity and profits of virtual currency scams. In: Böhme, R., Okamoto, T. (eds.) FC 2015. LNCS, vol. 8975, pp. 44–61. Springer, Heidelberg (2015). https://doi.org/10.1007/978-3-662-47854-7_4
7. Juels, A., Kosba, A., Shi, E.: The ring of Gyges: investigating the future of criminal smart contracts. In: Proceedings of the 2016 ACM SIGSAC Conference on Computer and Communications Security, pp. 283–295 (2016)
8. Bartoletti, M., Pes, B., Serusi, S.: Data mining for detecting bitcoin Ponzi schemes. In: 2018 Crypto Valley Conference on Blockchain Technology (CVCBT), pp. 75–84. IEEE (2018)
9. Chen, W., Zheng, Z., Cui, J., Ngai, E., Zheng, P., Zhou, Y.: Detecting Ponzi schemes on Ethereum: towards healthier blockchain technology. In: Proceedings of the 2018 World Wide Web Conference, pp. 1409–1418 (2018)
10. Chen, W., Zheng, Z., Ngai, E.C.-H., Zheng, P., Zhou, Y.: Exploiting blockchain data to detect smart Ponzi schemes on Ethereum. IEEE Access **7**, 37575–37586 (2019)
11. Hahn, C., Wons, A.: Initial Coin Offering (ICO): Unternehmensfinanzierung auf Basis der Blockchain-Technologie. Springer, Wiesbaden (2018). https://doi.org/10.1007/978-3-658-21787-7
12. Morris, D.Z.: The rise of cryptocurrency Ponzi Schemes. The Atlantic, 31 May 2017
13. Kondor, D., Pósfai, M., Csabai, I., Vattay, G.: Do the rich get richer? An empirical analysis of the bitcoin transaction network. PLOS ONE **9**(2), e86197 (2014)
14. Bartoletti, M., Carta, S., Cimoli, T., Saia, R.: Dissecting Ponzi schemes on Ethereum: identification, analysis, and impact. Fut. Gener. Comput. Syst. **102**, 259–277 (2020)
15. Fan, S., Fu, S., Xu, H., Zhu, C.: Expose your mask: smart Ponzi schemes detection on blockchain. In: 2020 International Joint Conference on Neural Networks (IJCNN), pp. 1–7. IEEE (2020)
16. Cai, H., Zheng, V.W., Chang, K.C.-C.: A comprehensive survey of graph embedding: problems, techniques, and applications. IEEE Trans. Knowl. Data Eng. **30**(9), 1616–1637 (2018)
17. Perozzi, B., Al-Rfou, R., Skiena, S.: DeepWalk: online learning of social representations. In: Proceedings of the 20th ACM SIGKDD International Conference on Knowledge Discovery and Data Mining, pp. 701–710 (2014)
18. Grover, A., Leskovec, J.: node2vec: scalable feature learning for networks. In: Proceedings of the 22nd ACM SIGKDD International Conference on Knowledge Discovery and Data Mining, pp. 855–864 (2016)
19. Kipf, T.N., Welling, M.: Semi-supervised classification with graph convolutional networks. In: International Conference on Learning Representations (ICLR) (2017)
20. Tang, J., Qu, J., Wang, M., Zhang, M., Yan, J., Mei, Q.: Line: large-scale information network embedding. In: Proceedings of the 24th International Conference on World Wide Web, pp. 1067–1077 (2015)

TSGN: Transaction Subgraph Networks for Identifying Ethereum Phishing Accounts

Jinhuan Wang[1,2], Pengtao Chen[1,2], Shanqing Yu[1,2], and Qi Xuan[1,2,3(✉)]

[1] Institute of Cyberspace Security, Zhejiang University of Technology,
Hangzhou 310023, China
`xuanqi@zjut.edu.cn`
[2] College of Information Engineering, Zhejiang University of Technology,
Hangzhou 310023, China
[3] PCL Research Center of Networks and Communications, Peng Cheng Laboratory,
Shenzhen 518000, China

Abstract. Blockchain technology and, in particular, blockchain-based transaction offers us information that has never been seen before in the financial world. In contrast to fiat currencies, transactions through virtual currencies like Bitcoin are completely public. And these transactions of cryptocurrencies are permanently recorded on Blockchain and are available at any time. Therefore, this allows us to build transaction networks (TN) to analyze illegal phenomenons such as phishing scams in blockchain from a network perspective. In this paper, we propose a Transaction SubGraph Network (TSGN) based classification model to identify phishing accounts in Ethereum. Firstly we extract transaction subgraphs for each address and then expand these subgraphs into corresponding TSGNs based on the different mapping mechanisms. We find that TSGNs can provide more potential information to benefit the identification of phishing accounts. Moreover, Directed-TSGNs, by introducing direction attributes, can retain the transaction flow information that captures the significant topological pattern of phishing scams. By comparing with the TSGN, Directed-TSGN indeed has much lower time complexity, benefiting the graph representation learning. Experimental results demonstrate that, combined with network representation algorithms, the TSGN model can capture more features to enhance the classification algorithm and improve phishing nodes' identification accuracy in the Ethereum networks.

Keywords: Ethereum · Phishing identification · Subgraph network · Network representation · Graph classification

1 Introduction

Blockchain is a distributed public ledger that is secured by blockchain technology. All transactions take place between two different public addresses and are

ⓒ Springer Nature Singapore Pte Ltd. 2021
H.-N. Dai et al. (Eds.): BlockSys 2021, CCIS 1490, pp. 187–200, 2021.
https://doi.org/10.1007/978-981-16-7993-3_15

permanently recorded on a specific blockchain built for Bitcoin. The process of securing these transactions is handled by Bitcoin miners, who use their computing power to solve complex encryption problems and validate blocks and transactions in the process [13]. There is no limit to the number of Bitcoin addresses that any individual or organization can create, and there is no need to verify the identity during the process of creating an address. With the above advantages, blockchain technology has been rapidly developed and naturally introduced into the financial field. In the digital currency scenarios, the most widely used application of blockchain is cryptocurrency technology [21], by which accounts can freely and conveniently conduct transactions with currency and information and do not have to rely on traditional third parties.

It's worth noting that the cryptocurrency market inevitably breeds many cybercrimes due to anonymity and unsupervised organization. Similarly, as the second-largest cryptocurrency platform next to Bitcoin, Ethereum has been affected by many entities/accounts engaging in illegal activities over the network, including smart Ponzi schemes, phishing, money laundering, fraud, and criminal-related activities. It is reported that phishing scams can break out periodically and are the most deceptive form of fraud [4]. Although the hash mechanism set up inside the blockchain can prevent transactions from being tampered with, so far, there are no available internal tools that can detect illegal accounts and suspicious transactions on the network. Thus it can be seen that cybercrimes, especially phishing scams, have become a critical issue on Ethereum and should be worthy of long-term attention and research to adopt effective countermeasures.

Generally, phishing is a social engineering attack that aims to exploit weaknesses caused by users in the system processes [9]. In traditional phishing attacks, the terminal consumers will receive emails or text messages containing a malicious website whose hostname is close to the legitimate domain from a trusted entity in disguise. Once the link is clicked, phishers will use the measures provided in the link to obtain the users sensitive information, such as usernames, passwords, and credit card details. Thus, existing researches on detecting phishing scams mainly focus on the suspected phishing website identification [5,16] and phishing text massages detection [1,7]. Compared with traditional phishing scenarios, blockchain's openness and transparency make the suspicious phishing addresses and fraudulent funds reportable and traceable. Therefore, traditional forms of phishing scams are difficult to implement on the Ethereum platform on a large scale, and the corresponding detection schemes are not suitable to migrate to the Ethereum phishing detection problem.

In order to identify phishing addresses on Ethereum, we construct transaction networks by transaction information recorded permanently on the Ethereum. Each account is accessible and their transaction history can be available freely. In the transaction networks, the nodes represent Ethereum addresses, while the edges indicate the transaction records with some attributes. Generally, each record between Ethereum accounts includes information such as transaction direction, transaction amount, and transaction timestamp. In this paper, we propose the TSGN model to identify phishing accounts. We think of transaction direction and transaction amount as the essential attributes to build transaction networks. Based on the above, we preproccess the weighted directed transaction networks and then map these networks to subgraph network structural space. According to different pre-processing and mapping strategies, we can obtain the corresponding TSGN and Directed-TSGN for the subsequent feature extraction and detection task. Specifically, our contributions can be concluded as follow:

- We propose a new transaction network model, transaction subgraph networks (TSGNs). Compared with original transaction networks, our TSGN can increase the diversity of features benefiting the subsequent network algorithms.
- We introduce different network mapping strategies to fully capture the potential structural topological information which can not be obtained easily from transaction networks.
- We build the problem of Ethereum phishing account identification as a graph classification task. Our TSGN model can be utilized to enhance various graph classification algorithms such as manual attributes, Graph2Vec, and Diffpool.
- We apply the new model to three transaction network datasets, and our experimental results demonstrate the effectiveness of TSGNs. The fusion of TN and TSGNs generated by different mapping strategies can increase the performance of graph classification algorithms. Directed-TSGN achieves the best performance in 7 of 9 cases. Especially, the classification result Directed-TSGN increases to 93.90% (93.25% for TSGN) when only Diffpool is considered, greatly improving the phishing account identification performance. More remarkably, compared with TSGN, generating Directed-TSGN needs much less time, reduced by almost one order of magnitude.

The rest of the paper is structured as follows. In Sect. 2, we make a brief description of the phishing identification and graph representation methods. In Sect. 3, we mainly introduce the definitions and construction methods of transaction subgraph networks. In Sect. 4, we give several feature extraction methods, which together with TSGN and Directed-TSGN are applied to three Ethereum transaction network datasets. Finally, we conclude our paper in Sect. 5.

2   Background and Related Work

In this section, to supply some necessary background information, we give a brief overview of phishing detection and graph representation algorithms in graph mining.

2.1   Phishing Identification

Phishing scams have become a major threat to the security of Ethereum transactions. To create a good investment environment in the Ethereum ecosystem, many researchers have paid lots of attention to study the effective detection methods for phishing scams. Different from the privacy of traditional financial transaction information, the transaction records of the blockchain are freely available and contain rich attributes. Therefore, many recent studies are mainly based on transaction records. Wu et al. [18] proposed an approach to detect phishing scams on Ethereum by mining its transaction records. By considering the transaction amount and timestamp, this work introduced a novel network embedding algorithm called trans2vec to extract the features of the addresses for subsequent phishing identification. Chen et al. [4] proposed a detecting method based on Graph Convolutional Network and autoencoder to precisely distinguish phishing accounts. One can see that these methods mentioned above mainly built phishing account detection as a node classification task, which can not capture more potential global structural features for phishing accounts. Yuan et al. [22] built phishing identification problem as the graph classification task, which used line graph to enhance the Graph2Vec method and achieved good performance. However, Yuan et al. only consider the structural features obtained from line graphs, ignoring the direction information, which plays a significant role in phishing scams' identification problem. As we know, in the process of phishing fraud, the phishing funds mostly flow from multiple accounts to a specific account. From the network's perspective, the phishing nodes' local topology may be more inclined to multiple inputs and a single output. Our method takes the direction information into consideration and builds the Directed-TSGN model, revealing the topological pattern of phishing scams.

2.2   Graph Representation

Network, as a general modeling approach, are frequently used to study various real world systems, such as social networks [19], traffic networks [15], protein interaction networks [3], literature citation networks [8], etc. Due to its unique structure characteristics, Blockchain ecosystem is naturally modeled as transaction networks to carry out related research. Simultaneously, many graph representation methods are applied to capture the dependency relationships between objects in the Blockchain network structure. Alarab et al. [2] adopted Graph Convolutional Networks (GCN) intertwined with linear layers to predict illicit transactions in the Bitcoin transaction graph and this method outperforms graph convolutional methods used in the original paper of the same data. Liu et al. [12] introduced an identify inference approach based on big graph analytics and learning, aiming to infer the identity of Blockchain addresses using the graph learning technique based on Graph Convolutional Networks. Zhang et al. [23] constructed a graph to represent both syntactic and semantic structures of an Ethereum smart contract function and introduced the graph neural network for smart contract vulnerability detection. According to the above works, one can find that graph representation methods can indeed be utilized to study blockchain networks and outperform in many different applications. In this work, we introduce three categories of graph representation methods such as handcrafted features [19], embedding method Graph2Vec [14], and deep learning method Diffpool [20], to extract the features of TNs, TSGNs, and Directed-TSGNs, preparing for the subsequent phishing account identification.

3   Methodology

In this section, we first formulate the problem description and then present the construction detail of the transaction subgraph network model.

3.1   Problem Description

Generally, given a set of addresses on Ethereum, we can construct transaction network $G = (V, E, W)$, where the node set V indicates the set of addresses, the edge set E represents the transaction from a source address to a destination address with the transaction amounts as the weight value set W.

Here, we construct a set of transaction graphs for each target address $\mathbf{G} = \{G_{add.1}, G_{add.2}, \cdots, G_{add.n}\}$, where $G_{add.i} = (V_{add.i}, E_{add.i}, W_{add.i}, D_{add.i}, y_{add.i})$ is a transaction graph of target address i, $V_{add.i}$ represents address i and it's neighbor addresses, $E_{add.i}$ is the directed transaction set between the addresses of $V_{add.i}$ with direction set $D_{add.i}$ and weight set $W_{add.i}$, and $y_{add.i} \in Y^{|\mathbf{G}| \times |\phi|}$ is the label of address i and it's corresponding transaction subgraph, where ϕ is the label set of all target addresses. In this work. our purpose is to learn a mapping function $\mathscr{F} : \mathbf{G} \to Y$ which can predict the labels of graphs in $\mathbf{G}$. The label set Y includes phishing addresses and normal addresses in the scenario of Ethereum phishing account identification.

3.2   Transaction Subgraph Networks

In this section, we introduce the detail of our transaction subgraph network model. Firstly, we give the definitions of TSGN and Directed-TSGNs as shown in the Definition 1 and Definition 2, and then we elaborate the construction methods of transaction subgraph networks (TSGNs) and directed transaction subgraph networks (Directed-TSGNs), respectively.

Definition 1 (TSGN). *Given a transaction graph $G = (V, E, W)$, the TSGN, indicated by $T = \mathscr{L}(G)$, is a mapping from G to $T = (V', E', W')$, with the node and edge sets indicated by $V' = \{t_i | i = 0, 1, 2, \cdots\}$ and $E' \subseteq (V' \times V')$. There will generate an edge between the transaction subgraphs t_a and t_b if they share the same addresses or transactions in the original transaction graph G. The W' will be calculated by a weight mapping function $W' \leftarrow f(W)$.*

Definition 2 (Directed-TSGN). *Given a directed transaction graph $G = (V, E, W, D)$, the Directed-TSGN, denoted by $T_D = \mathscr{F}(G)$, is a mapping from G to $T_D = (V^*, E^*, W^*, D^*)$, with the node and edge sets denoted by $V^* = \{d_i | i = 0, 1, 2, \cdots\}$ and $E^* \subseteq (V^* \times V^*)$. A directed edge will be built between two directed transaction subgraphs d_a and d_b when they meet the following conditions: In the original directed transaction graph G, (i) they share the common*

addresses or transactions, (ii) and form a path with the same direction. The W^*
will be calculated by a weight mapping function $W^* \leftarrow f'(W)$.

According to the above definitions, we can see that TSGN is a variant of SGN model [19] on Ethereum transaction networks. Different from SGN model, TSGN adds a network weight mapping mechanism, which can retain the transaction amount information in the original transaction network for downstream network analysis tasks. Based on TSGN model, Directed-TSGN introduces the direction information into the mapping mechanism which can capture the path of transaction behavior. Next, we will focus on demonstrating the specific construction methods.

3.3   Constructing TSGN

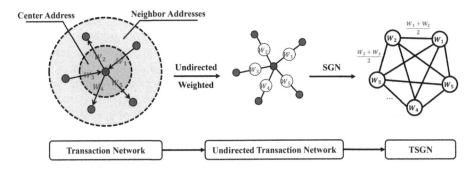

Fig. 1. A toy example of constructing TSGN.

Figure 1 shows the process of constructing TSGN. Given an original transaction network composed of a center address and it's neighbor addresses, we can firstly get a plain transaction network with weight values after undirected processing. And then, we map this network into TSGN structural space. Specifically, the edges in the undirected transaction network is mapping to the nodes W_1, W_2, W_3, W_4, W_5 of TSGN, and then new edges are built between nodes W_1, W_2, W_3, W_4, W_5 because the edges of undirected transaction network share the common (red) node. We choose the mean function $f(W_{ij}) = Mean(W_i, W_j)$ as weight mapping function in Definition 1, i.e., the weight of edge (W_1, W_2) can be calculated as $(W_1 + W_2)/2$. Of course, different weight mapping functions can be defined as required.

3.4   Constructing Directed-TSGN

According to the Sect. 3.3, we can find that the TSGN becomes more complex than the original transaction network, even a fully connected network, which may reduce graph mining algorithms' representation ability. Moreover, the mapping

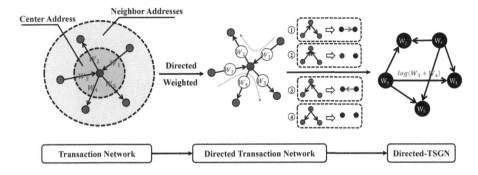

Fig. 2. A toy example of constructing Directed-TSGN.

mechanism of TSGN model can not retain the direction information, which may play an important role in the following tasks.

In response to the above problems, we propose the Directed-TSGN. As shown in Fig. 2, the directed transaction network remains the direction and weighted attributes of the original transaction network. Similarly, the edges are mapped into the black nodes W_1, W_2, W_3, W_4, W_5 of the Directed-TSGN. The two red directed dashed lines indicate that the transactions W_1 and W_2 and transactions W_3 and W_4 can be seen as two continuous transaction behaviors, respectively. In other words, the edges with weights W_1 and W_2 and the edges W_3 and W_4 can form two paths with the same direction, respectively. According to the four direction mapping strategies, we can build the new edges in the Directed-TSGN. Due to the fact that ② and ④ don't satisfy the requirements of constructing edges, the Directed-TSGN can limit the network size and get a relatively sparse transaction subgraph network. Here, $f'(W_{ij}) = log(W_i + W_j)$ is chosen as the weight mapping function in Definition 2.

4   Experimental Evaluations

4.1   Datasets

Ethereum, today's largest blockchain-based application, has fully open transaction data which can be easily accessed through the API of Etherscan(`etherscan.io`). Considering that the entire transaction network is enormous, we crawl some phishing addresses and normal addresses as the target nodes and only extract their first-order neighbor nodes from the Ethereum transaction records to construct transaction network datasets. After filtering and preprocessing the raw data, we finally got 1626 transaction networks centered on phishing nodes, and 1641 transaction networks centered on normal nodes. And then, these networks will be randomly divided so that we finally get three balanced datasets, each of which has 500 transaction networks of phishing addresses and 500 transaction networks of normal addresses. And the next experiments will be verified on these three datasets. The basic statistics of the three datasets are shown in Table 1.

Table 1. Statistics for the three datasets. N_G is the number of graphs, $\#C_{max}$ is the number of graphs belonging to the largest class, N_C is the number of classes, and #Nodes and #Edges are the average numbers of nodes and edges, respectively, of the graphs in the dataset.

Dataset	N_G	$\#C_{max}$	N_C	#Nodes	#Edges
EthereumG1	1000	500	2	26.003	25.031
EthereumG2	1000	500	2	31.650	30.673
EthereumG3	1000	500	2	26.338	25.369

4.2 Metrics

In order to accurately evaluate the quality of each classification model, in this paper, we will use *F1-Score* as a metric,

$$F_1 = \frac{2PR}{P+R}, \tag{1}$$

where P is precision and R is recall. *F1-Score* is the harmonic mean of precision and recall, so it can more comprehensively judge the pros and cons of the classification models.

4.3 Baselines and Experimental Setup

For the phishing account detection problem, we transform it into a graph classification task. In order to better verify the effect of the model proposed, we adopt three typical feature extraction methods to generate graph representation, namely handcrafted attributes, Graph2Vec, and Diffpool, which are introduced in the following.

Handcrafted Attributes. Many classic topological attributes can be utilized to analyze some important patterns in a complex network and can capture some basic information for graph classification [11,17,19], link prediction [6] and so on. In this paper, we aim to represent the networks by manually extracting the transaction network features, which are used in the downstream graph classification task. We mainly extracted 10 network features such as *the number of network nodes, the number of network edges* and *the average clustering coefficient*, etc. See the Appendix for details.

Graph2Vec. Graph2Vec [14] is the first embedding framework for the entire networks, which is relied on the embedding technique that has achieved impressive performances in NLP. Graph2Vec extracts some rooted subgraphs around different nodes and analogies them to Doc2Vec's context words and thus learns the graph representation [10]. Graph2Vec can learn the distributed representations of arbitrary sized graphs such that it can ignore the problem such as poor generalization.

Diffpool. This method [20] proposed a differentiable graph pool module, which can generate hierarchical representations of graphs and can be combined with various graph neural network architectures in an end-to-end manner. Diffpool learns the distinguishable soft cluster allocation of nodes on each layer of deep GNN and maps the nodes to a set of clusters, which then form the coarse input of the next GNN layer. This method mainly solves the problem that the traditional GNN methods are flat and can't learn the hierarchical representations of graphs.

Parameter Setting. The experimental part is mainly divided into two steps: the representation of the graph and the graph feature classification. In the graph feature representation part, we used the above three graph representation methods to extract features of TN, TSGN, and Directed-TSGN. For *Handcrafted Attributes*, there are no hyperparameters, just extract 10 features of each graph. For *Graph2Vec*, the parameter height of the WL kernel is set to 3. The embedding dimension is set to a commonly-used value of 1,024. For TN and Directed-TSGN, the parameters weight and direction are set to true. But for TSGN, we set the direction to false and the weight to true. We set the other parameters as: the learning rate is 0.025 and the epoch is 1000. For *Diffpool*, the parameter settings of the model are the same as in [20]. We also set corresponding initialization features for different networks. For TN, the node feature is a two-dimensional vector composed of in-degree and out-degree, while for TSGN and Directed-TSGN, the node feature is a one-dimensional vector composed of the weight of the corresponding link before graph mapping. In the graph feature classifier part, each dataset is randomly split into 9 folds for training and 1 fold for testing. To exclude the random effect of fold assignment, the experiment is repeated 500 times using the random forest classifier and then records the average F_1-*Score* and its standard deviation.

4.4   Results

According to the above setting, we conduct some experiments on the three Ethereum datasets, and the results of phishing account identification are shown in Table 2. We can find that, compared with the transaction networks (original), TSGN and Directed-TSGN models indeed has good performances in enhancing the phishing account identification. Interestingly, TSGN achieves the best classification performance 94.35% and 93.64%, in 2 of 9 cases based on the deep learning method Diffpool. Overall, Directed-TSGN increases the performance of the original classification results in 7 of 9 cases. Combined with the Handcrafted Attributes method, Directed-TSGN outperforms TN, leading to an increase of 1.11%. Directed-TSGN has an improvement over TN on all datasets, and it leads to an increase of 11.70% when considering the Graph2Vec method. We can see that TSGN and Directed-TSGN achieve the state-of-the-art results on the deep learning method Diffpool, which indicates that our TSGN model can further improve the representation capability of the deep learning method.

Table 2. The classification performance of different transaction subgraph network model.

Datasets	EthereumG1	EthereumG2	EthereumG3
Algorithm	Handcrafted		
TN(Original)	74.74±3.42	76.90±2.65	72.84±2.92
TSGN	75.25±1.63	76.94±2.29	73.04±2.43
Directed-TSGN	**75.35±3.88**	**77.50±2.25**	**73.95±2.31**
Algorithm	Graph2Vec		
TN(Original)	56.45±4.18	57.25±1.79	61.80±2.23
TSGN	56.95±2.42	57.85±2.72	62.05±3.02
Directed-TSGN	**68.15±2.26**	**68.10±1.28**	**64.15±2.48**
Algorithm	Diffpool		
TN(Original)	93.09±1.31	89.10±1.64	92.85±1.09
TSGN	**94.35±1.39**	**93.64±1.32**	93.25±1.49
Directed-TSGN	93.35±1.18	89.20±1.53	**93.90±2.43**

Furthermore, we record the computational times and compare the time consumption of constructing TSGN and Directed-TSGN on three datasets. The results are presented in Table 3, where one can see that, the computational time of Directed-TSGN is much less than that of TSGN on each dataset, decreasing from 3 hundred seconds to less than 70 s. Such results suggest that, Directed-TSGN can further enhance the performance of the algorithm for phishing account identification, while also greatly improve the efficiency of the algorithms.

Table 3. Time consumption (sec.) of constructing TSGNs and Directed-TSGNs.

Dataset	TSGN	Directed-TSGN
EthereumG1	1.355×10^2	7.3687
EthereumG2	3.650×10^2	56.9006
EthereumG3	1.264×10^2	65.3633

5   Conclusion

In this paper, we present a novel transaction subgraph network (TSGN) model for phishing account identification. By introducing different mapping mechanisms into the transaction networks, we built TSGN and Directed-TSGN models to enhance the classification algorithms. Compared with the TNs, our TSGN indeed provide more potential information to benefit the phishing account identification. Considering the direction attributes, the Directed-TSGNs can retain the transaction flow information that captures the significant topological pattern of phishing scams. By comparing with the TSGN, Directed-TSGN is of a controllable scale and indeed have much lower time complexity, benefiting the network feature extraction methods to learn the network structure with higher efficiency. Experimental results demonstrate that, combined with network representation algorithms, the TSGN and Directed-TSGN models can capture more features to enhance the classification algorithm and improve phishing nodes identification accuracy in the Ethereum networks. In particular, when deep learning methods Diffpool is adopted to extract the features of these networks, we can achieve the state-of-the-art results on all datasets.

Acknowledgments. This work was partially supported by the National Key R&D Program of China under Grant No. 2020YFB1006104, by the National Natural Science Foundation of China under Grant No. 61973273, and by the Zhejiang Provincial Natural Science Foundation of China under Grant No. LR19F030001.

7   Appendix

- **Number of Graph Nodes** (N): The number of nodes in the graph.
- **Number of Graph Edges** (E): The number of edges in the graph.
- **Average Degree** (D_A): The mean number of edges connected to a node in the graph.
- **Percentage of leaf nodes** (P): A node is defined as a leaf node if it's degree is 1. If there are l leaf nodes in the graph, the percentage of leaf nodes can be calculated as $P = l/N$.
- **Average Clustering Coefficient** (C_{coef}): The clustering coefficient is a classic measure to quantify the edge density of the ego-network. Given a graph, there are m_i neighbors of node v_i and they are connected by e_i edges. Then, the average clustering coefficient of the graph can be defined as

$$C_{coef} = \frac{1}{N} \sum_{i=1}^{N} \frac{2e_i}{m_i(m_i - 1)} . \tag{2}$$

- **Largest Eigenvalue of the Adjacency Matrix** (λ): Given a graph G, it can be represented as an adjacency matrix $A^{N \times N}$. As the isomorphic invariant, we can adopt the largest one λ of eigenvalues of A as the graph feature.
- **Network Density** (D_N): Given a network, the numbers of nodes and edges are N and E, then the network density can be defined as $D = 2E/N(N-1)$
- **Average Betweenness Centrality** (C_{betw}): For each pair of nodes in a connected network, there exists at least one shortest path between the nodes such that the number of edges that construct this path is minimized. The betweenness centrality of a node is a measure of centrality based on the shortest paths. So, the betweenness centrality of a node is defined as

$$C_{betw}(i) = \sum_{m \neq i \neq n} \frac{e_{mn}(i)}{e_{mn}} . \tag{3}$$

$C_{betw}(i)$ can reflect the importance of node i as a bridge node. Where e_{mn} is the number of shortest paths between v_m and v_n, and $e_{mn}(i)$ is the number of shortest paths between v_m and v_n that pass through v_i.

Then, the average betweenness centrality of the network can be calculated as

$$C_{betw} = \frac{1}{N} \sum_{i=1}^{N} C_{betw}(i) . \tag{4}$$

- **Average Closeness Centrality** (C_{close}): The closeness centrality is also a measure of centrality based on the shortest paths, which requires taking into account the shortest paths from each node to the other nodes. Given a connected network, the closeness centrality of a node is represented as the reciprocal of the sum of shortest path length between this node and the others. The average closeness centrality of the network is defined as

$$C_{close} = \frac{1}{N} \sum_{i=1}^{N} \frac{k-1}{\sum_{j=1}^{k} e_{ij}} , \tag{5}$$

where e_{ij} is the shortest path length between nodes v_i and v_j.
- **Average Neighbor Degree** ($D_{neighbor}$): The neighbor degree of a node is the average degree of all the neighbors of this node, which can capture the 2-hop information. We can calculate the neighbor degree of the node v_i as

$$D_{neighbor}(i) = \frac{1}{k_i} \sum_{v_j \in \mathcal{N}_i} k_j , \tag{6}$$

where $\mathcal{N}_i$ is the neighbor set of node v_i, and k_i and k_j are the degrees of node v_i and $v_j \in \Omega_i$. For a network, we can get the average neighbor degree

$$D_{neighbor} = \frac{1}{N} \sum_{i=1}^{N} D_{neighbor}(i) \tag{7}$$

References

1. Adebowale, M.A., Lwin, K.T., Sanchez, E., Hossain, M.A.: Intelligent web-phishing detection and protection scheme using integrated features of images, frames and text. Expert Syst. Appl. **115**, 300–313 (2019)
2. Alarab, I., Prakoonwit, S., Nacer, M.I.: Competence of graph convolutional networks for anti-money laundering in bitcoin blockchain. In: Proceedings of the 2020 5th International Conference on Machine Learning Technologies, pp. 23–27 (2020)
3. Borgwardt, K.M., Ong, C.S., Schönauer, S., Vishwanathan, S., Smola, A.J., Kriegel, H.P.: Protein function prediction via graph kernels. Bioinformatics **21**, i47–i56 (2005)

4. Chen, L., Peng, J., Liu, Y., Li, J., Xie, F., Zheng, Z.: Phishing scams detection in Ethereum transaction network. ACM Trans. Internet Technol. (TOIT) **21**(1), 1–16 (2020)
5. Feng, F., Zhou, Q., Shen, Z., Yang, X., Han, L., Wang, J.Q.: The application of a novel neural network in the detection of phishing websites. J. Ambient Intell. Humanized Comput. 1–15 (2018). https://doi.org/10.1007/s12652-018-0786-3
6. Fu, C., et al.: Link weight prediction using supervised learning methods and its application to yelp layered network. IEEE Trans. Knowl. Data Eng. **30**(8), 1507–1518 (2018)
7. Gualberto, E.S., De Sousa, R.T., Vieira, T.P.D.B., Da Costa, J.P.C.L., Duque, C.G.: The answer is in the text: multi-stage methods for phishing detection based on feature engineering. IEEE Access **8**, 223529–223547 (2020)
8. Hosseini, M.R., Maghrebi, M., Akbarnezhad, A., Martek, I., Arashpour, M.: Analysis of citation networks in building information modeling research. J. Constr. Eng. Manage. **144**(8), 04018064 (2018)
9. Khonji, M., Iraqi, Y., Jones, A.: Phishing detection: a literature survey. IEEE Commun. Surv. Tutorials **15**(4), 2091–2121 (2013)
10. Le, Q., Mikolov, T.: Distributed representations of sentences and documents. In: International Conference on Machine Learning, pp. 1188–1196 (2014)
11. Li, G., Semerci, M., Yener, B., Zaki, M.J.: Graph classification via topological and label attributes. In: Proceedings of the 9th International Workshop on Mining and Learning with Graphs (MLG), vol. 2, San Diego, USA (2011)
12. Liu, X., Tang, Z., Li, P., Guo, S., Fan, X., Zhang, J.: A graph learning based approach for identity inference in dapp platform blockchain. IEEE Trans. Emerg. Top. Comput. (2020)
13. Nakamoto, S.: Bitcoin: A peer-to-peer electronic cash system. Technical Report, Manubot (2019)
14. Narayanan, A., Chandramohan, M., Chen, L., Liu, Y., Saminathan, S.: subgraph2vec: Learning distributed representations of rooted sub-graphs from large graphs. In: International Workshop on Mining and Learning with Graphs (2016)
15. Ruan, Z., Song, C., Yang, X.H., Shen, G., Liu, Z.: Empirical analysis of urban road traffic network: a case study in Hangzhou city, china. Phys. Stat. Mech. Appl. **527**, 121287 (2019)
16. Sahingoz, O.K., Buber, E., Demir, O., Diri, B.: Machine learning based phishing detection from URLs. Expert Syst. Appl. **117**, 345–357 (2019)
17. Wang, J., et al.: Sampling subgraph network with application to graph classification. arXiv preprint arXiv:2102.05272 (2021)
18. Wu, J., et al.: Who are the phishers? phishing scam detection on Ethereum via network embedding. IEEE Trans. Syst. Man Cybern. Syst. (2020)
19. Xuan, Q., et al.: Subgraph networks with application to structural feature space expansion. IEEE Trans. Knowl. Data Eng. (2019). https://doi.org/10.1109/TKDE. 2019.2957755
20. Ying, R., You, J., Morris, C., Ren, X., Hamilton, W.L., Leskovec, J.: Hierarchical graph representation learning with differentiable pooling. In: Proceedings of the 32nd International Conference on Neural Information Processing Systems, pp. 4805–4815 (2018)

21. Yuan, Y., Wang, F.Y.: Blockchain and cryptocurrencies: model, techniques, and applications. IEEE Trans. Syst. Man Cybern. Syst. **48**(9), 1421–1428 (2018)
22. Yuan, Z., Yuan, Q., Wu, J.: Phishing detection on Ethereum via learning representation of transaction subgraphs. In: Zheng, Z., Dai, H.-N., Fu, X., Chen, B. (eds.) BlockSys 2020. CCIS, vol. 1267, pp. 178–191. Springer, Singapore (2020). https://doi.org/10.1007/978-981-15-9213-3_14
23. Zhuang, Y., Liu, Z., Qian, P., Liu, Q., Wang, X., He, Q.: Smart contract vulnerability detection using graph neural networks. In: Proceedings of the 2020 29th International Joint Conference on Artificial Intelligence, pp. 3283–3290 (2020)

Threat Prediction of Abnormal Transaction Behavior Based on Graph Convolutional Network in Blockchain Digital Currency

Meng Shen[1(✉)], Anqi Sang[2], Pengyu Duan[2], Hao Yu[1], and Liehuang Zhu[1]

[1] School of Cyberspace Science and Technology, Beijing Institute of Technology,
Beijing 100081, China
shenmeng@bit.edu.cn

[2] School of Computer Science, Beijing Institute of Technology, Beijing 100081, China

Abstract. There are some malicious traders in the current blockchain digital currency market, and their abnormal transaction behaviors have seriously threatened the security of a large number of users' assets. Therefore, the research on the threat prediction method of abnormal transaction behavior of blockchain digital currency is beneficial to actively prevent the threat of abnormal transaction behavior, and is of great significance to maintain the ecological environment health of blockchain digital currency. The representative Bitcoin is a currency with the highest market value among many blockchain digital currencies, with a huge number of users and transactions. The Bitcoin trading system is dynamic, and different types of abnormal transaction behaviors have different structures, so it is extremely challenging to predict the threat of abnormal transaction behaviors. This paper designs a new threat prediction method for abnormal transaction behavior. Specifically, through the analysis of the transaction relation pattern of typical abnormal transaction behaviors of Bitcoin, the abnormal transaction behaviors are uniformly modeled as an object-relation pattern. Then, the research proposes TSRGL framework, which uses R-GCN to learn the topology structure of the historical object-relation snapshot graph, and realizes the threat prediction of abnormal transaction behavior. To evaluate the effectiveness of this approach, we verified the effectiveness of the TSRGL framework based on real Bitcoin abnormal transaction behavior dataset. The experimental results show that TSRGL framework has better performance than the baseline methods and is currently the most suitable framework for the threat prediction of abnormal transaction behavior.

Keywords: Blockchain · Bitcoin · Abnormal transaction behavior · Graph convolutional network · Link prediction

1 Introduction

In recent years, blockchain digital currency has gradually become one of the most popular topics. A huge network of transactions is emerging based on the public ledger of blockchains. According to the statistics, as of November 2020, Bitcoin has more

ⓒ Springer Nature Singapore Pte Ltd. 2021
H.-N. Dai et al. (Eds.): BlockSys 2021, CCIS 1490, pp. 201–213, 2021.
https://doi.org/10.1007/978-981-16-7993-3_16

than 750 million addresses, which generated more than 580 million block transactions. As of October 2020, there are more than 800 million block transactions on Ethereum, and more than 500 million Ethereum transfers took place at more than 80 million addresses. But the abnormal users in the transaction network, their abnormal transactions and abnormal transaction behaviors are seriously affecting the ecological health of blockchain digital currency. In many blockchain digital currency, Bitcoin's market value is much higher than that of any other blockchain digital currency. The Bitcoin ecosystem faces serious challenges. On the one hand, because Bitcoin allows users to use pseudonyms that have nothing to do with their real identity without address reuse. Its anonymity makes it easier for users to hide their identities, thus the attack cost of the attacker is reduced, and the detection difficulty of the defender is increased. On the other hand, due to the continuous emergence of new attack methods such as airdrop and price manipulation [1], existing defense methods focus on post-hoc defense and fail to detect and prevent new or potential threats in a timely manner [2]. As a result, we need an effective method to take the initiative to predict threat in Bitcoin transaction network, so as to reduce the impact of the attacker's abnormal transaction behavior on the user.

This paper focuses on the threats generated by abnormal transaction behaviors such as "dust" injection, "airdrop" operation, extortion and schemes in the Bitcoin transaction network. These abnormal transaction behaviors are widespread, and seriously threaten the life and property safety of ordinary users. For example, between 2018 and 2019, the British police department alone had received more than 560 Bitcoin extortion incident reports, among them, 6 related incidents happened in 2018, and the number of related events had risen to 115 in 2019, surged by 1817%[1]. In the middle of 2019, a transaction platform called SOXex used fake airdrops and high-return schemes to cash out about 40 million yuan. Attackers can track the transaction behavior of the user by using "dust" injection, threatening the anonymity of users in Bitcoin transactions. Attackers can attract users' investment by airdrop operation, which may threaten the security of users' digital assets. Attackers launch extortion or schemes that threaten the security of a user's physical and virtual assets [3]. Therefore, it is important to take the initiative to further predict the threat of the above abnormal transaction behavior in the Bitcoin transaction networks, which not only helps to protect ordinary users from the attacker's attack, but also helps to better maintain the health of the blockchain digital currency ecosystem.

It is important to note that there are many challenges in predicting the threat of abnormal transaction behavior in Bitcoin. First, Bitcoin itself has the characteristics of large number of accounts, massive transactions and multiple relations, which will cause the threat prediction process based on transaction data to be subject to time and space, resulting in problems such as low efficiency and large amount of calculation. Second, the amount of ground-truth data of abnormal transaction behavior of Bitcoin is far less than the massive transaction data, and there is an imbalance between the number of true positive samples and true negative samples. Thirdly, different types of abnormal transaction behaviors of Bitcoin have different initiating objects, acting objects and interaction relations; that is the heterogeneity of the transaction relation pattern, and it is difficult to use a specific transaction relation pattern to predict different kinds of

---

[1] https://baijiahao.baidu.com/s?id=16616141112247744650wfr=spiderfor=pc.

threats. Fourthly, in each abnormal transaction behavior, the objects and the interaction relations generated or disappeared are dynamically changing over time, which brings great challenges to predict the threat of abnormal transaction behavior of Bitcoin.

Aiming at different types of abnormal transaction behaviors of Bitcoin, based on the historical transaction data records, this paper puts forward the corresponding transaction relation patterns of different kinds of abnormal transaction behaviors. Then all the transaction relation patterns are fused into a unified object-relation pattern, so as to represent the dependencies among different objects more completely. At the same time, in view of R-GCN's learning ability and applicable scenarios in graph structure, TSRGL for processing graph data is proposed, so as to predict the threat of abnormal transaction behavior. Finally, using the ground-truth set of abnormal transaction behavior of Bitcoin, the experiment verifies that TSRGL can effectively predict the threat of abnormal transaction behavior, and the performance of TSRGL are verified by comparing with the baseline method. The main contributions of this paper are as follows.

- This paper proposes the transaction relation patterns of different types of abnormal transaction behaviors of Bitcoin, and then abstracts them into the object-relation pattern diagram, which can effectively represent the object and dependency relation of heterogeneous abnormal transaction behaviors such as "dust" injection, "airdrop" operation, extortion and schemes.
- This paper proposes a framework TSRGL, which can transform the threat prediction of abnormal transaction behavior into directed graph link prediction. Based on the snapshot graph of historical object relation, it can effectively learn the structure features of threat network, and then predict the potential interaction relation between objects, and predict the threat of abnormal transaction behavior.
- The validity of TSRGL in the threat prediction task of abnormal transaction behavior is proved by experiments on the ground-truth set of abnormal transaction behavior of Bitcoin. The performance of TSRGL is evaluated by comparing with baseline methods, and the parameters are analyzed. The experimental results show that TSRGL is the most suitable architecture for the threat prediction task of abnormal transaction behavior of Bitcoin at present.

2   Methodology

2.1   Typical Abnormal Transaction Behavior of Bitcoin

"Dust" Injection and "Airdrop" Operation. "Dust" injection is where an attacker can track a large number of users' Bitcoin addresses and their related addresses by sending a small amount of coins (the value of which is much smaller than the value of a normal transaction) to them, thereby undermining the anonymity of Bitcoin. An "airdrop" operation is where an attacker sends a relatively fixed value of cryptocurrency to users Bitcoin address for free (or after the address is registered), in order to increase user usage and gain access to more digital assets. Their typical transaction relation pattern is shown in the Fig. 1(*a*), which involve the objects of attackers, such as blockchain-based services, transaction platforms, malicious organizations; and the execution address object generated by the attacker object, as well as the ordinary user object attacked by the "dust" injection attack and the "air drop" operation attack. That is, blockchain based services, transaction platforms and malicious organizations have an owner-member relation with the attacker object. There is a creation relation between the attacker object and the execution address object. And there is a dust or air-drop transaction relation between the execution address object and the ordinary user object. Specifically, the attacker object uses the created Bitcoin address to carry out a "dust injection" attack or an "airdrop" operation attack on the ordinary user object.

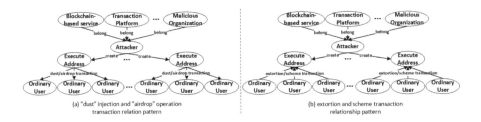

(a) "dust" injection and "airdrop" operation transaction relation pattern

(b) extortion and scheme transaction relationship pattern

Fig. 1. "Dust" injection and "airdrop" operation transaction relation pattern.

Extortion and Scheme. Extortion is when an attacker obtains cryptocurrency assets in an illegal way by demanding bitcoins as ransom from users in a heavy-handed way. A scheme is when a user is tricked into making money by an attacker and sends cryptocurrency to the attacker's Bitcoin address in an attempt to earn a high return on assets. Their typical transaction relation pattern is shown in the Fig. 1(b), which involve the objects of attackers, such as blockchain based services, transaction platforms, malicious organizations; and the execution address object generated by the attacker object, as well as the ordinary user object attacked by the "dust" injection attack and the "air drop" operation attack. That is, blockchain based services, transaction platforms and malicious organizations have an owner-member relation with the attacker object. There is a creation relation between the attacker object and the execution address object. And there is an extortion or scheme transaction relation between the execution address object and the ordinary user object. Specifically, the attacker object uses the created Bitcoin address to receive the value of the extortion or scheme transfer from the ordinary user object to complete the extortion attack and scheme attack.

2.2 Problem Definition

In order to better describe the object and interactive relation of different types of abnormal bitcoin transaction behaviors, we modeled the unified representation of the transaction relation pattern of the typical abnormal transaction behaviors as an object-relational pattern, as shown in the Fig. 2.

Definition 1. *Object-relation pattern. The object-relation pattern $G = (V, E, R, C)$ is a quadruple. Where V represents a set of nodes, means object, which contains six classes of objects, namely attacker type, attacker, attack types, user types, user, executive address. E represents a set of directed edges that represent the relation between*

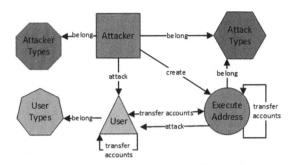

Fig. 2. Object-relation pattern.

nodes. R represents a group of relation types, including four relations, namely, owner-member relation, attack relation, creation relation, and transaction relation. C represents the weight function of a set of transaction edges, which only supports transaction relation, that represents the sum of the total transaction value between two nodes.

Definition 2. *Abnormal network. G_t is the snapshot of the object-relation at time t with the interactive adjacency matrix A_t. If, at time t, there is a directed edge from $v_i \in V_t$ to $v_j \in V_t$ between the two nodes v_i and v_j, then $A_t^{i,j} = 1$, and otherwise, $A_t^{i,j} = 0$.*

Figure 3 is a schematic diagram of abnormal network evolution based on the objectrelation pattern diagram, taking the attack type of "airdrop" operation as an example. The schematic diagram of the snapshot graphs of the object-relation at time t and time $t+1$ (G_t and G_{t+1}), and the schematic diagram of the corresponding interactive adjacency matrices (A_t and A_{t+1}) are shown in the figure respectively. As can be seen from the figure, at the time of $t+1$, the node 2 attacker and its created node 4 execution address have produced an "airdrop" operation attack on the node 7 user. That is, in the process of abnormal network evolution based on object-relation pattern diagram, directed edge $e_{2,7} \in E_{t+1}$ from nodes 2 to 7, and directed edge $e_{4,7} \in E_{t+1}$ from nodes 4 to 7 are generated. In the A_{t+1} schematic of the interactive adjacency matrix, these newly generated relations with a value of 1 are represented by red filled squares.

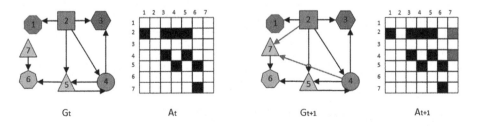

Fig. 3. Schematic diagram of abnormal network evolution. (Color fiugre online)

Definition 3. *Threat prediction. The threat prediction of abnormal transaction behaviors is learned to predict the object-relation snapshot $\widetilde{G_{t+1}}$ at time $t+1$. New relation links appear in the $\widetilde{G_{t+1}}$, indicating that some threat relations related to abnormal transaction behaviors are about to occur, such as the attacked users transfer money to the execution addresses, etc.*

2.3 TSRGL Framework

This paper proposes TSRGL, as shown in the Fig. 4, is suitable for the threat prediction of abnormal transaction behaviors of various blockchain digital currencies. It transforms the threat prediction task of heterogeneous abnormal transaction behaviors into a unified link prediction task based on directed graph, so as to reveal the potential threat relations of abnormal transaction behaviors through the predicted links. TSRGL is mainly composed of an encoder and a decoder. The historical object-relation of abnormal transaction behaviors at time $t+1$ are used as the input to the encoder, and then the encoder makes full use of R-GCN to mining the specific graph structure features. Then the DistMult factorization [4] decoder is used to decode, and finally, the link that is about to be generated, that is, the threat relations of abnormal transaction behavior are scored, and the score of predicted snapshot $\widetilde{G_{t+1}}$ of the object-relation is output.

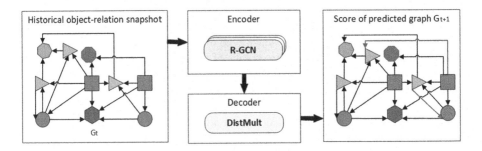

Fig. 4. TSRGL framework.

Encoder. In the encoder, we use R-GCN [5] to specifically realize the learning of the input graph topological features. Its defined forward update hierarchical propagation model for node $v_i \in V_t$ is shown in the Fig. 5, at time t, its formal representation is shown in the following Eq. (1).

$$h_{t,i}^{(l+1)} = \sigma \left(\sum_{r \in R} \sum_{j \in N_i^r} \frac{1}{c_{i,r}} W_r^{(l)} h_{t,j}^{(l)} + W_0^{(l)} h_{t,i}^{(l)} \right) \tag{1}$$

where $\sigma(\cdot)$ is the activation function, R represents the relation types between nodes, N_i^r represents the set of neighbor nodes of node i under relation r, $c_{i,r}$ is a normalized constant, $W_r^{(l)}$ is a shared weight matrix of l-layer relation type r, and its function is to prevent overfitting on rare relations and very large models. In the Fig. 5, the left half (*a*) is an object-relation snapshot for node $v_i \in V$, and the right half (*b*) is a forward update hierarchical propagation process for node $v_i \in V$. As shown in the figure, the filling node of yellow grid in (*a*) is $v_i \in V$, and the 5 nodes around it are adjacency nodes, there are a total of 8 relations. In (*b*), in order to ensure that the information of $v_i \in V$ node itself can be passed to the next layer, in addition to the three relation types that actually exist in (*a*), it also considers the self-loop relation, a special self-loop relation type that is applicable to each node. As can be seen from (*b*), node $v_i \in V$ carries out matrix operation with adjacent nodes, based on each relation, the type and direction of edges are transformed to obtain the normalized gray square. Then, the normalized adjacency information (feature vector) is accumulated in a sum, and the update is completed through the activation function transfer.

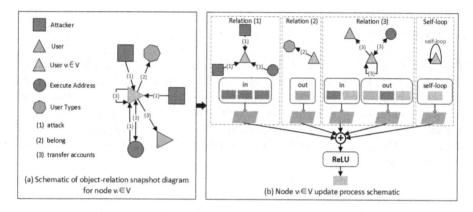

Fig. 5. Forward update hierarchical propagation model for node. (Color figure online)

The update of each layer of the graph neural network includes the parallel update of each node in the graph. At time t, the feature matrix of the hidden layer at layer l is composed of the combination of the hidden layer features of each node in G_t, and its formal representation is shown in the Eq. (2).

$$H_t^{(l)} = \left[h_{t,1}^{(l)}, h_{t,2}^{(l)}, ..., h_{t,i}^{(l)}, ..., h_{t,N}^{(l)} \right] \tag{2}$$

where N is the number of nodes in G_t, $H_t^0 = X_t$. R-GCN adopts stacked layer as a whole, that is, the output of the previous layer is used as the input of the next layer. The node features of each layer are obtained from the node features and node relations (edges) of the previous layer, and the feature matrix of each layer is also related to the feature matrix of the previous layer.

Decoder. In this paper, the threat prediction task of abnormal transaction behaviors is transformed into the task of predicting the topology structure of the dynamic directed graph and predicting the links that will be generated in the topology. And the DistMult decoder was used to score the predicted results. The formal definition of the final score is the following Eq. (3).

$$S_{i,j} = f(v_i, r, v_j) = m_i^T R_r m_j \tag{3}$$

where (v_i, r, v_j) is a triple, and $m_i = h_{t,i}^{(l)}$, R_r is a diagonal matrix, which every relation r associated with. We adopted the minimized loss function as shown in the Eq. (4).

$$L = \alpha \sum_{(v_i, r, v_j) \in G_t} y \log fl(S_{i,j}) + (1-y) \log(1 - fl(S_{i,j})) \tag{4}$$

where fl is the logistic sigmoid function, and y is an indicator set to $y = 1$ for positive triples and $y = 0$ for negative ones.

3   Experiment

This section conducts experiments on the effectiveness of TSRGL framework to predict the threat of abnormal transaction behaviors based on the real data set of abnormal transaction behaviors of Bitcoin. And compared with the widely used baseline methods, the performance of the architecture is verified, and the framework's parameters are analyzed. All experiments were implemented in Python, with a 3.7 GHz 8-core AMD Ryzen 7 2700X processor, 32 GB memory, Python 3.5 environment and 64-bit Windows 10 operating system.

3.1   Dataset

At present, the number of abnormal transactions in Bitcoin is still on the rise, but due to the large amount of manpower and resources required to mark the ground-truth of abnormal transactions in Bitcoin, there is no dataset available. Therefore, we conduct research based on the ground-truth set of abnormal transaction behaviors of Bitcoin provided by Ref. [3], which mainly includes the ground-truth of four kinds of abnormal transaction behaviors of Bitcoin, namely "dust" injection, "airdrop" operation, extortion and scheme. Considering the small number of ground-truth of scheme abnormal transaction behaviors provided by it, we introduce the ground-truth set of Ponzi scheme based on Bitcoin given in Ref. [6]. The Ref. [3] gives the ground-truth of 23 abnormal transaction behaviors of Bitcoin from May 1, 2017 to November 9, 2019. The Ref. [6] gives the addresses of 32 Bitcoin Ponzi schemes crawled from social networks.

As the ground-truth sets of the above abnormal transaction behaviors of Bitcoin are all independent Bitcoin addresses or clusters, there is no information about the transaction relation of abnormal transaction behaviors. We used the parsed record of Bitcoin historical transaction data obtained from BTC.com to construct the anomalous transaction behaviors threat network through Breadth First Search (BFS) for subsequent research. Here, for each abnormal transaction behaviors in the ground-truth set of abnormal transaction behaviors of Bitcoin, we respectively obtain a weighted directed abnormal transaction behaviors threat network through a layer of BFS. For each threat network with weighted directed abnormal transaction behaviors, it is obvious that the object-to-object relation in the threat network can be extracted according to the object-relation pattern diagram proposed in Definition 1, so as to form the object-relation graph of the threat network. Finally, based on all the threat networks in the ground-truth set of abnormal transaction behaviors of Bitcoin, we construct a largescale threat object-relation graph of abnormal transaction behaviors of Bitcoin with 424,130 threat objects and 1,755,334 threat relations as shown in Table 1.

Table 1. Statistics of the datasets.

Datasets	Entities	Train edges	Val. edges	Test edges
Abnormal transaction behaviors of Bitcoin [3]	177,538	751,231	13,800	13,800
Bitcoin Ponzi schemes [6]	246,592	1,004,103	192,000	192,000
Total	424,130	1,755,334	205,800	205,800

3.2 Baselines and Evaluation Metrics

In order to verify that TSRGL is currently the most suitable framework for the threat prediction task of abnormal transaction behaviors of Bitcoin, we took classic algorithms CP [7] and two link prediction models as the baseline for comparative evaluation. The two link prediction models are ComplEx [8] and HolE [9], in which, ComplEx facilitates modeling of asymmetric relations by generalizing DistMult to the complex domain, while HolE replaces the vector-matrix product with circular correlation. For each baseline methods, we used the author's publicly released source code and used the best parameter settings for the corresponding model.

And here, we adopted four widely used evaluation metrics, namely mean reciprocal rank (MRR), Hits at 1 (H@1), Hits at 3 (H@3) and Hits at 10 (H@10), which we report both filtered and raw.

3.3 Experimental Results and Analysis

Table 2 shows the overall prediction performance of the TSRGL framework compared to the baseline methods on the threat dataset of real-world Bitcoin abnormal transaction behaviors. Average the results of 10 experiments for each data in the table, which comprehensively display the average prediction performance of each method and threat type. The experimental results show that the proposed TSRGL framework is superior to the baseline methods in all four evaluation metrics, and TSRGL framework is the most suitable framework for the threat prediction task of abnormal transaction behaviors of Bitcoin at present.

Table 2. Overall performance comparison.

Model	MRR		Hits @ 1		Hits @ 3		Hits @ 10	
	Raw	Filtered	Raw	Filtered	Raw	Filtered	Raw	Filtered
R-GCN	0.287	0.438	0.233	0.409	0.325	0.461	0.382	0.481
CP	0.152	0.226	0.095	0.18	0.207	0.243	0.221	0.304
ComplEx	0.275	0.426	0.229	0.391	0.313	0.447	0.379	0.466
HolE	0.263	0.335	0.202	0.377	0.293	0.392	0.364	0.412

Framework Parameter Analysis. The topology learning ability of TSRGL framework is mainly based on the R-GCN model, therefore, we discuss the influence of R-GCN layer number on the prediction performance.

First of all, the effect of R-GCN layer number on prediction performance is shown in Fig. 6. Under the condition that other parameters are unchanged, the depth of the model is gradually changed from one layer to four layers, that is, the range of layers is $[1, 2, 3, 4]$. And the changing trends of the four evaluation metrics under different levels were recorded in the figure. As can be seen from the figure that when increasing the depth of R-GCN, the performance of the model is enhanced and peaks at number 3. However, as the number of convolutional layers continues to increase, the overall performance no longer rises but slightly reduces. We considered the reason is the obstacle of over-smoothing [10].

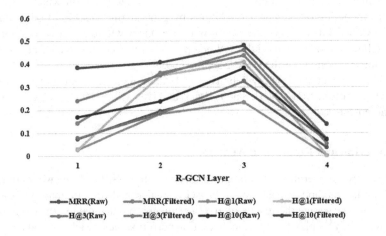

Fig. 6. Effect of R-GCN layer number.

4   Related Work

4.1   Abnormal Transaction Behaviors of Blockchain Digital Currencies

As the blockchain digital currencies are more and more well known by the public and the utilization rate is gradually increasing, the threat of abnormal transaction behaviors caused by the abuse of the characteristics of the blockchain digital currencies has brought great troubles to users. Therefore, many researchers are committed to the identification of abnormal transaction behaviors of blockchain digital currencies. These include the use of data-driven methods to identify extortion abnormal transaction behaviors in Bitcoin [11], identification of Ponzi Schemes in Bitcoin and Ethereum [6, 12], identifying illegal Bitcoin transactions in the dark web and tracking the flow of funds [13], based on cross-currency identification of abnormal transaction behaviors [14].

4.2   Graph Convolutional Network

Graph Convolutional Network (GCN) is a variant of Graph Neural Network (GNN) [15]. For example, the GCN model in Ref. [16] restricts the convolution operation layer by layer and mitigates the problem of overfitting. Moreover, the re-normalization operation is used to solve the problems of numerical instability and gradient explosion or disappearance. In addition, Graph Convolutional Network (GCN) can be applied to entity classification [17], link prediction [18] and other tasks. R-GCN [5] changed GCN from the dimensions of graph types to make it more suitable for large-scale graphs with edge information. At the same time, R-GCN can be further regarded as GCN under the differential message passing interpretation, that is, a subclass of GCN [19].

4.3   Network Link Prediction

Link prediction of networks is widely used in social networks [20] and other dynamic networks in the real world. Reference [21] proposed a new node representation learning method that can capture the evolution mode of dynamic networks. In this paper, the threat prediction task of abnormal transaction behaviors of blockchain digital currency is transformed into a unified link prediction task based on heterogeneous information network, so as to use a new method to reveal the potential threat relation of abnormal transaction behaviors through the predicted link.

5   Summary

The goal of this paper is to predict the threat of abnormal transaction behaviors of blockchain digital currency. In order to solve this problem, we analyze and summarize the typical transaction relation patterns of abnormal transaction behaviors of Bitcoin, and abstract the object-relation pattern used to uniformly represent abnormal transaction behaviors. Then the TSRGL framework, which takes the historical object-relation snapshot as input, is proposed to learn the structure information of threat network, so as to complete the task of link prediction for the threat of abnormal transaction behaviors. Finally, by using real abnormal transaction behaviors dataset of Bitcoin, the experiment proves the effectiveness of TSRGL framework in predicting the threat of abnormal transaction behaviors. At the same time, the performance experiment results of TSRGL framework are better than the baseline methods, and it is currently the most suitable framework for the threat prediction of abnormal transaction behaviors of blockchain digital currency. By predicting the threat relations of abnormal transaction behaviors, it can help prevent users from participating in abnormal transaction behaviors and protect users' digital assets.

In the future research, we will expand the research work from the following two aspects: (1) Reduce the overall complexity of TSRGL framework, so that it is more suitable for the link prediction task of large-scale heterogeneous information networks. (2) Explore more tasks that TSRGL framework can participate in, such as entity classification and subgraph matching.

Acknowledgments. This work is partially supported by National Key R&D Program of China under Grant 2020YFB1006101, Beijing Nova Program under Grant Z201100006820006, NSFC Projects under Grants 61972039 and 61872041, Beijing Natural Science Foundation under Grant 4192050, and Open Research Projects of Zhejiang Lab under Grant 2020AA3AB04.

References

1. Chen, W., Wu, J., Zheng, Z., Chen, C., Zhou, Y.: Market manipulation of bitcoin: evidence from mining the Mt. Gox transaction network. In: 2019 IEEE Conference on Computer Communications, INFOCOM 2019, Paris, France, 29 April–2 May 2019, pp. 964–972. IEEE (2019)
2. Zhou, S., Yang, Z., Xiang, J., Cao, Y., Yang, M., Zhang, Y.: An ever-evolving game: evaluation of real-world attacks and defenses in Ethereum ecosystem. In: Capkun, S., Roesner, F. (eds.) 29th USENIX Security Symposium, USENIX Security 2020, 12–14 August 2020, pp. 2793–2810. USENIX Association (2020)
3. Shen, M., Sang, A., Zhu, L., Sun, R., Zhang, C.: Abnormal transaction behavior recognition based on motivation analysis in blockchain digital currency. Chin. J. Comput. **44**(1), 193–208 (2021)
4. Yang, B., Yih, W., He, X., Gao, J., Deng, L.: Embedding entities and relations for learning and inference in knowledge bases. arXiv preprint arXiv:1412.6575 (2014)
5. Schlichtkrull, M., Kipf, T.N., Bloem, P., van den Berg, R., Titov, I., Welling, M., et al.: Modeling relational data with graph convolutional networks. In: Gangemi, A. (ed.) ESWC 2018. LNCS, vol. 10843, pp. 593–607. Springer, Cham (2018). https://doi.org/10.1007/978-3-319-93417-4_38
6. Bartoletti, M., Pes, B., Serusi, S.: Data mining for detecting bitcoin Ponzi schemes. In: Crypto Valley Conference on Blockchain Technology, CVCBT 2018, Zug, Switzerland, 20–22 June 2018, pp. 75–84. IEEE (2018)
7. Hitchcock, F.L.: The expression of a tensor or a polyadic as a sum of products. J. Math. Phys. **6**(1–4), 164–189 (1927)
8. Trouillon, T., Welbl, J., Riedel, S., Gaussier, É., Bouchard, G.: Complex embeddings for simple link prediction. In: International Conference on Machine Learning, pp. 2071–2080. PMLR (2016)

9. Nickel, M., Rosasco, L., Poggio, T.: Holographic embeddings of knowledge graphs. In: Proceedings of the AAAI Conference on Artificial Intelligence, vol. 30 (2016)

10. Rong, Y., Huang, W., Xu, T., Huang, J.: The truly deep graph convolutional networks for node classification. arXiv preprint arXiv:1907.10903 (May 2019)

11. Paquet-Clouston, M., Haslhofer, B., Dupont, B.: Ransomware payments in the bitcoin ecosystem. J. Cybersecur. 5(tyz003), 5 (2019)

12. Chen, W., Zheng, Z., Cui, J., Ngai, E.C.H., Zheng, P., Zhou, Y.: Detecting Ponzi schemes on Ethereum: towards healthier blockchain technology. In: Champin, P.-A., Gandon, F.L., Lalmas, M., Ipeirotis, P.G. (eds.) Proceedings of the 2018 World Wide Web Conference on World Wide Web, WWW 2018, Lyon, France, 23–27 April 2018, pp. 1409–1418. ACM (2018)

13. Lee, S., et al.: Cybercriminal minds: an investigative study of cryptocurrency abuses in the dark web. In: 26th Annual Network and Distributed System Security Symposium, NDSS 2019, San Diego, California, USA, 24–27 February 2019. The Internet Society (2019)

14. Yousaf, H., Kappos, G., Meiklejohn, S.: Tracing transactions across cryptocurrency ledgers. In: Heninger, N., Traynor, P. (eds.) 28th USENIX Security Symposium, USENIX Security 2019, Santa Clara, CA, USA, 14–16 August 2019, pp. 837–850. USENIX Association (2019)

15. Shen, M., Zhang, J., Zhu, L., Ke, X., Xiaojiang, D.: Accurate decentralized application identification via encrypted traffic analysis using graph neural networks. IEEE Trans. Inf. Forensics Secur. 16, 2367–2380 (2021)

16. Kipf, T.N., Welling, M.: Semi-supervised classification with graph convolutional networks. In: 5th International Conference on Learning Representations, ICLR 2017, Conference Track Proceedings, Toulon, France, 24–26 April 2017. OpenReview.net (2017)

17. Chen, L., Peng, J., Liu, Y., Li, J., Xie, F., Zheng, Z.: Phishing scams detection in Ethereum transaction network. ACM Trans. Internet Technol. (TOIT) 21(1), 1–16 (2020)

18. Chen, J., Xu, X., Wu, Y., Zheng, H.: GC-LSTM: graph convolution embedded LSTM for dynamic link prediction. CoRR, abs/1812.04206 (2018)

19. Gilmer, J., Schoenholz, S.S., Riley, P.F., Vinyals, O., Dahl, O:. Neural message passing for quantum chemistry. In: Precup, D., Teh, Y.W. (eds.) Proceedings of the 34th International Conference on Machine Learning, ICML 2017, Sydney, NSW, Australia, 6–11 August 2017, Volume 70 of Proceedings of Machine Learning Research, pp. 1263–1272. PMLR (2017)

20. Lu, Y., et al.: Social influence attentive neural network for friend-enhanced recommendation. In: Dong, Y., Mladenić, D., Saunders, C. (eds.) ECML PKDD 2020. LNCS (LNAI), vol. 12460, pp. 3–18. Springer, Cham (2021). https://doi.org/10.1007/978-3-030-67667-4_1

21. Trivedi, R., Farajtabar, M., Biswal, P., Zha, H.: DyRep: learning representations over dynamic graphs. In: 7th International Conference on Learning Representations, ICLR 2019, New Orleans, LA, USA, 6–9 May 2019. OpenReview.net (2019)

A Study on Bitcoin Price Volatility Based on the SVAR Model and Impulse Response Analysis

Hecong Xu[1], Xiaolei Xu[2($\boxtimes$)], Zhen Wu[2], Haifeng Guo[1], Yuxi Zhang[1], and Hongzhi Wang[3]

[1] Department of Finance, School of Management, Harbin Institute of Technology, Harbin 150001, China
[2] National Computer Network Emergency Response Technical Team/Coordination Center of China, Beijing 100094, China
xuxiaolei@cert.org.cn
[3] Computing Faulty, Harbin Institute of Technology, Harbin 150001, China

Abstract. Based on the monetary property and finance property of Bitcoin, this paper analyzed the influence factors of Bitcoin price volatility from the perspectives of Bitcoin's own and external factors. The structural vector autoregression (SVAR) model is applied to investigating the direction and strength of the effects of influence factors on Bitcoin prices and the variance decomposition approach is used to compare the contributions of these factors. The results show that the Bitcoin's own factors play fundamental roles in Bitcoin price volatility, and the speculation factors have significant impacts on Bitcoin price volatility, which reflects that the financial property of Bitcoin becomes increasingly important. Governments and investors should pay close attention to the financial property of Bitcoin.

Keywords: Bitcoin price volatility · Structural vector autoregression (SVAR) model · Impulse response · Variance decomposition · Influence factors

1 Introduction

Bitcoin, the most popular and typical digital currency, was proposed and constructed initially by Satoshi Nakamoto [1] in *Bitcoin: A Peer-to-Peer Electronic Cash System* in November 2008. Based on Blockchain technology, Bitcoin is a purely peer-to-peer electronic cash, which would allow online payments to be sent directly from one party to another without going through a financial institution.

Now, Bitcoin is used widely. Since Bitcoin has the special mechanism such as trading 24 h a day, no price limit and so on, its price rose rapidly accompanied by dramatic fluctuations, as shown in Fig. 1. Different from normal currencies or commodities, Bitcoin's price volatility is affected not only by the relationship between supply and demand, but also by many other factors, such as economic environment, capital market, international events, policies and so on, which gave not only great challenges but precious

© Springer Nature Singapore Pte Ltd. 2021
H.-N. Dai et al. (Eds.): BlockSys 2021, CCIS 1490, pp. 214–225, 2021.
https://doi.org/10.1007/978-981-16-7993-3_17

and scarce opportunities to economists, entrepreneurs, policy makers, and consumers [2]. Therefore, it is of great importance to research influence factors of Bitcoin price volatility.

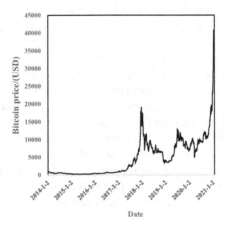

Fig. 1. Bitcoin prices from January 2nd 2014 to January 19th 2021.

2   Related Works

The study of the influence factors of Bitcoin is mainly from two aspects: Bitcoin's own factors and external factors.

In terms of Bitcoin's own factors, Kristoufek [3] investigated the dynamic relationship between Bitcoin price and currencies interests, and found that speculation factors are the key factors in Bitcoin price inflation. Kristoufek [4] also pointed out that conventional economic factors such as trade demand, supply and price level have important influence on the long-term development of Bitcoin. Guizani and Nafti [5] showed that demand factor has a significant impact on both Bitcoin's short-term and long-term prices, while the impact of supply factor is not significant in the short and long term, and the number of users and the difficulty of mining have positive impact in the short term. Donier and Bouchaud [6] indicated that the sharp price fluctuation of Bitcoin is caused by its own endogenous cycle, not by the latest information in the current market. Entrop, Frijns and Seruset [7] implied that the enhancement in market quality, such as lower trading costs and higher trading activity, has a positive causal effect on price discovery.

In terms of external factors, Jacobs [8] proved that Bitcoin may have regulatory, legal and other policy risks. Dyhrberg [9] analyzed different countries and regions' different effects on Bitcoin price, and pointed out that Bitcoin price react more strongly to the US dollar exchange rate than other currencies. Takaishi and Adachi [10] proved that Bitcoin prices have time sequence correlation. Dyhrberg [11] used the GARCH model, and found that Bitcoin and gold have the same property. Guizani and Nafti [5] pointed out that macroeconomic and financial factors have no significant impact in the short and long term. Gronwald [2] proved that Bitcoin prices are particularly affected by extreme prices changes, which are far greater than the crude oil and gold markets, which is caused by market immaturity and Bitcoin demand changes. Kalyvas, Papakyriakou, Sakkas and Urquhart [12] showed that economic uncertainty displays a negative and significant association with Bitcoin price crash risk, and suggested that investors can hedge economic uncertainty by investing in Bitcoin. Jin, Zhu, Yang and Wang [13] demonstrated that hedging the risk of fiat currencies might not be the key motivation for investing in Bitcoin.

The structural vector autoregression (SVAR) model, is beneficial to analyze the dynamic interactions between relevant time sequence variables, and has been widely used in the field of economic researches [14]. Therefore, in this paper, SVAR model is applied to analyzing the influence factors of Bitcoin price volatility.

Compared with the previous study, this paper's research perspective is more comprehensive, including Bitcoin's own factors and external factors, which avoids reaching incomplete conclusions due to consider only a single factor. Given that the recent change trend of the US dollar supply and Bitcoin prices is similar, this paper also creatively explores the impact of the US dollar supply on the Bitcoin price, which was rarely mentioned in the previous literature. Besides, the results of this paper are also valuable for predicting Bitcoin price.

3   Methodology

3.1   Data Specifications

Based on the past study, our data set consists of Bitcoin prices (BTC), the fees transferred to miners per transaction (FEE), the number of addresses (ADR), the number of Bitcoin in circulation (CIR), the volume of transaction (VOL), Standard and Poor's 500 Index (SPX), gold price (GOLD), and US dollar supply (M1). In consideration of the limited and effective data, it selects the daily data from January 2nd 2014 to January 19th 2021.

Bitcoin price data are selected from the website CoinMarketCap, whose data were most frequently cited all over the world. Whereas Bitcoin has been priced primarily in US dollar, we used the daily closing price denominated by US dollar.

This paper selects Bitcoin's own factors including both demand and supply factors as follows. Bitcoin's transaction demand factor is reflected by the fees transferred to miners per transaction based on daily data provided by the website coinmetrics. Bitcoin's speculation demand factor is represented by the number of addresses, whose daily data are selected from the website coinmetrics. Bitcoin's another speculation demand factor is represented by the volume of transaction selected based on daily data provided by the website coinmetrics. Bitcoin's supply factor is reflected by the number of Bitcoin in circulation selected based on daily data provided by the website coinmetrics.

This paper selects three external factors as follows. Standard and Poor's 500 Index daily closing prices, obtained from the website investing, are selected to represent one of the external factors. Gold daily closing prices, obtained from the website investing, are selected to represent another external factor. The third external factor, US dollar supply is represented by seasonal adjusted data M1, and obtained from the Federal Reserve Board. Because US dollar supply only has weekly data, this paper smoothly processes them into daily data.

Figure 2 shows the preliminary plot of seven influence factors of Bitcoin price volatility during the sample period.

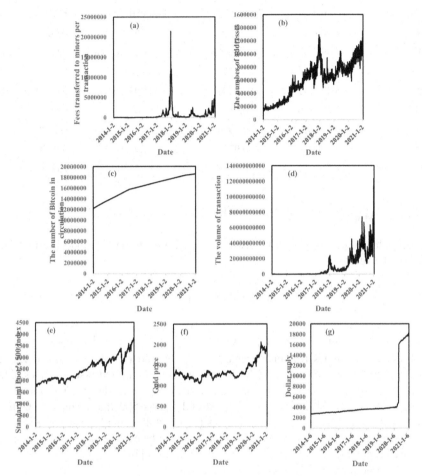

Fig. 2. Plots of the fees transferred to miners per transaction (a), the number of addresses (b), the number of bitcoin in circulation (c), the volume of transaction (d), standard and Poor's 500 Index (e), gold price (f), and US dollar supply (g) from January 2nd 2014 to January 19th 2021.

In order to examine the unit root test hypothesis, this paper performs the Augmented Dicky Fuller (ADF) tests. The results of the unit root tests are given in Table 1, which shows that the FEE and CIR are stationary at the 1% significance level for ADF test. ADR and VOL are stationary at the 5% significance level for ADF test. Other variables are not stationary, but stationary in terms of first differences.

To obtain the stationary variables, we select the first differences of Bitcoin prices, the fees transferred to miners per transaction, the number of addresses, the number of Bitcoin in circulation, the volume of transaction, Standard and Poor's 500 Index, gold price and US dollar supply as the empirical study data.

Table 1. ADF unit root tests

Variable	In level		In first difference	
	t-statistic	Prob.	t-statistic	Prob.
BTC	4.209905	1.0000	−11.66594	0.0000
FEE	−4.091008	0.0000	−21.02790	0.0000
ADR	−3.634242	0.0272	−26.72817	0.0000
CIR	−6.478351	0.0000	−3.20355	0.0200
VOL	−3.782596	0.0176	−28.56171	0.0000
SPX	−2.799443	0.1976	−12.55393	0.0000
GOLD	1.109925	0.9312	−42.09886	0.0000
M1	1.414967	0.9613	−42.07150	0.0001

3.2 SVAR Model

To analyze the influence factors of Bitcoin price volatility, the SVAR model is established based on the vector as

$$\Gamma_0 x_t = \delta + \sum_{i=1}^{p} \Gamma_i x_{t-i} + \mu_t \tag{1}$$

where $x_t = (BTC_t, FEE_t, ADR_t, CIR_t, VOL_t, SPX_t, GOLD_t, M1_t)^T$ is a vector of eight variables, BTC_t denotes Bitcoin prices changes, FEE_t denotes the fees transferred to miners per transaction changes, ADR_t denotes the number of addresses changes, CIR_t denotes the number of Bitcoin in circulation changes, VOL_t denotes the volume of transaction changes, SPX_t denotes Standard and Poor's 500 Index changes, $GOLD_t$ denotes gold price changes and $M1_t$ denotes the US dollar supply changes. δ, Γ_0 and Γ_i are the unknown coefficient vectors and matrices to be estimated; μ_t is the vector of serially and mutually uncorrelated structural innovations [14].

The normal form of the SVAR is represented as

$$x_t = \Gamma_0^{-1}\delta + \sum_{i=1}^{p} \Gamma_0^{-1}\Gamma_i x_{t-i} + e_t \tag{2}$$

where $e_t = \Gamma_0^{-1}\mu_t$ is the vector of the estimated residuals in the normal SVAR model.

When estimating the model, the first step is to determine the lag length of the SVAR model, which is selected through the Likelihood Ratio (LR), Final Prediction Error (FPE), Akaike Information Criterion (AIC), Schwarz Criterion (SC) and Hannan − Quinn Criterion (HQ). The lag length of 5 is selected according to the result in Table 2.

Then, the short-term restrictions on the model are transformed into the setting of matrix A and matrix B. The unknown elements to be estimated in the matrix are defined as NA, all non-default values are fixed as 0 or 1, and the matrix B is basically set as

Table 2. Selection of lag length for SVAR model

Lag	LogL	LR	FPE	AIC	SC	HQ
0	−142675.9	NA	1.90e + 60	161.4984	161.5232	161.5076
1	−142168.7	1009.202	1.15e + 60	160.9968	161.22	161.0793
2	−141970.4	392.7351	9.87e + 59	160.8448	161.2664	161.0006
3	−141796.5	342.9007	8.71e + 59	160.7204	161.3403	160.9495
4	−141614.5	357.1781	7.62e + 59	160.5869	161.4052	160.8892
5	−140731	1725.896*	3.02e + 59*	159.6594*	160.6760*	160.0350*

diagonal matrix. According to the causality between variables, the matrixes are set as follows:

$$A = \begin{pmatrix} 1 & NA & NA & 0 & NA & 0 & NA & 0 \\ 0 & 1 & 0 & NA & 0 & NA & 0 & 0 \\ 0 & NA & 1 & NA & NA & NA & 0 & 0 \\ 0 & 0 & 0 & 1 & 0 & 0 & 0 & 0 \\ 0 & 0 & 0 & 0 & 1 & NA & 0 & NA \\ 0 & 0 & 0 & 0 & 0 & 1 & NA & 0 \\ 0 & 0 & 0 & 0 & 0 & 0 & 1 & NA \\ 0 & 0 & 0 & 0 & 0 & 0 & 0 & 1 \end{pmatrix} \quad B = \begin{pmatrix} NA & 0 & 0 & 0 & 0 & 0 & 0 & 0 \\ 0 & NA & 0 & 0 & 0 & 0 & 0 & 0 \\ 0 & 0 & NA & 0 & 0 & 0 & 0 & 0 \\ 0 & 0 & 0 & NA & 0 & 0 & 0 & 0 \\ 0 & 0 & 0 & 0 & NA & 0 & 0 & 0 \\ 0 & 0 & 0 & 0 & 0 & NA & 0 & 0 \\ 0 & 0 & 0 & 0 & 0 & 0 & NA & 0 \\ 0 & 0 & 0 & 0 & 0 & 0 & 0 & NA \end{pmatrix}$$

Through multiple simulations, this paper obtains the most reliable restrictions of the SVAR(5) model as:

$$A = \begin{pmatrix} 1 & -0.0002 & -1.00e-05 & 0 & -1.14e-08 & 0 & -2.414 & 0 \\ 0 & 1 & 0 & -0.98 & 0 & -54.81 & 0 & 0 \\ 0 & -0.68 & 1 & 14.61 & -1.41e-05 & -121.86 & 0 & 0 \\ 0 & 0 & 0 & 1 & 0 & 0 & 0 & 0 \\ 0 & 0 & 0 & 0 & 1 & 2976914 & 0 & 1605057 \\ 0 & 0 & 0 & 0 & 0 & 1 & 0.044 & 0 \\ 0 & 0 & 0 & 0 & 0 & 0 & 1 & -0.004 \\ 0 & 0 & 0 & 0 & 0 & 0 & 0 & 1 \end{pmatrix}$$

$$B = \begin{pmatrix} 387.86 & 0 & 0 & 0 & 0 & 0 & 0 & 0 \\ 0 & 50633 & 0 & 0 & 0 & 0 & 0 & 0 \\ 0 & 0 & 340576 & 0 & 0 & 0 & 0 & 0 \\ 0 & 0 & 0 & 1710.71 & 0 & 0 & 0 & 0 \\ 0 & 0 & 0 & 0 & 3.44e+09 & 0 & 0 & 0 \\ 0 & 0 & 0 & 0 & 0 & 28.21 & 0 & 0 \\ 0 & 0 & 0 & 0 & 0 & 0 & 12.49 & 0 \\ 0 & 0 & 0 & 0 & 0 & 0 & 0 & 36.75 \end{pmatrix}$$

Next, the impulse response function of SVAR is applied to measuring the impact of one standard structural deviation from these influence factors on Bitcoin price volatility. The variance decomposition approach is used to measure the contribution of each structural impact to the changes of endogenous variables, and quantitatively evaluate the relative importance of each factor to Bitcoin price volatility.

4 Empirical Analysis

4.1 Impulse Response Analysis

To investigate the direction and strength of the effects of factors above on Bitcoin price volatility, the impulse response of the SVAR model is employed to conduct analysis. The impulse response functions of the impact of the fees transferred to miners per transaction shock, the number of addresses shock, the number of Bitcoin in circulation shock, the volume of transaction shock, Standard and Poor's 500 Index shock, gold price shock and US dollar supply shock on Bitcoin prices are plotted in Fig. 3.

Figure 3(a) shows the impulse response result of Bitcoin prices to one standard deviation of the number of addresses shock. As shown, Bitcoin prices respond to the number of addresses shock positively. The response is most significant in the second period but decreases soon, and essentially approaches to zero after thirteen period, which is in line with the law of supply and demand of general commodities. In addition, the positive impact of the number of addresses on Bitcoin price is long.

Figure 3(b) shows the impulse response result of Bitcoin prices to one standard deviation of the fees transferred to miners per transaction. As shown, Bitcoin prices respond to the fees transferred to miners per transaction positively on average. The response is positive in the first period. Then, in the second period, the response is negative but increases soon. The response is the most significant in the third period and decreases slowly to zero after ten period. In addition, the impact of the fees transferred to miners per transaction on Bitcoin price is long.

Figure 3(c) presents the impulse response result of Bitcoin prices to one standard deviation of the number of Bitcoin in circulation. As shown, Bitcoin prices respond to the number of Bitcoin in circulation negatively and constantly.

Figure 3(d) reports the impulse response result of Bitcoin prices to one standard deviation of the volume of transaction shock. As shown, Bitcoin prices respond to the volume of transaction shock positively. The response is most positively significant in the first period. Then, the response decreases to negative in fifth and sixth period. It essentially approaches to zero after thirteen period. For a long time, the impact of the volume of transaction is significant and long, which may be related to the irrational behavior of trading.

Figure 3(e) shows the impulse response result of Bitcoin prices to one standard deviation of the Standard and Poor's 500 Index shock. As shown, Bitcoin prices respond to the Standard and Poor's 500 Index shock positively. The response is most negatively significant in the first period. Then, the response increases to significantly positive in fifth period, and approaches to zero after ten period. The impact of the Standard and Poor's 500 Index on Bitcoin prices is negative in the short term. The reason may be that the Bitcoin market and the S&P 500 market are both investment markets. But compared to the S&P 500 market, since the Bitcoin market is small and less likely to have a substitution effect, it is affected by the same factors as S&P 500 market. In the long term, the S&P 500 index and Bitcoin prices change in the similar direction. In past studies, it can be considered that the S&P 500 index has a positive effect on Bitcoin. In this paper, the short-term negative impact of impulse response analysis confirms the fact that Bitcoin's investment market is expanding. It also shows that the impact of the S&P 500 on Bitcoin prices is relatively small.

Figure 3(f) reports the impulse response result of Bitcoin prices to one standard deviation of gold price shock. As shown, Bitcoin prices respond to gold price shock positively. The response is most positively significant in the first period. Then, the response decreases to the least negatively in the fifth period. It essentially approaches to zero after seven period. In addition, the impact of gold price is small. It shows that gold price is a positive impact in the short term. However, in the long term, it gradually becomes negative. The reason may be that gold prices' rising represents the active level of capital market, which makes Bitcoin prices rise. However, in the long term, because Bitcoin and gold both play important roles in the global financial system, and are noted as a store of wealth, medium of exchange and unit of value. To some extent, they are substitutes for each other, so that the positive impact will gradually decrease, which is consistent with the research findings of Dyhrberg [11]. It also shows that the impact of gold prices on Bitcoin prices is small.

Figure 3(g) shows the impulse response result of Bitcoin prices to one standard deviation of US dollar supply shock. As shown, Bitcoin prices respond to US dollar supply shock is small in the first and second period. Then, the response is positive in the third and fourth period. Then, the response is negative in the fifth, sixth and seventh period. It essentially approaches to zero after eight period. It indicates that the impact of US dollar supply is small, positive in the short term and negative in the long term.

Figure 3(h) shows the impulse response result of Bitcoin prices to one standard deviation of Bitcoin prices itself shock. As shown, Bitcoin prices respond to itself positively. The response is most significant in the first period, and decreases slowly to zero after six period. It indicates that the impact of Bitcoin prices is significant and long, which is consistent with the findings of Donier and Bouchaud [6].

4.2 Variance Decomposition

The variances of Bitcoin prices contain basic information that determines the price volatility, and the relative contribution of each factor's variance reflects the magnitude of the impact on price volatility [14]. In order to investigate the contributions of the above factors to Bitcoin price volatility, the Bitcoin price variances are decomposed to eight components using the variance decomposition approach and the results are given in Table 3 and Fig. 4. Since the variance decomposition results reach a stable state in Period 20, the decomposition results in Period 20 are finally used to compare the different factors' contributions to Bitcoin price volatility.

According to the results, the volume of transaction (2.834%) contributes most to Bitcoin price volatility in the sample period. The number of addresses (1.654%) shock's contribution ranks second among the influence factors. The Bitcoin's own factors including the volume of transaction and the number of addresses in circulation have significant

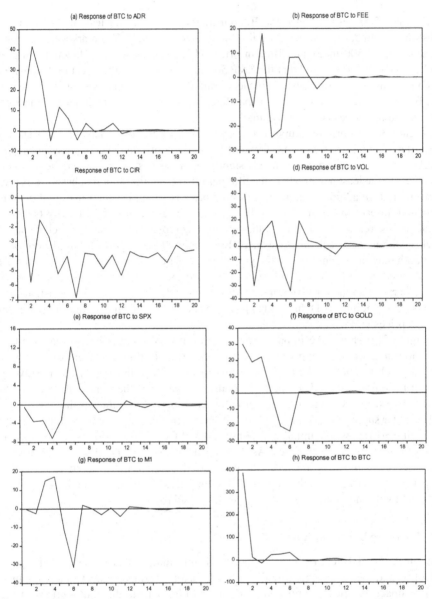

Fig. 3. Responses of bitcoin prices to structural one standard deviation shocks of the number of addresses (ADR) (a), the fees transferred to miners per transaction (FEE) (b), the number of bitcoin in circulation (CIR) (c), federal funds rate (VOL) (d), standard and Poor's 500 Index (SPX) (e), gold prices (GOLD) (f), US dollar supply shock (M1) (g), and itself (BTC) (h) respectively (Response period is fixed at 20 period).

impacts on Bitcoin price volatility, which indicates that Bitcoin's own factors play important roles in Bitcoin market. It shows that these two Bitcoin's own factors have significant
impact on Bitcoin prices volatility.

Besides, the volume of transaction (2.834%) and the number of addresses (1.654%)
representing speculation demand factors both contributes to Bitcoin price more than
the fees transferred to miners per transaction (1.020%) representing transaction demand
factor. It indicates that speculation factors have greater impact on Bitcoin prices than
transaction factors.

In addition, the number of Bitcoin in circulation (0.209%) is the second least, which
has shown that supply factors have weak impact on Bitcoin price, which is consistent
with the findings of Guizani and Nafti [5].

Standard and Poor's 500 Index (0.153%) contributes least to Bitcoin prices volatility.
Macroeconomic and financial factors have no significant impact, which is also consistent
with the findings of Guizani and Nafti [5].

In summary, Bitcoin's own factors including the volume of transaction, the number
of addresses and the fees transferred to miners per transaction play important roles in
Bitcoin price volatility. Speculation factors have greater impact on Bitcoin prices than

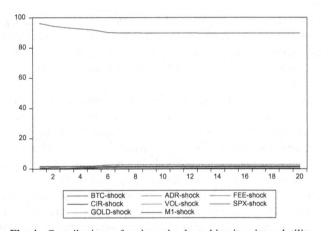

Fig. 4. Contributions of various shocks to bitcoin price volatility

Table 3. Contributions of various shocks to bitcoin price volatility

Period	BTC	ADR	FEE	CIR	VOL	SPX	GOLD	M1
1	98.267	0.105	0.008	0.000	1.026	0.000	0.594	0.000
5	93.590	1.653	0.952	0.043	1.946	0.054	1.349	0.413
10	91.601	1.648	1.022	0.112	2.812	0.151	1.647	1.008
15	91.508	1.655	1.021	0.166	2.834	0.153	1.646	1.018
20	91.467	1.654	1.020	0.209	2.834	0.153	1.645	1.018

transaction factors. Among the external factors, gold price has the greatest influence on Bitcoin price volatility.

5 Conclusions

In this paper, the structural vector autoregression (SVAR) model is established to analyze the influence factors of Bitcoin prices, and the impulse response analysis and variance decomposition approach are carried out. The following conclusions are concluded:

Bitcoin's own factors play important roles in Bitcoin price volatility. From the perspective of transaction demand factors, both transaction demand and speculation demand factors have positive impact on Bitcoin price volatility, but speculation demand is more significant than transaction demand. It proves that at least in the sample period, although Bitcoin may act as a general equivalent or currency in some special areas and special commodities, it plays an investment and speculation role more. Besides, the supply factor represented by the number of Bitcoin in circulation is weak. Therefore, the impact of "halving Bitcoin supply every four years" on Bitcoin price volatility is exaggerated. At the same time, Bitcoin price also has a great positive impact on itself, and it will last for a long period.

External factors also have impact on Bitcoin price volatility. Among them, gold price has the greatest impact, following is US dollar supply. These results show that with the financial development of digital currency market, these external factors become more and more important in the impact of Bitcoin price fluctuations due to the financial attributes of Bitcoin.

Bitcoin investors and traders ought to pay more attention to the changes of Bitcoin external factors, including the Standard and Poor's 500 Index, gold price, US dollar supply and so on. When the global economic environment changes greatly, investors can avoid investment losses and transaction conversion losses in time.

For the relevant departments, to curb and prevent price volatility caused by excessive speculation in digital currency market such as Bitcoin, the relevant departments should formulate restrictive policies on Bitcoin speculation and strengthen the regulation of speculation. At the same time, digital currencies that central banks are preparing should also draw on Blockchain technology and relevant experience and draft the policy formulation in advance.

Through the above research, this paper summarizes the influence factors that affect the price of Bitcoin, and provides some useful thoughts for Bitcoin traders, investors, and relevant departments. It can also offer some ideas for private or central banks' issuance of digital currency.

Acknowledgments. This work was supported by The National Key Research and Development Program of China (2020YFB1006104), The National Natural Science Foundation of China (NSFC 71773025 and NSFC U1866602).

References

1. Nakamoto, S.: Bitcoin: A Peer-to-Peer Electronic Cash System (2008)
2. Gronwald, M., Lothian, J.R.: Is bitcoin a commodity? On price jumps, demand shocks, and certainty of supply. J. Int. Money Finance **97**, 86–92 (2019)
3. Kristoufek, L.: Bitcoin meets Google trends and Wikipedia: quantifying the relationship between phenomena of the Internet era. Sci. Rep. **3**(1) (2013)
4. Kristoufek, L., Scalas, E.: What are the main drivers of the bitcoin price? Evidence from wavelet coherence analysis. Plos One **10**(4) (2014)
5. Guizani, S., Nafti, I.K.: The determinants of bitcoin price volatility: an investigation with ARDL model. Procedia Comput. Sci. **164**, 233–238 (2019)
6. Donier, J., Bouchaud, J.P.: Why do markets crash? Bitcoin data offers unprecedented insights. SSRN Electron. J. **10**(10) (2015)
7. Entrop, O., Frijns, B., Seruset, M.: The determinants of price discovery on bitcoin markets. J. Future Mark. **40**, 816–837 (2020)
8. Jacobs, E.: Bitcoin: a bit too far. J. Internet Bank. Commer. **16**(2), 2–4 (2011)
9. Dyhrberg, A.H.: Hedging capabilities of bitcoin. Is it the virtual gold? Finance Res. Lett. **16**, 139–144 (2016)
10. Tetsuya, T., Takanori, A.: Taylor effect in bitcoin time series. Econ. Lett. **172**, 5–7 (2018)
11. Dyhrberg, A.H.: Bitcoin, gold and the dollar–A GARCH volatility analysis. Finance Res. Lett. **16** (2016)
12. Kalyvas, A., Papakyriakou, P., Sakkas, A., Urquhart, A.: What drives bitcoin's price crash risk? Econ. Lett. **191**, 1–5 (2020)
13. Xuejun, J., Keer, Z., Xiaolan, Y., Shouyang, W.: Estimating the reaction of Bitcoin prices to the uncertainty of fiat currency. Res. Int. Bus. Finance **58**, 1–16 (2021)
14. Wang, H., Sheng, H., Zhang, H.W.: Influence factors of international gold futures price volatility. Trans. Nonferrous Met. Soc. China **29**(11), 2447–2454 (2019)

Research on DeepFakes to Ensure Social Information Security

Yang Zeng, Jialin Lin, Rui Zhan, Yufei Man, and Yu Yang[✉]

School of Cyberspace Security, Beijing University of Posts
and Telecommunications, Beijing 100876, China
{zengyang,linjialin19,zhanrui123,manyf,yangyu}@bupt.edu.cn

Abstract. AI face replacement technology - DeepFakes is often maliciously used to tamper with video faces. Deepfakes forges the access rights of face authentication confidential information or gains the trust of information carriers, which will bring great hidden danger to the information security in the field of social engineering. In order to promote the reasonable application of AI face replacement technology, the DeepFakes source code is analyzed to define the key technologies. And investigate the current status of DeepFakes research. Based on the principle of DeepFakes tampering, this paper summarizes and proposes the method of detecting DeepFakes tampering attacks from two aspects of image feature and combining depth learning. The robustness and accuracy of different detection methods are compared through experiments.

Keywords: DeepFakes · Social engineering · Image tamper detection · Deep learning · Image processing · CNN

1 Introduction

Face replacement technology for video or images has been studied before DeepFakes. Zhang [1] et al. proposed an algorithm to eliminate the boundary line of the replacement image caused by the color difference, illumination, and edge distortion caused by the face replacement process, which effectively improved the natural degree of the image after face replacement. Chou [2] et al. used a 3D model to replace the characters in the image and proposed a method to repair the damaged forehead skin texture during the replacement process. Koyuki [3] et al. used ASM (Active Shape Model) to acquire facial motions in chronological order and generate different expression components of each component of the human face, replacing the original facial features by matching facial expression features. Lin [4] et al. designed a 3D head model to more realistically generate replacement images that conform to facial features.

DeepFakes is a technology that uses the deep learning network to simultaneously replace the features of facial expressions, movements, hue, and brightness of people's faces in videos. It integrates existing research results and deep learning methods for face replacement, with a high degree of fit and simple operation. Other advantages have caused widespread concern in the community. But be aware that DeepFakes technology is also a

© Springer Nature Singapore Pte Ltd. 2021
H.-N. Dai et al. (Eds.): BlockSys 2021, CCIS 1490, pp. 226–240, 2021.
https://doi.org/10.1007/978-981-16-7993-3_18

serious security threat. With each day DeepFakes become more convincing, accessible, and easier to create and distribute. This makes DeepFakes more attainable to the average consumer and puts it in ready reach of potential attackers. For example, the criminals used artificial intelligence-based software to impersonate a chief executive's voice and fraudulently transferred of €220,000 ($243,000) in March 2019. A voice call that sounds like an executive adds another layer of credibility to a request. DeepFakes videos are more likely to be maliciously used by criminals to make victims more convinced in similar ways. It demonstrates that deepfake video can become another tool in an attacker's social engineering arsenal.

In August 2019, a mobile app "ZAO" for making DeepFakes video was launched, and the download volume rose to first place in one day. The agreement was allegedly infringed by the Ministry of Industry and Information Technology. However, DeepFakes itself has great research and application potential, such as in video image restoration, film production, and other fields. Although the development of DeepFakes has been improperly applied, it is a bold attempt at artificial intelligence, which has far-reaching significance for the future development of artificial intelligence.

According to the DeepFakes source code, this paper first analyzes its implementation architecture and clarifies the technical characteristics of the main aspects of DeepFakes. Then it investigates the research status of detection image tampering at home and abroad and proposes different methods for DeepFakes detection based on the existing detection technology and DeepFakes technology characteristics. Finally, Test methods were compared and evaluated. The research on image tamper detection comes down to two directions, manual extraction of features and combined depth learning for classification. The detection angles are summarized in Fig. 1.

In this paper, the DeepFakes structure and its detection methods are mainly divided into five parts. The first part analyzes the overall architecture and main principles of DeepFakes. The second part sorts out the detection methods that have been proposed. The third part proposes different angles for the implementation of DeepFakes. The method and the method are evaluated. The fourth part analyzes the main factors affecting

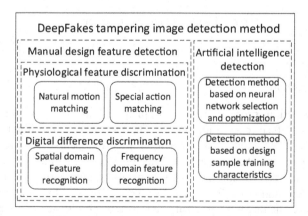

Fig. 1. DeepFakes detection angle induction

the detection effect of DeepFakes and compares the advantages and disadvantages of different methods. The fifth part summarizes the research done.

2   DeepFakes Analysis

The DeepFakes implementation is divided into three main parts: face extraction, model training, and face replacement. This section is based on the DeepFakes open source project to analyze its main framework and processing methods.

The conversion process of DeepFakes first converts the target video into a video frame image set or collects a material image set of the target face, and then performs face clipping and feature extraction on the frame image set to obtain a sample for training the replacement model in the neural network; The sample is input into the training face model in the GAN (Generation Against Network); the original video frame image is replaced by the face-changing model to obtain the frame image set containing the target face; finally, the frame image set is converted into the video output (in the original video) The face part will be replaced, and the face part of the target video will be replaced in the original video. All the "original video", "target video", "original face" and "target face" appearing in this article have the same meaning). Figure 2 shows the main steps and processes of DeepFakes throughout the conversion process.

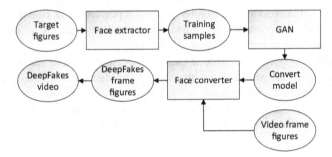

Fig. 2. DeepFakes implementation process

2.1   Face Extraction

The face recognition process in the DeepFakes framework is done using the "face_recognition" face recognition library. The face_recognition library is based on the deep learning CNN model development in the C++ open-source library dlib. The recognition process uses the frontal_face_detector() method in dlib.

DeepFakes face positioning includes face detection and feature point localization. The bilinear interpolation method is used to reduce the workload of sliding window detection images. The direction gradient histogram method is used to optimize the effi-ciency of sliding window detection of face position and face detection. For face feature point location, DeepFakes uses the face feature model trained by the ResNet network to mark the face position. Finally, a uniform-size face image sample is obtained by image scaling, cropping, and rotation. Sample Heading (Third Level). Only two levels of headings should be numbered. Lower level headings remain unnumbered; they are formatted as run-in headings.

2.2 Face Change Model Network Structure

DeepFakes uses GAN (Generative Adversarial Networks) to train face-changing models, mainly including image codec training. The performance of the codec determines the face-changing effect.

Encoder and Decoder. The encoder and decoder in DeepFakes encode the original video face and decode it into the target face. The encoder expresses the input face samples as features and encodes them using the AutoEncoder algorithm model. The decoder reconstructs a target sample having the same characteristics as the original face sample according to the encoding rule of the encoder and the sample feature data output by the encoder. Figure 3 shows the process of the GAN training decoder model.

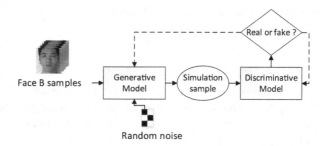

Fig. 3. GAN training decoder model process

The generated model generates simulation samples according to the target face samples and random noise training, and determines whether the generated simulation samples are qualified target faces, and generates feedback to the generated model and the self, and generates and models the training models according to the feedback.

Generative Adversarial Networks. DeepFakes uses the face sample feature training encoder and uses the GAN generation network G and the discriminant network D to train the target face decoder. When the discriminant network D determines that the virtual face output by the decoder according to the input facial feature is substantially the same as the target face, the training is completed.

The GAN network uses different structures to train codecs. DeepFakes sets a variety of models for the network (dfaker, dfl_h128, iae, lightweight, original, unbalanced, villain). By default, the original model is selected for training. Table 1 shows the DeepFakes original model structure.

The convolution layer in the network basically uses the ReLU activation function, and the last layer of the convolution layer uses the sigmoid activation function to reduce

Table 1. Training codec network structure

Encoder Training network structure	Decoder Training network structure	
input(64 × 64 RGB image)	var_x	var_y
conv2-128	input(8*8*512 vector)	input(8*8*512 vector)
conv2-128*2	conv2-256	conv2-256
conv2-128*4	PixelShuffler	PixelShuffler
conv2-128*6-	conv2-128	conv2-128
Flatten	PixelShuffler	PixelShuffler
Dense(4*4*1024)	conv2-64	conv2-64
conv2–512	PixelShuffler	PixelShuffler
PixelShuffler	conv2	conv2
Output	Output = append(var_x,var_y)	

the model gradient. The use of inter-layer upsampling in the network ensures that the training is not distorted and the over-fitting condition is alleviated.

2.3 Face Replacement

DeepFakes encodes the original video face as a feature tensor (marking face contour, facial features, and motion), and uses the decoder trained by the target face sample to decode the feature tensor to generate a target face that conforms to the original video face motion feature.

The original video face sample A input is extracted by the encoder trained by the training sample of A to extract the facial features of the face A (including facial expressions, facial orientation, facial features, and facial contour positions, etc.), and obtain low-dimensional data capable of accurately describing the A features. Then, the decoder trained by the target face B decodes the low-dimensional data containing the face A feature and obtains the false face image of B which is the same as the A feature.

Face Calibration. The face calibration corrects the position and orientation of the fake face and the original face. DeepFakes uses procrustes analysis to implement face calibration.

Platts analysis uses the least-squares method to determine the affine transformation from A shape to B shape, compares the feature points of the original face and the fake face, and uses the least-squares method to calculate the original face and false face features after rotation, translation, and scaling in the replacement process. Find the best alternative to the minimum distance of the point.

The face calibration process is a process of describing the transformation and decomposition of the face feature matrix. Finally, a false face image with consistent expressions is obtained by matrix fitting.

Edge Blur. The fake face is pasted in the original image and the edge part is obvious. DeepFakes blurs the edge of the fake face. The blurring process is done using a filter. Considering the actual effect, DeepFakes uses Gaussian blur to process the face edges. Since the fake face only contains facial features, DeepFakes splicing the edges of the fake face without affecting the overall effect.

Hue and Brightness. DeepFakes generally works with color images and uses a color histogram that represents different layers of the image to adjust the image tones. Deep-Fakes uses a color intensity histogram matching method to unify the tones of the fake face and the original face. By comparing the color intensity histogram data distribution between the fake face and the original video image, the difference between the false face and the original video image color is adjusted, and the difference between the color information of the surrounding area is used to replace the difference data, thereby narrowing the difference., adjust the effect of hue and brightness.

3   Existing Detection Methods

3.1   Detection Method Based on Blink Frequency

In the case of insufficient samples containing blinking movements, the samples trained by DeepFakes showed almost no blinking or less blinking. The blinking action time is periodic and usually has a stable blink frequency and the longest blink interval. Li [5] and so on extracted the eye action sequence diagram from the video and entered it into the trained LRCN (Long-term Recurrent Convolutional Networks) model. The LRCN uses a labeled normal blink image training sample for training to predict the normal occurrence of blinking. The DeepFakes tampering behavior is detected by detecting whether the blinking frequency of the face in the video is normal.

There is an obvious problem with this method. If the sample of the DeepFakes face-changing model is sufficient, DeepFakes can simulate the blinking action of the face in the original video, and the generated fake face video and the original video have the blinking action of the same frequency. In this case, the method is not able to recognize the DeepFakes tampering behavior, which is also ineffective for local replacement.

3.2   Detection Method Based on Face Orientation

DeepFakes' face changing process is only for face areas, ignoring the overall characteristics of the head contour, which may cause differences in face orientation and head orientation. Yang [6] et al. calculated a feature vector reflecting the face orientation and a feature vector reflecting the head orientation by a 3D Head Pose Estimation algorithm. The natural image character face and head orientation are consistent, and the images falsified by DeepFakes cannot match the features of the face toward such whole integrity. This method is not valid for local tampering.

3.3 Detection Method Based on Specific Expression Habits

In response to DeepFakes' forgery of public opinion with a certain influence and the creation of public opinion-oriented news, Gu [7] et al.proposed a method to detect DeepFakes based on the specific expression behavior of a particular individual. The method first inputs the real video samples of a specific detection object (generally a public figure) and uses the open-source facial motion tracking analysis package OpenFace2 to perform tracking analysis on the facial actions of the characters in the sample. According to the action unit of different positions on the face set in OpenFace2, the actions of raising, swinging, and pulling down the eyebrows, eyes, nose, mouth, and jaw are analyzed, and the feature values of different positions are obtained, and the correlation between the feature values is calculated. Sexually get a special facial action for a specific test subject. The same method is used to detect whether the facial expression of the specific detection object in the video sample to be tested contains its unique action.

The flaws of this detection method are obvious, and can only be used to detect a small number of video samples containing well-known public figures, which is not universal; at the same time, the resistance to local tampering is poor.

3.4 Comparison of Existing Detection Methods

The existing detection methods mainly combine manual features and deep learning network discrimination, including certain limitations. Table 2 shows the comparison results of the existing detection methods.

Table 2. Comparison of existing detection methods

Method description		Detection accuracy	Scope of application
Based on blink frequency	LRCN network	0.99	Applicable to the lack of blink samples in the face model training data; not applicable to partial replacement
	CNN network	0.98	
	EAR network	0.79	
Based on Face orientation	UADFV data set	0.89	Not suitable for partial replacement
	DARPA GAN data set	0.84	
Based on specific expression habits	Full face replacement detection	0.93 ~ 0.96	Not for random samples; not for local replacement
	Partial replacement detection	0.95 ~ 0.99	
	Head replacement detection	0.98 ~ 1.00	

4 Feasible Detection Method Research

According to the research status of image forensics, image recognition, and other fields, the feasibility of detecting DeepFakes is proposed from three angles: detection of the defects in the techniques and operations of DeepFakes technology; local differences and tampering of images caused by tampering Traces are used for evidence; DeepFakes tampering images and natural images are classified using deep learning neural networks.

4.1 Data Set

Data sets that can be used to study the DeepFakes method include Columbia University's Public Figures Face Database; Colorferet; YouTube Faces and others.

This paper uses the DeepFakes research dataset released by the University of Queensland's VidTIMIT audio and video database. The dataset contains 44 types of faces, each with head-up, head-down, left-turn, and right-turn actions, totaling more than 132,000 samples. Table 3 shows the comparison of the different data sets suitable for DeepFakes research.

Table 3. Comparison of different data sets

Data set	Number of faces	Number of samples	Characteristics
Public Figures Face Database	200	58000 +	Suitable for face recognition in unrestricted scenes
Colorferet	1000 +	10000 +	Universal face library, with universal testing standards, each with photos of different expressions, lighting, gestures and ages
YouTube Faces	1595	3425 video	Suitable for face recognition in unrestricted scenes
VidTIMIT	44	132000 +	DeepFakes research data set, each face has a head up, head down, left turn, right turn action

4.2 Detection Method for GAN

Wang [8] et al. investigated the development status and application fields of GAN, and analyzed the advantages and disadvantages of GAN. Wu [9] et al. analyzed the synthesis and editing principles of GAN network, including texture synthesis and image restoration. Based on the principle of GAN image processing This section presents a feasible detection method.

The image generated by the GAN network is different from the natural image. For each frame image in the fake face video, the face details cannot be completely restored. In the video that has been tampered with by DeepFakes, the adjacent two frame images are basically maintained in the character motion. In the case of constant, the fake face is extremely similar at the pixel level due to the lack of detail features, and the corresponding image in the original video often has a certain difference because of the difference in detail.

It is worth noting that in the original video, there are also cases where the faces of two adjacent frames are extremely similar at the pixel level, but in this case, the similarity of the facial features and the contours of the characters are consistent. Since DeepFakes only replaces the facial features of the face (the generated fake face may contain a part of the jaw edge), DeepFakes tampering with the image face still maintains high similarity in the case where the contours of the adjacent two frames are different. Figure 4 shows the comparison of the different images of two adjacent frames of a video frame image set.

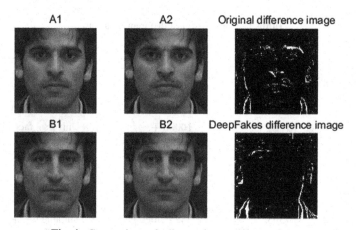

Fig. 4. Comparison of adjacent frame difference maps

A1 and A2 represent images of two adjacent frames in the original video; B1 and B2 represent images of two frames corresponding to A1 and A2 in the video after falsification by DeepFakes. The difference of the face part of the image that has been tampered with by DeepFakes is closer to 0, and the difference image of the face part of the original video frame image can clearly distinguish the facial features.

4.3 Detection Method for Image Features

Copy-Paste Detection. Warif [10] et al. investigated the image copy-and-paste tamper detection method and clarified the characteristics of copy-and-paste tampering. There are many researches on copy-and-paste tamper detection. The feature matching detection method is usually used. SIFT and SURF are commonly used image feature matching algorithms. Ma [11] et al. And so on are improved based on sift algorithm, and the image feature vector is reduced by using the perceptual hash. Combined with K-means clustering, the locating trend tends to be. Image feature matching detection methods often copy-paste tampering for the same image, while DeepFakes face-changing operations belong to different image copy-and-paste tampering, so such methods are not effective. Huang [12] et al. Performed homomorphic processing on the image and detected the non-constant feature of the illumination component of the copy-and-paste image. However, this method does not work well for retouched tampering images. Huang [13] et al. Identify copy-and-paste tampering by detecting the image-compressed block-effect grid, but this method cannot detect images that have not undergone block-compression (Fig. 5).

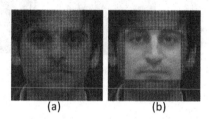

(a)   (b)

Fig. 5. Block effect grid comparison

(a) represents the original image block effect grid mark; (b) represents the DeepFakes image block effect grid mark. The block effect detection method is used to detect that DeepFakes requires the image to be subjected to block compression. This method is not universal and cannot cope with the case where the image is subjected to multiple compression coding.

Fuzzy Retouch Detection. DeepFakes uses Gaussian blur to retouch the fake face image and hide the tampering traces.

The gray level range at the edge of the false face that has been blurred is reduced, and the gray level dynamic range of the unblurred image portion is large. Zhou [14] et al. proposed a fuzzy detection algorithm based on the edge feature of mathematical morphology. The fuzzy operation of DeepFakes on the edge of the false face corresponds to the reflection component of the image. The homomorphic filtering operation can compress the illumination component, extend the reflection component, and enhance the blurred image face. Edge. The fuzzy operation can be regarded as the mathematical morphological expansion operation. By performing the etch operation in the morphological filtering on the binary image of the homomorphic filtered face-changing image, the edge of the tampering region in the image is amplified and enhanced, thereby detecting Tampered with the section. This method does not work well for lower-quality images.

There is a quality difference between the DeepFakes tampering part and the original image. Farid [15] and others proposed that the difference between the image undergoing JPEG secondary compression and the one-time compression is small, JPEG compression is mainly low-pass filtering operation, and the image blurring is also low-pass filtering in the frequency domain angle, so image 2 can be used. Sub-fuzzy characteristics are detected [16] (Fig. 6).

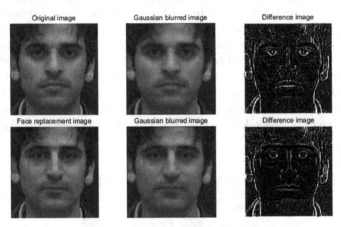

Fig. 6. Comparison of quadratic blur difference mapping

Resampling Detection. The face-changing process requires re-sampling operations such as zooming, rotating, and panning the fake face. The resampling operation does not affect the image visually, but it will destroy the special correlation between the image data. Prasad [17] et al. pass the detection. Resampling identifies image tampering. suppose an image undergoes a resampling operation with a parameter of $M/N \geq 2$, and the interpolation process selects bilinear interpolation or cubic convolution. The first-order difference between the two original elements in the sequence is equal, and the second-order difference zero, so a zero value will appear in every M element in the sequence after resampling, and the position of the zero value will appear periodic in the sequence. Zuo [18] et al. calculated the feature quantity for image segmentation and used the feature quantity inconsistency to detect resampling tampering. However, this method is prone to misjudgment in the face of tampering with an image with a large area. In this section, combined with the existing research, the method of calculating the resampling probability by block is proposed. According to the resampling periodicity, the probability of resampling of the image block is calculated, and the resampling tampering is judged according to the overall shape of the probability image (Fig. 7).

4.4 Deep Learning Detection Method

DeepFakes generates realistic false faces through deep learning networks, and the accuracy of general feature detection methods is greatly affected. The deep learning network can extract more detailed features of the sample and can process a large amount of sample data to improve the detection accuracy.

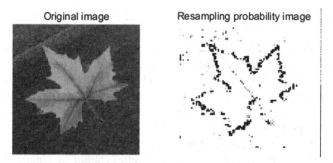

Fig. 7. Block resampling probability detection effect

Sample Pretreatment. The purpose of the pre-processing is to offset some of the Deep-Fakes retouching operations on the tampering traces, making the sample features easily recognizable by the detection network. According to the characteristics of DeepFakes technology, the pre-processing operation can be sharpened. after sharpening, the difference in image quality between the fake face and other parts of the image can be better reflected. Figure 8 shows the front-to-back comparison of the image after Sharpening, (a) showing the image face region sharpening result without tampering; and (b) showing the image face region sharpening result falsified by DeepFakes.

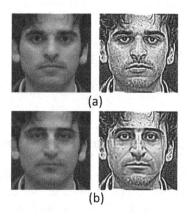

Fig. 8. Sharpened sample

Deep Learning Classification Model. The DeepFakes tamper detection problem is a fine-grained image classification problem, usually processed using a better-performing convolutional neural network (CNN). This section compares several network models that are suitable for detecting DeepFakes.

The VGG model focuses on the impact of network depth on performance. Since the VGG model greatly reduces the convolution kernel size of the AlexNet model and increases the number of layers of convolution, it is advantageous to extract more detailed features of the image. The GoogLeNet team proposed that the Inception network structure transforms the network full connection into a sparse connection, clustering the sparse matrix calculation into a denser sub-matrix calculation to improve performance, to solve the problem of gradient dispersion, and difficulty in optimization caused by deepening of the network depth. The VGG and GoogLeNet models are based on the idea that the number of network layers is deepened to improve network performance. After the number of network layers reaches a certain depth, the increase in the number of layers no longer has a positive impact on performance, resulting in network convergence becoming difficult and the classification accuracy rate correspondingly decreasing. The ResNet model applies the concept of "residual representation" in computer vision to a deep learning network. Each layer improves the learning performance by learning the residual representation between input and output, making it deeper in network deep extraction. At the same time as the depth feature of the face, avoid the problem caused by too deep depth [19]. Table 4 shows the structure comparison of VGG, GoogLeNet, and ResNet, Y means inclusion, and N means not included.

Table 4. Model Structure Comparison

Model name	layers	Top-5 error	Convolution layers	Convolution kernel size	Fully connected layer	Dropout
VGG	19	7.30%	16	3	3	Y
GoogLeNet	22	6.70%	21	5	1	Y
ResNet	152	3.57%	151	5	1	Y

5 Detection Results and Influencing Factors Analysis

The factors affecting the detection effect are mainly the quality of the feature detection sample, the quality of the model training sample, and the deep learning model. Sample quality factors include lighting, hue, compression coding, resolution, and sample size. Table 5 shows the sensitivity of the detection methods and deep learning models mentioned in this paper to various influencing factors. " +" indicates degree level and robustness; "\" means unaffected.

The detection method for DeepFakes tampering image features is less robust and has a clear scope of application. Using deep learning methods to detect DeepFakes has higher requirements on the quantity and quality of training samples, but better robustness. The accuracy is higher.

Table 5. Comparison of detection methods

Method name		illumination	tone	coding	Resolution	Number of samples	Robustness	Accuracy
Copy-paste detection		+	\	++	++	\	+	0.32
Fuzzy retouch detection		+	\	\	+++	\	++	0.52
Resampling detection		++	+	++	+	\	+	0.54
Deep learning detection method	VGG	+++	++	+	++	+++	++	0.88
	GoogLeNet	++	+	+	+	++	+++	0.92
	ResNet	++	+	+	++	+	+++	0.97

6 Conclusion

DeepFakes will have a great impact on social engineering. The face produced by Deep-Fakes through deep learning conforms to the digital features of a real face. It can unlock the access control system of face recognition. Forgery video can be used to cheat the holder of secret information, cheat the trust to steal confidential information. This paper studies DeepFakes, on the one hand, in order to explore the detection method, on the other hand, to prove its impact on the information security in the field of social engineering through its implementation principle.

The research of DeepFakes detection technology is lacking, and it is based on the recognition of certain features of DeepFakes image, which is less robust. The detection technology combined with deep learning has good robustness and accuracy but requires high training samples. Different training sets may affect the detection accuracy. The next step should be carried out in terms of improving the universality and accuracy of the test methods.

Acknowledgments. This research was supported by "the National Key R&D Program of China (No. 2017YFB0802803)".

References

1. Zhang, X.: The image blending method for face swapping. In: IEEE Beijing Section. Proceedings of 2014 4th IEEE International Conference on Network Infrastructure and Digital Content, IEEE Beijing Section, p. 4 (2014)
2. Chou, J.-K., Yang, C.-K.: Simulation of face/hairstyle swapping in photographs with skin texture synthesis. Multimedia Tools Appl. **63**(3) (2013)
3. Hayakawa, K., Takahashi, H.: Video face swapping based on time-sequential coherence in facial expression transformations. ITE Tech. Rep.**36**, 16 (2012)
4. Lin, Y., Wang, S., Lin, Q., Tang, F.: Face swapping under large pose variations: a 3D model based approach. In: Multimedia and Expo (ICME), 2012 IEEE International Conference (2012)
5. Li, Y., Chang, M.C., Lyu, S.: In ICTU Oculi: exposing AI created fake videos by detecting eye blinking (2018)
6. Yang, X., Li, Y., Lyu, S.: Exposing deep fakes using inconsistent head poses (2018)

7. Gu, Y., He, M., Nagano, K., Li H.: Protecting world leaders against deep fakes (2019)
8. Wang, K., Gou, C., Duan, Y., Lin, Y., Zhen, X., Wang, F.: Research progress and prospect of generating against network GAN. J. Autom. **43**(3), 321–332 (2017)
9. Wu, X., Xu, K., Hall, P.: A survey of image synthesis and editing with generative adversarial networks. Tsinghua Sci. Technol. **22**(6), 660–674 (2017)
10. Warif, N.B.A., Wahab, A.W.A., Idris, M.Y.I., Ramli, R.
11. Ma, W., Lin, M., Wu, Y., Huang, G.: Image copy and paste tamper detection method based on SIFT and perceptual hash. Mod. Comput. **2019**(15), 56–59
12. Huang, H.-Y., Ciou, A.-J.: Copy-move forgery detection for image forensics using the super-pixel segmentation and the Helmert transformation. EURASIP J. Image Video Process. **2019**(1)
13. Huang, W., Huang, T., Zhang, X., Xiao, H.: Re-acquisition JPEG image tamper detection based on block effect grid offset. J. Netw. Inf. Secur. **3**(12), 24–30 (2017)
14. Zhou, L.: Research on Digital Image Blind Forensics Technology. Beijing University of Posts and Telecommunications (2007)
15. Farid, H.: Exposing digital forgeries from JPEG ghosts. IEEE Trans. Inf. Forensics Secur. **4**(1), 154–160 (2009)
16. Li, X.: Forged image blind discriminant algorithm based on edge fuzzy detection. Comput. Appl. **33**(S2), 159–161 (2013)
17. Prasad, S., Ramakrishnan, K.R..: On resampling detection and its application to detect image tampering. In: Multimedia and Expo, 2006 IEEE International Conference (2006)
18. Zuo, J., Den, J.: Image forgery detection based on resampling traces. Comput. Appl. Softw. **33**(10), 328–333 (2016)
19. He, K., Zhang, X., Ren, S., et al.: Deep residual learning for image recognition. In: 2016 IEEE Conference on Computer Vision and Pattern Recognition (CVPR), IEEE Computer Society (2016)

Blockchain Phishing Scam Detection via Multi-channel Graph Classification

Dunjie Zhang[1]([⊠]), Jinyin Chen[1,2], and Xiaosong Lu[3]

[1] College of Information Engineering, Zhejiang University of Technology,
Hangzhou 310023, China
chenjinyin@zjut.edu.cn
[2] Institute of Cyberspace Security, Zhejiang University of Technology,
Hangzhou 310023, China
[3] Ningbo Shiruidi Optoelectronics Co., Ltd., Ningbo 315000, China

Abstract. With the popularity of blockchain technology, the financial security issues of blockchain transaction networks have become increasingly serious. Phishing scam detectors will protect possible victims and build a healthier blockchain ecosystem. Usually, the existing works define phishing scam detection as a node classification by learning the users' potential features by graph embedding methods such as random walk or graph neural network (GNN). However, these detectors are suffered from high complexity due to the blockchain transaction networks' large scale. Addressing this problem, we defined the transaction pattern graphs for users and transformed the phishing scam detection into a graph classification. To extract richer information, we proposed a multi-channel graph classification model (MCGC) with multiple feature extraction channels for GNN. The transaction pattern graphs and MCGC are more able to detect potential phishing scammers by extracting the transaction pattern features of the target users. Extensive experiments on seven benchmark and Ethereum datasets demonstrate that the proposed MCGC can not only achieve state-of-the-art performance in the graph classification task but also achieve effective phishing scam detection based on the target users' transaction pattern graphs.

Keywords: Blockchain · Ethereum · Phishing detection · Graph neural network · Graph classification

1 Introduction

As one of the most successful applications of blockchain [1], cryptocurrency [2,3] has promoted the rapid development of blockchain technology. The financial security [4,5] of cryptocurrency has also become an important prerequisite for the healthy development of blockchain technology. According to a report of *Chainalysis*, 30,287 victims encountered financial scams on the Ethereum platform in the first half of 2017, including phishing scams, Ponzi schemes, ransomware, etc., with a total economic loss of $225 million [6]. Among these scams, more than

© Springer Nature Singapore Pte Ltd. 2021
H.-N. Dai et al. (Eds.): BlockSys 2021, CCIS 1490, pp. 241–256, 2021.
https://doi.org/10.1007/978-981-16-7993-3_19

50% can be classified as phishing scams that take the cryptocurrency as the phishing target.

Traditional phishing scam detection methods [7] are usually applied to the identification of phishing emails or phishing webpages, to reduce the possibility of scams by warning users or directly blocking content. Due to the openness of the blockchain [1], the transaction records of all users are publicly available. By extracting the transaction records on blockchain, we can construct a large graph-structured transaction data, benefits from which it is possible to discover the identity features of different users from the blockchain transaction data through graph analysis methods [8]. Modeling as different graph analysis tasks, such as node classification [9,10], graph classification [11,12], and link prediction [13, 14], can help us identify potential scammers and provide assistance in solving financial scam on the blockchain.

Existing works [15–18] regard the phishing scam detection task as a node classification. They extract the target user's identity feature from the transaction information according to the transaction records, such as transaction address, transaction amount, and timestamp. The unsupervised graph embedding methods [15,16] based on random walk determine the process of the random walk according to the transaction amount and timestamp. Based on graph neural network (GNN), [17] and [18] transform phishing scam detection task into a supervised dynamic node classification problem by learning the structural and dynamic features of the blockchain transaction network. It is worth noting that although these methods have achieved satisfying performance on blockchain phishing scam detection, they are suffered from high computational complexity since the node classification task often takes the transaction network containing all user nodes and transaction records as the input.

Considering the high complexity of graph analysis on large-scale data, it is still a challenge to propose a low-complexity phishing scam detection model. From the perspective of the graph-structured data, the two nodes with a larger shortest path length can affect each other by transmitting messages through the edges. However, for the target node, it is often the node-set in its neighborhood that has the greatest impact on it. Since the GNN-based graph classification methods [11,12] have achieved satisfying performance in the real-world datasets. It may be a feasible solution to construct transaction pattern graphs based on the neighbor transaction records of the target user. We transform the node classification task with the whole large-scale transaction network as input into a graph classification task with multiple small-scale transaction pattern graphs as input, which helps to achieve efficient phishing scam detection. The main contributions of our work are summarized as follows:

- We firstly defined the transaction pattern graphs for blockchain transaction users. Each user has its own small-scale transaction pattern graph, which makes it possible to detect potential phishing scammers with less computational complexity through graph classification.

- We proposed a multi-channel graph classification model, namely MCGC. The proposed MCGC has a multi-channel GNN architecture, which can automatically extract richer information from the different pooling graphs.
- Extensive experiments conducted on seven benchmarks and an Ethereum datasets demonstrate that the MCGC achieves state-of-the-art performance in graph classification task and can effectively detect the phishing nodes according to the transaction pattern graphs.

2   Related Work

Our work builds upon two categories of recent research: phishing scam detection and graph classification.

2.1   Phishing Scam Detection

Phishing scam detection methods can identify phishing scammers before the scam occurs, or provide early warning for possible victims. In this section, we briefly review phishing scam detection methods, mainly categorized into random walk-based methods and GNN-based methods.

Random Walk-Based Methods. Wu et al. [16] proposed a novel network embedding algorithm called trans2vec, which is composed of random walk sampling and node sequence embedding. According to the transaction amount and timestamp, trans2vec performs biased random walk in the network to obtain a large number of node sequences, which are used to extract the users' node features. Wu et al. [15] further proposed T-EDGE, whose main structure is similar to the main structure of trans2vec. The main improvement of T-EDGE is to ensure the sequence of nodes during the random walk, and it also solves the problem of multiple edges in the transaction network.

GNN-Based Methods. To make full use of the powerful learning representation ability of GNN, Pareja et al. [17] proposed EvolveGCN, which adapts the graph convolutional network (GCN) model along the temporal dimension without resorting to node embeddings. EvolveGCN captures the dynamism of the graph sequence by using a recurrent neural network (RNN) to evolve the GCN parameters. Tam et al. [19] proposed a new message passing mechanism named EdgeProp, which allows multi-dimensional continuous edge features propagating into node embeddings when performing node classification task.

In summary, whether it is a random walk or a GNN-based method, existing work regards phishing scam detection as a node classification task. When applied to the blockchain transaction network, the huge number of nodes and transaction records lead to the high complexity of these detection methods.

2.2 Graph Classification

Graph classification can predict the graph-level labels of small-scale graphs, which has achieved satisfying performance in real-world datasets such as bioinformatics and chem-otherapy informatics. Here we briefly introduce graph classifiers.

Narayanan et al. [20] proposed a neural embedding framework named Graph2vec to learn data-driven distributed representations of arbitrary-sized graphs. Graph2vec can solve the problem of the poor generalization ability of graph kernel methods [21,22] in an unsupervised manner. Ying et al. [11] proposed a differentiable graph pooling method named Diffpool, which aggregates the nodes into a new cluster as the input of the next layer by the cluster assignment matrix. Due to the high complexity of the learning cluster assignment matrix, the self-attention graph pooling (SAGPool) [23] considers both node features and graph topology. SAGPool selects top-K nodes based on a self-attention mechanism to form the induced subgraph for the next input layer. OTCOARS-ENING proposed by Ma et al. [24] designs a coarsening strategy based on hierarchical abstraction through minimizing discrepancy along the hierarchy, which can be combined with unsupervised learning methods. GMN [25] introduces an efficient memory layer for GNNs that can jointly learn node representations and coarsen the graph.

3 Preliminary

This section introduces the problem definition of the graph classification and the phishing scam detection on the blockchain. We represent a graph as $G = (V, E, A)$, where V is the node set with $|V| = N$, $e_{i,j} =< v_i, v_j >\in E$ is the edge between the node v_i and v_j. $A \in \mathbb{R}^{N \times N}$ is the adjacency matrix, where $A_{i,j} \neq 0$ denotes node v_i directly connected with v_j while $A_{i,j} = 0$ otherwise. The graph G may contain an attribute vector of each node in some case, here we denote the attribute vector of graph G as $A \in \mathbb{R}^{N \times D}$, where D is the dimension of X. Generally, the adjacency matrix A contains the information of V and E on graph G, so we use $G = (A, X)$ to represent a graph more concisely.

Definition 1 (Graph classification). For a graph classification dataset G_{set}, it includes M graphs $\{G_1, G_2, ..., G_M\}$. The graph classification task aims to predict the categories of unlabeled graph $G_u \subset G_{set}$ through the model $f_\theta^{graph}(\cdot)$ trained by the labeled graphs $G_l = G_{set} - G_u$ with its corresponding label $Y = [y_1, \cdots, y_{|G_l|}]$.

Definition 2 (Phishing scam detection on blockchain). On blockchain transaction network, the node set V represents the users of the blockchain trading platform, and E represents the transaction record set between different users. Here, there may be n transactions $\{e_{i,j}^0, e_{i,j}^1, ..., e_{i,j}^n\}$ between users v_i and v_j. The phishing scam detection task aims to predict the categories of unlabeled nodes $V_u \subset V$ $f_\theta^{phishing}(\cdot)$ trained by the labeled nodes $V_l = V - V_u$ with its corresponding label $F = [\tau_1, \cdots, \tau_l]$, where τ_i is the ground truth label of v_i. $\tau_i = 1$ denotes the node v_i is a phishing node while $\tau_i = 0$ otherwise.

4   Methodology

To transform the high complexity node classification task into a lower complexity graph classification task on a blockchain transaction network, we define the user transaction pattern graphs for the first time. Specifically, we take the whole graph-level representation of the transaction pattern graph as the target user's transaction pattern feature, which provides a more efficient method for phishing node detection. Additionally, to extract richer information from the transaction pattern graphs, we propose MCGC, a graph classification model with a multi-channel GNN architecture, which aggregates the information of pooling graphs in multiple channels in a trainable manner, thus achieving better graph classification performance.

4.1   Transaction Pattern Graph Construction

In this part, we introduced the construction process of the transaction pattern graphs for the Ethereum trading platform. We collected Ethereum transaction data from the Ethereum trading platform (https://etherscan.io/) through Ethereum clients Geth and Parity. Each transaction data in this website contains dozens of attributes, among which the transaction timestamp, transaction sending and receiving address, and transaction amount are the key information for constructing a transaction network. The sending address and receiving address correspond to the nodes in the transaction network, the transaction timestamp and the transaction amount indicate the existence edges and their information between the corresponding node pairs. We reserve this transaction information from the original data to construct the transaction pattern graphs. The partial transaction records and the process of constructing a transaction pattern graph are shown in Fig. 1. Figure 1(a) shows the partial transaction records of the target node v_0 that is marked in red, and Fig. 1(b) shows the construction process of the first-order transaction pattern graph of v_0. The 4 transaction records in Fig. 1(a) contain 4 different addresses, corresponding to 4 edges and 4 nodes in the transaction graph.

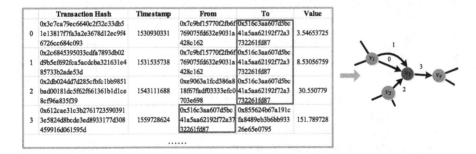

Fig. 1. The process of Ethereum transaction pattern graph construction. (Color figure online)

Through the above steps, we took the target node v_0 as the central node and extracted the user address of the other party as the first-order transaction node based on the transaction records. Then, the first-order transaction nodes are regarded as the central nodes, the second-order transaction nodes are extracted according to the same method. Repeat this step until the designated K-order transaction pattern graph is constructed. Different from a large-scale Ethereum transaction network used for the node classification task, we constructed an independent small-scale transaction pattern graph for each node. There may be multiple transaction records between two transaction addresses on blockchain transaction data, In this case, we merge multiple transaction records into one transaction, taking the summed transaction amount as a new transaction amount information, and the average timestamp as the new edge information.

Here, we choose the 1259 phishing nodes marked in [16] and the same number of active normal nodes randomly selected in the same period as our target node set. Besides, we set $K = 4$ to ensure that the transaction pattern graphs still contain enough information after merging multiple transaction records.

4.2 Multi-channel Graph Classification

Our proposed approach, MCGC, utilizes a multi-channel architecture to fuse the node-level representations of different pooling graphs. The specific architecture of multi-channel architecture is shown in Fig. 2. The key intuition is that for each hierarchical graph pooling layer of MCGC, we introduce trainable node importance weights to aggregate the node-level representations to the graph-level. Thus, we can capture the important structural information for graph classification from different pooling graphs. After that, MCGC learns effective features from these structural information and outputs the final graph classification results.

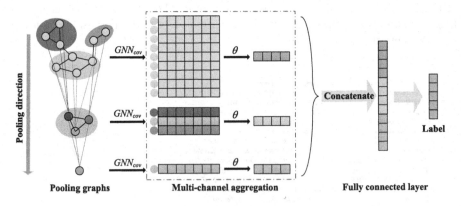

Fig. 2. The specific illustration of multi-channel architecture in MCGC.

Hierarchical Graph Pooling. MCGC aggregates the nodes in the input graph into a new node cluster through the node aggregation operation of the graph pooling layer, thus obtaining the coarsened pooling graph structure. Multiple graph pooling layers can extract different crucial hierarchical structure information of the input graph, which helps us extract multi-level user transaction pattern information. In addition, the pooling layer can be combined with GNNs to form an end-to-end training model and has demonstrated good performance on many real-world graph classification datasets.

Specifically, MCGC employs the propagation function to implement the convolution layer for extracting the l-th node-level representation, which can be expressed as:

$$H^{l,k} = \sigma(\hat{A}^l H^{l,k-1} W^{l,k}) \tag{1}$$

where $\hat{A}^l = \tilde{D}^{-\frac{1}{2}} \tilde{A}^l \tilde{D}^{-\frac{1}{2}}$, A^l is the l-th adjacency matrix of input graph G, and $\tilde{A}^l = A^l + I_N^l$ is the adjacency matrix of the l-th pooling graph G^l with self-connections. I_N^l is the identity matrix and $\tilde{D}_{ii} = \sum_j \tilde{A}^l_{ij}$ denotes the degree matrices of $\tilde{A}^l$. $W^{l,k}$ is the parameters of the k-th propagation function in the l-th architecture. σ is the Relu active function. When $k = 1$, $H^{l,0}$ is the node attribute X^l of the l-th architecture.

The $(l+1)$-th node-level representation H^{l+1} is usually obtained by running K iterations of Eq. 1. To achieve effective graph convolution with lower complexity, here we choose $K = 3$. The convolution layer of the l-th architecture is denoted as:

$$H^{l+1} = GNN_{cov}(A^l, X^l; \theta^l) \tag{2}$$

where H^{l+1} is computed from the l-th adjacency matrix A^l and node attribute X^l. θ^l is the parameters set of the l-th architecture. The input A^0 and X^0 are the original adjacency matrix and node attributes on graph, i.e., $A^0 = A$, $X^0 = X$, respectively.

For the pooling layer, it calculates the cluster assignment matrix $C^l \in \mathbb{R}^{n_l \times n_{l+1}}$ according to the topological structure and node representation of the current graph. The cluster assignment matrix of the l-th architecture is:

$$C^l = softmax\left(GNN_{pool}(A^l, X^l)\right) \tag{3}$$

where GNN_{pool} has the same structure as GNN_{cov}. n_l and n_{l+1} represent the number of nodes in the l-th and the $(l+1)$-th pooling graphs, respectively. Each row in the C^l represents the probability that the node is assigned to each node cluster in the $l + 1$-th layer. Generally, $n_l > n_{l+1}$, the pooling layer can coarsen the graph into a pooling graph with a smaller number of nodes, which helps extract the crucial structure of the original graph.

According to the adjacency matrix A^l and node attribute X^l of the l-th pooling graph, the convolutional layer and the pooling layer obtain the node-level representation H^l and cluster assignment matrix C^l of the l-th layer, respectively. Then the pooling adjacency matrix A^{l+1} and the node attribute X^{l+1} of $(l+1)$-th layer are calculated by:

$$X^{l+1} = C^{l^T} H^l \in \mathbb{R}^{n_{l+1} \times d} \tag{4}$$

$$A^{l+1} = C^{l^T} A^l C^l \in \mathbb{R}^{n_{l+1} \times n_{l+1}} \tag{5}$$

where d denotes the feature dimension of each node. Equation 4 aggregates the H^l according to the cluster assignments C^l, generating a new pooling node attribute for each of n_{l+1} clusters. Similarly, Eq. 5 generates a new pooling adjacency matrix based on the adjacency matrix A^l, denoting the connectivity strength between each pair of clusters.

Multi-channel Structure. MCGC extracts L pooling graphs $\{G^1(A^1, X^1), ..., G^L(A^L, X^L)\}$ from the original graph $G(A, X)$ through L hierarchical graph pooling layers. The topological structure and node-level representations of these pooling graphs reflect the multiple channel representations of G. Intuitively, the crucial graph structures learned by the pooling graphs of different channels are also different. We hope to capture the relationship between different channels and graph-level representations in a learnable manner, instead of simply using mean-pooling or max-pooling to obtain graph-level representation.

For the above considerations, we introduce a trainable node importance weight for each pooling graph to learn its graph-level representation. Specifically, for the l-th pooling graph, MCGC obtains its node-level representation through the graph convolutional layer GNN_{cov}. The importance values of different nodes in the current pooling graph are learned by the proposed trainable node importance weights, and then we aggregate the node-level representation of the pooling graph into the graph-level by weighted summation, which can be expressed as:

$$S_l = \frac{\sum \theta_l(i) \cdot Z_l(i)}{\sum \theta_l} \tag{6}$$

where $S_l \in \mathbb{R}^d$ denotes the graph-level representation of the l-th pooling graph.

Then, we combine the graph-level representations of the original graph and the pooling graphs. MCGC preserves the multi-channel information of the graph as much as possible by concatenating the graph-level representations of different pooling graphs together. The global-level representation $S \in \mathbb{R}^{(L+1)d}$ is denoted as:

$$S = concat(normal(S_0), ...normal(S_L)) \tag{7}$$

where $concat(\cdot)$ denotes the concatenate function, which stitches the graph-level representations of the original graph and the $L - 1$ pooling graphs. $normal(S_l) = S_l / \sum S_l$ is a normalization function, which converts the graph-level representation of each pooling graph into an identity vector. It can avoid the inconsistency of the scope of graph-level representations caused by the difference in the number of nodes.

Finally, we get the prediction probability of the input graph through the fully connected layer with a softmax classifier:

$$O = softmax(SW + b) \tag{8}$$

where $W \in \mathbb{R}^{(L+1)|Y|}$ and $b \in \mathbb{R}^{|Y|}$ denote the weight and bias of the fully connected layer, respectively. $|Y|$ is the number of labels in the graph dataset G_{set}.

Training Procedure. The entire MCGC is an end-to-end model that can be trained by stochastic gradient descent. For a set of graphs G_{set}, we employ the following loss function $\mathcal{L}$ to train our MCGC, which can be represented as:

$$\mathcal{L} = - \sum_{G_i \in G_{set}}^{|G_{set}|} \sum_{j=1}^{|Y|} Q_{ij} \ln O_{ij} (A_i, X_i) + \sum_{l=1}^{L} \sum_{i=1}^{n_l} \frac{1}{n_l} H(C_l(i)) \qquad (9)$$

where $Y = \{y_1, ..., y_{|Y|}\}$ is the category set of the graphs, Q_{ij} is the ground truth with $Q_{ij} = 1$ if graph G_i belongs to category y_j and $Q_{ij} = 0$ otherwise. O_{ij} denotes the predicted probability that graph G_i belongs to y_j, which is calculated by Eq. 8 and can be considered as a function of A_i and X_i, thus we denote it as $O_{ij}(A_i, X_i)$. $H(\cdot)$ denotes the information entropy function.

$\mathcal{L}$ consists of two parts. The first part represents the cross-entropy of the classification prediction probability and the ground truth label, which can guide the prediction probability to be closer to the ground truth label. The second part represents the information entropy constraint of the cluster assignment matrix of the l-th layer, which helps the row vector of the cluster assignment matrix to approach the ont-hot vector and better learn the mapping relationship between nodes.

5   Experiments

To verify the performance of MCGC, we conducted graph classification experiments on several benchmark graph classification and Ethereum transaction datasets. For each dataset, we perform 10-fold cross-validation and report the average accuracy. In our MCGC, we implement three hierarchical graph pooling layers, i.e., we set $L = 3$. We use the Adam optimizer to optimize the model, and the learning rate is searched in 0.1,0.01,0.001. The feature dimension d is set by a hyper-parameter search in $\{32, 64, 128, 256, 512\}$. We implement our proposed MCGC with PyTorch, and our experimental environment consists of i7-7700K 3.5 GHzx8 (CPU), TITAN Xp 12 GiB (GPU), 16 GBx4 memory (DDR4), and Ubuntu 16.04 (OS).

5.1   Datasets

To verify whether the multi-channel structure can better aggregate node-level representation and the phishing node detection performance of MCGC, we select seven benchmark and Ethereum transaction datasets for our graph classification experiments. Among the benchmark datasets, two datasets are social network datasets, including IMDB-BINARY and REDDIT-BINARY. The others are about bio-informatics and chemo-informatics. Each dataset is composed of two classes of graphs. The basic statistics are summarized in Table 1.

5.2 Baselines

To verify the performance of MCGC, we compare it with 5 advanced graph classification methods including Graph2vec [20], Diffpool [11], SAGPool [23], OTCOARSENING [24] and GMN [25]. The specific method is introduced as follows:

Graph2vec. It establishes the relationship between a network and the rooted subgraphs. It extracts rooted subgraphs and provides corresponding labels into the vocabulary, and then trains a skip-gram model to obtain the representation of the network.

DIFFPOOL. It learns a differentiable soft cluster assignment for nodes at each layer and generates hierarchical representations of graphs in an end-to-end manner.

SAGPool. Based on self-attention, It uses graph convolution to capture both node features and graph topology. Compared with DIFFPOOL, this algorithm can learn hierarchical representations of graphs with fewer parameters.

OTCOARSENING. It designs a coarsening strategy based on hierarchical abstraction through minimizing discrepancy along the hierarchy, which can be combined with unsupervised learning methods.

GMN. It designs an efficient memory layer for GNNs that can jointly learn node representations and coarsen the graph. It consists of a multi-head array of memory keys and a convolution operator to aggregate the soft cluster assignments from different heads.

Table 1. The basic statistics of eight datasets.

Dataset	#Graphs	#Classes	#Ave_nodes	#Ave_edges
MUTAG [26]	188	2	17.92	20.42
PTC [27]	344	2	14.29	14.69
PROTEINS [28]	1113	2	39.06	72.82
NCI1 [29]	4110	2	29.87	32.30
NCI109 [29]	4127	2	29.69	32.13
IMDB-BINARY [21]	1000	2	19.77	96.53
REDDIT-BINARY [21]	2000	2	429.63	497.75
Ethereum	2518	2	120.43	130.08

5.3 Evaluation Metrics

The datasets in our experiment are all binary datasets, in which the number ratio of positive examples to negative examples tends to 1. Therefore, we only use the accuracy to evaluate the performance of the different algorithm, which can be expressed as:

$$Accuracy = \frac{TP + TN}{TP + TN + FP + FN} \tag{10}$$

where TP and TN are the numbers of positive and negative examples predicted correctly, respectively. FP and FN are the numbers of positive and negative examples predicted incorrectly, respectively.

5.4   Graph Classification Performance

To better detect phishing nodes on blockchain transaction network through the powerful learning representation ability of GNN, we transform the phishing detection task into a graph classification task with a smaller graph scale and lower training complexity. We first verify the performance of the proposed MCGC in the benchmark graph classification datasets. Compared with the baselines in Table 2, the proposed MCGC achieves state-of-the-art performance among all benchmark datasets. Additionally, the performance improvement of MCGC on the REDDIT-BINARY is more obvious. This may be due to the most intuitive connection between the label of REDDIT-BINARY and the topological structure of the graph. The graph structure generated by Q & A interaction is usually similar to a star network, while the graphs of user discussion interaction usually have no obvious central node.

Table 2. The graph classification performance of seven datasets by various methods.

Methods	MUTAG	PTC	PROTEINS	NCI1	NCI109	IMDB-BINARY	REDDIT-BINARY
Graph2vec	83.15	61.59	73.30	73.22	74.26	62.74	59.07
Diffpool	80.60	62.00	75.90	74.29	74.10	75.20	86.19
SAGPool	78.60	61.39	73.30	74.18	74.06	72.20	73.90
OTCOARSENING	85.60	63.57	74.90	76.18	68.50	74.60	76.53
GMN	90.53	64.59	75.78	73.17	73.26	77.00	87.36
MCGC	91.67	64.71	78.91	76.54	76.36	77.00	91.00

Generally, the graph classification performance of various graph classification methods is different on bioinformatics datasets and social network datasets. For bioinformatics datasets, the classification results obtained by different methods are relatively close. Since MUTAG, PTC, PROTEINS, NCI1, and NCI109 are all small-scale graphs, they usually only contain dozens of nodes. The simple topology makes it easy to extract the structure information of these graphs. However, the hierarchical representation learning of graphs begins to show its advantages for social network datasets with complex structure. The classification accuracy of Diffpool and other hierarchical graph classification methods on IMDB-BINARY and REDDIT-BINARY is 8%–10% higher than Graph2vec. Since MCGC is based on the hierarchical structure of Diffpool, it aggregates multi-channel hierarchical graph structure information in a learning manner, which helps to better aggregate the node-level representation of hierarchical pooling graphs into the graph-level, thus obtaining better graph classification performance.

5.5 Phishing Node Detection on Blockchain Network

The blockchain account information based on the hash value of the public key makes users further obscure the identity attribute information on the basis of pseudonyms. This makes it difficult to define a user's identity features based on information other than his account transaction records. Considering that it is still a huge challenge to analyze large-scale data in deep GNN models, we transform the phishing scam detection into a small-scale graph classification task. We learn the potential features of the users by building transaction pattern graphs centered on these user nodes. In this part, we conduct the graph classification experiments on the transaction pattern graphs of phishing and normal nodes. The performance of the proposed MCGC and baselines are shown in Fig. 3. We can see that in the Ethereum transaction network, MCGC can still achieve state-of-the-art performance, which indicates that the proposed MCGC can better extract the potential identity features of the transaction users.

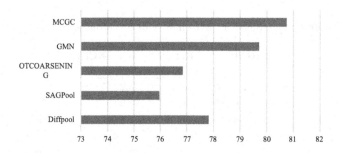

Fig. 3. The graph classification accuracy of the Ethereum dataset.

To further investigate the reason why the hierarchical graph classification methods perform well on the Ethereum dataset, we visualize the topological structure of the transaction pattern graphs of phishing nodes and normal nodes, respectively. Figure 4(a) are two transaction pattern examples of phishing nodes, and (b) are two transaction pattern examples of normal nodes. The red node is the target user, the gray node is its neighboring node, the red edge are the transaction records of the target user, and the gray edges are the transaction records between neighboring nodes. Compared with normal users, phishing users have fewer direct trading users. The nodes directly connected to the phishing nodes often have a larger node degree value. They are usually exchange addresses, which are used for asset management, currency exchange, and so on.

Hierarchical graph classification methods such as MCGC can effectively aggregate the nodes with a larger node degree value and their neighbor node sets. Normal nodes are more likely to be aggregated, while phishing nodes tend to exist as independent nodes in the next pooling graph. When the node-level representations are aggregated into the graph-level, the feature vector of the phishing node tends to account for a larger proportion, which instructs the graph classifier to classify the input graph into the phishing transaction pattern class.

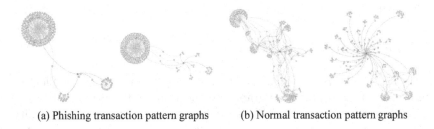

(a) Phishing transaction pattern graphs   (b) Normal transaction pattern graphs

Fig. 4. The visualization of phishing and normal transaction mode graphs.

5.6 Time Efficiency of Phishing Detection

In this part, we verify the time efficiency of the GNN-based phishing detector and MCGC on the blockchain transaction network. Since EvolveGCN [17] and EdgeProp [19] consider dynamic information or edge information based on GCN, respectively. They have higher complexity than the traditional GCN. Therefore, we take the simplest GCN [9] as an example to detect phishing scams on the blockchain transaction network. Specifically, we select multiple nodes as the central nodes at the same time and construct the whole K-order transaction graph by the construction process in Sect. 4.1, which is used in the GCN-based phishing scam detector.

Figure 5 shows the time efficiency of phishing scam detection under different node scales for GCN and MCGC. When the number of nodes is small, GCN has higher time efficiency. However, as the number of nodes increases, the computational complexity of GCN increases rapidly. When the number of nodes exceeds 40k, the complexity of MCGC is relatively lower. In addition, facing users newly added to the transaction network, the phishing scam detectors based on node classification may need to reconstruct the transaction graph for retraining, while our MCGC can detect any newly added user transaction pattern graph without retraining.

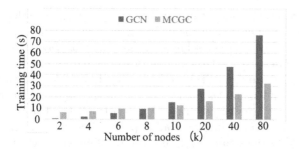

Fig. 5. The training time in each iteration when detecting different sizes of the transaction network.

6   Conclusion

In this paper, we firstly define the transaction pattern graphs for blockchain transaction data and propose a graph classification model with a multi-channel GNN architecture, named MCGC. To reduce the computational complexity of the phishing scam detection, we transform the blockchain phishing scam detector into a graph classification task and build the independent transaction pattern graphs for the target blockchain transaction users. Moreover, to extract richer transaction pattern features from the transaction pattern graphs, we regard the pooling graphs learned from different hierarchical graph pooling layers as the multi-channel representations and introduce trainable node importance weights to better aggregate the information of multi-channel pooling graphs. Experiments on seven benchmark and Ethereum datasets demonstrate that MCGC can not only achieve the state-of-the-art performance in graph classification task, but also achieve effective phishing scam detection based on the target users transaction pattern graphs.

Acknowledgments. The authors would like to thank the National Natural Science Foundation of China under Grant No. 62072406, the Natural Science Foundation of Zhejiang Province under Grant No. LY19F020025, the Major Special Funding for Science and Technology Innovation 2025 in Ningbo under Grant No. 2018B10063.

References

1. Iansiti, M., Lakhani, K.R.: The truth about blockchain. Harv. Bus. Rev. **95**(1), 118–127 (2017)
2. Yuan, Y., Wang, F.Y.: Blockchain and cryptocurrencies: model, techniques, and applications. IEEE Trans. Syst. Man Cybern. Syst. **48**(9), 1421–1428 (2018)
3. Wood, G., et al.: Ethereum: a secure decentralised generalised transaction ledger. Ethereum project yellow paper, vol. 151, no. 2014, pp. 1–32 (2014)
4. Chen, W., Zheng, Z., Cui, J., Ngai, E., Zheng, P., Zhou, Y.: Detecting Ponzi schemes on Ethereum: towards healthier blockchain technology. In: 2018 Proceedings of the 2018 World Wide Web Conference, pp. 1409–1418 (2018)

5. Bartoletti, M., Carta, S., Cimoli, T., Saia, R.: Dissecting Ponzi schemes on Ethereum: identification, analysis, and impact. Futur. Gener. Comput. Syst. **102**, 259–277 (2020)
6. EtherScamDB: Etherscamdb. https://blog.chainalysis.com/reports/therise-of-cybercrime-on-ethereum
7. Khonji, M., Iraqi, Y., Jones, A.: Phishing detection: a literature survey. IEEE Commun. Surv. Tutor. **15**(4), 2091–2121 (2013)
8. Wu, Z., Pan, S., Chen, F., Long, G., Zhang, C., Philip, S.Y.: A comprehensive survey on graph neural networks. IEEE Trans. Neural Netw. Learn. Syst. **32**, 4–24 (2020)
9. Kipf, T.N., Welling, M.: Semi-supervised classification with graph convolutional networks. In: International Conference on Learning Representations, Toulon, France (2017)
10. Wang, X., Zhu, M., Bo, D., Cui, P., Shi, C., Pei, J.: AM-GCN: adaptive multi-channel graph convolutional networks. Association for Computing Machinery, New York (2020)
11. Ying, R., You, J., Morris, C., Ren, X., Hamilton, W.L., Leskovec, J.: Hierarchical graph representation learning with differentiable pooling. In: Proceedings of the 32nd International Conference on Neural Information Processing Systems, ser. NIPS 2018, p. 4805C4815. Curran Associates Inc., Red Hook, NY, USA (2018)
12. Wang, H., et al.: Incremental subgraph feature selection for graph classification. IEEE Trans. Knowl. Data Eng. **29**(1), 128–142 (2016)
13. Duan, L., Ma, S., Aggarwal, C., Ma, T., Huai, J.: An ensemble approach to link prediction. IEEE Trans. Knowl. Data Eng. **29**(11), 2402–2416 (2017)
14. Fu, C., et al.: Link weight prediction using supervised learning methods and its application to yelp layered network. IEEE Trans. Knowl. Data Eng. **30**(8), 1507–1518 (2018)
15. Wu, J., Lin, D., Zheng, Z., Yuan, Q.: T-edge: temporal weighted multidigraph embedding for Ethereum transaction network analysis. arXiv preprint arXiv:1905.08038 (2019)
16. Wu, J., et al.: Who are the phishers? Phishing scam detection on Ethereum via network embedding. IEEE Trans. Syst. Man Cybern. Syst. (2020)
17. Pareja, A., et al.: EvolveGCN: evolving graph convolutional networks for dynamic graphs. In: Proceedings of the AAAI Conference on Artificial Intelligence, vol. 34, no. 04, pp. 5363–5370 (2020)
18. Chen, W., Guo, X., Chen, Z., Zheng, Z., Lu, Y.: Phishing scam detection on Ethereum: towards financial security for blockchain ecosystem. In: International Joint Conferences on Artificial Intelligence Organization, pp. 4506–4512 (2020)
19. Handason Tam, D.S., et al.: Identifying illicit accounts in large scale e-payment networks-a graph representation learning approach. arXiv arXiv:1906.05546 (2019)
20. Narayanan, A., Chandramohan, M., Venkatesan, R., Chen, L., Liu, Y., Jaiswal, S.: graph2vec: learning distributed representations of graphs. arXiv preprint arXiv:1707.05005 (2017)
21. Yanardag, P., Vishwanathan, S.: Deep graph kernels. In: 2015 Proceedings of the 21th ACM SIGKDD International Conference on Knowledge Discovery and Data Mining, pp. 1365–1374 (2015)
22. Vishwanathan, S.V.N., Schraudolph, N.N., Kondor, R., Borgwardt, K.M.: Graph kernels. J. Mach. Learn. Res. **11**, 1201–1242 (2010)
23. Lee, J., Lee, I., Kang, J.: Self-attention graph pooling. In: International Conference on Machine Learning, pp. 3734–3743 (2019)

24. Ma, T., Chen, J.: Unsupervised learning of graph hierarchical abstractions with differentiable coarsening and optimal transport. arXiv preprint arXiv:1912.11176 (2019)
25. Khasahmadi, A.H., Hassani, K., Moradi, P., Lee, L., Morris, Q.: Memory-based graph networks. arXiv preprint arXiv:2002.09518 (2020)
26. Debnath, A.K., Lopez de Compadre, R.L., Debnath, G., Shusterman, A.J., Hansch, C.: Structure-activity relationship of mutagenic aromatic and heteroaromatic nitro compounds. Correlation with molecular orbital energies and hydrophobicity. J. Med. Chem. 34(2), 786–797 (1991)
27. Toivonen, H., Srinivasan, A., King, R.D., Kramer, S., Helma, C.: Statistical evaluation of the predictive toxicology challenge 2000–2001. Bioinformatics 19(10), 1183–1193 (2003)
28. Borgwardt, K.M., Ong, C.S., Schönauer, S., Vishwanathan, S., Smola, A.J., Kriegel, H.-P.: Protein function prediction via graph kernels. Bioinformatics 21(Suppl 1), i47–i56 (2005)
29. Shervashidze, N., Schweitzer, P., Van Leeuwen, E.J., Mehlhorn, K., Borgwardt, K.M.: Weisfeiler-Lehman graph kernels. J. Mach. Learn. Res. 12(9), 2539–2561 (2011)

Transparency to the Extreme: An In-Depth Study of the Bitcoin Exchange Ecosystem

Gengsheng Xue[1]($\boxtimes$), Yang Li[1], and Zibin Zheng[1,2]

[1] School of Data and Computer Science, Sun Yat-sen University,
Guangzhou 510275, China
{xuegsh,liyang99}@mail2.sysu.edu.cn
[2] National Engineering Research Center of Digital Life, Sun Yat-sen University,
Guangzhou 510275, China
zhzibin@mail.sysu.edu.cn

Abstract. Bitcoin exchanges, which are digital platforms for investors to trade Bitcoins freely, operate between digital and fiat currency networks. Thus they provide an opportunity to connect real-world identities to pseudonymous Bitcoin addresses, which is critical to anti-money laundering efforts. To this end, in this paper, we conduct a systematic investigation on the whole Bitcoin exchange ecosystem and seek to characterize, understand, and identify patterns around exchanges (including exchanges' internal wallet structure and transfer activity). Specifically, we first construct the Bitcoin Transfer Graph (BTG) using the on-chain transaction records and propose an approach to identify the Bitcoin addresses belonging to Bitcoin exchanges. Then, based on the found addresses, we conduct a preliminary analysis of mainstream Bitcoin exchanges and provide an overview of their internal wallet architecture. Lastly, we obtain many observations and findings by analyzing these graphs, which help us obtain a deep understanding of the Bitcoin exchange ecosystem.

Keywords: Blockchain · Bitcoin · Exchange · Wallet · Graph analysis

1 Introduction

Bitcoin is the first and widest spread cryptocurrency which was proposed in 2008 and released in 2009 [1]. According to *coinmarketcap.com*, it is now the largest cryptocurrency by market capitalization. Unlike traditional currencies, Bitcoin operates on a peer-to-peer network with no central authority, thus making Bitcoin fully decentralized and public [2]. Today Bitcoin has developed an extensive ecosystem, including applications like exchanges, pools, gambling, etc. The most popular application is Bitcoin exchanges, which account for approximately 40% of the addresses in the Bitcoin network according to *walletexplorer.com*.

© Springer Nature Singapore Pte Ltd. 2021
H.-N. Dai et al. (Eds.): BlockSys 2021, CCIS 1490, pp. 257–271, 2021.
https://doi.org/10.1007/978-981-16-7993-3_20

A Bitcoin exchange is a digital marketplace where investors can transact freely with Bitcoins. Currently, there are numerous Bitcoin exchanges on the market and most of them are centralized online platforms requiring pre-paid assets (e.g., Bitcoins) from users, facilitating that exchanges are usually in charge of thousands of Bitcoins. Therefore, exchanges are usually suffering from external attacks. It is estimated that Bitcoin exchanges lose $2.7 million on average every day and the amount is continuously growing. Specially, Binance, one of the largest cryptocurrency exchanges, has confirmed a large scale data breach from hackers in 2019, resulting in a loss of about 7,000 Bitcoins. Besides, we know that the trading volume can be regarded as an essential indicator for measuring an exchange. But in fact, SEC (Securities and Exchange Commission) discloses that many cryptocurrency exchanges exaggerate their trading volumes aiming to swindle investors.

The influence of the attacks and frauds shown above is harsh for the whole ecosystem. Undoubtedly the exchanges have become an indispensable component of the Bitcoin ecosystem. Meanwhile, there is no denying that exchanges are usually black-box to users since users know few true information about them. Hence, it's necessary to solve the problem of information asymmetry between users and exchanges. Nowadays it has drawn attention among researchers to study the new exchange ecosystem. However, most of these studies focus on matchmaking trading like market manipulation [3], etc. There is little analysis of the exchange itself, especially on aspects like security, wallet structure.

In an attempt to fill the gap in research, this paper proposes a framework for analyzing the Bitcoin exchange ecosystem. Specifically, our approach consists of three phases: 1) *Data Collection*, we collect transactions, scripts and addresses' tags for further analysis (Sect. 2); 2) *Exchange Address Identification*, we construct the Bitcoin Transfer Graph (BTG) using the proposed algorithm and characterize the BTG to help identify the exchange wallets (Sect. 3); 3) *Exchange Analysis*, we focus our analysis on the mainstream Bitcoin exchanges to reveal their unique features (Sect. 4). In summary, we make the following contributions:

1. We conduct a systematic investigation on the whole Bitcoin exchange ecosystem via graph analysis and provide an overview of their internal wallet architecture. To the best of our knowledge, this is the first work to make an in-depth study of the Bitcoin exchange ecosystem.
2. We propose an algorithm to identify addresses controlled by Bitcoin exchanges based on the on-chain data and graph analysis. The validation result shows that our algorithm can effectively filter out exchanges' addresses from thousands of pseudonymous addresses.
3. We obtain many new observations and findings of Bitcoin exchange ecosystem by adopting graph analysis and other methods, which help us obtain a new understanding of the Bitcoin exchange ecosystem. In particular, we further analyze why some exchanges are suffering from external attacks.

2   Data Collection

We first launch a full node (i.e., Bitcoin Core) on our server and then synchronize the node to the network by downloading all the blocks. We download all the blocks before June 4th, 2020 (from the very first block to block 633,000). Then, we use the BlockSci parser to extract the transaction records from the blocks for further analysis. From the extracted information, we can get all transactions of an address. By scanning these transactions, we can calculate the current balance of this address. Through this method, we can figure out which address has the most Bitcoins (i.e., the rich list).

3   Exchange Address Identification

3.1   Exchange Wallet Structure

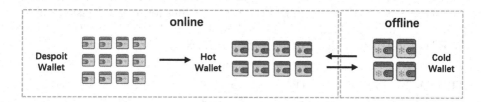

Fig. 1. Standard structure of exchange wallet.

Figure 1 shows the standard structure of exchanges wallet [4]. Users can deposit Bitcoins to exchanges by transferring to the deposit wallet address, which is created and owned by Bitcoin exchanges. Hot wallets collect Bitcoins from deposit wallets and transfer the extra Bitcoins to cold wallets. Besides, hot wallets are also responsible for meeting users' withdrawal demand. Hot wallets usually have access to the Internet, which carries potential risks since most computer systems have hidden vulnerabilities that can be used by hackers to break into the system and steal the Bitcoins. Cold wallets are usually disconnected to the Internet, thus it is safe and reliable but inconvenient for users to transfer Bitcoins compared to hot wallets. Furthermore, hot wallets are usually used for frequent and constant transactions (i.e., active trading), while cold wallets are used for long-term holdings with minimal interaction with other wallets.

3.2   Exchange Address Mining

To mine the set of addresses controlled by an exchange, it is reasonable to start with the cold wallet addresses since: 1) cold wallets usually have large balances, thus we can easily find them on the rich list of Bitcoin; 2) cold wallets are relatively infrequent involved in transactions, making it less complexity to analyze.

Starting with a cold wallet address, the question remains on how to figure out more addresses that are controlled by the same person. Clustering based on multi-input heuristics may help but it also shows some limits. Considering these two transactions[1,2], 88,888 Bitcoins were first transferred from address *34xp*[3] to *3Qjv* and then back to *34xp*. The funds transferring process here strongly suggests that address *34xp* and *3Qjv* are controlled by the same entity. However, the clustering methods [5] divide these two addresses into different groups.

Based on this, a reasonable method is to take the fund transfer process into account. Thus, we propose our exchanges address identification method based on fund transfer analysis and multi-input heuristics. In our algorithm, we assume that if an exchange address A receives hundreds of Bitcoins from address B, then there is a controlling relationship between A and B. That is to say, address A and B may be controlled by the same entity in this situation. Therefore, by traversing all transactions of the start address A (i.e., the cold wallet address of an exchange) where A appears as an output in the transaction, we can figure out where A's funds come from and which addresses are having a controlling relationship with A. Similarly, by recursively backtracking a series of transfer transactions, more addresses will be revealed and thus forming a transfer graph. To this end, we first define the Bitcoin Transfer Graph (BTG) and then detail the BTG construction algorithm together with the pruning strategy.

BTG Definition. BTG $= (V, E, w)$, where V is a set of addresses and E is a set of edges. $E = \{(v_i, v_j) | v_i, v_j \in V\}$ is a set of ordered pairs of nodes, where the order of the edge indicates the transferring relationship. $w : (v_i, v_j) \rightarrow \mathbb{R}^+$ associates each edge with a weight representing that v_i totally transfers w Bitcoins to address v_j. Hence, BTG is a weighted directed graph.

BTG Construction. To construct the graph, we follow the process described in Algorithm 1. The input is an addresses (A) in rich list and the list of transactions (T) where A appeared in an output. By using the proposed algorithm, we aim to build up the Bitcoin transfer graph and reveal the relationship of the addresses on the graph. Note that we also need to provide a parameter N to specify the number of steps to track the funds. N is usually address-dependent (i.e., addresses with a simpler transferring pattern need a smaller value of N; otherwise, a larger value of N). The larger N, the higher the complexity.

Stop Criteria. As described above, our process traces exchanges' funds transferring step by step. A stop criterion is needed to stop the process and prevent useless tracing. One simple solution is to use the multi-input heuristics. That is, if *input* (line 8) and *output* (line 7) violate multi-input heuristics, then we stop tracing in this branch (line 9–10). However, the above case shows that it doesn't

---

[1] 1e4968cac36d91c4a4294810e9d384e4b52bb73695dc23feb9459c5d89ab6e9c.

[2] 74fb65a24350ef3b9380e8232e734416224cd6a2f12cacb66eee9e176b9e337c.

[3] For writing convenience, we use the first four character to represent an address.

Algorithm 1: Backward Address Mining Algorithm

Input: A, an address in richlist; T, the list of transactions where address A
appeared in an output; N, number of steps to trace back; p, the ratio to
determine whether to prune an input.

Output: G, the Bitcoin transfer graph start with address A.

1 initialize a directed graph G and add a node for address A;

2 **foreach** $tx \in T$ **do**

3    $address\_list = [A]$, $tx\_list = [tx]$;

4   **for** $i = 1$ to N **do**

5       $expand\_address\_list = expand\_tx\_list = []$;

6   **foreach** $t \in tx\_list$ **do**

7          $output = address\_list[index]$, where $index$ is t's index in tx_list;

8   **foreach** $input \in t$ **do**

9   **if** $amount_{input} < p * amount_t$ *or stop conditions are met* **then**

10   continue

11   **if** $G.has\_edge(input, output)$ **then**

12                $w_{(input,output)} += amount_{input} * \frac{amount_{output}}{amount_t}$;

13   **else**

14                $G.add\_edge(input, output, amount_{input} * \frac{amount_{output}}{amount_t})$;

15             $expand\_address\_list += input$'s address;

16             $expand\_tx\_list +=$ the transaction that this $input$ spent;

17       $address\_list, tx\_list = expand\_address\_list, expand\_tx\_list$;

18 **return** graph G;

---

fit well. Thus, we refine it by weakening the constraint as follows (considering
the case that A received funds from B):

Heuristic 1: If A receives hundreds of Bitcoins from B, then A and B are
considered to be controlled by the same exchange.

Heuristic 2: If B and one of the addresses that have been added to BTG
before this transaction conform to multi-input heuristic, then A and B are considered to be controlled by the same exchange.

Heuristic 1 is based on the reasonable assumption that if A receives hundreds
of Bitcoins from B, then A and B are highly likely to be controlled by the same
entity. Since we construct BTG based on the multi-input heuristic and Heuristic
1, the addresses on BTG are supposed to be controlled by the same entity. Hence,
here we propose the Heuristic 2. In Heuristic 2, we suggest that A and B are
belong to the same entity as long as B and one of the addresses on BTG conform
to the multi-input heuristic.

BTG Pruning. Considering the transaction (see footnote 2), address *34xp*
receives 90,530 BTC mainly from two inputs: *3Qjv* (88,888 BTC) and *37JX*
(1,642 BTC). However, according to Algorithm 1 (line 8–16), we need to traverse all the inputs and expand them, including another five inputs with less than

0.0001 BTC. Intuitively these small value inputs contribute little to this transaction, thus ignoring them has little impact on our purpose. Besides, expanding them leads to a heavy cost since the complexity of the backtracking process grows exponentially as N increase. Therefore, to make the BTG construction reliable while efficient, we introduce the pruning part (line 9). Note that pruning aims at inputs of transactions rather than addresses. Here we use parameter p to determine whether to prune an input. Larger p means filtering out more small value inputs.

3.3   Overview of Bitcoin Transfer Graph

We apply Algorithm 1 to each address on the rich list, thus we can get a complete BTG. In this section, we provide an overview of the constructed BTG before analyzing special Bitcoin exchanges.

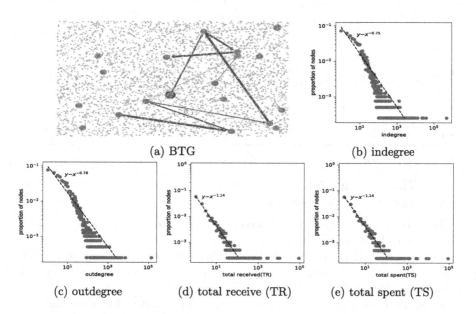

(a) BTG   (b) indegree

(c) outdegree   (d) total receive (TR)   (e) total spent (TS)

Fig. 2. Visualization and nodes distribution of BTG. (Color figure online)

Figure 2a shows a part of the BTG. The nodes denote Bitcoin addresses and the directed edges represent the transactions between the two addresses.

The thickness of the edges indicates the total amount of Bitcoins transferred between two addresses. We also highlight some uncommon addresses (the blue and orange nodes). These uncommon addresses have a big gap on behavior patterns compared with the majority (the gray nodes) since most nodes are connected with quite thin edges while highlighted nodes are connected with thick edges (the thickest edge in Fig. 2a represents a transfer of more than 80,000

Bitcoins). This indicates that the large funds are mainly in the hands of few addresses and are transferred around them. In addition, nearly all nodes are connected with few edges while the orange node is pointed at by a bunch of edges with different sources. Meanwhile, the orange node has one thick edge which points out at another address. The orange node acts like an address that collects small changes from a lot of addresses and then aggregate the money to a new place, which behaves quite similar to a hot wallet address.

To further analyze BTG, we plot some distributions of the nodes in Fig. 2, including indegree, outdegree, total received and total spent distributions. As can be seen, all of them follow the power-law distribution, suggesting that the majority of the nodes behave quite similarly whereas a small part behave quite differently. The fitted line $y \backsim x^{-\alpha}$ for each distribution is plotted. Generally, the larger the α, the less variable of the nodes' behavior.

As shown in Fig. 2b, almost half of the addresses (45.9%) have less than 10 money-receiving transactions. 99.8% of the addresses have no more than 10,000 transactions. Similarly, in Fig. 2c, the outdegree distribution also conforms to the power law. 46.8% of the addresses are involved in ten moneypaying transactions or less. 99.9% of the addresses have no more than 10,000 transactions. These statistics show from another angle that most addresses are not active whereas a small number of addresses are frequently reused for collecting and transferring funds.

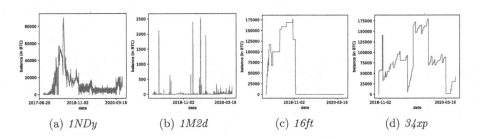

(a) *1NDy*   (b) *1M2d*   (c) *16ft*   (d) *34xp*

Fig. 3. Balance of addresses sampled from the above distributions.

Since some nodes are connected with a rather large weight (large weight means large capital flow), we further investigate the total amount of Bitcoins that addresses have received/sent and draw their distributions in Fig. 2d and 2e. As can be seen, 49.2% of the addresses received less than 10 Bitcoins in total and only 1.3% of the addresses received more than 10,000 Bitcoins. Besides, 49.3% of the addresses sent less than 10 Bitcoins in total while only 1.2% of the addresses sent more than 10,000 Bitcoins. An insight from these two distributions is that the funds are concentrated in the hands of only a few addresses.

As discussed above, the minority of nodes (mainly the nodes distributed at the tail of the above distributions) show very different behavior patterns. Thus, to further reveal the characteristic of these nodes, we simply delve deeper into their involved transactions. Figure 3 shows the balance curve of addresses[4] sampled from the tail of the above distributions. As can be seen in Fig. 3a and 3b, the balance of both address sampled from indegree and outdegree distribution rise and fall frequently, indicating that they are possibly used for hot wallets. Whereas addresses sampled from TR and TS distribution (Fig. 3c and 3d) show a very different pattern. They keep a larger balance and meanwhile their balances are relatively more stable, which conforms to the pattern of cold wallets.

3.4   External Validation

The constructed BTG starting at address S guarantees with a high degree of confidence that all the addresses on the graph are controlled by the same entity with S. Further, the characteristics described in Sect. 3.3 show that the potential hot/cold wallet addresses distribute mainly in the tail of the above distributions. Hence, we first pick out the addresses from the tail of the above distributions and then we simply tag the addresses in the tail of the indegree/outdegree distribution as hot wallet addresses and the addresses in the tail of the TR/TS distribution as cold wallet addresses. Finally, the cold and hot wallet addresses are aggregated into different exchanges.

To verify our tagging results, we compare them with the tagged addresses we have collected from exchange announcements, public forums and online websites (like *bitinfocharts.com*). As the result shows, our method obtains a high *recall* (nearly 94%), which indicates that we have precisely identified almost all the addresses we collect. Meanwhile, the *precision* is a little bit low (86%). Through further analysis, we conclude that we have found more true hot/cold addresses than the collected data (especially some deprecated addresses and the *Temporary Hot Wallet* addresses we define below), thus resulting in a lower *precision* value.

4   Mainstream Exchanges Analysis

In this section, we conduct a preliminary analysis of Bitcoin exchanges (including Binance, Bittrex, Bitfinex, Bitflyer, Bitstam, Huobi, Kraken, Poloniex, OKEX and Coinbase) and provide an overview of their internal architecture of fund management. In the following, we focus our study on the exchange addresses found in previous section and try to answer the following research questions:

- **RQ1:** What is the wallet structures of the exchanges mentioned above like?
- **RQ2:** What security considerations do these exchanges take in funds management?
- **RQ3:** Are there any other interesting insights of these exchanges?

---

[4] They are *1NDyJtNTjmwk5xPNhjgAMu4HDHigtobu1s*, *1M2dx2YFaYGdnthCcP-Efv LJhinwnGrNxXx*, *16ftSEQ4ctQFDtVZiUBusQUjRrGhM3JYwe*, *34xp4vRoCGJym-3xR7yCVPFHoCNxv4Twseo* respectively.

4.1   Wallet Structures (RQ1)

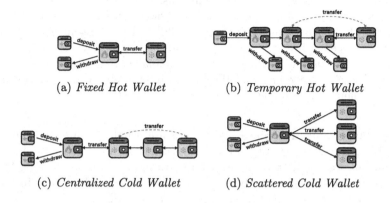

(a) *Fixed Hot Wallet*   (b) *Temporary Hot Wallet*

(c) *Centralized Cold Wallet*   (d) *Scattered Cold Wallet*

Fig. 4. Variants of hot/cold wallet structure.

Based on our exploration, we find that not all of the surveyed exchanges are using standard wallet structures (see Sect. 3.1). In practical use, exchanges might modify the standard wallet model to better meet their requirements. In the following, we will introduce some variants of the wallet structures.

Hot Wallet Structure. Figure 4a and 4b show the two variants of hot wallet structure, namely *Fixed Hot Wallet* and *Temporary Hot Wallet*.

Fixed Hot Wallet is widely adopted by exchanges (e.g., Binance, Bittrex, Bitfinex, Bitflyer, Bitstamp). As shown above, *Fixed Hot Wallet* handles users' deposit, thus having a lot of UTXOs. Meanwhile, it also transfers to users' wallet (for withdrawal) and to cold wallets (for cold storage). One of its distinguishing features is that although *Fixed Hot Wallet* handles hundreds of transactions every day, it always maintains its balance at a certain level. For explanation, we simply take a *Fixed Hot Wallet* address *1NDy* (belongs to Binance) as example and plot its balance curve in Fig. 3a. As the balance curve shows, address *1NDy* has remained its balance in the range of 5,000 to 20,000 Bitcoins since Nov. 2018. Whereas another address *bc1q*[5] (belongs to Bitflyer) keeps at around 200 Bitcoins for two years. Note that the quantity of funds in *Fixed Hot Wallet* is not usually at the same level, it is dependent on the scale of the exchanges' business. In addition, those exchanges adopting this variant usually use only one *Fixed Hot Wallet* rather than many, leading to an easier management.

Temporary Hot Wallet is more complicated. Base on our analysis, we find that Huobi and Bitstamp are managing their hot wallets in this manner. Similarly, we take address *1M2d* (belongs to Huobi) as an example and plot its balance curve in Fig. 3b. As can be seen, between the two structure variants, there is a clear distinction: *Temporary Hot Wallet* has a balance of zero most of the time. Hence, we carefully analyze the transaction records and summarize the

---

[5]   bc1qwqdg6squsna38e46795at95yu9atm8azzmyvckulcc7kytlcckxswvvzej.

characteristics of this scheme as follows: 1) Every time *Temporary Hot Wallet* receives some Bitcoins, the funds are then transferred to another *Temporary Hot Wallet* (as a change address) in a couple of hours. This accounts for the zero balance and the sharp balance change in Fig. 3b; 2) The *Temporary Hot Wallets* with zero balance are further reused. The funds are frequently traveling through these wallets. In this way, exchanges have to manage a series of *Temporary Hot Wallets*; 3) Each *Temporary Hot Wallet* has interactions with users, whereas only few of them have interactions with the cold wallets.

Cold Wallet Structure. Since cold wallets are usually off-line and have less transactions, the structure of cold wallets seems much simpler. As shown in Fig. 4c and 4d, we classify the cold wallet structures into *Centralized Cold Wallet* and *Scattered Cold Wallet*. For better comprehension, we select some instances of the two structures and plot their balance curves in Fig. 5.

Centralized Cold Wallet. In this scheme, the exchanges save their massive funds in only a few (usually a dozen) cold wallets. Hence, each *Centralized Cold Wallet* keeps a quite large balance throughout its lifetime, usually at the level of 100,000 Bitcoins. Due to its advantage of easy implement and convenient management, this scheme is extensively adopted by exchanges, such as Huobi, Bittrex, etc. As shown in Fig. 5a, Huobi now has two *Centralized Cold Wallets* in use, whose balances are around 250,000 and 70,000 Bitcoins respectively.

Scattered Cold Wallet. By contrast, exchanges following the *Scattered Cold Wallet* scheme usually split their massive funds into many (usually dozens) cold wallets, each of which owns a relatively small quantity of Bitcoins (approximately 1,000 to 10,000). This structure places a higher requirement on the management, because more private keys need to be carefully safeguarded. Therefore, few exchanges adopt this structure. In our analysis, we discover that only Bitflyer, OKEX and Coinbase are using this structure. As Fig. 5b shows, Bitflyer maintains a series of *Scattered Cold Wallets* and distributes its massive funds evenly to these wallets (1,000 Bitcoins each). Meanwhile, due to the decentralized storage of funds, *Scattered Cold Wallet* usually has less interaction with hot wallets (dozens of times) than *Centralized Cold Wallet* (hundreds of times).

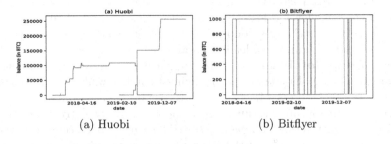

(a) Huobi   (b) Bitflyer

Fig. 5. Balance chart of the two cold wallet structure variants.

4.2   Security for Cold/Hot Wallets (RQ2)

In this section, we try to answer RQ2 from the perspective of hot wallets and cold wallets respectively.

Security for Hot Wallets. Hot wallets are usually held in an online server, thus leading to a higher exposure and risk. Especially, *Fixed Hot Wallets* suffer a lot from this. For example, Bitfinex has confirmed that roughly 120,000 BTC (more than $60 million) was stolen[6] in 2016 and meanwhile Bitstamp claims 19,000 BTC (about $5.1 million) lost in hot wallet hack[7]. As seen in both cases, Bitfinex and Bitstamp hold thousands of Bitcoins in their *Fixed Hot Wallets*. Therefore, to mitigate the high risk of *Fixed Hot Wallets*, exchanges had better take the following security considerations:

- **Consideration 1:** Reduce the amount of funds held in *Fixed Hot Wallets* while allowing them to maintain a sufficient balance for online service.
- **Consideration 2:** Periodically move extra funds to cold storage so that a compromise of the servers does not result in a lost of the majority of the funds.

In contrast, according to the information we have, there have not been a massive theft on *Temporary Hot Wallets*. This can be attributed to the zero balance and lower exposure of *Temporary Hot Wallets*. Compared with *Fixed Hot Wallet*, exchanges adopting the *Temporary Hot Wallet* scheme usually controls a series of *Temporary Hot Wallets* (i.e., based on our identification, Huobi has more than 1,000 *Temporary Hot Wallets*) and most of them are of zero balance, thus it is difficult for hackers to find the correct target (i.e., the wallet of non-zero balance). Besides, lower exposure enables *Temporary Hot Wallet* to conceal itself better thus increase the difficulty of being detected. The security consideration behind *Temporary Hot Wallet* can be summarized as follows:

- **Consideration 3:** Manage a series of *Temporary Hot Wallets* to achieve lower exposure and better concealment, thus reducing the security risk.

Security for Cold Wallets. Exchanges usually isolate the private keys of cold wallets physically (i.e., disconnect to Internet, or shut down the computer). Technically speaking, it can prevent the cold wallets from being hacked and stolen. Thus, unlike hot wallets facing risks from external attacks, the risks of cold wallets mainly come from internal management and inside jobs. To this end, exchanges mostly adopt Multisignature to ensure the security of cold wallets.

Multisignature (*multisig*) refers to that multiple private keys are required to authorize a Bitcoin transaction, rather than a single signature from one key. These transactions are referred to as M-of-N transactions, which means M of the N keys are needed to spend a UTXO. It is widely applied to divide the

---

[6] http://coindesk.com/Bitcoin-drops-12-exchange-hack-amplifies-price-decline.
[7] http://coindesk.com/bitstamp-claims-roughly-19000-btc-lost-hot-wallet-hack.

responsibility for possession of Bitcoins among multiple people (usually the corporate executives) and avoid a single-point of failure, making it substantially more difficult for the wallet to be compromised.

According to our statistics, for nearly all of the *Scattered Cold Wallets* we found, they adopt Pay-to-Public-Key-Hash (P2PKH) or Pay-to-Witness-Public-Key-Hash (P2WPKH), in which only one key is required to sign a transaction. From the perspective of management, this phenomenon is reasonable since: 1) the funds in each *Scattered Cold Wallet* is relatively small; 2) the number of *Scattered Cold Wallets* that an exchange holds is usually quite large; 3) using *multisig* for them results in too many private keys to manage, which is quite challenging. Hence, this is more of a trade-off.

For *Centralized Cold Wallet*, the situation is more complicated. Due to the usually large balance in *Centralized Cold Wallets*, exchanges (like Huobi, Bitfinex, Bitstamp, Bittrex) widely adopt *multisig* to manage their cold wallets. However, Binance unusually adopts P2PKH and P2WPKH on all its cold wallets. Meanwhile, Bitstamp and Bittrex still own some P2PKH or P2WPKH cold wallet addresses, which we infer that these addresses are responsible for the interaction with hot wallets. We summarize the security consideration as:

- **Consideration 4:** Split the massive funds into dozens of *Scattered Cold Wallets* or employ *multisig* to ensure the security of exchanges' Bitcoin reserves.

4.3   Other Insights (RQ3)

The hot wallets of exchanges generate hundreds of transactions every day in order to service the users' withdrawal. While initializing a transaction in Bitcoin, one needs to pay an extra fee to the miners. For this reason, miners have a financial incentive to prioritize the validation of transactions that pay a higher fee. The transaction fee depends on a number of factors (i.e., network conditions at the time and the size of your transaction) and hence varies greatly over time. Generally, the higher fee you pay, the sooner your transaction receives a confirmation. Note that setting the fee too low may cause your transaction to remain unconfirmed for a long time and even possibly to be rejected.

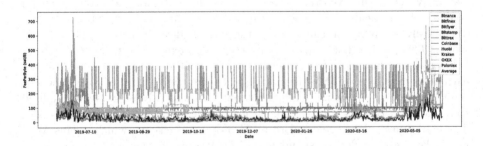

Fig. 6. Transaction fees of ten Bitcoin exchanges.

Usually the transaction fee is relatively small (around 10–1,000 satoshi/Byte), however, for hot wallets, the daily expense of fees is quite large due to a lot of transactions. Directly reducing the fee to cut down expenditures requires careful consideration, since the confirmation for a transaction that pays a lower fee will typically take more than several hours, which results in poor user experience. Thus, an appropriate fee decision strategy to balance expenses and experiences is necessary. To this end, in this section, we conduct a fee analysis on these mainstream exchanges. Figure 6 shows the transaction fees paid by these exchanges in the past year. The black line represents the average transaction fee at that moment, which somehow depicts the degree of crowdedness in the Bitcoin network. As demonstrated in Fig. 6, it is clear that these exchanges adopt different fee strategies and we summarize them into three categories as follows:

- **Dynamic Fees Strategy:** Dynamic fees mean that exchanges will take the current network conditions into account when calculate an appropriate fee for the transaction. The dynamic fee is set to get your transaction included in a block within few hours. As can be seen, the curves of Bitfinex, Bitstamp, Bittrex and Kraken are highly consistent with the *Average* curve, indicating that they are using this strategy.
- **Stable Fees Strategy:** Stable fees suggest that exchanges set a stable fee rate range for most of the time. However, this does not mean the strategy is static. Instead, exchanges are supposed to adjust the fee rate when the pre-set fee rate is out-of-date. Three of the ten exchanges (Binance, Huobi, OKEX) conform to this scheme. As the curves shows, they adopt a relatively stable fee (usually a bit higher than *Average*, about 100 satoshi per byte) for most of the time. Nonetheless, in June 2020, the pre-set fee (100 sat/B) is lower than the average fee rate, thus these exchanges simultaneously increase their transaction fees.
- **Higher Fees Strategy:** Higher fees imply that exchanges pay a much higher fee rate than the market. Bitflyer and Poloniex are using this strategy and both remain their fee rate in a stable range ([60 sat/B, 230 sat/B], [100 sat/B, 400 sat/B] respectively), which is several times the *Average*. Similar to Stable Fees Strategy, Bitflyer and Poloniex also revise the stable range to adapt to the changes in the fee market and meet the requirement of faster confirmation.

5 Related Work

Recently, a lot of literatures based on Bitcoin have emerged. Three kinds of research are closely related to our study. The first type focuses on mining the blockchain to reveal the characteristics of users in the system, from discussing user privacy issues [6–8], identifying various user behaviors [9–11], to revealing illegal activities [12–15]. The second type mainly discusses the Bitcoin exchanges. For example, the work [16] presents an empirical analysis of Bitcoin exchange risk. The work [17] conducts a theory-driven empirical study of the Bitcoin exchange rate (against USD) determination with technology and economic factors. Other related works include [4,18,19]. The third type, which is also the most relevant to our research, aims to deanonymize the Bitcoin system, from detecting mixing services [20,21], detecting illicit entities [22], to Bitcoin addresses clustering [5,6,23]. Works of Bitcoin addresses clustering usually use common behavior pattern analysis to cluster Bitcoin addresses, and divide Bitcoin addresses into several categories (e.g., gambling, mixer, exchange, pool, etc.). In contrast, our work aims at the addresses in Bitcoin exchanges and we make an in-depth analysis of the structure and security of different Bitcoin exchanges.

6   Conclusion

We conduct a systematic study to transparentize the Bitcoin exchange ecosystem. By using the Bitcoin-Core client, we collect all transactions and scripts on the Bitcoin blockchain and then construct the Bitcoin Transfer Graph. We then provide an overview of the constructed graph and characterize the hot and cold wallet addresses. Moreover, we further analyze some mainstream Bitcoin exchanges. Throughout these studies, we obtain many observations and findings, which help us obtain a deep understanding of the Bitcoin exchange ecosystem. This study raises, but still has not answered yet, many interesting and important questions. Hence we will conduct a more thorough study of the ecosystem in the future.

References

1. Nakamoto, S.: Bitcoin: a peer-to-peer electronic cash system. Technical report, Manubot (2019)
2. Zheng, Z., Xie, S., Dai, H.-N., Chen, X., Wang, H.: Blockchain challenges and opportunities: a survey. Int. J. Web Grid Serv. **14**(4), 352–375 (2018)
3. Chen, W., Wu, J., Zheng, Z., Chen, C., Zhou, Y.: Market manipulation of bitcoin: Evidence from mining the Mt. Gox transaction network. CoRR, abs/1902.01941 (2019)
4. Li, Y., Liu, Z., Zheng, Z.: Quantitative analysis of bitcoin transferred in bitcoin exchange. In: Zheng, Z., Dai, H.-N., Tang, M., Chen, X. (eds.) BlockSys 2019. CCIS, vol. 1156, pp. 549–562. Springer, Singapore (2020). https://doi.org/10.1007/978-981-15-2777-7_44
5. Ermilov, D., Panov, M., Yanovich, Y.: Automatic bitcoin address clustering. In: 2017 16th IEEE International Conference on Machine Learning and Applications (ICMLA), pp. 461–466. IEEE (2017)
6. Jourdan, M., Blandin, S., Wynter, L., Deshpande, P.: Characterizing entities in the bitcoin blockchain. In: 2018 IEEE International Conference on Data Mining Workshops (ICDMW), pp. 55–62. IEEE (2018)
7. Khalilov, M.C.K., Levi, A.: A survey on anonymity and privacy in bitcoin-like digital cash systems. IEEE Commun. Surv. Tutor. **20**(3), 2543–2585 (2018)
8. Reid, F., Harrigan, M.: An analysis of anonymity in the bitcoin system. In: Altshuler, Y., Elovici, Y., Cremers, A., Aharony, N., Pentland, A. (eds.) Security and Privacy in Social Networks, pp. 197–223. Springer, New York (2013). https://doi.org/10.1007/978-1-4614-4139-7_10

9. Di Francesco Maesa, D., Marino, A., Ricci, L.: An analysis of the Bitcoin users graph: inferring unusual behaviours. In: COMPLEX NETWORKS 2016 2016. SCI, vol. 693, pp. 749–760. Springer, Cham (2017). https://doi.org/10.1007/978-3-319-50901-3_59

10. Di Francesco, D., Maesa, A.M., Ricci, L.: Detecting artificial behaviours in the bitcoin users graph. Online Soc. Netw. Media **3**, 63–74 (2017)

11. McGinn, D., Birch, D., Akroyd, D., Molina-Solana, M., Guo, Y., Knottenbelt, W.J.: Visualizing dynamic bitcoin transaction patterns. Big Data **4**(2), 109–119 (2016)

12. Bartoletti, M., Carta, S., Cimoli, T., Saia, R.: Dissecting Ponzi schemes on Ethereum: identification, analysis, and impact. Futur. Gener. Comput. Syst. **102**, 259–277 (2020)

13. Bartoletti, M., Pes, B., Serusi, S.: Data mining for detecting bitcoin Ponzi schemes. In: 2018 Crypto Valley Conference on Blockchain Technology (CVCBT), pp. 75–84. IEEE (2018)

14. Chen, W., Zheng, Z., Cui, J., Ngai, E., Zheng, P., Zhou, Y.: Detecting Ponzi schemes on Ethereum: towards healthier blockchain technology. In: Proceedings of the 2018 World Wide Web Conference, pp. 1409–1418 (2018)

15. Vasek, M., Moore, T.: Analyzing the bitcoin Ponzi scheme ecosystem. In: Zohar, A., et al. (eds.) FC 2018. LNCS, vol. 10958, pp. 101–112. Springer, Heidelberg (2019). https://doi.org/10.1007/978-3-662-58820-8_8

16. Moore, T., Christin, N.: Beware the middleman: empirical analysis of bitcoin-exchange risk. In: Sadeghi, A.-R. (ed.) FC 2013. LNCS, vol. 7859, pp. 25–33. Springer, Heidelberg (2013). https://doi.org/10.1007/978-3-642-39884-1_3

17. Li, X., Wang, C.A.: The technology and economic determinants of cryptocurrency exchange rates: the case of bitcoin. Decis. Support Syst. **95**, 49–60 (2017)

18. Giudici, P., Abu-Hashish, I.: What determines bitcoin exchange prices? A network VAR approach. Financ. Res. Lett. **28**, 309–318 (2019)

19. Wang, H., He, D., Ji, Y.: Designated-verifier proof of assets for bitcoin exchange using elliptic curve cryptography. Futur. Gener. Comput. Syst. **107**, 854–862 (2020)

20. Wu, J., Liu, J., Chen, W., Huang, H., Zheng, Z., Zhang, Y.: Detecting mixing services via mining bitcoin transaction network with hybrid motifs. arXiv preprint arXiv:2001.05233 (2020)

21. Gaihre, A., Pandey, S., Liu, H.: Deanonymizing cryptocurrency with graph learning: the promises and challenges. In: 2019 IEEE Conference on Communications and Network Security (CNS), pp. 1–3. IEEE (2019)

22. Cui, J., Wu, H., Fu, L., Gan, X.: De-anonymizing bitcoin networks: an IP matching method via heuristic approach: poster. In: Proceedings of the ACM Turing Celebration Conference-China, pp. 1–2 (2019)

23. Meiklejohn, S., et al.: A fistful of bitcoins: characterizing payments among men with no names. In: Proceedings of the 2013 Conference on Internet Measurement Conference, pp. 127–140 (2013)

Theories and Algorithms for Blockchain

Modeling and Analysis of Blockchain Trading Network Based on Directed Time Weighted Random Walk

Miao Wang, Ruizhi Sun$^{(\boxtimes)}$, and HuiYu Mu

College of Information and Electrical Engineering, China Agricultural University, Beijing, China
{s20193081360,sunruizhi,b20183080630}@cau.edu.cn

Abstract. Blockchain technology as an emerging technology is widely concerned by researchers. However, the unique characteristics of blockchain data make the blockchain data analysis full of challenges. Blockchain data has not only spatial characteristics, but also temporal characteristics. The blockchain trading network is greatly different from the traditional network, and the modeling method based on simple graph cannot accurately describe the blockchain trading network. In order to more accurately describe the transaction information between entities in the blockchain trading network, the time weighted multigraph is used to model the blockchain trading network. According to the characteristics of blockchain trading network, this paper designs a new random walk strategy for blockchain trading network, directed time weighted random walk strategy. By introducing the concept of candidate neighbor node in the transaction network, different candidate neighbor nodes can be generated according to different parameters, and different candidate neighbor nodes of the same node can be studied. The random walk is evaluated by using link prediction the graph embedded downstream task on the real dataset. Finally, the sensitivity of the introduced parameters is analyzed. The experimental results show that the AUC value and AP value of the proposed directed time weighted random walk are 87.44 and 85.57 in link prediction, which prove the effectiveness of the proposed method.

Keywords: Blockchain trading network · Complex network · Time weighted multigraph · Random walk · Link prediction

1 Introduction

Blockchain is a popular integrated technology in recent years. Since its birth, it has been widely welcomed by people from all walks of life and known as a new technology that triggers social changes. Blockchain has the characteristics of decentralization, openness, tamper resistance, anonymity, traceability and so on, which improves the security of data. Blockchain is widely used in various industries. For instance, Blockchain theory builds an integrated platform based on mobile fingerprint recognition [1] to prevent hackers from changing fingerprint information. The blockchain technology is expected to improve the security, immutability, and decentralization of wireless communication through smart

© Springer Nature Singapore Pte Ltd. 2021
H.-N. Dai et al. (Eds.): BlockSys 2021, CCIS 1490, pp. 275–286, 2021.
https://doi.org/10.1007/978-981-16-7993-3_21

contract and distributed ledgers [2] and promotes the development of the autonomous driving industry. A typical example of blockchain application is digital currency. Since the birth of Blockchain 1.0, represented by Bitcoin [3], it has accumulated a large amount of user transaction data. Since the birth of blockchain 2.0, represented by Ethereum [4], it has enriched the data types of blockchain. With the continuous development of blockchain technology, the data in blockchain is constantly increasing, but only the data obtained after data analysis is the valuable data.

Complex networks are a general tool for analyzing actual working systems in different fields and have been used to model and analyze huge transactional networks in various fields, such as future avionics system [5], heatwave patterns and propagations over the USA [6], scenarios for cascade water reservoirs for mitigating drought and flood impacts [7], etc. Complex networks are also used to model and analyze huge networks of blockchain systems. In 2018, Chen [8] et al. conducted the first systematic study on Ethereum by leveraging graph analysis to characterize three major activities on Ethereum, namely money transfer, smart contract creation, and smart contract invocation. Alqassem [3] et al. analyzed the evolution of the Bitcoin exchange graph, showing the general dynamics of typical social networks.

In the blockchain trading network, each edge represents a specific transaction event. The transaction information includes transaction hash, timestamp, transaction input address, transaction output address, total transaction input amount, total transaction output amount, and so on. In order to accurately model and describe transaction events on the blockchain, it is extremely important to accurately integrate transaction information. Multigraph is more suitable for modeling blockchain trading networks than simple graph. Multigraph is a graph that allows a self-loop and multiple parallel edges, as opposed to a simple graph. Modeling the transaction events of the blockchain network as multigraph can more accurately capture the temporal nature of the network and the characteristics of multiple transactions.

Random walk [9] is a mathematical statistical model used to represent irregular variation forms, which has been proved to be an effective technique to measure the local similarity of networks. As an ideal mathematical state of Brownian motion, random walk is close to Brownian motion and has become a common sampling method in graph representation [10], so as to represent a large number of network nodes in a low-dimensional space and be used for graph analysis and graph data mining. Most graph representation learning methods are used to mine social networks [11] etc.

To solve the above problems, we represent the blockchain trading network based on the graph representation learning method of random walk. Firstly, we model the trading events in the blockchain trading network based on time weighted multigraph. Secondly, we propose a new time weighted graph sampling and representation method with control conditions. Finally, we conduct network structure statistical experiment and link prediction experiment to prove the effectiveness of the graph modeling and graph mining methods.

2 Related Research

2.1 Complex Networks

Complex network [12] originated from graph theory and topology in the field of mathematics. Complex network abstracts entities in real life into nodes in the network and abstracts the relations between entities into edges in the network. The parameters commonly used in complex networks are degree, degree distribution, clustering coefficient, intermediate number and so on. Degree reflects the number of relationships established between this node and other nodes, and further reflects the importance of this node. The probability distribution of node degree in the network is the degree distribution of the complex network, that is, the probability that the degree value of node vi is K.

2.2 Time Weighted Multigraph

A graph [13] is composed of a finite non-empty set of vertices and a set of edges between vertices, which is usually expressed as: $G = (V, E)$, where G represents a graph, V is the set of vertices in G, and E is the set of edges in G. Graphs can be divided into simple graphs and multiple graphs. A simple graph is one that does not contain self-ring and parallel edges. A time-weighted multiplex with time attribute and weight attribute.

Definition 1: Time Weighted Multigraph (TWMDG)

Given a graph G, $G = (V, E)$, V represents the nodes that make up the complex network, E represents the edges that make up the complex network, and each edge is unique. It is expressed as $e = (s, d, w, t)$ where s represents the start node, d represents the target node, w represents the weight, and t represents the timestamp.

2.3 Random Walk

The definition of time random walk [14] is as follows.

Given a source node and simulating a time random walk of fixed length L, the distribution of its nodes is shown in Formula 1.

$$p(v_v = d | v_{i-1} = s) = \begin{cases} \dfrac{\pi vxf(e(t))}{Z \sum_{e \in ner(v_{i-1})} f(e(t))} & \textbf{if}(d, s) \in E \\ \quad 0 & \textbf{otherwise} \end{cases} \tag{1}$$

Where, e(t) represents the time of edge e, f(e(t)) means that t is sorted according to certain principles, and ner(v_{i-1}) represents the neighbor node with time continuous edge of the current node. Πvx represents the de-normalized transition probability between d and s, and Z is the normalization constant.

Weighted random walk [15] is defined as follows.

Given a source node, and simulated a weight random walk of fixed length L, the distribution of its nodes is shown in Eq. 2.

$$p(v_v = d | v_{i-1} = s) = \begin{cases} \dfrac{\pi vxg(e(w))}{Z \sum_{e \in ner(v_{i-1})} \sum_{e \in ner(v_{i-1})} g(e(w))} & \textbf{if}(d, s) \in E \\ \quad 0 & \textbf{otherwise} \end{cases} \tag{2}$$

Where e(w) is the weight of edge e, and g(e(w)) is the mapping function of e(w).

3   Network Construction

Ethereum, the poster child for blockchain 2.0, has amassed a rich record of transactions. However, the complex topology of Ethereum trading network makes it difficult to analyze and study the network. A large number of studies have shown that complex networks can well simulate complex systems in real life. Therefore, we use complex network theory to study the transaction network of block chain. In a transaction, the transaction entity is represented by the address of the transaction input and the address of the transaction output. In this way, blockchain transaction is abstracted into a network, which is symbolically represented as $G = (V, E)$, where $V = \{v_1, v_2, \ldots v_i\}$ represents the entity of the transaction, represented by a node in the network, $E = \{e_{i1}, e_{i2\ldots}e_{ij}\}$ represents a successful transaction between two parties to the transaction and is represented by an edge between node v_i and node v_j in the network. G stands for the entire network diagram, blockchain trading network.

Blockchain trading network has a complex topology and a large number of transaction data. A situation where there are multiple transactions between entities. Thus, the transaction entity cannot be used as a unique identification of a transaction. As shown in the Fig. 1, $\{v_2, v_3\}$ can represent the relevant information of transaction ⑥, $\{v_2, v_4\}$ can represent the relevant information of transaction ⑦, $\{v_2, v_5\}$ can represent the relevant information of transaction ⑧, but, transactions ①②③④⑤ can not be simply expressed by $\{v_1, v_2\}$. In order to better describe the transaction information, a time weighted multigraph is adopted to model the blockchain trading network.

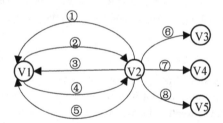

Fig. 1. Schematic diagram of a typical blockchain trading network

In the blockchain trading network, there is a huge amount of information flowing. The general transaction information includes the transaction hash, time stamp, the transaction input address, the transaction output address, the transaction total input amount, the transaction total output amount, etc. The transaction hash is the unique identification of the transaction, the timestamp indicates the time of the transaction, the address of the transaction input is the seller, the address of the transaction output is the buyer, the difference between the total transaction input and the total transaction output is the amount of the transaction. Thus, Blockchain trading network abstraction for quad (sellers, purchasers, money, time), purchasers use money to trade with sellers at time. A quad can be used as a unique identifier for a transaction. In order to study the transaction information of the blockchain trading network, the blockchain trading network is abstracted into a time weighted multigraph. We define a TWMDG where each node represents the unique entity participating in the transaction and each edge represents the unique transaction of the blockchain. Modeling blockchain transactions based on complex networks can more clearly describe the transaction information.

4   Graph Representation Learning Based on Random Walk

Through the analysis of the characteristics of the blockchain trading network, it is found that, regardless of the size of the network, the degree distribution of the nodes in the network is mainly concentrated in the small degree value part. With the increase of the degree value, the probability of degree distribution becomes smaller. This indicates that most entities do not have extensive business connections, and the degree distribution pattern is in the form of power law, as shown in Fig. 2. The graph representation learning method based on random walk has been proved to be extensible and effective for large graphs. The sampling method based on random walk can effectively preserve the power law property of graph.

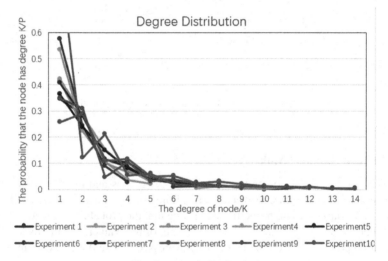

Fig. 2. Degree distribution

4.1   Time Random Walk

In the graph structure, the time walk from node V1 to VL is an l-length path traversed in non-decreasing timestamps. For example, a time walk is a set of nodes, $l = \{v_1, v_2, \ldots, v_l\}$, the corresponding edge is a set of edges, $e = \{e_1, e_2, \ldots, e_{l-1}\}$, $\text{Sre}(e_i) = v_i$, $\text{Dst}(e_i) = v_{i+1}$, $\{1 \leq i \leq (l-1)\}$, $\text{T}(e_i) = \text{T}(e_{i+1})$, $\{1 \leq i \leq (l-2)\}$.

Blockchain transaction network is a chronological network, as shown in Fig. 3. Cur represents the current node, and T represents the time when the transaction takes place. The larger the value of T, the later the transaction takes place. In the random walk method, if the current node is cur, then the probability that the next node is V2, V3 and V4 is the same. However, if the last travel path of the current node cur is ②, the probability that the path of ③④⑦⑧ is the next travel path is 0 because the occurrence time of path ② is later than the path ③④⑦⑧, then the probability that the next node is V2 and V3 is 0. Therefore, the time random walk approach is more suitable for the transaction network of blockchain. Thus, a time random walk is adopted, and the sequence of sampling nodes is a time continuous edge, that is, the time of the edge through which the walk goes is an ascending sequence or a descending sequence.

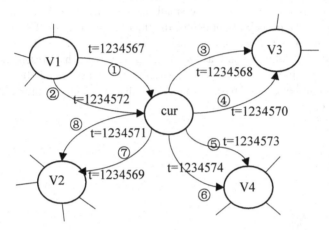

Fig. 3. Schematic diagram of network with time attribute

4.2 Weighted Random Walk

In the network, the theory of finite discrete Markov chains and the theory of random walk are essentially the same, so every discrete finite Markov chain is considered to be a random walk. Markov chain properties determine that the probability of a node moving to a neighbor node is independent of the past state of the walker. In Markov's process, the transition probability from node S to E is expressed by Pse (t), as shown in Eq. 3.

$$\mathbf{P_{se}} = \frac{\mathbf{A_{se}}}{\sum_{i \in V} \mathbf{A_{si}}} \tag{3}$$

Where, s,e ∈ V,V represents the set composed of nodes, and A_{se} represents the weight between nodes s and e. The greater the weight between nodes s and e, the greater the probability of transition between the two points.

Blockchain trading network is a weighted network, as shown in Fig. 4, where cur represents the current node and M represents the transaction amount. The larger the value of M, the greater the transaction volume. In the random walk method, if the current node is CUR, then the probability of the next random walk node is V2, V3 and V4 is the same, which does not conform to the definition of Formula 3. Therefore, the weighted random walk method is more suitable for the trading network of blockchain. Weighted random walk is adopted, and trading volume is used as the weight of probability transfer.

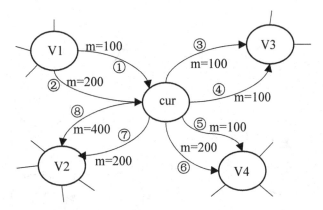

Fig. 4. Schematic diagram of network with weight attribute

4.3 Directed Time Weighted Random Walk

In all of the above methods, there is a common variable, which is the neighbor node. In different traversal methods of the graph, the same node has different neighbor nodes. As shown in Fig. 5, cur is the current node. If the previous node of the current node is V1, the current node is reached through the path ①. When traversing with depth-first search, the neighbor nodes of cur are {V4, V5, V6}; when traversing with breadth-first search, the neighbor nodes of cur are {V3, V4}. The results of the breadth-first search are the immediate neighbors of the current node, and the local features of the node are extracted. The result of depth-first search is the depth node of the current node, and the global features of the node are extracted. Breadth-first search mainly reflects the isomorphism of nodes, while depth-first search mainly reflects the homogeneity of nodes. In order to conduct sampling more flexibly, the direction parameter β is added on the basis of the time weighted random walk, so that the isomorphism and homogeneity of the network can be studied in the sampling. The definition of β is shown in Formula 4.

$$\beta(\text{pre, des}) = \begin{cases} 1 & \text{if hop(pre, des)} = 1 \\ \frac{1}{k} & \text{if hop(pre, des)} = 2 \end{cases} \tag{4}$$

Where, pre represents the previous node of the current node, and des represents the next node of the current node, $hop(pre, des)$ is the number of hops between pre and des. K is the control parameter of the search mode. When k > 1, it means that the current search mode is breadth-first search, and when 0 < k < 1, it means that the current search mode is depth-first search.

Based on the analysis of block chain trading network, a directed time weighted random walk for blockchain trading network is proposed.

Directed time weighted random walk is defined as follows.

Given a source node and simulating a directed time random wk of fixed length L, the distribution of its nodes is shown in Formula 5.

$$p(v_v = d | v_{i-1} = s) = \begin{cases} \dfrac{\pi\, vxf(e(t))g(e(w))\beta}{Z\sum_{e\in ner(v_{i-1})} f(e(t)) \sum_{e\in ner(v_{i-1})} g(e(w))} & \text{if}(d,s)\epsilon E \\ 0 & \text{otherwise} \end{cases} \tag{5}$$

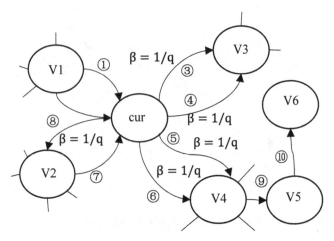

Fig. 5. A network schematic with direction

5   Experimental Analysis

Different random walk strategies are adopted in order to better retain the attributes of the network and provide basic preparation for downstream tasks. In general, the downstream tasks of evaluation graph representation learning are link prediction and node classification. The task of link prediction aims to predict the occurrence of links in a given graph based on observed information. Embedding explicitly or implicitly captures the inherent dynamics of the network, enabling applications to link predictions. Wang et al. [16] predicted the links represented by learning nodes on publicly accessible collaborations and social networks. Grover et al. [17] applied it to biological networks. They show that on these data sets, the link using embedded prediction is more accurate than the traditional similarity based link prediction method described above. In this section, link prediction is used to evaluate our proposed graph embedding model.

5.1   Dataset

We use the transaction data of Ethereum as the real data of the experiment. This dataset contains timestamp, transaction input address, transaction output address, total transaction input amount, total transaction output amount and other information. The dataset used in this paper has a total of 67,954 records, each of which is composed of four elements, namely, the starting address, the ending address, the transaction amount and the transaction time, and a total of 271,816 data.

5.2   Evaluation Index

The selected evaluation indexes are AUC [18], average accuracy (AP), precision (P), recall rate (R) and F1 value. Where, AUC is the area under the ROC curve, and AP is the graphic area enclosed by the PR curve and the X axis. P is the proportion of correct numbers among the results predicted as positive classes. R is the proportion of samples that are actually positive and correctly judged to be positive. F1 is the weighted harmonic mean of P and R, and is a comprehensive index to balance the influence of P and R. Definitions are shown in Formula (6–10).

$$AUC = S(ROC) \tag{6}$$

$$AP = S(TPR) \tag{7}$$

$$P = \frac{TP}{TP + FP} \times 100\% \tag{8}$$

$$R = \frac{TP}{TP + FN} \times 100\% \tag{9}$$

$$F1 = \frac{2 \times P \times R}{P + R} \times 100\% \tag{10}$$

Where, TP, Predict the positive case to be true; FN, The positive example is predicted to be false; FP, Predict the counter example to be true; TN, The counter example is predicted to be false.

5.3 Link Prediction

The experiments are carried out based on random walk, time random walk, weighted random walk, time weighted random walk and directed time weighted random walk. The dataset is randomly divided into test set and training set. 1 means there are edges between nodes, and 0 means there are no edges between nodes. We use the same kind of support vector machine method (SVM) for prediction. The SVM is fitted according to the given training set. The results are shown in Table 1.

The results show that the best result is obtained based on the directed time weighted random walk. The specific analysis is as follows: AUC, AP, 0-P, 0-F1, 1-P, 1-R, 1-F1 get the maximum value based on directed time weighted random walk method, and 0-R get the maximum value based on random walk method. The results obtained by the time random walk method and the weighted random walk method are better than those obtained by the random walk method. It is proved that time attribute and volume attribute are relatively important characteristics in the blockchain trading network. The combination of time attribute and trading volume attribute can take into account the characteristics of blockchain trading network in a more comprehensive way, so the result based on time weighted random walk is better than the first three. The transaction network of blockchain not only has the isomorphism of the network, but also has the homogeneity of the network. Isomorphism refers to the entities that act as a bridge in the blockchain trading network, while homogeneity refers to the communities that frequently trade entities in the blockchain trading network. Thus, the best result is obtained on the directed time weighted random walk.

Table 1. Resulting data

Method	AUC	AP	0-P	0-R	0-F1	1-P	1-R	1-F1
Time random walk	77.37	75.68	0.70	0.96	0.81	0.94	0.59	0.72
Weighted random walk	77.46	75.85	0.70	0.96	0.81	0.94	0.59	0.72
Time weighted random walk	79.27	77.48	0.72	0.96	0.82	0.94	0.63	0.75
Directed time weighted random walk	87.44	85.57	0.82	0.96	0.88	0.95	0.79	0.86

5.4 Parameter Sensitivity

In order to obtain the isomorphism and homogeneity of the blockchain trading network flexibly, we put forward the control parameter β. According to Eq. (3), when k > 1, it ndicates that the current search method is breadth-first search, when 0 < k < 1, it means the current search method is depth-first search. When all other parameters are fixed, the influence of K on the model performance is studied. Macro average [1, 19, 20] is used as a performance indicator. The macro average is the arithmetic average of the performance metrics for each class. Macro-Precision($\overline{P}$), Macro-Recall($\overline{R}$), Macro-F1($\overline{F_1}$) is the evaluation index. The calculation formula is shown in (11–13). When 0 < k < 1, the K value is 0.1, 0.2, 3,0.4, 0.5, 0.6, 7,0.8, 0.9. When k > 1, the K value is 2,3,4,5,6,7,8. When K = 1, the control parameters are in an invalid state, and the search mode cannot be controlled. The experimental results are shown in Fig. 6.

$$\overline{P} = \frac{\sum_{c_i \in C} P_C}{|C|} \tag{11}$$

$$\overline{R} = \frac{\sum_{c_i \in C} R_C}{|C|} \tag{12}$$

$$\overline{F_1} = \frac{\sum_{c_i \in C} F_{1C}}{|C|} \tag{13}$$

The results show that the introduced direction parameter β has a certain disturbance to the experimental results. Specific analysis is as follows. When k > 1, it indicates that the current search method is breadth-first search. With the change of k value, the macro average value is in a state of fluctuation with a small fluctuation range. Thus, local features have less impact on the blockchain trading network. When 0 < k < 1, it indicates that the current search method is depth-first search. With the change of k value, the macro average value is in a wide range of fluctuations. Thus, global features have a greater impact on the blockchain trading network. Throughout the chart, the maximum values appear more frequently in the 0 < k < 1 section. When k = 0.3, the macro average value reaches the peak. Thus, global features are more important than local features in the blockchain trading network.

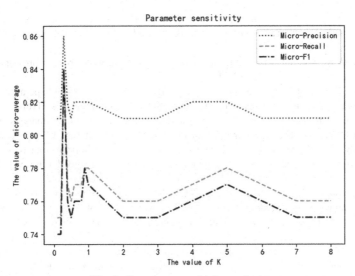

Fig. 6. Parameter sensitivity analysis

6 Conclusion

In this paper, the dynamic characteristics of complex network are used to model the blockchain trading network. A modeling method based on time weighted multigraph is adopted to distinguish the multiple transactions between the two sides of the transaction, and to describe the blockchain trading network more accurately. The feature learning of network is divided into local feature and global feature by using different graph searching methods. Depth-first search can obtain the global characteristics of the network, while breadth-first search can obtain the local characteristics of the network. Based on the modeling, a directed time weighted random walk algorithm is proposed to obtain more accurate graph features, which lays a foundation for blockchain transaction tracking.

Acknowledgement. This research was funded in part by Collaborative Precision Location Service Application for Mass Users (2016YFB0501805-1) and National Development and Reform Commission Integrated Data Service System Foundation Platform Construction Project (JZNYYY001).

References

1. Huh, J.H., Seo, K.: Blockchain-based mobile fingerprint verification and automatic log-in platform for future computing. J. Supercomput. (2019)
2. Jameel, F., Javed, M.A., Zeadally, S., et al.: Efficient mining cluster selection for blockchain-based cellular V2X communications. IEEE Trans. Intell. Transp. Syst. (2020)
3. Alqassem, I., Rahwan, I., Svetinovic, D.: The anti-social system properties: bitcoin network data analysis. IEEE Trans. Syst. Man Cybern. Syst. 1–11 (2018)
4. Corbet, S., Lucey, B.M., Yarovaya, L.: Datestamping the bitcoin and ethereum bubbles. Soc. Sci. Electron. Publ. (2017)

5. Huo, D., Ouyang, R., Sun, B., et al.: Complex network of aviation e-services in the belt and road initiative: a heuristic study of small data based on block modeling. Emerg. Markets Financ. Trade (2019)

6. Mishra, A.K., Mondal, S.: Complex networks reveal heatwave patterns and propagations over the USA. Geophys. Res. Lett. (2020)

7. Ren, K., Huang, Q., Huang, S., et al.: Identifying complex networks and operating scenarios for cascade water reservoirs for mitigating drought and flood impacts. J. Hydrol. (2021)

8. Chen, T., Zhu, Y., Li, Z., et al.: Understanding Ethereum via graph analysis. In: 'IEEE INFOCOM 2018 - IEEE Conference on Computer Communications. IEEE (2018)

9. Chen, X., Xu, M., An, Y.: Identifying the essential nodes in network pharmacology based on multilayer network combined with random walk algorithm. J. Biomed. Inform. **114**, 103666 (2020)

10. Angstmann, C.N., Henry, B.I., Mcgann, A.V.: Time-fractional geometric Brownian motion from continuous time random walks. Phys. A: Stat. Mech. Appl. 526 (2019)

11. Sweet, T.M., Flynt, A., Choi, D.: Clustering ensembles of social networks. Netw. Sci. 1–19 (2019)

12. Lu, W., Wen, B.: Construction and research of education emergency network model based on complex network-a case study of child abuse incident in Beijing RYB education pre-school. In: 2020 IEEE 2nd International Conference on Computer Science and Educational Informatization (CSEI). IEEE (2020)

13. Alolaiyan, H., Yousaf, A., Ameer, M., et al.: Non-conjugate graphs associated with finite groups. IEEE Access (2019)

14. Klamut, J., Gubiec, T.: Directed continuous-time random walk with memory. Phys. Condens. Matter **92**(4), 69 (2019)

15. Xu, B., Guan, J., Wang, Y., et al.: Essential protein detection by random walk on weighted protein-protein interaction networks. IEEE/ACM Trans. Comput. Biol. Bioinf. **16**(2), 377–387 (2019)

16. Wang, D., Cui, P., Zhu, W.: Structural deep network embedding. In: Proceedings of the 22nd International Conference on Knowledge Discovery and Data Mining, ACM, pp. 1225–1234 (2016)

17. Grover, A., Leskovec, J.: node2vec: scalable feature learning for net-works. In: Proceedings of the 22nd International Conference on Knowledge Discovery and Data Mining, ACM, pp. 855–864 (2016)

18. Cheng, F., Fu, G., Zhang, X., et al.: Multi-objective evolutionary algorithm for optimizing the partial area under the ROC curve. Knowl.-Based Syst. **170**(Apr 15), 61–69 (2019)

19. Kim, K.M., Kim, Y., Lee, J., et al.: From Small-scale to large-scale text classification. In: The World Wide Web Conference (2019)

20. Eason, G., Noble, B., Sneddon, I.N.: On certain integrals of Lipschitz-Hankel type involving products of Bessel functions. Phil. Trans. Roy. Soc. London **A247**, 529–551, Apr 1955

A Scalable and Secure Consensus Scheme Based on Proof of Stake in Blockchain

Fayuan Zhu[1], Jie Yin[1(✉)], Lei Liu[2], Jie Feng[2], and Zhangquan Wang[3]

[1] State Key Laboratory of ISN, School of Telecommunications Engineering, Xidian University, Xi'an 710126, China
yinjie0003@stu.xidian.edu.cn
[2] Shaanxi Key Laboratory of Blockchain and Secure Computing, Xi'an 710071, China
[3] The 601th Institute, the 6th Academy, China Aerospace Science and Industry Corporation, Hohhot 010076, China

Abstract. As a decentralized database, the public blockchain has broad application prospects in many fields such as finance, healthcare, and supply chain, so it is getting more and more attention. The current mainstream public blockchain protocol based on Proof of Work (PoW) cannot be applied to various extendable application scenarios with performance requirements due to performance bottlenecks. Proof of Stake (PoS) circumvents the performance bottleneck of PoW by utilizing equity instead of computing power. However, ordinary PoS protocols still have security problems for they are vulnerable to nothing-at-stake attacks, and rely on third parties to support dynamic availability. In this paper, we propose a novel scalable and secure PoS consensus scheme to support the application of public blockchain in various extendable scenarios. We classify nodes in different states and perform node state transitions through different protocols. Combining stake mechanism with consensus schemes and using dynamic stake proportion table to support dynamic stake scenario, we propose a block compression method to reduce the communication consumption of consensus. We propose a chain selection rule based on Verifiable Random Function (VRF) nonce and longest chain rule, which supports dynamic availability without third parties. In addition, we prove the security of our scheme and analyze its performance at general security threats. Finally, experimental results show that our scheme have better system performance and better scalability under the same condition.

Keywords: Blockchain · Consensus · PoS · Chain selection · Scalability

1 Introduction

Consensus mechanism is the core and cornerstone of public chain. PoW has become the prevailate consensus mechanism of public chain because of its simplicity, practicality and provable security, such as Bitcoin [1] et al. However,

© Springer Nature Singapore Pte Ltd. 2021
H.-N. Dai et al. (Eds.): BlockSys 2021, CCIS 1490, pp. 287–301, 2021.
https://doi.org/10.1007/978-981-16-7993-3_22

energy consumption and performance barrier make it hard to apply to various extendable scenarios. PoS [2] is an energy-efficient public chain consensus framework, it uses stake to replace computing power for leader election. PoS overcomes the shortcomings of PoW and is a popular alternative of it. However, PoS chain is more susceptible to nothing-at-stake attacks from malicious nodes, so its security cannot be ascertained.

Related work about PoS protocol is mainly based on Byzantine Fault Tolerance (BFT) and the longest-chain-rule [17]. BFT-based PoS protocol [3,4] selects candidates to form a committee based on nodes' stake and guarantees the security of the protocol by BFT, therefore increases the communication consumption of the consensus. In addition, the scalability of the protocol is also limited by BFT. The longest-chain-rule-based PoS protocol [5–9] uses stake proportion for leader election and longest-chain rule for block synchronization. It avoids the scalability limitation of the front and its communication consumption is low. However, its security cannot be guaranteed, and nodes are vulnerable to bribery attacks [4], and it relys on a third party to support dynamic availability, which reduces the decentralized property of public chain.

In this paper, we propose a novel scalable and secure PoS consensus scheme which has an independent equity mechanism and does not rely on third parties to satisfy dynamic availability. We utilize a block compression method to enhance the efficiency of consensus, which increases the system performance of public blockchain. Meanwhile, it has a provable security under the standard blockchain attributes and could defend other threats.

Our contributions are as follows:

1) We propose a novel blockchain protocol based on PoS, which combines stake mechanism and consensus scheme, applies dynamic stake proportion table to support dynamic stake scenario, and utilizes a block compression method to reduce the consumption of the block propagation in a distributed network, which could improve the system performance efficiently.
2) We present a chain selection rule based on VRF nonce and longest-chain rule, and then propose a block synchronization protocol based on it, which can support dynamic availability without trusted third parties, further strengthen the decentralization attribute, and effectively circumvent single point effects.
3) We propose a scalable and secure PoS consensus scheme with an independent stake mechanism, which has a stronger provable security and better scalability. It has been proven to meet the security attributes of the blockchain, and the proportion of stake fault tolerance of the protocol also performs well.

The rest of this paper is as follows. The tools and model assumptions will be introduced in the next section. Section 3 illustrates the system model and detailed design of the scheme. Security analysis is given in Sect. 4, and Sect. 5 presents the experiments and results. Section 6 introduces the related works and Sect. 7 gives the conclusion and discussion.

2   Tools and Model Assumptions

In this Section, we introduce the VRF and KES tools used in our scheme, and explain the clock model, communication model and security model assumptions, and finally give our design goals, which could better expound our scheme.

Tools. We use two tools to improve the security of our scheme.

Verifiable Random Function (VRF). VRF [11] is a non-interactive verifiable nonce algorithm based on an asymmetric encryption algorithm, which guarantees the uniformity, verifiability and security of the generated nonce. It has two participants: prover uses secret key SK and a random seed to calculate VRF nonce and proof, verifiers use the homologous verifiable key VK and other public information to verify it. VRF was applied to PoS scheme design in [3,6–8,16].

Key Evolving Signature schemes (KES). KES [12] is a forward signature scheme, which periodically generates a new key pair based on the original key and destroys the old key. It can effectively prevent malicious nodes from modifying the transaction information of stored blocks, and ensure that the security of data.

Models. Public chain is an open and distributed network and its clock is uncertain. To avoid other interferences, we have 3 models below:

Clock Model. We assume the consensus time (the time of each round of the block generation protocol) is determinate, and the consensus node could get the same current timestamp when its network is normal.

Network Model. The communication between nodes is partially synchronized, that means messages sent by nodes can arrive within the maximum delay Δt_{delay}, and the messages are invalid when their reachable time beyond Δt_{delay}.

Security Model. The security threats of our scheme mainly come from Byzantine [11] nodes. The biggest security threat is nothing-at-stake attack [4], which malicious nodes could expand various chains at a extremely low cost to make chain diverges. Bribery attacks is also a inevitable problem, we assume that it's only feasible to few honest nodes.

Goals. Based on the tools and models above, our PoS consensus scheme should have dynamic availability, scalability, and provable security.

Dynamic Availability. The public chain is an open network that nodes can join and exit at any time. Unsynchronized honest nodes could synchronize the longest chain dominated by honest nodes by executing our protocol.

Scalability. The communication consumption of distributed networks increases rapidly with the increase of the number of nodes, our scheme needs to enhance the efficiency of consensus and have a high system performance to make public chain more scalable.

Provable Safety. our scheme should have provable security under the models above, which means it meets the three standard security attributes of the blockchain chain growth, common prefix and chain quality.

3   Scalable Consensus Scheme Based on Proof-of-Stake

In this Section, we specifically introduce our PoS consensus scheme. We classify the nodes in the network into 3 types: new nodes, unsynchronized nodes and synchronized nodes according to their states. Then we propose three protocols: node registration, block generation and block synchronization, which node could execute them for state transition. In order to combine stake mechanism with our scheme, we initialize the stake value in node's registration transaction in *NodeRegistration* protocol. We propose a candidate block compression method in *BlockGeneration* protocol to reduce the communication consumption of consensus. In *BlockSynchronization* protocol, we use the longest-chain-rule and VRF nonce to propose a new chain selection rule, so that our scheme supports dynamic availability without third parties.

3.1   System Model

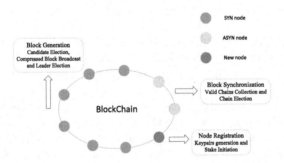

Fig. 1. Overview of system model.

Figure 1 is an overview of our model, there is a peer-to-peer network in our system model, it includes three types of new nodes: synchronized nodes, and unsynchronized nodes. And our scheme involves three protocols: *NodeRegistration*, *BlockGeneration* and *BlockSynchronization*. Synchronized nodes have synchronized to the latest block and have the longest chain, while unsynchronized nodes doesn't synchronize to the latest block due to network failures or other additions. Only synchronous nodes can participate in the consensus to compete to become the leader to generate new blocks.

NodeRegistration protocol includes two stages: key pair generation and equity initialization. *BlockGeneration* protocol includes three stages: candidate election, compressed block broadcast and leader election. *BlockSynchronization* protocol includes two stages: legal chain collection and chain selection.

3.2   Scheme Design

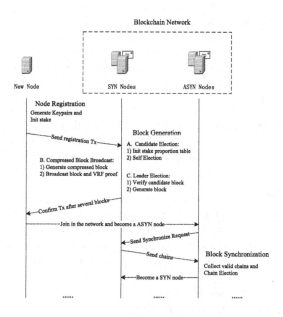

Fig. 2. Scheme overview.

Scheme Overview. Figure 2 is the overview of our view, the state of the nodes in the system is as dynamic as the real scene, and can transform to another state by executing the homologous protocol, or keep the original state:

1) The new node executes the node registration protocol to join the network. After the transaction is confirmed, the node registers successfully and becomes an unsynchronized node.
2) The unsynchronized node executes the block synchronization protocol to become a synchronized node. After the synchronization is completed, it become a synchronized node.
3) The synchronization node executes the block generation protocol to maintain the synchronization state. If the execution is successful, it will remain synchronized state, otherwise it will become an unsynchronized node.

Node Registration. In the original PoS protocol, stake is the token in the incentive mechanism, which is negative to the development of public chains. We separate the stake mechanism from the incentive mechanism and make it a independent part of our PoS consensus scheme. For each new node N_i, it performs the following initialization processing respectively.

Init. Generate Keypairs and Init Stake. N_i generate KES keypairs PK_i^{kes} and SK_i^{kes} to sign and verify the node information to ensure the authenticity of it. Then it uses random input 1^k and $KeyGen(*)$ to generate VRF keypairs VK_i^{vrf} and SK_i^{vrf}. Nodes use SK_i^{vrf} to generate nonces and proofs for candidate election, use VK_i^{vrf} to verify the proof to ensure the unforgeability of VRF nonces. N_i inits its stake value w_i^{init}.

Send Registration Transaction. N_i sends the registration transaction with w_i^{init}, its PK_i^{kes}, VK_i^{vrf} and other public information to the consensus network. The node registers successfully when the new block containing the transaction is generated and confirmed.

Node Stake. The changes of nodes' stake will record in a transaction and store in the block, stake is valid only when it's recorded in the blockchain. We set the stake mechanism as a open setting in this paper, which makes it more flexible.

3.3   Block Generation

We use stake proportion table to support dynamic stake scenario with our stake mechanism in this part. And the communication of broadcasting messages in large-scale distributed networks is costly, we use a block compression method to reduce communication consumption and increase the efficiency of consensus. Then we use VRF nonce to select the leader, which is impartial and secure.

For each participant node N_i with local chain $Chain_l^{local}$, and its chain length is $l(>1)$ after r rounds. The latest block is

$$Block_l = \left((root_l^{trans}|nonce_l|Other) \, |BlockBody_l \right) \tag{1}$$

for $r+1th$ round, our consensus performs below:

Candidate Election. Every node in our scheme could compete to be the leader, we use self election to save communication consumption. It's divided into 2 stages:

1) Generate Node Stake Proportion Table. N_i reads stake transactions from $Chain_l^{local}$ and calculates the stake value w_i^l of each node, then generates the node stake proportion table W_l^{local}. For the stake proportion s_i^l of each node is $s_i^l = \frac{w_i^l}{\sum_{j=1}^n w_j^l}$.

2) Self Election. Consensus node uses $nonce_l$ from $Block_l$, consensus round $r+1$, nonce $index$ and SK_i^{vrf} to generate $nonce_i^{r+1}$ and $proof_i^{r+1}$, then uses $nonce_i^{r+1}$ and its stake proportion s_i^l for candidate election, the condition is $nonce_i^{r+1} \leq s_i^l \times 2^{len}$, len is the binary length of VRF nonce. The node meets the condition becomes a candidate and executes the next protocol.

Compressed Block Broadcast. In a general blockchain, transaction data is actually broadcast twice, the first time is in the transaction broadcast stage, for the second time in the block broadcast stage. Different with PoW, the hash calculation time of the PoS protocol is almost 0, and the block broadcast time is a big factor of consensus efficiency.

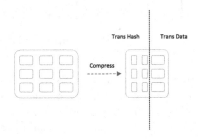

Fig. 3. Candidate block compression.

1) Generate compressed block. For the received transaction, node N_i first verifies its validity, then saves the valid one in $TransPool_i$. The transactions that have been broadcast are deposited in $Trans_i^{broadcast}$, others are deposited in $Trans_i^{local}$. The candidate node only packs the broadcast transaction's unique identifier (such as transaction hash). Figure 3 shows the diminution of the block size with the same number of transactions after compression.

2) Broadcast block and VRF proof. After the candidate node generates the compressed candidate block, it packages them as

$$Candidate_i^{l+1} = \left(Trans_i^{l+1}|\left(nonce_i^{l+1}|proof_i^{l+1}|VK_i^{vrf}|Other\right)\right) \quad (2)$$

then broadcast it to other nodes in the network.

Leader Election.   *i)* Verify Messages. For each candidate message $Candidate_{j(j\neq i)}^{l+1}$, node N_i firstly verifies the validity of the VRF nonce $nonce_j^{r+1}$, and then verify the validity of candidate according to W_l^i. If both the results are true, N_i adds it to candidate pool $Candidates_i^{l+1}$. *ii)* Generate Block. If the number of candidates in $Candidates_i^{l+1}$ is more than 1, N_i chooses the one with the smallest VRF *nonce* as leader, and generates a new block based on it; if it is 0, then no block will be generated. The next round will begin at the end of this consensus.

Empty Block. Assume that a total of n participates in one round of consensus, and the stake of node N_i is s_i. It has been proved that the VRF *nonce* is uniform and satisfies the law of distribution in [3]. Therefore, it can set the probability of node N_i self-elected successfully is s_i when n is big enough. The probability of generating empty block θ_{empty} when a node only generates one nonce is

$$\theta_{empty} = \prod_{i=1}^{n} (1 - s_i) \tag{3}$$

it have $\sum_{i=1}^{n} s_i \leq 1$, when n is big enough, $\prod_{i=1}^{n} (1 - s_i) \leq \prod_{i=1}^{n} \left(1 - \frac{1}{n}\right)$ and $\lim_{n \to \infty} \left(1 - \frac{1}{n}\right)^n = \frac{1}{e}$ thus

$$\theta_{empty} = \prod_{i=1}^{n} (1 - s_i) \leq \prod_{i=1}^{n} \left(1 - \frac{1}{n}\right) = \frac{1}{e} \tag{4}$$

which means the phenomenon of generating empty blocks is inevitable.

Block Synchronization. In the original PoS protocol, it obtains dynamic availability through "checking point", which decreases the decentralized attribute of the blockchain. In Block Synchronization protocol, honest nodes only need genesis block and current timestamp and then they could synchronize to the valid chain, which supports dynamic availability without a third party.

Chain Selection Rules. i) If there are two chains with different lengths, choose the longer one; *ii)* if their length is equal, choose the one with the earlier consensus round after their divergence point firstly; *iii)* If their round is the same, choose the one with the smaller VRF nonce of the block after the divergence point.

The chain selection rule is a special longest chain rule, which guarantees that the honest nodes will choose the same longest chain. Although malicious nodes may successfully attacks in new blocks, honest nodes would still dominate the longest main chain while their stake proportion is big enough.

We assume that the local chain of node N_i is $Chain_local$ and the current timestamp is T. The protocol steps are as follows:

1) Calculate the consensus round. The node N_i get the initial timestamp t from genesis block, and then uses current timestamp T to calculate the current consensus round R.

2) Collect legal chains. N_i requests other nodes for their local chain $Chain_i$ and verifies its validity. Firstly, it verify whether the consensus round is smaller than R, then the validity of genesis block, and finally verify the legality of the chain and block. All valid chains are collected into $Chains_i^{syn}$.

3) Chain selection. For each $Chain_i$ from $Chains_i^{syn}$, N_i uses chain selection rules to select one chain as its new local chain.

Besides the chain length, we also use consensus round R and VRF *nonce* to upgrade our Chain Selection Rule. That is to ensure that the node would select only one chain among multiple chains. Any honest node can finally synchronize the longest chain dominated by honest nodes with executing the block synchronization protocol. Therefore, our scheme can support dynamic availability when the stake proportion of malicious nodes is less than a certain value.

4 Security Analysis

In order to ensure the feasibility of our scheme, we firstly prove its security under a standard security model, then we analyze the stake fault tolerance proportion of the protocol and its performance under other security threats.

4.1 Security Attributes

Definition. Blockchain has three key security attributes: chain growth [13], common prefix [14,15] and chain quality [14]. These three attributes are used for security analysis in PoS protocols such as [6–9,16]. We also use them to analyze our protocol's security. We firstly give their definitions and then prove that our protocol satisfies them under our assumptions and security model.

Definition 1. *Chain growth. There is a PoS protocol Pos with a set of participants P_*. The chain growth properties are described as follows: there is a parameter $\sigma \in R$, for any honest participant P_i with local chain C_i and chain length L_i when the round of consensus is R_i, and honest participant P_j with local chain C_j and chain length L_j when the round of consensus is R_j. when $P_i, P_j \in P^*, R_i > R_j$, there is $L_i - L_j \geq \sigma(R_i - R_j)$ in the execution of Pos.*

Definition 2. *Common prefix. There is a PoS protocol Pos with a set of participants P_*. The public prefix attributes are described as follows: there is a parameter $k \in N_+$, for any honest participant P_i with local chain C_i and chain length L_i, and honest participant P_j with local chain C_j and chain length L_j. When $P_i, P_j \in P_*, L_i > L_j$, there is $Chain_j [\neg k] \subseteq Chain_i$ in the execution of Pos.*

Definition 3. *Chain quality. There is a PoS protocol Pos with a set of participants P_*. The chain quality attribute is described as follows: there are two parameter $\mu \in R \, (0 < \mu < 1), L \in N_+$, for any honest participant P_i with local chain C_i and chain length L_i. When L_i is large enough, the proportion of blocks generated by honest nodes in C_i is at least μ in the execution of Pos.*

Proof. In order to prove that our scheme satisfies these three security attributes, we have tree preconditions below: i) The stake proportion α of all honest nodes is greater than that of all malicious nodes β, it means $\alpha = \lambda\beta, \lambda > 1$; ii) Honest nodes generate a every r rounds on average, $r = e/(e-1), r \in R$, e is the natural exponential; iii) Protocol executes in the $NetworkModel$ of Sect. 2.

We assume that there is a honest node N_i with local chain $Chain_i$ and chain length l_i when the round of consensus is r_i, a honest node N_j with local chain $Chain_j$ and chain length l_j when the round of consensus is r_j, and a node N with local chain $Chain_{local}$ and chain length l.

Proof. Chaingrowth. In the worst case, the malicious node does not generate new blocks. The stake proportion of honest nodes is α, and on average at least one block is generated every $r' = e^\alpha / (e^\alpha - 1)$ round, then there is $l_i - l_j \geq (r_i - r_j)/r'$. It's obvious that $1/r' \in R$, so it satisfies the chain growth attribute.

Proof. Commonprefix. For honest nodes N_i and $N_j, l_i > l_j$, we know that their genesis blocks are generated when the blockchain is initialized, so at least $Chain_j[\neg k] \subseteq Chain_i$. According to the chain selection rules, we know that all honest nodes will eventually choose a chain as the main chain. So we have $Chain_j[\neg l_j - h] \subseteq Chain_i, h > 1$. so it satisfies the common prefix attribute.

Proof. Chainquality. The chain length l of the honest node's local chain $Chain_{local}$ will be long enough after the protocol has been executed for a long time. And the probability of a consensus node being elected as a leader to generate a new block is positively correlated with its stake proportion. Since we assume that the stake proportion of honest nodes is α, that of malicious nodes is β, and $\alpha = \lambda\beta, \lambda > 1$. We proved that the worst-case inflation rate [9] of malicious nodes will eventually converge to a certain value $ratio^{full-greedy}$ in next segment, then the proportion of blocks generated by honest nodes $\mu' \approx \alpha / (\alpha + \beta \times ratio^{full-greedy}) = \lambda/(\lambda + ratio^{full-greedy})$. we have $0 < \mu' < 1$ when $\lambda > 1$, so it satisfies the chain quality attribute.

4.2 Security Threats

Stake Fault Tolerance Proportion. The PoS protocol is vulnerable to nothing-at-stake attacks because its low computation consumption. Malicious nodes can expand on multiple chain branches of a consensus at a very low cost. We use the amplification ratio [9] to analyze the stake fault tolerance proportion of our protocol. Similarly, we have the following analysis:

For the chain $Chain'$ with length l' and consensus rounds r', the stake proportion of the malicious nodes $N_{adversary}$ is *beta*, and the max probability of generating a block each round is also β. Let $f(t, l)$ be the number of chains with chain length $l' + l$ and consensus time $r' + t$ which extends from $Chain'$, we have $f(t, l) = f(t - 1, l) + f(t, l - 1)\beta = \binom{t}{l}\beta^l = \frac{t!}{l!(t-l)!}\beta^l$. we know $t! \approx \sqrt{2\pi t}t^t$ when t is large enough, combine (10) and $t = rl$ we have

$$f(t, l) \approx \frac{\sqrt{2\pi rl}(rl)^{rl}}{\sqrt{2\pi l}l^l\sqrt{2\pi(t-l)}(t-l)^{t-l}} = \sqrt{\frac{r}{2\pi(r-1)l}}\left[\frac{r^r}{(r-1)^{r-1}}\beta\right]^l,$$ and we know that

$f(t, l) \geq 1$ when l is big enough, then combine $t = rl$ we have $\frac{r^r}{(r-1)^{r-1}}\beta > 1 \Rightarrow l < \left[\frac{r}{r-1}\right]^{r-1}\beta t$. we know that l is the length of $Chain'$ with full-greedy [9] strategy extends after time t, so the amplification ratio is $ratio^{full-greedy} < \left[\frac{r}{r-1}\right]^{r-1}$.

When malicious nodes implement the full-greedy strategy and honest nodes not, our stake fault tolerance proportion $\rho = \frac{1}{1 + ratio^{full-greedy}}$.

Prediction Window. The results of [17] show that it needs higher stake proportion to guarantee security when the prediction window is larger, because it's more vulnerable to bribery attacks (BA) [4]. The random seed of generating VRF nonce will change in each round in our protocol, so our prediction window size is 1, which can be regarded as unpredictable when ignoring network delays, so it defends BA well.

Table 1. Secure attributes of PoS consensus schemes.

	Ourobros	Algorand	Nakamoto-Pos	Our scheme
Window size	κ	$\Theta(\kappa)$	1	1
Faulr tolerance	50%	33%	27%	36%/42%/46%
Threat of BA	High	Medium	Low	Low

Table 1 shows the comparison of our scheme and other schemes. κ is a security parameter in [5–7] and its value is 2160. The stake fault tolerance proportion is about 36% in our scheme when there is only one nonce generated in each round, it would be 42% while there is 2 and 46% while it's 3.

5   Experiments and Results

In our scheme, the candidate block broadcast time is the main part of the block generation protocol. Therefore, we implemented the prototype of the candidate block compression module and used the Bitcoin network in [16] to simulate it. Te block header size is 100B, the size of ordinary transaction is 256B, and the transaction hash size is 32B. Our simulation runs on a quad-core machine (Intel core i5-4590, 3.3 GHz, 8 GB RAM), and evaluated the average time of 100 block broadcasts on 75% and 90% of a 3000-node Bitcoin simulation network while the transaction compression proportion is 100%, 75% and 50%, 0% represents the original PoS scheme. We mainly evaluate the relationship between the *BlockSize, BlockBroadcastTime* and *SystemPerformance* and the transaction compression proportion.

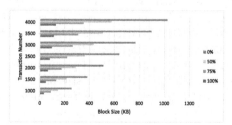

Fig. 4. Block size with different tx numbers and compression proportions.

Block Size. Figure 4 is the block size of the number of transactions ranges from 1000 to 4000. When the compression proportion is 100%, 75% and 50%, the size of block is from 32 KB to 128 KB, 88 KB to 352 KB, 144 KB to 576 KB, it's about 13%, 35%, and 56% of the original one. And it will be more efficient when the transaction size is larger than the ordinary ones.

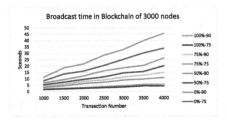

Fig. 5. Broadcast time with different number of transactions.

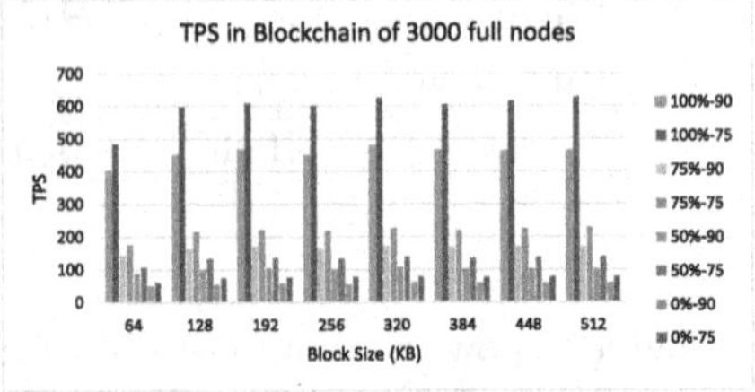

Fig. 6. System performance with different tx sizes.

Block Broadcast Time. Figure 5 is also the block broadcast time of the number of transactions ranges from 1000 to 4000. The time of block broadcasting to 75% nodes is about 15%, 35%, and 57% of original one; while 90% is about 14%, 33%, and 56%, and it grows faster with lower compression proportion. In addition, it takes about more than 26–34% of time to broadcast the block to 90% nodes than 75% when other conditions are the same.

System Performance. Figure 6 is the system performance of the block size ranges from 64 KB to 512 KB. When the compression proportion is 100%, 75% and 50%, TPS (transactions per second) is approximately 400–630, 140–230 and 90–140. It's about 8 times, 2.9 times, and 1.8 times of the ordinary PoS schemes. In addition, the TPS of the block broadcast to 90% of the network nodes is about 24% lower than that of 75% when other conditions are the same.

Due to the message delay of the distributed network, even the performance of the blockchain system of a 100% compressed block has an upper limit, but compared to the ordinary PoS system, the TPS of our solution is significantly improved, and there are also some optimized aspects. In general, the block compression method we proposed can reduce the size of the block under the same number of transactions and save the communication consumption of block broadcasting, it indeed improves the TPS of public chain.

6   Related Work

Review the work of the current public chain consensus protocols, Algorand [3] uses the VRF and BFT mechanisms in the PoS protocol for the first time. Hotstuff [4] optimizes the BFT protocol, and uses a pipeline method to optimize the protocol execution to improve efficiency. Libra [18] is a more robust and efficient consensus mechanism designed based on Hotstuff. However, the scalability of these schemes is limited by BFT, and the consensus consumption will increase rapidly when the number of nodes in the network increases. Snow White [5] firstly proposes the framework of the provably secure PoS protocol, and analyzed the security of the protocol in an open network environment. Ouroboros [6–8] divides the longest chain PoS protocol into two stages, epoch and slot, which makes the stake fault tolerance proportion close to 50%. However it's vulnerable to bribery attacks. [9] proposes a new security property *chainsoundness* of blockchain. [17] discusses the impact of predictability on security of PoS protocols. These schemes are mainly concerned the security instead of the system performance of the protocol [19,20].

7   Conclusion and Discussion

In this paper, we propose a scalable and provably secure PoS protocol to support the application of public chains in extendable scenarios. We propose an independent stake mechanism that binds stake to nodes with transactions, and uses stake proportion table to support dynamic stake scenario. We propose a method of candidate block compression to decrease the communication consumption of block broadcast. We propose a new longest-chain rule, which supports the dynamic availability without a third party. In addition, we prove the security of our protocol and analyze its stake fault tolerance proportion. Our experimental results show that our communication consumption is lower with the same number of transactions, and the system performance is indeed better than other solutions. Furthermore, we plan to increase the stake fault tolerance proportion of this scheme, and prove its security in a more realistic and complex network environment. On the other hand, we will continue to research the public chain consensus schemes that have higher system performance.

Acknowledgments. This work is supported by the National Key Research and Development Program of China (2020YFB1807500), in part by Guangdong Basic and Applied Basic Research Foundation (2020A1515110496, 2020A1515110079).

References

1. Nakamoto, S.: Bitcoin: A peer-to-peer electronic cash system (2009). https://bitcoin.org/bitcoin.pdf
2. Quantum Mechanic. Proof of Stake (2011). https://bitcointalk.org/index.php?topic=27787.0
3. Gilad, Y., Hemo, R., Micali, S., et al.: Algorand: scaling byzantine agreements for cryptocurrencies. In: Proceedings of the 26th Symposium on Operating Systems Principles, pp. 51–68. ACM (2017). https://doi.org/10.1145/3132747.3132757

4. Brown-Cohen, J., Narayanan, A., Psomas, A., et al.: Formal barriers to longest-chain proof-of-stake protocols. In: Proceedings of the 2019 ACM Conference on Economics and Computation, pp. 459–473 (2019). https://doi.org/10.1145/3328526.3329567

5. Bentov, I., Pass, R., Shi, E.: Snow white: provably secure proofs of stake. IACR Cryptology ePrint Archive 2016:919 (2016)

6. Kiayias, A., Russell, A., David, B., Oliynykov, R.: Ouroboros: a provably secure proof-of-stake blockchain protocol. In: Katz, J., Shacham, H. (eds.) CRYPTO 2017. LNCS, vol. 10401, pp. 357–388. Springer, Cham (2017). https://doi.org/10.1007/978-3-319-63688-7_12

7. David, B., Gaži, P., Kiayias, A., Russell, A.: Ouroboros Praos: an adaptively-secure, semi-synchronous proof-of-stake blockchain. In: Nielsen, J.B., Rijmen, V. (eds.) EUROCRYPT 2018. LNCS, vol. 10821, pp. 66–98. Springer, Cham (2018). https://doi.org/10.1007/978-3-319-78375-8_3

8. Badertscher, C., Gaži, P., Kiayias, A., et al.: Ouroboros genesis: composable proof-of-stake blockchains with dynamic availability. In: Proceedings of the 2018 ACM SIGSAC Conference on Computer and Communications Security, pp. 913–930 (2018). https://doi.org/10.1145/3243734.3243848

9. Fan, L., Zhou, H.S.: A scalable proof-of-stake blockchain in the open setting (or, how to mimic Nakamoto's design via proof-of-stake). Cryptology ePrint Archive, Report 2017/656 (2017). Version 20180425:201821

10. Micali, S., Rabin, M., Vadhan, S.: Verifiable random functions. In: 40th Annual Symposium on Foundations of Computer Science (Cat. No. 99CB37039), pp. 120–130. IEEE (1999). https://doi.org/10.1109/SFFCS.1999.814584

11. Lamport, L., Shostak, R., Pease, M.: The Byzantine generals problem. ACM Trans. Program. Lang. Syst. **4**(3), 382–401 (1982). https://doi.org/10.1145/3335772.3335936

12. Bellare, M., Miner, S.K.: A forward-secure digital signature scheme. In: Wiener, M. (ed.) CRYPTO 1999. LNCS, vol. 1666, pp. 431–448. Springer, Heidelberg (1999). https://doi.org/10.1007/3-540-48405-1_28

13. Kiayias, A., Panagiotakos, G.: Speed-security tradeoffs in blockchain protocols. IACR Cryptology ePrint Archive 2015:1019 (2015)

14. Garay, J., Kiayias, A., Leonardos, N.: The bitcoin backbone protocol: analysis and applications. In: Oswald, E., Fischlin, M. (eds.) EUROCRYPT 2015. LNCS, vol. 9057, pp. 281–310. Springer, Heidelberg (2015). https://doi.org/10.1007/978-3-662-46803-6_10

15. Pass, R., Seeman, L., Shelat, A.: Analysis of the blockchain protocol in asynchronous networks. In: Coron, J.-S., Nielsen, J.B. (eds.) EUROCRYPT 2017. LNCS, vol. 10211, pp. 643–673. Springer, Cham (2017). https://doi.org/10.1007/978-3-319-56614-6_22

16. Gervais, A., Karame, G.O., Wüst, K., et al.: On the security and performance of proof of work blockchains. In: ACM SIGSAC Conference on Computer and Communications Security, pp. 3–16. ACM (2016). https://doi.org/10.1145/2976749.2978341

17. Bagaria, V., Dembo, A., Kannan, S., et al.: Proof-of-stake longest chain protocols: security vs predictability. arXiv preprint arXiv:1910.02218 (2019)

18. Bano, S., Baudet, M., Ching, A., et al.: State machine replication in the Libra Blockchain (2020). https://developers.libra.org/docs/state-machine-replication-paper. (Consulted on December 19, 2020)

19. Liu, L., Feng, J., Pei, Q., et al.: Blockchain-enabled secure data sharing scheme in mobile edge computing: an asynchronous advantage actor-critic learning approach. IEEE Internet Things J. **8**(4), 2342–2353 (2021). https://doi.org/10.1109/JIOT.2020.3048345

20. Feng, J., Yu, F.R., Pei, Q., et al.: Cooperative computation offloading and resource allocation for blockchain-enabled mobile-edge computing: a deep reinforcement learning approach. IEEE Internet Things J. **7**(7), 6214–6228 (2020). https://doi.org/10.1109/JIOT.2019.2961707

Redactable Blockchain Technology Based on Distributed Key Management and Trusted Execution Environment

Lisha Liu[1], Lin Tan[2], Jun Liu[3], Jing Xiao[1(✉)], Haibo Yin[2], and Shuang Tan[4]

[1] College of Electrical and Information Engineering, Hunan University, Changsha 410082, China
jxiao1985@hnu.edu.cn
[2] Hunan Tianhe Guoyun Technology Co., Ltd., Changsha 410100, China
[3] The 723 Institute of CSIC, Yangzhou 225101, China
[4] National Defense Science and Technology University, Changsha 410003, China

Abstract. Proponents view the blockchain technology as transformative because its emergence has solved many security problems in the open environment. However, it is necessary to study redactable blockchain in specific circumstances to remove the limitations brought by its immutability. This paper presents a secure redactable blockchain using distributed key management and Trusted Execution Environment (TEE). We first realizes hash collision by replacing the hash function in the blockchain with the distributed chameleon hash. The distributed key management is then adopted to ensure the security of the trapdoor, which is the core of chameleon hash. And the security of the trapdoor-related calculation is strengthened through TEE, which can ensure confidentiality and integrity of data and computations by putting code and data in a secure region. Moreover, we analyze the security of the scheme in several attack scenarios and implement a redactable blockchain based on EOS testnet. Our results demonstrate that the average time cost of distributed chameleon hash we used is more than that of the standard chameleon hash but within 15%. Nevertheless, the harm is negligible for the hash calculation time on the order of milliseconds while the security is greatly improved.

Keywords: Redactable blockchain · Distributed key management · Trusted execution environment · Chameleon hash · Decentralization

1 Introduction

Since the explosion of technologies such as big data, artificial intelligence and 5G, the massive growth of data has brought greater storage requirements [1]. The traditional storage methods are generally centralized storage, which is unreliable for putting the sovereignty of data in the hands of the administrator [2]. Once centralized storage is damaged, it may affect millions of users in the network

© Springer Nature Singapore Pte Ltd. 2021
H.-N. Dai et al. (Eds.): BlockSys 2021, CCIS 1490, pp. 302–315, 2021.
https://doi.org/10.1007/978-981-16-7993-3_23

[3]. The above defect has led to a boom in decentralized technology [4]. As a representative technology of decentralization, the blockchain has gradually entered the public view with the popularity of bitcoin [5].

Blockchain is a brand-new decentralized infrastructure and distributed computing paradigm [6]. It is characterized by traceable and tamper-proof [7]. The append-only feature of blockchain is the key to ensuring the security of the system [8]. The transaction will be permanently stored on a distributed ledger, which cannot be tampered with or deleted [7]. Applied in the field of digital currency, blockchain can trace each transaction at any time effectively and avoid double spending [9]. However, the recent practice has made people realize that decentralization and non-tampering are double-edged swords [10]. While laying a solid foundation of blockchain security, smart contracts and overlay applications may not work or scale for the immutability [11]. In the blockchain system, once outdated or harmful information is uploaded, it cannot be eliminated [12]. In the meantime, the immutability of blockchain violates the principle of the right to be forgotten under the General Data Protection Regulation (GDPR) [13]. Therefore, it is valuable to study how the blockchain edit its content under special conditions.

At present, scholars have put a lot of researches and investment in developing redactable blockchain technology [14]. The existing methods are mainly chameleon hashing, block pruning, etc. To calculate hash collisions, the hash function in our scheme is replaced by the chameleon hash. Therefore, we can delete invalid data or modify incorrect information without affecting the blockchain structure. In the redactable blockchain system based on chameleon hash, the critical thing is to manage the trapdoor well [11]. Many of current redactable blockchains adopt centralized key management, which conflicts with the decentralized idea of blockchain. Even decentralized solutions have security risks at the stage of key synthesis. To solve this problem, the Trusted Execution Environment (TEE) is introduced [15]. TEE establishes a secure and isolated computing medium through hardware technology [16]. It can be trusted by multiple parties to further strengthen the security of the redactable blockchain system [17]. Based on TEE and the distributed key management, this paper carries out a redactable blockchain technology. Our contributions can be summarized as follows:

1) We have designed a distributed redactable blockchain. By defining nodes with three roles and separating the trapdoor, we have reduced the risk of being controlled by malicious nodes, which is also in line with the feature of decentralization. The function we have used is the Distributed Chameleon Hash (DCH), which outputs the shards of the trapdoor directly from inputting the threshold at the algorithm initialization stage.
2) We have introduced TEE technology to the trapdoor shard management of redactable blockchain. The code and data related to trapdoor shards are all done in TEE. Therefore, no nodes can get the complete plaintext information of the trapdoor, which greatly reduces the possibility of trapdoor leakage.

3) We have carried out security analysis and simulations to validate our hypothesis. Our solution is able to resist security attacks in several situations, such as attacks on different types of nodes. As for the performance, the average time cost of distributed chameleon hash we have used is 6–15% higher than that of a standard chameleon hash, and the result turns out that the redactable blockchain works well. As for the low-frequency modification behavior, the value it brings in security enhancement is far greater than the time loss it causes in the order of a millisecond.

This paper is organized as follows: We introduce the background and related works in Section one and Section two respectively. Then we elaborate the scheme of the redactable blockchain in Section three and analyze its security in Section four. The fifth section shows our experimental results while Section six draws a conclusion.

2   Related Work

Since redactable blockchain is regarded to expand the application of blockchain, a variety of solutions of realizing the redactable blockchain have been implemented and conceptualized, most of which are based on the chameleon hash function. In the next part, we will list how existing researches implement redactable blockchain and analyze its associated limitations.

In 1998, Krawczyk and Rabin [18] first proposed the chameleon hash algorithm in *Chameleon Hashing and Signatures*. Chameleon hash is defined as a one-way hash function that carries the characteristics of strong collision resistance, trapdoor collisions, and uniformity. The algorithm is divided into four parts, including Setup, KeyGen, Hash, and Forge. In 2017, Ateniese et al. proposed the redactable blockchain utilizing the chameleon hash for the first time in their work [11]. They defined an administrator in the public chain to control the trapdoor. It is obvious that centralized storage of trapdoor violates the characteristics of blockchain. After that, there were more researches on trapdoor preservation. Puddu et al. used the Multi-Party Computation (MPC) protocol in the process of key segmentations and reconstructions [19]. Also using the MPC protocol, Ashritha et al. proposed an ephemeral trapdoor key mechanism to limit the modification of the verifier [20]. But due to the high complexity and low performance of MPC, these schemes are difficult to implement and are not suitable for public chains. Then Huang et al. [21] proposed the first Threshold Chameleon Hash (TCH) as well as Accountable-and Sanitizable Chameleon Signature (ASCS) schemes. According to their experimental results, TCH is more efficient than MPC even in case that too much nodes existing in the system. However, previous studies did not use TEE technology to ensure the security of the trapdoor during the calculation.

In conclusion, the redactable blockchain implemented by the chameleon hash can be modified without affecting the overall structure. Based on the above studies, this paper intends to implement a more secure redactable blockchain.

Compared with the scheme of Ateniese et al. [11], we does not require the administrator to keep the trapdoor, and a single node cannot edit the block. Moreover, we have not adopted a complicated MPC protocol for distributed key management. Instead, we have optimized the chameleon hash function like Huang et al. [21] We fragment the trapdoor through secret sharing and isolate the calculations related to the shards in TEE. As a result, the blockchain security of the editing process is enhanced.

3   Proposed Solution

Our scheme implements a redactable blockchain through the chameleon hash function. The function has a feature of trapdoor collision, which makes it easy to calculate the hash collision for the node that controls the trapdoor, but it is still safe for the nodes that do not know any trapdoor information. With the hash collision, we can modify the transaction content without changing its hash value. As shown in Fig. 1, when the memo field in a transaction needs to be modified, we can calculate a new nonce value through the chameleon hash and get the same hash value as the original one. Then we implement distributed management for the trapdoor of the chameleon hash, which means that the trapdoor is divided into multiple parts through secret sharing algorithm. Finally, the trapdoor-related calculations are put into the TEE environment of randomly selected computing nodes, which provides better protection for the trapdoor synthesis process.

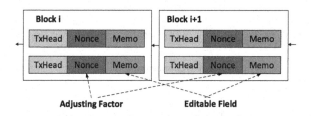

Fig. 1. Fields of a transaction

3.1   Node Function

As shown in Fig. 2, we set the blockchain nodes into three roles:

Key Holding Node (KHN): Saving a shard of the trapdoor.

Computing Node (CompN): Calculating the nonce value of the transaction for generating a hash collision.

Consensus Node (ConsN): Voting and verifying each editing request and result.

When the blockchain system is established, a fixed number of KHNs are determined. At the same time, the distributed chameleon hash function is initialized, and trapdoor fragments are randomly sent to KHNs. CompNs are required to possess some reputation and deploy TEE. In each round of view, a CompN is randomly selected to calculate the hash collision. ConsN participates in each voting of editing request and result. The consensus mechanism adopts PBFT. If there are f-crashed nodes, as long as the number of ConsN is greater than or equal to 3f+1, the system can still operate stably.

On top of that, the role of the node can be adjusted dynamically. After ConsN deployed TEE locally, it can become a computing node. If the TEE of CompN is damaged, it can only be a ConsN. In principle, a KHN cannot be changed. But under special conditions, we can update the trapdoor fragments. If the KHN is malicious or the trapdoor fragment is lost, the function should be recalculated through hard fork. The cost of the recalculation is relatively high, but it is still a low probability event that could be neglected.

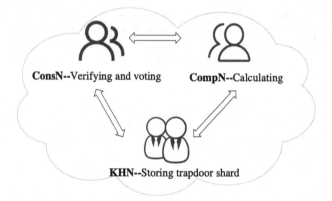

Fig. 2. Node function in the system

3.2 System Model

This scheme divides the entire process of redaction into seven stages. The following are the descriptions of each stage we designed, which are shown in Fig. 3.

Stage 1 Initialization: Assigning roles to each node in the process of generating the genesis block. We define a node with TEE as a CompN, and initialize the distribution chameleon hash function. During the process, KHNs get the shard of the trapdoor randomly. The blockchain then operates in the usual way.

Stage 2 Request Generation: When it is detected that there is wrong, harmful or expired information in the blockchain, one node sends a modification request $Req = \{num, content\}$ and broadcasts it to the entire network. Req represents the request, num stands for the block number that needs to be modified, and $content$ refers to the data content in the transaction.

Stage 3 Consensus Voting: All ConsNs verify whether the request is reasonable. After that, they broadcast the proposal $Res=0/1$ to the network. 1 means accepting the Req, and 0 stands for disagreeing with it. PBFT is adopted as the consensus mechanism. When 2/3 of ConsNs agree, the request is passed. Otherwise, the request is rejected. The voting result will be published on the blockchain.

Stage 4 CompN Selection: When a CompN detects a passed Req on the blockchain, it generates a random number locally and divides the number into multiple shards by secret sharing. Then it sends them to other CompNs. Each CompN computes a hash value with the shards they received and its public key. The smart contract on the blockchain will automatically select the CompN with the largest hash value to modify the blockchain for this round. The selection mechanism ensures the randomization of the CompN selected for each round.

Stage 5 Calculation: The selected CompN initializes the TEE and generates a certification σTEE to prove the correctness of the TEE initialization. Then it contacts the certification service center to obtain a $Quote$. This $Quote$ is bundled with the σTEE into a report π, and the report is sent to the blockchain. The process is the remote authentication service, which can prove the identity of the TEE. After the security check, each KHN encrypts the trapdoor segment with the public key of the selected CompN and sends it to its TEE. Here, we require KHN to attach their signature. The CompN then enters the private key and calculates the nonce value in the TEE that can produce hash collision. The selected CompN can get nothing except the nonce value. Based on this value, the CompN can calculate a new block with a timestamp.

Stage 6 Verification: The ConsNs check the modified content and corresponding report π. The modified block can be put into block pool only after 2/3 of ConsNs agree, otherwise this block will be discarded.

Stage 7 Blockchain Updating: All nodes replace the original block with the new blocks in the block pool to ensure the consistency of blockchain ledger.

3.3 Algorithm

Here we introduce the Distributed Chameleon Hash algorithm. In this paper, we combined the standard chameleon hash algorithm proposed by Krawczyk and

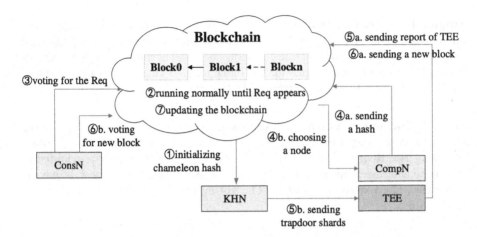

Fig. 3. The working process of redactable blockchain

Rabin and the (k, n) secret sharing algorithm proposed by Shamir to form the Distributed Chameleon Hash, which differs from standard chameleon hash in several parts. In the Setup stage of DCH, the parameters passed in are added with the threshold (k, n) of the Shamir secret sharing algorithm. Therefore, in the KeyGen stage, DCH can randomly divides the trapdoor into n parts through the Shamir algorithm, while the standard chameleon hash generates complete private key sk. The hash calculation methods of the standard chameleon hash and DCH are the same. And in the Forge stage, DCH can calculate the random number according to k copies of sk and Shamir decryption algorithm. The complete trapdoor information is not disclosed in the whole process. The details are as follows:

1) $(param) \leftarrow DCH.Setup(\lambda, (k,n))$: on input a security parameter $\lambda \in \mathbb{N}$, the threshold *(k,n)* of secret sharing, output system parameter *param*.
2) $((tk_1, ..., tk_n), hk) \leftarrow DCH.KeyGen(param)$: on input system parameter *param*, output a set of threshold trapdoor keys $(tk_1, \cdots, tk_n)$ and a public key *hk*.
3) $(h) \leftarrow DCH.Hash(hk, m, r, s)$: on input the public key *hk*, a message *m*, and (r, s), where *r* and *s* denote the random number used to generate the hash value, output a chameleon hash *h*.
4) $(r', s') \leftarrow DCH.Forge((tk_1, \cdots, tk_k), m', h)$: on input a set of threshold trapdoor keys $(tk_1, \cdots, tk_k)$ (k¡n), a new message *m'*, chameleon hash *h*, output a new random tuple *(r',s')*.

4   Security Analysis

This paper implements a redactable blockchain through the chameleon hash. Our scheme seems to go against the original intention and destroys security mechanism of blockchain. In reality, we take into account the importance of the trapdoor and adopt a distributed key management to keep the trapdoor from being controlled by one malicious node.

The redactable blockchains proposed by Puddu and Ashritha used Muti-Party Computation (MPC) [19,20] for distributed management of trapdoors, but such method did not consider how to ensure security during the reconstruction process, and got low performance due to the complexity of the MPC protocol. We use threshold secret sharing to distribute trapdoors and isolate trapdoor-related calculations in TEE. First, when the trapdoor is initialized, it is divided into n pieces and is sent to the KHNs directly. Neither can any nodes obtain the trapdoor information, nor can a single KHN obtain the complete trapdoor. Second, each operation requires a majority of ConsNs to vote and verify. Moreover, the selection of the CompN is random, and the computing process is placed in TEE that has passed remote service authentication. The TEE ensures the security of programs and data through permission control and encryption. For the following possible situations, the security analysis is also carried out:

Attacks on the KHN: The attacker may invade a KHN and sends the wrong trapdoor shard. Our scheme requires the KHN to attach a signature when sending the trapdoor segment, and the selected CompN can perform signature verification on the received segment.

Attacks on the ConsN: The ConsN is of the largest number in the blockchain system. And we adopt PBFT as the consensus mechanism. Even if an adversary attacks consensus nodes with total amount of f, according to the PBFT protocol, the blockchain system can operate normally as long as there are more than $2f+1$ normal ConsNs.

Attacks on the CompN: When calculating random numbers in TEE, the attacker may attack the selected CompN. Suppose an adversary attacks a CompN, generally, he cannot obtain the trapdoor fragments to synthesize a complete trapdoor due to the isolation of the TEE. Even if the adversary controls the TEE machine, if TEE deviates from the original protocol and does not have the correct signature of the selected CompN, he cannot generate a valid certification report which needs to be uploaded to the blockchain to prove its authenticity. Besides, even if he maliciously calculates a new block, it cannot be on the chain as long as it does not obtain the consent of 2/3 of ConsNs.

Attacks on the Key Shards: When the KHN sends the trapdoor to the selected CompN, an attacker may steal or intercept the key shards. In this paper, the KHN is required to encrypt the trapdoor with the public key of the selected CompN, and only the corresponding CompN can decrypt it with its private key. Therefore, even if the attacker steals the fragments, he cannot obtain the plaintext. Moreover, if the adversary intercepts the sending of the trapdoor shards, a complete trapdoor can be synthesized as long as at least k shards are received. Since our scheme uses (k, n) threshold secret sharing, the complete trapdoor can be synthesized as long as t fragments are received. Even if the trapdoor leaks at a number of more than n-k, it means that the trapdoor synthesis fails, and we can enter the next round without safety hazard.

Replay Attack: To ensure that each editing operation is not exposed to replay attacks, it is necessary to add a timestamp to the newly modified block. When the ConsN verifies the block, it first checks the timestamp and rejects the old request. In addition, the modified content must be the task specified in the request Req. Therefore, only one legitimate request will be accepted.

All in all, our scheme takes into account the various attacks that may occur in the process of modifying the blockchain. It can prevent attacks on the KHN, the ConsN, the CompN, the key shards as well as replay attacks. Therefore, it is able to ensure the security of the blockchain environment.

5   Implementation

The experiment environment is a standard 64-bit Ubuntu 18.04.5 LTS, Linux version 4.15.0-117-generic with Intel (R) Core (TM) i5-4210U, 3.60 GHz processor. All the evaluations were performed by programs in C++ and go.

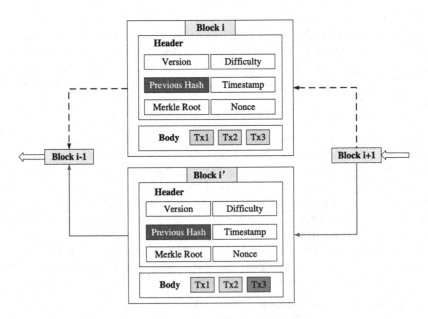

Fig. 4. The theory process of block revision

Our scheme is based on the data structure of EOS. The principle of this scheme is that the transaction hash remains unchanged when the field memo is modified. As shown in Fig. 4, Transaction 3 has been edited, and a new random number is found through the chameleon hash. Therefore, the original block i can be replaced with the new block i', and the data structure of the entire blockchain is guaranteed not to be affected.

In this experiment, suppose that in the current blockchain, the information of block 1076 was shown in Fig. 5 (a). The data contained in the memo field of

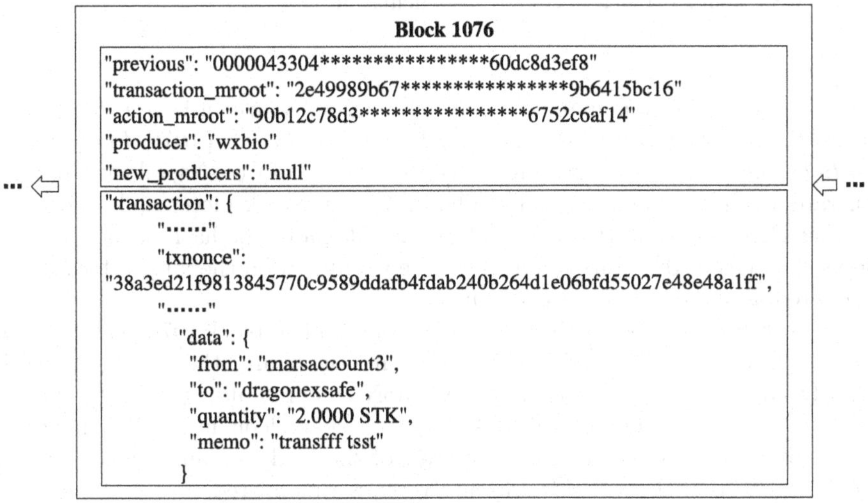

Block 1076

"previous": "0000043304****************60dc8d3ef8"
"transaction_mroot": "2e49989b67****************9b6415bc16"
"action_mroot": "90b12c78d3****************6752c6af14"
"producer": "wxbio"
"new_producers": "null"

"transaction": {
    "......"
     "txnonce":
"38a3ed21f9813845770c9589ddafb4fdab240b264d1e06bfd55027e48e48a1ff",
    "......"
     "data": {
     "from": "marsaccount3",
     "to": "dragonexsafe",
     "quantity": "2.0000 STK",
     "memo": "transfff tsst"
    }

(a) before modifying

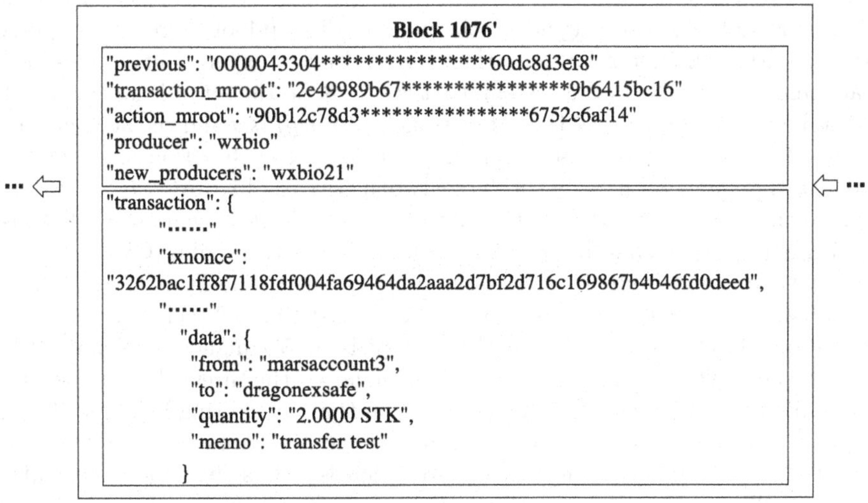

Block 1076'

"previous": "0000043304****************60dc8d3ef8"
"transaction_mroot": "2e49989b67****************9b6415bc16"
"action_mroot": "90b12c78d3****************6752c6af14"
"producer": "wxbio"
"new_producers": "wxbio21"

"transaction": {
    "......"
     "txnonce":
"3262bac1ff8f7118fdf004fa69464da2aaa2d7bf2d716c169867b4b46fd0deed",
    "......"
     "data": {
     "from": "marsaccount3",
     "to": "dragonexsafe",
     "quantity": "2.0000 STK",
     "memo": "transfer test"
    }

(b) after modifying

Fig. 5. The information of block1076 before and after modifying

Table 1. Comparison of standard chameleon hash and DCH in terms of the perfomance

Function	Average time cost	Percentage of increased time
Standard CH	0.1865 ms	–
DCH (k = 5)	0.1993 ms	6.86%
DCH (k = 6)	0.2021 ms	8.36%
DCH (k = 7)	0.2141 ms	14.80%
DCH (less than k)	Return errors when calculating	–

the first transaction was manually entered incorrectly, which is *transfff tsst*. To ensure the accuracy of the system, a node initiates *Req1* = {*1076, from transfff tsst to transfer test*}. After getting the consent of 2/3 of ConsNs, all the CompNs generate a random number locally. They divide it into k pieces and send them to other CompNs respectively. Each CompN calculates the hash of the sum of k pieces they received and its public key. The CompN with the largest hash value is selected as the producer of this round.

Figure 5(b) below shows the information of modified block 1076. The changed fields have been highlighted. As is shown in the figure, the *new_producer* is a newly added field, representing the CompN that modifies the block. The *tx nonce* is a random number calculated by the chameleon hash. And memo is the editable field for transactions. The rest of the fields remain unchanged. For simplicity, fields such as timestamp and version are omitted.

In blockchain applications, the editing process is a low-frequency behavior. We can only consider the performance of the hash calculation. Therefore, we analyzed the performance of DCH. In order to ensure the security of editing operations and trapdoor fragments, the number of trapdoor fragments required for reconstruction should be more than a half. In this experiment, we assumed that there are 8 KHNs in the system, that is $n = 8$. So the set of legal thresholds should be $k = (5, 6, 7)$. We set the old message as *transfff tsst* and the new message as *transfer test*. Then we use different chameleon hash functions to calculate and get the same hash value of these two messages. Figure 6 (a) shows the average time of distribution of standard chameleon hash to generate collisions, and Fig. 6 (b, c, d) shows that of DCH under different thresholds. Obviously, the average time cost is gradually increasing from (a) to (d). The Table 1 below shows the average time cost and percentage of increased time of each function. The percentage of increased time of DCH we adopt is 6–15% higher than that of the standard chameleon hash. It turns out that the larger the threshold becomes, the longer the calculation time is. In consideration that the editing behavior is low-frequent, the use of DCH has little impact on the performance while it assures security. Besides, if the number of received shards is less than the threshold k, an error will be returned when calculating.

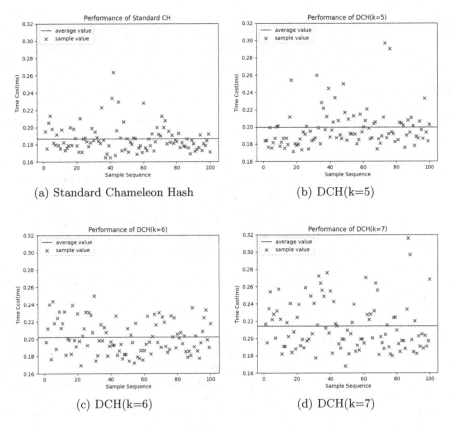

Fig. 6. The performance of the standard chameleon hash and the distributed chameleon hash under different threshold (k = 5, 6, 7)

6   Conclusion

This paper proposes a redactable blockchain scheme with distributed key management and TEE. We can quickly calculate the hash collision with the help of chameleon hash. Distributed key management is adopted to ensure the security of the trapdoor. Meanwhile, a selection mechanism is defined to randomly choose a computing node to reduce the risk of being attacked. TEE can protect the synthesis of the trapdoor and the hash collision calculation to prevent malicious nodes from controlling the trapdoor and arbitrarily modifying the blockchain system. Therefore, our scheme meets editing requirements under the premise of keeping the security of the blockchain system. Looking ahead, we still need to improve this scheme to reduce hard forks that may be caused by malicious actions of the keys holding nodes.

Acknowledgments. This work was supported by Program for Young Scholars of Colleges and Universities in Hunan Province and Leading Program of High-tech Industry Technology Innovation for Science and Technology Development (2020GK2005).

References

1. Yueyue Dai, D.X., Maharjan, S., Chen, Z., He, Q., Zhang, Y.: Blockchain and deep reinforcement learning empowered intelligent 5G beyond. IEEE Netw. **33**(3), 10–17 (2019)
2. Wang, C.-X., Di Renzo, M., Stanczak, S., Wang, S., Larsson, E.G.: Artificial intelligence enabled wireless networking for 5G and beyond: recent advances and future challenges. IEEE Wireless Commun. **27**(1), 16–23 (2020)
3. Zwitter, A., Hazenberg, J.: Decentralized network governance: blockchain technology and the future of regulation. Front. Blockchain-Blockchain Good **3**, 12 (2020)
4. Debe, M., Salah, K., Rehman, M.H.U., Svetinovic, D.: IoT public fog nodes reputation system: a decentralized solution using Ethereum blockchain. IEEE Access **7**, 178082–178093 (2019)
5. Nakamoto, S.: Bitcoin: a peer-to-peer electronic cash system. Technical report, Manubot (2019)
6. Yaga, D., Mell, P., Roby, N., Scarfone, K.: Blockchain technology overview. arXiv preprint arXiv:1906.11078 (2019)
7. Zheng, Z., Xie, S., Dai, H., Chen, X., Wang, H.: An overview of blockchain technology: architecture, consensus, and future trends. In: 2017 IEEE International Congress on Big Data (BigData Congress), pp. 557–564. IEEE (2017)
8. Henry, R., Herzberg, A., Kate, A.: Blockchain access privacy: challenges and directions. IEEE Secur. Priv. **16**(4), 38–45 (2018)
9. Karame, G.O., Androulaki, E., Capkun, S.: Double-spending fast payments in bitcoin. In: Proceedings of the 2012 ACM Conference on Computer and Communications Security, pp. 906–917 (2012)
10. Budish, E.: The economic limits of bitcoin and the blockchain. Technical report, National Bureau of Economic Research (2018)
11. Ateniese, G., Magri, B., Venturi, D., Andrade, E.: Redactable blockchain-or-rewriting history in bitcoin and friends. In: 2017 IEEE European Symposium on Security and Privacy (EuroS&P), pp. 111–126. IEEE (2017)
12. Agrawal, R., et al.: Continuous security in IoT using blockchain. In: 2018 IEEE International Conference on Acoustics, Speech and Signal Processing (ICASSP), pp. 6423–6427. IEEE (2018)
13. Berberich, M., Steiner, M.: Blockchain technology and the GDPR-how to reconcile privacy and distributed ledgers. Eur. Data Prot. L. Rev. **2**, 422 (2016)
14. Politou, E., Casino, F., Alepis, E., Patsakis, C.: Blockchain mutability: challenges and proposed solutions. IEEE Trans. Emerg. Top. Comput. (2019)
15. Sabt, M., Achemlal, M., Bouabdallah, A.: Trusted execution environment: what it is, and what it is not. In: 2015 IEEE Trustcom/BigDataSE/ISPA, vol. 1, pp. 57–64. IEEE (2015)
16. Ayoade, G., Karande, V., Khan, L., Hamlen, K.: Decentralized IoT data management using blockchain and trusted execution environment. In: 2018 IEEE International Conference on Information Reuse and Integration (IRI), pp. 15–22. IEEE (2018)

17. Cheng, R., et al.: Ekiden: a platform for confidentiality-preserving, trustworthy, and performant smart contracts. In: 2019 IEEE European Symposium on Security and Privacy (EuroS&P), pp. 185–200. IEEE (2019)
18. Krawczyk, H., Rabin, T.: Chameleon hashing and signatures (1998)
19. Puddu, I., Dmitrienko, A., Capkun, S.: muchain: how to forget without hard forks. IACR Cryptology ePrint Archive, 2017:106 (2017)
20. Ashritha, K., Sindhu, M., Lakshmy, K.V.: Redactable blockchain using enhanced chameleon hash function. In: 2019 5th International Conference on Advanced Computing & Communication Systems (ICACCS), pp. 323–328. IEEE (2019)
21. Huang, K., et al.: Building redactable consortium blockchain for industrial Internet-of-Things. IEEE Trans. Industr. Inf. **15**(6), 3670–3679 (2019)

Trustworthy Blockchain Data Sharing Model Based on Multi-authority ABE and zk-SNARK

Yang Li[1,2], Guangzong Zhang[1(✉)], Jianming Zhu[1,2], Xiuli Wang[1,2], and Youwei Wang[1,2]

[1] School of Information, Central University of Finance and Economics, Beijing 100081, China
[2] Engineering Research Center of State Financial Security, Ministry of Education, China, Central University of Finance and Economics, Beijing 102206, China

Abstract. With the advent of the era of big data, data sharing has become a widespread demand. However, the process of data sharing is faced with problems such as privacy leakage, access control ambiguity and data reliability uncertainty. The blockchain data sharing model based on attributed based encryption (ABE) is an existing solution to data sharing, this model enables each node of the blockchain to share fine-grained data in a weak trust environment. However, it puts the access policy and attributes directly on the blockchain, so every one in the blockchain can access these access policies and attributes, which will cause privacy leakage. A privacy protection model based on zk-SNARK was proposed in this article to solve this privacy leakage problem. This model uses the blockchain double-chain structure, and realizes the fine-grained access control of data sharing based on Multi-authoirty ABE scheme. At the same time, this model adopts zk-SNARK technologies to protect sensitive access policies and sensitive attributes from disclosure, effectively defending the privacy of users when data sharing in blockchain, avoiding the risk of single authorization.

Keywords: Blockchain · Data sharing · Multi-authority · ABE · zk-SNARK · Privacy protection

1 Introduction

With the advent of the information age, data has become a new strategic resource. However, many data are currently isolated and fragmented and cannot be effectively used. Therefore, how to collect and use data to generate new economic benefits has become a matter of widespread concern from all walks of life. Data sharing is an effective solution to break data islands, promote data exchanges in all walks of life, and enhance data availability and integrity. However, there are many problems in the process of data sharing. For example, how to ensure the authenticity of the shared data and the reliability of the source; how can the data demander find the data sharer; how the two parties can exchange data to ensure privacy and obtain reliable data.

Blockchain is an effective way to solve the above problems. The use of blockchain for data sharing can truly record the past data sharing records, prevent betrayers from

H.-N. Dai et al. (Eds.): BlockSys 2021, CCIS 1490, pp. 316–328, 2021.
https://doi.org/10.1007/978-981-16-7993-3_24

changing records, increase trust among data sharers, and break data islands. At present, various industries have proposed blockchain data sharing solutions based on business scenarios. Many schemes use CP-ABE scheme for encryption to meet the fine-grained access control requirements of business scenarios. However, direct use of the CP-ABE scheme without privacy protection may lead to the leakage of some sensitive information. For example, when the access strategy involves the company's income attributes, project attributes, business attributes, or expense attributes, etc., if competitors on the same blockchain obtain this information, it may have a negative impact on the company. It can be seen that when data is shared in the blockchain, how to meet the needs of fine-grained access control while protecting the privacy of user nodes is a problem worthy of study.

Zero-knowledge proof and attribute-based encryption have been widely used in data sharing privacy protection. Zero-knowledge proof is a rapidly developing technology in recent years. This technology has been widely used in blockchain, such as data privacy protection of blockchain, data compression on blockchain, and off-chain expansion of blockchain, etc. The range of proofs continues to expand, from simple proof of the transaction path, such as ZeroCash, to proof of correctness, such as Filecoin, that the data down the chain is being handled correctly. Attribute-based encryption is also widely used in privacy protection. Especially in the ciphertext policy attribute-based encryption scheme, this CP-ABE scheme encrypts ciphertext by using access structure and generates user key through attribute set. Only users with specified attributes in the access policy can decrypt and access ciphertext.

At present, there are few researches on the privacy protection of data sharing on the blockchain. The zero-knowledge proof technology zk-SNARK has the characteristics of proof-shortness and zero-knowledge. So it can be used for sensitive access policy and sensitive attributes hiding in data sharing. This paper proposes a privacy protection model for blockchain data sharing that applies zero-knowledge technology zk-SNARK to the field of multi-authority attribute-based encryption. Using this scheme can effectively protect the privacy of the sensitive attributes and sensitive access policy of the MA-ABE scheme and realize the fine-grained access control, avoiding the risk of single authorization.

2   Related Works

There are many researches on blockchain models for data sharing.Wang Xiuli et al. [19] have studied the application of attribute-based encryption in combination with the blockchain system, they applied this model to data sharing between enterprises. However, their model directly put access policies and attributes on the blockchain, which may cause privacy risks since some access policies are very sensitive. If privacy protection is not carried out, this may leak the privacy of users who share data [20].

In attribute-based encryption and access policy hiding, there are many research solutions. Sahai et al. [17] first proposed a cryptosystem based on identity encryption, which is the basis for subsequent derivative attribute-based encryption. Melissa Chase [5] proposed the first multi-authoirty attribute based encrytion scheme, this scheme avoided the risk of single authorization. Brent waters [3] proposed an attribute-based encryption method based on a ciphertext strategy, which transforms the access strategy to LSSS matrix so as to encrypt the plaintext and uses an attribute set to decrypt. Goyal et al. [10] proposed a fine-grained access control scheme, and many subsequent attribute-based encryption schemes are based on this scheme. Chen et al. [6] proposed an Inner Product Predicate Encryption (IPE) scheme with adaptive security and complete attribute hiding. Katz et al. [14] studied the application of predicate encryption in attribute-based encryption. Many current strategy hiding and attribute hiding are based on this technology. Cui et al. [7] proposed a CP-ABE scheme that partially hides the access strategy. This scheme has better access efficiency than the scheme that completely hides the access strategy.

As a key technology of blockchain privacy protection, zero-knowledge proof has a variety of implementation schemes. The current technologies that realize zero-knowledge proof mainly include zk-SNARK [16], zk-STARK [1], Bullet proof [4], etc. Among which zk-SNARK is due to its short proof, it is easy to verify and widely used. The current typical technical blochchain solution based on zk-SNARK technology is Zcash [2]. In addition, PLONK [9] and Sonic [18] schemes are also based on zk-SNARK technology. These two schemes achieve complete simplicity and linearity in terms of circuit and proof size. Groth et al. [12] proposed an updatable CRS model, so that the public reference string does not need to be set multiple times. Besides, Groth [11] proposed an efficient NIZK scheme based on zk-SNARK, which is known as Groth 16.

There are also a lot of research on the specific application of zk-SNARK technology. Guan Zhangshuang [13] designed a blockchain trading system based on account model based on zk-SNARK zero-knowledge proof technology, which can effectively protect the transaction privacy of users. Wei Xiaosong [21] designed an anonymous electronic survey system based on NSE-NIZK technology, which can realize the anonymity of questionnaire fillers. Li Gongliang [15] proposed a blockchain privacy protection method based on zero knowledge proof, which satisfied zero knowledge when verifying the blockchain amount. Fu Yonggui [8] studied the information sharing mechanism and management mode of blockchain based on the scene of supply chain.

In general, scholars in recent years have focused on applying zk-SNARK to different business scenarios and improving the efficiency of zero-knowledge proof technology. Besides, these researches are optimizing the size of the proof, expanding the scope of proof, and applying the zero-knowledge proof technology to appropriate scenarios, and researching attribute-based encryption to solve blockchain privacy issues and so on. However, there are few researches and models that use zero-knowledge proof technology for blockchain data sharing, and most of them are the application of attribute-based encryption combined with the blockchain model. The zero-knowledge proof technology zk-SNARK is increasingly used in the construction of blockchain models due to its good proof performance. Combining the zero-knowledge proof technology with the multi-authority attribute-based encryption scheme can effectively protect sensitive access policies and attributes on blockchain, while meeting the requirements of fine-grained access control.

3 Preliminaries

The truthworthy data sharing model in this paper is mainly based on zk-SNARK and Multi-authority ABE to realize privacy protection in the process of blockchain data sharing.

3.1 Multi-authority ABE

Multi-authoirty ABE is a widely used encryption scheme that satisfies fine-grained access control by setting access policies. MA-ABE use multiple authorities to authorize the attributes. In this scheme, access policy is used to encrypt plaintext into ciphertext, and attribute set is used to generate key, so that data owners can make unique access structure according to their own data, so that members with attributes can access. Only the properties of the key that meet the ciphertext access structure can be decrypted.

In the MA-ABE scheme, we need to construct Bilinear pairing. Let $\mathbb{G}_0$ be a addition cyclic group of prime order q, let $\mathbb{G}_M$ be a factorial cyclic group of prime order q, let g_0 be a generator of $\mathbb{G}_0$. In addition, let $\hat{e} : \mathbb{G}_0 \times \mathbb{G}_0 \to \mathbb{G}_M$ denote the bilinear map. In addition, $\mathbb{G}_0 \times \mathbb{G}_0 \neq 1_{\mathbb{G}_t}$, $\hat{e}(ag, bg) = \hat{e}(g, g)^{ab}$.

3.2 Access Structure

Access structure is the key to attribute base encryption. Currently, there are mainly the following three access structures. In the AND gate access structure, all threshold nodes are AND. The threshold node in the access tree is AND, OR, which is converted to polynomial in the design. The LSSS matrix transforms the threshold nodes in the access policy into matrix form. In this model we adopts the access tree as the access policy structure. As it is shown in Fig. 1, in the first threshold node, 2/3 of the attributes are needed to satisfy the access structure.

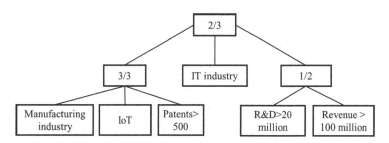

Fig. 1. Alliance chain

3.3 zk-SNARK

zk-SNARK is a technology of zero-knowledge proof, which has the characteristics of proof-shortness and zero-knowledge. The full name of zk-SNARK technology is Zero

Knowledge Succinct Non-interactive ARgument of Knowledge. zk-SNARK first needs to generate a public parameter, that is, a public character reference string, and then send the parameters to the prover and the verifier. The prover uses the public parameters to generate the proof, and then sends the proof to the verifier. The verifier can use the public parameters and the sent proof to verify whether the prover has knowledge. But in this verification process, the verifier does not get any information about the knowledge proven, which is zero knowledge. The proof generated by the prover that needs to be verified is very concise, and the verifier can verify it in a very short time to determine whether it is correct. The formula is from (1) to (5).

$$Setup(1^\lambda) \rightarrow pp_z \tag{1}$$

$$KeyGen(C) \rightarrow (pk_z, vk_z) \tag{2}$$

$$GenProof(pk_z, C, K) \rightarrow \pi \tag{3}$$

$$VerProof(vk_z, C, \pi) \rightarrow result \tag{4}$$

$$Pr\left\{VerProof(vk_z, C, \pi) \rightarrow 1 \middle| \begin{array}{l} KeyGen(C) \rightarrow (pk_z, vk_z) \\ GenProof(pk_z, C, K) \rightarrow \pi \end{array}\right\} = 1 \tag{5}$$

3.4 Blockchain Data Sharing Model

The blockchain data sharing scheme in this paper adopts the double-chain structure in the alliance chain, public chain, and private chain. The public chain has the major nodes of the blockchain, including all of the authorities, and the authorities nodes are first-level nodes. The private chain is a data chain that stores data shared by users. Only when data visitors pass the zero-knowledge smart contract of the public chain can they access the private chain. All data access records are recorded on the public chain by all the nodes. The verification of the proof of the user attribute set is carried out through the MA-ABE smart contract of the public chain. When constructing the blockchain, set up the authoritative user node, and the user's attributes is set by all the authoritative user node.

4 Trustworthy Data Sharing Model Based on Blockchain and zk-SNARK

4.1 Data Sharing Model

The model in this article is based on the blockchain model, the Chase07 scheme and the zk-SNARK scheme. The blockchain data sharing system adopts the structure of alliance chain, which is open to specific user nodes, and data can be shared among user nodes. User nodes can be divided into first-level nodes, which is the same as authoritative nodes, second-level sub-nodes, and third-level sub-nodes. As it is shown in Fig. 2, the child node can apply for the authorization to access the data of the upper node through the upper node. The data of each node is encrypted by MA-ABE, and users who meet the attributes of the access policy can access and decrypt the data. All the user nodes on the blockchain can verify and check the proof.

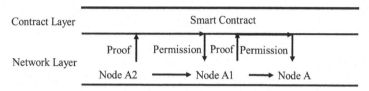

Fig. 2. User node structure

This model mainly has three layers, the smart contract layer, the network layer, and the data layer.

The smart contract layer includes zk-SNARK smart contracts and MA-ABE smart contracts. The zero-knowledge proof smart contract based on zk-SNARK technology is used to receive the access strategy submitted by the user node to generate zero-knowledge proof parameters, and to verify the zero-knowledge proof file submitted by the node, and return the result to the node and broadcast it to the whole public chain.The MA-ABE smart contract plays the role of the attribute authority center. First, it is responsible for assigning attribute management authority to all authoritative nodes. The user submits the attribute set to it, and the MA-ABE smart contract returns the attribute set decryption key for decryption through a secure channel. Users who want to access the data shared need to pass the zk-SNARK smart contract verification, and then they can access the MA-ABE smart contract.

The network layer contains all user nodes, sub-nodes, and authoritative nodes in the blockchain. All of these nodes communicate, authenticate, and exchange information through the network layer. The data layer contains the data of the user node, the data collection encrypted by the attribute base, and all data access records. The data of the data layer can be accessed through smart contracts.

As shown in Fig. 3, node A wants to share data. First, node A submits the access structure and data, returns the attribute-based encryption parameters, encrypts the data, and places it in the data layer. At the same time, the smart contract generates zk-SNARK parameters based on the access structure. Node B who wants to obtain the data of node A obtains the zk-SNARK parameters from the smart contract layer and uses its own attribute set to generate the zero-knowledge proof. After the verification is passed, the smart contract layer distributes the private key to node B, and node B can use the private key access the data shared by Node A and broadcast the access record to the entire blockchain. In the whole process, the attribute set of node A has not been leaked, and the access strategy of node B has not been disclosed, which hides the attributes and access strategy.

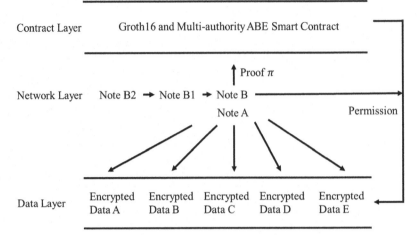

Fig. 3. Privacy protection model for blockchain data sharing

4.2 zk-SNARK and Multi-authority ABE Algorithms

In this model, we use zk-SNARK to design a general circuit and automatically generate the corresponding circuit when the user defines the access strategy. For example, assume access policy (income or revenue) and (expense or staff number). In this access policy, there are four kinds of user node can access. However, some attribures are sensitive attributes such as income expense, user node do not want to make this public. So we carry out zero-knowledge proof to protect this sensitive information.

First, we initialize the blockchain and establish a double-chain blockchain structure. We set up three level user node from first level to third level and set up the authority node. The authority nodes have the right to set up attributes for each level nodes, and these attributes are updatable. Second, we initialize zk-SNARK smart contract and multi-authority attribute-based encryption smart contract.

For zk-SNARK smart contract. Given secuirty parameter, initializes the algorithm settings, generates PK_z, VK_z. The data demander uses proving key and attribute set to generate proof. The blockchain smart contract layer uses the verification key to verify the proof. The data provider uses the access policy to encrypt data. After getting permission, the data demander uses the attribute set to decrypt the encrypted data.

Our zero-knowledge protocol is based on Groth16 [11], there are four steps as the followings.

Definition$(G_1, G_2, G_T, \dots)$: First set up three finite group G_1, G_2, G_T, their generators are $g, h, e(g, h)$ respectively. The calculation for G_1 is $|d|_1 = g^d$, for G_2 is $|d|_2 = h^d$. Then set up *public statements* $= (a_1, \dots, a_l)$ and transform the knowledge, which is known as the attributes set $U = \{u_1, u_2, u_3, \dots, u_j\}$ (j equals to $(m - l)$), into *serect knowledge* $= (a_{l+1}, \dots, a_m)$. The a_i satisfy the polynomial commitment as the formula (6), $u_i(X)$, $v_i(X)$, $w_i(X)$ are polynomials.

$$\sum_{i=0}^{m} a_i u_i(X) \cdot \sum_{i=0}^{m} a_i v_i(X) = \sum_{i=0}^{m} a_i w_i(X) + h(X)t(X) \qquad (6)$$

Setup(σ, τ) : Randomly select $\alpha, \beta, \gamma, \delta, x \leftarrow F^*$, generate $PP = \sigma, \tau$, the formulas are from (7) to (10).

$$\tau = (\alpha, \beta, \gamma, \delta, x) \tag{7}$$

$$\sigma = (|\sigma_1|_1, |\sigma_2|_2) \tag{8}$$

$$\sigma_1 = \left(\alpha, \beta, \gamma, \delta, \left\{x^i\right\}_{i=0}^{n-1}, \left\{\frac{\beta u_i(x) + \alpha v_i(x) + w_i(x)}{\gamma}\right\}_{i=0}^{l}\right.$$

$$\left.\left\{\frac{\beta u_i(x) + \alpha v_i(x) + w_i(x)}{\beta}\right\}_{i=l+1}^{m}, \left\{\frac{x^i t(x)}{\delta}\right\}_{i=0}^{n-2}\right) \tag{9}$$

$$\sigma_2 = \left(\beta, \gamma, \delta, \left\{x^i\right\}_{i=0}^{n-1}\right) \tag{10}$$

GenProof (A, B, C) : Randomly select r and s from F^*, calculate $\pi = \prod \sigma = (|A|_1, |C|_1, |B|_2)$, the formulas are from (11) to (13).

$$A = \alpha + \sum_{i=0}^{m} a_i u_i(x) + r\delta \tag{11}$$

$$B = \beta + \sum_{i=0}^{m} a_i v_i(x) + s\delta \tag{12}$$

$$C = \frac{\sum_{i=l+1}^{m} a_i(\beta u_i(x) + \alpha v_i(x) + w_i(x)) + h(x)t(x))}{\delta} + As + rB - rs\delta \tag{13}$$

VerProof (π, σ, τ) : Verify the following equation, the formula is (14).

$$|A|_1 \cdot |B|_2 = |\alpha|_1 \cdot |\beta|_2 + \frac{\sum_{i=0}^{l} a_i|(\beta u_i(x) + \alpha v_i(x) + w_i(x))|_1}{(|\gamma|_1/|\gamma|_2)} \cdot + |C|_1 \cdot |\delta|_2 \tag{14}$$

Proof of completeness : The following calculation is the proof of completeness of formula (14). Since $g \cdot \leq h = e(g, h)$, we can simply the formula (14) to the following equations.

$$e(|A|_1, |B|_2) = e(|\alpha|_1, |\beta|_2) \cdot e\left(\frac{\sum_{i=0}^{l} a_i|(\beta u_i(x) + \alpha v_i(x) + w_i(x))|_1}{|\gamma|_1}, |\gamma|_2\right) \cdot e(|C|_1 \cdot |\delta|_2)$$

$$A \cdot B = \left(\alpha + \sum_{i=0}^{m} a_i u_i(x) + r\delta\right) \cdot \left(\beta + \sum_{i=0}^{m} a_i v_i(x) + s\delta\right)$$

$$= \alpha \cdot \beta + \alpha \cdot \sum_{i=0}^{m} a_i v_i(x) + \alpha s\delta + \beta \cdot \sum_{i=0}^{m} a_i u_i(x) + \sum_{i=0}^{m} a_i u_i(x) \cdot$$
$$\sum_{i=0}^{m} a_i v_i(x) + s\delta \cdot \sum_{i=0}^{m} a_i u_i(x) + r\delta\beta + r\delta \cdot \sum_{i=0}^{m} a_i v_i(x) + rs\delta^2$$

$$= a \cdot \beta + \sum_{i=0}^{l} a_i(\beta u_i(x) + \alpha v_i(x) + w_i(x)) + \sum_{i=l+1}^{m} a_i(\beta u_i(x)$$
$$+ \alpha v_i(x) + w_i(x)) + h(x)t(x) + \alpha s\delta + s\delta \cdot \sum_{i=0}^{m} a_i u_i(x) + rs\delta^2$$

$$+ r\delta\beta + r\delta \cdot \sum_{i=0}^{m} a_i v_i(x) + rs\delta^2 - rs\delta^2$$

$$= \alpha \cdot \beta + \sum_{i=0}^{l} a_i(\beta u_i(x) + \alpha v_i(x) + w_i(x)) + \sum_{i=l+1}^{m} a_i(\beta u_i(x)$$
$$+ \alpha v_i(x) + w_i(x)) + h(x)t(x) + As\delta + rB\delta - rs\delta^2$$

$$= \alpha \cdot \beta + \frac{\sum_{i=0}^{l} a_i(\beta u_i(x) + \alpha v_i(x) + w_i(x))}{\gamma} \cdot \gamma + C \cdot \delta$$

Our data encryption scheme is based on Chase07 scheme [5], there are four steps as the followings.

Setup : For MA-ABE smart contract. First set up two finite group G_0, G_M, their generators are g_0, $g_M = e(g_0, g_0)$ respectively. When the node user data provider submit the access policy, it first generates the master key, the formula is (15). Then generates authority public key, the formula is (16), $s_1 \ldots s_k$, y_0 are randomly selected from $\mathbb{Z}_p$.

$$MK = \left(y_0, g_0 = g^{y_0}\right) \tag{15}$$

$$APK = \left(t_{k,1} \ldots t_{k,n+1}, T_k(x) = g_M^{x^n} g^{h(x)} = g_M^{x^n} \prod_{i=1}^{n+1} t_{k,i}^{\Delta i(x)}\right) \tag{16}$$

Encrypt(APK, M, ϕ) : The the MA-ABE smart contract encrypt the data with access policy ϕ, the formula is (17), choose a polynomial q_x for each node x in ϕ and the root node is R. There are $q_R(0) = s$ and $q_x(0) = q_{parent(x)}$.

$$CT = \left(\phi, \tilde{C} = Me(g_0, g_0)^s, C = g_0^s, \{E_{k,i} = T_k(i)^s\}_{i \in U}\right) \tag{17}$$

KeyGen(MK, U) : Then the smart contract use attributes set $U = \{u_1, u_2, u_3, \ldots, u_j\}$ from data demander to generate the serect key SK. The formula is (18).

$$SK = \left(D = g_M^{(y_0 - \sum_{i=0}^{K} y_{k,u})}, y_{k,u} = q_x(0), D_{k,x} = g_2^{q_x(0)} T(i)^{r_{k,x}}\right) \tag{18}$$

Decrypt(CT, SK) : The demander use the secret key to decrypt the data, the formula is (19). x is the node of access policy ϕ.

$$\frac{\tilde{C}}{e(C, D)} \cdot \frac{e\left(D_{k,x}, E'\right)}{e\left(R_{k,x}, E_{k,i}\right)} = \frac{Me(g, g)^s \cdot e(g, g)^{rs}}{e(g^{rs}, g^r)} = M \tag{19}$$

4.3 Privacy Protection Model Algorithms

In order to achieve the above requirements, we design the following four algorithms, and their relationship is shown in Fig. 4.

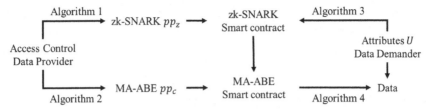

Fig. 4. Privacy protection algorithms

Algorithm 1 is mainly used to generate zero-knowledge proof public parameters. It executed once when the data provider submits the access policy. The set of attributes $U = \{u_1, u_2, u_3, \ldots, u_j\}$ used for validation is guaranteed to meet the access policy requirements. The detailed process is as follows.

Algorithm 1 zk-SNARK Smart contract Setup

Inputs: Access Policy, A security parameter λ
Outputs: zk-SNARK public parameters pp_z
pp_z = **Function** Setup (1^λ)
For each policy p **in** Access Policy:
   Construct a circuit C_p
   Compute $(pk_z, vk_z) = KeyGen(C_p)$
Set $PK_z = \cup pk_z$ and $VK_z = \cup vk_z$
Output $pp_z = (PK_z, VK_z)$

Algorithm 2 is used to generate MA-ABE public parameter list, which is mainly used for attribute base encryption of data. The detailed process is as follows.

Algorithm 2 Mulit-authority ABE Smart contract Setup

Inputs: Access Control, A security parameter κ
Outputs: MA-ABE parameters pp_c
pp_c = Function Setup (1^κ)
For parameter 1^κ:
   Compute MK_c
   Compute APK_c
Output: $pp_c = (PK_c)$

Algorithm 3 is used to generate and verify the proof in zk-SNARK. The data demander obtains the proof parameters from the smart contract layer of zk-SNARK, and then input the attribute set and the zk-SNARK proof parameters to generate the proof, and submit the proof to the smart contract layer of zk-SNRAK for verification. After the smart contract layer verification is passed, the data visitor will get the right to access MA-ABE smart contract. The detailed process is as follows.

Algorithm 3 Proof Generation and Verification

Inputs: Attributes U, PK_z, VK_z
Outputs: Proof, Permission or Denial
For pk_z in PK_z:
  Compute $proof_z = Genproof(Attributes\ U, pk)$
  $Proof_z = \cup\ proof_z$
For $proof_z$ in $Proof_z$:
  Compute $Verproof(proof_z, vk_z)$
  If $Verproof(proof_z, vk_z)$ succeed:
    Give right to access MA-ABE Smart Contract
  If $Verproof(proof_z, vk_z)$ fail:
    Deny access request
Output: Permission or Denial

Algorithm 4 is mainly used for data encryption and decryption. When the data provider access policy is submitted to the MA-ABE smart contract layer, it will obtain a *SK* that can be used for attribute-based encryption of the data. After being verified by the zk-SNARK smart contract layer, the data visitor can submit the attribute set to the MA-ABE smart contract layer to obtain the SK, which is used to decryption the data stored in the private chain. The detailed process is as follows.

Algorithm 4 Data Encryption and Decryption

Inputs: Access policy, Permission, Attributes U, Data
Outputs: Encrypted Data
For Data, PK, Access policy:
  Compute $Encrypted\ data = Encrypt(APK, Access\ Policy, Data)$
For Permission, MK and Attributes U:
  Compute SK_c
For SK and Encrypted data:
  Compute $Data = Decrypt(SK,\ Encypted\ Data)$
Output: Data

The above Algorithm 1 to 4 realizes the protection of sensitive access policy and sensitive attributes in this process of blockchain data sharing. It also meets the requirements of confidentiality and zero-knowledge. For confidentiality, the multi-authority attribute-based encryption can effectively protect the data. Users who do not own the set of attributes specified by the access policy cannot obtain any information about the plaintext from the ciphertext. Besides, this scheme avoids the risk of setting single authorization. For zero-knowledge, other ondes cannot obtain any information about access policies and user attribute sets from the access records or certificates in the public chain.

5 Conclusion

Based on the blockchain data sharing model using MA-ABE encryption, this article uses zero-knowledge proof to propose a blockchain data sharing privacy protection model based on zk-SNARK technology. This model not only satisfies the fine-grained access control requirements of data sharing, but also effectively protects the privacy protection problems that occur when user nodes adopt multi-authority attribute-based encryption on blockchain data sharing, preventing the risk of sensitive access strategies and sensitive attribute leakage, avoiding the risk of single authorization.

There are still many improvements in this article. This paper adopts zero knowledge proof scheme is not for general updatable zk-SNARK, so for different access strategy and data sharing scheme, blockchain intelligent contract parameters need to reset the zero knowledge proof, this will affect the efficiency of data sharing, to some extent, further work to set up general renewable zk-SNARK scheme. In addition, the security assumption of the multi-authority attribute-based encryption scheme is simple, and the security is low. The further work is to update the multi-authority attribute-based encryption scheme by adopting the difficult problem with high security, so as to achieve higher security.

Acknowledgments. This work is supported by the Emerging Interdisciplinary Project of CUFE, Ministry of education of Humanities and Social Science project (No. 19YJCZH178), the National Natural Science Foundation of China (No.61906220).

References

1. Ben-Sasson, E., Bentov, I., Horesh, Y., Riabzev, M.: Scalable, transparent, and post-quantum secure computational integrity. Eprint. Iacr. Org **693423**, 1–83 (2018)
2. Ben-Sasson, E., et al.: Zerocash: Decentralized anonymous payments from bitcoin. In: Proceedings - IEEE Symposium on Security and Privacy, pp. 459–474 (2014)
3. Waters, B.: Ciphertext-policy attribute-based encryption: an expressive, efficient, and provably secure realization. In: International Workshop on Public Key Cryptography, pp. 53–70 (2011)
4. Bunz, B., Bootle, J., Boneh, D., Poelstra, A., Wuille, P., Maxwell, G.: Bulletproofs: short proofs for confidential transactions and more. In: Proceedings - IEEE Symposium on Security and Privacy, pp. 315–334, May 2018

5. Chase, M.: Multi-authority attribute based encryption. In: Vadhan, S.P. (ed.) TCC 2007. LNCS, vol. 4392, pp. 515–534. Springer, Heidelberg (2007). https://doi.org/10.1007/978-3-540-70936-7_28

6. Chen, J., Gong, J., Wee, H.: Improved inner-product encryption with adaptive security and full attribute-hiding. In: Peyrin, T., Galbraith, S. (eds.) ASIACRYPT 2018. LNCS, vol. 11273, pp. 673–702. Springer, Cham (2018). https://doi.org/10.1007/978-3-030-03329-3_23

7. Cui, H., Deng, R.H., Lai, J., Yi, X., Nepal, S.: An efficient and expressive ciphertext-policy attribute-based encryption scheme with partially hidden access structures, revisited. Comput. Netw. **133**, 157–165 (2018)

8. Fu, Y.: Research on supply chain information sharing mechanism and management mode based on blockchain. Doctor Level of Thesis, Central University of Finance and Economics (2018)

9. Gabizon, A., Williamson, Z.J., Ciobotaru, O.: PLONK : permutations over lagrange-bases for oecumenical noninteractive arguments of knowledge. In: Stanford Blockchain Conference, pp. 1–33 (2020)

10. Goyal, V., Pandey, O., Sahai, A., Waters, B.: Attribute-based encryption for fine-grained access control of encrypted data. In: Proceedings of the ACM Conference on Computer and Communications Security, pp. 89–98 (2006)

11. Groth, J.: On the size of pairing-based non-interactive arguments. IACR, pp. 1–25 (2016)

12. Groth, J., Kohlweiss, M., Maller, M., Meiklejohn, S., Miers, I.: Updatable and universal common reference strings with Applications to zk-SNARKs. In: Shacham, H., Boldyreva, A. (eds.) CRYPTO 2018. LNCS, vol. 10993, pp. 698–728. Springer, Cham (2018). https://doi.org/10.1007/978-3-319-96878-0_24

13. Guan, Z.: Efficient privacy-preserving account-model blockchain based on zero-knowledge proof. Master Level of Thesis, ShanDong University (2020)

14. Katz, J., Sahai, A., Waters, B.: Predicate encryption supporting disjunctions, polynomial equations, and inner products. In: Smart, N. (ed.) EUROCRYPT 2008. LNCS, vol. 4965, pp. 146–162. Springer, Heidelberg (2008). https://doi.org/10.1007/978-3-540-78967-3_9

15. Li, G., He, D., Guo, B., Lu, S.: Blockchain privacy protection algorithms based on zero knowledge proof. J. Huazhong Univ. Sci. Technol. (Natural Science Edition), **48**, 7 (2020)

16. Petkus, M.: Why and How zk-SNARK Works, pp. 1–65 (2019). http://arxiv.org/abs/1906.07221

17. Sahai, A., Waters, B.R.: Fuzzy identity based encryption. In: Proceedings of the 24th Annual International Conference on Theory and Applications of Cryptographic Techniques, pp. 1–9 (2005)

18. Sandborn, W., et al.: Sonic. Am. J. Gastroenterol. **103**, S436 (2008)

19. Wang, X., Jiang, X., Li, Y.: Model for data access control and sharing based on blockchain. J. Softw. **30**(6), 1661–1669 (2019)

20. Wang, Y., Fan, K.: Effective CP-ABE with hidden access policy. J. Comput. Res. Dev. **56**(10), 2151–2159 (2019)

21. Wei, X.: Research and implementation of anonymous electronic survey system based on non-interactive zero knowledge. Master Level of Thesis, Northeastern University (2015)

Multi-scene Classification of Blockchain Encrypted Traffic

Yu Wang[1,2], Chencheng Wang[1,2], Gang Xiong[1,2(✉)], and Zhen Li[1,2]

[1] Institute of Information Engineering, Chinese Academy of Sciences, Beijing, China
{wangyu1996,wangchencheng,xionggang,lizhen}@iie.ac.cn
[2] School of Cyber Security, University of Chinese Academy of Sciences,
Beijing, China

Abstract. The functions carried by the blockchain are gradually increasing, and the types of services are diverse. Users use blockchain by synchronizing block data, query balances or trade through the trading platform, use decentralized applications (DApps), which are deployed on different blockchains. Blockchain uses different proprietary encryption protocols to let users communicate with others. The trading platform and DApps adopt SSL/TLS encryption protocol, making blockchain's encrypted traffic classification difficult. In this paper, we conduct a multi-scene classification of blockchain, including synchronizing block data, user behavior on DApps, and user behavior on the trading platform. We use deep learning and machine learning to solve different problems and verify the methods through the real traffic data because of the different encrypted protocols. The results show that our methods can perform well in the multi-scene classification of blockchain encrypted traffic.

Keywords: Blockchain · Synchronizing block data · Trading platform · Dapps user behavior · Encrypted traffic · Classification

1 Introduction

Ethereum is the second most valuable cryptocurrency and is the first major blockchain to support Turing-complete scripting via smart contracts. As of March 2021, there are more than three thousand DApps, and DApps based on Ethereum occupy above 81%. So we choose Ethereum to study. Ethereum's network communication is comprised of three different protocols, which run on top of UDP and TCP: RLPx for node discovery and secure transport, DEVp2p for application session establishment, and the Ethereum application-level protocol (henceforth referred to as Ethereum subprotocol). DApps and the trading platform use the SSL/TLS protocol to encrypt transmission data.

Many methods of full traffic analysis become useless, such as deep packet inspection (dpi). There are lots of researches on application identification [1,2,5]. Due to the improvement of technology, existing methods can not meet people's demands. So many researchers study the classification of application

© Springer Nature Singapore Pte Ltd. 2021
H.-N. Dai et al. (Eds.): BlockSys 2021, CCIS 1490, pp. 329–337, 2021.
https://doi.org/10.1007/978-981-16-7993-3_25

user behaviors [3]. But DApps are different from Apps, many features performed unsatisfying. Although Shen et al. [4] classified DApps application traffic to distinguish different DApps, this may be too coarse-grained. Aiolli et al. [1] used time statistics features to identify user behaviors in the bitcoin wallet with high accuracy, but there is a terrible performance of our research point.

In this paper, we consider the multi-scene classification of blockchain encrypted traffic and proposed different methods to solve different application scenarios. The contributions are as follows: first, We propose different methods to classify blockchain encrypted traffic in multiple scenarios, synchronizing block data, user behavior on DApps, and user behavior on the trading platform, including proprietary encryption protocol and TLS encryption protocol; Second, for the features, we use DApps' encrypted traffic to characterize the features for visualization. And it can be seen from the figure that the characteristics are distinguishable under different behaviors; Third, we collect the encrypted traffic generated by blockchain in different scenarios. Multi-datasets are collected in the real environment. Experimental results in the multiple scenarios achieve good performance.

2   Related Work

According to our research points, we will review the related work from three aspects: Web application encrypted traffic classification, mobile application encrypted traffic classification, and network traffic analysis of blockchain.

Web Application Encrypted Traffic Classification. Chen et al. [1] showed that despite encryption, such a side-channel information leak is a realistic and serious threat to user privacy, such as stateful communication, low entropy input, and significant traffic distinction. Cai et al. [2] used an SVM with a custom kernel based on an edit-distance. The web fingerprinting attack achieved more than 86% accuracy for 100 sites.

Mobile Application Encrypted Traffic Classification. Vincent et al. used [5] side-channel data, such as packet size and direction is still leaked from encrypted connections, identified 110 applications with 96% accuracy, and proved that app fingerprints persist to varying extents across devices and app versions. Conti et al. [3] first clustered the application's user behavior streams by clustering. They calculated the dynamic warping distance between different streams for each stream's through packet length features, but they experimented with each app, eliminating the effects between apps.

Network Traffic Analysis of Blockchain. Shen et al. [4] fused time series, packet length series and burst series into high-dimensional features. The accuracy of DApps traffic classification is 90% through SVM, KNN, and RF. Aiolli et al. [1] used time statistics features of different stream directions such as length, maximum, minimum, average, etc., the user behavior in the bitcoin wallet is trained by SVM and random forest, and the accuracy of the final recognition of user behavior is above 95%.

3   Methodology

In this section, we introduce the dataset used in our experiments. The system framework is shown in Fig. 1. First, we collect the encrypted traffic generated in three application scenarios. Then we preprocess flows. Finally, we send different features to different classifiers.

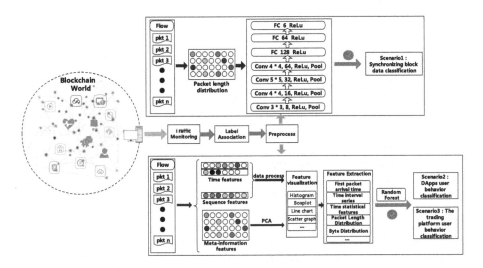

Fig. 1. Multi-scene classification framework.

3.1   Datasets

As for the block synchronization dataset, we choose three ways to synchronize data on Ethereum, including full (or public), fast, and light. And two clients (i.e., Geth, Parity) with the most significant number of users are selected for traffic collection. As seen in Table 1, Each behavior corresponds to a specific explanation.

As for the user behavior classification of DApps and trading platforms, we selected 11 DApps based on Ethereum and two trading platforms. Most of them are close to our lives and have lots of transactions. By analyzing these DApps and trading platforms, we extract 88 user behaviors on DApps and 12 user behaviors on the trading platforms.

We analyze the two trading platforms and DApps, and identify the behaviors available on them. Due to space limitations, some of the behaviors are explained as follows.

Table 1. Flow of the block synchronization

Behaviors	Specific explanation	Flows
Geth-Full	The Geth client synchronizes data in full mode, obtains header and body of the block, and verifies the information of each block from the genesis block	965
Geth-Fast	The Geth client synchronizes data in fast mode, only obtains header and body of the block	474
Geth-Light	The Geth client synchronizes data in light mode and only obtains the state	5518
Parity-Public	The Parity client synchronizes data in light mode, only the block header is synchronized	3388
Parity-Light	The Parity client synchronizes data in Public mode and obtains header and body of the block	5500
Background	Background traffic	31544

- **Register:** Open the webpage, click Register, enter the email address, and complete the registration as required.
- **Login:** open the webpage, click Login, enter the user name and password.
- **View sellers:** Open the webpage, choose to buy, select the payment method and purchase amount, and click Buy Now to view eligible sellers.
- **Buy cryptocurrency:** On the seller's page, check the seller's offer and restrictions, select the seller, click Buy, enter the amount, and complete the purchase.
- **View detail:** Users open things and view detailed information of them.
- **Follow someone:** Users follow a person in the DApps. The person in different DApps represents different identities, such as author, publisher.
- **Like something:** Users give artwork or other things a like or dislike.
- **create project:** Users can publish some different projects in different DApps. We can create payment request for rent in Staybit DApp; We can create a task to find suitable worker; We can upload the local video to draft and describe it.
- **activities:** Users browse activities that occur in DApps.

We collected about two hundred thousand flows and millions of packets. Before extracting information from pcap files, we first perform the preprocessing operation. 1) For each data stream, we filter other traffic streams by the extension field named Server Name Identification in the Client Hello packet. 2) We filter packets in streams that may affect classification accuracy, such as ACK packets and retransmission packets, which may affect the similarity between the two data streams. Finally, from Wireshark capture files, we extracted data from the data streams to form Json files.

3.2   Feature Extraction

We consider practical traffic features from four aspects: time feature, series feature, and meta-information feature. We visualize some of the features on DApps encrypted traffic to show the difference between the features.

Time Features

The First Packet Arrival Time from Server To Client. DApps backend runs on Ethereum through the smart contract, and the data is stored on Ethereum nodes. When a user opens the DApps through the browser, because the resource size of each page is different, different size data needed to be retrieved from the nodes on Ethereum, then transmitted to the front-end through API and displayed on the interface. Figure 2 shows that each behavior has a time interval that includes more than 80% of streams. The histogram straight-line represents this interval, indicating that different user behaviors have differences in the first packet arrival time from server to client.

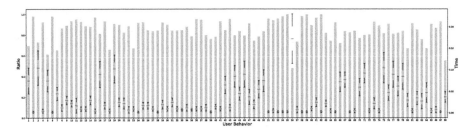

Fig. 2. First packet arrival time from server to client of 88 user behavior. The Interval in histogram means the first arrival time of most packets, and the histogram represent the percentage in this interval.

Time Statistical Features. We have also processed the following features and represented them with figures. The mean of total time per-flow and the average arrival time of packets, the ratio of the sum of each flow packets arrival time and the sum of packets per flow.

Figure 3 compares these two statistical features in 88 DApps user actions. The conspicuous differences in the means of total time and the average arrival time indicate that these time statistical features can be used as useful features of the classifier.

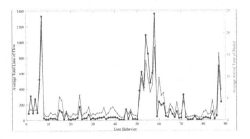

Fig. 3. The mean of total time per flow and the average arrival time of packets.

Sequence Feature

Packet Length Distribution. For many DApps user behaviors, such as Staybit DApp, which is a Decentralized Short-Term Rental Payment System, users can create applications to get rent by describing what they can provide, when other users see the application and want to rent this item, you need to check this application and pay through Ethereum account. The data that needed to be transferred to Ethereum for the two behaviors is not identical, so we consider the packet length feature. Each subplot of Fig. 4 represents a DApp, and each small chart has different user behaviors. From the shape of the polyline, we can find that there are significant differences in the distribution characteristics of packet length between different DApps

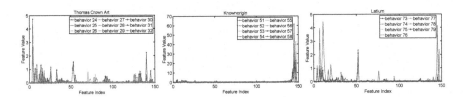

Fig. 4. Packet length distribution of different DApps user behaviors.

3.3   Classification

In our experiments, we used the Random forest classifier. The classifier is trained using 100 estimators (or weak learners).

4   Performance Evaluation

4.1   Classification Performance of Synchronizing Block Data.

As for this classification, We use the packet length distribution as input to classify six types of encrypted traffic through the CNN model. As seen in Table 2, precision, recall, F1-metrics are reported.

Table 2. Classification performance for synchronizing block data

Behaviors	Precision	Recall	F1
Geth-Full	0.8365	0.9171	0.8749
Geth-Fast	0.8428	0.6561	0.7378
Geth-Light	0.9978	0.9922	0.995
Parity-Public	0.9556	0.6488	0.7729
Parity-Light	0.8197	0.9891	0.8932
Background	0.9983	0.9998	0.9991

4.2 Classification Performance of User Behavior on DApps

The Classification Performance of DApps User behavior is shown in Fig. 5

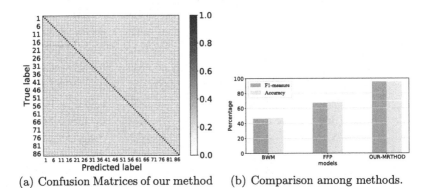

(a) Confusion Matrices of our method   (b) Comparison among methods.

Fig. 5. Classification performance of DApps user behavior

Compared with Previous Work. To confirm the validity of the proposed approach, we compared the results achieved by the proposed features with two other methods. Shen [4] fuse three sequence features by a kernel function (named FFP). We also extracted the features proposed by [1] (named BWM).

Figure 5(b) shows the results. The accuracy of our method is 95.66%. Compared to BWM and FFP. The improvement effect is very obvious.

4.3 Classification Performance of User Behavior on the Trading Platform

As for the classification of user behavior encryption traffic on the trading platform, we select the main functions on the two platforms, among which Blockchain is a transaction query platform, and Paxful is a trading platform. As seen in

Table 3. For Blockchain, the precision is above 92%, while the classification result of trading platform user behavior is lower, the precision is 83%. The precision rate of buying and selling cryptocurrency is lower than the average level. We guess it may be because of the two similar behavior. The only difference is whether Bitcoin is bought or sold, so the website's encrypted traffic confuses the classifier.

Table 3. Classification performance for synchronizing block data

Platform	User behavior	Precision	Recall	F1
Blockchain	View market quotations	0.9166	0.8667	0.891
	View Blockchain	0.9239	0.9444	0.9341
	View unconfirmed transactions	0.8989	0.8889	0.8939
	View api	1	0.9889	0.9944
	View diagram about Blockchain	0.9139	0.9222	0.918
	Average	0.9298	0.9234	0.9265
Paxful	Register	0.9333	0.8796	0.9057
	Login	0.8182	0.9	0.8571
	View sellers	0.8469	0.8827	0.8644
	View buyers	0.7732	0.7234	0.7474
	Buy cryptocurrency	0.7993	0.7625	0.7805
	Sell cryptocurrency	0.7652	0.7321	0.7483
	View notification messages	0.8842	0.8653	0.8746
	Average	0.83	0.8198	0.8214

5   Conclusion

In this paper, we conduct a multi-scene classification of blockchain, including synchronizing block data, user behavior on DApps, and user behavior on the trading platform. We use deep learning and machine learning to solve different problems and verify the methods through the real traffic data. We use DApps' encrypted traffic to characterize features to visualize features. The results show that our methods can perform well in the multi-scene classification of blockchain encrypted traffic. In future work, we plan to propose a method that balances the supervision and user privacy in the DApps world.

Acknowledgment. This work is supported by The National Key Research and Development Program of China (No. 2020YFB1006100, No. 2020YFE0200500 and No. 2018YFB1800200) and Key research and Development Program for Guangdong Province under grant No. 2019B010137003.

References

1. Aiolli, F., Conti, M., Gangwal, A., Polato, M.: Mind your wallet's privacy: identifying bitcoin wallet apps and user's actions through network traffic analysis. In: Proceedings of the 34th ACM/SIGAPP Symposium on Applied Computing, SAC 2019, Limassol, Cyprus, 8–12 April 2019, pp. 1484–1491 (2019). https://doi.org/10.1145/3297280.3297430
2. Cai, X., Zhang, X.C., Joshi, B., Johnson, R.: Touching from a distance: website fingerprinting attacks and defenses. In: the ACM Conference on Computer and Communications Security, CCS, pp. 605–616 (2012)
3. Conti, M., Mancini, L.V., Spolaor, R., Verde, N.V.: Analyzing android encrypted network traffic to identify user actions. IEEE Trans. Inf. Forensics Secur. $11(1)$, 114–125 (2016). https://doi.org/10.1109/TIFS.2015.2478741
4. Shen, M., Zhang, J., Zhu, L., Xu, K., Du, X., Liu, Y.: Encrypted traffic classification of decentralized applications on Ethereum using feature fusion. In: Proceedings of the International Symposium on Quality of Service, IWQoS, pp. 18:1–18:10 (2019)
5. Taylor, V.F., Spolaor, R., Conti, M., Martinovic, I.: AppScanner: automatic fingerprinting of smartphone apps from encrypted network traffic. In: IEEE European Symposium on Security and Privacy, EuroS&P, pp. 439–454 (2016)

Combination of Certificateless Message Authentication and Blockchain Incentives for Traffic Event Reporting in VANETs

Li Zhang[1], Jianbo Xu[1(✉)], and Mingdong Tang[2]

[1] School of Computer Science and Engineering,
Hunan University of Science and Technology, Xiangtan 411201, China
jbxu@hnust.edu.cn
[2] School of Information Science and Technology,
Guangdong University of Foreign Studies, Guangzhou 510006, China
mdtang@gdufs.edu.cn

Abstract. The application of vehicle ad-hoc networks has brought huge potential to the development of intelligent transportation systems. By traffic event reporting, traffic efficiency can be significantly improved. However, people usually lack the motivation for reporting traffic events or driving violations, because once the identity of the reporter is leaked, he or she may be tracked by malicious attackers or be retaliated by violators. However, if the reporter is anonymous, it is difficult to guarantee the accuracy and authenticity of the reports. In order to solve this contradiction, a mechanism that combines certificateless message authentication and blockchain incentives is proposed in this paper. A certificateless message signature algorithm is designed to provide anonymity and non-repudiation for traffic-related message reporters. Simultaneously, an adaptive t-threshold multi-signature mechanism is introduced in our scheme. Similar to crowdsourcing, it requires multiple participants to witness the authenticity of the message together. Aggregation signature verification improves message authentication efficiency. A trust currency is introduced to motivate reporters' enthusiasm for participation in intelligent transportation, and it is also taken as a report dissemination network. The simulation results show that our scheme is secure and effective in the intelligent transportation system.

Keywords: Intelligent transportation system · Blockchain incentives · Certificateless identity authentication · Aggregation verification

1 Introduction

For decades, with the development of the economy and technology, the number of vehicles has increased year by year. Intelligent transportation systems (ITS) are playing an increasingly important role in transportation networks. The popularization of ITS will create a fundamental revolution in the management of urban transportation. The development of wireless communication

H.-N. Dai et al. (Eds.): BlockSys 2021, CCIS 1490, pp. 338–351, 2021.
https://doi.org/10.1007/978-981-16-7993-3_26

technology makes it easier for vehicle manufacturers to install wireless communication equipment in vehicles. Under this circumstance, the vehicular ad-hoc network (VANET) emerges, which significantly facilitates the communication among vehicles, or between vehicles and roadside units (RSU). Simultaneously, VANET also provides convenience for broadcasting traffic reports, such as traffic jams, traffic accidents, road conditions, even traffic violations. According to these traffic reports, drivers can be cautious with road conditions or change their driving route. The traffic management department can restrain and punish traffic violations, all of which can guarantee traffic safety.

Although the VANET has many advantages and can bring great convenience to traffic management, the open, dynamic wireless network environment and the high mobility of vehicles bring considerable challenges to the safe transmission of traffic reports and the privacy protection of vehicles [2]. Adversaries can easily launch various attacks through wireless networks, such as tampering with the emergency level of traffic accidents or the location of traffic jams, tracking the trajectory of vehicles according to the messages sent by vehicles, etc. The information security issues in the VANET have become the bottleneck of the further development of the VANET. Improving the information security of VANET has become a prevalent issue in the fields of academic research and industrial application.

Although traditional cryptography can ensure integrity and confidentiality of messages during transmission, it still has certain limitations and cannot effectively prevent malicious attackers from masquerading legitimate reporters to spread fake or wrong messages to other vehicles intentionally. These fake messages will reduce traffic efficiency and even impose a huge threat on people's lives. Furthermore, the disclosure of identity information also causes disturbance to reporters and decreases their activeness. Therefore, the authenticity of reports, identity privacy preservation, and participation enthusiasm are primarily aims needed to be achieved in our proposed scheme.

To accomplish the objectives mentioned above, we propose a traffic event reporting scheme based on the combination of certificateless message authentication and blockchain incentive mechanism in this paper. The main contributions of this paper are as follows:

(1) A network model which is consisted of vehicles, roadside units (RSUs), trust authority is designed for message reporting system in VANET. With the help of vehicles and roadside infrastructure, the dissemination of traffic events and the report of violations can be implemented.
(2) A novel certificateless signature algorithm on the basis of the hash function, bilinear pairing operation, and elliptic curve cryptography (ECC) is proposed. As asymmetric cryptography, the signature algorithm ensures the legitimacy and non-repudiation of message reporters. Hash function is utilized to generate message digests to check the integrity of the message. At the same time, a pseudonym is adopted in the message signature process to realize anonymity. When a malicious vehicle releases a fake message, its real identity can be tracked, which provides conditional privacy protection for the message reporters.

(3) Inspired by the crowdsourcing model, we propose an adaptive t-threshold multi-signature and aggregation signature verification scheme in this paper. The opinions of multiple witnesses are taken to judge the authenticity and accuracy of the reported events. In the message signature verification process, the aggregation verification is adopted to replace verification one by one, which significantly improves the message authentication efficiency. Considering the real traffic circumstances, the number of witnesses needed to participate in message signature, i.e., threshold t can be assumed to vary with the time and location in which traffic events occur.

(4) In order to increase the enthusiasm of message reporters, a blockchain-based TCoin incentive mechanism is proposed. Reporters and witnesses who join in the verification process can get TCoin as a reward for their active participation, and they can also spend TCoin in real life. Similar to blockchain cryptocurrency, all TCoin transactions are recorded in the blockchain. Furthermore, the reported messages can be broadcasted through nodes in the blockchain.

2   Related Work

The authentication and privacy for VANETs are very broad terms related to different security requirements. They are usually achieved by using the cryptographic method. PKI-based authentication is a simple and effective solution proposed earlier to implement security for VANETs. PKI mechanism can not only guarantee integrity, confidentiality, and non-repudiation of messages, but also solve the secret key distribution problem that existed in symmetric cryptography [10]. In existing literature, RSA algorithm [8], ElGamal algorithm [3] and Elliptic Curve Cryptography (ECC) [5] are usually adopted to ensure data security. However, it needs to consume large computational and storage resources to manage certificates in PKI mechanism, which probably makes a bottleneck in performance [14]. In order to overcome the defects of the PKI mechanism, Identity-based public key cryptography (ID-PKC) [12] is proposed, which has been widely applied for secure authentication in VANETs.

As a unique part responsible for generating private keys for all entities, the key generator center (KGC) perhaps uses these private keys to forge signatures known as the key escrow problem. To address this problem, the concept of certificateless public key cryptography (CL-PKC) was introduced by Al-Riyami and Paterson in 2003 [1]. Subsequently, many certificateless signature schemes have been proposed successively [7]. Most of them use the bilinear pairing method to realize signature and verification with different computational costs and communication costs. In these schemes, the pseudonym is usually combined with a signature algorithm to implement privacy preservation.

Cryptographic methods mentioned above are just prerequisites for traffic-related messages to be accepted. They can only guarantee that the messages are sent by authorized entities and not tampered by malicious attackers [2]. However, adversaries perhaps impersonate legitimate entities to broadcast fake messages by cracking the cryptosystem and forge signatures. How to check the authenticity of messages, many scholars have proposed threshold verification method. If a message is confirmed by a certain number of entities together, it can be considered as a valid message [9]. Shamir [11] originally introduced threshold thought into cryptography for sharing messages among group members. However, each member in the group should believe each other, which is obviously not appropriate for non-fully trusted VANET networks. Bresson et al. [4] designed a threshold ring signature, only more than t numbers of entities participate in the signature process, the signed message can be valid. Zhang et al. [16] proposed a scheme called APPA, which utilized a group signature to address the problem of authentication for VANET. However, all members need to use the same private key. Both two schemes inevitably bring significant security risks, such as the well-known Sybil attack.

Recently, blockchain has already been applied in many Internet of Things (IoTs) applications [13]. The development of blockchain techniques facilitates decentralized trust management in VANETs. The trust value of the source can be used as important evidence to judge whether the message is credible. Goka et al. [6] designed a distributed management system for trust and reward. The system can reduce the passive impact between non-cooperative nodes in mobile ad hoc networks. Yang et al. [15] presented a traffic event verification scheme based on blockchain, in which the Proof-of-Event (PoE) consensus mechanism is designed instead of PoW approach for saving computational power. As a research hot, blockchain is anticipated to address many issues that existed in VANET due to its various properties such as decentralization, openness, tamper-resistance, data consistency, etc. In this paper, we propose a concept of taking reward coins as trust value, which benefits trust management and also provides profit-driven incentives.

3 Proposed Traffic Event Reporting Scheme

3.1 System Model

In this section, we describe the model of traffic event reporting system, as shown in Fig. 1. It mainly includes three entities, namely, Trust Authority (TA), RSUs, and vehicles. Their specific functions are illustrated as follows:

(1) TA: It is the highest authority in VANET, which is consisting of three parts: key generation center (KGC), identity trace center (TRA), and traffic management department (TMD). KGC is responsible for system initialization and registration for vehicles and RSUs; TRA performs identity management for all entities in VANET. It can track real identities of malicious vehicles when the vehicles are found to do some misbehaviors; TMD is in charge of processing traffic events and driving violations. It possesses confirmation right on the authenticity of reports when event reports have not enough witnesses.

(2) RSUs: They are widely distributed on roadsides or at crossroads, with stable computing power and a certain storage capacity. They can be regarded as routers between vehicle nodes or as edge nodes in VANET, providing remote

network access services for vehicles. In our proposed scheme, when RSU receives a traffic event report submitted by a vehicle, it needs to collect feedback opinions from event witnesses within its communication range to evaluate the report's authenticity. RSU broadcasts it in the entire VANET and rewards trust coin, namely TCoin, to vehicles if the report is credible. For example, there is no witness in some particular circumstances, the report would be resubmitted to the TMD for judgment. The blockchain proposed in this paper is also composed of RSUs. After partially authorized RSU nodes execute the consensus algorithm, all RSUs jointly maintain a distributed TCoin currency ledger. Here, we assume that attackers are not capable of attacking the majority of RSUs even if RSUs work in a non-full trusted environment. Therefore, most RSUs are supposed to be credible.

(3) Vehicles: Each vehicle is deployed with an on-board unit (OBU). Due to the limited communication capability of OBU, Vehicle-to-Vehicle (V2V) and Vehicle-to-Infrastructure (V2I) communication adopt dedicated short-range communication (DSRC) protocol or C-V2X protocol. With DSRC, each vehicle can disseminate a traffic-related message within a time interval (100–300 ms) to other vehicles or RSUs. The vehicle identity and some confidential parameters needed in cryptographic operations are also stored in the OBU's tamper-proof device (TPD).

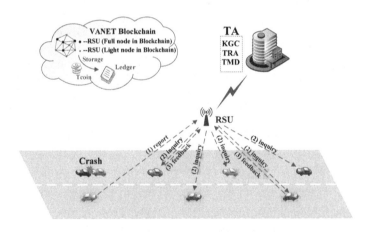

Fig. 1. Network architecture based on blockchain in VANET.

In order to simplify the description, we define three types of roles in our proposed reporting scheme. They are report initiator, responder and verifier, which are denoted as $\mathcal{I}$, $\mathcal{R}$ and $\mathcal{V}$, respectively. Role $\mathcal{I}$ is a vehicle that is willing to submit a report to RSU when it encounters a traffic event or violation. RSU act as role $\mathcal{V}$. When the RSU receives a report from vehicle $\mathcal{I}$, it broadcasts the inquiring message to other vehicles driving in its communication coverage so as to collect responses for verifying the authenticity of the report. Responder $\mathcal{R}$ is the event witness; it is a vehicle that voluntarily gives a feedback opinion to $\mathcal{V}$.

Messages transmitted in the communication process are also categorized into three forms, including report initiating packet ($\mathcal{RIP}$), opinion inquiring packet ($\mathcal{OIP}$), and opinion feedback packet ($\mathcal{OFP}$). $\mathcal{RIP}$ represents a type of packet sent from initiator $\mathcal{I}$ to verifier $\mathcal{V}$. When the initiator decides to submit an event report to the verifier, it first creates the event content, including event ID, event type, location, time, etc., then generates the corresponding signature according to the content, finally packs the content, signature, its own pseudonym and timestamp as $\mathcal{RIP}$. $\mathcal{OIP}$ is a type of opinion inquiry packet that is broadcasted from verifier $\mathcal{V}$ to multiple vehicles. $\mathcal{OIP}$ consists of event content, the hash value of content, and timestamp. $\mathcal{OFP}$ is a type of opinion feedback packet that witnesses response to the verifier. It includes the opinion of the responder, pseudonym, signature, and timestamp.

Here, taking the timeliness of the report into account, we assume that initiator $\mathcal{I}$ needs to submit the report near the site of the event rather than far away. In this case, there are no cross-domain issues. Furthermore, we should consider the actual situation in VANET that multiple vehicles submit reports within a short period, and some of the reports probably refer to the same events.

3.2   Algorithm Description

The protocol process mainly includes five stages:

1. **Setup**: It is the system initialization stage in which system parameters and public-private key pairs of all roles are generated.
2. **Report**: When a vehicle encounters a traffic event and is willing to report it, the vehicle then transforms its identity into report initiator $\mathcal{I}$. It generates a report initiating packet $\mathcal{RIP}$ and forwards this packet to the nearest RSU, i.e., verifier $\mathcal{V}$.
3. **Inquiry**: After receiving $\mathcal{RIP}$, $\mathcal{V}$ check timestamp and signature, if correct, it broadcasts opinion inquiry packet $\mathcal{OIP}$ to the witnesses for feedback.
4. **Feedback**: When a vehicle receives $\mathcal{OIP}$, it is indeed the witness of the event and pleasure to give feedback to $\mathcal{V}$, it becomes responder $\mathcal{R}$ and response an opinion feedback packet $\mathcal{OFP}$ to $\mathcal{V}$.
5. **Verification**: $\mathcal{V}$ verifies the authenticity of the report after it collects more than threshold t $\mathcal{OFP}$s.

The specific algorithm is described as follows:

(1) Setup phase

Step 1: *System initialization.* As a trusted authority, TA is the executor of system initialization. In this phase, the two departments of TA, namely KGC and TRA, are in charge of generating the necessary system parameters.

(a) First of all, KGC chooses a safety parameter l^n, $n \in N$ as an input of ECC algorithm, and then the algorithm outputs (G_1, G_2, e), where $(G_1, +)$ and $(G_2, \cdot)$ are the additive group and the multiplicative group with the order of a large prime q, respectively, All elements in the group are the points in discrete elliptic curve. Function $\hat{e} : G_1 \times G_1 \to G_2$ represents a bilinear pairing operation. KGC randomly selects a point P as the generator of G_1 and calculates $g = \hat{e}(P, P)$.

(b) TRA randomly selects a number $s \in Z_q^*$ as the master private key and calculates $P_{pub} = s \cdot P$ as the public key, keeping s not leaking.

(c) KGC randomly selects a number $k \in Z_q^*$ as the master private key and sets $P_k = (P_{k1}, P_{k2}) = ((\frac{1}{k})P, kP)$ as the public key, keeping k safe.

(d) KGC chooses three different secure hash functions $H_1, H_2, H_3 : \{0,1\}^* \rightarrow Z_q^*$. After all processes mentioned above are completed, KGC announces the following system public parameters $params = \{p, q, G_1, G_2, \hat{e}, g, P, P_{pub}, P_k, H_1, H_2, H_3\}$.

Step 2: *Vehicle pseudonym registration*. The vehicle submits a registration request through a secure channel. For example, the vehicle performs an offline registration using tamper-proof devices.

(a) Vehicles V_i submits relevant materials such as the owner's ID card and vehicle license. After verification by TRA, the real identity of the vehicle RID_i is generated according to certain functions such as hash-to-point operation, and then pseudonym is generated for V_i through $PID_i = RID_i \oplus H_1(s, T_{reg})$, where T_{reg} is the vehicle registration time.

(b) TRA records (PID_i, T_{reg}) in the vehicle registration information table, which is used to track the real identity of the vehicle, and (PID_i, T_{reg}) is also returned to the vehicle and written into the TPD of the vehicle.

Step 3: *Vehicle partial public and private key generation*. KGC selects a random number $b_i \in Z_q^*$, lets $A_i = b_i \cdot P$, then calculates $\alpha_i = H_2(PID_i, A_i)$, $\beta_i = (b_i + k\alpha_i) \mod q$ and $B_i = \beta_i \cdot P_{k2}$. Sets B_i and (A_i, β_i) are the partial public key and the partial private key of the vehicle respectively. KGC sends (B_i, A_i, β_i) back to the vehicle, and then, they are written into the TPD.

Step 4: *Vehicle public and private key generation*. After receiving partial public and private keys, the vehicle verifies them by the equation $\beta_i P = A_i + \alpha_i P_{k2}$. The correctness is proved as follows:

$$\begin{aligned} \beta_i P &= (b_i + k\alpha_i \mod q) \cdot P \\ &= b_i \cdot P + k\alpha_i \cdot P \\ &= A_i + \alpha_i P_{k2} \end{aligned} \tag{1}$$

If the equation holds, the vehicle selects a random number $x_i \in Z_q^*$, then calculates $X_i = x_i \cdot P_{k2}$, sets $PK_i = (B_i, X_i)$ and $SK_i = (\beta_i, x_i)$ as the public key and the private key of the vehicle respectively. Then, the vehicle submits PID_i and PK_i to KGC, so that KGC publishes them in the blockchain.

Step 5: *Vehicle information publishment*. After KGC receives PID_i and PK_i, it initializes the trust coin $TCoin_i = 0$ for the vehicle, then requests RSU to record PID_i, PK_i and $TCoin_i$ in the blockchain. Subsequently, authorized RSUs execute consensus algorithm and publishes these parameters to the blockchain. The specific block generation process in the blockchain is illustrated in Sect. 4.

(2) Report phase

After completing information publishment in blockchain, the vehicle can join in the smart transportation system. When it encounters a traffic event and willing to report the event, it begins to act as $\mathcal{I}$). It firstly creates the message M_i including event ID, event type, location and time, then calculates $h_i = H_3(M_i, PID_i, PK_i, T_i)$ and the signature Sig_i according to the following Eq. (2), finally packs (M_i, PID_i, Sig_i, T_i) as $\mathcal{RIP}$ and sends $\mathcal{RIP}$ to nearest RSU.

$$Sig_i = \left(\frac{1}{h_i \cdot x_i + \beta_i} \right) \cdot P_{k1} \tag{2}$$

In our system, reporting an event will cost a certain amount of TCoins. Once this message is successfully responded to, the vehicle will get the corresponding rewards after confirming transactions. The amount of reward TCoins is usually higher than that of expenditure. Thus, if reports from a malicious vehicle cannot be recognized as true reporting in the end, it will lose TCoins.

(3) Inquiry phase

When the RSU receives the $\mathcal{RIP}$, it becomes $\mathcal{V}$. It firstly judges inequation $T_c - T_i \leq \Delta T$, where T_c is the current time, ΔT is a reasonable time interval. When the time expires, the $\mathcal{RIP}$ is directly discarded. Otherwise, it checks whether the event involved in $\mathcal{RIP}$ is duplicate according to Algorithm 1. If not, the RSU searches PK_i and $TCoin_i$ in blockchain through the pseudonym PID_i. If the $TCoin_i < 0$, reporter $\mathcal{I}$ is considered as an invalid vehicle and the $\mathcal{RIP}$ is discarded. Otherwise, $\mathcal{V}$ uses $\mathcal{RIP}$ and PK_i to calculate $h_i = H_3(M_i, PID_i, PK_i, T_i)$, and then verifies whether the signature Sig_i is correct by the following equation.

$$\hat{e}\left(Sig_i, \ h_iX_i + B_i\right) = g \tag{3}$$

If the equation does not hold, $\mathcal{V}$ rejects $\mathcal{RIP}$. Otherwise, $\mathcal{V}$ accepts $\mathcal{RIP}$ and calculates $h_v = H_3(M_i, PID_v, T_v)$, where PID_v is pseudonym of verifier $\mathcal{V}$, T_v is timestamp. Next, $\mathcal{V}$ packs (M_i, h_v, PID_v, T_v) as $\mathcal{OIP}$ and broadcasts the $\mathcal{OIP}$ in its own communication range. The correctness proof of Eq. (3) is as follows:

$$\begin{aligned}
\hat{e}\left(Sig_i \ , \ h_iX_i + B_i\right) &= \hat{e}\left(\left(\tfrac{1}{h_i \cdot x_i + \beta_i} \right) P_{k1} \ , \ h_i \, X_i + B_i \right) \\
&= \hat{e}\left(\left(\tfrac{1}{h_i \, x_i + \beta_i} \right) P_{k1} \ , \ h_i \, x_i P_{k2} + \beta_i P_{k2} \right) \\
&= \hat{e}\left(\left(\tfrac{1}{h_i \, x_i + \beta_i} \right) \left(\tfrac{1}{k} \right) P \ , \ (h_i \, x_i + \beta_i) \, kP \right) \\
&= \hat{e}\left(P, P \right)^{\left(\frac{1}{h_i \, x_i k + \beta_i k} \right)(h_i \, x_i k + \beta_i k)} \\
&= \hat{e}\left(P, P \right) \\
&= g
\end{aligned} \tag{4}$$

(4) Feedback phase

After receiving $\mathcal{RIP}$, if vehicle is the witness of the event referred in M_i and voluntarily participate in reporting system, it transforms into Responder $\mathcal{R}$. At first, $\mathcal{R}$ check whether $\mathcal{OIP}$ is expired by timestamp T_v. If expired, $\mathcal{OIP}$ is neglected. Otherwise, $\mathcal{R}$ calculates $h'_v = H_3(M_i, PID_v, T_v)$ and judge whether the equation $h'_v = h_v$ holds. If equals, $\mathcal{R}$ computes $h_r = H_3(M_i, PID_r, PK_r, OP, T_r)$, here,

PID_r and PK_r are respectively pseudonym and public key of $\mathcal{R}$, T_r is timestamp, OP represents witness opinion which is set to 1 in our proposed scheme. Subsequently, $\mathcal{R}$ generates signature Sig_r with its own private key SK_r, message digest h_r and a part of KGC's public key P_{k1} according to the Eq. (3), and packs $(Sig_r, M_i, PID_r, OP, T_r)$ as $\mathcal{OFP}$, then transmits the $\mathcal{OFP}$ to $\mathcal{V}$. It should be noted that malicious vehicles may also respond as $OP = 1$ in our proposed scheme.

(5) Verification phase
As the verifier $\mathcal{V}$, if the RSU receives multiple $\mathcal{OFP}$s within a certain period, it can search in blockchain for the public keys and trust coins according to pseudonym set $\{PID_r | r = 1, 2, ..., m\}$ of the multiple responders. After the related information set $\{PK_r, TCoin_r | r = 1, 2, ..., m\}$ is found, $\mathcal{V}$ firstly discards the $\mathcal{OFP}$s corresponding to PID_r with $TCoin_r < 0$, because the inequation $TCoin_r < 0$ represents the vehicle is incredible. Next, the signatures transmitted by credible responders are verified through aggregation verification. Similar to the single signature verification mentioned in inquiry phase, $\mathcal{V}$ calculates $h_r = H_3(M_i, PID_r, PK_r, OP, T_r)$, $r = 1, 2, 3, ..., n$, and then judge whether the following equation holds.

$$\hat{e}\left(\sum_{i=1}^{n}(Sig_r, \; h_r X_r + B_r)\right) = g \tag{5}$$

If it is true, it indicates the authenticity of the signature and the integrity of the $\mathcal{OFP}$s. The correctness proof of Eq. (5) is as follows:

$$\hat{e}\left(\sum_{i=1}^{n}(Sig_r, \; h_r X_r + B_r)\right) = \hat{e}\left(\sum_{i=1}^{n}\left(\left(\frac{1}{h_r \cdot x_r + \beta_r}\right) P_{k1} \; , \; h_r X_r + B_r\right)\right)$$
$$= \hat{e}\left(\sum_{i=1}^{n}\left(\left(\frac{1}{h_r \cdot x_r + \beta_r}\right) P_{k1} \; , \; h_r x_r P_{k2} + \beta_r P_{k2}\right)\right)$$
$$= \hat{e}\left(\sum_{i=1}^{n}\left(\left(\frac{1}{h_r \cdot x_r + \beta_r}\right)\left(\tfrac{1}{k}\right) P \; , \; (h_r x_r + \beta_r) kP\right)\right) \tag{6}$$
$$= \hat{e}(P, P)^{\sum_{i=1}^{n}\left(\frac{1}{h_r x_r k + \beta_r k}\right)(h_r x_r k + \beta_r k)}$$
$$= \hat{e}(P, P)$$
$$= g$$

When the number n of valid signatures is larger than preset threshold t, i.e. $n > t$, verifier $\mathcal{V}$ considers the event reported in $\mathcal{RIP}$ is authentic and valid. Reporter $\mathcal{I}$ and credible responder $\mathcal{R}$ would obtain different rewards $TCoin_i$ which are used in daily life, such as exchanging commodities, enjoying services. However, although this kind of threshold method can provide a simple and effective way to acquire reliable report results, there are still some special circumstances in which the authenticity of reported events is difficult to verify. For example, when $\mathcal{OIP}$ is broadcasted at midnight in a remote area, there are rare vehicles passing by. Thus no $\mathcal{OFP}$s can be collected for judging the validity of the event. In order to address this issue, we design an adaptive t-threshold scheme. Depending on time and location, threshold t is set to different values. Considering people's travel habits, we express the time as a piecewise linear function with dividing points 0:00, 8:00, 10:00, 12:00, 15:00, 18:00 and 24:00. The specific time function is as follows:

$$f(x) = bx + k \ (x_i < x \le x_j, \ x_i, x_j \in [0, 24]) \tag{7}$$

Here, x is time with range from 0:00 to 24:00, $f(x)$ is time coefficient with maximum value 1 and minimum value 0. Meanwhile, we divide the location into five different levels from crowd to remote, the corresponding location coefficient λ is set to value $\{1, 0.75, 0.5, 0.25, 0\}$. Weight parameters for time and location are set to η and α, respectively, and $\eta + \alpha = 1$. Generally, α should be set larger than η because the number of vehicles passing by a certain area is usually more influenced by location than time. For instance, there may be many cars passing by a prosperous intersection in the middle of the night, while there is no car in a remote location even during the rush hour. Thus, the threshold t can be computed by the following formula:

$$t_{threshold} = [\eta f(x) + \alpha \lambda] \times t_{baseline} \tag{8}$$

In the formula, $t_{baseline}$ is a preset baseline value for the number of vehicles, $t_{threshold}$ is the expected number of vehicles, i.e., the threshold t. The formula shows the relationship between threshold and time-location pair. According to the formula, the maximum value of threshold t is $t_{baseline}$, the minimum value is 0. When an $\mathcal{OIP}$ is broadcasted at midnight in a remote area, the threshold t is the minimum value 0. While in a downtown area at 12:00, the threshold t can reach the maximum value $t_{baseline}$. It is noted that the verification task of the reported event should be transferred to the traffic management department to complete when the threshold t is small, so that the reliability of the verification result is guaranteed.

3.3 Blockchain Incentive Mechanism

In order to increase the enthusiasm of message reporters, a blockchain-based TCoin incentive mechanism is proposed. Reporters and witnesses who join in the verification process can get TCoin as a reward for their active participation, and they can also spend TCoin in real life. Similar to blockchain cryptocurrency, all TCoin transactions are recorded in the blockchain. Furthermore, the reported messages can be broadcasted through nodes in the blockchain.

RSU broadcasts it in the entire VANET and rewards trust coin, namely TCoin, to vehicles if the report is credible. For example, in some special circumstances, there is no witness, the report would be resubmitted to the TMD for judgment. The blockchain proposed in this paper is also composed of RSUs. After partially authorized RSU nodes execute the consensus algorithm, all RSUs jointly maintain a distributed TCoin currency ledger. Here, we assume that attackers are not capable of attacking the majority of RSUs even if RSUs work in a non-full trusted environment. Therefore, most RSUs are supposed to be credible. If the $TCoin_i < 0$, reporter $\mathcal{I}$ is considered as an invalid vehicle and the $\mathcal{RIP}$ is discarded.

The structure of the block is shown as $B \equiv (B_h, B_t, B_u)$. Let B_h be the block header information. Let B_t be the transaction within the block. Let B_u be the block header list of the uncle node. The block header comprises the following data items: the Version Number, the Previous Block Hash, the Timestamp, the Random Number, the Target Hash, etc. Merkle Patricia Tree is used in TCoin. The Merkle Patricia Tree is calculated using the transaction set to form the last block to date. The new block $Block_{new}$ is constructed by generating the block header B_h, the transaction B_t in the block, and the block header list B_u of the uncle node.

Each vehicle's address corresponds to an account in the blockchain system, which stores $(nonce, balance)$, the $nonce$ is the transaction counter, and the $balance$ is the balance information. We could select the appropriate block difficulty and initial block user beneficiary to build the creation block $Block_0$.

Users use addresses for transactions without revealing real identities. The transaction is a signed data packet of a message sent from an account. Let $nonce$ be the transaction counter. Let $addr\_from$ be the sender of the message. Let $addr\_to$ be the receiver. Let $value$ be the transaction value. Let $data$ be the transmitted data. Let sig be the signature for confirming the sender. We describe a simple transaction format for TCoin, as follows:

$$T := (nonce, addr\_from, addr\_to, value, data, sig) \tag{9}$$

Feedback to Reporting: After witnesses feedback successfully, the smart contract will be called to generate the transaction $T_{feedback}$ from public to $\mathcal{R}$, the change will be transferred to $\mathcal{R}$. $T_{feedback}$ contains as follows:

$$(nonce_{public}, addr_{public}, addr_r, value_{feedback}, data_{feedback}, sig_{public}) \tag{10}$$

Finish a Reporting Verification: After finishing reporting, a smart contract will be called to generate the transaction T_{reward} from public to $\mathcal{I}$, the change will be transferred to $\mathcal{I}$. T_{reward} contains as follows:

$$(nonce_{public}, addr_{public}, addr_i, value_{reward}, data_{reward}, sig_{public}) \tag{11}$$

By storing the state in the tree structure, only a small portion of the tree structure needs to be changed for each additional block. In general, most of the tree structures of two adjacent blocks should be the same, so storing data once can be referenced twice with a pointer (i.e., a subtree hash). In addition, since all state information is part of the last block, it is unnecessary to store all of the block histories, saving a lot of storage space.

4   Performance Analysis

We evaluate the feasibility and performance of the proposed system through simulations in this section. The simulation experiments are conducted on a PC. The experimental environment is as follows: the CPU is Intel i5-8250U, the memory is 16G, and Windows 10 is the operating system. We simulated a smart city, and the size is 30 km * 30 km. The number of vehicles is increased from 500 to 2000, and the average vehicle speed is around 45 km in the city. We simulate the movement of these vehicles in 3 days (72 h). RSUs are distributed in this city, and the coverage of each RSU is 300 m. The maximal percentage of malicious vehicles is 60%.

Figure 2 presents the average computation time of verification as the increase of the threshold of the vehicle number. It is the aggregate verification time of multiple vehicles that send feedbacks. The incremental changes in time can be clearly seen.

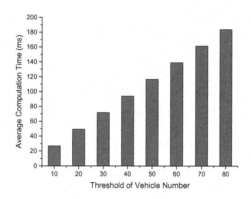

Fig. 2. The average computation time of verification.

As can be seen, Fig. 3 demonstrates the verification rate of the traffic management department under two situations, adaptive threshold method and fixed threshold method. We consider the location and time of reporting, so the adaptive threshold method is more flexible, making the verification less reliant on traffic management department verification.

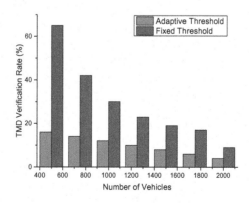

Fig. 3. Traffic management department verification rate as the increase of vehicle number.

Figure 4 presents reporting success rate when the percentage of malicious vehicles is increasing. It can be seen that the probability that false reporting from malicious vehicles being verified to become true event reporting is increasing. The success rate is reached only 35% when the malicious vehicles grow to 60%, which also makes our system reliable.

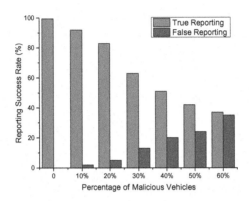

Fig. 4. Reporting success rate as the increase of the percentage of malicious vehicles.

5   Conclusion

In this paper, we proposed a mechanism that combines certificateless message authentication and blockchain incentives. A certificateless message signature algorithm is designed to provide anonymity and non-repudiation for traffic-related message reporters. Simultaneously, an adaptive t-threshold multi-signature mechanism is introduced in our scheme. Similar to crowdsourcing, it requires multiple participants to witness the authenticity of the message together. Aggregation signature verification improves message authentication efficiency. TCoin is introduced as a trusted currency to motivate reporters' enthusiasm for participation in intelligent transportation, where the blockchain records TCoin transactions, and it is also taken as a report dissemination network. We conducted the simulation experiments under the varied vehicle number, varied threshold, and varied percentage of malicious vehicles. The simulation results show that our scheme is secure and effective for VANETs.

Acknowledgments. This work is supported by the National Natural Science Foundation of China under grant no. 61872138.

References

1. Al-Riyami, S.S., Paterson, K.G.: Certificateless public key cryptography. In: Laih, C.-S. (ed.) ASIACRYPT 2003. LNCS, vol. 2894, pp. 452–473. Springer, Heidelberg (2003). https://doi.org/10.1007/978-3-540-40061-5_29

2. Ali, I., Hassan, A., Li, F.: Authentication and privacy schemes for vehicular ad hoc networks (VANETs): a survey. Veh. Commun. **16**, 45–61 (2019)
3. Ara, A., Al-Rodhaan, M., Tian, Y., Al-Dhelaan, A.: A secure privacy-preserving data aggregation scheme based on bilinear ELGamal cryptosystem for remote health monitoring systems. IEEE Access **5**, 12601–12617 (2017)
4. Bresson, E., Stern, J., Szydlo, M.: Threshold ring signatures and applications to ad-hoc groups. In: Yung, M. (ed.) CRYPTO 2002. LNCS, vol. 2442, pp. 465–480. Springer, Heidelberg (2002). https://doi.org/10.1007/3-540-45708-9_30
5. Dinarvand, N., Barati, H.: An efficient and secure RFID authentication protocol using elliptic curve cryptography. Wireless Netw. **25**(1), 415–428 (2017). https://doi.org/10.1007/s11276-017-1565-3
6. Goka, S., Shigeno, H.: Distributed management system for trust and reward in mobile ad hoc networks. In: 15th IEEE Annual Consumer Communications & Networking Conference, CCNC 2018, Las Vegas, NV, USA, 12–15 January 2018, pp. 1–6. IEEE (2018)
7. Malhi, A.K., Batra, S.: An efficient certificateless aggregate signature scheme for vehicular ad-hoc networks. Discrete Math. Theor. Comput. Sci. **17**(1), 317–338 (2015)
8. Mondal, H.S., Hasan, M.T., Hossain, M.M., Arifin, M.M., Saha, R.
9. Raya, M., Aziz, A., Hubaux, J.: Efficient secure aggregation in VANETs. In: Holfelder, W., Johnson, D.B., Hartenstein, H., Bahl, V. (eds.) Proceedings of the Third International Workshop on Vehicular Ad Hoc Networks, VANET 2006, Los Angeles, CA, USA, 29 September 2007, pp. 67–75. ACM (2006)
10. Salem, A.H., Abdel-Hamid, A., El-Nasr, M.A.: The case for dynamic key distribution for PKI-based vanets. CoRR abs/1605.04696 (2016)
11. Shamir, A.: How to share a secret. Commun. ACM **22**(11), 612–613 (1979)
12. Shamir, A.: Identity-based cryptosystems and signature schemes. In: Blakley, G.R., Chaum, D. (eds.) CRYPTO 1984. LNCS, vol. 196, pp. 47–53. Springer, Heidelberg (1985). https://doi.org/10.1007/3-540-39568-7_5
13. Shi, S., He, D., Li, L., Kumar, N., Khan, M.K., Choo, K.R.: Applications of blockchain in ensuring the security and privacy of electronic health record systems: a survey. Comput. Secur. **97**, 101966 (2020)
14. Slagell, A.J., Bonilla, R., Yurcik, W.: A survey of PKI components and scalability issues. In: Proceedings of the 25th IEEE International Performance Computing and Communications Conference, IPCCC 2006, Phoenix, Arizona, USA, 10–12 April 2006. IEEE (2006)
15. Yang, Y., Chou, L., Tseng, C., Tseng, F., Liu, C.: Blockchain-based traffic event validation and trust verification for VANETs. IEEE Access **7**, 30868–30877 (2019)
16. Zhang, L., Wu, Q., Qin, B., Domingo-Ferrer, J.: APPA: aggregate privacy-preserving authentication in vehicular ad hoc networks. In: Lai, X., Zhou, J., Li, H. (eds.) ISC 2011. LNCS, vol. 7001, pp. 293–308. Springer, Heidelberg (2011). https://doi.org/10.1007/978-3-642-24861-0_20

Blockchain and Internet of Things

Classification Method of Blockchain and IoT Devices Based on LSTM

Pengyu Duan[1], Ruiguang Li[2], Liehuang Zhu[1(✉)], and Hao Yu[1]

[1] School of Computer Science, Beijing Institute of Technology, Beijing 100081, China
liehuangz@bit.edu.cn
[2] National Internet Emergency Response Center, Beijing 100029, China

Abstract. With the development of the technology, more and more blockchain devices and Internet of Things devices are deployed around us. In order to manage these devices more conveniently, it is necessary to classify the devices according to the flow rate. The existing classification methods of devices are divided into active detection and passive detection. Active detection needs to send messages to them. Passive detection only needs to get the flow information of the devices, and existing passive detection needs to do so. The methods are all based on complete flow. We propose a method based on the previous part of the flow, using LSTM and random forest algorithm to classify. The f1-score of our method is 0.89. Compared with the existing methods, our method improves by 8%–30%, and our method can classify devices more effectively .

Keywords: Blockchain · Internet of things · Network traffic · Random forest · LSTM

1 Introduction

Blockchain is a new application combining distributed storage, point-to-point transmission, encryption algorithm and other technologies [1–3]. In essence, it is a decentralized database. The device can verify and store the block by accessing the blockchain network.

Internet of Things (IoT) technology is a technology that connects sensors to the Internet, uses devices and technologies such as radio frequency identification technology, global positioning system, etc. to collect objects or processes that need to be monitored, connected and interacted in real time, to collect information about them, and to access them through various networks, and to achieve the interconnection of people and objects.

Now more and more blockchain device and Internet of Things devices are applied in homes, campuses, enterprises and cities [4], such as blockchain nodes, smart speakers, smart light bulbs and other devices. At the same time, the increase of devices poses a challenge to management. Network administrators need to know which devices are in the network, so as to adjust the network accordingly. Because different devices and devices are usually installed and managed by different people, it is difficult to integrate related information uniformly, and often a large number of devices make it difficult to enter device information manually. How to accurately identify devices has become an important issue.

© Springer Nature Singapore Pte Ltd. 2021
H.-N. Dai et al. (Eds.): BlockSys 2021, CCIS 1490, pp. 355–367, 2021.
https://doi.org/10.1007/978-981-16-7993-3_27

Device classification is a technology that identifies the kind, manufacturer, model and other information of devices based on the characteristics of devices on the network, that is, the traffic sent and received by devices. It can solve the problem that devices are difficult to manage. There are two main categories of device classification methods: active detection and passive detection. The active detection method is to send packets to some IP addresses, determine if the other party is specific type device based on the returned information, and send more packets, identify specific fields in the packets returned by the device to classify the device in more detail [2–5].Passive detection is to collect packets sent and received by devices at gateways, classify them according to their characteristics, and use machine learning methods [6–14].

Most of the existing passive detection methods use complete TCP/UDP streams, but also use the first few packets of HTTPS protocol to classify. The previous part of TCP/UDP streams has been less studied. Since classifying using a complete stream requires more storage space and does not recognize devices in real time, classifying using the previous part of the stream can avoid these shortcomings.

To this end, our main contributions can be summarized as follows:

Based on the in-depth investigation of the existing classification methods of Internet of things, this paper analyzes and summarizes the defects and shortcomings of the existing classification methods, and summarizes the key reasons for the poor performance of the existing methods: active detection methods need to send messages actively, passive measurement methods use the complete flow of equipment.

This paper presents an innovative classification method of Internet of things devices, which is classified by using the former part of the device to generate traffic. The data packet head information and statistical information in the traffic are extracted, and the model is established by using LSTM algorithm and random forest algorithm. This method makes up for the shortcomings of the existing technology, and realizes the high-precision classification of Internet of things devices.

This paper verifies the function and performance of the method based on the actual network traffic data set. In this scheme, 32 kinds of devices are used in 21 days of flow, including 600000 traffic. The experimental results based on the above data set show that F1 score can reach 0.89 and can effectively classify the equipment.

2   Related Work

In this section, we classify the existing device classification methods into two categories: active detection-based and passive detection-based. And we introduce network traffic classification.

2.1   Activate-Based Device Classifying

Feng [5] and others use the format and information of Modbus and S7 protocol slogans to identify the manufacturer and device version of the industrial control device, Li et al. use the device's login page to extract keywords to identify the device [6], measure the concentration of words on the page, use the results returned by search engines as device fingerprints [7], Leonard [8] et al. use TCP ACK to detect if the host is alive, and use the response of DNS, HTTP, SMTP protocols to identify the device type and operating system of the host.

Active detection can intuitively get information about the device and is easier to identify, but because of the need for probes to send messages to network segments, there are performance problems in large-scale scanning, which is easy to be intercepted by firewalls, and also need to adapt for each protocol, which is more difficult to achieve.

2.2 Passive Detection-Based Device Classifying

Kohno. T. [9] et al. use clock offsets of multiple protocols, i.e. the difference between clock time and actual time for device identification, and Aneja [10] et al. use the arrival interval time (IAT) graph as a feature to classify using CNN algorithm. Husak [11] and others use the SSL/TLS handshake information in the HTTPS protocol as device fingerprints to classify user agents. Sivanathan [12] and others use streaming information and DNS, NTP number of requests, request interval to classify. Msadek [13] and others classify port numbers into recognized ports, registered ports, dynamic ports, and classify devices using protocol types and streaming statistics. Aksoy [14] extracts all possible features and uses genetic algorithms to build all types of classifiers for classification. Desai [15] and others use only stream statistics, including mean, median, variance, distribution similarity, to classify. Meidan [16] uses other data besides stream information, including Alexa ranking and GeoIP information for classification, Shahid [17] and others use the size and IAT of the first N packets sent and received.

Passive detection does not need to send messages to the device. It is so concealed that it is difficult to be found by the target device. However, it does not get the model and version of the device directly. It needs to use algorithms such as machine learning to train the model. At present, the more popular method is passive detection.

The passive detection of devices uses network traffic classification technology, which classifies the traffic generated by the devices as input. The traffic of the devices includes different protocols for the communication between the devices and the outside world, from which you can know how much data the devices send at what time and address, and the contents of the data (if not encrypted), which can be characterized by the use of multiple machines. Machine learning algorithms classify devices. At present, the commonly used machine learning algorithms are SVM, LR, CNN, etc. Sivanathan [12] et al. used random forests to classify traffic. Msadek [13] et al. compared the performance of k-NN, SVM, RF, ET and other algorithms in traffic classification. Manuel [18] et al. used CNN and CNN + RNN to classify traffic. Shen [19, 20] et al. use packet length information to identify web pages and applications, and use Markov chain to identify applications. The existing passive detection methods are based on complete traffic, which need large storage space and cannot be classified in real time.

3 The Proposed Approach

In this section, we outline the proposed device classification methods, and then describe in detail the specific methods, including (i) traffic collection (ii) flow separation and feature extraction (iii) device classification.

3.1 Traffic Collection

After connecting to the network, devices can get the traffic of all devices in the network at the gateway. Different devices have different services, use different protocols and ports, communicate with different rules and servers, and can collect and classify these traffic to identify the type of device. We collected the original traffic through the gateway, which is in pcap format, including every data packet sent by each device, from the physical layer to the application layer.

3.2 Flow Separation and Feature Extraction

Since each original traffic file includes all the traffic for all devices in a day, for the sake of extracting features, we split the traffic by device, first breaking up the traffic for the first device. For each packet, if the source or destination MAC address is the MAC address for the device, the package is extracted, and finally all the packages for the device in a day are combined into one Traffic file. Same method for other devices.

From the IP header information, we can get the source ip address, destination ip address, message length, TTL, and upper-layer protocol type. From the TCP header information, we can get the source port, destination port, TCP message length, window size, and maximum segment size.

We use the joy tool to extract streams and related statistics, which splits streams in a traffic file and generates a JSON data for each stream, including information about the source address, source port, destination address, destination port, protocol, start time, end time, length and interval of each packet. We extract the corresponding stream statistical characteristics from the JSON file and the packet length time series of each stream. Specific features include:

Statistical characteristics, including the number of streams generated in 10 min, the number of protocols used, the most commonly used protocols, the types of ports used, the most commonly used ports, the length of incoming traffic, the number of incoming packets, the number of outgoing traffic length and packets, the TTL, MSS of input and output, and the window size.

Packet length time series, a sequence of the packet length for each stream, and the time interval between the previous packet.

3.3 Device Classification

Since we have the sequence of packets sent by each device, we can use the statistical information and sequence information to classify the devices. RNN algorithm is a kind of algorithm for sequence classification. LSTM is a variant of RNN, which enhances its ability to classify long sequences. So we use LSTM to classify the packet length time series, and classify the result of classification together with other statistical information as random. The input and output of a forest classifier are predicted device types. The output of dense layer is part of the feature, and the statistical characteristics of flow are another part of the feature, which is input into the random forest classifier to output the probability of each category, with the label with the highest probability as the final prediction result.

The overall structure of the model is shown in Fig. 1.

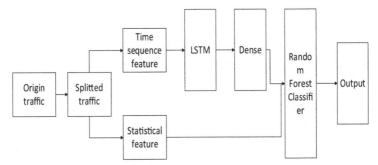

Fig. 1. The overall structure of the model

3.4 Implementations

We collected the traffic of Bitcoin and Ethereum. For the traffic of other devices, we used dataset collected by arunan et al., which is the traffic they acquired on the school network from September to October 2016, including the original traffic of 22 Internet of things devices and some non internet of things devices and MAC address of each device The device name, MAC address, and device type are shown in Table 1.

Each file in the original data contains all the traffic of all devices in a day. We use tshark tool to separate the original traffic file by device according to the MAC address, and each file after segmentation contains all the traffic of a device in a day.

We then use the joy tool to extract information for each stream, including source IP, destination IP, protocol, port, start time, end time, packet length and interval time for the first 50 packets, as shown in Table 2.

The data extracted by the joy tool is in JSON format, with each stream being a row. We traverse each row, extracting data from the first 10 min of each active device as a feature, because most devices can interact in less than 10 min, and assume that the device is active at this time if it has at least one stream, the algorithm is shown in algorithm 1 and algorithm 2.

Algorithm 1 Stream Merge

input: The traffic of device $S = \{s_1, s_2, s_3, \cdots, s_n\}$
output: Merged traffic $S = \{s_1, s_2, s_3, \cdots, s_n\}$
1. Record the start time and the end time of first stream s_1 as t_{1start} and t_{1end}.
2. Record the start time and the end time of next stream s_2 as t_{2start} and t_{2end}.
3. If $t_{2start} > t_{1end}$, output merged traffic $\{s_1, \cdots, s_2\}$
4. If $t_{2start} \leq t_{1end}$ and $t_{2end} > t_{1end}$, $t_{1end} = t_{2end}$ and come back to step 2.
5. If $t_{2start} \leq t_{1end}$ and $t_{2end} \leq t_{1end}$, come back to step 2.

Algorithm 2 Extract Features

input: Merged traffic $S = \{s_1, s_2, s_3, \cdots, s_n\}$

output: Features $F = \{f_1, f_2, f_3, \cdots, f_q\}$, q is the number of device activations

1. For each stream in S do:
2. Extract features of s_i
3. End
4. Computing Statistically Related Features
5. Output $\{f_1, f_2, f_3, \cdots, f_q\}$

Algorithm 3 Extract Time Sequence

input: Merged traffic $S = \{s_1, s_2, s_3, \cdots, s_n\}$,

$s_1 = \{p_1, p_2, p_3, \cdots, p_n\}$, max packets m_p

output: Sequence of packet length and time

$$(L, T) = \{(l_1, t_1), (l_2, t_2), (l_3, t_3), \cdots, (l_n, t_n)\}$$

1. For each packet p_i in s_1 do:
2. If $I > m_p$, end
3. If i = 1, record the end time of p_i as t_0
4. Else, record the start time of p_i as t_{start}
5. The length of p_i is l_i
6. $t_i = t_{start} - t_0$
7. Record the end time of p_i as t_0
8. End
9. Output the sequence $\{(l_1, t_1), (l_2, t_2), (l_3, t_3), \cdots, (l_n, t_n)\}$

After extracting the statistical features, we also extract sequence of packet length and time as input to LSTM. When there are multiple streams during the active period of the device, we extract sequence of packet length and time from the first stream, as shown in algorithm 3.

Table 1. Device list

Device type	Name
Blockchain	BTC, ETH
IoT	Smart Things, Amazon Echo, Netatmo Welcome, TP-Link Day Night Cloud camera, Samsung SmartCam, Dropcam, Insteon Camera, Withings Smart Baby Monitor, Belkin Wemo switch, TP-Link Smart plug, iHome, Belkin wemo motion sensor, NEST Protect smoke alarm, Netatmo weather station, Withings Smart scale, Blipcare Blood Pressure meter, Withings Aura smart sleep sensor, Light Bulbs LiFX Smart Bulb, Triby Speaker, PIX-STAR Photo-frame, HP Printer
Others	Samsung Galaxy Tab, Nest Dropcam, Android Phone, Laptop, MacBook, Android Phone, IPhone, MacBook/Iphone, TPLink Router Bridge LAN (Gateway)

10% of the data from each device is selected to form the test set, and the other data is used to model the training set. The time series extracted by algorithm 3 is used as input to LSTM, and the output and other characteristics of LSTM are used as input to random forest classifier for training.

For comparison, we use the Random Forest algorithm mentioned by Arunan [12] and the Deep Learning algorithm mentioned by Manuel et al. [18]. As a comparison, we use the traffic divided by algorithm 1 and algorithm 2 to classify.

Table 2. Feature list

Type	Feature
Stream	stream number, max stream duration, avg stream duration
Protocol	protocol types, protocol most used, port types, port most used
Length	bytes in, max bytes in stream, packets in, max packets in stream, bytes out, max bytes out stream, packets out, max packets out stream
IP protocol	ttl in, ttl out
TCP protocol	mss in, mss out, first window size in, first window size out
Time sequence	sequence of packet length and interval

4   Experimental Setup

In our scenario, the first 10 min of a device activity are recorded during each device activity, and the statistical information of the flow and the packet length time series are extracted. The relevant parameters are shown in the Table 3.

Table 3. The relevant parameters

No	Parameter	Value
1	Time threshold	10 min
2	Number of merged traffic	603992
3	Max number of packets	50
4	Train batch of LSTM	10
5	Train epochs of LSTM	30

We first introduce the two algorithms as a comparison, then introduce the partition of training set and test set, and then compare the performance of these two algorithms and the algorithm proposed in this paper.

We have about 600,000 traffic data sets, and the number of traffic data for each device is shown in Fig. 2.

As a comparison, we use the traffic statistical characteristics proposed by Arunan and the classification method of random forest algorithm, and compare the packet length time series proposed by Manuel et al. And CNN + RNN classification method. These two methods have good classification results when using complete streams for classification. We now evaluate the classification effects of these two algorithms on the segmented data set.

In this experiment, we use weighted F1-score as the evaluation criterion of the model. For multi-classification problems, the formula of F1-score is as follows.

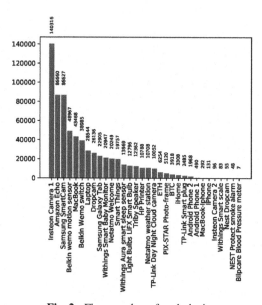

Fig. 2. Flow number of each device

For device D,The number of predicted device D and actual device D is TP, the number of predicted device D but actual other devices is FP, the number of predicted device D but actual device D is FN, and the number of predicted device D and actual other devices is TN.

$$\Pr ecision = \frac{TP}{TP + FP}$$

$$Recall = \frac{TP}{TP + FN}$$

$$Weighted - \Pr ecision = \sum W_i \Pr ecision_i$$

$$Weighted - Recall = \sum W_i Recall_i$$

$$Weighted - F1 = \frac{2 \cdot Weighted - \Pr ecision \cdot Weighted - Recall}{Weighted - \Pr ecision + Weighted - Recall}$$

We use 10% cross validation method, stratified sampling 10% of the data as the test set, that is, 10% of the data is taken from each label category, grouped into a test set, and

90% as a training set. This sampling method can be used without increasing The sample size reduces the sampling error, and the performance on the test set can better represent the algorithm performance in the actual situation.

5 Performance Evaluation

The performance comparison between our algorithm and the algorithm proposed in the literature is shown in Table 4.The confusion matrix of each method is shown in Fig. 4. The vertical axis is the actual classification, and the horizontal axis is the predicted classification. The color of the j column in row I represents the number of devices that are actually classified as I into class J. the darker the color at the diagonal and the lighter the color in other places, the higher the accuracy of the classifier. The F1-score of classification results is 0.89.

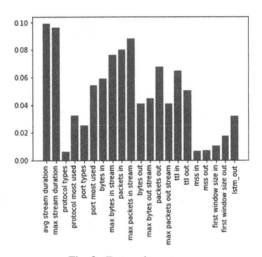

Fig. 3. Feature importance

In terms of running time, the training time of random forest algorithm is 42 s and the classification time is 14 s. The training time of the proposed scheme is 1921 s and the classification time is 136 s. The training time of CNN + RNN algorithm is 9952 s and the classification time is 215.2 s. The running time of the algorithm proposed in this paper is longer than random forest algorithm, but shorter than CNN + RNN algorithm. The running time comparison of the three schemes is shown in Table 5. It can be seen that the proposed scheme achieves the balance between classification efficiency and running time.

The feature importance of the random forest classifier is shown in Fig. 3.

From Table 4, we can see that the performance of our proposed methods is significantly better than that of the existing methods, and the classification of different IoT devices is better. From the confusion matrix, we can see that our proposed method has significantly fewer classification errors than other methods. However, the classification

Table 4. Model performance

Algorithm	Weighted-F1 score	Train time	Classification time
Random forest	0.56	42	14
CNN + RNN	0.81	9952	215.2
LSTM + Random Forest	0.89	1921	136

Table 5. Model performance

Device	Precision	Recall	F1-score
Amazon Echo	1	1	1
Android Phone 1	0.65	0.41	0.5
Android Phone 2	0.86	0.53	0.65
BTC	0.92	0.91	0.91
Belkin wemo switch	0.58	0.59	0.58
Belkin wemo motion sensor	0.58	0.57	0.58
Blipcare blood pressure meter	0	0	0
Dropcam	1	1	1
ETH	0.95	0.93	0.94
HP Printer	0.97	0.95	0.96
IPhone	0.5	0.23	0.32
Insteon Camera 1	0.91	0.91	0.91
Insteon Camera 2	0.67	0.89	0.76
Laptop	0.92	0.94	0.93
Light Bulbs LiFX Smart Bulb	1	1	1
MacBook	0.7	0.69	0.7
MacBook-Iphone	0.7	0.48	0.57
NEST Protect smoke alarm	1	1	1
Nest Dropcam	0.5	0.4	0.44
Netatmo Welcome	1	0.99	1
Netatmo weather station	1	1	1
PIX-STAR Photo-frame	0.99	0.99	0.99
Samsung Galaxy Tab	0.94	0.97	0.95
Samsung SmartCam	0.94	0.94	0.94
Smart Things	1	1	1

(continued)

Table 5. (*continued*)

Device	Precision	Recall	F1-score
TP-Link Day Night Cloud camera	0.99	1	0.99
TP-Link Smart plug	0.97	0.95	0.96
Triby Speaker	0.98	0.98	0.98
Withings Aura smart sleep sensor	1	1	1
Withings Smart Baby Monitor	1	1	1
Withings Smart scale	1	1	1
iHome	1	0.99	1

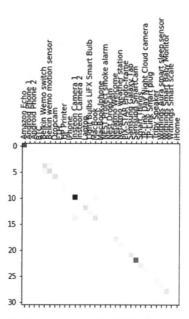

Fig. 4. Confusion matrix of LSTM + Random Forest

errors of Belkin Wemo switch and Belkin wemo motion are more obvious. This may be due to the same brand of equipment using some of the same services, resulting in similar traffic characteristics, difficult to classify.

6 Conclusions

The existing classification methods of Internet of things devices based on passive detection need to use complete flow or long-time traffic for classification, which is difficult to obtain, process or manage the equipment in real time according to the classification results. In this paper, we propose a traffic classification method using LSTM and random forest algorithm in the scenario of using the flow of a certain time before the equipment activity. Compared with the existing algorithms based on the complete flow, our proposed algorithm has a F1 score of 0.89, which is greatly improved compared with the existing methods. At the same time, using some new data to update the model can make the model perform better for subsequent data classification.

Acknowledgments. This work is supported by National Key R&D Program of China with No. 2020YFB1006101.

References

1. Zheng, Z., Xie, S., Dai, H., Wang, H., Chen, X.: Blockchain challenges and opportunities: a survey. Int. J. Web Grid Services (IJWGS) **14**(4), 352–375 (2018)
2. Dai, H.-N., Zheng, Z., Zhang, Y.: Blockchain for Internet of Things: a survey. IEEE Internet of Things J. (IoT-J **6**(5), 8076–8094.7 (2019)
3. Huang, Y., Kong, Q., Jia, N., Chen, X., Zheng, Z.: Recommending differentiated code to support smart contract update. In: 2019 IEEE/ACM 27th International Conference on Program Comprehension (ICPC), pp. 260–270, May 2019
4. Huang, K-Q., Chen, X.-T., Kang, Y.-F., Tan, T.-N.: Intelligent visual surveillance: a review. Chin. J. Comput. **38**(6), 1093–1118(2015)
5. Feng, X., Li, Q.: Han, Q., et al.: Identification of visible industrial control devices at Internet scale. In: IEEE International Conference on Communications. IEEE (2016)
6. Li, Q., Feng, X., Wang, H., et al.: Automatically discovering surveillance devices in the cyberspace. In: The 8th ACM. ACM (2017)
7. Feng, X., Li, Q., Wang, H., et al.: Acquisitional rule-based engine for discovering internet-of-thing devices. In: 27th USENIX Security Symposium (2018)
8. Leonard, D., Loguinov, D.: Demystifying service discovery: implementing an internet-wide scanner. In: Proceedings of the 10th ACM SIGCOMM Conference on Internet Measurement 2010. ACM, Melbourne (2010)
9. Kohno, T., Broido, A., Claffy, K.C.: Remote physical device fingerprinting. IEEE Trans. Dependable Secure Comput. **2**(2), 93–108 (2005)
10. Aneja, S., Aneja, N., Islam, M.S.: IoT device fingerprint using deep learning. In: 2018 IEEE International Conference on Internet of Things and Intelligence System. IEEE (2018)
11. Husák, M., Cermák, M., Jirsík, T., et al.: HTTPS traffic analysis and client identification using passive SSL/TLS fingerprinting. Eurasip J. Inf. Secur. **2016**(1), 6 (2016)
12. Arunan, S., Hassan, H.G., Franco, L., et al.: Classifying IoT devices in smart environments using network traffic characteristics. IEEE Trans. Mob. Comput. **1** (2018)
13. Msadek, N., Soua, R., Engel, T.: IoT Device fingerprinting: machine learning based encrypted traffic analysis. In: 2019 IEEE Wireless Communications and Networking Conference. IEEE (2019)
14. Aneja, S., Aneja, N., Islam, M.S.: IoT Device fingerprint using deep learning. In: 2018 IEEE International Conference on Internet of Things and Intelligence System. IEEE (2018)
15. Desai, B.A., Divakaran, D.M., Nevat, I., et al.: A feature-ranking framework for IoT device classification. In: International Conference on Communication Systems and Networks (2019)
16. Meidan, Y., Bohadana, M., Shabtai, A., et al.: ProfilIoT: a machine learning approach for IoT device identification based on network traffic analysis. In: Proceedings of the Symposium on Applied Computing, pp. 506–509 (2017)

17. Shahid, M.R., Blanc, G., Zhang, Z., et al.: IoT devices recognition through network traffic analysis. In: IEEE International Conference on Big Data. IEEE (2018)
18. Sivanathan, A., Sherratt, D., Gharakheili, H.H., et al.: Characterizing and classifying IoT traffic in smart cities and campuses. In: IEEE INFOCOM 2017 -IEEE Conference on Computer Communications Workshops. IEEE (2017)
19. Shen, M., Liu, Y., Zhu, L., Du, X., Hu, J.: Fine-grained webpage fingerprinting using only packet length information of encrypted traffic. IEEE Trans. Inf. Forensics Secur. **16,** 2046–2059 (2021)
20. Shen, M., Zhang, J., Zhu, L., Xu, K., Du, X.: Accurate decentralized application identification via encrypted traffic analysis using graph neural networks. IEEE Trans. Inf. Forensics Secur. 16, 2367–2380 (2021)
21. Shen, M., Wei, M., Zhu, L., Wang, M.: Classification of encrypted traffic with second-order Markov chains and application attribute bigrams. IEEE Trans. Inf. Forensics Secur. **12**(8), 1830–1843 (2017)

A Privacy Enhancement Scheme Based on Blockchain and Blind Signature for Internet of Vehicles

Huajie Wang, Jin Gan, Yong Feng$^{(\boxtimes)}$, Yingna Li, and Xiaodong Fu

Yunnan Key Laboratory of Computer Technology Applications, Kunming University of Science and Technology, Kunming, Yunnan 650500, China

Abstract. In Internet of Vehicles (IoV), it is getting increasing interests how to enhance the privacy of vehicles while commucating with other vehicles or Infrastructres. This paper proposes a vehicle privacy protection scheme based on blockchain and blind signature. Each vehicle has its own private key, and uses it to generate the correspongding public key. Then the vehicle obtains a digital certicate from the certicate authority (CA) through a blind signature algorithm, which ensures that the real identity information of the vehicle is strictly condential. When CA issues a certicate to a vehicle, the public key of the vehicle is stored in the blockchain. In vehicle-to-vehicle communication, the receiver can perform a hash operation with the sender's public key to obtain a Merkel's root value, and compare it with the root in the blockchain to confirm the legitimacy of the sender's identity. Simulation experiment results verify the effectiveness and applicability of the proposed scheme.

Keywords: Internet of vehicles · Privacy enhancement · Anonymous authentication · Blockchain · Blind signature

1 Introduction

The Internet of Vehicles(IoV) [1] is a large system network which is based on the intranet, the inter vehicle network and the mobile Internet on the vehicle, and conducts wireless communication and information exchange between vehicles, roads, pedestrians and the Internet according to the agreed communication protocol and data interaction standards. There are two types of communication in IoV, namely, vehicle to vehicle (V2V) communication and vehicle to infrastructure (V2I) communication [2]. By means of special short distance communication (DSRC) radio communication, nearby vehicles exchange messages in V2V and communicate directly with roadside unit (RSU) in V2I [3]. However, due to the unique features of IoV (such as high mobility and variability), it is vulnerable to various attacks. Therefore, the safety and privacy of vehicles should be considered in IoV.

According to the DSRC protocol in IoV [1], the vehicle will broadcast its own traffic status information and identity information every 100–300 ms in the

© Springer Nature Singapore Pte Ltd. 2021
H.-N. Dai et al. (Eds.): BlockSys 2021, CCIS 1490, pp. 368–387, 2021.
https://doi.org/10.1007/978-981-16-7993-3_28

process of driving. By using the information, the vehicle, RSU and traffic control center can achieve vehicle collision avoidance and road optimization, thus improving road safety and traffic efficiency. At the same time, the attacker can also attack the traffic state information and identity information broadcast by the vehicle to reconstruct the vehicle trajectory. In order to protect the identity privacy and location privacy of vehicles, each vehicle should have a corresponding pseudonym. Documents [4–6] proposed a pseudonym authentication scheme to assign digital certificates to vehicles. However, these schemes need to equip vehicles with a large number of digital certificates, and the management and storage of certificates is a complex problem, which is not suitable for traditional IoV.

In order to solve the problems of storage and management of digital certificates and anonymous authentication of vehicle identity information in IoV, the anonymous authentication scheme based on public key infrastructure (PKI) is proposed in references [7–9]. Vehicles have their own public/private key pairs, and use public key certificate as the method to verify vehicle identity. The public key certificate is applied by the vehicle to the CA. In the process of applying for the certificate, the vehicle uses the key and short-term pseudonym to generate the signature. If the CA is broken by the attacker, the privacy information of the user's vehicle will be leaked. In references [10–12], identity based signature (IBS) is proposed. IBS uses the identity identifier of each vehicle as the public key, and uses the identity identifier to generate the private key to sign the message. When the vehicle needs to verify its identity information, that is to verify its identity identifier signature, no digital certificate is needed. Compared with PKI, IBS saves the requirement of digital certificate when verifying vehicle identity. But IBS only solves the problem of communication between vehicles. When vehicles communicate with CA, there is no digital certificate to verify the legitimacy of vehicles.

This paper proposes a vehicle privacy enhancement scheme based on blind signature and blockchain. The vehicle uses blind signature to apply for digital certificate from CA and store the digital certificate in blockchain. Because the blockchain is decentralized, it is used to store and manage digital certificates and anonymous authentication of vehicle identity information. Finally, the vehicle identity information will not be leaked when the vehicle communicates with V2I and V2V. To sum up, the main contributions of this paper are as follows:

(1) In this paper, blind signature and blockchain technology are applied to IoV to enhance the privacy of vehicle identity information, the storage of vehicle certificate and the authentication of vehicle identity.
(2) In order to ensure the authenticity of this scheme, a large number of simulation experiments are carried out in this paper. Compared with the privacy protection scheme BARS under law enforcement authority (LEA), the performance of this scheme is more significant.

The organizational structure of this paper is as follows, Sect. 2 describes the current related work, and Sect. 3 introduces the system model and the related definitions of the terms used in this paper. Section 4 introduces the workflow of this scheme and the related algorithms of blockchain. Section 5 evaluates the performance of the scheme through simulation experiments. Section 6 summarizes the work of this paper.

2   Related Work

In recent years, the automobile industry has developed rapidly, and the number of vehicles has increased dramatically. It is estimated that the number of registered vehicles will reach 2 billion in the next 10 to 20 years [12]. The security of vehicle identity privacy has become the focus of scholars' research.

Choi [13] first uses the knowledge of symmetric cryptography to verify the vehicle's identity privacy. He combines symmetric authentication with short-term pseudonyms in IoV. Each vehicle receives a unique identifier and a short-term pseudonym. Personal key is managed by RSU. When there is message communication between vehicles, the authenticity of the message can only be verified by RSU. Due to the fact that RSU is not decentralized, RSU can not reveal the identity of the vehicle correctly when there is a vehicle dispute, so it does not meet the requirements of conditional privacy.

Based on PKI, Schaub [14] proposes a marking method to solve the problem of vehicle identity information disclosure caused by CA being attacked by malicious users. This method is to embed the tag information into the pseudonym accessed by each authority to prevent the authority from being attacked and cause information disclosure. Since each vehicle has a corresponding vehicle pseudonym certificate, the vehicle cannot obtain a new kana from the CA when the vehicle's kana certificate is revoked. If the vehicle wants to obtain a new kana certificate, it needs to be confirmed in the certificate revocation list. Because of the huge capacity of certificate revocation list, it is very expensive to confirm the certificate.

Karati [15] proposed a provably secure identity signature scheme based on IBS, in which the private key generator (PKG) is responsible for generating the private key. PKG first calculates the parameters of master key and public key, and then sends the public address of the parameters to the privacy protection entity. When each entity needs to communicate, the message sending entity uses the private key and signature algorithm to generate a signature for the message, and the message receiver determines whether the signature is valid through the verification method. In this scheme, the verification method eliminates the requirement of certificate, so it does not need to issue relevant certificate. However, all private keys are generated by PKG, which means that PKG knows the private keys of all entities, that is, there is a key escrow problem.

Al Riyami and Paterson [16] proposed a certificateless signature (CLS), which solves the problems of certificate management and key escrow in IBS. Compared with the traditional PKI and IBS schemes, the authenticity of the public key does not need to be guaranteed by a certificate, but acts as a semi trust institution through a third party, namely the key generation center (KGC). KGC uses the vehicle information to calculate part of the private key and send it to the vehicle. The vehicle receives part of the private key and generates the real private key according to the secret value provided by KGC. Compared with IBS, KGC can't get the public key of the vehicle. CLS is a promising solution in IoV, but its efficiency and cost still need to be solved.

Group signature authentication scheme is also one of the effective methods to protect vehicle privacy. The scheme allows any group member to sign the message, and only the group manager (GM) can identify the real identity of the sender. On the basis of group signature scheme, Zhang [17] proposed a scheme in which RSU acts as GM to solve the efficiency problem of group signature scheme and the selection problem of GM. In this scheme, when the vehicle enters the communication range of RSU for the first time or the private key of the vehicle is expired, the vehicle can apply for a new member private key. On the basis of Zhang's scheme, Park [18] and others proposed a distributed group key management method. RSU manages the key according to the distributed key management protocol instead of setting a unique GM to manage the key. However, it is difficult to find group administrators and maintain the stability of the group in a specific IoV scenario.

3   System Model

3.1   System Architecture

A typical IoV consists of three layers: Vehicle subnet, network operator and service infrastructure. Vehicle subnet is composed of on-board unit (OBU). Each vehicle can communicate with other vehicles or roadside infrastructure. Network operators provide corresponding network operation services for vehicles and service infrastructure. The service infrastructure consists of three parts: CA (certificate authority), SP (service provider) and RSU (road side unit). Therefore, in the Internet of vehicles, communication types can be divided into two categories: V2V and V2I communication, as shown in Fig. 1.

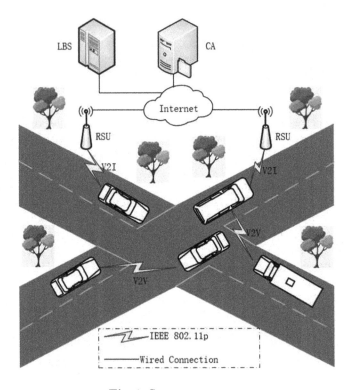

Fig. 1. System structure.

Among them, CA is responsible for managing the issue and revocation of vehicle identity and vehicle certificate in the local area. In this process, CA does not know the identity information of the vehicle and the association information of the public key. RSU is responsible for receiving certificate application and forwarding it to CA. After receiving the certificate application, CA processes it, and then forwards the reply to OBU. In addition, RSU can broadcast road information and safety information received from other RSUs or collected by itself. Due to economic reasons, RSUs are rarely set up in sparsely populated areas. It is assumed that each RSU has strong physical security and is not easy to be broken. The last part of the system is OBU. Each vehicle is equipped with an OBU and allows data communication with other vehicles and roadside infrastructure. For each vehicle equipped with OBU, every legal vehicle V_i have a unique real identity ID_i, A public key of its own PK_i, the private key generated with its own public key SK_i and certificate $Cert_i$ applied from CA.

3.2 Blockchain Model

Blockchain [19,20] is a new application mode of computer technology, and its core is distributed data storage, point-to-point transmission, consensus mechanism and encryption algorithm. The essence of blockchain is a series of series transactions, that is, blocks, which use cryptography to connect and protect their contents. Each block includes hash values of the previous block, the time when the block was generated, and all the data of the transaction, and the Merkel tree is used to store the transaction data.

The infrastructure model of blockchain can be divided into six layers [21], namely data layer, network layer, consensus layer, incentive layer, contract layer and application layer. The data layer encapsulates the chain structure of the underlying data blocks, as well as the related asymmetric public private key data encryption technology and time stamp technology. The network layer includes distributed networking mechanism, data transmission mechanism and data verification mechanism. The consensus layer mainly encapsulates all kinds of consensus mechanism algorithms of network nodes. The main consensus algorithms include proof of work (POW), proof of stack (POS), delegated proof of stack (DPOS) [22–24], etc. The incentive layer integrates economic factors into the blockchain technology system, mainly including the issuance mechanism and distribution mechanism of economic incentives. The contract layer mainly encapsulates all kinds of scripts, algorithms and smart contracts, which is the basis of the programmable characteristics of blockchain. The application layer encapsulates various application scenarios and cases of blockchain.

In blockchain, each data block is a chain data structure which is connected and combined in time order. All transactions will be recorded permanently on the chain in time order. Each block contains the following: current block hash value, previous block hash value, random number, timestamp and Merkel root value. Since hash values of the previous block are included in each block, all blocks are connected to each other to form a blockchain. Each block has a Merkel tree [25,26]. Each node is composed of hash of its two sub nodes, and the final root node is also formed by the hash of its two nodes. The purpose of the Merkel tree is to allow data in a block to be scattered and ensure that all data is correct.

3.3   Blind Signature Model

The concept of blind signature [27] was proposed by D. Chaum at the American Society of cryptography in 1982. This signature requires that the signer can sign the message without knowing the contents of the signed file. In addition, even if the signer sees the message and signature in the future, he cannot judge when the signature was generated.

In blind signature scheme, the message owner needs the entity U of blind signature service, which is called user here, and the entity S providing blind signature service is called signer. When user U needs signer S to sign the message, follow the following steps:

1) User U first blinds the signed message, so that the specific content of the message is garbled for signer S, also known as blind message.
2) User U sends the transformed blind message to signer S.
3) Signer S digitally signs all received blind messages.
4) The signer S gives the blind message and its signature to the user U.

5) User U verifies the received signature and then performs deblinding processing to obtain the original message's signature by signer S.

Blind signature schemes can be divided into many kinds, including blind signature based on discrete logarithm, blind signature based on elliptic encryption algorithm, blind signature based on RSA [28–30], etc. The blind signature scheme adopted in this paper is based on RSA. For each signer S, he has his own public key e, private key d and a public modulus m. suppose that user U signs to signer S in this process, the process is as follows:

1) User U selects blind factor k and encrypts information m. Where t is the encrypted blind information.

$$t = mk^e (mod\ n) \tag{1}$$

2) The signer S signs the blind information t

$$t^d = (mk^e)^d (mod\ n) \tag{2}$$

3) The signer S returns the blind information after signature to the user, and the user U obtains the blind information after signature through calculation.

$$s = \frac{t^d}{k} (mod\ n) \tag{3}$$

The decrypted information obtained by calculation is as follows:

$$s = m^d (mod\ n) \tag{4}$$

4) User U verifies whether the signature information is accurate. The verification process is as follows:

$$t^d \equiv (mk^e)^d \equiv m^d k (mod\ n) \tag{5}$$

$$t^d * k^{-1} = m^d * k * k^{-1} \equiv m^d (mod\ n) \tag{6}$$

4   Anonymous Authentication Scheme Based on Blockchain and Blind Signature

4.1   Problem Posing

In the traditional vehicular ad hoc network, vehicles need real-time and accurate traffic information. Therefore, for each vehicle, the vehicle will periodically broadcast its own beacon information, including the vehicle's identity information and driving status information. Due to the open characteristics of IoV, attackers can intercept beacon information broadcast in real time. By analyzing the intercepted beacon information, we can obtain the driver's habits, vehicle trajectory, driver's identity and other privacy information. Therefore, vehicle identity privacy needs to be protected. On the other hand, when a vehicle applies for a digital certificate from a CA, it needs to provide its own identity information to the CA. in this process, if an attacker attacks the CA, the vehicle information will also be leaked. Therefore, in the traditional vehicular ad hoc network, there are two hidden dangers, namely, the privacy of vehicle driving state information and identity information, as shown in Fig. 2 below.

4.2   Initialization Model

Each vehicle V_i has its own private key SK_i. Due to vehicle V_i want to enter the vehicular ad hoc network to apply for digital certificate, V_i first use the private key SK_i generate its own public key PK_i through asymmetric encryption algorithm. And then submit their own public key and identity information to RSU for digital certificate application. In the application process, the vehicle's identity information is not encrypted, so there may be malicious attackers who want to attack the CA to obtain the user's identity privacy information, which is not secure. In this model, each vehicle applies for digital certificate from CA through blind signature algorithm. In the previous process, CA uses its own private key to encrypt the vehicle identity information. Because the blind signature is blind, it can effectively protect the specific content of the signed message, so even if the attacker attacks the CA, he can not get the privacy information of the vehicle. After the CA issues the certificate to the vehicle, it will store the current

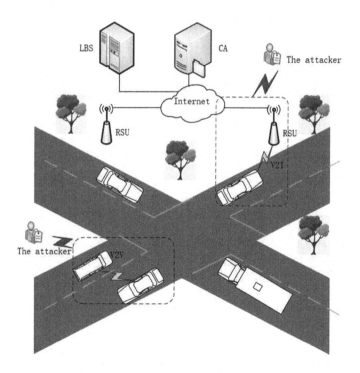

Fig. 2. IoV vehicle privacy threat model.

transaction information and public key in the blockchain. The blind signature algorithm is as follows:

Algorithm 1. Blind signature

Input: The message of vehicle
Output: The Vehicle signature
 1: **for** each $V_i \in V$ **do**
 2:     V_i use e produce m, d
 3:     **if** V_i want to get $Cert_i$ **then**
 4:         V_i caculateMu(message,m,e)
 5:         V_i send message to CA
 6:         **if** message is legal **then**
 7:             CA signatureCaculate(message)
 8:             CA send message to V_i
 9:         **end if**
10:         V_i.verrify(message)
11:         V_i.get($Cert_i$)
12:     **end if**
13: **end for**

4.3   Digital Certificate Issuance

After receiving the application from vehicle V_i, CA issues the transaction $Cert_{CA}$ and issues the certificate to vehicle V_i. The process is as follows:

$$Cert_{CA} = [PK_{CA}, PK_{V_i}, AE_{CA}(PK_{V_i}, ID_{V_i}), T, BSig_{CA}] \qquad (7)$$

where PK_i is the public key of V_i, $BSig_{CA}$ is the signature of CA and T is the time stamp. $AE_{CA} PK_{v_i}, ID_{v_i}$ is the public key and real identity of vehicle V_i after asymmetric encryption of CA. The certificate issuing process is as follows:

1) Vehicle V_i generates its own key pair (PK_{V_i}, SK_{v_i}) through asymmetric encryption algorithm according to its private key SK_{V_i}.
2) Vehicle V_i submits its public key PK_{v_i} and legal materials proving its identity to CA.
3) CA to vehicle V_i perform blind signature and use my private key SK_{CA} encrypts the public key and identity information of the vehicle.
4) CA issues digital certificate to vehicle after encrypting relevant information of vehicle V_i.
5) All transaction information of CA, identity information of vehicle and public key of vehicle are stored in blockchain.

The overall process of certificate issuance is shown in Fig. 3, and the numbers in the figure correspond to the above steps.

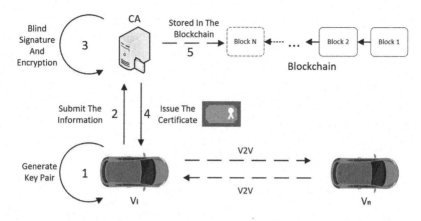

Fig. 3. IoV vehicle vertificate issuance model.

4.4 Anonymous Authentication

When the vehicle is moving, it needs to broadcast beacon messages periodically, including the identity information and driving status information of the vehicle. When the vehicle receives the broadcast beacon information from another vehicle, it must first verify the legitimacy of the information to prevent false information.

In V2V communication, the sender sends data and the receiver receives data to verify the validity of the data. When the sender sends the data, it also provides the sender with the public key for anonymous authentication. The process of anonymous authentication is the proof of the existence of the vehicle. The receiver uses the public key provided by the sender to calculate the root of the Merkel tree storing the public key, and then compares the root with the root of the Merkel tree. If the two values are consistent with the values stored in the block, it means that the sender is legal.

Improvement of Merkel Tree. For the traditional Merkel tree, the hash value of two adjacent nodes is combined into a string, and then the hash value of the string is calculated to get the hash value of the parent node of the two nodes. The hash value of the root node is also obtained by the hash operation of its two child nodes. In the Internet of vehicles, it takes a lot of time for CA to store the public key of each vehicle in the blockchain. At the same time, when the vehicle receives the information sent by the sender's vehicle, it also takes a lot of time to find the public key of the vehicle in the blockchain and carry out anonymous authentication of the vehicle. Therefore, using the traditional Merkel tree for storage will consume a lot of time.

In Ethereum, there is a data structure called Patricia tree. Patricia tree [31] is also called prefix tree or dictionary tree. The content of each node of Patricia tree is usually string. The position of each node in the tree is usually determined by the key value of the node. Compared with Merkle tree, Patricia tree is very efficient in finding key values with the same prefix. For example,to find a word with the prefix of Bu, in Merkle tree, we need to go through the whole Merkle tree, while in Patricia tree, we only need to find the node with the prefix of Bu, and then traverse the subtree of the node to find the key value. But Patricia tree has two disadvantages:

1) Low efficiency of direct search

If n is the length of the key value of the lookup node, the efficiency of Patricia tree is $O(n)$. In the process of one lookup, there will be n times of IO overhead. Compared with direct lookup, the pressure on disk is greater.

2) It's a waste of space

If there is a node with a long content and no matching prefix, in order to store the node, many non leaf nodes need to be created to construct the path from the node to the root node, which results in a waste of space.

In Ethereum [33], Merkle tree and Patricia tree are combined and improved to get Merkle Patricia tree. Merkle Patricia tree is based on Patricia tree, and key values are generated based on Merkle tree. Merkle Patricia tree introduces many new node types, including null node, branch node, leaf node and extension node. Among them, the structure of leaf node is the list of key value pairs. The extension node is also a list of key value pairs, and value is the hash value of other nodes. The branch node is a list with a length of 17. The first 16 items correspond to the 16 possible values of traversing the key.

Public Key Insertion. In the Internet of vehicles, the process of issuing certificate is the process of storing new public key into Merkle Patricia tree, that is, the insert operation of Merkle Patricia tree. In the process of inserting a node, it is necessary to find the current node with the longest prefix as the new insertion node, and the public key to be inserted as PK_{v_i}. In the process of inserting a node, different operations should be performed according to the shared nibbles relationship between node and PK_{v_i}, as follows:

1) Node is the extension node

When inserting PK_{v_i}, first find the longest prefix node that matches it. At this point, judge whether the shared nibbles value of the node matches the newly inserted node. If it matches, replace the newly inserted node PK_{v_i} with the original node. If the inserted nodes do not match exactly, point the next node to the corresponding extended node of shared nibbles, and insert the PK_{v_i} node.

2) Node is a branch node and the next node does not have the same shared nibbles.

When inserting PK_{v_i}, the longest prefix node is found to be a branch node. If the next node does not have the same shared nibbles, a new branch node will be generated, the previous branch node will point to the newly generated branch node, and then PK_{v_i} will be inserted into the new branch node.

3) Node is a branch node and the next node has the same shared nibbles.

When inserting PK_{v_i}, find that the longest prefix node is just the branch node. If the next node has the same shared nibbles, directly point the node to the extension node with the same shared nibbles, and finally insert PK_{v_i} node.

The algorithm of public key insertion is shown below:

Algorithm 2. Public key insertion

Input: Public key of each vehicle
Output: Adjust the tree and caculate time
 1: Initialize Merkle Patricia Tree
 2: **for** each $PK_{V_i} \in PK$ **do**
 3:     find the same longest prefix node as Node
 4:     **if** Node is extended node **then**
 5:         **if** Node.nibbles $== PK_{V_i}$.nibbles **then**
 6:             Add PK_{V_i} into Merkle Patricia Tree
 7:         **else**
 8:             Node $- >$ next node
 9:             Add PK_{V_i} into Merkle Patricia Tree
10:         **end if**
11:     **end if**
12:     **if** Node is branch node and Node.nibbles $!=$ next node.nibbles **then**
13:         creat new branch node as NewNode
14:         Node $- >$ NewNode
15:         Add PK_{V_i} into Merkle Patricia Tree
16:     **else**
17:         Node $- >$ next node
18:         Add PK_{V_i} into Merkle Patricia Tree
19:     **end if**
20: **end for**

Anonymous Certification of Vehicle Information. When vehicles communicate with each other in V2V, the receiver must verify the validity of the sender's public key to confirm the identity of the vehicle. To verify the legitimacy of vehicle identity is to verify the existence of the sender's public key, that is, whether the public key exists in Merkle Patricia tree. The process of verification is to verify the shared of Merkle Patricia tree related nodes Whether nibbles can form the hash value of the public key, calculate the hash value of its parent node at the same time, calculate the hash value of the root node layer by layer, and finally verify the hash value of the root node. Compare the calculated hash value with the hash value of the root node in the block. If the hash value is consistent, that is, verify the legitimacy of the vehicle, and communicate with it in V2V. The algorithm is as follows.

Algorithm 3. Vehicle information anonymous authentication

Input: Public keys of two authenticated vehicles
Output: Judging the authenticity of vehicle identity information
1: Initialize V_i and V_j
2: **if** $V_i -> V_j$ **then**
3:     $PK_{V_i} = V_j.getPublicKey(V_i)$
4:     Node $= PK_{V_i}$.leaf node
5:     **while** Node $!=$ root node **do**
6:         Hash $=$ CaculateHash(Node)
7:             **if** Hash $==$ Node.prefix.hash **then**
8:                 Node $->$ Node.prefix
9:             **else**
10:                 V_i is illegal
11:                 break
12:             **end if**
13:     **end while**
14:     **if** Node.prefix $!=$ null and Node.hash $==$ root.hash **then**
15:         V_i is legal
16:     **else**
17:         V_i is illegal
18:     **end if**
19: **end if**

4.5   Safety Analysis

Certificate Security. The essence of blockchain is to ensure the security requirements of certificates. When a vehicle applies for a certificate, it needs a CA to perform blind signature. After the vehicle obtains the certificate, the CA will insert the public key of the vehicle into the blockchain in chronological order. Because the blockchain is decentralized, all the added information can not be modified unless the attacker has more than 51% of the computing power of the blockchain. At the same time, the certificate is transparent, and all the inserted public key information can be verified.

Beacon Information Security. The proof of vehicle identity is to verify the public key of the vehicle. Vehicles should broadcast beacon information to surrounding vehicles all the time. The receiver receives the information from the sender and uses the public key of the sender's vehicle for anonymous authentication to judge the legitimacy of the vehicle's identity. Anonymous authentication is to verify whether the root value of Merkle Patricia tree where the public key is located is the same as that calculated by the vehicle. Because the blockchain is decentralized, the legitimacy of the sender's vehicle is guaranteed when the vehicle is anonymous authenticated, that is, the beacon information is secure.

Vehicle Privacy Security. Each vehicle has its own private key, and the vehicle generates the public key through its own private key. When the vehicle carries out V2V communication, the sending information needs to be verified. When an attacker wants to publish false information, it is not feasible. When a vehicle applies for a certificate, the material provided by CA is encrypted with its own public key, and the signature algorithm of CA is blind signature algorithm. In V2I communication, even if the attacker attacks CA, the identity information of the vehicle cannot be obtained.

5   Experimental Results and Analysis

The vehicle privacy protection scheme based on blockchain and blind signature mainly realizes the communication security of vehicle V2V and V2I through blockchain and blind signature. In this paper, assuming that the communication quality of V2V and V2I meets the requirements of this scheme, the experimental environment is deployed in Java environment, and the computer is configured with 2.3 GHz Intel i5 processor and 8 GB memory. The experiment is divided into three parts: blind signature, public key insertion and anonymous authentication. The time consumption of blind signature is evaluated from the perspective of CA, the time consumption of public key insertion and anonymous authentication is evaluated from the perspective of a single vehicle, and finally the storage space consumption is evaluated.

5.1   Blind Signature

In this scheme, the first thing to consider is the process of blind signature. Each vehicle needs to submit its identity information to CA for blind signature when applying for digital certificate. In order to ensure the randomness and authenticity of the experiment, a vehicle is randomly selected to perform blind signature to CA. the signature process runs 300 times, and the time consumption of each signature is calculated. Figure 4 shows the time consumption of blind

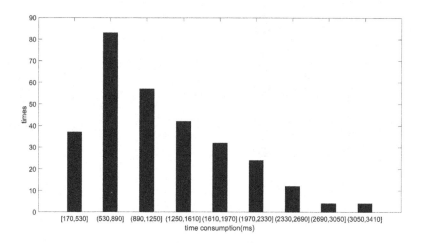

Fig. 4. Blind signature time consumption.

signature. It can be seen from the figure that the time consumption of blind signature is mostly less than 1250 ms. Considering that the computing power of digital certificate authority is much higher than the experimental conditions in this paper, the time cost of CA is completely acceptable.

5.2   Experimental Settings

The main parameters N and S of the second part of the experiment. N is the number of current legal public keys, that is, the number of leaf nodes in the Merkle Patricia tree, and S is the size of other nodes in Merkle Patricia tree except leaf nodes. In this experiment, N is taken as [25000,50000,75000,100000], and S is [128 bytes, 256 bytes, 512 bytes]. Due to the limitation of experimental conditions, the values of N and S are taken to 100000 and 512 bytes respectively.

Issue of Certificate. The certificate issuing process is the process of inserting leaf nodes in Merkle Patricia tree. Before public key insertion, SHA-256 is encrypted to ensure the security of public key. In order to ensure the randomness of the experiment, N takes three values for S corresponding to one value each time, and calculates the average time consumption 300 times each time the experiment runs. Figure 5 is the time consumption of N inserting public key each time with different values. As can be seen from Fig. 6, with the increase of the number of public keys, the time consumption is basically linear. This is because the number of public keys is also linearly increased. When the number of public keys is the same, the time consumption of inserting public key is similar under different node sizes. When hash operation is carried out, the size of node is independent of the speed of hash operation, so the time consumption is close to the number of public keys but different node sizes. Finally, when the public key scale reaches 100000, the insertion time of public key is less than 2500 ms.

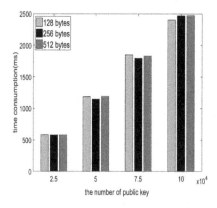

Fig. 5. Public key insertion.

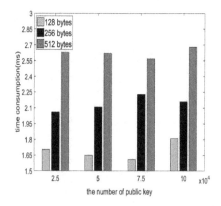

Fig. 6. The time consumption of anonymous authentication when N and S take different values.

Considering the limitation of the experimental environment and the calculation of CA, the time consumption of certificate issuing is completely acceptable.

Anonymous Authentication. In the process of anonymous authentication, the sender sends the public key anonymously, and the receiver performs multiple hash operations after receiving the data to verify whether the public key exists in the Merkle Patricia tree. The same as the certificate issuing experiment, N takes three values for S corresponding to one value each time, and calculates the average time loss 300 times each time. Figure 6 is the time consumption of anonymous authentication when N and S take different values. As can be seen from Fig. 6, with the increase of public key, the time consumption of anonymous authentication is not very volatile, because the process of anonymous authentication is the process of hash operation to calculate the root value of Merkle Patricia tree, which is related to the storage space size of Merkle Patricia tree, and has nothing to do with the number of public keys. When the public key is fixed, the time consumption increases with the increase of the size of the Merkle Patricia tree node. This is because the size of the node affects the operation speed of hash operation, so as the size of the node increases, the time consumption increases. Finally, considering the limitation of the experimental environment, under the condition of 100000 public key, the time of anonymous authentication is less than 3 ms. Considering the computing ability of the actual CA, the time consumption of anonymous authentication is completely acceptable.

Storage Space. In addition to time consumption, storage cost should also be considered. As mentioned above, each time N takes a value, the corresponding S takes three values to calculate the storage consumption of Merkle Patricia tree and public key. Figure 7 shows the consumption of storage space when N and S take different values. As can be seen from the figure, with the increase of the number of public keys, the storage space also increases, but the increase is not large. This is because after SHA-256 operation, the public key will become a 256 bit hash string, which has little impact on the storage space. When the number of public keys is fixed, the space consumption increases with the increase of node size. On the whole, when the public key size reaches 100000 and S takes 512 bytes, the storage space consumption is about 70 mb. Considering the storage capacity of the actual CA, the storage consumption under the experimental conditions is completely acceptable.

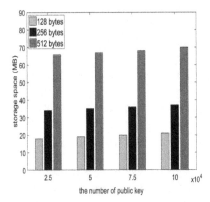
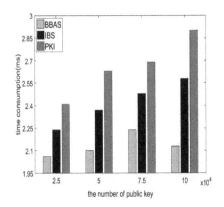

Fig. 7. Storage space cost.

Fig. 8. Comparison of anonymous authentication time of different schemes.

5.3 Experimental Comparison

In this part, we compare the existing vehicle anonymous authentication schemes, public key infrastructure (PKI) anonymous authentication scheme and identity based signature (IBS) anonymous authentication scheme to verify the feasibility of this scheme. The comparison is made from three aspects: signature time and anonymous authentication time.

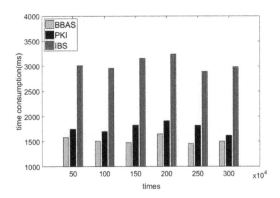

Fig. 9. Comparison of signature time of different schemes.

In the PKI scheme, the vehicle is equipped with a public key/private key pair for pseudonymous communication, and the public key digital certificate is used as a safe and reliable method of verifying the vehicle. When a CA issues a digital certificate to a vehicle, it needs to detect the public key and private key generated by the vehicle through a pseudonymous channel, and verify the public key digital certificate for signature. Generate the private key identifier of the message and use it as the identity of the node in the IBS scheme. Using the identifier of the message sender is sufficient to verify the signature. In addition to considering the time consumption of anonymous authentication, we should also consider the time consumption of PKI and IBS under the same public key, as shown in Fig. 8. Randomly select vehicles to use the PKI scheme and the IBS scheme for signature authorization in the process. The entire program is run 300 times, and the current average consumption time is calculated every 50 times, as shown in Fig. 9. In summary, the BBAS scheme is superior to the other two schemes.

6   Conclusion

This paper proposes a privacy enhancement scheme based on blockchain and blind signature. Through the combination of blockchain and blind signature technology, the privacy of vehicle identity in V2V communication and V2I communication is realized. In V2I communication, vehicle applies for digital certificate from digital certificate authority through blind signature. In V2V communication, vehicles ensure the privacy of communication between vehicles through the consensus mechanism of blockchain. At the same time, Merkle Patricia tree in Ethereum is improved to realize the distributed and efficient authentication process between vehicles, which ensures the scalability of the whole anonymous authentication scheme managed by digital certificate authority. Finally, the experimental results show that the time and space cost of this scheme is feasible. With the help of this model, the privacy protection of vehicle identity information can be realized in different communication scenarios.

Acknowledgments. This work is Supported by the National Natural Science Foundation of China (62062047, 61662042).

References

1. Butt, T.A., Iqbal, R., Shah, S.C., et al.: Social internet of vehicles: architecture and enabling technologies. Comput. Electric. Eng. **69**, 68–84 (2018)
2. Butakov, V.A., Ioannou, P.: Personalized driver assistance for signalized intersections using V2I communication. IEEE Trans. Intell. Transp. Syst. **17**(7), 1910–1919 (2016)
3. Lu, Z., Qu, G., Liu, Z.: A survey on recent advances in vehicular network security, trust, and privacy. IEEE Trans. Intell. Transp. Syst. **20**(2), 760–776 (2018)
4. Akhtar, N., Ergen, S.C., Ozkasap, O.: Vehicle mobility and communication channel models for realistic and efficient highway VANET simulation. IEEE Trans. Veh. Technol **64**(1), 248–262 (2014)
5. Zeng, Y., Xiang, K., Li, D., et al.: Directional routing and scheduling for green vehicular delay tolerant networks. Wirel. Netw. **19**(2), 161–173 (2013)

6. Freudiger, J., Jadliwala, M., Hubaux, J.P., et al.: Privacy of community pseudonyms in wireless peer-to-peer networks. Mob. Netw. Appl **18**(3), 413–428 (2013)

7. Kondareddy, Y., Di Crescenzo, G., Agrawal, P.: Analysis of certificate revocation list distribution protocols for vehicular networks. In: 2010 IEEE Global Telecommunications Conference GLOBECOM 2010, IEEE 2010, pp. 1–5. IEEE, Miami (2010). https://doi.org/10.1109/GLOCOM.2010.5683985

8. Azees, M., Vijayakumar, P., Deboarh, L.J.: EAAP: efficient anonymous authentication with conditional privacy-preserving scheme for vehicular ad hoc networks. IEEE Trans. Intell. Transp. Syst. **18**(9), 2467–2476 (2017)

9. Eichler, S.: Strategies for pseudonym changes in vehicular ad hoc networks depending on node mobility. In: 2007 IEEE Intelligent Vehicles Symposium, IEEE 2007, pp. 541–546. IEEE, Turkey (2007). https://doi.org/10.1109/IVS.2007.4290171

10. Lu, H., Li, J., Guizani, M.: A novel ID-based authentication framework with adaptive privacy preservation for VANETs. In: 2012 Computing, Communications and Applications Conference, IEEE 2012, pp. 345–350. IEEE, Hong Kong (2012). https://doi.org/10.1109/ComComAp.2012.6154869

11. Zhang, L., Wu, Q., Domingo-Ferrer, J., et al.: Distributed aggregate privacy-preserving authentication in VANETs. IEEE Trans. Intell. Transp. Syst. **18**(9), 516–526 (2016)

12. Choi, J.Y., Jakobsson, M., Wetzel, S.: Balancing auditability and privacy in vehicular networks. Proceedings of the 1st ACM International Workshop on Quality of Service & Security in Wireless and Mobile Networks, ACM 2005, pp. 79–87. Association for Computing Machinery, Montreal (2005). https://doi.org/10.1145/1089761.1089775

13. Schaub, F., Kargl, F., Ma, Z., et al.: V-tokens for conditional pseudonymity in VANETs. In: 2010 IEEE Wireless Communication and Networking Conference, IEEE 2010, pp. 1–6. IEEE, Sydney (2010). https://doi.org/10.1109/WCNC.2010.5506126

14. Karati, A., Islam, S.K.H., Biswas, G.P., et al.: Provably secure identity-based signcryption scheme for crowdsourced industrial Internet of Things environments. IEEE Internet Things J. **5**(4), 2904–2914 (2017)

15. Al-Riyami, S.S., Paterson, K.G.: Certificateless public key cryptography. In: Laih, C.-S. (ed.) ASIACRYPT 2003. LNCS, vol. 2894, pp. 452–473. Springer, Heidelberg (2003). https://doi.org/10.1007/978-3-540-40061-5_29

16. Zhang, L., Wu, Q., Solanas, A., et al.: A scalable robust authentication protocol for secure vehicular communications. IEEE Trans. Veh. Technol. **59**(4), 1606–1617 (2009)

17. Park, M.H., Gwon, G.P., Seo, S.W., et al.: RSU-based distributed key management (RDKM) for secure vehicular multicast communications. IEEE J. Sel. Areas Commun. **29**(3), 644–658 (2011)

18. Nakamoto, S.: Bitcoin: a peer-to-peer electronic cash system. Manubot (2019)

19. Kang, J., Yu, R., Huang, X., et al.: Enabling localized peer-to-peer electricity trading among plug-in hybrid electric vehicles using consortium blockchains. IEEE Trans. Ind. Inf. **13**(6), 3154–3164 (2017)

20. Frey, R.M., Bühler, P., Gerdes, A., et al.: The effect of a blockchain-supported, privacy-preserving system on disclosure of personal data. In: 2017 IEEE 16th International Symposium on Network Computing and Applications (NCA), IEEE 2017, pp. 1–5. IEEE, Cambridge (2017). https://doi.org/10.1109/NCA.2017.8171385

21. King, S., Nadal, S.: Ppcoin: peer-to-peer crypto-currency with proof-of-stake. self-published paper 19 (2012)

22. Larimer, D.: DPOS Consensus Algorithm-The Missing White Paper 19 (2017)
23. Larimer, D.: Delegated proof-of-stake (dpos). Bitshare whitepaper (2014)
24. Wang, Y., Shen, Y., Wang, H., et al.: MtMR: ensuring mapreduce computation integrity with merkle tree-based verifications. IEEE Trans. Big Data **4**(3), 418–431 (2016)
25. Koo, D., Shin, Y., Yun, J., et al.: An online data-oriented authentication based on merkle tree with improved reliability. In: 2017 IEEE International Conference on Web Services (ICWS), IEEE 2017, pp. 840–843. IEEE, Honolulu (2017). https://doi.org/10.1109/ICWS.2017.102
26. Chaum, D.: Blind signatures for untraceable payments. In: Chaum, D., Rivest, R.L., Sherman, A.T. (eds.) Advances in Cryptology, pp. 199–203. Springer, Boston, MA (1983). https://doi.org/10.1007/978-1-4757-0602-4_18
27. Camenisch, J.L., Piveteau, J.-M., Stadler, M.A.: Blind signatures based on the discrete logarithm problem. In: De Santis, A. (ed.) EUROCRYPT 1994. LNCS, vol. 950, pp. 428–432. Springer, Heidelberg (1995). https://doi.org/10.1007/BFb0053458
28. Zhang, F., Safavi-Naini, R., Susilo, W.: Efficient verifiably encrypted signature and partially blind signature from bilinear pairings. In: Johansson, T., Maitra, S. (eds.) INDOCRYPT 2003. LNCS, vol. 2904, pp. 191–204. Springer, Heidelberg (2003). https://doi.org/10.1007/978-3-540-24582-7_14
29. Chien, H.Y., Jan, J.K., Tseng, Y.M.: RSA-based partially blind signature with low computation. In: Proceedings Eighth International Conference on Parallel and Distributed Systems, ICPADS 2001, IEEE 2002, pp. 385–389. IEEE, Kyongju (2002). https://doi.org/10.1109/ICPADS.2001.934844
30. Karame, G., Gruber, D., Li, W.: Method and system for providing a transaction forwarding service in blockchain implementations: U.S. Patent Application, Heidelberg (2018)
31. Fenu, G., Marchesi, L., Marchesi, M., et al.: The ICO phenomenon and its relationships with ethereum smart contract environment. In: 2018 International Workshop on Blockchain Oriented Software Engineering (IWBOSE), IEEE 2018, pp. 26–32. IEEE, Campobasso (2018). https://doi.org/10.1109/IWBOSE.2018.8327568

Research on the Security of Beyond-the-Sight Services Based on Blockchain

Xuefei Duan[1(✉)], Hua Lu[1], Lejin Bai[2], and Zixuan Guo[2]

[1] GuangDong Communications and Networks Institute, Huangpu District, Guangzhou City, Guangdong Province, China
{duanxuefei,luhua}@gdcni.cn

[2] State Key Laboratory of Networking and Switching Technology, Beijing University of Posts and Telecommunications, Beijing, China
{bailejin,zx_guo}@bupt.edu.cn

Abstract. In 2008, blockchain was proposed as the basic technology of Bitcoin, and it is essentially a decentralized database. This technology is widely used in financial industry, data storage, edge computing and other scenarios. With the rapid increase of the number of devices connected to the Internet of Things (IoT), the traditional centralized cloud computing system is unable to satisfy the Quality of Service (QoS) of many IoT applications, especially for areas with real-time. IoT services based on Mobile Edge Computing (MEC) are gradually becoming popular, and the characteristics of the distributed accounting and consensus mechanism of the blockchain can ensure the security of MEC-based IoT services. In this paper, we first summarize the existing blockchain and MEC related technologies, and then propose a future-oriented Internet of Vehicles (IoV) service: beyond-the-sight service. At last, we specifically discuss how the blockchain can ensure the security of beyond-the-sight service in terms of terminal equipment identification and data transmission.

Keywords: Blockchain · Mobile edge computing · Internet of Vehicles · Internet of Things · Beyond-the-sight service

1 Blockchain Overview

1.1 Introduction of Blockchain

The concept of blockchain first appeared in digital currency, the purpose is to solve the problem of users' high dependence on banks, and to build a shared and autonomous ledger. In the traditional transaction scenario, since the bank is credible, users can directly conduct transactions through cash. However, with the development of the Internet, online payment services have gradually emerged, and clearing and settlement is no longer only related to banks. Since there is no shared database of mutual trust, all business parties that access the bank need

© Springer Nature Singapore Pte Ltd. 2021
H.-N. Dai et al. (Eds.): BlockSys 2021, CCIS 1490, pp. 388–396, 2021.
https://doi.org/10.1007/978-981-16-7993-3_29

to provide their own relevant data, which greatly increases the cost of communication and maintenance. In this scenario, if the blockchain is used as a method of data storage, business parties can obtain and maintain data information.

Blockchain technology is based on cryptography combined with a hash algorithm to encrypt and record user transaction data. Each data block contains valid and complete transaction information with a timestamp, as well as the information of the previous block. The blocks are connected together in chronological order to construct a peer-to-peer (P2P) distributed electronic cash ledger, which is jointly maintained by participating users. On this basis, combining the Merkle tree and consensus mechanism and other mechanisms to jointly ensure the immutability, anonymity, information transparency, and self-control of the blockchain, which is essentially a decentralized database [1]. Due to the above characteristics, blockchain is widely used in financial industry, data storage, smart contracts [2], IoT and other scenarios. Bitcoin [3] is the most successful application of blockchain in the financial field, and most of the digital currencies that have been proposed later also use distributed accounting to break away from the dependence on third parties. Blockchain can be used as a way of data storage, because it is essentially a distributed database, and because of its decentralized and highly redundant features, it can ensure data security. At present, Storj cloud [4] storage has been applied, which utilizes scattered storage space to reduce storage costs while ensuring performance and security. For the application of smart contracts, Ethereum has a good combination with it, which can be used in scenarios such as securities, voting, and smart wills. The combination of blockchain and the IoT is also very popular. Sharma et al. proposed a blockchain-based distributed cloud architecture with a Software Defined Networking (SDN) with blockchain technologies [5]. It can solve many problems of the traditional cloud computing such as real-time data transmission, scalability, security and high availability.

1.2   Architecture of Blockchain

The blockchain platform represented by Bitcoin can usually be divided into five layers from bottom to top: data layer, network layer, consensus layer, smart contract layer, and application layer [6].

The data layer includes the blockchain's regulations on data structure and processing methods. The original transaction data stores the information of each transaction in a fixed data structure. The transaction data is encrypted using asymmetric encryption methods such as SHA256 and stored in a Merkle tree to form a block body. The block header carries the hash value of the previous block, the current Merkle tree root, and the timestamp, etc., adding time dimension information to the blockchain. These data are organized together in time to form a chain structure, which ensures that the blockchain can trace historical data and cannot be tampered with.

The network layer determines that the blockchain based on distributed data uses a P2P network. Each node in the network has the dual identity of the producer and consumer of the data to ensure equality between nodes. Data

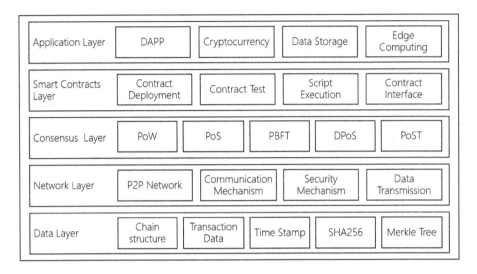

Fig. 1. Architecture of blockchain

sharing is achieved by publishing transaction information between nodes through a broadcast mechanism, and each node has to undertake network routing, data transmission, security assurance, and data verification.

The consensus layer includes the consensus algorithm used by the blockchain. On the one hand, the purpose is to ensure that the data in the distributed network is consistent, and the entire network users recognize the current packaged data. On the other hand, it is to encourage all nodes to participate in the consensus process through economic reward in. At present, the basically mature algorihms include Proof of Work (PoW) [7] used in Bitcoin, Proof of Stake (PoS) [7], Proof of Space-Time (PoST) [8], Delegate Proof of Stake (DPoS) [9], improved based on PoW, etc. There are also a series of algorithms such as Practical Byzantine Fault Tolerance (PBFT) [10] to solve the Byzantine fault tolerance problem. Taking the original PoW algorithm as an example, all participants participate in a calculation process to prove their workload. This process needs to obtain a random number and get a number with the first N bits all being 0. With the continuous growth of the blockchain, the number of N also needs to be gradually increased to ensure the difficulty of calculation. Participants who calculate first have the right to pack data on blocks and get corresponding rewards.

The smart contract layer is used to deploy smart contracts and test. Smart contracts refer to contract terms defined in digital form. All parties can use the corresponding interface to execute the contract, reducing reliance on trusted third parties. The code and data of the smart contract deployed on the blockchain are tamper-proof. In addition, the response result of the smart contract is deterministic, that is, running a script on the same data will get a consistent result. Users in the blockchain network can rely on smart contracts to send data and process to ensure the trustworthiness of the blockchain.

The top layer is the application layer, which includes the current services and application scenarios that can be provided based on blockchain technology. At present, it has been widely used in decentralized application (DAPP), Cryptocurrency, data storage and edge computing, etc.

2   Internet of Vehicles Based on MEC

2.1   Mobile Edge Computing Overview

MEC is a network architecture that enables IT and cloud-computing capabilities at the edge of the cellular network [11]. It can reduce network congestion and improve applications by performing related processing tasks closer to the end-user. The technology is designed to be implemented at cellular base stations, providing rapid deployment of applications and other customer services.

The core idea of edge computing is to complete the computational program near the edge of the data source. Edge computing can push the frontier of computing applications, the privacy data storage and real-time data processing and analysis away from centralized cloud to the edge servers of the network, which can retain the core advantages of cloud computing and transfer the realtime control and sensitive data storage to the edge servers [12].

2.2   IoV Combined with MEC

Nowadays, existing IoT applications require more timely computing responses. In the context of IoV, the beyond-the-sight service is to provide a view of the road conditions outside the line of sight for vehicles in the network. For example, pedestrians crossing the road will be blocked by car B when car A and car B are meeting. So pedestrians are out of sight for car A. If car A cannot detect pedestrians crossing the road, it is likely to cause a traffic accident. For another example, the road condition information after a 90-degree turn is also very important information but out of sight for the vehicle. The beyond-the-sight service must return traffic information to the vehicles in time, otherwise, it will lose the meaning of the service and may even cause a safety accident. Based on the characteristics of edge computing mentioned in the previous paragraph, the calculate ability of edge computing nodes can satisfy IoT services. So the deployment and operation of IoT- related services often rely on mobile edge computing to get a more timely response.

For the beyond-the-sight service in the IoV, it is very important to avoid malicious attacks and data tampering. A maliciously attacked node can paralyze the entire IoV network and invalidate the entire beyond-the-sight service. For example, the Sybil attack [13] is an Internet of Vehicles attack method based on fake identities. The fake node controls the vehicle by forging the car ID, sending false information, and forging the traffic scene to affect the normal judgment of the vehicle.

Most of the existing terminal equipment access authentication relies on a third-party trusted center. Wang Qun proposed a method for identifying vehicle identity based on radio frequency identification (RFID). When the vehicle passes through the area covered by the reader, its electronic tag is activated and recognized by the reader. The reader sends the identified vehicle information via the network to the central database for identification and verification [14]. VIJAYAKUMAR P proposed an identity authentication scheme based on identity signature [15]. In the scheme, a private key generator (PKG) is used as a trusted third party for private key generation and distribution. The private keys of all vehicles are generated by PKG. And PKG can know the private key and scheme of each vehicle. It has a key escrow problem. The authentication mechanism that relies on a third party is not completely reliable. Once the trusted center is attacked, the service will paralyze.

3   Blockchain in Beyond-the-sight Service

3.1   Architecture of Beyond-the-sight Service

Beyond-the-sight service aims to avoid traffic accidents. It can be used in automatic driving to help vehicles predict and plan routes in advance. 3D object detection is the core function of the beyond-the-sight service which estimates 3D bounding boxes specifying the size, 3D pose (position and orientation), and class of the objects in the environment [16]. The traditional structure consists of vehicle nodes, roadside units (RSU), MEC nodes and a third-party trusted center. Vehicle nodes has certain computing capabilities and data transmission capabilities. RSU is used to capture original information. It is the information exchange hub for sensing the characteristics of the road network and road participants. MEC nodes provide computing power. They process the original information collected by the vehicle nodes and RSU, detect 3D objects and return the view of road conditions to the vehicle nodes. The third-party trusted center provides node access authentication services by providing certificates.

Recently, blockchain has found many applications in various networks and distributed systems today [17], one of them is IoV. Introducing the blockchain into the beyond-the-sight service in the IoV can improve the availability and security of the service. IoV based on MEC naturally has the characteristics of a distributed network structure. Each micro-computing node is formed by the vehicle as a unit. So, they form a point-to-point network structure, which is very consistent with the application scenarios of the blockchain. Blockchain can ensure safety in the beyond-the-sight service from the two aspects of vehicle access authentication and information transmission. After the introduction of blockchain, the beyond-the-sight service system consists of intelligent vehicle nodes, RSU, MEC nodes, and two levels of blockchain.

The service is often used in scenarios shown in Fig. 2. And the structure is shown in Fig. 3.

Vehicle nodes will have a certain amount of intelligent computing capabilities. They can autonomously detect objects in simple road conditions. They also do

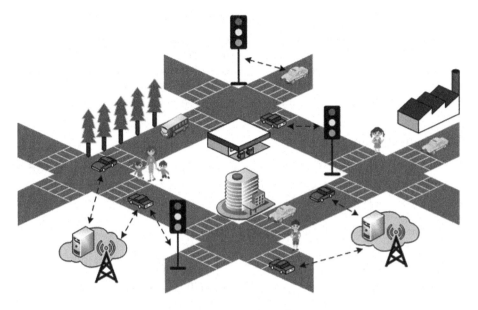

Fig. 2. Beyond-the-sight service scenarios

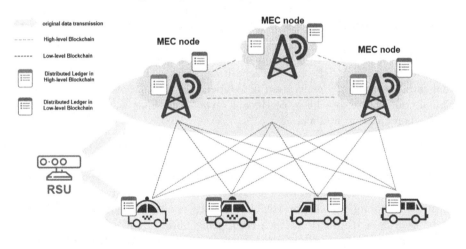

Fig. 3. Framework of beyond-the-sight service system with blockchain

some preprocessing for complex scenes and then transmit it to the MEC nodes. Intelligent vehicle nodes make the service response faster. It will provide a view of the road conditions around the vehicle at a certain moment in near real time. MEC nodes and vehicle nodes will form two distributed networks. The high-level blockchain is located in the network formed by the MEC nodes, which is used to replace the function of the third-party trusted center and provide vehicle access authentication services. Every nodes hold a distributed ledger.

Each distributed ledger record the registration information of all vehicles. The low-level blockchain is located in a distributed network formed by intelligent vehicle nodes and MEC nodes. The pre-processed road condition information and the final road condition view will be transmitted between nodes. Blocks record information passed between nodes. The low-level blockchain is used to ensure the correctness of information transmission among network nodes.

3.2 Security Guaranty

The identity verification of vehicles entering the network is very important. Strict identity verification can avoid malicious attacks from the source. Besides, in the entire process of service provision, Information transmission between nodes may also be maliciously tampered with, resulting in invalid services, even paralyzing the operation of the traffic network or causing traffic accidents.

Decentralized Authentication. High-level blockchain can replace the function of a third-party trusted center. When IoT devices leaves the factory, a public key, private key and a self-signed digital certificate are generated, which are written into the device by the manufacturer. And then submit a release application to the blockchain identity authentication system. The blockchain identity authentication system is located in each mobile edge computing nodes, and uses its computing power. After the blockchain identity authentication system checks the certificate, it records the certificate in the blockchain. There is no certificate revocation list (CRL) for blockchain certificates. If you want to revoke a certificate, you can only generate a new blockchain transaction to overwrite the original transaction to achieve certificate revocation. That is, you can add data status when creating a block.

Data Transmission. The data consistency and anti-tampering features of the low-level blockchain can be used to ensure the integrity of the beyond-the-sight information. In the network, the basic communication primitive for exchanging information among vehicles or vehicles to MEC nodes or among MEC nodes, can be seen as a transaction. Each computing node in the network maintains the same transaction records. Each transaction will be presented in the form of a block. Once a block is formed, the hash value of the previous block will be added to the block header and connected to the blockchain. Once the attacker modifies the information contained in the block, the hash value of the block will change, causing the hash pointer to become invalid. Then the attacker must modify the information of the next block, and so on to modify the information of each block. This is almost impossible to achieve. Therefore, once the data is generated, the block is tamper-proof. So we can realize the safe synchronization and transmission of beyond-the-sight data in IoV.

4   Conclusion

In this paper, we first explore the contribution of blockchain to IoV services in the MEC environment, and propose a future-oriented IoV service: the beyond-the-sight service. Then we discuss the application of blockchain in the beyond-the-sight service in detail. Based on the indestructibility and immutability of the data block, the terminal access authentication is realized, and malicious nodes are denied access to the network from the source. Using the characteristics of distributed accounting and consensus mechanism, interoperability can be formed between all participants in the MEC organization ecology. At the same time, MEC provides an efficient computing guarantee for beyond-the-sight service and blockchain.

The combination of MEC-based IoV and blockchain is a new cross-cutting field. Large-scale applications still face many challenges: the maturity of technology has yet to be improved, and the scarcity of talents in cross-cutting fields are all urgent problems to be solved. But we still have reasons to believe that the blockchain can use its characteristics to bring new developments to IoT.

Acknowledgments. We thank all the researchers providing support for the paper. This work was partially supported by the Key-Area Research and Development Program of Guangdong Province (No.2018B010113001).

References

1. Yaga, D., Mell, P., Roby, N., Scarfone, K.: Blockchain technology overview (2019). arXiv preprint arXiv:1906.11078
2. Buterin, V.: Ethereum: a next-generation smart contract and decentralized application platform (2014). https://github.com/ethereum/wiki/wiki/%5BEnglish%5D-White-Paper7
3. Nakamoto, S., Bitcoin, A.: A peer-to-peer electronic cash system. Bitcoin (2008). https://bitcoin.org/bitcoin.pdf4
4. Wilkinson, S., Boshevski, T., Brandoff, J., Buterin, V.: Storj a peer-to-peer cloud storage network (2014)
5. Sharma, P.K., Park, J.H.: Blockchain based hybrid network architecture for the smart city. Future Gener. Comput. Syst. **86**, 650–655 (2018)
6. Shao, Q.F., Zhang, Z., Zhu, Y.C., Zhou, A.Y.: Survey of enterprise blockchains. J. Softw. **30**, 2571–2592 (2019)
7. King, S., Nadal, S.: Ppcoin: Peer-to-peer crypto-currency with proof-of-stake. Self-published paper, August 19, 1 (2012)
8. Moran, T., Orlov, I.: Simple proofs of space-time and rational proofs of storage. In: Boldyreva, A., Micciancio, D. (eds.) CRYPTO 2019. LNCS, vol. 11692, pp. 381–409. Springer, Cham (2019). https://doi.org/10.1007/978-3-030-26948-7_14
9. Larimer, D.: Delegated proof-of-stake (dpos). Bitshare Whitepaper **81**, 85 (2014)
10. Castro, M., Liskov, B., et al.: Practical byzantine fault tolerance. In: OSDI, vol. 99, pp.173–186 (1999)
11. Paymard, P., Mokari, N.: Resource allocation in pd-noma–based mobile edge computing system: multiuser and multitask priority. Transactions on Emerging Telecommun. Technol. (1), e3631 (2019)

12. Luo, C., Xu, L., Li, D., Wu, W.: Edge computing integrated with blockchain technologies. In: Du, D.-Z., Wang, J. (eds.) Complexity and Approximation. LNCS, vol. 12000, pp. 268–288. Springer, Cham (2020). https://doi.org/10.1007/978-3-030-41672-0_17

13. Druschel, P., Kaashoek, M.F., Rowstron, A.I.: Revised papers from the first international workshop on peer-to-peer systems (2002)

14. Yong, L., Fei, L., Lulu, G., Xiang, X.: Feasibility study of automotive identity based on blockchain technology. Autom. Technol **513**(6), 20–25 (2018)

15. Vijayakumar, P., Chang, V., Deborah, L.J., Balusamy, B., Shynu, P.: Computationally efficient privacy preserving anonymous mutual and batch authentication schemes for vehicular ad hoc networks. Fut. Gener. Comput. Syst **78**, 943–955 (2018)

16. Arnold, E., Dianati, M., de Temple, R., Fallah, S.: Cooperative perception for 3d object detection in driving scenarios using infrastructure sensors. IEEE Trans. Intell. Transp. Syst (2020)

17. Christidis, K., Devetsikiotis, M.: Blockchains and smart contracts for the internet of things. IEEE Access **4**, 2292–2303 (2016)

Blockchain and Smart Contracts

An Automated Modeling Method and Visualization Implementation of Smart Contracts

Jie Meng, Zheng Li, Ruiliang Zhao, and Ying Shang[✉]

Department of Computer Science, Beijing University of Chemical Technology Beijing,
Beijing 100029, China
Shangy@mail.buct.edu.cn

Abstract. Smart contracts are one of the core components of the blockchain system and have been widely used across various fields. Since
a smart contract cannot be easily changed or updated once instanti-
ated, one has to be absolutely sure that the program code works as
expected. However, there are no uniform definitions for smart contracts,
and the programming of smart contracts requires professional developers
with expert domain knowledge. This paper proposed a formal modeling
method for start contracts. First, the formal definition of smart contracts
is proposed. Second, we introduce an EFSM based modeling method for
smart contracts. Finally, we design a visual modeling tool EFSMSolid
for creating EFSM on an easy-to-use graphical platform. To verify the
effectiveness of the method, we conduct experiments on smart contracts
of five blockchain applications, and the experimental results show that
the proposed method can automatically and effectively create smart contracts models.

Keywords: Blockchain · Smart contracts · EFSM · Formal
definition · EFSMSolid

1 Introduction

Relying on the advantages of transparency, decentralization, security, blockchain
is regarded as the core technology that has the most potential to trigger the fifth
wave of the Industrial revolution after the steam engine, electricity, information,
and Internet technology [1]. Smart contracts are the core component of current
blockchain technology. The security incident of The DAO [2] attack in 2016
made researchers from both academic and industrial communities start to focus
their attention to the concept and implementation technology of smart contracts,
especially the formal methods for verification of smart contracts before they are
deployed on the blockchain.

The National Natural Science Foundation of China under Grant No. 62077003 supports
the work described in this paper.

H.-N. Dai et al. (Eds.): BlockSys 2021, CCIS 1490, pp. 399–406, 2021.
https://doi.org/10.1007/978-981-16-7993-3_30

Smart contracts technologies enable users to form decentralized digital agreements without the need for a third party [4]. At present, there are few studies on building a formal model of smart contracts based on business contracts. In [6] the authors take a smart contract of a gambling application as an example and point out that all parties involved, whether it's the contract maker or the code writer, have reasons to worry that there may be some vague ways for others to make use of the contract for their benefit with the increasing complexity of smart contract. In [7] the author proposes an FSM-based approach for the design of secure smart contracts. They developed the FsolidM tool which allows users to design their contract as an FSM (Finite State Machine) which is then automatically transformed into a Solidity smart contract. In [8] the authors present VeriSolid, the improved version of FsolidM, adding formal operational semantics to the proposed FSolidM model.

However, related researches all use the FSM model. Since the FSM model cannot take into account any variables, it is impossible to verify the evolution of the value of the variable during the execution of the smart contract. We propose a contract-oriented modeling method based on the EFSM model, which enables users to automatically create a smart contract model. And we have designed the model integrity verification algorithm and implements a visual modeling tool EFSMSolid.

The main contribution of this paper:

1. Define the smart contract, describing the status of business contracts terms and the relevant conditions and operations involved in the transition between the status of the terms;
2. Propose an EFSM-based smart contract modeling method that enables users to automatically create a smart contract formal model;
3. Develop visual modeling tools to facilitate users to verify and modify EFSM;

The rest of this paper is organized as follows. In Sect. 2 related work is discussed. Section 3 introduces our proposed method. In Sect. 4, we design experiments and analyze experimental results. Section 5 introduces the EFSMSolid tool we developed. Finally, we conclude our work and suggest directions for future work.

2   Related Work

Formal methods include formal description, formal verification, automatic code generation, and conformance testing [9]. This article mainly discusses the formal description and formal verification methods of smart contracts.

The Extended Finite State Machine (EFSM) model is an extension of the FSM model. Based on the FSM model, it adds variables, transition preconditions, and operations caused by the transition, and enhances the dynamic description ability of the system. The EFSM model is widely used in various fields. The system described by EFSM can be easily transformed into other descriptive languages. Zhao et al. used the EFSM model to characterize the behavior of Web application clients [10], which can accurately describe the control flow, data flow information, and state transition conditions of the target system. The EFSM model is often expressed as a Sextuple: $\langle S, S_0, I, O, T, V \rangle$

Among them, S is the non-empty state set; S_0 is the initial state; I, O and V respectively represent the non-empty input set, output event set, and variable set; T represents the non- empty transition set, and the transition $t \in T$ It can be expressed as a five-tuple $\langle \text{Head}(t), \text{Event}(t), \text{Cond}(t), \text{Action}(t), \text{Tail}(t) \rangle$, where Head(t) is the source state of the transition t; Event(t) is the stimulus event of the transition t or NULL; Cond(t) is the precondition for the execution of the transition t or NULL; Action(t) is the operation caused by the transition t, which is composed of a series of variable assignment statements or output statements or is empty; Tail(t) represents the target state of transition t.

3   Model Construction and Verification

Based on the above analysis and the characteristics of the EFSM model, we propose a method for automatically constructing a smart contract model based on EFSM. In this section, we first give a formal definition of terms in the contract based on the business contract. Then, we design algorithms based on formal terms, which automatically identify and analyze the states involved in the terms and the migrations between states. Through the above, we build an EFSM model of smart contracts. This method supports both the smart contract modeling of a single contract and composite contracts.Fig. 1 shows the overall framework of the method:

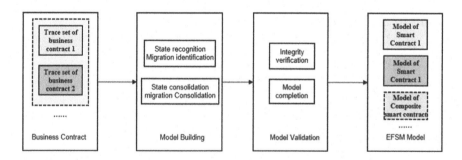

Fig. 1. Smart contract automation modeling method based on EFSM

3.1   A Subsection Sample

Definition 1. *Trace: A trace can be expressed as Trace*$=< IA_0, ..., IA_j, ...IA_{n-1} >$

We define the clauses in the commercial contract as Trace. Taking the classic aviation delay insurance contract [5] as an example, it contains five traces.According to the delay insurance process, the following states can be derived: start, insured, purchase, effective, settlement, and end. According to the formal definition of the terms in this article, the aircraft delay insurance can be converted into a set of Trace.

3.2   Smart Contract Model Construction

According to the trace set of the smart contract, we can obtain the state list S and the migration list T of the EFSM model. However, because different traces may have the same migration and migrate to the same state, the obtained state list and the migration list will contain the same state or migration.

In addition to modeling a single contract, this article also targets other modeling of smart contracts in the same context, such as a scenario where passengers both purchase air ticket insurance and baggage insurance at the same time. At this time, the status and migration in the status list and migration list will be more complicated. Therefore, how to merge state and migration is the key to constructing the EFSM model.

In order to realize the effective merging of migrations in the migration list T, this paper proposes the concepts of equivalent migration and weakly equivalent migration, which are defined as follows:

Definition 2. *Equivalent Migration:*
There are $t_1 =< Head(t_1), lb(t_1), Tail(t_1) >$ and $t_2 =< Head(t_2), lb(t_2), Tail(t_2) >$, where the label $lb(t) =< Event(t), Cond(t), Action(t) >$, $Cond(t) = [VC, TC]$, if and only if $Head(t_1) = Head(t_2)$, $lb(t_1) = lb(t_2)$, and $Tail(t_1) = Tail(t_2)$, then migration t_1 and t_2 are equivalent.

Definition 3. *Weakly Equivalent Migration:*
There are $t_1 =< Head(t_1), lb(t_1), Tail(t_1) >$ and $t_2 =< Head(t_2), lb(t_2), Tail(t_2) >$, where the label $lb(t) =< Event(t), Cond(t), Action(t) >$, $Cond(t) = [VC, TC]$, if and only if $Head(t_1) = Head(t_2)$, $lb(t_1) \sim lb(t_2)$, and $Tail(t_1) = Tail(t_2)$, then migration t_1 and t_2 are weakly equivalent. Among them, $lb(t_1) \sim lb(t_2)$ means that in the tag information, except for the different values of the same clock variable and counter variable of $Cond(t)$, the rest of the components including $Cond(t)$ are all equal.

The algorithm for building an EFSM model based on smart contracts is shown in Algorithm 1.

4   Experiment and Analysis

4.1   Experimental Design

In order to verify the effectiveness of the method proposed in this article, we conduct empirical studies on five smart contracts: Aircraft Delay Insurance, Betting Transaction, Auction Contract [11], Baggage Insurance, and Combination contract of aircraft delay insurance and baggage insurance the study.

Algorithm 1. EFSM model construction algorithm

Input: Smart contract standardized Trace set: Traces
Output: EFSM$< S', T'' >$

    S,T ← getTransState(Traces)
    S' ← meargeStateByStateName(S)
    T' ← reviseSourceTarget(T,S')
    while True **do**
        WeakEqList,EqList ← getAllEquiTrans(T')
        if WeakEqList or EqList ont empty **then**
            EqList2 ← mergeWkEqL(WeakEqList)
            EqList ← Add(EqList,EqList2)
            mergeEqList ← (T',EqList)
        else WeakEqList and EqList is empty
        break
    return S', T''

Table 1 shows the detailed information of the five smart contracts converted into the Trace set, including the name of the contract (Subject), the number of terms constructed (TN), the total number of interactions in the trace (IA), the total number of states (State), and the total number of events (Event).

4.2 Experimental Results and Analysis

This paper conducts experiments and analysis on the following two research questions:
RQ1: Does our method automate the construction of smart contract EFSM models?
RQ2: Is our method be applied to the application scenarios of multiple sets of smart contracts?

RQ1. This article builds an EFSM model based on the Trace collection of five smart contracts. Table 2 shows the migration information of the model. Through the model construction method in this article, the 22 states obtained from the set Trace can be finally merged into 6 states. START is the initial state, S1 is Insured, S2 is the End, S3 is the Purchase, S4 is the Insurance Effective, and S5 is the Settlement. According to statistics, the migration has been merged from the original 17 to 11.The algorithm realizes the effective combination of state and migration.

RQ2. Cai [3] pointed out that with the development of blockchain technology, later smart contracts will become more and more difficult to apply, and it will not be the application of a single smart contract, but the application of a group of smart contracts. For this reason, the design experiment puts the aircraft delay insurance and baggage insurance in the same application scenario and constructs

Table 1. Details of smart contract trace set

Subject	TN	IA	State	Event
Aircraft delay insurance	5	17	22	5
Betting transaction	3	6	11	3
Auction contract	2	7	9	2
Baggage insurance	5	17	22	5
Combination contract of aircraft delay insurance and baggage insurance	10	34	44	10

Table 2. EFSM model migration information for aircraft delay insurance

Trans	Head(t)	Tail(t)	Event(t)	Cond(t)	Action(t)
t1	S3	S2	Deposit(company)	$y > 60$	Passenger $=$ Passenger $+ 10$, y $= 0$
t2	START	S1	Buy(ticket, x)	$Null$	x$=$0
t3	S5	S2	Transfer()	$Null$	Company $=$ Company$+10$, Passenger $=$ passenger $+ 1000$
...	...	...	...	...	...
t11	S1	S2	Null	$x > 30$	x $= 0$

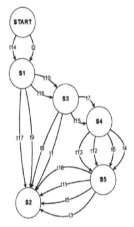

Fig. 2. Combination contract of aircraft delay insurance and baggage insurance EFSM Model

a unified symbolic trace set as the model input. After verification, our method can build a composite smart contract. The model is shown in Fig. 2.

5   EFSMSolid Tool

We developed the EFSMSolid tool based on the modeling method described in this article. EFSMSolid is a visualized, business contract-oriented smart contract tool, includes automatic EFSM model generation and verification. It enables multi-users to jointly maintain the formal description of the business contract, and edit the business contract trace set by importing one-by-one or one-click mode and then automatically build the smart contract EFSM model. At the same time, it supports online editing of the visual EFSM models and displays the results of model integrity verification.

EFSMSolid software based on B/S architecture, using front-end and back-end separation technology, can be deployed in Linux and ubuntu, front-end uses nginx+vue technology for development, back-end uses sqlite3+Django technology to develop. We also apply docker technology to facilitate deployment. Part of the tool interface is shown in Fig. 3.

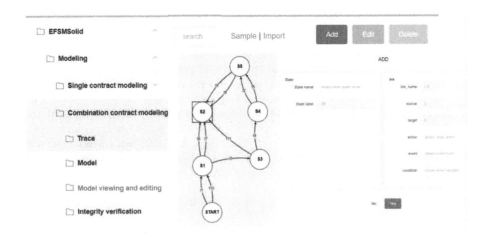

Fig. 3. EFSMSolid tool

6   Conclusions and Prospects

This paper proposes an EFSM based modeling method for smart contracts from business contracts, which automatically recognizes the states involved in the analysis clauses and the migration between states. EFSMSolid is a Web pages-based visualized smart contract modeling tool, which enables users to complete the construction, edit and certificate the smart contract models using UI controls. This visualized editing mode reduces the complexity of smart contract modeling. At the same time, it facilitates the communication between smart contract developers and business contract creators. It also helps eliminate the inconsistency of smart contracts and business contract intentions. Experiment on 5 blockchain applications proved that our method suitable for composite smart contract application scenarios.

The method in this paper can accurately describe the smart contract of complex business logic and lay a good foundation for model-based testing. In the future, we will focus on the research of model-based smart contracts vulnerability detection and model-based automatic smart contract code generation.

References

1. https://www.mckinsey.com/industries/financial-services/ourinsights/blockchain-in-insurance-opportunity-or-threat, Accessed 10 Apr 2021
2. https://www.8btc.com/media/326359, Accessed 10 Apr 2021
3. CAI Weide.: Reconstruction of Social Contract. Law Press (2020)
4. Sayeed, S., Marco-Gisbert, H., Caira, T.: Smart contract: attacks and protections. IEEE Access **6**, 24416–24427 (2020)
5. Wang, P.W., Yang, H.T., Meng, J., Chen, J.C., Du, X.Y.: Formal definition for classical smart contracts and a reference implementation. Ruan Jian Xue Bao/J. Softw. **30**, 2608–2619 (2019)
6. Ellul, J., Pace, G.J.: Runtime verification of ethereum smart contracts. In: 2018 14th European Dependable Computing Conference (EDCC), Iasi, Romania, pp. 158–163 (2018). https://doi.org/10.1109/EDCC.2018.00036
7. Mavridou, A., Laszka, A.: Designing secure ethereum smart contracts: a finite state machine based approach. In: Financial Cryptography and Data Security - 22nd International Conference, FC 2018, Nieuwpoort, Curaçao, 26 February–2 March 2018 (2018)
8. Mavridou, A., Laszka, A., Stachtiari, E., Dubey, A.: VeriSolid: correct-by-design smart contracts for ethereum. In: Goldberg, I., Moore, T. (eds.) FC 2019. LNCS, vol. 11598, pp. 446–465. Springer, Cham (2019). https://doi.org/10.1007/978-3-030-32101-7_27
9. Hu, K., Bai, X.M., Gao, L.C., Dong, A.Q.: Formal verification method of smart contract. J. Inf. Secur. Res., 1080–1089 (2016)
10. Zhao, R., Gou, X., Wang, W., Shang, Y.: Client-side EFSM test case generation based on the server-side sensitive path coverage for web applications. J. Harbin Eng. Univ., 884–891 (2019)
11. Mavridou, A., Laszka, A.: Designing secure ethereum smart contracts: a finite state machine based approach. In: Meiklejohn, S., Sako, K. (eds.) FC 2018. LNCS, vol. 10957, pp. 523–540. Springer, Heidelberg (2018). https://doi.org/10.1007/978-3-662-58387-6_28

A New Electronic Contract System Model Based on Blockchain

Haihong Zhao[1]($\boxtimes$), Ziqiang Zhu[1], Changfeng Pan[2], Zhongyuan Yao[1], Weihua Zhu[1], and Xueming Si[1,3]

[1] Research Institute of Frontier Information Technology,
Zhongyuan University of Technology, Zhengzhou 450007, Henan, China
[2] New Huadu Business School, Minjiang University, Fuzhou 350101, China
[3] School of Computer Science, Fudan University, Shanghai 201203, China
`sxm@fudan.edu.cn`

Abstract. In order to solve the problems of easy loss, tampering and difficulty in fine-grained sharing in the storage and sharing of the electronic contract (EC), a new electronic contract system model based on blockchain is proposed. The system allows registered users to perform related operations such as uploading, querying, authorizing, and verifying, etc., among Ordinary Users (OUs), Lawyer Users (LUs), and Court Users (CUs). By assigning user attribute sets to registered users, the system initiates the smart contract automatically to check whether user attributes match the EC access rules to achieve fine-grained sharing. Finally, the system was prototyped using Fabric as the underlying framework and the demonstration proved that the system can solve the above problems well.

Keywords: Electronic contract · Blockchain · Smart contract · Access control · Fabric

1 Introduction

Contracts play an important role in people's economic life, it binds two signed parties to perform their responsibilities and obligations. When a contract is violated, relevant procedures are carried out following the signed agreement. Paper contracts are easily lost, damaged, and can be time-consuming to find. With the continuous development of technology, paper contracts have gradually evolved into electronic contracts. However, it has caused a series of problems while overcoming the shortcomings of paper contracts: (1) The EC storage is vulnerable to attack, which leads to the leakage of contract contents; (2) The EC is stored centrally, and the contents may be leaked by internal personnel. Moreover, it may require more manpower and time to verify the authenticity; (3) The owner doesn't possess the sharing ownership of the EC and cannot decide who can access it. (4) It's time-consuming for the court to verify the authenticity when disputes occur.

The emergence of blockchain technology provides a new way to solve the aforementioned problems. The concept of blockchain was first proposed by a scholar named Satoshi Nakamoto [1]. It is a chained data structure that combines data

© Springer Nature Singapore Pte Ltd. 2021
H.-N. Dai et al. (Eds.): BlockSys 2021, CCIS 1490, pp. 407–417, 2021.
https://doi.org/10.1007/978-981-16-7993-3_31

blocks sequentially in time sequence and a distributed ledger that cannot be tampered with or forged through cryptography [2], with the characteristics of decentralization, immutability and data traceability. Therefore, the combination of blockchain provides an effective solution for the safe storage and sharing of EC.

2   Related Work

Due to the superior characteristics of blockchain itself, related researches combining with blockchain have been widely used in various scenarios [3–5]. In the data storage and sharing, Ekblaw proposed a MedRec prototype based on blockchain to address the problem of safe storage and improved system operability and adaptability [6]. Xue presented a sharing model for medical data based on blockchain [7], which uses DPOS to realize rapid consensus verification. Proxy re-encryption is adopted to realize access control and security sharing. Feng proposed a medical and health data security model based on Alliance blockchain [8], storing data hash and description on blockchain and encrypted medical data in the distributed database to facilitate safe storage.

In access control, Zhang put forward an access control framework based on the smart contract [9], which includes multiple access control contracts, a judge contract and a registration contract. Each contract has a predefined static and dynamic access rights validation policy. The judging contract can assess the access control contract through the improper behavior judgment method to realize the trusted access control of the system. Wang proposed a data access control and sharing model based on blockchain [10]. This scheme takes the access control policy tree formulated by attributes as the encryption condition, enabling attribute matches to decrypt and obtain data, and gain access control as well as secured sharing. Liu bases on the ABAC model to realize a big data access control mechanism [11]. By improving the storage structure of blockchain transactions, the distributed management of access control policies can be achieved by using blockchain transactions. At the same time, the automatic access control can be realized for the policies published on the blockchain through smart contracts.

In application development, Ding designed an electronic certificate depository scheme based on Hyperledger Fabric to solve problems like tampering, low data trust and unguaranteed security [12]. It combined smart contracts and IPFS to make electronic evidence credible and traceable. Sun proposed an electronic data depositing system based on blockchain [13], storing key information of electronic data on the blockchain and electronic files in distributed database, and introducing user integral mechanism to increase the reliability of the system. Hou designed an electronic evidence system architecture model based on blockchain [14], realizing the storage and issuance of data and ensure authenticity at the same time. Batching packaging of electronic evidence was introduced into the model to improve the efficiency of storage. However, these above articles didn't consider the users' ownership of the electronic contract, nor involve the transfer process of the electronic contract in the real environment.

Based on this, this paper proposes a new electronic contract system model based on blockchain. This system takes Hyperledger Fabric as the underlying framework of the system and mainly provides services for OUs, LUs, and CUs.

The system can provide the basic functional requirements of EC, including on-chain certificate storage, on-chain query, access control and contract verification. The ciphertext of EC is stored in the cloud server while the hash value of it is stored in the blockchain to reduce the pressure on the blockchain data storage as well as ensuring safe storage. Each user in the system has its attributes and the owner of the EC sets the access right by them. The smart contract can automatically analyze whether the visitor's attributes meet the set requirements, realizing the automatic authorization sharing and also ensuring the sharing dominant right of the EC. To avoid EC tampering, users can compare it with the information on the blockchain through the verification function. Meanwhile, the verification results should be stored in the blockchain to confirm the authenticity.

3 System Architecture

3.1 Logical Architecture

There are three kinds of users in the system: OUs, LUs and CUs, which can be selected when registering the system. OUs are the uploader and owner of the EC with the dominant right. EC needs to be encrypted before storing in the blockchain to ensure security. Then, the cloud server returns the index address of the EC to OUs. If LUs or other users in this system need to access EC, they can apply for it. They will be authorized only if their attributes meet the access rules set by OUs, thus, they can decrypt and then obtain the EC. After receiving the arbitration application from LUs, CUs can verify the authenticity of EC and sync the result to the blockchain. The logical architecture diagram of the system is shown in the Fig. 1 below:

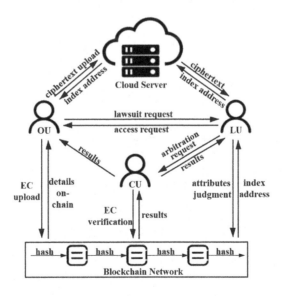

Fig. 1. Logical architecture diagram

OUs are the signee of the contract and are responsible for encrypting and uploading the signed EC. Before uploading to the blockchain, OUs set the access control rules for it through the attributes and only the system users who match the attribute requirements can view the EC. Through this system, users can query the EC information on the blockchain, including the block number, hash value, uploaded date and so on.

LUs provide services for OUs who have contract disputes. Then LUs apply for access of the EC after receiving the lawsuit request from OUs. The system initiates the smart contract automatically to check the visitor's attributes and determine its authority. If the attributes meet the requirements, then the visitor can obtain the EC plaintext through the decryption key.

As the enforcement officers, CUs file the contract disputes after receiving the LUs' arbitration application. If there are doubts about the authenticity of the EC, it can be verified through the system. Meanwhile, the verification results need to be recorded on the blockchain, and then the arbitration results will be broadcast to the blockchain network.

The cloud server is used to store encrypted EC. OUs encrypt and upload EC and the cloud server returns the index address of the storage. Through the index address, the applicant can get the EC ciphertext on-chain and then decrypt it to obtain the plaintext information.

3.2 Functional Architecture

This system uses Hyperledger Fabric as the blockchain platform and interacts with the blockchain network through the Web front-end. The functional hierarchy of the system is as shown in the Fig. 2, which is divided into the application layer, interface layer, smart contract layer and blockchain platform layer from top to bottom.

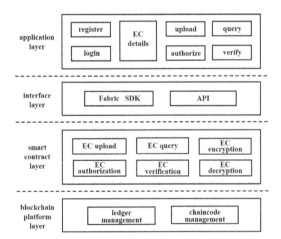

Fig. 2. Functional hierarchy architecture diagram

The application layer uses the VUE framework to realize the interactive Web front-end interface, which can realize users' login and registration functions as well as loading, querying, access control and verification functions. The results are intuitively fed back to users. The interface layer interacts with the front-end and the blockchain network through the Fabric SDK and API, facilitating the call of smart contract and providing basic functions such as retrieval and transaction. The smart contract layer designs several key smart contracts in the system, which interact with the underlying platform of blockchain through the GRPC interface, including the functions of EC loading, querying, authorizing and verifying, which will be introduced in the next chapter. Blockchain platform layer manages ledgers and smart contracts and provides support for system data processing.

4 System Design

4.1 Smart Contract Design

The smart contract is also known as chaincode, is a piece of code running in a Docker container. It is the core part of the blockchain and can automatically follow the set rules to avoid human errors when it is triggered. A smart contract can be developed through a variety of programming languages, and this system uses Go language.

Fabric can read and modify ledger data through the smart contract, and the interaction between the two needs a shim package, which is the system package provided by Fabric. The shim package provides an interactive ChaincodeStubInterface, through which ledger data in Fabric can be conveniently manipulated [15]. This system mainly designs four smart contracts, including EC upload, EC query, EC authorization and EC verification. The specific processes are as follows:

EC Upload. After users log to the system and upload the EC, the system will automatically generate the hash value of it. The smart contract firstly acquires parameter information through the interface of the shim package. If it meets the requirements, it will be converted to JSON format. Then, smart contract initiates the PutState method in the Fabric to write it into the ledger and returns the information on the blockchain. The algorithm is as follows:

Algorithm 1: Upload

Input: ID, ContractName, hash, Timestamp
Output: display the uploaded results
1 **while** *contract ID doesn't exist* **do**
2   jsons←json.Marshal(Contract) (convert EC information into JSON format)
3   **if** *parameters input are correct* **then**
4   contract←stub.PutState(args[0],jsons) (initiate the PutState method to upload)
5   return EC details on-chain
6   **else**
7   return an error message
8   **end**
9 **end**

EC Query. The smart contract searches through the unique ID value of the EC. After it is analyzed base on the set requirements, it obtains data from the ledger through the GetState method and finally returns the query result. The algorithm is as follows:

Algorithm 2: Query

Input: ID
Output: display the query results
1 **if** *parameters input are correct* **then**
2   Avalbytes←stub.GetState(ID) (get data through GetState(ID))
3   return query results
4 **else**
5   return an error message
6 **end**

EC Authorization. Fabric can refine the access control through an attribute-based approach. Permission control in smart contracts needs to be carried out through the client identity library, which provides relevant methods to obtain the identity attributes of visitors [16]. In this example, the EC authorization smart contract determines whether the visitors have the Att.init attribute through the cid.AssertAttributeValue method. The specific design of access control will be described in detail in the next chapter. The algorithm is as follows:

Algorithm 3: Authorization

Input: attribute information
Output: display authorization results
1 **while** *err←cid.AssertAttributeValue(stub,"Att.init","ture")   (get*
  visitors' attributes) **do**
2 │   judge the attributes **if** *attributes meet the requirement* **then**
3 │   │   return the authorization results
4 │   **else**
5 │   │   deny the authorization
6 │   **end**
7 **end**

EC Verification. CUs or LUs upload obtained EC to the system, the system will return the hash value of the EC. By comparing with the EC information on-chain, the authenticity of the current EC can be verified. The EC verification smart contract acquires the historical record on the blockchain through the GetHistoryForKey method, compares the obtained hash value on-chain with the uploaded file hash value and returns the verification result. The algorithm is as follows:

Algorithm 4: Verification

Input: ID
Output: display the verification results
1 **if** *parameters input are correct* **then**
2 │   resultsIterator←stub.GetHistoryForKey(ID)   (get history
  │   information)
3 │   use the hash value as a condition to query whether there is a
  │   corresponding hash value on-chain return verification results
4 **else**
5 │   return an error message
6 **end**

4.2   Access Control Design

There is no need for identity management and access control in the public blockchain because it allows anyone to join. However, this system uses the Alliance blockchain, which is required to carry out the access control to ensure data security [17]. The system users' attributes will be defined at the time of registration and cannot be changed freely. Before uploading the EC ciphertext, OUs set the access control according to the attributes and only following the attribute requirements shall the visitors be granted access to the EC.

The EC ciphertext is stored in the data body, while the data head is used to describe access control information, which is public to all system users who can see what attributes are needed to access the ciphertext. When system users apply to access the EC, the system can automatically initiate the smart contract to check the visitors' attributes and then decide whether the EC can be accessed.

The specific steps of access control are as follows:

1. Initialization: CA generates public key and private key and then sends them to all system users. Users can download the keys and save them to the local database.

2. EC Encryption: To ensure data security, EC need to be encrypted before uploading to the blockchain. OUs use the temporary key k generated by random numbers to encrypt the EC plaintext M. OUs can set the valid duration of k. When the date is exceeded, k becomes invalid and the ciphertext cannot be decrypted by it again. OUs use the public key P_a to encrypt k to avoid forgetting it, and then simply call the private key S_a to find the k. The encryption algorithm is as follows:

$$Enc(k, M) \rightarrow cph \tag{1}$$

$$Enc(P_a, k) \rightarrow K \tag{2}$$

3. Data Access: Visitors need to send their public key P_b when accessing EC and the system can automatically initiate the smart contract to verify the visitor's attributes. If it meets the requirements set by OUs, the smart contract can send the data or deny the authorization.

4. Data Sending: The smart contract calls the private key S_a of OU to decrypt and obtain the temporary key k, and then encrypts k and index address with the public key P_b sent by the visitor. Finally, it sends K' to the visitor.

$$Dec(S_a, K) \rightarrow k \tag{3}$$

$$Enc(P_b, k, index) \rightarrow K' \tag{4}$$

5. Data Decryption: After receiving the K', the visitor can decrypt it with his private key S_b to obtain the $index$ and k, so as to obtain EC ciphertext on-chain and decrypt to get the plaintext. The algorithm is as follows:

$$Dec(S_b, K') \rightarrow k, index \tag{5}$$

$$Dec(k, cph) \rightarrow M \tag{6}$$

5   System Test

5.1   Upload Function Test

After logging to the system, OUs click to enter the upload interface, type the name of EC, select the EC file and input some descriptions. Then the system will automatically return the hash value of the EC and retrieve the interface of the back-end to upload EC information. The record is as shown in the Fig. 3.

Fig. 3. EC upload diagram

5.2 Query Function Test

OUs can query the contract details and on-chain information through this system, including the EC name, block number, hash value, previous block hash value and so on. Visitors who meet the attribute requirements set by OUs can further decrypt and obtain plaintext after downloading the file to the local. The test results are shown in the Fig. 4.

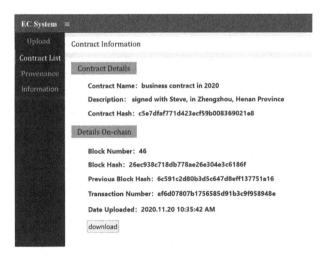

Fig. 4. EC query diagram

5.3 Verification Function Test

After logging to the system, OUs or LUs upload the EC that they have received for verification. The system compares the newly generated hash value with that on-chain. If the hash value is inconsistent, the result will be rejected. Otherwise, if the value is accepted, it will reflect the information, such as the block number, hash value, the previous block hash and so on. The test results are shown in the Fig. 5.

Fig. 5. EC verification diagram

6   Conclusion

Aiming at a series of problems encountered in EC, a new electronic contract system based on blockchain is proposed. This system adopts a storage mode combining blockchain and cloud server to relieve the storage pressure of blockchain. The access control rules of EC are set by OUs themselves, which can not only dominate the EC but also protect the data privacy. The system test results show that this system can realize the functions of EC well.

Acknowledgements. This work is supported by National Key R&D Program of China(SQ2020YFB100050), Major Project Fund of Higher Education of Henan Province (No.19A520047), and Major Science and Technology Project of Henan Province (project number 20130021030).

References

1. Nakamoto, S.: Bitcoin: A peer-to-peer electronic cash system [OL] (2008). https://bitcoin.org/bitcoin.pdf.
2. Yuan, Y., Wang, F.Y.: Blockchain: the state of the art and future trends. Acta Automatica Sinica **42**(4), 481–494 (2016)
3. Li, H., Tian, H., Zhang, F., He, J.: Blockchain-based searchable symmetric encryption scheme. Comput. Electric. Eng. **73**, 32–45 (2019)

4. Kang, J., et al.: Blockchain for secure and efficient data sharing in vehicular edge computing and networks. IEEE Internet Things J. **6**(3), 4660–4670 (2018)
5. Qian, W., Shao, Q., Zhu, Y., Jin, C., Zhou, A.: Research problems and methods in blockchain and trusted data management. J. Softw **29**(1), 150–159 (2018)
6. Ekblaw, A., Azaria, A., Halamka, J.D., Lippman, A.: A case study for blockchain in healthcare: "MedRec" prototype for electronic health records and medical research data. In: Proceedings of IEEE Open & Big Data Conference, vol. 13, p. 13 (2016)
7. Xue, T., Fu, Q., Wang, C., Wang, X.: A medical data sharing model via blockchain. Acta Automatica Sinica **43**(9), 1555–1562 (2017)
8. Feng, T., Jiao, Y., Fang, J., Tian, Y.: Medical health data security model based on alliance blockchain. Comput. Sci. **47**(04), 305–311 (2020)
9. Zhang, Y., Kasahara, S., Shen, Y., Jiang, X., Wan, J.: Smart contract-based access control for the internet of things. IEEE Internet Things J. **6**(2), 1594–1605 (2018)
10. Wang, X.L., Jiang, X.Z., Li, Y.: Model for data access control and sharing based on blockchain. J. Softw. **30**(6), 1661–1669 (2019)
11. Liu, A., Du, X., Wang, N., Li, S.: A blockchain-based access control mechanism for big data. J. Softw. **30**(9), 2636–2654 (2019)
12. Ding, Y., Xiang, H., Luo, D., et al.: Scheme for electronic certificate storage by combining fabric technology. J. Xidian Univ. **47**(5), 113–121 (2020)
13. Sun, G., Mao, X., Chen, D., et al.: Electronic data storage and certificate system based on blockchain. J. Xi'an Univ. Posts Telecommun. **23**(4), 78–83 (2018)
14. Hou, Y., Liang, X., Zhan, X.: Block chain based architecture model of electronic evidence system. Comput. Sci. **45**(S1), 348–351 (2018)
15. Feng, X., Liu, T., et al.: Blockchain in Action: Key Technology and Case Analysis for Hyperledger Fabric. China Machine Press, Beijing (2018)
16. Yang, B., Chen, C., et al.: Principle, Design and Application of Blockchain, 2nd edn. China Machine Press, Beijing (2020)
17. Huang, L., Wu, S., Cao, F., et al.: Security Technology Guide for Blockchain. China Machine Press, Beijing (2018)

M-A-R: a Dynamic Symbol Execution Detection Method for Smart Contract Reentry Vulnerability

Zexu Wang[1], Bin Wen[1,2,3(✉)], Ziqiang Luo[2,3], and Shaojie Liu[1]

[1] School of Information Science and Technology, Hainan Normal University, Haikou 571158, China
binwen@hainnu.edu.cn
[2] Cloud Computing and Big Data Research Center, Hainan Normal University, Haikou 571158, China
[3] Key Laboratory of Data Science and Intelligence Education of Ministry of Education, Hainan Normal University, Haikou 571158, China

Abstract. The original intention of smart contract design is to execute every transaction in the blockchain spontaneously, efficiently and fairly, meanwhile, smart contract plays an important role in the blockchain activities. With the development of blockchain, the vulnerability of smart contract becomes more and more obvious. The security vulnerability detection of smart contract is very important. This paper proposes M-A-R, a dynamic symbol execution method focusing on efficient detection for reentry vulnerability, realizes the security detection of the source code of smart contract, optimizes the design of its implementation method, then compares it with the existing related tools. The results show that M-A-R approach can detect the reentry vulnerability efficiently and has good universality and scalability.

Keywords: Smart contract · Dynamic symbolic execution · Reentry attack · Vulnerability detection · Blockchain

1 Introduction

Whether in the public blockchain or consortium blockchain, smart contract plays a very important role in the correct execution of transactions in the blockchain. As the blockchain, once a transaction is chained, it cannot be tampered with, that is: code is law. The design concept of smart contract is another form of human will, so the security problem of smart contract is inevitable, the incorrect use of syntax rules by programmers, the characteristics of blockchain, and the security of code change with the development of blockchain. In short, smart contracts with defects will make assets and transactions vulnerable and vulnerable, seriously affecting the normal operation of blockchain transactions. At present, the number of tools for smart contract vulnerability detection is small, and few tools can achieve high accuracy and efficient detection. The existing smart contract vulnerability detection technologies mainly include symbol execution,

© Springer Nature Singapore Pte Ltd. 2021
H.-N. Dai et al. (Eds.): BlockSys 2021, CCIS 1490, pp. 418–429, 2021.
https://doi.org/10.1007/978-981-16-7993-3_32

fuzzy testing, formal verification, program analysis and taint analysis. The main idea of symbolic execution is to convert the uncertain input values into symbolic values to promote the analysis of program execution. The method of dynamic symbol execution can maximize the code coverage. In this paper, we will use the improved method of dynamic symbol execution to detect reentry attacks, simplify the operation process of dynamic symbol execution, and maximize the code coverage in a short time.

The main contributions of this paper are as follows:

Novel Idea: we introduce M-A-R, which tracks transactions by simulating transactions to detect whether reentry attacks occur. At the same time, we simplify the process of solving constraints to improve the speed of operation and ensure the reliability and applicability of detection;

Comprehensive Evaluation: the effectiveness of M-A-R in detecting the vulnerability of reentry attack is evaluated by experiments with existing detection tools with good performance;

High Reliability: the new idea of dynamic symbol execution detection in this method can greatly simplify the process of solving dynamic symbol execution constraints and make the detection process more efficient and reliable;

Open Source: in order to facilitate the follow-up research, upload the experimental source code and experimental cases to GitHub.[1] .

The organization of the remaining sections is as follows. In Sect. 2, we will introduce some background knowledge, attack mechanism and the advantages and disadvantages of existing detection tools.In Sect. 3, we review reentrancy attack of Ethereum smart contracts.In Sect. 4,we will talk about Main research methods and deficiencies for reentry attack detection. Then in Sect. 5, we will introduce the detection principle and implementation method of dynamic symbol execution. In Sect. 6, we will introduce the experiment and evaluation. Finally, In Sect. 7, we will summarize the experimental results and propose future works.

2   Reentry Attack

Smart contract is a piece of code running on the blockchain platform. It has three cache units for storage: stack, memory and storage. Stack operations will disappear with the end of the transaction, and will not be stored. Memory is the address area of bytes allocated at run time. Both of them are easy to lose. Therefore, the balance of the account information that needs to be saved after the transaction is saved by the storage unit. At the same time, the gas price higher than stack and memory calculation is needed to calculate the storage.

When a smart contract performs a program call, the stack is needed to record the return address at the end of the call. It can be used directly when calling the function inside the contract. When calling the function of other contracts outside the contract, it is called externally. Call instruction can send information to the outside, but there is no gas consumption limit when calling the call

---

[1] https://github.com/woods1060/M-A-R.

instruction of the external function. By default, all the remaining gas will be used to execute this command. Using the call instruction to call and transfer the external contract, the risk of reentry attack will be greatly increased.

Reentry attack is the most typical vulnerability in high level language of smart contract vulnerability, and it is also one of the most serious vulnerabilities under attack, resulting in huge losses. Although most of the existing vulnerability detection tools support the detection of reentry attacks, there is still a long way to go for the great results and efficiency of vulnerability detection and the influence of comprehensive factors to achieve large-scale popularization and use.

3   Attack Mechanism

From the perspective of transaction, reentry vulnerability ultimately achieves the result of multiple transfers, but only sends a transfer request once. When contract A calls the function in contract B through external call, contract A calls contract B again in the same transaction, thus it continues to loop until the remaining gas is exhausted. This type of attack is reentry attack. The most notorious attack is Dao attack. Attackers steal more than 50 million dollars worth of ether from Dao contracts, causing huge economic losses.

```
contract Bank{

    ...

    function withdrawBalance(uint amount){
        if(!(msg.sender.call.value(amount)())){
        revert();
    }
        userBalance[msg.sender]-= amount;
    }

    ...

}
```

The function *withdrawBalance*() of Bank contract is to let the registered account withdraw its assets. When the user calls this function, the contract first checks whether the user's balance is greater than the amount of funds withdrawn. If the check is passed, the assets requested to be withdrawn will be transferred to the user in the form of eth, and the corresponding balance will be deducted from the user's account.

Due to the operation mechanism of Ethereum smart contract, if the received transfer address is a contract address, the fallback function of the address will be triggered. This mechanism may be used by malicious attackers to launch reentry attacks. Attack is an attack contract, and as code shows:

```
contract Attack{

    ...

    function Attack() public{
       Bank.withdrawBalance(100000000000000000);
    }
    function() public payble{
       Bank.withdrawBalance(1000000000000000000);
    }

    ...

}
```

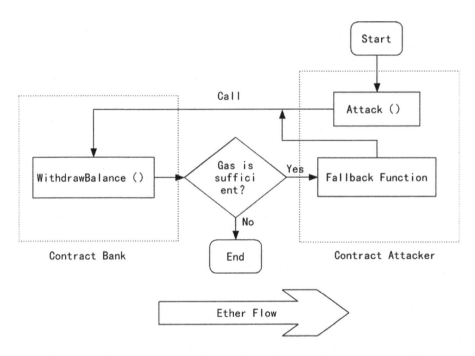

Fig. 1. Flow chart of reentry attack

The attacker only needs to call the victim contract's *withdrawbalance*() function through the function *attack*(), and the victim contract's function *withdraw − balance*() of *mag.sender.call.value*(*amount*)() statement is executed, the fallback function in the attack contract will be triggered. If the attacker launches a call to the victim contract withdraw again in this function, before the user's balance is reduced, Recursion calls are made repeatedly until gas is exhausted, and ether assets in the victim contract are stolen continuously. The whole attack process is shown in Flow chart of reentry attack (see Fig. 1).

The attacker constructs a loop to continuously steal ether in the victim contract. Reentry vulnerabilities need to meet a number of conditions, that is, transfer and storage modification, logical atomic binding, transfer ahead, and transfer using call instruction. Although the reentry vulnerability can be avoided by developers modifying the operation order at the high-level language level, its root cause is the gas mechanism of Ethereum virtual machine call instruction call, fallback function mechanism, recursive access to allow low-level calls and other features.

4   Main Research Methods and Deficiencies

4.1   Program Analysis

Program analysis is a common technology. For smart contract vulnerability detection, it is usually divided into static program analysis and dynamic program analysis [1]. Static program analysis mainly uses the static control flow and data flow information of the program for analysis, while dynamic program analysis can further collect the runtime information of the program [3]. In static analysis, slither [2] performs data flow analysis and taint analysis to detect vulnerabilities in entity programs, but slither execution is limited by other static tools;

4.2   Formal Verification

Formal verification technology is an effective technology to verify whether the program meets the expected design properties and security specifications. Hirai et al.[9,10] use $Isabelle/hol$ to formalize the instruction semantics in Ethereum virtual machine, so as to use it to manually prove the security of a program. It only supports part of the instructions, and it can not fully express the semantics of the supported instructions.

Kevm [12] uses K framework to formalize the semantics of smart contract. K framework is a verification framework based on Reachability logic and independent of high-level language [11]. Kevm tries to use it to implement some semantic related analysis tools on smart contracts [12]. It is difficult for kevm to complete relatively complete program analysis, and it consumes a lot of human work investment, which makes its scalability poor. At the same time, the $f*$ language tried by bhargavan et al. [3] also faces the same problem.

Zeus [13] translates the Solidity source code into the intermediate language of LLVM, uses XACML on it to complete the formulation of verification rules, finally completes the formal verification work through SeaHorn. Although converting Solidity to LLVM as an intermediate language, traditional methods and tools can be used to complete the automatic detection of the program. However, in the process of completing the conversion, whether the semantics of the smart contract can be correctly converted is an object that needs to be studied, and the Solidity language has some unique properties of its own, which may not be supported by the traditional LLVM intermediate language.

Securify [14] is a typical automated security attribute verification tool, which mainly analyzes the bytecode of the smart contract and makes semantic factual inferences, expresses it through the DataLog language. Securify uses the security attribute verification code defined by DataLog for rule verification. By matching semantic facts with verification rules, the security of smart contracts is determined.

4.3   Symbol Execution

Oyente [16] implements a symbolic execution engine for smart contracts, which is one of the earliest work of automatic vulnerability mining for smart contracts. Oyente includes four components, CFG Builder, Explorer, Core Analysis, and Validator, mainly analyzes bytecode files. CFG Builder analyzes the contract in advance and creates a basic control flow chart to form a topological structure with basic blocks as nodes and jump relationships as edges. And add symbolic execution to solve the problem that the jump relationship between some blocks cannot be determined. Therefore, the main work of symbolic execution is to complete the missing transfer relationship. Explorer is mainly to complete the work of symbolic execution, mainly to traverse the code of each basic block in the control flowchart, and determine the jump relationship between each block. In the process of symbolic execution, the Z3 constraint solver is mainly used to solve the conditions, and Explorer determines the jump relationship according to the results of the constraint solver. Core Analysis is also an important component of Oyente. It completes the design of the model based on the information collected by Explorer and realizes the identification of vulnerabilities in smart contracts. Finally, the Validator filters the analysis results of Core Analysis.

However, some of Oyente's detection schemes are not perfect. In the actual smart contract detection work, a large number of false positives be reported, and the vulnerabilities involved are not comprehensive enough. Only several contract vulnerabilities detection schemes such as conditional competition, timestamp dependency, unchecked return value, and reentrance vulnerabilities are implemented. At the same time, the tool also lacks maintenance and updates by related developers, which can no longer meet the current needs of smart contract development for security vulnerability detection.

After that, more and more researches on automatic vulnerability mining of smart contracts, such as Osiris [4], Mythril [5], Manticore [6], SmartCheck [7], Securify [8], etc., which use symbolic execution technology, begin to appear. They mainly increase the transaction depth of symbolic execution analysis to simulate more real contract execution and explore deeper state space, To achieve more accurate vulnerability detection, but symbol execution faces the problems of path explosion and not easy to expand.

The main idea of symbolic execution is to convert the uncertain input in the process of program execution into symbolic value to promote program execution and analysis [15]. Due to the influence of branches, loops and other structures, symbolic execution often faces problems such as path explosion. However, compared with traditional applications, smart contract has less code, fewer paths and shorter length, which is more suitable for symbolic execution analysis. However, because the constraints of smart contract are transferred between different paths, the traditional symbolic execution approach can only collect the constraints on a single contract path, not the global constraints. This also brings challenges to the symbolic execution of smart contracts.

5   Detection Method of Dynamic Symbol Execution

This paper proposes a dynamic symbolic execution detection method named M-A-R for smart contract vulnerabilities. It not only combines the advantages of symbolic execution method to solve the security problem of smart contract, but also uses the idea of dynamic symbol to solve the problem of path explosion caused by too large constraint or too deep execution in the process of symbol execution, which greatly saves the time cost and computing resources of detection work. The improvement of M-A-R algorithm makes M-A-R perform well in the efficiency of vulnerability detection.

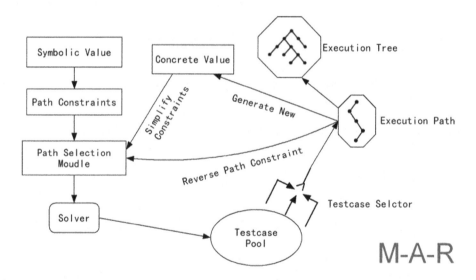

Fig. 2. M-A-R traversal process

The main idea is to use the given or randomly generated initial value to execute the program, but the input is still a symbolic value and form a path constraint. The program needs to select the appropriate branch according to the given or randomly generated initial value, and collect the symbolic constraints associated with the input at the path branch. Finally, according to the set path search algorithm, the constraint solver is used to reverse the path constraint to get a new input. In theory, the new input value can make the program execute along different paths. This process is then repeated until the program path is explored or the end of exploration condition is reached, or after the scheduled test time has passed. M-A-R traversal process is shown in Fig. 2. The process is briefly described as follows:

    I. Enter the Initial Value. The input value is still a symbol value, but the actual value and the symbol value are executed in parallel and enter the path selection module;

    II. Path Selection. Input the initial input symbol value or the result of the path constraint inversion into the path selection module to select a path for execution;

    III. Generate Path Constraints. Execute the current path to the stop of the leaf node of the path, and generate the constraint conditions of the path;

    IV. Solving Path Constraints. Input the path constraint conditions into the constraint solver for solution, and input the actual value of the path to simplify the constraint solution and avoid problems such as path explosion;

    V. Generate New Execution Path. After the execution path of a certain path is generated through constraint solving, the constraint conditions are reversed to generate a new execution path;

    VI. Generate Execution Tree. Traverse each execution path in turn to finally generate an execution tree;

    VII. Attribute verification. Based on the generated execution tree, the verification of smart contract attributes is completed, and the code audit is realized.

M-A-R combines the characteristics of high precision and high coverage of dynamic symbolic execution technology, which can achieve the advantage of zero rate in theory. Therefore, it can well solve the problem of path explosion faced by existing symbolic execution methods in smart contract vulnerability detection. The technology of dynamic symbolic execution has been paid more and more attention in the automatic generation and utilization of test cases, and it also has a certain practical value in practical application.

6   Experiment and Evaluation

The M-A-R algorithm is implemented in Python. Based on the syntax environment of Manticore, the dynamic symbolic execution method is used to simulate the transaction and complete the attribute verification. The existing six smart contract detection tools that support reentry vulnerability detection and perform well are compared with M-A-R synchronously, and the key data such as vulnerability detection results and detection time are recorded, the experimental data set has been uploaded to GitHub (see footnote 1).

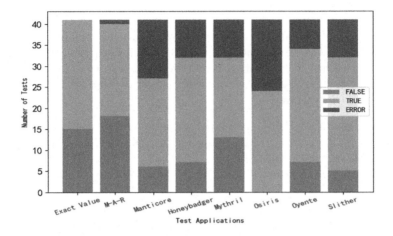

Fig. 3. Proportion of test results

6.1   Simulation Experiment

In vulnerability detection, the error rate will directly affect the test results, so the classification of test results is the most intuitive way.

As shown in Fig. 3, the red part represents the number and proportion of errors reported in the experimental results of vulnerability detection. As can be seen from the figure, Osiris has a higher error reporting rate, while M-A-R has the lowest error reporting rate, and the proportion of detection results is closest to the accurate value, indicating that M-A-R has high practicability and good scalability.

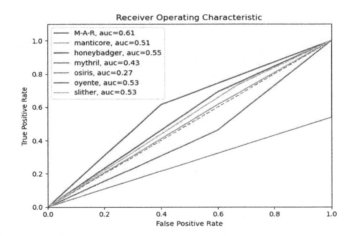

Fig. 4. ROC curve of tools

Receiver operating characteristic curve, referred to as ROC curve, can well show the same sensitivity of each point on the curve. AUC, the area under the ROC curve, is a more stable index reflecting the quality of the model. It can be seen from the figure below(see Fig. 4). that M-A-R has the best detection performance for reentry vulnerabilities and osiris model has the worst detection performance under the condition of maintaining high TPR.

6.2   Time Delay Test

The running time of vulnerability detection also has a certain impact on the practicability of vulnerability detection tools, Compared with the traditional formal verification and static analysis, the time cost of M-A-R is much higher.

In this work, will focus on the comparative test between M-A-R and Manticore tools, as M-A-R uses the same language environment as Manticore, and manticoe is also the main tool for vulnerability detection using traditional symbolic execution. It can be seen from the figure that in the face of the same experimental data set, dynamic symbolic execution well shows its advantages and characteristics compared with traditional symbolic execution. Dynamic symbolic execution greatly improves the efficiency of program operation by solving evolutionary constraints.

M-A-R ensures the high reliability of the test results and the superiority of the performance by simulating the real transaction, and adopts the method of dynamic symbolic execution to simplify the constraint solving process, which greatly improves the running time and efficiency of practical application (Fig. 5).

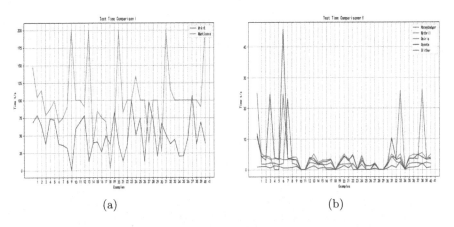

(a)   (b)

Fig. 5. Time comparison chart

7   Conclusions and Future Works

The most important feature of M-A-R is to use simulated transaction to verify attribute proof. The experimental data show that: compared with the existing smart contract vulnerability detection tools, M-A-R model has outstanding reentry vulnerability detection results, which is 30% higher than the average detection results. Compared with the traditional symbolic execution, M-A-R model reflects the advantages of dynamic symbolic execution, and its running speed is 2–3 times of its execution.

To sum up: M-A-R model can greatly reduce the consumption of time and resources, enhance the efficiency of M-A-R, and ensure the high reliability of test results through the characteristics of dynamic symbol execution and the way of testing while verifying when simulating reentry vulnerability transactions.

The dynamic symbolic execution method can simplify the constraint solution and improve the speed of symbolic execution. On this basis, the further works are as follows:

1. It is of great significance to solve other security problems with the idea of dynamic symbol execution for the detection of reentry attacks;
2. The speed of dynamic symbol execution is optimized by improving the path search strategy;
3. Research and implementation of blockchain security audit assistant tool.

Acknowledgements. This research has been supported by the Natural Science Foundation of Hainan Province (No. 620RC605) and Postgraduates' Innovative Research Projects of Hainan Province (No. Hys2020-332).

References

1. Grishchenko, I., Maffei, M., Schneidewind, C.: A semantic framework for the security analysis of ethereum smart contracts. In: Bauer, L., Küsters, R. (eds.) POST 2018. LNCS, vol. 10804, pp. 243–269. Springer, Cham (2018). https://doi.org/10.1007/978-3-319-89722-6_10
2. Crytic. Slither (2018).https://github.com/crytic/slither
3. Bhargavan, K., Delignat-Lavaud, A., Fournet, C., et al.: Formal verification of smart contracts: short paper. In: The 2016 ACM Workshop on Programming Languages and Analysis for Security, pp. 91–96 (2016)
4. Ferreira, C.O.: (2018). https://github.com/christoftorres/Osiris
5. ConsenSys. Mythril (2017). https://github.com/ConsenSys/mythril-classic
6. Manticore. https://github.com/trailofbits/manticore
7. SmartDec. SmartCheck (2017). https://github.com/smartdec/smartcheck
8. SRI Lab. Securify (2018). https://github.com/eth-sri/securify
9. Hirai, Y., et al.: Defining the ethereum virtual machine for interactive theorem provers. In: Brenner, M. (ed.) FC 2017. LNCS, vol. 10323, pp. 520–535. Springer, Cham (2017). https://doi.org/10.1007/978-3-319-70278-0_33
10. Hirai, Y.: Formal verification of deed contract in ethereum name service. In: 2019 10th IFIP International Conference on New Technologies, Mobility and Security (NTMS), pp. 1–6 (2019)
11. SeaHorn | A Verification Framework. https://seahorn.github.io/
12. Hildenbrandt, E., Saxena, M., Rodrigues, N., et al.: KEVM: a complete formal semantics of the ethereum virtual machine. In: 2018 IEEE 31st Computer Security Foundations Symposium (CSF), 9–12 July 2018, pp. 204–217. IEEE, Oxford (2018)

13. Kalra, S., Goel, S., Dhawan, M., et al.: ZEUS: analyzing safety of smart contracts. In: Network and Distributed System Security Symposium, pp. 26–35 (2018)
14. Tsankov, P., Dan, A., Cohen, D.D., et al.: Securify: practical security analysis of smart contracts (2018). ArXiv180601143 Cs
15. Angr/angr. GitHub. https://github.com/angr/angr
16. Luu, L., Chu, D.-H., et al.: Making smart contracts smarter, pp. 254–269 (2016)

Using Blockchain to Promote the Construction of Smart Court

Zhanli Sun[1](✉), Yuhonglin Ran[2](✉), and Zheliang Cai[2]

[1] Institute of Rule of Law and Economic Development, School of Law, Guangdong University of Finance and Economics, Guangzhou 510320, China
[2] School of Law, Guangdong University of Finance and Economics, Guangzhou 510320, China

Abstract. This Blockchain is considered to be a new technology to reshape the world, and China has listed the blockchain as an integral part of its national strategy. The smart court is a court information system with the characteristics of networking, transparency, and intelligence. Private blockchain, Consortium blockchain, and Public blockchain each have their characteristics, and the corresponding scenarios should be selected to be used in the construction of a unified, whole-process, integrated smart court system across the country. Cooperate with other judicial agencies to create a full-process and integrated judicial blockchain system centered on trials, actively explore the construction of a blockchain system for international judicial cooperation. Give full play to the traceability and immutability of the distributed ledgers, smart contracts and the data generated by the blockchain, information symmetry and transparency, technical credit, automatic processing, and other unique functions to ensure judicial justice, improve judicial efficiency and enhance judicial credibility..

Keywords: Blockchain · Smart court · Judicial justice · Judicial efficiency · Judicial credibility

1 Technical Characteristics of Blockchain and Construction of Smart Court

1.1 Technical Characteristics of Blockchain

In 2008, Satoshi Nakamoto designed an electronic cash system without a trusted third party in *Bitcoin: A Peer-to-Peer Electronic Cash System* and put forward the concept of Bitcoin. As the underlying technology of Bitcoin is blockchain, this paper is recognized as the theoretical origin of blockchain. In January 2009, Satoshi Nakamoto, inventor of blockchain, created the first block (The foundation block), and the blockchain moved from theoretical design to practical application. Melanie Swan, the founder of American Blockchain Research Institute, divided the blockchain into three stages in her book *Blockchain: Blueprint of New Economy.* blockchain 1.0 represented by digital currency, blockchain 2.0 represented by smart contract, and blockchain 3.0 which transcends currency, economy, and market in the fields of justice, government management, and

© Springer Nature Singapore Pte Ltd. 2021
H.-N. Dai et al. (Eds.): BlockSys 2021, CCIS 1490, pp. 430–440, 2021.
https://doi.org/10.1007/978-981-16-7993-3_33

notarization [1]. Blockchain has entered the 2.0 stage and is moving towards the 3.0 stage.

Blockchain does not change the TCP/IP protocol of the Internet, so why not link these ledgers with the Internet? The answer lies in the technical characteristics of the blockchain and the unique advantages. It is generally believed that blockchain technology has the following characteristics: First, it is decentralized. The blockchain has no central control. Through distributed accounting and storage, each node realizes self-verification, transmission and management of information. Decentralization is the most prominent and essential feature of blockchain. The second is openness. The foundation of blockchain technology is open source. Except that the private information of all parties to the transaction is encrypted, the data of the blockchain is open to everyone. Anyone can query blockchain data and develop related applications through the public interface. The entire system Information is highly transparent. The third is independence. Based on consensus specifications and agreements, the entire blockchain system does not rely on other third parties, and all nodes can automatically and safely verify and exchange data in the system without any human intervention. The fourth is safety. If you cannot control more than 51% of the data nodes, you cannot modify the network data, which makes the blockchain itself relatively safe [2]. The above description provides a concise summary of the main characteristics of the blockchain, and is also suitable for observing and understanding the blockchain from the perspective of the rule of law.

Regarding the characteristics of the blockchain, a multi-angle observation will lead to different conclusions. From the perspective of the equality of rights and obligations, the blockchain uses distributed accounting and storage, and there is no centralized management agency. Therefore, the rights and obligations of each node are equal, and the data blocks in the system are jointly maintained by all nodes with maintenance functions in the entire system. From the perspective of autonomy, the blockchain does not require any human intervention. It uses consensus-based specifications and protocols to enable all nodes in the entire system to automatically and securely verify and exchange data. The reason why the blockchain automatically verifies and exchanges data without human intervention is because of the characteristic functions of smart contracts. The concept of smart contract was first proposed by Nick Szabo in 1993. It refers to an agreement that is automatically executed according to the conditions set on the blockchain. In the transaction, the smart contract can automatically calculate the amount to be paid by the parties to the contract and arrange the payment, and the payment behavior of the party will automatically trigger the other party to perform the corresponding obligations. For example, the ownership or use right of the subject matter is automatically transferred through electronic records.

In summary, the technical characteristics of the blockchain can be summarized in the order of legal logic: the anonymity of the subject, the intelligence of transactions or management, the decentralization of management, the autonomy of the rules on the chain, the immutability of data, and automation of rewards and punishments.

It should be noted that blockchain does not exclude the application of artificial intelligence, big data, cloud computing, and the Internet of Things. Moreover, blockchain can and needs to be integrated with these technologies, and the construction of smart court is no exception. As for the relationship between the Internet and blockchain, simply speaking, blockchain does not change the TCP/IP protocol of the Internet but is only the top-level application of the Internet, but blockchain has the above-mentioned technical characteristics completely different from the Internet.

1.2 Blockchain Helps to Promote the Goal of Building a Smart Court

On January 29, 2016, Zhou Qiang, President of the Supreme People's Court, first proposed the development goal of building a smart court. At the end of 2017, the People's Court Information Construction Version 3.0 came to a perfect conclusion, and the pattern of smart court has taken shape. The informatization construction of the people's court is divided into three stages, version 1.0, version 2.0 and version 3.0. In version 1.0, the informatization construction of the People's Court has realized paperless regular office, electronic file management, networked process monitoring, and computerized trial records. In version 2.0, the People's Court has realized online case filing, case handling, enforcement, letters and visits, and disclosure. In addition, it has built a platform for public trial procedures, public trial activities, public judgment documents, and implementation information disclosure platforms (referred to as the "Four Major Public Platforms") to achieve full supervision of trials and implementation work, and effectively promote the trial system and trial capabilities modernization.

The Opinions on Accelerating the Construction of Smart Courts issued by the Supreme People's Court in April 2017 pointed out that smart courts are a form of organization, construction and operation in which people's courts make full use of advanced informatization system to support online handling of all businesses, lawful openness of whole process and all-around intelligent services and to realize impartial justice and justice for the people. It can be considered that smart court are a new type of organization, construction, and operation based on the informatization of the people's courts. It is an informatization system of the people's courts that is networked, transparent, and intelligent. The People's Court Information Construction Version 2.0 has basically achieved networking and transparency. The focus of the construction of smart court (People's Court Information Construction Version 3.0) is to further transform and enhance network and transparency through intelligence, or smart court. The networking and transparency of the smart court will be intelligent networking and transparency, and the three will complement each other and work together in the construction of smart court.

In the process of intelligent social development, the Internet of Things, blockchain and artificial intelligence are all important means of intelligence. The construction of smart court also needs and should integrate and use these technologies to promote the construction of smart court. Blockchain has gradually been widely recognized, and future blockchain applications will be expanded to various social fields, including the judicial field. We should fully tap the judicial value of blockchain and actively expand the judicial practice functions of blockchain, and make full use of the technical characteristics of blockchain to promote the construction of smart court.

2 Practice and Application Status of Blockchain in Smart Court Construction

How to link to form a smart judicial system faces two choices, the Internet of Things and blockchain (the Internet of Things can be linked to the Internet or blockchain). Compared with blockchain, the construction cost of the Internet is lower and the construction difficulty is smaller. The completion of parole cases handled by the Guangzhou Intermediate People's Court with the public security organs and procuratorial organs through the Internet is a useful exploration in this field. The application of blockchain is not widespread, but it has special advantages. In the practice of building a smart court, the judicial application of blockchain has achieved positive results.

On September 7, 2018, the Supreme People's Court issued *Provisions of the Supreme People's Court on Several Issues Concerning the Trial of Cases by Internet Courts*, which recognized blockchain as a technical means to collect, fix, and tamper-proof data, and affirmed the legal effect of the evidence of blockchain deposit. In August 2019, the Supreme People's Court announced the establishment of a unified judicial blockchain platform. At present, 27 nodes of the Supreme People's Court and 20 local courts, multiple dispute mediation platforms, notary offices, and judicial authentication centers have been completed.

Hangzhou Internet Court has officially launched the first judicial blockchain on September 18, 2018. Judicial blockchain makes the whole process of electronic data generation, storage, dissemination, and uses credible. The blockchain consists of three layers: First, the blockchain program, users can directly record the whole process of operation behavior in the blockchain through the program, such as submitting electronic evidence such as electronic contract, rights protection process, and service process details online; The second is the blockchain full link capability layer, which mainly provides real-name authentication, electronic signature, timestamp, data deposit certificate and trusted services of the whole blockchain process; The third is the judicial alliance layer, which uses blockchain technology to connect notary offices, CA/RA institutions, judicial authentication centers, and courts, and each unit becomes a node in the chain. Through the whole and complete structure, it can solve the generation, storage, dissemination, and use of electronic data in the whole life cycle on the Internet, especially the whole process credibility of the generation end [3]. In October 2019, Hangzhou internet court began to implement the first judicial application of blockchain intelligent contract ("version 2.0" of judicial blockchain). by creating a closed-loop of the whole process of network behavior "voluntary signing-automatic performance-performance cannot be intelligently filed-intelligent trial-intelligent execution", it designed judicial governance mechanism and dispute resolution to boost the execution efficiency of intelligent contracts and efficiently handle a few default behaviors. Reduce the interference of human factors and uncontrollable factors, build a new form of contract signing and performance in the Internet era, and truly realize the whole process recording of network data and network behavior, full link credibility, full node witness, and all-round cooperation [4].

The current judicial application of blockchain is mainly concentrated in the field of evidence. Evidence is called the "king of court". The collection, fixation, review and judgment of electronic data evidence are more difficult, so the credibility of the entire process of electronic data undoubtedly has extremely high judicial value. However, the judicial application of blockchain should not be limited to electronic data evidence. Some courts and related companies are also actively exploring, such as the first blockchain smart contract judicial application promoted by the Hangzhou Internet Court. In general, the judicial application of blockchain is still in its infancy, and the unique rule of law function of "blockchain + justice" should be fully exploited and fully and effectively applied to the construction of smart court.

3 The General Idea of Using Blockchain to Promote the Construction of Smart Court

On July 31, 2019, the Supreme People's Court issued the *Opinions of the Supreme People's Court on Building One-stop Diversified Dispute Resolution Mechanisms and One-stop Litigant Service Centers*, which specifically stated: "Promoting the building of smart litigation services. A new mode of "smart litigation services" relying on big data, cloud computing, artificial intelligence, the Internet of Things, and other information technology, integrating service halls, hotlines, websites, and mobile terminals, permitting litigation business in the whole process to be transacted, shall be shaped. Online service functions shall be expanded, the China Mobile Micro Court shall be fully applied, the channel for authentication of parties shall be unblocked, and one-stop services such as online guidance, case docketing, payment and refunding of fees, check, consulting, file consultation, preservation, trial, and petition shall be provided. The construction of lawyer service platforms shall be strengthened to provide services such as online case docketing, check, file consultation, submission of materials, contacting judges, evidence exchange, mediation, court in session, representing petitioners, and application for enforcement. Intelligent equipment such as all-in-one computers for facilitative services shall be assigned to litigation service halls. The 12368 litigation service hotline intelligent answering system shall be improved. The integration of service platforms including "service halls, websites, hotlines, and circuits" shall be promoted to achieve the mutual accessibility and automated linking of information resources and provide the public with litigation services by harmonized standards, based on data from the same source." The overall vision of the blockchain in this regard is as follows:

3.1 Classification of Blockchain and Its Application Scenarios in the Construction of Smart Court

From the application form, blockchain can be divided into public blockchain, consortium blockchain, and private blockchain, and different types of blockchain are suitable for different application scenarios. Public blockchain is a completely open blockchain, and its participants can enter the system at any time for data reading, transaction sending and confirmation, competitive accounting, and system maintenance. Common applications of public blockchain include Bitcoin and Ethereum. Consortium blockchain is a blockchain managed by several institutions, which belongs to a hybrid blockchain between public blockchain and private blockchain. Each institution runs and manages one or more nodes in the chain, and its data can only be read and written by the institutions in the alliance. All institutions can send transactions and record transaction data together. Typical applications include super ledger, enterprise Ethereum and so on. Private blockchain refers to a blockchain whose write permission is controlled by an organization or institution, and whose read permission can be opened to the outside world or restricted to a certain extent [5]. In the construction of smart court, we can choose to build specific judicial blockchain according to different needs. Among them, private blockchain can be used to build the internal system of smart court, consortium blockchain can be used to build smart judicial system, smart international judicial cooperation system and external cooperation system between smart courts and banks, and public blockchain can be used in court litigation services, publicity of rule of law, judicial openness and other scenes open to public participation.

3.2 Using Blockchain to Build a National Unified Whole Process and Integrated Smart Court System

The mode of informatization construction of the People's Court is that the Supreme People's Court carries out the overall design and solves important issues at the same time. The local courts actively explore and develop various system platforms with local characteristics. The advantage of this construction mode is that it can mobilize the enthusiasm of local courts and make concerted efforts to build. It was a suitable choice in the past informatization construction of the People's Court and actually achieved the expected results, but it is not necessary to follow this mode in the future construction of smart court. The shortcomings of this model are mainly as follows: the repeated construction of local courts will lead to a huge waste of manpower, financial resources, and material resources; Constrained by factors such as construction conditions, the construction quality is uneven; There are many system platforms, which are often incompatible, and have poor synergy and sharing; Excellent construction achievements are inconvenient to be fully popularized in the national court system.

The construction of smart court is a complex systematic project. According to the construction goal and current situation of smart court, the construction of smart court should focus on building a unified whole-process and integrated smart court system, that is, relying on the Internet or blockchain. The construction of smart court is a complex systematic project. According to the construction goals and status quo of the smart court, the focus of the construction of the smart court is to build a unified, whole-process and integrated smart court system across the country. Relying on the internal and external systems of smart court based on the Internet or blockchain, a smart litigation system with "smart judges" (smart court artificial intelligence systems) as the core is established for smart case filing, trial, judgment, and execution. Connected with intelligent prosecution and intelligent policing to form a trial-centric smart judicial system to fully realize the systematic litigation function between smart court. For example, after a party submits an appeal petition and pays the appeal fee, the system will automatically transmit the electronic file of the court of first instance to the court of second instance. Some local courts are exploring the construction of an integrated litigation platform based on the Internet. Blockchain has incomparable advantages over the Internet. It is suggested that under the unified deployment of the Supreme Court, the internal system of smart court in the chain should be built, which is based on the interconnection of intelligent litigation systems of all courts in China. When conditions are mature, it can be expanded to form a blockchain integrated business processing platform with arbitration, administrative law enforcement and mediation, and insurance claims.

3.3 Using Blockchain to Build a Smart Judicial System Centered on Trial

China's intelligent prosecution and intelligent policing services are also under active construction. The interconnection of smart court with intelligent prosecution and intelligent policing systems is an inevitable trend, thus forming a full-process smart judicial system with smart court as the core node. How to link to form a smart judicial system faces two choices, namely the Internet and the blockchain (the Internet of Things can be linked to the Internet or the blockchain). Compared with the blockchain, the construction cost of the Internet is lower, and the construction difficulty is also less. The current application of blockchain is not widespread, but it has special advantages. The whole process and integrated litigation system based on the blockchain helps to place the entire litigation process in the technical guarantee of the information transparency, the data unchanged, and the credible evidence of the blockchain, especially helping to solve the problem of evidence collection. The stage of tampering, damage and concealment. At present, investigative agencies, prosecutive agencies, and judicial agencies are actively exploring and trying to apply blockchain to solve some judicial problems. There are no obstacles in policies, technologies, systems, etc., in the use of blockchain to build a smart judicial system centered on trials. Therefore, the use of blockchain to build a full-process and integrated judicial system centered on trials can begin preparations.

3.4 Using Blockchain to Build a Smart International Judicial Cooperation System

On February 1, 2018, the European Commission announced the launch of a new mechanism aimed at promoting the development of blockchain technology in Europe and helping Europe benefit from it. This mechanism has the functions of collecting information related to blockchain, monitoring and analyzing related trends, exploring the socio-economic potential of blockchain technology, and coping with related challenges. According to the European Commission, blockchain technology can make online transactions have high traceability and security, which is regarded as a major technological breakthrough. This technology will affect digital services and change the modes in the fields of medical care, insurance, finance, energy, logistics, and government services [6]. Some countries or regions have started to build smart court or electronic courts, and the construction of smart court of people's courts will also strengthen the smart judicial cooperation function with overseas smart court or electronic courts in international judicial assistance and other work, thus building a smart international judicial cooperation system. Limited by external conditions, it is difficult to build a smart international judicial cooperation system. The possible mode is to connect with the smart court system of individual countries on a pilot basis, and then sum up experience based on the pilot and gradually advance.

4 The Judicial Practice Function and Significance of Using Blockchain to Promote the Construction of Smart Court

4.1 Using Blockchain to Promote the Construction of Smart Court Is Conducive to Ensuring Judicial Justice

In order to unify the judgment criteria and prevent "the different verdict in the same kind case" and "unjust and wrong cases", the Supreme People's Court has created a mechanism for searching similar cases and correlated cases. In the trial of a case, a judge handling the case shall, on the case handling platform, file system, China Judgments Online, www.faxin.cn, the Intelligent Trial System, etc., comprehensively search the similar cases and correlated cases closed concluded or under trial and develop a report on the searching of similar cases and correlated cases. Where upon research, similar cases and correlated cases fall under the following circumstances, a judge handling the case shall handle the case as needed under the following provisions: (a)Where new adjudication criteria will be formed for the judgment intended to be rendered in the handling of a new-type case, they shall be submitted to the professional judge meeting for discussion and shall be submitted to the judicial committee for discussion upon decision or suggestion of the president or the chief judge of the court. (b) Where significant differences in the adjudication criteria for similar effective cases of the court are found, the trial management office shall be notified after a request is submitted to the chief judge for research, and the trial management office shall submit a report to the president and submit it to the judicial committee for discussion after cooperating with the relevant trial business tribunal for reviewing the issues on the application of law. This mechanism and the "four major public platforms" (especially the platforms for the publication of judgment documents) have a significant effect on solving legal application errors in the judgment process, effectively curbing obvious legal errors and fraud in the judgment documents. However, these measures cannot completely solve this problem. Blockchain smart contracts can reduce manual intervention during the execution of the agreement. When applied to the construction of smart court, the opinions or grounds of litigation participants will be automatically imported into the judgment document, thereby preventing the phenomenon of selective quotation of opinions or grounds.

"Take facts as the basis and laws as the yardstick" is one of the basic principles of law application, and it is also the basic guarantee of judicial justice. Measures such as searching similar cases and correlated cases, reporting differences between higher courts and the "four major public platforms" can solve the problem of error in fact determination, but they cannot completely solve this problem from the source of evidence. Therefore, the distributed ledger of the blockchain, data traceability, immutability, information transparency and information symmetry, as well as the time stamp function, can effectively prevent the phenomenon of tampering or concealing evidence. From the source of evidence, it can effectively prevent the phenomenon of "different verdict in the same kind case" and "unjust and wrong cases".

4.2 Using Blockchain to Promote the Construction of Smart Court Will Help Improve Judicial Efficiency

"Difficulty in enforcement" is one of the problems that the People's Court at all levels have been trying to solve in recent years, and the implementation of online investigation and control and online enforcement through the Internet are important results among them. The Supreme People's Court has established an online inspection and control system, which can query 16 categories of 25 items of information (real estate, deposits, online funds, etc.) of the enforced nationwide. It can basically realize the effective coverage of the main property forms and related information of the person subject to execution. However, the Internet cannot completely solve the phenomenon of executives delaying execution within the execution deadline. Although the use of the Internet for online investigation and control and online enforcement has brought great convenience, whether or not to take enforcement measures still depends on the initiative of the enforcement judge and the external constraints of the system.

The automatic execution of the smart contract of the blockchain can solve this problem, using blockchain technology to establish Consortium Blockchain with banks and other institutions. As long as there is property available for execution, execution measures such as freezing and transfer can be automatically completed in accordance with the consensus mechanism of the blockchain and smart contracts, which not only improves execution efficiency, but also effectively solves the phenomenon of long-term delay. Specifically, after the applicant applies for enforcement, the blockchain system will intelligently review whether it meets the conditions for applying for enforcement. If the conditions are met, the system will automatically initiate network checks, transfers, punishments and other measures of the bank account of the person subject to enforcement, without the intervention of the enforcement judge, thereby improving judicial effectiveness. Blockchain smart contracts are not only embodied in automatic enforcement without human intervention, but also can automatically complete tasks such as case filing, court formation, and trial process management. However, this is only the function of the smart contract in the blockchain. The use of the blockchain for electronic data storage can pre-verify the electronic data evidence, which can also improve the judicial efficiency in the aspect of proof, cross-examination, and identification of evidence. It is foreseeable that with the in-depth application of blockchain in the construction of smart court, it will greatly improve judicial efficiency in judicial litigation, judicial services, and judicial management.

4.3 Using Blockchain to Promote the Construction of Smart Court Will Help Improve Judicial Credibility

Blockchain technology fundamentally changes the traditional centralized credit establishment model. It uses a set of mathematical algorithms based on a collective consensus reached in advance agreement, replaces dependence on centralized institutions with data blocks, and establishes credit through machine technology endorsements rather than signatures of centralized institutions. The credit supported by blockchain technology is a purely mathematical method to establish a trust relationship between all parties. The use of all nodes to book accounts through the entire network can quickly establish global credit, and it can also automatically eliminate false and fraudulent information [7]. Different from the traditional manual credit evaluation system, there is no credit evaluation and credit verification institution in blockchain, but distributed account books are used to ensure the immutability and transparency of block data, thus establishing a credit evaluation system with technology as an endorsement. In other words, each user's transaction will form credit data or constitute the basis for credit evaluation, thereby establishing a unique credit system. Unlike the traditional manual credit evaluation system, the blockchain does not have a credit evaluation and credit verification agency, but uses a distributed ledger to ensure the immutability and transparency of block data, thereby establishing a credit evaluation system with technology as an endorsement. In other words, each user's transaction will form the basis of credit data or credit evaluation, thereby establishing a unique credit system.

In the blockchain area, it is smart contracts that completely dispel the worries of transaction parties about transaction risks. Moreover, this trust can also be passed on to third parties on the chain. According to the *2018 China Blockchain Industry White Paper* of the Ministry of Industry and Information Technology, the use of blockchain to realize information sharing can achieve "trust transfer" or "trust spillover."

From the perspective of consensus, law is the result of social consensus. The law also promotes and guarantees the stability of social consensus through the adjustment of social relations. It is generally believed that the difficulty of social consensus lies mainly in the diversification of values. In the market environment, the scarcity of resources and the normalized zero-sum game make it more difficult to reach a consensus. The technology credit, trust transmission and consensus mechanism of the blockchain has created a unique way to provide a novel solution for the formation of social consensus. Blockchain can credibly promote social governance innovation in terms of traceability, voting, rights registration, transfer, decision-making and supervision.

In the blockchain, it is smart contracts that completely dispel the worries of transaction parties about transaction risks. Smart contract with its automatic execution mechanism eliminates both parties' concerns about contract performance risks. It is the unique credit evaluation system of blockchain and the automatic execution mechanism of smart contracts that provide a new trust model. If the function of the Internet is mainly information transmission and information interaction, the characteristic function of the blockchain is to form value transmission. From the perspective of the construction of smart court, the technical credit of blockchain (to establish a credit foundation from a technical level through a consistent technical agreement or specification), consensus mechanism, and information transparency can also help prevent the formation and spread of rumors, thereby effectively improving justice Credibility.

5   Conclusion

China's smart court have established a model with the most comprehensive network coverage, the largest data stock, the strongest openness, the widest scope of collaboration, and the latest smart services in the world. In the future, we will promote the development of smart court from initial formation to comprehensive construction. Looking back on the history of the informatization construction of the people's courts, the development of information technology has provided strong support for the people's courts to ensure judicial fairness and improve the quality of trials. The informatization construction of the people's courts has made great achievements, and we look forward to the new type of smart court to continue to promote judicial reform, advance the modernization of judicial capabilities and judicial systems, and set a model for the construction of smart court in countries around the world.

Acknowledgments. This paper is supported by the Special Project of "System Theory Research" of Guangdong Planning Office of Philosophy and Social Science: Research on the Coupling of Information Technology and the Rule of Law to Improve the System of Social Fairness, and Justice. (No. GD20ZD16).

References

1. Swan, M.: Blockchain: Blueprint for a New Economy. O'Reilly Media (2015)
2. Jiang, R., Wei, C.: Application progress and value discussion of blockchain. Gansu Financ. **2**, 19–21 (2016)
3. Hangzhou Internet Court: Our hospital held the first press conference on the launch of judicial blockchain in China. http://hztl.zjcourt.cn/art/2018/9/19/art_1225222_25457534.html. Accessed 6 Nov 2019
4. Yu, J., Wu, W., Zhang, M.: The judicial application of blockchain intelligent contract in Hangzhou internet court goes online. https://www.chinacourt.org/article/detail/2019/10/id/459 1024.shtml. Accessed 6 Nov 2019
5. China Communications Standards Association., ZTE Corporation., China Unicom.: The White Paper on the application and development of internet of things + blockchain. https://res-www.zte.com.cn/bigmediafiles/zte/Files/PDF/white_book/201911071548.pdf. Accessed 7 Nov 2019
6. Wang, Z.: EU launches new mechanism to embrace blockchain technology. https://www.cailianpress.com/roll/21151410. Accessed 10 Sept 2018
7. Feng, W., Shen, F.: Blockchain: subversion of traditional finance. Gansu Soc. Sci. **5**, 239–244 (2017)

Value of Blockchain in Rule of Law

Wei Liu[1]([✉]), Jing Bian[2], and Cui-Ting Zeng[3]

[1] Institute of Law and Economic Development, Guangdong University
of Finance and Economics, Guangzhou 510320, China
[2] School of Software Engineering, Sun Yat-Senen University, Guangzhou 510006, China
[3] Guangdong University of Finance and Economics, Guangzhou 510320, China

Abstract. Blockchain is considered as a new technology to reshape the world, which characterized by anonymity of subject, intelligence of transaction, decentralization of management, autonomy of on-chain rules, data immutability, transparency and symmetry of information, and automation of incentive (or reward and punishment) from the perspective of law. The significance of "blockchain + rule of law" is mainly the technical credit, trust transfer, new consensus mechanism, the coupling effect of code norms and legal norms.

Keywords: Blockchain · Smart contracts · Rule of law · Social governance · Intelligence

1 Problem Presentation

In 2016, the Notice of the 13th Five-Year Plan for National Informatization which was issued by the State Council, listed blockchain as a key cutting-edge technology for the first time and clearly proposed that the innovation, experiment and application of blockchain and other new technologies should be strengthened in order to seize the dominance of the new generation of information technology. The current legal research mainly focuses on the legal issues caused by blockchain, such as digital currency, blockchain finance and smart contracts. This paper intends to observe and discuss the legal significance of blockchain, hoping that the legal circle will pay more attention to the legal significance of blockchain and promote the legal practice and application of blockchain.

2 Blockchain "Stigmatized" by Bitcoin: The Perspective of Technology and Law

2.1 Concept and Characteristics of Blockchain

In 2008, Satoshi Nakamoto designed an electronic cash system without a trusted third party and proposed the concept of Bitcoin. As its underlying technology is blockchain, it is considered to be the theoretical origin of blockchain. Then, in January 2009, he created the first block (the "creation block"), and the blockchain went into practical use. According to Melanie Swan's classification, blockchain is divided into three stages:

H.-N. Dai et al. (Eds.): BlockSys 2021, CCIS 1490, pp. 441–446, 2021.
https://doi.org/10.1007/978-981-16-7993-3_34

blockchain 1.0 represented by digital currency, 2.0 represented by smart contract, and 3.0 beyond the expanded application of currency, economy and market in judicial, government management, notarization and other fields. At present, it has entered the 2.0 era and is moving towards the 3.0 stage [1].

Blockchain essentially is a decentralized distributed ledger. When it applied to different scenarios, it will bring significance to transaction participants in the following four aspects: 1. To eliminate the necessity of the existence of transaction intermediaries so as to reduce transaction costs. 2. The settlement of trades is almost real-time, which improves the trading efficiency and greatly improves the utilization of assets. 3. The immutability of information on blockchain and the decentralized way of data storage make it the best carrier for data and information recording. 4. The programmable blockchain makes the transaction process fully automated, that is, by embedding the preset transaction rules in blockchain, the transaction will be automatically completed when the predetermined conditions are met, which can improve the degree of automation of the transaction. It actually refers to a smart contract [2]. Although blockchain will not change the TCP/IP protocol of the Internet, the reason why it is still not applicable to the Internet link ledger is exactly what the advantages of blockchain are: decentralization, openness, independence, security and anonymity.

2.2   Legal Dimension of Blockchain

The above description provides a concise summary of the concept and main characteristics of blockchain, and is also suitable for observing and understanding blockchain from the perspective of the rule of law. Therefore, what kind of chain reaction "blockchain + rule of law" will produce and how to give full play to the unique function of blockchain in the practice of rule of law have become issues worthy of study.

The basic problem is to observe blockchain and its application as a new legal phenomenon. The characteristics of this legal phenomenon can be summarized in the order of legal logic as follows: Subject anonymity (authentication that protects privacy but does not affect identity), intelligentization of transaction (the function of smart contracts, the word "transaction" should be extended to management and other fields with the expansion of the application field of blockchain), decentralization of management (no hardware facilities such as servers and the management center hosted by them), autonomy of on-chain rules (achieving consensus through consistent protocols or technical arrangements), immutability of data, transparency and symmetry of information, automation of incentive (the function of smart contracts), which will inevitably bring new challenges to the rule of law, but also provides new opportunities for the modernization of the rule of law.

3   Value Interconnection: Technical Credit, Trust Transfer, New Consensus Mechanism, Coupling Effect of Code Norms and Legal Norms

Legal circles generally believe that market economy is essentially a legal economy. It is also generally believed that the market economy is a credit economy from the perspective of economics. Bona fide doctrine is known as the "imperial principle" of civil and commercial laws, and it is also the core requirement of the rule of law for economic activities. If the market economy generally presents the form of honesty or the sincerity of the counterparty is high, the transaction cost will be directly reduced and legal resources will be saved. On the contrary, it will increase the corresponding transaction and social governance costs. So, is there an ideal model for solving related problems?

Blockchain technology fundamentally changes the traditional centralized credit establishment mode, adopts a set of mathematical algorithms based on the collective consensus reached by prior agreements and specifications, uses data blocks instead of relying on centralized institutions, establishes trust between machines. Different from the traditional manual credit evaluation system, blockchain does not have credit evaluation and credit verification institutions. Instead, distributed ledger is adopted to ensure the immutability and transparency of block data, so as to establish a credit evaluation system with technology as endorsement. Although credit can produce trust, it is only a necessary condition of trust but not a sufficient condition in logic. In blockchain, it is smart contracts that with its automatic execution mechanism eliminate the concerns of both parties on the risk of contract performance. Based on blockchain technology, "trust transfer" or "trust spillover" can be realized to form group trust between participants. And it is the unique credit evaluation system of blockchain and the self-execution mechanism of smart contracts that provide us with a new trust model.

The stable operation of blockchain system and mutual trust of nodes depend on consensus mechanism. Consensus mechanism can be divided into algorithm consensus and decision-making consensus. The former is equivalent to the consistency and correct expression of distributed nodes, while the latter studies the problem of how to reach a consensus on the optimal decision in no-centered group decision making, which also requires all nodes to believe that "the expressed content is correct". Consensus algorithm of blockchain belongs to the subset of the branch of algorithmic consensus, which is essentially "machine consensus". Decision-making consensus is mostly seen in the field of distributed artificial intelligence, and its essence is "human consensus", which is simply a way for a diverse group to make decisions without conflict. According to Edward Shils' concensus concept, it needs to meet three conditions: member's common acceptance of norms, member's unanimous recognition of implementing agencies and identity. [3] In any case, the charm of blockchain has gradually been widely recognized, its application fields are constantly expanding, the maturity of technology is also promoting the continuous improvement of its application efficiency, and the gradual upgrading from networking to blockchain has gradually become a trend. If the main function of the Internet is information transmission and information interaction, the application of blockchain promotes value transmission, which is why blockchain is called the Internet of value.

From the perspective of consensus, law is not only the result of social consensus, but also promotes and guarantees the stability and predictability of social consensus through the dynamic adjustment of social relations, so as to guarantee the harmony and development of society. In general, the difficulty of social consensus lies in the diversification of value. In the market, the contradiction of interests, especially the scarcity of resources and the normalized zero sum game make it more difficult to reach consensus. Blockchain's technology credit, trust transfer and consensus mechanism are unique, providing a novel solution for the formation mechanism of social consensus, and can credibly promote social governance innovation in the aspects of traceability, voting, right registration and transfer, decision-making, supervision and so on. "Core socialist values should be integrated into all aspects of social development, and transformed into people's thinking and behavior" was put forward at 19th National Congress of the Communist Party of China. The unique mechanism of blockchain helps to realize the mutual trust between the transaction parties, and can produce trust transfer, so as to complete the transaction safely in the distrust environment, replace the traditional artificial credit with technical credit, thus credibility mode supporting multi-party verification is used in place of the traditional witness, authentication and notarization to realize technology substitution.

4   The Rise of Technical Norms and Its Coupling with Legal Norms

Rimavera De Filippi and Samer Hassan argue that in recent years, as the Internet has become more widely available and our reliance on digital technology has increased, the trend to replace existing laws and regulations with technical rules has slowly begun to develop. Because laws and regulations can only be rescued after the intervention of the state, while technical rules can be prevented in advance by code. "Code is law" means that with the emergence of digital technology, code has gradually become the main way to regulate the behavior of Internet users. Code can enforce rules more effectively than law, but because of the ambiguity and flexibility of legal rules, it is sometimes difficult to translate them into code form. However, with the development of blockchain technology and smart contracts, code will play a greater role than law in regulating the behavior of Internet users in the long run [4].

We agree that the trend of technical rules replacing the existing laws and regulations is gradually forming and that technical rules can prevent in advance through codes, but at the same time, the view that laws and regulations can only provide post-hoc incentive through state intervention is untenable. The value of law is more important to provide predictability for the legal result of the actor's behavior, so as to prevent the occurrence of disputes (rather than incentive or settlement of disputes) and promote the maximization of the actor's interests under the premise of legalization, so as to achieve the legislative purpose of building an orderly social order and promoting social development expected by legislators. However, the relationship between code and law is indeed a legal issue worth exploring.

Compared with the uniqueness of the code, the fuzziness of the legal norms (even causing ambiguity) and its uncertainty are indeed the inherent defects of the legal norms. However, it may be a false proposition to discuss the role of code versus law, because the relationship between them is not suitable to discuss from the size of the role, and in fact, it is impossible to make a quantitative comparison. The relationship between code and law has been raised in the computer era. The relationship between code and law has been raised in the computer age. The mutual trust mechanism and autonomy generated by the unique mechanism of blockchain give new connotation and provide new evidence for the view that "code is law". The view that blockchain produces anarchism is not worth worrying, but the view that "code is law" (or code replaces law in the blockchain world) is also questionable.

Blockchain and law are essentially both trust mechanisms, and the uncertainty of their relationship leads to the polarized evaluation of blockchain in Kevin warbach's opinion. Though both of them have their own governance limitations. The solution is to integrate governance, which can be achieved through two modes of legal encoding and code legalizing. [5] Though her ideas are consistent and original, the conclusions are not the same as the viewpoints put forward after the specific analysis of the relevant issues. But the relevant discussion is still helpful to clarify the relationship between code and law and analyze its coupling effect.

5   Conclusion

The significance of "blockchain + rule of law" is mainly the technical credit, trust transfer, new consensus mechanism, the coupling effect of code norms and legal norms. We will refine and summarize the coupling effect and its enlightenment into the following four points.

1. **Normative Value of Code.** In blockchain, the user's assets and behaviors are digitized, and the data is automatically executed according to the instructions of the code, and the code is the technical specification. The essence of blockchain is to establish a mutual trust mechanism. Users agree on the specific contents of their rights, obligations and responsibilities through the smart contract, which needs to be written as code. Code is neither direct nor indirect specification, but it can still eliminate the possibility of user's choice of action or inaction based on the fact that the parties cannot change the agreed code of conduct in the smart contract.

2. **Law Encoding and Code Legalizing.** It is mentioned representative as the interaction and effect between multiple norms will inevitably be transmitted to other norms, which will lead to interaction and adjustment from the form and content, and finally form the normative system of collaborative governance of multiple norms. This is the so-called integrated governance. However, this does not mean the equality of the effectiveness of norms. We should still strive to explore the path of the integration of scientific and technological rationality and legal rationality in response to the coupling of technical norms and legal norms.

3. **Value of Legal Norms Has Not Been Weakened by the Rise of Codes.** The value of legal norms is not reflected in the breadth and depth of its intervention, but through the maintenance of social order and the strengthening of social functions to reflect its effectiveness and further highlight its value. The value lies in the co-governance of multiple norms under the control of legal norms, and the concept of "collaboration, participation and common interests" will also play its unique value guiding function in the network society from the perspective of normative governance.

4. **Collaborative Governance of Multiple Norms.** The integration rule of virtue, rule of law and autonomy has become the consensus of modern social governance, which is manifested as opinions issued by the State Council of the CPC Central Committee

"giving full play to the positive role of autonomy regulations, village rules and residents' conventions in urban and rural community governance, and promoting public order and good customs". In blockchain, there are also online communities and corresponding autonomy norms similar to urban and rural communities, which realize decentralized autonomy through consensus technical norms. Therefore, the autonomy model of blockchain also provides a new observation sample for the enrichment and development of autonomy theory.

Acknowledgments. This paper is supported by the Major Program of the National Social Science Fund of China "Theoretical Model and Practical Approach of Integrating Socialist Core Values into the Construction of Rule of Law in Smart Society" (No. 20VHJ009) and Research on Innovation Mode of Nurturing High Quality Legal Talents for the Guangdong-Hong Kong-Macao Greater Bay (No.GXJK090).

References

1. Swan, M.: Blockchain: Blueprint for a New Economy, 1st edn. O'Reilly Media, California (2015)
2. Caria, R.D.: A digital revolution in international trade? The international legal framework for blockchain technologies, virtual currencies and smart contracts: challenges and opportunities. In: Proceedings of the Congress of the United Nations Commission on International Trade Law, vol. 4, pp.105–107. United Nations, Vienna (2017)
3. KPMG's Report: "Blockchain consensus–immutable agreement for the internet of value". https://assets.kpmg/content/dam/kpmg/cn/pdf/en/2016/09/blockchain-consensus.pdf. Accessed 30 May 2021
4. Filippi, P.D., Hassan, S.: Blockchain technology as a regulatory technology: from code is law to law is code. Soc. Sci. Electron. Publ. **21,** 12 (2018)
5. Werbach, K.: The Blockchain and the New Architecture of Trust, 1st edn. MIT Press, Cambridge (2018)

"Blockchain + Rule of Law" and Modernization of Social Governance

Zhenyu Li[1]([✉]), Jing Bian[2], and Ping Wu[2]

[1] School of Law, Guangdong University of Finance & Economics,
Guangzhou 510320, GD, China
[2] School of Software Engineering, Sun Yat-Sen University, Guangzhou 510006, GD, China

Abstract. Due to the unique advantages of blockchain and the continuous maturity of technology, blockchain has rapidly extended from bitcoin and finance to other fields. Blockchain can be used in legislation, law enforcement, judicature, law-abiding and other activities to boost the modernization of the rule of law and further improve the intelligent and legal level of social governance. "Blockchain + rule of law has value on social governance in three ways: information transparency and symmetry, uncertainty and predictability and safety and efficiency. In terms of social governance function, distributed verifiable databases and smart contracts promoted by blockchain technology have the potential to change the boundary between technology and law and form a new governance model. The value of blockchain in social governance or the significance of the rule of law should not be negated. The full-process litigation system on the chain helps to place the entire litigation process in the technical guarantee of blockchain information transparency, constant data, credible evidence, and automatic triggering of relevant judicial actions. In particular, it helps to solve the problem of tampering, destruction and concealment of evidence in the investigation stage.

Keywords: Blockchain · Social governance · Blockchain + rule of law · Information transparency · Information symmetry

China has listed blockchain as an integral part of its national strategy. Developed countries in Europe and America, Australia, Japan, South Korea and other countries also attach great importance to the technical value and social application of blockchain. The latest important information is that on February 1, 2018, the European Commission announced the launch of a new mechanism aimed at promoting the development of blockchain technology in Europe and helping Europe benefit from it. The mechanism has the functions of collecting information related to blockchain, monitoring and analyzing related trends, exploring the socio-economic potential of blockchain technology and coping with related challenges. The commission said blockchain technology, which allows online transactions to be highly traceable and secure, is seen as a major technological breakthrough. The technology will affect digital services and change modes in the fields of medical care, insurance, finance, energy, logistics and government services. According to the comprehensive relevant data, the unique technical advantages of blockchain and its social application value have been widely recognized. The application

© Springer Nature Singapore Pte Ltd. 2021
H.-N. Dai et al. (Eds.): BlockSys 2021, CCIS 1490, pp. 447–456, 2021.
https://doi.org/10.1007/978-981-16-7993-3_35

of blockchain in the future will be extended to various social fields, that is, "blockchain + ", and the legal field is no exception.

1 Intelligent and Legalization of Blockchain and Social Governance

Melanie Swan, founder of American Blockchain Research Institute, divided the blockchain into three stages in his book *Blockchain: Blueprint of New Economy*, namely, blockchain 1.0 represented by digital currency, blockchain 2.0 represented by smart contract, and blockchain 3.0 which transcends currency, economy and market to the fields of justice, government management and notarization,etc. Blockchain has entered the 2.0 era and is moving towards the 3.0 stage [1]. After General Secretary Xi's speech, the central and local governments have issued policies to promote blockchain technology and innovation. Blockchain has entered the industry application stage in an all-round way. It is worth mentioning that China's blockchain service network (BSN), which has attracted much attention from the industry, officially entered the commercial stage on April 25, 2020 and launched the overseas version of public beta. BSN allows developers to easily develop various applications on it at a very low cost and has opened more than 120 public city nodes on six continents.

Due to the unique advantages of blockchain and the continuous maturity of technology, blockchain has rapidly extended from bitcoin and finance to other fields. According to *the 2018 White Paper on China's Blockchain Industry* issued by the Ministry of Industry and Information Technology, blockchain is distributed, tamper-resistant, highly transparent and traceable, which meets the business needs of the entire financial system. Therefore, it has been applied in payment and clearing, credit financing, financial transactions, securities, insurance, leasing and other sub-fields. With the gradual maturity of blockchain technology innovation and development, the actual effect of its industrial application has become more apparent. The application of blockchain has extended from the financial field to the physical field, such as electronic information depository, copyright management and transaction, product traceability, digital asset transaction, Internet of Things, intelligent manufacturing, supply chain management and other fields. Blockchain technology can be applied in almost all industrial scenes because almost all industrial scenes involve transactions and there is a need to reduce costs, improve efficiency and optimize the industrial integrity environment, which is the role that Blockchain technology can play quickly after it is applied. From the perspective of epistemology, blockchain is the link bridge between the real world and the virtual world and its significance lies in reconstructing a trust mechanism to enhance the order of the real world; From the perspective of technical characteristics, blockchain has the characteristics of data immutability, smart contract, information traceability, decentralization and trust consensus mechanism [2]. Blockchain has strong economic value, legal value, management value and application value, but it not only brings opportunities for national development and social convenience, but also has certain risks [3].

The Third Plenary Session of the Eighteenth Central Committee of the Communist Party of China pointed out that the overall goal of comprehensively deepening reform is to improve and develop the socialist system with Chinese characteristics and promote the modernization of the national governance system and governance capacity. *The report of the 19th National Congress of the Communist Party of China* further pointed out that it is necessary to strengthen the construction of social governance system, improve the social governance system with the leadership of the Party Committee, government responsibility, social coordination, public participation and legal guarantee, and improve the level of socialization, legalization, intelligence and specialization of social governance. Xi Jinping emphasized: "The difference between governance and management reflects system governance, legal governance, source governance, and comprehensive policy."

At the first meeting of the Central Leading Group for Cyber Security and Informatization in 2014, Xi Jinping pointed out: " Without informatization, there will be no modernization". General Secretary Xi's famous assertion clarifies the relationship between informatization and modernization, which promotes the informatization strategy to an unprecedented height. To promote the modernization of national governance system and capacity and to improve the socialization, legalization, intelligence and specialization of social governance, it is necessary to use modern information technology and promote modernization through informationization. The process of informatization in our country has completed electronization, and basically realized the network. The key point of the next step is intellectualization. Intelligentization not only comes from the technical application of artificial intelligence, but also the Internet of Things, which is famous for its smart city construction, and the blockchain represented by distributed ledger and smart contract, which are important intelligent technologies. With the help of multi-node backup data, the distributed ledger of blockchain ensures that the data cannot be changed, and enables multiple parties to participate in verification, which can realize the transparency, traceability and auditability of the transaction process, and the intelligent contract does not need human intervention so that it can automatically conduct safe transactions in a distrustful environment, which is the concrete embodiment of its intelligent characteristics.

Meng Jianzhu pointed out: "As the best model of social governance, the rule of law has the advantages of clear rights and responsibilities, open procedures and stable expectations." To strengthen and innovate social governance, it is necessary to deepen the reform of social governance system by law, improve the level of social governance by law, and improve the efficiency of social governance through modernization of the rule of law. Modernization of the rule of law is an important part of the modernization of social governance and it also provides modern legal protection for the modernization of social governance. Looking back at the modernization of the rule of law from the perspective of social governance, the modernization of the rule of law should also improve the level of intelligence and specialization. It may be argued that the modernization of the rule of law should take the rule of law as the body, with intelligence and specialization as the wings, which synergically resonate and interact with each other, and promote the realization of the modernization of the rule of law in the information age by its resonance effect.

China has traditionally been a government-led social management system, which is currently promoting the transformation from social management to social governance. In social governance, it emphasizes "co-construction, co-governance and sharing", pays more attention to fairness and people-oriented, strengthens the government's public service function, and realizes the transformation from a regulated government to a service-oriented government. As a subsystem of the social governance system, the decentralized management mode in the blockchain system echoes the essential requirements of social governance based on society. The distributed ledger, traceability of data and self-execution mechanism embody the "source governance", while the characteristics of information transparency, information symmetry, technical credit and trust transmission provide a reference governance model for the "comprehensive policy" in the new social governance. Blockchain can be used in legislation, law enforcement, judicature, law-abiding and other activities. At present, it has made some achievements and is expanding new practical functions, thus boosting the modernization of the rule of law and further improving the intelligent and legal level of social governance.

2 The Social Governance Value of "Blockchain + Rule of Law"

From the perspective of legal culture, the establishment and development of market economy in China, as well as the impact of economic globalization, make the ancient Chinese traditional legal culture is undergoing modern transformation. From the institutional level, China's traditional legal culture needs to complete the following transformation: from penal-centered to people-centered, from procedural instrumentalism to procedural justice, from public law to private law, from the closed legal system to the open, from the separation of judicature and administration to judicial independence. In terms of value, we should complete the transformation from group standard to individual standard, from ethics to rationalization, from the spirit of law to the rule of law, and from "non-litigation" to justice [4]. With the promotion of informatization to the modernization process, the modernization of legal culture has made new development in the information age, which has important value for solving the conflict of legal culture and building new legal culture. From the perspective of blockchain, honesty and credit, social standard, pluralistic governance, information transparency, information symmetry, legal certainty and predictability all provide new "nutrition" for reshaping legal culture in the information age, and will also give new connotations to legal values such as fairness, justice, security and efficiency. Due to limited space, this paper only discusses the social governance value directly related to it.

2.1 Information Transparency and Symmetry

According to *the 2018 White Paper on China's Blockchain Industry* issued by the Ministry of Industry and Information Technology, the centralized ledger proves the feasibility of eliminating the need for any third party intermediary for share transactions. For example, on December 30, 2015, NASDAQ announced that its partner Chain had for the first time used NASDAQ's blockchain technology trading platform LINQ in an offering of shares to a private investor. NASDAQ said the deal will replace its paper-based voucher system with blockchain technology. After the information of each equity transaction of each company is put on the blockchain, the amount of financing and valuation of the company can be clear at a glance. The transaction becomes open and transparent, which solves the problem of information asymmetry and makes the investment decision more simple and efficient. Although this is a commercial application of blockchain, it can vividly illustrate the practical functions of information transparency and information symmetry.

In the rule of man, the power holders "say what the law says", the decision-making process is "black box", and the information is not transparent. Sunshine is the best preservative, and the purpose of sunshine is to prevent judicial corruption and promote judicial justice through openness or information transparency. In administrative management, since the implementation of *the Regulations on the Disclosure of Government Information in China* and the strengthening of the construction of a sunny government, the transparency of administrative management has effectively prevented power rent-seeking and enhanced the public's trust in the government. The Supreme People's Court is actively promoting the construction of a smart court, which aims to be networked, sunny and intelligent. In terms of sunshine, there are now open platforms for trial process, trial activities, judgment documents and execution information (usually referred to as "four platforms"). In general, the sunshine of the current administration and justice is based on the Internet. Blockchain implements the whole network bookkeeping and the information is highly transparent, which can more effectively build the sunshine court and the sunshine government.

Michel Foucault introduced Bentham's "Panoramic Prison" theory and believed that in traditional society, social managers mainly realized lower cost and higher efficiency of social management by means of information asymmetry. The information dissemination in the era of Internet makes the "panoramic prison" style social management on the basis of information asymmetry meet with crisis, and the "common view prison" on the basis of symmetrical information will promote the innovation of power structure and management mode. In the world of blockchain, information is highly transparent and there is no human involvement or intervention in the whole process. The information is traceable and auditable, and complete information symmetry can be achieved.

2.2 Uncertainty and Predictability

The reason why the law has the function of preventing disputes is that the certainty of the law provides legal predictability for the result of the actor's behavior. In the same way, the actor can prevent legal risks and seek the maximization of legal interests, and the prohibition, restriction, permission and encouragement of the law can be realized by the rational choice of the actor. However, this is only an ideal state. In fact, the foreseeability of the actor's behavior result may be affected by legislative gaps and defects (such as the fuzziness of legislation), and the legal consequences of his behavior cannot be foreseen due to the uncertainty of judicature (law enforcement). At present, there is no sufficient practice to prove the legislative value of blockchain, but the judicial blockchain of Hangzhou Internet Court shows that blockchain can resolve the judicial uncertainty, and its principle mainly lies in: The factors that affect the result of judicial judgment are law and fact. For judges, law is certain (there is no judge to make law), which belongs to the invariable item. Variable item is the change of case fact caused by the different determination of the proof force of evidence. Blockchain uses the immutability and traceability of its data to fix the evidence on the blockchain, which effectively prevents judicial arbitrariness and blocks the possible space of judicial corruption, thus helping to resolve judicial uncertainty and improve the predictability of actors' behavior results, as well as administrative law enforcement.

2.3 Safety and Efficiency

Safety and efficiency are the basic principles of commercial law as well as the value requirements of the rule of law. Generally speaking, there is a contradiction between safety and efficiency, that is, efficiency will be damaged when pursuing safety, and vice versa. The legislation of market economy has always been committed to coordinating the relationship between the two from the perspective of balance. However, this balance is an ideal state, which is constantly challenged by new formats and new models such as sharing economy and sharing economy. Blockchain is just a new mode to solve the contradiction between security and efficiency from technology and trading mechanism. In blockchain transactions, contracts are stored in the blockchain in the form of smart contracts. Blockchain technology ensures that contracts shall not be tampered with and contract performance behaviors such as payment and delivery can be automatically and real-time completed during the performance of contracts, thus improving transaction security and efficiency. The security and efficiency value of blockchain is more evident in its commercial application, but it has also been applied creatively in the practice of the rule of law, and has attracted the high attention of some countries. According to *the 2018 White Paper on China's Blockchain Industry* issued by the Ministry of Industry and Information Technology, Annie's blockchain-based copyright certification service has provided rights confirmation services for millions of works, partially solving the pain points and difficulties of content creators. Give full play to the massive, rapid and immediate characteristics of block chain technology in the process of rights confirmation, authorization and rights protection, and gradually realize "creation is right confirmation, use is authorization, discovery is right protection". It can be seen that the innovative application of blockchain solves the historical problem of intellectual property rights confirmation, authorization and rights protection. Of course, the function of blockchain is not limited to the field of intellectual property. In September 2018, 133 representatives of the Spanish People's Party submitted proposals related to blockchain to the lower house of the Spanish Parliament. According to the public documents, the proposal suggests that the government introduce blockchain to improve internal processes and provide traceability, robustness and transparency of decision-making. According to the document, the introduction of blockchain—in administrative concessions, contracts or internal procedures—will encourage greater control, traceability and transparency in the process. The use of this technology can also bring additional income to the administrative authorities by promoting the new model, and exchanging rights in logistics, tourism or infrastructure. In addition, legislators suggested establishing public and private blockchain models to benefit the secondary market of goods and services, thereby reducing costs, improving productivity and encouraging the creation of specialized jobs [5]. From the perspective of organizational behavior, blockchain can be seen as a new organizational behavior model, thus demonstrating its added value in terms of safety and efficiency.

3   The Social Governance Function of "Blockchain + Rule of Law"

There are also doubts about the social governance function of blockchain. For example, in the field of national governance and social governance, technology and law are mutually substitutable. If the cost of technical solutions is lower than that of legal solutions in a certain social scenario, technical tools may replace legal forms as the main means of order generation. Distributed verifiable databases and smart contracts promoted by blockchain technology have the potential to change the boundary between technology and law and form a new governance model. However, technical solutions can not only improve efficiency and certainty, but also threaten the inefficient value of law, such as equality and justice [6]. There are also views that blockchain technology cannot effectively solve the problems of community building, free rider, wealth gap and equity, so it is almost impossible to replace the existing centralized governance system [7].

Admittedly, blockchain cannot solve all the problems (such as the "wealth gap problem"), nor can it replace the existing centralized governance system (in fact, it does not need to), but this does not negate the value of blockchain in social governance or the significance of the rule of law. Of course, we can't misunderstand the blockchain. In a decentralized public blockchain, where there is a governance mechanism agreed upon by all participants of the chain, and where tokens act as negotiable, encrypted digital proof of interest mechanisms, each block is equal (or not superior), the idea that blockchain is inconsistent with equality or justice is untenable. From the current practice, full link sharing and co-governance is the development trend; "Let the data run more, people less errands" has become a basic consensus; It is the established direction of e-government development to continuously improve the level of equalization, universal benefit and convenience of public services. New things should be looked at scientifically, comprehensively and objectively. "Make use of its strengths and avoid its weaknesses" is the right way; "Encouraging innovation and being inclusive and prudent" should be a rational choice.

At present, China is committed to establishing a modern legal system of scientific legislation, strict law enforcement, fair justice and law-abiding for all people. The practical function of "blockchain + rule of law" needs to be further explored. However, from the legal characteristics of blockchain, the application of blockchain may promote the construction of modern rule of law system and further promote the modernization of social governance in the following aspects: to promote democratic legislation with its advantages such as consensus mechanism and then promote scientific legislation, to build an integrated law enforcement supervision system with transparency, efficiency and information symmetry, to build a trial-centered whole-process judicial blockchain system in the construction of intelligent justice, and to promote the independent protection and automatic relief of intellectual property rights and other rights. As mentioned above, the blockchain is used to protect intellectual property rights. The protection of other rights such as real estate property rights is also being actively explored. The automatic execution of smart contracts can effectively complete automatic relief. The following is a brief discussion on the application of blockchain in legislation, law enforcement and justice.

There has been very little discussion about blockchain advancing legislation but there are studies that touch on the issue. For example, the medical block chain for the distributed transmission, aggregation, storage and analysis of patients' clinical and diagnosis and treatment data, through the confirmation of the mutual trust agreement to reach a consensus to maintain the security and trust of the data, so as to achieve the sharing and opening of health and medical big data on the basis of safety and legality. Therefore, medical blockchain is the fundamental technical guarantee to break the bottleneck of health and medical big data legislation and ensure the legislation and enforcement of health and medical big data [8]. This study is from the perspective of big data analysis and decision-making under blockchain. The application of blockchain in the legislative field may also be extended to anonymous solicitation of opinions, analysis of social conditions and public opinion, coordination and cooperation of legislative participants, and voting, etc., so as to promote democratic legislation and further promote scientific legislation through modernization of legislative methods.

According to *the 2018 United Nations E-government Survey Report*, China's e-government development index EGDI is 0.6811, ranking 65th in the world. On July 25,2018, the State Council issued *the Guiding Opinions on Accelerating the Construction of National Integrated Online Government Service Platform*, which is based on "Internet + Government Service" and does not mention the application of blockchain, which is directly related to the insufficient application practice of blockchain. Fortunately, departments such as finance, taxation, public security and auditing have recognized the unique advantages of blockchain, and are actively exploring or landing the practical application of blockchain. For example, Hu Guangjun, deputy director of the Information Security Department of the First Research Institute of the Ministry of Public Security, said in an interview that the physical world and the relationship with people will be brought into the whole blockchain ecosystem in the future. At present, the department is considering how to apply blockchain technology to the public security field, for example, using blockchain technology to store case evidence chains, and using the unchangeable property of blockchain to run through the whole process of identity entry, etc. [9]. Some local governments are also actively promoting the application of blockchain in government affairs, for example, "Shaanxi Digital Link" (a provincial integrated government affairs cloud platform based on blockchain), which won the annual best practice case and best practice achievement award for digital China construction in 2018. According to *the 2018 China Blockchain E-Government Research Report*, there are seven main application scenarios of China's blockchain in e-government: government audit, digital identity, data sharing, public-related supervision, electronic bill, electronic certificate deposit and export supervision [10]. On the whole, the consensus on the application of blockchain in government affairs is mainly the traceability and charitable management of food, drugs and dangerous goods. However, from the technical characteristics of blockchain, it also has unique advantages in citizen information management, social credit, network security, data sharing, information disclosure, automatic approval or punishment, law enforcement supervision, etc., which provides a new technical solution for improving the development level of e-government in China and building an integrated law enforcement supervision system with transparency, high efficiency and symmetrical information.

As for the judicial application of blockchain, the Procuratorial Technology Information Research Center of the Supreme People's Procuratorate has established a

"Blockchain Technology Laboratory" to explore the establishment of a system platform for the application of blockchain technology in procuratorial work and to study solutions to problems such as lack of trust in the process of data sharing in the industry. In August 2018, initiated by the Supreme Inspection, the Wuhan Municipal Prosecutor's Office of Hubei Province and Wuhan University, Wuhan Fire Information Integration Technology Co., Ltd., Zhejiang Nuqin Technology Co., Ltd. and other five units set up a "Intelligent Inspection Innovation Research Institute Inspection Blockchain Joint Laboratory". The laboratory takes procurator blockchain research as the main direction and explores the applications of blockchain technology in the procuratorate, such as blockchain technology in the storage, information system identity management and other applications [11]. Hangzhou Internet Court officially launched the first judicial blockchain in China on September 18, 2018, after it pronounced the first case in China with blockchain as the deposit certificate. The blockchain consists of three layers of structure: one is the blockchain program.Users can record the whole process of operation behavior on the blockchain directly through the program, such as online submission of electronic contract, rights protection process, details of service process and other electronic evidence;The second is the full link capability layer of blockchain. It mainly provides trusted services for real-name authentication, electronic signature, timestamp, data storage and the whole process of block chain; Third, the judicial alliance layer. Blockchain technology is used to connect notary offices, CA/RA institutions, judicial authentication centers and courts, and each unit becomes a node in the chain. The judicial blockchain makes the entire process of the generation, storage, dissemination, and use of electronic data credible [12]. The credibility of electronic data evidence is undoubtedly the key issue of judicial justice and the innovation of Hangzhou Internet Court is undoubtedly worthy of recognition. At the same time, it should be noted that the judicial application space of blockchain is very large, which should not be limited to the civil field, and its functions have yet to be developed and applied to judicial practice. At present, public security organs, procuratorial organs and judicial organs are discussing and trying to apply blockchain to solve some judicial problems. It can be put on the agenda to use block chain to build the whole process of criminal litigation system on the chain with trial as the center. The full-process litigation system on this chain helps to place the entire litigation process in the technical guarantee of blockchain information transparency, constant data, credible evidence, and automatic triggering of relevant judicial actions. In particular, it helps to solve the problem of tampering, destruction and concealment of evidence in the investigation stage, so as to prevent unjust, false and wrong cases.

4   Conclusion

Blockchain is called "the technology that is most likely to change the business model in the next decade", but it is also called a haven for criminal activities, Ponzi schemes, anarchy and authoritarianism [13]. In addition, the current blockchain still has high power consumption, high storage, high latency (relative to real-time), high cost, low application, low privacy, low throughput, and no modification (error elimination) performance defects. The idea of blockchain reshaping the world may be exaggerated, but with the further application of blockchain in the future, its foresight will gradually become apparent. From the perspective of the rule of law, it is necessary to evaluate the value of the rule of law of block chain objectively, actively expand the practical function of the rule of law of block chain, and make full use of the technical characteristics of block chain to promote the modernization of the rule of law.

Acknowledgments. This paper is supported by the Major Program of the National Social Science Fund of China "Theoretical Model and Practical Approach of Integrating Socialist Core Values into the Construction of Rule of Law in Smart Society" (No.20VHJ009).

References

1. The official Xinhua News Agency: EU Launches New Mechanism to 'Embrace' Blockchain Technology. Financial Times. https://www.cailianpress.com/roll/211514. Accessed 10 Sept 2018
2. Li, D., Long, H., Lu, Y.: Construction of academic journal publishing integrity system based on block chain technology. J. Chongqing Technol. Business Univ. (Soc. Sci. Edn.) **37**(5), 116–121 (2020)
3. Liu, J., Sun, C., Yuan, Y.: Hot blockchain fields and frontier paths in China — based on citespace econometric analysis. J. Chongqing Univ. Posts Telecommun. (Soc. Sci. Edn.) (6), 121–129 (2020)
4. Hu, L., Yang, Z.: The modern transformation of traditional Chinese legal culture. J. Xi'an Jiaotong Univ. (Soc. Sci. Edn.) (1) (2004)
5. Wu, J.: Spanish Legislation Promotes Blockchain Applications in Public Governance, on Giant Push Chain. https://www.jutuilian.com/article-62541-1.html. Accessed 20 Sept 2018
6. Zheng, G.: Blockchain and future rule of law. Oriental Law J. (5) (2018)
7. Zhang, L.: Blockchain technology can't replace centralized governance. Democracy Sci. (4) (2018)
8. Xue, X.: Breaking the legislation bottleneck with blockchain. https://www.sohu.com/a/220894983_100091728. Accessed 10 Sept 2018
9. Liang, Q.: Blockchain standards will be formulated. Econ. Inf. Daily A01, May 10 2018
10. Chain Tower Think Tank: 2018 China blockchain e-government research report, on the China e-government network. http://www.e-gov.org.cn/article-167531.html. Accessed 10 Oct 2018
11. Wen, Q.: Wuhan: procuratorial blockchain laboratory signs cooperation agreement with several units, tencent. https://mp.weixin.qq.com/s/dmSuIjZZPLhWv_DQFNqIng. Accessed 20 Aug 2018
12. Wang, C., Zhang, M., Wu, W.: Hangzhou internet court judicial blockchain online. Legal Daily, 3rd edn, 20 Sept 2018
13. Warbach, K.: Trust but verification: why blockchain needs law, translated by Lin Shaowai, East. Law J. (4) (2018)

Blockchain Services and Applications

PolyChain: A Generic Blockchain as a Service Platform

Shan Jiang$^{(\boxtimes)}$, Jiannong Cao, Juncen Zhu, and Yinfeng Cao

Department of Computing, The Hong Kong Polytechnic University,
Hong Kong, China
{cssjiang,csjcao,csjzhu1,csyfcao}@comp.polyu.edu.hk

Abstract. In recent years, blockchain technology has been attracting intensive attention from both the industries and academia because of its capability of rebuilding trust in trustless environments. There are increasing demands for developing and delivering blockchain applications and services in an agile and continuous way. To this end, Blockchain as a Service (BaaS) emerges which refers to cloud-based blockchain infrastructure developed by a vendor allowing users to develop, host, and use their own blockchain components, functions, and applications. There are many BaaS platforms developed by industries and academia, e.g., Bitcoin, Ethereum, and Hyperledger Fabric. However, they are either limited in scalability or difficult for configuration and customization. In this paper, we propose and develop PolyChain, a generic BaaS platform with high modularity, flexibility, scalability, reliability, and security, which are achieved with the following three design principles. First, each blockchain node is designed as four modularized components, e.g., network, storage, consensus, and application, based on the functionalities. Second, the components in a logic blockchain node interact via communication interfaces and can be deployed on different physical nodes. Finally, the component deployment is optimized based on the capabilities of the physical nodes. We believe PolyChain may benefit the industries and academia in agile development and continuous delivery of blockchain prototypes and applications.

Keywords: Blockchain · Blockchain as a Service · Blockchain platform · Blockchain architecture · Blockchain applications

1 Introduction

Blockchain is a technology of distributed ledger for trustless data management with auditability. In 2008, Nakamoto developed Bitcoin [10], which is a kind of cryptocurrency and also the first application of blockchain. Later on, the academic and industries have developed a wide range of applications based on blockchain leveraging its distinctive features of decentralization, transparency, and immutability. The application domains range from cryptocurrencies [14], education [13], healthcare [7], to manufacturing [6], etc.

The development of blockchain technology mainly experienced three stages: 1.0, 2.0, and 3.0+. blockchain 1.0 is a programmable currency, e.g., Bitcoin [10],

© Springer Nature Singapore Pte Ltd. 2021
H.-N. Dai et al. (Eds.): BlockSys 2021, CCIS 1490, pp. 459–472, 2021.
https://doi.org/10.1007/978-981-16-7993-3_36

related to money transfer, remittance, and digital payment. With the integration of smart contracts in blockchain systems, the blockchain technology enters the 2.0 era, in which the representative application is Ethereum [14]. Since the 2.0 era, blockchain has received unprecedented attention all around the world, and enterprises began to develop blockchain-based applications. As a result, enterprise-customized blockchain solutions (blockchain 3.0+) began to appear, in which Hyperledger Fabric [1] is an outstanding project.

With the popularity of blockchain technology, there are increasing demands for developing and delivering blockchain applications and services agilely and continuously. Moreover, many start-ups are eager to promote blockchain-related entrepreneurship even without enough hardware. The technology push and market pull give birth to the concept of blockchain as a service (BaaS), which refers to cloud-based blockchain infrastructure developed by a vendor allowing users to develop, host, and use their blockchain components, functions, and applications.

At present, many enterprises have launched the BaaS platforms, among which Bitcoin, Ethereum, and Hyperledger Fabric are the most popular ones. However, they are either limited in scalability or difficult for configuration and customization. In academia, the researchers have proposed several BaaS solutions, however, they are either conceptual [11,12], for specific applications [2–4,8], not deployed in real-world applications [9,17]. The evolution of blockchain demands a generic BaaS platform while existing platforms can hardly provide.

In this paper, we propose PolyChain, a generic BaaS platform with distinctive advantages of flexibility, scalability, reliability, security, and modularity. The main contributions of this paper are as follows:

– We design PolyChain, a generic BaaS platform that may benefit the industries and academia in agile development and continuous delivery of blockchain prototypes and applications.
– We evaluate PolyChain extensively in terms of flexibility, scalability, reliability, security, and modularity.
– We deploy PolyChain with three example applications in authenticable transcripts, big data sharing, and food traceability.

The rest of this paper is organized as follows. In Sect. 2, we introduce the related work and articulate the motivations of this work. In Sect. 3, we introduce the five design goals and three design principles of PolyChain. Section 4 presents the system architecture and component design of PolyChain. Three example applications based on PolyChain are demonstrated in Sect. 5. Finally, Sect. 6 concludes the paper.

2   Related Work

In this section, we introduce the existing BaaS platforms in industry and academia separately and analyze their shortcomings.

In industry, Bitcoin [10], Ethereum [14], and Hyperledger Fabric [1] are the three representative BaaS platforms in blockchain 1.0, 2.0, and 3.0+, respectively. Bitcoin, a cryptocurrency invented in 2008, is the first application of blockchain. Although Bitcoin is a great success whose market capitalization hit 1 trillion US dollars in 2021, it suffers from the issues of poor scalability, no support for smart contracts, and difficulties in customization. As a result, the enterprises seldom employ Bitcoin as the BaaS platform.

In 2014, Ethereum was initiated with the support of smart contracts. The developers can freely develop decentralized applications by writing smart contracts on Ethereum. Microsoft announced in November 2015 that it provides Ethereum Blockchain as a Service (EBaaS) on Microsoft Azure. EBaaS allows financial service customers and partners to quickly build and test their applications at a low cost in a ready-made development/test/production environment. It allows users to use industry-leading frameworks to quickly create private, public, and consortium-based blockchain environments and distribute their blockchain products through Azure's World Wide distributed platform. This makes Azure an excellent development/test/production environment for blockchain applications. However, they still have shortcomings, such as insufficient scalability and difficulties to customize the consensus mechanism.

Hyperledger Fabric is a permissioned blockchain infrastructure providing a modular architecture with a delineation of roles among the nodes in the infrastructure, smart contract execution environments, and configurable consensus and membership services. For example, the IBM blockchain network is built on the Hyperledger Fabric stack. Although Hyperledger Fabric is developing very fast, it merely supports public blockchain, provides insufficient native consensus mechanisms, and is very difficult for inexperienced developers to use.

Besides Bitcoin, Ethereum, and Hyperledger Fabric, large enterprises such as Amazon, Baidu, and Alibaba are also developing their BaaS platforms as parts of their cloud services.

In academia, the researchers have been developing BaaS solutions. In [11], Samaniego et al. propose BaaS for the first time. However, it is conceptual and only shows a set of experimental results. Singh et al. analyze the management, governance, and trust issues of BaaS platforms while merely touch the technical details [12]. In [2] and [3], Alia et al. and Aujla et al. consider the integration of BaaS with end-edge-cloud networks and software-defined networks for applications in unmanned aerial vehicles and smart city, receptively, which are pioneer but lacks design details of BaaS.

The two recent research works introduce two BaaS platforms, i.e., NutBaaS [17] and uBaaS [9]. NutBaaS is a BaaS platform providing blockchain service over cloud computing environments, such as network deployment and system monitoring, smart contracts analysis, and testing. Based on these services, developers can focus on the business code to explore how to apply blockchain technology more appropriately to their business scenarios, without bothering to maintain and monitor the system. Although NutBaaS has a clear system architecture with technical approaches to enhance reliability and security, the design of the different layers remains unclear. In uBaaS, various services including deployment as a service, design pattern as a service, and auxiliary services are provided. The deployment of uBaaS is not bound to the cloud service providers or the blockchain platform. The proposed solutions are evaluated using a real-world quality tracing use case in terms of feasibility and scalability. UBaaS focuses on the vendor-irrelevant design and provides the implementation details. However, the advantages of uBaaS in terms of security, flexibility, etc. over existing BaaS platforms are unclear.

To conclude, the existing BaaS platforms from academia and industry are not enough in terms of modularity, flexibility, scalability, reliability, and security. The evolution of blockchain technology demands a generic BaaS platform.

3   PolyChain Design Goals and Principles

In this section, we introduce five primary goals of PolyChain and three design principles to meet the goals.

3.1   Design Goals

PolyChain pursues the following five goals:

- *Modularity*: refers to the degree of decomposition of the components. High modularity makes it possible to reuse the developed components, reduces the development costs, and enables transplantation of the components.
- *Flexibility*: refers to the degree of support for diversified customization. Users can flexibly choose system parameters, components, consensus protocols to build a blockchain system that meets their own development requirements.
- *Scalability*: refers to the ability of the system to remain high-performance when the workload increases. It is embodied in the reasonable arrangement of resources and the optimal allocation of hardware.
- *Reliability*: means that the ability of the system to run continuously and stably even with internal faults.
- *Security*: means that the ability of the system to resist various external attacks. In particular, in the BaaS platform, the main resistance is the single point of failure, that is, the broken of one component will not cause the failure of the entire system.

3.2   Design Principles

PolyChain employs three design principles, component modularization, distributed deployment, and resource optimization, to achieve the five design goals.

Component Modularization. In a blockchain system, normally there are many fixed components and layers for different functionalities that make the entire system complex, bloated and hard to develop, thus making it harder to design applications over it. In Ethereum, there are Ethereum virtual machines, miners, blocks, transactions, consensus algorithms, accounts, smart contracts, mining nodes, etc. The developers almost only can design applications through smart contracts instead of modifying every component they need like consensus. In Hyperledger Fabric, there are also many fixed components and relationships like peer, orderer, endorser, and membership service provider. The design space of developers is also very limited since they need to choose and combine these components to form their network, which means it is hard to change the consensus algorithm or database choices.

The reason why there are many fixed components, and most of them are unmodifiable is that they do not separate various functionalities well within the entire blockchain system, which brings difficulties and costs for developers to design the application they want.

We address the issue by decomposing each blockchain node into four components, namely application component, consensus component, network component, and storage component, based on the functionalities. Each component focus on one dedicated group of functionality. Such an approach achieves modularity and makes the system easy to understand, develop, and maintain. Meanwhile, since the interface of each module is well-defined, their implementation can be changed independently according to different application/experiment need without rebuilding the rest of the system which achieves flexibility. Because the functions are divided into various components, each component does not affect each other, the security of the system is also guaranteed.

Distributed Deployment. Deployment is another key issue for the current blockchain platform. In Ethereum, for the smart contract, developers need to compile their Solidity code into byte-codes, use APIs for deployment, and finally use the web3 library to call the contracts. Such procedures are unfriendly for those who not familiar with blockchain.

As a BaaS platform, we provide multiple deployment methods through web interfaces. Developers can transform the components they design into an executable program, install script or Docker image then upload and configure them, and finally form a blockchain network. In this way, developers can also Initialize or update their components or nodes in platforms, with monitoring of them. This deployment method ensures the flexibility of the platform.

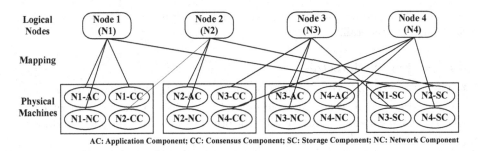

AC: Application Component; CC: Consensus Component; SC: Storage Component; NC: Network Component

Fig. 1. PolyChain deployment model

We propose a novel distributed deployment scheme to ensure the reliability and security of the system. First, we identify the concepts of logical nodes and physical machines. Each logical node consists of four components while the components of a logical node can be deployed in different physical machines. As shown in Fig. 1, the application component, network component, and consensus component of logical node 1 are in physical machine 1 while the storage component of logical node 1 is in physical machine 4.

The advantage of the deployment scheme is that it can resist single-point attacks very well. The damage of one component will not affect the operation of the entire blockchain network. Moreover, the physical machines may have different specialized capabilities and are good at hosting different components. For example, storage components can be deployed in physical machines with a high capability of storage.

Resource Optimization. Finally, we optimize the component deployment based on the functions of physical nodes. We mainly use the following two methods to ensure the scalability of the platform.

Each major component is also a portable distributed sub-system, which means that the components can be implemented in different threads/processes or hosts. Some components, e.g. application component and consensus component, may be implemented in a parallelized manner to maximize transaction processing throughput. In contrast, some components, e.g. storage component, may be implemented in a distributed manner to scale for intensive and complex querying and supporting the huge data volume. The components communicate with each other with fixed protocols and frameworks. Such an approach also enables the scalability and cross-platform capability of the system.

Meanwhile, the components in the platform are reusable. We provide some pre-defined components, e.g., proof-of-work consensus component for developers to use and form their network at the beginning. Developers can also reuse their components built by themselves. This approach will reduce the development cost and make the design of applications more flexible.

4   System Architecture and Component Design

In this section, we demonstrate the system architecture and component design of PolyChain in detail.

4.1   System Architecture

In PolyChain, there are two kinds of entities, i.e., users and PolyChain nodes. The users generate application data and enjoy the services provided by PolyChain. The PolyChain nodes interact with each other to maintain the blockchain and provide services to the users.

Figure 2 depicts the system architecture of PolyChain. The blockchain is maintained by a network of nodes connecting with each other. Each PolyChain node consists of four components with functionalities as follows:

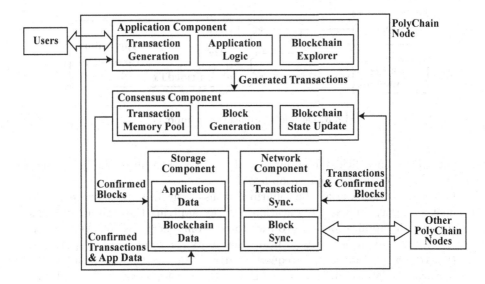

Fig. 2. PolyChain system architecture

- *Application component* (AC) manages the application logic interacting with the users. Particularly, it interacts with the users through predefined application interfaces, generates raw transactions, and applies the confirmed transactions to execute the application logic. Furthermore, it provides interfaces to display the blockchain data, i.e., confirmed blockchain and transactions.
- *Consensus component* (CC) packs the raw transactions into a linked chain of blocks agreed by the PolyChain network. Such a component maintains the pool of raw transactions, packs transactions into blocks, and updates the blockchain state given the blocks from other nodes.
- *Storage component* (SC) manages the application data and blockchain data, which implies the application states and blockchain states, respectively.
- *Network component* (NC) connects the PolyChain node with other ones and synchronizes the transactions and blocks.

The PolyChain system architecture allows the components to be implemented separately. In the following, we explain the design of the four components.

4.2 Application Component

As shown in Fig. 3, there are three APIs in the application component: TxGEN (invokable by users), ONCONFIRMEDTX (invokable by the storage component), and GETDATA (invokable by users).

- TxGEN takes data from the users as input, generates a transaction based on pre-defined formats, and sends the generated transaction to the consensus component (CC.ONNEWTX). In PolyChain, a transaction is a dictionary

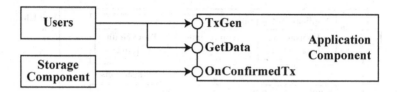

Fig. 3. Design of application component

with pre-defined fields. The purpose of TxGen is to fill in the fields based on the user data and application logic.

– OnConfirmedTx takes the confirmed transactions from the storage component as input, generates application data by applying the transactions, and submits the application data to the storage component (SC.OnAppData).
– GetData takes parameters from the users as input and responds to the requested data. The requested data can be the application and blockchain data requested from the storage component (SC.GetData, and even the transaction memory pool from the consensus component (CC.GetMemPool) depending on the willingness of the developers.

4.3   Consensus Component

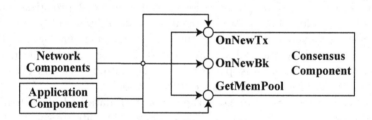

Fig. 4. Design of consensus component

As shown in Fig. 4, there are three APIs in the consensus component: OnNewTx (invokable by the application and network components), OnNewBk (invokable by the network component), and GetMemPool (invokable by the application and network components).

– OnNewTx takes a new transaction tx as input and updates the transaction memory pool. It checks whether tx is already in the memory pool or the blockchain. If not, it will send tx to the network component (NC.OnNewTx) for broadcasting in the blockchain network.
– OnNewBk takes a new block bk as input and updates the blockchain state. It checks whether the block height is correct and whether the hash values match. If yes, it will store bk in the storage component (SC.OnConfirmedBk) and

send *bk* to the network component (NC.ONNEWBK) for broadcasting in the blockchain network.

– GETMEMPOOL responds to the requests with the set of unconfirmed transactions in the memory pool. Such an API is useful for transaction synchronization and state debug.

4.4 Storage Component

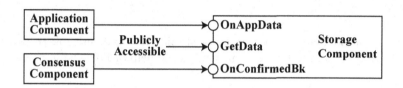

Fig. 5. Design of storage component

As shown in Fig. 5, there are three APIs in the storage component: ONCONFIRMEDBK (invokable by the consensus component), ONAPPDATA (invokable by the application component), and GETDATA (publicly accessible).

– ONCONFIRMEDBK takes a block as input, updates the blockchain data, and sends the confirmed transactions in the block to the application component (AC.ONCONFIRMEDTX).
– ONAPPDATA takes the application data as input for storage.
– GETDATA responds with the corresponding data based on the parameters.

4.5 Network Component

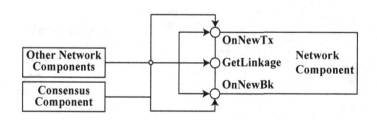

Fig. 6. Design of network component

As shown in Fig. 6, there are three APIs in the network component: ONNEWTX (invokable by the consensus component and other network components), ONNEWBK (invokable by the consensus component and other network components), and GETLINKAGE (invokable by other network components).

– ONNEWTX takes a transaction as input and sends it to the consensus component (CC.ONNEWTX) and other network components (NC.ONNEWTX) for broadcasting purpose.
– ONNEWBK takes a block as input and sends it to the consensus component (CC.ONNEWBK) and other network components (NC.ONNEWBK) for broadcasting purpose.
– GETLINKAGE responds to the request with the set of connected network components of other blockchain nodes.

5   Case Studies

In this section, we demonstrate three case studies, i.e., authenticable transcripts, big data sharing, and food traceability, with the help of PolyChain.

5.1   PolyScript: Authenticable University Record Management

In almost all universities, many procedures are complicated and time-consuming because of the numerous data distributed among departments. For example, the confirmation of the examination results may go through the lecturers, departmental general office, faculty general office, research office, and finally the student portal. Blockchain can serve as a secure communication platform connecting various university offices, which can improve the time efficiency of university affairs. Moreover, electronic transcripts and certificates can be generated on the blockchain, which is environmental-friendly, convenient, and anti-counterfeiting. To this end, we propose PolyScript, a PolyChain-based system for authenticable management of university records.

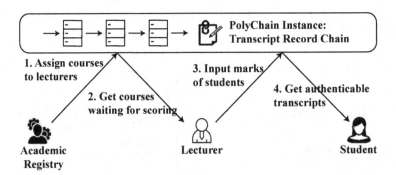

Fig. 7. PolyScript system architecture

Figure 7 depicts the system architecture of PolyScript. The university (or multiple universities as an alliance) will maintain the PolyChain instance, which is responsible for storing the university records, e.g., student registration information, course information, and examination results.

Each transaction on the PolyChain instance contains the following fields:

- TIME: the timestamp when the piece of record is submitted.
- STUID: the unique identifier of the student.
- COURSEID: the unique identifier of the course.
- LECTURERID: the unique identifier of the lecturer.
- YEARSEM: the academic year and semester of the piece of record.
- GRADE: the examination result.

With PolyChain, a set of university record management functions can be supported as follows:

- *Course assignment* (open to the academic registry): assigning courses to the corresponding lecturers.
- *Marking* (open to the lecturers): input marking results of the students.
- *Transcript generation* (open to the students): generating authenticable transcripts based on the marking results stored on PolyChain.

5.2   AI3: PolyChain Enabled Big Data Sharing

Big data sharing refers to the act of the data sharers to share big data so that the sharees can find, access, and use it in the agreed ways. In recent years, big data sharing is more and more popular due to its wide applications such as big data trading and cross-domain data analytics. Traditional big data sharing platforms can be classified into data hosting centers and data aggregation centers. However, they suffer from either privacy or authenticity issues. To this end, we cooperate with Huawei Technologies Co., Ltd. to develop AI3, a PolyChain-based big data sharing platform [5,15]. In AI3, we propose to leverage two loosely-coupled blockchains, metadata chain and sharing data chain, to guarantee the privacy of the original data and the authenticity of the sharing records.

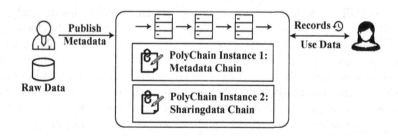

Fig. 8. AI3 system architecture

Figure 8 depicts the AI3 system architecture. All the data sharers and sharees join the blockchain network and maintain two PolyChain instances, i.e., metadata chain and sharing data chain, which are responsible for storing the shared metadata and sharing records, respectively. Note that only the metadata will be publicly accessible while the original data is stored by the data sharers locally.

Each transaction on the metadata chain contains fields as follows:

- TIME: the timestamp when the metadata is published.
- PUBLISHER: the one who published the metadata.
- URL: a publicly accessible web address to the metadata.
- DATAHASH: the hash value of the original data.
- FILETYPE: the type of the original file.

Each transaction on the sharing data chain contains the following fields:

- TIMEREQUEST: the timestamp of requesting data.
- TIMESHARING: the timestamp of sharing data.
- SHARER: the one who share the data.
- SHAREE: the one who use the data.
- METADATAHASH: the unique identifier of the metadata to be shared (linked with metdata chain).

With the above two PolyChain instances, a set of big data sharing functions can be supported within AI3:

- *Data publishing*: the data sharers publish their data using metadata chain.
- *Data searching*: the data sharees use keywords to search the available data on the metadata chain.
- *Data transfer*: the data sharers transfer the requested data to data sharees with records on sharing data chain.
- *Nearline computation*: the data sharees use predefined functions to perform the calculation on the shared data with permissions from the data sharers. The data sharing records are also stored on sharing data chain.

5.3 Food Traceability

Food traceability refers to the ability to follow the trajectories of food products and their ingredients through all steps along the food supply chain. Food traceability helps the stakeholders to better manage the food supply chain and increase of confidence of the customers. Blockchain technology has been widely adopted in food traceability because the transparent and immutable data on blockchain makes the product tracing results remarkably reliable. We cooperate with Alibaba Group Holding Limited to develop a federated blockchain-based solution for ensuring the provenance and authenticity of food items [16].

Figure 9 depicts the system architecture of the PolyChain-based food traceability system. The stakeholders along the food supply chain will join the blockchain network as federated members and maintain the PolyChain instance, which is responsible for storing the food transactional records and providing query services. There are three kinds of roles, i.e., federated member, administrator, and customer, who have different authorities for querying the blockchain data.

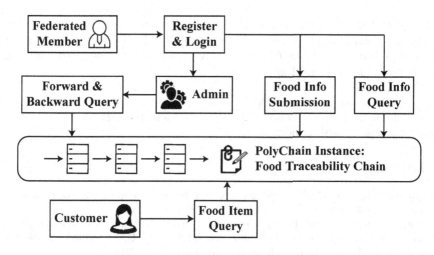

Fig. 9. System architecture of blockchain food traceability

Each transaction on the PolyChain instance contains the following fields:

- TIME: the timestamp when the record is submitted.
- LOCATION: the location when the record is submitted.
- PUBLISHER: the one who submitted the record.
- SRCITEMS: the unique identifiers of the source food items.
- DSTITEMS: the unique identifiers of the result food items.
- DESCRIPTION: description information, e.g., access control info, submitted by the publisher.

With PolyChain, a set of food traceability functions can be supported:

- *Food item query* (open to the customers): given the identifier of a food item, query the origin.
- *Food info submission* (open to the federated members): submit the food product records.
- *Food info query* (open to the federated members): given the identifier of a food item, query all the related information along the food supply chain.
- *Forward and backward query* (open to the administrators): given the identifier of an item (it is not necessarily a food item, e.g., can be the ingredients), query all the records about the source and result items.

6   Conclusion

In this paper, we propose and develop PolyChain, a BaaS platform with flexibility, scalability, reliability, security, and modularity. We employ the design principles of component modularization, distributed deployment, and resource optimization to provide the above distinctive features. PolyChain is implemented and deployed with applications of authenticable transcripts, big data sharing, and food traceability, which shows its practicability. In the future, we will evaluate the performance of PolyChain extensively, add support of smart contracts, and deploy more real-world applications.

Acknowledgments. This research is supported by GDSTC Key Technologies R&D Programme with project number 2020B010164002 and Hong Kong RGC Research Impact Fund (RIF) with project number R5034-18.

References

1. Androulaki, E., et al.: Hyperledger fabric: a distributed operating system for permissioned blockchains. In: ACM EuroSys, pp. 1–15 (2018)
2. Asheralieva, A., Niyato, D.: Distributed dynamic resource management and pricing in the IoT systems with blockchain-as-a-service and UAV-enabled mobile edge computing. IEEE Internet Things J. **7**(3), 1974–1993 (2019)
3. Aujla, G.S., Singh, M., Bose, A., Kumar, N., Han, G., Buyya, R.: Blocksdn: blockchain-as-a-service for software defined networking in smart city applications. IEEE Network **34**(2), 83–91 (2020)
4. Chen, Y., Gu, J., Chen, S., Huang, S., Wang, X.S.: A full-spectrum blockchain-as-a-service for business collaboration. In: IEEE ICWS, pp. 219–223 (2019)
5. Jiang, S., et al.: Privacy-preserving and efficient multi-keyword search over encrypted data on blockchain. In: IEEE Blockchain, pp. 405–410 (2019)
6. Jiang, S., Cao, J., Wu, H., Yang, Y.: Fairness-based packing of industrial IoT data in permissioned blockchains. IEEE Trans. Ind. Inf. **17**(11), 7639–7649 (2020)
7. Jiang, S., Cao, J., Wu, H., Yang, Y., Ma, M., He, J.: Blochie: a blockchain-based platform for healthcare information exchange. In: IEEE SMARTCOMP, pp. 49–56 (2018)
8. Li, D., Deng, L., Cai, Z., Souri, A.: Blockchain as a service models in the internet of things management: systematic review. Trans. Emerg. Telecommun. Technol., e4139 (2020). https://doi.org/10.1002/ett.4139
9. Lu, Q., Xu, X., Liu, Y., Weber, I., Zhu, L., Zhang, W.: Ubaas: a unified blockchain as a service platform. Future Gener. Comput. Syst. **101**, 564–575 (2019)
10. Nakamoto, S.: Bitcoin: a peer-to-peer electronic cash system. Technical Report (2019)
11. Samaniego, M., Jamsrandorj, U., Deters, R.: Blockchain as a service for IoT. In: IEEE iThings/GreenCom/CPSCom/SmartData, pp. 433–436 (2016)
12. Singh, J., Michels, J.D.: Blockchain as a service (baas): providers and trust. In: IEEE EuroSP Workshops, pp. 67–74 (2018)
13. Turkanovic, M., Holbl, M., Kosic, K., Hericko, M., Kamisalic, A.: Eductx: a blockchain-based higher education credit platform. IEEE Access **6**, 5112–5127 (2018)
14. Wood, G., et al.: Ethereum: a secure decentralised generalised transaction ledger. Ethereum Project Yellow Paper **151**(2014), 1–32 (2014)
15. Wu, H., Cao, J., Jiang, S., Yang, R., Yang, Y., Hey, J.: Tsar: a fully-distributed trustless data sharing platform. In: IEEE SMARTCOMP, pp. 350–355 (2018)
16. Wu, H., et al.: Data management in supply chain using blockchain: challenges and a case study. In: IEEE ICCCN, pp. 1–8 (2019)
17. Zheng, W., Zheng, Z., Chen, X., Dai, K., Li, P., Chen, R.: Nutbaas: a blockchain-as-a-service platform. IEEE Access **7**, 134422–134433 (2019)

Incremental Forensics Snapshot of Digital Evidence Method Using Differencing Algorithm and Blockchain

Fanjin Meng[1], Yong Ding[1,2,3(✉)], Dewei Chen[4], Fang Yuan[5], and Zhenyu Li[1]

[1] School of Computer Science and Information Security, Guilin University of Electronic Technology, Guilin 541004, China
[2] Cyberspace Security Research Center, Peng Cheng Laboratory, Shenzhen 518055, China
[3] Guilin 541004, China
[4] School of Electronics and Information, Chongqing Institute of Engineering, Chongqing 400056, China
[5] Communications Bureau of the Ministry of Foreign Affairs, Beijing 100045, China

Abstract. The application of the E-government has been improving the quality of public service in many countries. The emergence of blockchain technology with the characteristics of tamper-proof, traceability and decentralization has brought new opportunities for E-government development. As one of the most suitable technical solutions for E-government, consortium blockchain has the advantages of better controllability, faster transaction speed, and access control. However, considering consortium blockchain's partial decentralization, there is a possibility of collusion among multiple participants. Therefore it is necessary to find effective regulatory methods to enhance the credibility of consortium blockchain. This paper presents a blockchain snapshot forensics method based on blockchain and the differencing algorithm. By extracting incremental information of digital forensics content through the differencing algorithm, we can significantly improve the storage performance of the supervision blockchain. Our method can generate multiple versions of forensics data for each original data in the business blockchain and check out the specified version of digital forensics according to every forensics data. Compared with the full data storage scheme, our scheme can reduce the storage cost of blockchain by about seven times on average. Furthermore, compared with the summary information storage scheme, our scheme can recover complete evidence data. And the time consuming of incremental data extraction and recovery are within the acceptable range for the supervision blockchain.

Keywords: Blockchain · Differencing algorithm · Digital forensics · Fisco bcos · Consortium chain

© Springer Nature Singapore Pte Ltd. 2021
H.-N. Dai et al. (Eds.): BlockSys 2021, CCIS 1490, pp. 473–485, 2021.
https://doi.org/10.1007/978-981-16-7993-3_37

1   Introduction

With the increasing demand for government services [1], E-government has been widely used and proved to have a tremendously positive effect [6] as one of the relatively maturely forms of government service. E-government, both in developed and developing countries, has proven to improve efficiency and transparency, reduce corruption and operating costs, facilitate government departments' operation [2,7,17]. E-government systems also play a significant role in some mega-events. During the outbreak of the COVID-19, governments and international organizations disclosed epidemic prevention information through E-government systems and provided online health services to the public, which has played a positive role in controlling the epidemic [19].

At present, how to prompt the credibility of E-government is one of the main problems to be solved. The premise for citizens to use E-services is to establish a foundation of trust. Otherwise, people are more willing to handle business through offline channels [3]. Therefore, the credibility of E-government is particularly critical. Increasing information openness and setting up regulatory measures are effective measures to enhance credibility.

Blockchain is a kind of distributed ledger in a peer-to-peer network, in which each node follows the consensus protocol. It maintains a growing list of public access records protected by encryption and are not tampered with or modified. Blockchain has characteristics of tamper-proof, traceability and de-neutralization, which can improve the quality and capacity of government services, and improve the transparency and accessibility of government information. Government services' credibility are the main aspects of people's evaluation of the quality of government services [10]. With the rapid development of blockchain technology and blockchain technology's gradual maturity, blockchain technology, mainly the consortium blockchain, is gradually applied to E-government services. In order to improve the credibility of E-government services, it is necessary to improve the efficient regulatory mechanism.

1.1   Our Solution

This paper proposes the following solutions for the supervision blockchain forensics based on blockchain, differencing algorithm, compression algorithm, and other technologies:

1. The differencing algorithm is used to extract incremental data for creating, retrieve, update, and delete(CRUD) operation on the business chain, the differencing algorithm is used to reduce the storage space of the supervision blockchain occupied by the forensics data, and blockchain as an immutable data source is used to store these different data. The last block's data is the change of the previous data, and each update will be added as a new block in the chain.
2. The compression algorithm is used to compress the incremental data further to reduce the storage space consumption of redundant data. Especially in

extreme cases, the differencing algorithm can not reduce the storage space consumption very well, and the compression algorithm will also play a maximum effect.

3. We present a solution for recovering each version of full evidence data by incremental data which saved in the supervision blockchain.

1.2   Our Construction

The remainder of this paper is organized as follows. Section 2 summarizes the related work. Section 3 presents the design of our system model. Section 4 describes key aspects of the implementation of digital forensics. Section 5 presents system performance analysis. Section 6 concludes the paper.

2   Related Work

Blockchain has gradually begun to be applied to E-government, such as applying it to Value Added Tax(VAT) systems to provide more efficient services [13]. Providers of E-government services are mainly government departments and organizations. The characteristics of consortium blockchain well meet the needs of E-government, which makes it a feasible solution to improve the service quality of E-government [5,20]. A consortium blockchain is that several pre-selected institutions or organizations participate in the management of the near blockchain. Each participating institution or organization is running one or more nodes in the blockchain. Consortium blockchain's each participating institution or organization runs one or more nodes in it. The data only allows different organizations in the system to read, write, send transactions, and joint record transaction data. Consortium blockchain implementation in the field of E-government requires safe and reliable supervision technology.

In order to realize the supervision of the business chain, the existing primary method is to use a double-chain structure to save the critical information of the business chain to the supervision blockchain [9]. There are three main ways to obtain and save forensics data for such a regulatory structure. One way is to extract digital abstract of evidence and then store evidence and abstract separately. Another way is to store evidence's abstracts in blockchain only [15]. In this way, the original evidence can not be restored only according to the summary information. Meanwhile, there are potential collision problems [4,18], which may cause the validity of the evidence information can not be effectively guaranteed. And the third way is whole evidence copy data storage [9]. However, for the business chain with large data size and lots of CRUD operations, storing whole copy data in the supervision chain every modification will result in a large amount of redundant data in the supervision chain. All nodes participating in the consensus network need to maintain a complete copy of the supervision blockchain, which requires vast storage space. Huge storage requirements also lead to endless ledger problems, such as adding new nodes to the blockchain takes too much time to download and validate the blockchain. Reduces storage performance and presents performance challenges to nodes in supervision blockchain networks [14].

Differencing algorithm is used to generate the shortest edit path of the string. The commonly used differencing algorithm has satisfactory performance, such as Myers' diff algorithm's time complexity is O(ND) which D is the size of the minimum edit script for two strings and N is the sum of the lengths of two strings, better than decision process algorithm [11]. Incremental data can be stored economically with differencing algorithms because the data change usually occupies only a tiny part of the complete copy. This way saves much storage [16], and the difference information can directly show what changes have been made to efficiently track data evolution through the difference section [8]. This kind of algorithm has been widely used in version control systems such as Git.

3   System Model

Blockchain can be regarded as a distributed ledger, which uses cryptography to generate data blocks. Each data block contains transaction information, and the data blocks are linked with each other. The main participants of E-government are government agencies and related enterprises, which correspond to the business chain in our model. The supervision blockchain provides regulators with relevant functional interfaces, access rights, and data with complete and verifiable for audit analysis. A dual blockchain structure for supervision of consortium chain is shown in Fig. 1. The forensics module collects forensics data through the world state of the business chain. The world state is a database that stores the current state of the ledger. By default, the ledger state is represented by key-value pairs. The program can query the ledger's current state directly through the world state without traversing the entire log to obtain the current value. The forensics module can query the business chain's current world state and does not need to traverse blocks to calculate the current state results. The forensics module processes and stores the data obtained from the business chain in the supervision chain, and the supervisor can read and parse the data stored in the supervision chain through the relevant interface. In dealing with the data on the supervision blockchain, we also use the word state.

Block is the minimum data unit on the supervision blockchain. Each time the evidence's incremental data is collected, a new block will be added to the supervision blockchain. The data structure of supervision blockchain is shown in Table 1.

4   Our Proposal

This section proposes a method that can generate multiple versions of incremental information for each original data in the business chain. To review some original evidence, it can recovery the specified version of digital forensics according to each incremental data.

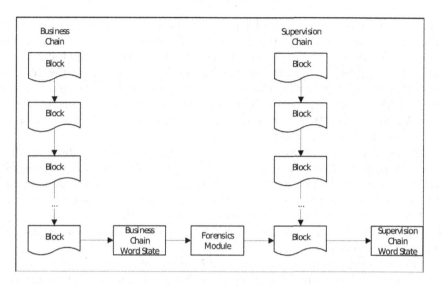

Fig. 1. Dual b lockchain architecture

Table 1. Data structure of block

Field	Explanation
HashAddress	Hash address of current block
PrimaryKey	Identification of file corresponding to evidence
Version	Forensic data's version number, the initial value is 0
BaseHash	The original evidence's hash address of same file
PreviousHash	The previous version's hash address of same file
NodeSignature	The digital signature of the node that submitted this incremental data
TimeStamp	Forensic time stamp
Data	Forensic data in binary format

4.1   Incremental Data Extraction Module

The problem of extracting and storing incremental forensics data can be abstracted as finding the minimum editing distance between two texts. In other words, it is how to find the longest common subsequence (LCS). There are many algorithms to solve these problems, such as the gestalt pattern matching algorithm, which is now used in Python's difflib library [16]. And Myers' diff algorithm, which is now used in Git. We adopt Myers' diff algorithm in this paper. Myers'diff algorithm directly solved the equivalent problem of LCS, i.e., the minimum edit distance (MED) problem. This algorithm can generate the minimum edit script (SES) to describe the differences between two texts. The time complexity is O (ND). Taking two strings A and B as examples, N is the sum of the lengths of A and B, and D is the sum of the lengths of the different parts of two strings. Assuming that B is the new version of A, the algorithm will generate SES to convert A to B. The SES contains only two commands: delete from A and insert in B. The modification operation will be decomposed into a delete and insert operation [11].

In this paper, some optimization methods are added based on the algorithm. First, the prefix and suffix are compared, the same prefix and suffix are marked, and the prefixes and suffixes are excluded in the subsequent operation. Second, the module will determine whether there is an inclusion relationship between the two texts and if there is, the module will directly return the corresponding result. The Myers' diff algorithm generates three kinds of incremental data: unchanged, deleted, and inserted.

Unchangeable and deleted content will be discarded in the output of the differencing algorithm. Only the edit position, the deleted length, and the inserted content will be recorded. The increment information format is '[(edit position,(operation type, operation value)]', the edit position specifies which byte in the source file to start editing, the operation type '1' is inserted, '-n' is deleted n byte, the operation value specifies the inserted text content. The process of incremental data extraction is shown in left of Fig. 2. For the original text "abcdefghijklmn1234567890" and the modified text "acderpqijopklmn124566890", the approximate format of incremental information generation is as follows: "[(1, (−1,)), (4, (−5,)), (4, (1, 'rpqijop')), (17, (−1,)), (20, (−1,)), (20, (1, '6'))]".

4.2 Full Data Recovery Module

In general, the edited text is more similar to the first edition. The existing version control system solution based on blockchain compares the current text version with the content submitted last time [12]. Considering the possibility of the same part between the editing information is very low, leading to inefficient incremental data extraction. Moreover, it is necessary to restore all the editing information on the path when checking out to get the specified version. Correspondingly, we compare with the first version of the data instead of the previous version. All subsequent versions associate with the original version that is easy to visit. Furthermore, the incremental data can restore to complete evidence by visiting the original version hash address in the chain block.

The client builds a request to query the target evidence data. After receiving the request, the evidence recovery module compares the request's information with the supervision blockchain's current world state. If the request dost not have a version number or the version number is larger than the maximum version number of the corresponding document in the world state, the query will fail. Otherwise, the evidence recovery module will firstly get the latest version of the corresponding document and then find the requested version's hash address recursively in the world state. According to the hash address recorded in the requested version's block, the next step visits the original evidence. And then use the recovery of Myers' diff algorithm to process original evidence and incremental data to recover the requested evidence. The process of recover target evidence is shown in right of Fig. 2.

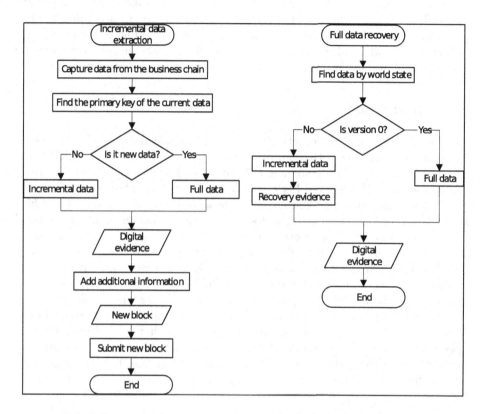

Fig. 2. Incremental data extraction and full data recovery flowchart

4.3 Version Control

Mainstream version control systems need to consider version bifurcation. However, in the application scenario of forensics data management, there will only single editing route of the incremental data. When writing incremental data to the supervision blockchain, the version control module first obtains the supervision blockchain's world state to determine whether the current version number exists. If not, the version control module will write full evidence into the supervision blockchain. Otherwise, the version control module will extract incremental data by Myers' diff algorithm, get the hash address and version number of corresponding original evidence and previous incremental data by querying the world state, and then package those data to writing into the supervision blockchain.

The supervision blockchain's form example is shown in Fig. 3. Only the block data fields related to version control are listed in the figure, "/" indicating the field value is null. In this figure, there are two version branches of two evidence data. The primary keys are text1 and text2, respectively. Supervision blockchain's world state records information for blocks 3 and 4. Assuming that we need to obtain version 1 of text1 data, block 2 is found according to the previous hash in block 4. And then, block 0 is found according to the base hash in block 4. Finally, full evidence data is recovered by original data in block 0 and incremental data in block 2 through the evidence recovery module.

5   Experiments

The core part of the incremental data extraction module and the full data recovery module are written in Python, version 3.7.1, running in windows 1020H2 On 64-bit systems. The test system is configured as I5-8400 3.8GHz 6C6T, 16G DDR4 2666Mhz. We selected Fisco bcos as the blockchain platform.

To determine running efficiency of our proposed model we designed test file specifically targeting two main modules of our model viz incremental data extraction module and full data recovery module. We uses Chinese and English text data sets to analyze the system's storage performance, intercepts the text with 10000 - 100000 characters as the original data, and generates the corresponding modified file according to each intercepted text. There are two parameters of the modified file: the modification radio and the statistical dispersion. Modification radio value the percentage of modified text to the original text. Statistical dispersion refers to the maximum number of characters that a word modification operation can edit. For example, statistical dispersion 10 means the maximum number of characters that can be continuously deleted, inserted, and replaced. The performance of the proposed solutions has been measured as illustrated below.

5.1   Performance Evaluation

We designed 100 rounds of test for two different modes under the condition of 100000 Chinese words text, 15% modification radio, and 100 statistical dispersion. Text in each experiment was modified randomly, and the execution time of critical modules was calculated. The results are shown in Fig. 4 and Fig. 5. The two modes are Line mode and Word mode. Line mode will split two texts into an array of strings and then reduce the texts to a string of hashes where each Unicode character represents one line. Do it in this way can indicate the speed of operation, but it will reduce the compression ratio. Word mode will run a line-level diff first to identify the changed areas, then rediff the parts for greater accuracy.

Performance evaluation results show that for the incremental data extraction module, line mode has better performance. In word mode, there are some timeout situations. When calculating the incremental data, if the execution time exceeds

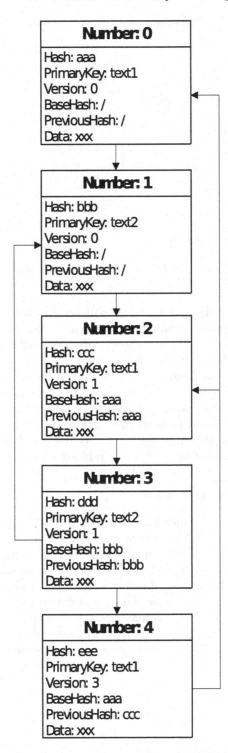

Fig. 3. Version control structure example

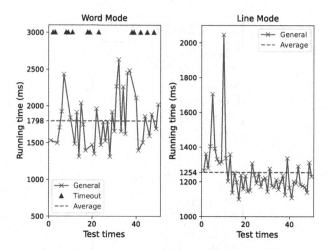

Fig. 4. Running time of incremental data extraction module in multiple experiments

the set abandonment time, the module will return the result that has been calculated. It is guaranteed that the results can always be calculated. In the phase of full data recovery, the average execution time of word mode is shorter, which is 3.37 times that of line mode.

We also calculate the corresponding data compression ratio, and the results are shown in Fig. 6. In general, compared with line mode, word mode has a better data compression ratio and average compression ratio. Generally speaking, word mode has better all-around performance. Although there are timeouts in word mode, the execution time can be limited by setting the abandonment time, and a better compression ratio can still be guaranteed.

5.2   The Size of the Blockchain

We implemented the basic blockchain system under the framework of Fisco bcos. Under the conditions of 10000 - 100000 words text, 1% - 90% modification rate and 10 - 1000 statistical dispersion, we designed 1667 rounds of test, and each time the text was randomly modified. We record and compare the average value of data on the blockchain under different conditions, and the results are shown in Fig. 7. Compared with incremental data, full data occupies 6.62 to 7.95 times of blockchain storage space. Experimental data show that incremental data can effectively reduce the storage space consumption of blockchain compared with the full data storage method of the evidence storage system based on blockchain.

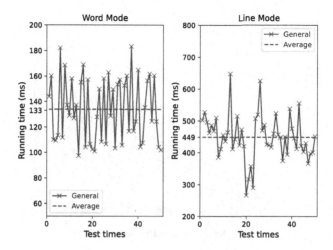

Fig. 5. Running time of full data recovery module in multiple experiments

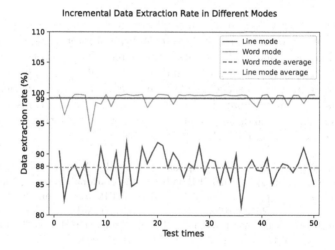

Fig. 6. Incremental data extraction rate in different modes

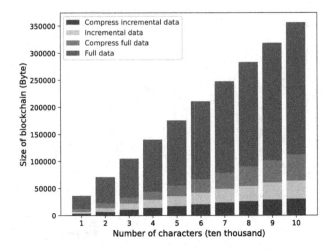

Fig. 7. Average size of blockchain in multiple experiments

6   Conclusion

In this paper, we provided an incremental snapshot forensics method based on blockchain storage, and we provided the prototype of forensic blockchain model based on Fisco bcos and evaluated its performance. The prototype has shown acceptable overhead in running time and resource utilization. The incremental data generated by the differencing algorithm saved a lot of storage space on the supervision chain compared with the full data. Simultaneously, the time consuming of incremental data extraction and recovery are within the acceptable range for the supervision blockchain.

Acknowledgments. This article is supported in part by the National Key R&D Program of China under project 2020YFB1006003, the National Natural Science Foundation of China under projects 61772150 and 61962012, the Guangdong Key R&D Program under project 2020B0101090002, the Guangxi Natural Science Foundation under grants 2018GXNSFDA281054 and 2019GXNSFGA245004, and the Peng Cheng Laboratory Project of Guangdong Province PCL2018KP004.

References

1. Arayankalam, J., Khan, A., Krishnan, S.: How to deal with corruption? examining the roles of e-government maturity, government administrative effectiveness, and virtual social networks diffusion. Int. J. Inf. Manage. **58**, 102203 (2021)
2. Baguma, R., Lubega, J.: Factors for success and failure of e-government projects: the case of e-government projects in Uganda. In: Proceedings of the 7th International Conference on Theory and Practice of Electronic Governance, pp. 194–197. ICEGOV (2013)
3. Bélanger, F., Carter, L.: Trust and risk in e-government adoption. J. Strateg. Inf. Syst. **17**(2), 165–176 (2008)

4. Dolhansky, B., Ferrer, C.C.: Adversarial collision attacks on image hashing functions. arXiv preprint arXiv:2011.09473 (2020)
5. Elisa, N., Yang, L., Li, H., Chao, F., Naik, N.: Consortium blockchain for security and privacy-preserving in e-government systems. arXiv preprint arXiv:2006.14234 (2020)
6. Grönlund, Å.: Ten years of e-government: the 'End of History' and new beginning. In: Wimmer, M.A., Chappelet, J.-L., Janssen, M., Scholl, H.J. (eds.) EGOV 2010. LNCS, vol. 6228, pp. 13–24. Springer, Heidelberg (2010). https://doi.org/10.1007/978-3-642-14799-9_2
7. Hou, H.: The application of blockchain technology in e-government in china. In: 2017 26th International Conference on Computer Communication and Networks (ICCCN), pp. 1–4. IEEE (2017)
8. Hunt, J.W., MacIlroy, M.D.: An Algorithm for Differential File Comparison. Bell Laboratories Murray Hill, New York (1976)
9. Košt'ál, K., Helebrandt, P., Belluš, M., Ries, M., Kotuliak, I.: Management and monitoring of IoT devices using blockchain. Sensors 19(4), 856 (2019)
10. Mensah, I.K., Zeng, G., Luo, C.: E-government services adoption: an extension of the unified model of electronic government adoption. SAGE Open 10(2), 2158244020933593 (2020)
11. Myers, E.W.: Ano (nd) difference algorithm and its variations. Algorithmica 1(1–4), 251–266 (1986)
12. Nizamuddin, N., Salah, K., Azad, M.A., Arshad, J., Rehman, M.: Decentralized document version control using ethereum blockchain and IPFS. Comput. Electr. Eng. 76, 183–197 (2019)
13. Setyowati, M.S., Utami, N.D., Saragih, A.H., Hendrawan, A.: Blockchain technology application for value-added tax systems. J. Open Innov. Technol. Mark. Complex. 6(4), 156 (2020)
14. Thakkar, P., Nathan, S., Viswanathan, B.: Performance benchmarking and optimizing hyperledger fabric blockchain platform. In: 2018 IEEE 26th International Symposium on Modeling, Analysis, and Simulation of Computer and Telecommunication Systems (MASCOTS), pp. 264–276. IEEE (2018)
15. Tian, Z., Li, M., Qiu, M., Sun, Y., Su, S.: Block-def: a secure digital evidence framework using blockchain. Inf. Sci. 491, 151–165 (2019)
16. Tichy, W.F.: The string-to-string correction problem with block moves. ACM Trans. Comput. Syst. (TOCS) 2(4), 309–321 (1984)
17. Tolbert, C.J., Mossberger, K.: The effects of e-government on trust and confidence in government. Public Adm. Rev. 66(3), 354–369 (2006)
18. Wang, X., Yu, H.: How to break MD5 and other hash functions. In: Cramer, R. (ed.) EUROCRYPT 2005. LNCS, vol. 3494, pp. 19–35. Springer, Heidelberg (2005). https://doi.org/10.1007/11426639_2
19. Yasir, A., Hu, X., Ahmad, M., Rauf, A., Shi, J., Ali Nasir, S.: Modeling impact of word of mouth and e-government on online social presence during covid-19 outbreak: a multi-mediation approach. Int. J. Environ. Res. Public Health 17(8), 2954 (2020)
20. Zhang, Y., Deng, S., Zhang, Y., Kong, J.: Research on government information sharing model using blockchain technology. In: 2019 10th International Conference on Information Technology in Medicine and Education (ITME), pp. 726–729. IEEE (2019)

A Digital Copyright Protection Method Based on Blockchain

Zhigang Song[1], Zaifu Yu[2], Wenqian Shang[2,3](✉), and YaXuan Li[3]

[1] Academy of Digital China (Fujian), Fuzhou University, Fuzhou, China
[2] State Key Laboratory of Media Convergence and Communication, Communication University of China, Beijing, China
yzf-ccs@cuc.edu.cn
[3] School of Computer and Cyber Sciences, Communication University of China, Beijing, China

Abstract. Traditional centralized digital copyright protection is weak in security and difficult to manage. In order to protect digital assets from unauthorized use and to solve the centralized regulatory challenges, blockchain technology is used to enhance the protection of digital works copyrights. This paper proposed a digital works copyright protection architecture based on the Consortium Blockchain, and elaborate on the security problems and solutions faced by the architecture. Moreover, the Diffie-Hellman algorithm is improved based on the Shamir algorithm to make it more suitable for the characteristics of blockchain. Finally, a smart contract is written according to the characteristics and process of digital copyright protection, and a Fabric-based digital copyright protection solution is implemented. The feasibility and effectiveness of using blockchain for digital copyright protection proposed in this paper are proved through experiments, Furthermore, the extensibility of the solution is discussed.

Keywords: Digital copyright · Blockchain · Sharmir · Diffie-Hellman · Consortium blockchain

1 Introduction

Digital copyright is enrichment and addition to copyright in the digital age. Digital copyright is the author's right to preserve, reproduce and distribute digital works in a digital way. Digital works include two major categories: one is the digitization of traditional works. The other category is naturally existing digital code works. The acquisition of copyright includes both automatic acquisition and registered acquisition. At present, there are many problems in the digital copyright industry, such as difficulties in copyright confirmation, infringement monitoring, evidence maintenance, royalty settlement, and restricted content dissemination.

Blockchain is applied to the protection of digital copyright, mainly through encryption to ensure the safety of storage and distribution of digital works [1, 10, 13, 17], and through smart contracts for the transaction of digital copyright. In addition, blockchain will record the attribution of digital copyrights in the form of transactions and hide the identity information of copyright holders.

© Springer Nature Singapore Pte Ltd. 2021
H.-N. Dai et al. (Eds.): BlockSys 2021, CCIS 1490, pp. 486–498, 2021.
https://doi.org/10.1007/978-981-16-7993-3_38

Many enterprises have explored a lot in the use of blockchain for digital copyright protection. Baidu and The Whole Family have relatively perfect solutions for digital copyright protection respectively, However, it is currently in a state of centralization, which is contrary to the distributed consensus of blockchain. Digital Qin Technology and Ziggurat Internet Technology also have their own solutions for digital copyright protection, but they are not perfect. For example, they can only do copyright acknowledgment and lack copyright transaction function. The Blockai and Primas adopt similar technical approaches to digital copyright protection, both of which are only symbolic proof of digital copyright and lack practical value. It can be seen that there is no more perfect blockchain-based digital copyright protection architecture yet.

There has also been a lot of research on digital copyright protection using blockchain by scholars around the world. Ma et al. [2] proposed a blockchain-based digital rights management scheme that supports the right content for the right users in the right way. However, this paper mainly presents the principles of some encryption algorithms. Sun et al. [3] use blockchain and homomorphic cryptography to implement a copyright auction system. However, this paper mainly compares the performance of homomorphic encryption with other algorithms. Sheng et al. [4] proposed a blockchain-based framework for crowdsourcing data transactions for copyright protection and designed an auction algorithm based on semantic similarity. However, this paper focuses on the semantic similarity-based auction algorithm. Mehta et al. [5] proposed a decentralized peer-to-peer photo sharing marketplace based on Ethereum. However, this paper focuses on the application of perceptual hashing algorithms in image detection. Li et al. [6] designed an efficient system to accurately analyze data and information protection. However, this paper mainly discusses some technologies, such as hybrid network address technology. Muwafaq et al. [7] used a perceptual hashing algorithm for image verification by exploiting the advantages of IPFS to store the copyright owner's images and text files in a decentralized file system. However, this paper focuses on the application of IPFS and perceptual hashing algorithms in image processing. Meng et al. [8] proposed a digital watermarking-based copyright management system that combines digital watermarking, blockchain, perceptual hashing, QR codes, and IPFS. However, this paper focuses on the algorithm that uses QR codes for digital watermark encryption and decryption. Wang et al. [9] proposed a secure digital copyright management system based on Ether. However, this paper focuses on improving the ElGamal encryption algorithm.

The research results of the above scholars mainly focus on the encryption and decryption algorithms, while there is a lack of discussion on the architecture of blockchain-based digital copyright protection. Liang et al. [11] proposed a digital copyright registration and transaction system with a dual-chain architecture. However, this paper mainly focuses on the performance of the proposed architecture without a comprehensive discussion of the architecture of blockchain for digital copyright protection. Lu et al. [12] propose a scheme for digital copyright management of design works using blockchain. However, this paper mainly discusses part of the structure of blockchain-based digital copyright management and lacks a discussion of the overall architecture. Chen et al. [14] propose a reliable blockchain-based copyright detection architecture. However, this paper mainly focuses on hashing algorithms, including verification tests, and generally lacks a discussion on digital copyright protection architecture. Miao et al. [15] designed a model of a digital copyright trading system based on a consortium blockchain and implemented copyright registration and trading. However, this paper mainly focuses on copyright transactions and does not describe other processes such as copyright registration. It can be seen that none of the above scholars' research results have fully described the blockchain-based digital copyright protection architecture.

The structure of this paper is as follows. The second part mainly introduces the architecture of digital copyright protection based on a consortium blockchain. The third part mainly introduces the improved core algorithm of this paper. The fourth part is the experiment of digital copyright protection based on Fabric, and finally the conclusion of this paper.

2 Architecture

The digital copyright protection architecture based on the consortium blockchain can be divided into three layers: the data layer represented by the blockchain, the intermediate functional layer, and the front-end representation layer. Unlike the public blockchain, the consortium blockchain belongs to a semi-centralized structure as a whole. The core idea of the digital copyright protection architecture based on the consortium blockchain proposed in this paper is to reduce the load of the blockchain, balance the load of the consortium nodes and strive for maximum distributed decentralization, which also means that the consortium nodes can negotiate among themselves to run each sub-function. Figure 1 shows the architecture of this paper is presented.

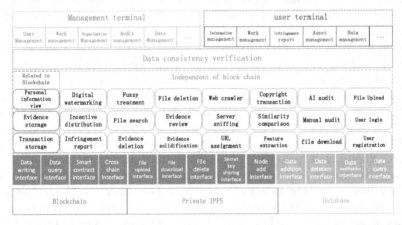

Fig. 1. The architecture of digital copyright protection based on consortium blockchain

- Data layer: Private IPFS is used to store digital works, blockchain is used to store user information, transaction information, etc. Database is mainly used to backup blockchain data and also record other data independently of blockchain.
- Middle Function Layer: This layer mainly has two functions, the first function is to act as middleware to provide data interaction between data layer and representation layer, and the second function is to provide external service API.

- Representation layer: This layer mainly provides visual operations for users and administrators, and also provides some encryption and decryption functions using technologies such as JavaScript.

To distribute the functions in the architecture to different consortium nodes, Docker technology will be used, and to balance the load of different consortium federated nodes and prevent server downtime, sniffing technology and function distribution technology will be used. Also, the technology is used to assign URLs for crawlers.

In order to ensure the security of data communication, Channel technology is introduced to create a channel based on peer-to-peer communication to ensure the closure of information interaction. Of course, the use of this technique also increases the overhead of the system. Figure 2 shows the Docker for load balancing.

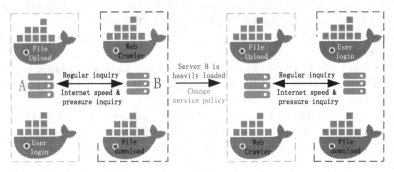

Fig. 2. The server load balancing based on docker technology

2.1 Decentralized Identity

Decentralized identity system, which is the user identity in the blockchain world. DID is a verifiable, hard-to-tamper autonomous identity system that is the embodiment of user value in the blockchain world. In contrast to PKI, DID prevents identity data from being controlled by a single central authority.

DID Generation Algorithm In this paper, we propose to encrypt the public key using SHA3-256 and Base-58 encryption algorithms. A total of six steps are required to generate DID by adding identity type identifiers and other operations, where identity type identifiers are used to distinguish different types of identities. Figure 3 shows the generation of DID.

DID-Based Registration and Login *The identity registration process is as follows:*

a. The user generates the public and private key pairs locally.
b. The user scans the QR code using the DID-APP. the QR code includes: the random ID, the server's DID and the request URL.

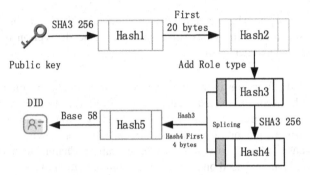

Fig. 3. The process of DID generation

c. The user uses the URL to generate a registration request, and then uses the server's DID to query the server's public key from the blockchain.
d. The user encrypts his own public key using the server's public key and then sends the encryption result to the server.
e. The server uses its private key to decrypt the result, then generates the user's DID based on the user's public key and saves the DID and other information in the blockchain.
f. The server uses its private key to encrypt the user's DID, generates a digital certificate, and then sends the digital certificate and the user's DID to the user after are encrypted by random ID, and the registration is completed.

Figure 4 shows the process of user identity registration.

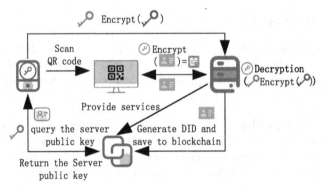

Fig. 4. The process of user identity registration

The identity login process is as follows:

a. The user scans the QR code using the DID-APP. the QR code includes: the random ID, the server's DID and the request URL.

b. The user uses the URL to generate a login request, and then uses the server's DID to query the server's public key from the blockchain.

c. The user encrypts the requested data using the server's public key, and then sends the encrypted result to the server. The request data includes the digital certificate issued by the server to the user and the digital signature generated by the user using his private key and the random ID.

d. The server uses its private key to decrypt the requested data and then uses the public key to verify the digital certificate to obtain the user's DID.

e. The server queries the user's public key from the blockchain according to the user's DID.

f. The server uses the user's public key to verify the digital signature, and then verifies the random ID and the login is completed.

Figure 5 shows the process of user identity login.

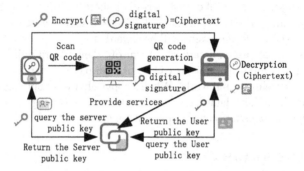

Fig. 5. The process of user identity login

2.2 Uploading and Reviewing Digital Works

Uploading and reviewing digital works is the first step in digital copyright protection. Figure 6 shows the process of uploading and reviewing digital works.

Fig. 6. The process of uploading and reviewing digital works

In order to ensure the security of digital works during the uploading process and prevent the files from being intercepted during transmission, the public key of the server is used to encrypt the digital works at the front end, and the server uses its private key to decrypt the digital works when they are securely transmitted to the server.

To prevent reviewers from stealing unencrypted digital works, digital works are added with a digital watermark before submission for review. For the review of digital works, artificial intelligence review is used first. Artificial intelligence auditing mainly extracts the features of digital works and then calculates the similarity with the already stored digital works. It also checks whether the digital works contain pornographic and violent content. After the AI review is completed, it will be submitted to human review.

After the review is approved, the required processing fee will be calculated based on the size of the digital works. After the digital works uploader pays the processing fee, the server will encrypt the digital works and eventually store them in a private IPFS. The fee charged is mainly to pay the service fee to the consortium nodes and also to prevent attackers from uploading a large number of digital works. To prevent attackers from uploading a large number of digital works in a short period of time for the purpose of the attack. The more digital works are uploaded in a short period of time, the more fees will be paid and the fewer tokens will be rewarded.

In order to motivate users, a certain amount of token reward will be given to the uploaders of digital works. The tokens can be used to pay a certain percentage of the service fee or to purchase digital works. When a copyright owner uploads digital works, both the blockchain and the database will record the corresponding information for the purpose of copyright registration and copyright confirmation.

2.3   Trading of Digital Works

Trading of digital works is the core of the digital copyright protection architecture. Without copyright transactions, digital works would lack value. Figure 7 shows the process of digital works trading.

Fig. 7. The process of digital works trading

A purchaser of a digital works requests a service from a server and uses the hash of that works to request a file from a dedicated IPFS. Since the goal of the architecture proposed in this paper is to strive for maximum distributed security, the use of distributed encryption and decryption when uploading, purchasing, and downloading digital works ensures that the file and key do not exist in the same server.

When the complete existence of a digital works file is determined, the purchaser pays a royalty to the copyright owner. After the payment is completed, the server stores the corresponding information in the blockchain and database, respectively.

At the end of each transaction, different token rewards will be provided to the copyright owner and the purchaser to encourage the trading of digital works. To prevent malicious purchases, a transaction fee will be charged for each transaction based on the transaction amount and the size of the digital works. Similarly, to prevent malicious large-scale purchases of underpriced digital works, the size of short-term transactions of digital works will be limited. The larger the transaction volume, the higher the transaction fee and the lower the token reward.

2.4 Distribution and Download of Digital Works

Digital works downloading is the process by which a copyright owner obtains ownership files from a digital works copyright protection platform. Figure 8 shows the process of downloading digital works.

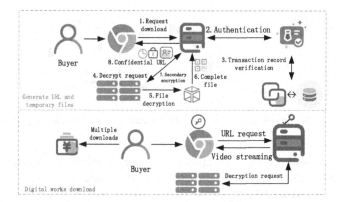

Fig. 8. The process of downloading digital works

The copyright owner requests the download service, which contains the hash of the digital works and the DID of the applicant. The server first verifies the identity of the applicant, queries the corresponding information of the user stored in the database and blockchain after authentication, and then checks the consistency of the information. After passing the information consistency check, the server will request the distributed decryption of the file in IPFS. After successful decryption, a digital watermark is added, and then a secondary distributed encryption is executed and stored temporarily in the server. Finally, an encrypted URL is generated based on the file address, timestamp, and user identity.

After the user obtains the download URL, it will request the digital works file from the server. Since the digital works file is distributed and encrypted, it needs to be decrypted in a distributed manner. After decryption, the file will be encrypted using the user's public key to ensure the secure transmission of the file. After the file is downloaded, the temporary file will be deleted.

Mass submission of download requests is a common method of attack. To solve this problem, when the number of download requests submitted by a user in a short period of time exceeds a set threshold, a fee will be charged based on the file size. The preservation and deletion of temporary files should also be considered. For works with a large number of downloads, they can be considered as more popular works, and therefore the temporary storage time of the works will be extended appropriately.

2.5 Digital Works Infringement and Reporting

Digital works infringement management is mainly carried out in two aspects: artificial intelligence supervision and user supervision. Figure 9 shows the process of digital works infringement supervision and reporting.

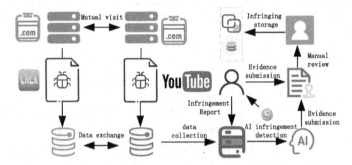

Fig. 9. The process of digital works infringement supervision and reporting

After digital works is uploaded, artificial intelligence infringement detection is first performed. When new digital works are uploaded, AI infringement detection comes into effect. It is mainly used to check whether the uploaded works are suspected of infringing the rights and interests of the stored works. There are two main forms of digital works infringement: infringement by external digital works against digital works stored in this system, and infringement by digital works stored in this system against external digital works.

Artificial intelligence infringement detection requires access to a large data set, which requires the use of crawler technology. However, it is impractical to crawl all digital works on the entire web. Considering that digital works are more widely distributed on large websites, it is necessary to obtain data from large websites only. However, the storage size of digital works on large websites is also very large, and it is not suitable for fetching all digital works. Therefore, it is necessary to use tag-based crawling, and the timestamp of digital works is also an important basis for determining whether they constitute infringement.

It is not enough to rely on artificial intelligence for infringement detection alone; therefore, it is necessary to rely on users to govern the blockchain. Users can report an infringement, and a certain amount of reward will be given for qualified reports. To prevent false reports, a fee is required upfront when reporting infringement of digital works.

The fee will be refunded when the administrator has reviewed the user's infringement report and passed. In order to keep copyright holders from selling during the infringement review period, all proceeds from digital works will be temporarily deposited in the consortium's public account.

3 Core Algorithm

3.1 Shamir Secret Sharing Algorithm

The Shamir secret sharing algorithm divides the secret into n sub-secrets. Any k sub-secrets can recover the original secret, but any $k-1$ sub-secrets cannot recover the original secret.

The encryption process is as follows:

a. Suppose there is a secret S, choose random numbers $a_1, a_2, \ldots, a_{k-1}$ and p, p, is a large prime, and $S < p$. Construct a polynomial (1), where $a_0 = S$.

$$f(x) = a_0 + a_1 x + a_2 x^2 + \ldots + a_{k-1} x^{k-1} \bmod (p) \tag{1}$$

b. Randomly select n numbers $x_1, x_2, \ldots x_n$, Then substitute them into the polynomial (1) to obtain $f(x_1), f(x_2), \ldots f(x_n)$. Finally, store $(x_1, f(x_1)), (x_2, f(x_2)), \ldots, (x_n, f(x_n))$ in n servers.

The decryption process is as follows:

a. Select data $(x_1, f(x_1)), (x_2, f(x_2)), \ldots, (x_k, f(x_k))$ from k servers arbitrarily, and replace it with polynomial (1), obtaining polynomials (2).

$$\begin{pmatrix} 1 & x_1 & \cdots & x_1^{k-1} \\ 1 & x_2 & \cdots & x_2^{k-1} \\ \vdots & \vdots & \ddots & \vdots \\ 1 & x_k & \cdots & x_k^{k-1} \end{pmatrix} \begin{pmatrix} a_0 \\ a_1 \\ \vdots \\ a_{k-1} \end{pmatrix} = \begin{pmatrix} f(x_1) \\ f(x_2) \\ \vdots \\ f(x_{k-1}) \end{pmatrix} \rightarrow \begin{pmatrix} a_0 \\ a_1 \\ \vdots \\ a_{k-1} \end{pmatrix} = \begin{pmatrix} 1 & x_1 & \cdots & x_1^{k-1} \\ 1 & x_2 & \cdots & x_2^{k-1} \\ \vdots & \vdots & \ddots & \vdots \\ 1 & x_k & \cdots & x_k^{k-1} \end{pmatrix}^{-1} \begin{pmatrix} f(x_1) \\ f(x_2) \\ \vdots \\ f(x_{k-1}) \end{pmatrix} \tag{2}$$

b. Solve the polynomial (2) to get $a_0, a_1, a_2, \ldots, a_{k-1}$, and substitute them into the polynomial (1). Let $x = 0$ to get the original secret $S = a_0$.

3.2 Improved Diffie Hellman Key Agreement Protocol

Diffie-Hellman key exchange algorithm means that two communicating parties can generate a shared secret key by exchanging only some information that can be made public. The Diffie-Hellman algorithm will face Flooding attacks, Replay attacks, and Man-in-the-Middle attacks due to the uncertain identity information of the communicating parties.

The improved Diffie-Hellman algorithm is as follows:

a. The user and the server negotiate to obtain a large prime number p and a generator G of the p, $2 \leq G \leq p-1$. At the same time, use p to generate Q and $Q^{-1}\mathrm{mod}(p-1)$, Q and $Q^{-1}\mathrm{mod}(p-1)$ are coprime. In order to suitable for the characteristics of blockchain, p and Q are generated by Shamir algorithm.

b. The user generates a random number A that satisfies the condition $1 \leq A \leq p-1$. Then calculate $X_1 = G^{A \cdot Q}\mathrm{mod}\ P$ and $X_2 = G^{A^2 \cdot Q}\ \mathrm{mod}\ P$, send the calculation results to server. The server generates a private random number B, $1 \leq B \leq p-1$. Then calculate $Y_1 = G^{B \cdot Q}\mathrm{mod}\ P$ and $Y_2 = G^{B^2 \cdot Q}\ \mathrm{mod}\ P$, send the calculation results to user.

c. The user calculates $X = Y_1^{Q^{-1}}$ and $K_a = X^A\mathrm{mod}\ P$ to get the secret key K_a. Then calculation $Key_a = ((Y_2^{Q^{-1}})^A)^{Q^{-1}}\ \mathrm{mod}\ p$, send $Hash(Key_a)$ to server. The server calculates $Y = X_1^{Q^{-1}}\ \mathrm{mod}\ p$ and $K_b = Y^B\mathrm{mod}\ P$ to get the secret key K_b. Then calculation $Key_b = ((X_2^{Q^{-1}})^B)^{Q^{-1}}\ \mathrm{mod}\ p$, send $Hash(Key_b)$ to user.

d. The user verifies that $Hash(Key_b)$ and $Hash((K_a)^{A \cdot Q^{-1}})\ \mathrm{mod}\ p$ are equal. The server verifies that $Hash(Key_a)$ and $Hash((K_b)^{B \cdot Q^{-1}})\ \mathrm{mod}\ p$ are equal.

The improved Diffie-Hellman algorithm is more suitable for blockchain characteristics, and, prevents Man-in-the-Middle attacks. The reciprocal cookie mechanism is used for blocking attacks, which can prevent forged IP addresses and port numbers [16]. The secret key obtained by the Diffie-Hellman algorithm can be used as the secret key for other symmetric encryptions, which can efficiently encrypt larger digital works and can also be used for encrypting other communication information. All operations of blockchain require a signature mechanism, so many insecurity problems are solved at the bottom of blockchain.

4   Experiment Results and Analysis

The experiments are built based on Fabric, a single machine multi node network containing one Orderer node and multiple Peer nodes is established, and then the smart contract for digital copyright protection is run on this network. The smart contract includes all the sub-functions described above. Figure 10 shows Digital copyright transaction results.

Fig. 10. Digital copyright transaction

4.1   Performance Analysis of Architecture

In order to verify the performance of Fabric-based digital copyright protection system, Postman was used to test each of the six operation interfaces for 30 times. Figure 11 shows the performance test results of the system.

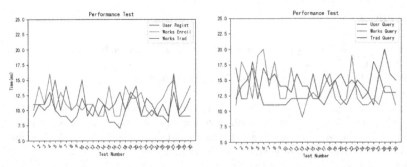

Fig. 11. Performance test

As shown in Fig. 11, a write operation to the blockchain takes about 7.5 ms – 15 ms, and a read operation takes about 10 ms – 17.5 ms. This time consumption can prove that the response time of the architecture is acceptable.

4.2 Scalability Analysis of Architecture

The architecture proposed in this article is distributed, it has minimal coupling and will not affect the original structure when new functions are added. In addition, the server can automatically adjust the load according to its own resource conditions, and flexibly set the business scale and throughput. This architecture can be applied not only in the fixed application scenario of digital copyright protection, but also in scenarios that require the use of blockchain technology to achieve credible data sharing.

The feasibility of the consortium blockchain-based digital copyright protection system proposed in this paper is demonstrated through experiments. Although, at this stage, it is in Solo mode, it can be easily deployed to Kafka mode in the future. The experiment of Fabric-based digital copyright protection implemented in this section can prove the integrity and reliability of the system proposed in this paper, both in terms of the overall process of copyright protection and transaction speed.

5 Conclusion

This paper proposes a digital copyright protection solution based on a consortium blockchain. Compared with previous studies, this paper is the first time to propose a complete blockchain-based digital copyright protection architecture, and, the Diffie-Hellman algorithm is suitably improved to make it more suitable for blockchain characteristics. Finally, the feasibility of the consortium blockchain-based digital copyright solution proposed in this paper is verified based on Fabric. The reliability of data and its secure distribution in the external system of blockchain will be studied and a relevant solution will be studied in the future.

Acknowledgement. This work was supported by National Key R&D Program of China (2018YFB0803701-1) and Fundamental Research Funds for the Central Universities (CUC210A003).

References

1. Fan, Y.K., et al.: Privacy preserving based logistic regression on big data. J. Netw. Comput. Appl. **171**, 102769 (2020)
2. Ma, Z.F., Jiang, M., Gao, H.M., Wang, Z.: Blockchain for digital rights management. Future Gener. Comput. Syst. **89**, 746–764 (2018)
3. Sun, W.Y., Fang, H.K., Zheng, S.S., Qian, Q.: Blockchain and homomorphic encryption for digital copyright protection. In: IEEE International Conference on Parallel & Distributed Processing with Applications, Big Data and Cloud Computing, Sustainable Computing and Communications, Social Computing and Networking, pp. 754–761 (2020)
4. Sheng, D.J., et al.: CPchain: a copyright-preserving crowdsourcing data trading framework based on blockchain. In: 29th International Conference on Computer Communications and Networks (ICCCN), pp. 1–9. IEEE (2020)
5. Mehta, R., Kapoor, N., Sourav, S., Shorey, R.: Decentralised image sharing and copyright protection using blockchain and perceptual hashes. In: 11th International Conference on Communication Systems & Networks (COMSNETS), pp. 1–6. IEEE (2019)
6. Li, D.M., Liu, W.J., Deng, L.B., Qin, B.: Design of multimedia blockchain privacy protection system based on distributed trusted communication. In: Transactions on Emerging Telecommunications Technologies, vol. 32, p. e3938. Wiley Online Library (2021)
7. Muwafaq, A., Alsaad, S.N.: Design scheme for copyright management system using blockchain and IPFS. In: International Journal of Computing and Digital Systems, vol. 9, pp. 1–6. University of Bahrain (2020)
8. Meng, Z.X., Morizumi, T., Miyata, S., Kinoshita, H.: Design scheme of copyright management system based on digital watermarking and blockchain. In: 42nd Annual Computer Software and Applications Conference (COMPSAC), vol. 2, pp.359–364. IEEE (2018)
9. Wang, P., Li, Y., Li, F., Dong, X.H, Chen, P.: Secure and traceable copyright management system based on blockchain. In: 5th International Conference on Computer and Communications (ICCC), pp. 1243–1247. IEEE (2019)
10. Fan, Y.K., Liu, J.X., Li, K.C., Lei, X., Tan, G., Tang, M.D.: One enhanced secure access scheme for outsourced data. Inf. Sci. **561**, 230–242 (2021)
11. Liang, W., Lei, X., Li, K.C., Fan, Y.K., Cai, J.H.: A dual-chain digital copyright registration and transaction system based on blockchain technology. In: International Conference on Blockchain and Trustworthy Systems, pp. 702–714. Springer (2019)
12. Lu, Z.H., Shi, Y.Q., Tao, R., Zhang, Z.H.: Blockchain for digital rights management of design works. In: 10th International Conference on Software Engineering and Service Science (ICSESS), pp. 596–603. IEEE (2019)
13. Fan, Y.K., Zhao, G.Q., Lei, X., Liang, W., Li, K.C.: SBBS: a secure blockchain-based scheme for IoT data credibility in fog environment. In: IEEE Internet of Things Journal, vol. 8, pp. 9268–9277. IEEE (2021)
14. Chen, Z.L., Wang, Y.T., Ni, T.J., Zhong, H.: DCDChain: A Credible Architecture of Digital Copyright Detection Based on Blockchain. arXiv preprint. arXiv:2010.01235 (2020)
15. Miao, F., et al.: Digital copyright works management system based on DOSA. In: Proceedings of the 2nd International Conference on Computer Science and Application Engineering, pp. 1–9 (2018)
16. Wei, W., Chen, J.Z., Li, D., Zhang, B.F.: Research on the Bit security of Elliptic curve Diffie-Hellman. J Electron. Inf. Technol. **42**, 1820–1827 (2020)
17. Fan, Y.K., Bai, J.R., Lei, X., Lin, W.G., Hu, Q., Wu, G.D.: PPMCK: privacy-preserving multi-party computing for K-means clustering. J. Parallel Distrib. Comput. **154**, 54–63 (2021)

A Dynamic Group Signature Scheme for Blockchain-Based Traceability Bulletin Board

Manman Hou[1], Kaiyi Zhao[1], Ruizhi Sun[1,2(✉)], and Gang Yuan[1(✉)]

[1] College of Information and Electrical Engineering, China Agricultural University, Beijing, China
{S20193081359,zhaokaiyi1204,sunruizhi}@cau.edu.cn, yuangang_cau@163.com
[2] Scientific Research Base for Integrated Technologies of Precision Agriculture (Animal Husbandry), The Ministry of Agriculture Tiergartenstr, Beijing, China

Abstract. The traceability system plays a vital role in tracing the supply records of products with quality problems. The application of blockchain in the traceability system solves the problems of easy information tampering and centralization of data storage during the traceability process, but it also brings problems such as easy information leakage, i.e., the real identity of the corresponding user can be found through the address. The characteristics of data integrity, fairness, verifiability, anonymity, and irrevocability in group signatures are of great significance for protecting the privacy of blockchain traceable transaction data. Therefore, this paper proposes a blockchain-based traceability bulletin board group signature scheme, where the bulletin board provides a direct interaction platform for users and departments. In the group signature scheme proposed in this paper, the role is re-divided for traceability, in which department members can dynamically join or withdraw, and the signature information of department members is stored on the traceability bulletin board of the blockchain and hidden department personnel's signature information on traceability documents.

Keywords: Blockchain · Traceability · Bulletin board · Group signature · RSA

1 Introduction

With the development of the economy and the complexity of the production process, the supply chain in the production process has grown rapidly, and the factors have also increased rapidly [8]. Unstable factors of product safety exist in the entire life cycle of the product supply chain, including raw material production, product processing, logistics transportation, and sales [9]. Faced with constantly emerging product safety issues, consumers urgently need a safe product traceability system to ensure product safety [2]. The main purpose of the traceability system is to record and store the relevant information of the product in the supply process. When there is a quality problem, it can quickly and

H.-N. Dai et al. (Eds.): BlockSys 2021, CCIS 1490, pp. 499–511, 2021.
https://doi.org/10.1007/978-981-16-7993-3_39

effectively trace the problematic link, implement targeted rescue measures, and recall the product when necessary. In this way, the quality and safety of products are guaranteed [7].

Traditional product traceability solutions mostly use centralized storage models, which are vulnerable to internal and external attacks [6,14,16]. The blockchain was first proposed by Satoshi Nakamoto in 2008 as the distributed accounting technology of the electronic cash payment system, and the Bitcoin network was founded in 2009 and has been running until now. Blockchain technology is a distributed, Internet-based decentralized trust management mechanism developed with the Bitcoin system. The blockchain is a reliable database technology solution that is jointly maintained by the collective.

At present, the global application of blockchain technology involves many fields [11], including financial transactions, medical protection, and anti-counterfeiting traceability. In 2015, the R3 Blockchain Alliance was established by a number of international banking organizations. Currently, more than 40 banking organizations around the world have participated. The R3 Alliance uses Ethereum and Microsoft Azure technologies to connect 11 banks to distributed ledgers and establish distribution Corda, i.e., a private ledger, researches experimental blockchain applications. In 2016, the US Department of Health and Human Services [4] proposed to combine medical treatment with blockchain technology to hold a blockchain medical research challenge to ensure the integrity of data such as patient treatment and identity information. In recent years, domestic blockchain applications have gradually begun to land. In 2018, JD.com launched the self-developed blockchain project JD Chain. JD.com uses this project to accurately trace the source of food and medicine, and build a digital depository and credit network.

In order to better realize the anti-counterfeiting traceability of commodities, many researchers have proposed supply chain solutions based on blockchain technology. Feng Tian [12] built a traceability system based on radio frequency identification (RFID) and blockchain technology, which collected information from production, processing, warehousing, distribution, and sales to transmit and share agricultural food data, and the BigchainDB database is introduced to relieve the pressure on blockchain storage. Zeng Xiaoqing et al. [17] established a food safety traceability system architecture based on the Internet of Things and blockchain combined with radio frequency technology to monitor agricultural products and pharmaceutical cold chains in real time, and improve the efficiency and transparency of the food supply chain. Xu Xiwei et al. [15] designed a blockchain-based traceability system origin chain, which replaces the central database with a blockchain, and provides high-availability, transparent, tamper-proof, and traceable data.

With the continuous development and wide application of blockchain-based traceability, its drawbacks have become increasingly obvious. First of all, the formation of a blockchain decentralized consensus requires the support of user transaction information. The transaction records of many blockchain traceability projects are open to the entire network, which brings users the risk of information leakage [1]. Secondly, transactions in a typical blockchain system are all based on addresses, and addresses are randomly generated and stored by users, and no third party is required to participate. In addition, the address space is large enough, each user can have multiple transaction addresses at random, and the address itself has nothing to do with the user's identity information. Operational interaction through the address will destroy the relevance of the operation behavior and usage information. The anonymous way of using simple addresses to replace accounts for transactions is unreliable in the face of analysis techniques such as pattern recognition of large amounts of data and link analysis graphs. Finally, publicity and immutability bring the risk of analyzing and inferring the relevance. All transaction information in the blockchain system will be recorded on the public ledger. While ensuring that the information cannot be tampered with, it also provides the original data for the attacker to analyze and infer the relevance of the transaction information. By tracking and analyzing the input and output in the transaction record, you can Gradually reduce the anonymity of the transaction address, and even discover that the address corresponds to the user's real identity [10]. Group signature technology plays an important role in data integrity, identity authentication, non-repudiation, and user anonymity, so the group signature scheme can reduce the occurrence of these problems [3].

Generally speaking, a group signature scheme consists of a group, group members, group administrators or group center and signature recipients, and has the following three properties [13]:

(1) The signer who signs the message must be a member of the group.
(2) Although the validity of the signature can be verified by the recipient of the signature, the true identity of the signer cannot be identified through this process.
(3) In the event of a dispute, the group administrator (or a joint group of members) can identify the true identity of the signer.

With group signatures, the system exposes its own public key, so any user can verify the correctness of the transaction record. In this way, externally, the system hides the transaction records of the blockchain traceability project; internally, when the product has a problem, the system can still trace the problematic link [5].

The contribution of this paper is as follows: A blockchain-based traceability bulletin board group signature scheme is proposed. First, all traceable transaction information records are stored in the blockchain, so all transactions are checked by decentralized nodes, and any untrusted transactions can be detected and rejected. Second, we use a storage bulletin board, which provides a direct interaction platform for users and authorized institutions. Using different storage bulletin boards can prevent storage centralization problems. Third, the scheme re-divides the traceability-oriented role in the group signature scheme, in which members of the production unit will often enter and exit the traceability system. Fourth, the group signature scheme is dynamic. The vector space secret sharing technology is used to use a given secret, when department members are added or deleted, the sub-secret of each group member will be changed accordingly, while the group public key remains unchanged, which makes the group signature scheme dynamic. Among them, the member signature is valid after the production unit is added and before the withdrawal. Finally, security analysis shows that the scheme can prevent key leakage, effectively protect the privacy of all aspects of the signature, and meet other specific requirements of the signature scheme. Therefore, analyzing the signature scheme of the traceable bulletin board group based on the blockchain is of great significance to the development of the privacy protection of blockchain traceable transaction data.

The other parts of this paper are as follows: In Sect. 2, we introduce the RSA public key cryptosystem, hash function, and pairing-based cryptography used in the scheme. In Sect. 3, we will introduce the traceability-oriented participating departments and the corresponding functions of the departments, and analyze the construction process of the dynamic group signature scheme. In Sect. 4, we will discuss the security analysis of our scheme. In Sect. 5, we will summarize the scheme, and introduce the future work.

2   Preliminaries

The main symbols are used in this paper have been summarized in Table 1.

Table 1. Description of the main symbols used in this paper

Symbol	Description
n, e	Secret key
d	Public key
m	Information
$H(m)$	Hash function
E	Mapping function
G_i	Cyclic group
Z	Integer
q	Prime order
U	Users
D	Competent authority
P_i	Production unit
R_A	Regulatory Authority
A	Signature set
W_i	Sub-secret
ψ	Mapping function
K	A finite element set

2.1   RSA

RSA (Rivest-Shamir-Adleman) is a public key cryptosystem, which has been widely used in secure data transmission. RSA algorithm includes four steps: key generation, key distribution, encryption, and decryption. A basic principle behind RSA is to find that three very large positive integers e, d, and n are feasible. Therefore, modular exponentiation is performed for all integers m $(0 \leq m < n)$:

$$(m^e)^d \equiv m(\text{mod n}) \tag{1}$$

Here, mod denotes modular operation, "$\equiv$" denotes the congruence of $(m^e)^d$ and m to module n. RSA contains a public key and a private key. The public key is known to everyone and is used to decrypt messages. The purpose is that messages encrypted by private keys can only be decrypted by public keys in a reasonable time. The private key is represented by integers n and e, the public key is represented by integers d, and m is the message.

2.2 Hash Function

The hash function is a function that maps data of arbitrary size to fixed-size values. A good hash function satisfies three basic properties: 1) the computational complexity of the function should be very low; 2) it should minimize the repetition of the output value; 3) its reverse calculation is very difficult, even impossible to achieve. The hash function is defined as follows:

$$y = H(m) \tag{2}$$

Here, $H(\cdot)$ is any hash function, m is message, y is function value, i.e., hash value. The commonly used hash functions are identity hash function, trivial hash function, division hashing, multiplicative hashing, Fibonacci hashing, and so on.

2.3 Pairing-Based Cryptography

Pairing-based cryptography is to construct a cryptosystem by pairing elements of two cryptography groups to the third group with a mapping $E : G_1 \times G_2 \rightarrow G_T$. Here G_1, G_2 are two additive cyclic groups of prime order q, G_T is the multiplicative cyclic group of order q. The mapping E meets the following properties:

- Bilinearity: $\forall a, b \in Z_q^*, \forall P \in G_1, Q \in G_2 \Rightarrow E(aP, bQ) = E(P, Q)^{ab}$.
- Non-degeneracy: $e \neq 1$.
- Computability: There must be an efficient algorithm to calculate E.

When the first two groups use the same group(i.e. $G_1 = G_2$), pairing is called symmetry, which is a mapping from two elements of one group G_1 to elements of the second group G_T.

3 Dynamic Group Signature Scheme for Block Chain-Based Traceability Bulletin Board

In order to make the transaction records and information in the blockchain traceability project clearer and more reliable, we first introduce the competent department D in the scheme: generate and distribute keys, help signers generate respective signatures, and gather individuals together to generate group signatures; production unit P_i: use the sub-secret sent to it by D and his private key sign the message m; user U: verify the signature; regulatory authority R_A: as an arbitration, when a dispute occurs, it can distinguish which signer generates the signature. Some additional information is added to the signature information, so that the unauthorized user can only verify whether the signature is valid, and the authorized department can obtain additional information through the subliminal channels. It can not only verify the validity of the signature, but also "open" the signature in case of dispute to find out which group member signed the signature. The schematic diagram of group signature based on blockchain traceability is shown in Fig. 1.

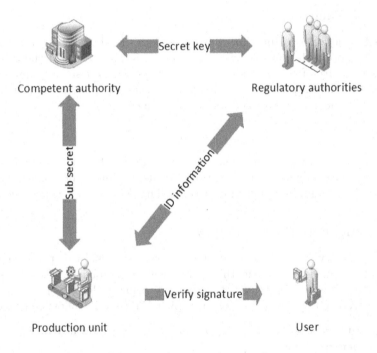

Fig. 1. Schematic diagram of group signature.

The group signature scheme makes the information of traceable transaction records unable to be viewed by users, and members who have obtained sub-secrets on the bulletin board can not only view the information of traceable transaction records, but also quickly find out which department appears when there is a problem with the product issues. Group signature is a digital signature technology with both anonymity and traceability, but the length of the group signature and the length of the group public key are related to the number of members in the group, and the addition of new members requires redistribution of the member private key and changes group public key. However, for a large group, the addition or deletion of members is a frequent operation, so the signature private key and group public key are changed due to the addition or deletion of members, which is obviously extremely impractical. Therefore, this paper proposes the dynamic group signature scheme of traceability for practical application. In view of the non-dynamic characteristics of the original signature scheme, given secrets, when a department member joins or exits a project with a time stamp, the sub-secrets of each department member will change accordingly, which makes the scheme dynamic.

When the group signature scheme is not dynamic, it is impossible to add or delete group members. Only when it is dynamic can it be applied to the actual traceability process. The dynamic group signature scheme based on the blockchain-based traceability bulletin board proposed in this paper has four parts: the competent authority, the production unit, the user, and the regulatory authority. The competent department, production unit, and supervisory department all have the right to view product traceability information and sign product traceability documents, but users can only verify the signature and learn about the product without knowing the specific traceability information. When a department signs the product traceability document, each member of the department can get a sub-secret, which can be used to obtain the right to view the traceability information. If one of the members does not obtain the sub-secret, that is, if there is no such right, then the department's signature could not be generated. In this way, it can be ensured that every member has the right to participate in the department's project activities. If a member of a department leaves or joins, the original sub-secret of each member of the Department will be invalid, and a new sub-secret needs to be sent to each member. In this way, new members can be added to the department activities, and the departing members can be prevented from forging the Department signature.

3.1 Initialization

Suppose the information to be signed is m, an additive cyclic group is G_1, the product unit is P, and a multiplicative cyclic group is G_T, and their orders are all prime numbers q. The discrete logarithm problems on the groups G_1 and G_T are both difficult. Define the bilinear pair $E : G_1 \times G_1 \rightarrow G_T$. The password one-way hash function H is defined as: $H : \{0,1\}^* \rightarrow G_1$. Suppose the set of n participants is $P = \{p_1, p_2, ..., p_n\}$, and there is an access structure $\Gamma = \{A_1, A_2, ..., A_\lambda\}$, where $A_i \in \Gamma$ is the authorized subset, $1 \leq i \leq \lambda$.

D first randomly selects $n \in Z_q, e \in Z_q$ as the key jointly owned by it itself and the regulatory agency R_A, and uses d as the corresponding public key and announce the value of d. Assuming that there are l group members in the group signature set A, the l group members first submit their own identity information (ID_i) to the regulatory agency R_A separately, and the regulatory agency R_A calculates and publishes $h_i = eH(ID_i)$, given the secret $k \in K$, D randomly select $v_2, v_3, ..., v_l \in K$. Let $V = (v_1, v_2, v_3, ..., v_l)$, where $v_1 = k$, ψ is the mapping function between P_i production unit and R_A regulatory authority. K is a finite element set. Among them $c_i \in K$ can be calculated by each participant.

$$V \cdot \psi(D) = V \cdot \left(\sum_{i=1}^{l} c_i \psi(p_i) \right)$$

$$= \sum_{i=1}^{l} c_i (V \cdot \psi(p_i)) \tag{3}$$

$$= \sum_{i=1}^{l} c_i w_i$$

D sends a sub-secret to each production unit P_i through the secure channel.

3.2   The Production Units Join

If the production unit P_{l+1} wants to become a member of the signature authorization set A, he must secretly submit his identity information ID_{l+1} to the regulatory agency R_A. The regulatory agency R_A calculates and publishes $h_{l+1} = xH(ID_l + 1)$, then there are $l + 1$ group members in the group signature set A, given the secret $k \in K$, D randomly chooses $v_2, v_3, ..., v_{l+1} \in K$, let $v = (v_1, v_2, ..., v_{l+1})$, among them, $v_1 = k$. Secret $k = \sum_{i=1}^{l+1} c_i w_i$. Through the secure channel, D distributes the new sub-secret w_i to each production unit, and stamps the time stamp T_{join} at the same time.

3.3   Withdrawal of Production Units

If the production unit P_j wants to withdraw from the signature authorization set A, its identity information (ID_j) will be deleted from the regulatory agency R_A. This makes the group signature set A have $l - 1$ group members, let $v = (v_1, v_2, ..., v_l)$, among them,$v_1 = k, v_2, v_3, ..., v_l \in K, k = \sum_{i=1}^{l} c_i w_i$. D redistributes new sub-secrets to each production unit, and stamps the revocation time stamp $T_{revocation}$ at the same time.

3.4   Generate User Signature

Each production unit $P_i \in A$ chooses a random number $b_i \in Z_q^*$, calculates the value of $y_i = b_i P$, and sends y_i to D secretly. D randomly selects α_i, calculates $r_i = \alpha_i P$, and then calculates $U_i = n(y_i + r_i) + neH(ID_i), z_i = n(y_i + r_i), v_i = n(w_i P + y_i)$. D sends r_i, U_i, z_i, v_i to p_i through a secure channel, and p_i does the following calculation: $s_i = (w_i + b_i)H(m), T_i = d_i + U_i, \hat{h}_i = r_i + y_i + h_i$. Then the individual signature generated by p_i is $(U_i, s_i, y_i, z_i, v_i, \hat{h}_i, T_i, m, t)$, where t is the signature time stamp, and the individual signature secret is sent to D to publish the value of $w_i P$.

3.5   User Verification Signature

First find out whether the production unit P_i has a revocation time stamp, if not, verify the formula Eq. (4). Whether it is established or not, if established, the signature is valid; if the production unit P_i has a revocation time stamp, compare the order of the revocation time stamp and the signature time stamp. If the former is before the latter, the signature is invalid.

$$\begin{cases} E(T_i, P) = E(H(m), w_i P)E(\hat{h}_i, d)\dot{E}(H(m), y_i) \\ E(s_i, d) = E(H(m), v_i) \\ E(U_i, P) = E(\hat{h}_i, d) \\ T_{join} < t < T_{revocation} \end{cases} \tag{4}$$

3.6   Generate Group Signature

The individual signature submitted by each production unit $P_i \in A$ must be verified by the user. After the verification is passed, the D can be calculated at this time: $\hat{h} = \sum_{i=1}^{l} \hat{h}_i, s = \sum_{i=1}^{l} c_i d_i, U = \sum_{i=1}^{l} U_i, T = s+U, Z = \sum_{i=1}^{l} z_i, g = \sum_{i=1}^{l} c_i y_i$, the group signature is $(U, \hat{h}, s, g, T, z, m)$.

3.7   Verify Group Signature

By the following formula: $E(T, P) = E(H(m), kP + g)E(\hat{h}, d)$. The user can verify the group signature. If this formula holds, the group signature is considered valid, otherwise, the signature is considered invalid.

3.8   The "opening" Process of the Discriminator

Once a dispute occurs, through the key n and the secret value e, the regulatory agency R_A can "open" the signature to identify the identity, and thus can determine which authorized subset of the group signature is signed. For example, for authorized subset A, calculate $\sum_{i \in A} H(ID_i), (ne)^{-1}(U - Z)$, if the two formulas are equal, the signature authorization subset is A (Note: There are l elements in A).

$$\sum_{i \in A} H(ID_i) = \sum_{i=1}^{l} H(ID_i) \tag{5}$$

4   Safety Analysis

No matter which group signature scheme, there are a series of attacks, and many attacks on the product traceability system are relatively close. So we analyze each one according to the requirements of the group signature scheme.

Integrity: Only authorized department members can sign. In our scheme, the initiator of the signature can disclose his private key e, the nodes of the entire network can verify the validity of the signature on the traceability bulletin board, and all illegal signatures are recorded on the storage bulletin board.

Privacy: All signatures must be kept confidential. Firstly, in the signing phase, the signer can use a different address to sign. Secondly, members cannot associate the signature with the signer. The signer who uses the group signature is from this group, but cannot distinguish which specific member made the signature. Therefore, the group signature effectively protects the privacy of the signer.

Eligibility: People who are not qualified to sign are not allowed to sign. In the initial stage of signing, the competent authority uses its own key to sign the name, and will publish a signature plan, which includes all the signer's information. If this information is added or deleted in the later stage, it will be considered that the previously published signature plan is illegal, where illegal nodes cannot obtain signature qualifications.

Fairness: Nothing can hinder the signature. For the members of each department in the traceability system, all their actions are recorded in this block. If there are any illegal actions, they will be recorded, and other members will stop this illegal signature plan. For miners, their behavior is constrained by other miners in the entire network. Any information recorded by the miners in the blockchain will be verified by the entire network. If illegal behavior is found, the block will be discarded. For the bulletin board, it stores all the signature information, no one can forge the signature result, and no one has the right to modify the signature that already exists on the bulletin board.

Verifiability: No one can tamper with the signature result, all signature information is stored in the bulletin board, and no one can modify the signature information in the bulletin board. At the same time, all traceable transaction record information is recorded in the block, and the miner checks all product information before writing it into the block, and the product in question will be discovered and discarded.

Revocability: It can be seen from this scheme that when the exited production unit signs again, the signature is invalid, because the signature time stamp is after the time stamp is added but before the time stamp is revoked. If the time stamp is revoked, the signature stamp is invalid. In addition, the retired production unit will not receive new sub-secrets from the competent department D, and is not satisfied with $k = \sum_{i=1}^{l} c_i w_i$.

Anonymity: Only the regulator R_A can determine the actual group signer, and no one else has this right. In this scheme, only R_A owns the key e and the secret value n, can get the signature authorization set A, and others want to obtain the values of n and e through $h_i = eH(ID_i)$ and d will face the difficulty of solving the discrete logarithm.

Traceability: In the event of a problem with the product, revealing the true identity of the signatory must be done by the regulator R_A. R_A has the key n and the secret value e, so it can trace the signature authorization set to achieve traceability.

Unforgeability: A production unit cannot generate a signature on behalf of another production unit. Each production unit p_i chooses a random number b_i, so different production units have different b_i, and different production units get sub-secret w_i from the competent department D is also different, and the generated $s_i = (w_i + b_i)H(m)$ is also different.

In addition, although w_iP and kP are published, based on the difficulty of discrete logarithms, it is impossible for an attacker to calculate w_i and k from w_iP and kP. Since different group signature sets have the same public key, it is impossible to verify whether the group signature is done by the same group member, that is, this scheme satisfies non-correlation.

5 Conclusion and Outlook

This paper mainly introduces the traceability bulletin board group signature scheme based on blockchain. First, the blockchain is used to store traceable transaction information, all transactions are checked by nodes on the blockchain. When an untrusted transaction is detected, the transaction is rejected. Second, we use the storage bulletin board to provide a direct interaction platform for users and authorized institutions to prevent storage centralization problems. Third, we redefine the traceability-oriented role in the group signature scheme, and hide the signatures of the traceability information of department members. Fourth, the group signature scheme is dynamic. The vector space secret sharing technology uses a given secret, when department members are added or deleted, the sub-secret of each group member will be changed accordingly, and the group public key will remain unchanged, so that department members can dynamically join or leave the production department. Make the group signature scheme dynamic. Finally, security analysis shows that the scheme can prevent key leakage, effectively protect the privacy of all aspects of the signature, and improve the robustness of the dynamic group signature scheme. At the same time, this scheme can meet other specific signature schemes.

Of course, the research results designed in this article are not yet perfect, and the technology is being updated day by day. The actual implementation is bound to bring many unconsidered problems. This article is just a preliminary attempt at the application of group signatures in blockchain traceability. The following mainly looks forward to the future research work in this field:

(1) Due to the complexity of blockchain programming and the difficulty of constructing distributed systems, this paper conducts theoretical research. In the future, there will be many problems that need to be solved in actual programming, testing, and going online.
(2) In the traceability application based on the blockchain, the group signature technology is used to protect the privacy of the signer. The privacy protections of the signer's IP address and the realization of comprehensive anonymity protection are the focus of future research.

(3) Many current group signature schemes are not dynamic, and the schemes are very poor in terms of security and efficiency. Therefore, how to safely and efficiently join or delete a group member becomes a problem worthy of study.

(4) Some existing safe and efficient group signature algorithms basically rely on some difficult problems, such as the discrete logarithm difficulty problem, the RSA signature system and the Schnoor signature system, etc. The efficiency of the signature algorithm and the open algorithm is not high. Therefore, it is necessary to design some new, safer, and more efficient group signature schemes.

Acknowledgments. This research was funded by Application of collaborative precision positioning service for mass users (2016YFB0501805-1) and National Development and Reform Commission integrated data service system infrastructure platform construction project (JZNYYY001).

References

1. Aune, R.T., Krellenstein, A., O'Hara, M., Slama, O.: Footprints on a blockchain: trading and information leakage in distributed ledgers. J. Portfolio Manage. **45**(1App.), 60–64 (2018)
2. Bevilacqua, M., Ciarapica, F., Giacchetta, G.: Business process reengineering of a supply chain and a traceability system: a case study. J. Food Eng. **93**, 13–22 (2009). https://doi.org/10.1016/j.jfoodeng.2008.12.020
3. Boneh, D., Boyen, X., Shacham, H.: Short group signatures. **3152**, 227–242 (2004). https://doi.org/10.1007/978-3-540-28628-8_3
4. Brodersen, C., et al.: Blockchain: Securing a newhealth interoperability experience (2016)
5. Cao, Y., Li, Y., Sun, Y., Wang, S.: Decentralized group signature scheme based on blockchain, pp. 566–569 (July 2019). https://doi.org/10.1109/CISCE.2019.00131
6. Damle, A., Bangera, M., Tripathi, S., Meena, M.: Blockchain technology: An overview (2020)
7. Hobbs, J.: Information asymmetry and the role of traceability system. Agribusiness **20**, 397–415 (2004). https://doi.org/10.1002/agr.20020
8. Krichen, S., Ben Jouida, S.: Introduction to supply chain management. pp. 13–23 (December 2015). https://doi.org/10.1002/9781119261469.ch2
9. Marucheck, A., Greis, N., Mena, C., Cai, L.: Product safety and security in the global supply chain: issues, challenges and research opportunities. J. Oper. Manage. **29**, 707–720 (2011). https://doi.org/10.1016/j.jom.2011.06.007
10. Moubarak, J., Filiol, E., Maroun, C.: On blockchain security and relevant attacks. pp. 1–6 (April 2018). https://doi.org/10.1109/MENACOMM.2018.8371010
11. Mueller, P.: Application of blockchain technology. it - Inf. Technol. 60 (November 2018). https://doi.org/10.1515/itit-2018-0035
12. Tian, F.: An Agri-food supply chain traceability system for china based on RFID & blockchain technology, pp. 1–6 (June 2016). https://doi.org/10.1109/ICSSSM.2016.7538424
13. Vidali, J.: Group signatures, vol. 547 (April 1991). https://doi.org/10.1007/3-540-46416-6_22

14. Xie, C., Xiao, X.: Traceability of agricultural product quality and safety based on blockchain – taking fresh e-commerce as an example. In: Abawajy, J.H., Choo, K.-K.R., Xu, Z., Atiquzzaman, M. (eds.) ATCI 2020. AISC, vol. 1244, pp. 288–294. Springer, Cham (2021). https://doi.org/10.1007/978-3-030-53980-1_43

15. Xu, X., Lu, Q., Liu, Y., Zhu, L., Yao, H., Vasilakos, A.V.: Designing blockchain-based applications a case study for imported product traceability. Future Gener. Comput. Syst. **92**, 399–406 (2019)

16. Yao, L.U., Wen, J.: Scheme of supply chain control and traceability based on bitcoin technology. Computer Engineering (2018)

17. Zeng, X.Q., Peng, Y., Wang, Q.: Research on food safety traceability system based on IoT and blockchain technology. Food Mach. **34**(09), 100–105 (2018)

Absorptive Capacity, Blockchain and Food Traceability: An Empirical Invetigation

Kai Wu[1], Baiqing Sun[2(✉)], and Haifeng Guo[2]

[1] Business School, Harbin Commercial Univeristy, Harbin 150028, China
[2] Management School, Harbin Institute of Technology, Harbin 150001, China
`baiqingsun@hit.edu.cn, guohaifeng1981@msn.com`

Abstract. Food holds a major role in human societies and involved from different essential actors, such as farmers, distributers, retailers, consumers, etc., which forms the food supply chain and argues as one of the most complex and challenge systems. Although traceability forms basis of its food supply chain, but it still faces some fundamental problems. Current research indicates that blockchain is a promising technology for handling these problems, in which various nodes (actors) are connected through the blockchain traceability system with efficiency, feasibility and trust. However, many mysteries are still existing in the blockchain food traceability system, such as the dynamic interactions among the nodes and the responses for the frequent contextual changes are still waiting for discover urgently. In this study adopted absorptive capacity, as the theoretical lens, for discovering the blockchain traceability system node's capability for absorbing the blockchain as new knowledge, the interaction among the chain nodes, and the chain nodes' absorption on the contextual changes. This study contributes to the IS literature by providing an account of the blockchain about absorptive capacity of these loose-connected chain nodes on the new knowledge, and responsibility of these chain nodes collectively on the frequent contextual changes?

Keywords: Absorptive capacity · Blockchain · Food supply chain · Traceability

1 Introduction

Food supply chain is the primary section in human societies, in which the food quality, safe and trust have become a major issue in public health in the last twenty years, such as the foot-and-mouth Disease in Europe in 2001, the *Escherichia Coli* outbreak in Spinach in 2006 in USA, the South African listeriosis outbreak in 2017, and even the COVID-19 spread in 2019. Moreover, the supply chain is highly multi-actor based and distributed, with numerous different actors involved, such as farmers, logistic companies, distributor, and retailers. During these food epidemic incidents, lack of traceability among these actors for building up the trust, transparency and traceability has been identified as a major challenge for controlling these incidents (Manski 2017, Ringsberg 2014, Marabelli and Newell 2019). The blockchain offer a faceable solution to these existing challenge, as its traceability systems take the advantages providing the transparency and reliability

© Springer Nature Singapore Pte Ltd. 2021
H.-N. Dai et al. (Eds.): BlockSys 2021, CCIS 1490, pp. 512–529, 2021.
https://doi.org/10.1007/978-981-16-7993-3_40

(Demestichas et al. 2020), which have been considered as the fundamental attribute in the current supply chain system.

The blockchain's transparency and fault tolerance make it gains the success in cryptocurrencies, and, nowadays, the application of blockchain in food traceability has got significant attention (Kouhizadeh et al. 2021). It is widely adopted by both research and business for providing the 'Farm to Fork' traceability service, and the blockchain is a promising technology towards a transparent traceability. The blockchain provides us a trust mechanism, as any one is trying to tamper or corrupt the data in one specific block, who must alter the following tampered actor of the chain. For the constantly added blocks, it is practically impossible to change a single actor in the chain (Demestichas et al. 2020, Ruoti et al. 2019). Therefore, blockchain, as the reliable tracking solution, has been adopted for the food supply chain tracking system (Esmaeilian et al. 2020, Kamilaris et al. 2019). However, as a novel technology, it is remained the mystery, such as the interacting among the chain linked nodes (actors), and the nodes' collaborative respondence to the contextual changes (Demestichas et al. 2020, Esmaeilian et al. 2020). For exploring the mystery, absorptive capacity (AC) provides us a solid theoretical support.

AC has its prominent role in IS research and adopted by scholar to explain how organizations learn from external source of knowledge (e.g. other firms, systems, and technology), integrate this knowledge within the organization and turn it into internal capability (Van Den Bosch et al. 1999, Todorova and Durisin 2007, Mariano and Walter 2015), response to the contextual changes with proper activities (Vasconcelos et al. 2019, Zahra and Hayton 2008), and creates the competitive advantage (Patterson and Ambrosini 2015, Zou et al. 2016). Especially for the modern company, at the heart of the construct is the external knowledge which is the source of the internal knowledge and basis for achieving the alliance and collaboration (Tzokas et al. 2015, Saad et al. 2017). This suggests that using the AC to investigate the blockchain food supply chain might shed light on the interactions among the loose connected actors that organizations are still struggling. There is an awareness that AC is context sensitive and that changes in context could act as triggers lead to the action and the change about AC (Marabelli and Newell 2019, Zahra and Hayton 2008). Moreover, these contextual change leaded AC evolution and development has been less focused (Omidvar et al. 2017, Ferreras-Méndez et al. 2015). Indeed, how it develops in a loose connected context, such as the blockchain, has never been touched. This paper presents such an empirical study that invest the collective activities among the blockchain connected actors for responding to the contextual change.

Our methodological approach to AC analysis and food traceability system practice in synthesizing this framework is qualitative. Compared to quantitative methods commonly used AC analysis (Gao et al. 2017), qualitative analysis allows an in-depth analysis of learning and practice over time (Neuman 2010, Denicolai et al. 2016). The rest of this paper is structured as follows: Section two provides a review of literature and highlights critical gaps. Section three presents the chosen case study and offers some in-depth insights about the role of AC in the blockchain food traceability system. A timeline is adopted to show the interplay and syntheses between AC, traceability system and work practice. Section four presents the indeed analyses dynamics among the blockchain connected nodes in a traceability system. The final section presents conclusions and identifies avenues for future research.

2 Literature Review

Traceability is described as the ability to trace the history, application, or location of that is under consideration (GalvÃ£o et al. 2010, Mann et al. 2018), which received wide application, such as the mining, software, manufacture and even food (Maouchi et al. 2019, Mann et al. 2018, Lin et al. 2018b). Nowadays, due to the food crisis, the traceability aspect of the food supply chain has been highlighted, as it includes all the information about food through its entire life circle with the identification. Moreover, traceability also relates to the ability to track and trace along the supply chain, as it allows the supply chain shareholders to follow the downstream path of a product, tracing enables identification of the origins (Maouchi et al. 2019). In summary, the food traceability includes all the information about the food ingredients, sources, processing, transportation, and storage and so on. The food traceability ensures the safety in food supply chains at least for four major areas: 1) information management for transparency and interpretability, 2) quality management for food quality and safety requirements, 3) production management for in-house production and outsourcing, and 4) logistics management for food supply chain complexity (Ringsberg 2014, GalvÃ£o et al. 2010, Demestichas et al. 2020). The blockchain based food traceability is a combination of interconnecting process and a re-constructing procedure of certain food (Aung and Chang 2014). Subsequently, all actors in the food supply chain must coordinate with the others to produce a trustworthy outcome in terms of traceability.

A blockchain was initially introduced by Stuart Haber and W. Scott Stornetta in 1991 in their article "How to Time-Stamp a Digital Documen", and well recognized since 2008, as Satoshi Nakamoto (a name used by an unknown person or group of people) defined it a cryptocurrency and developed the first blockchain database (Luther 2019). A general defined and accepted concept of blockchain is "digital transaction ledger, maintained by a network of multiple computing machines that are not relaying on a trusted third party" (Kamilaris et al. 2019), which generate a key feature of a blockchain is its ability to keep a consistence, tractability and agreement among the nodes. The agriculture traceability system contains the food information from "farm to fork", requires the information in the secure, transparent and immutable. Therefore, the blockchain network is well accepted and further developed in this area for guaranteeing food safety and quality throughout entire supply chain (GalvÃ£o et al. 2010, Ringsberg 2014). In agriculture traceability, the blockchain is suggested in HACCP (Hazard Analysis Critical Control Point) system for food production, transportation, and preservation (Tian 2017). A blockchain based food supply chain system was developed in China for improving food safety by providing the information and transaction security between all involved parties (Tse et al. 2017). Since 2018 more research applied the blockchain in agriculture supply chain and traceability system were conducted, such as the Food Trading System with Consortium blockchain (FTSCON) for improving transaction security and privacy (Mao et al. 2018); applying the blockchain technology into the existing (enterprise resource planning) ERP project for improving the traditional agri-food supply chain (Lin et al. 2018a); adopt the blockchain in supply chain for achieving the future industry 4.0 (Esmaeilian et al. 2020). Blockchain received more attention in traceability section, but still leak of research on its inside dynamics among the nodes and its interactions with continuous contextual changes (Demestichas et al. 2020), which play the essential roles for organization's long-term IS project success (Saad et al. 2017, Ranjan et al. 2016). Therefore, it is necessary for scholars to conduct the blockchain traceability research on the dynamic interaction and contextual change aspects.

During the last two decades years, absorptive capacity (AC) has been accepted as an important construction for IS scholars to study how firms capture external knowledge and learn from it to fits into the business environment and generate the new knowledge. Cohen and Levinthal (1990) first introduced AC as "the ability of a firm to recognize the value of new, external information, assimilate it, and apply it to commercial ends". Later AC has been defined as a substantive organizational capability (a high-level routine or set of routines) that relates to the gain and release of resources (Zou et al. 2016). AC, as an important theory to understanding the knowledge processing processes in organization, clearly plays an important role in studying IS. By focusing the construct of AC, Dyer and Singh (1998) propose a method that contrasts with the single-loop learning process described by Cohen and Levinthal. They view AC as an iterative process of exchange (modifying assumptions). Lane and Lubatkin (1998) develop the idea of "relative absorptive capacity". They assess AC as a learning dyad – in which a firm's ability to learn from another firm depends on similarities in their knowledge bases, organizational structures, and dominant logics. Zahra and George (2002) provide a procedural view of AC as a dynamic capability and suggest that the construct has potentially two general states. One is when firms acquire and assimilate new knowledge, and another is when firms transform and exploit new knowledge. The construct of AC has been widely adopted in IS study for understanding organization capability for knowledge processing capacity and contextual change respondence (Grandinetti 2016, Mariano and Walter 2015, Liu et al. 2013, Agramunt et al. 2020), and it is also adopted in this study for uncovering the mystery of blockchain traceability system.

Despite the population of the blockchain technology on both research and industry, only few studies briefly touched the blockchain's dynamic internal interaction and co-responding to the contextual changes. The AC has been well adopted for understanding the inter-organizational knowledge processing capacity and organization's capability for processing the contextual changes (Vasconcelos et al. 2019, Zahra and George 2002), which is also applicable for us to understand what are the interactions among the blockchain connected nodes and how these nodes collaboratively response to the contextual changes.

3 Research Setting and Method

In line with Walsham (1993), this study adopts an approach that assumes that reality, including the organizational actor domain, is a social construct. This approach is consistent with our aims in the study. The study regards AC as an essential dynamic capacity of an organization and aims to move beyond the traditional view that treats AC as an objective reality (defining antecedents and drivers) with predictable outcomes that contribute to organizational learning (measuring the outcomes). We believe that observing the blockchain traceability system provides an insightful way to understand the role of AC in the loose connected inter-organizational context and underpins the co-evolving between AC and blockchain system in a dynamic context.

During the period 2019–2020, we collected data about a blockchain food traceability system project from Alpha, Beta and Omega. Alpha is blockchain technology company and particularly providing the service in the food supply chain. It has developed a blockchain technology-based food traceability system and named ETS in this study. Beta is a local company supermarket company with about 3,000 employees. It has ten supermarkets and about 100 mini supermarkets in one city. Omega is a farm with about 2,000 pig, 3,000 duck and 1,500 chicken, and most of its pig supply to Beta. In 2019 ETS was being rolled out and the system is continuously updated as the new functionalities were added; in particular, these functions are for meeting the predictable and unpredictable requirements come from internal demanding and external force. For meeting the research purpose, we regarding these three actors as a single case and have the close observation of daily practice (Klein and Myers 1999, Doolin and McLeod 2012). Also we adopt the interpretive approach for data collection and analysis (Walsham 1993, Walsham 2006).

We found this case extremely interesting and appropriate as an object for this research aim, as it is providing us a unique opportunity to access the data from 'farm to fork' to cover the entire food circle and food supply chain. The data are collected primary qualitative from several sources, such as interview, non-participant observations, official documents, meeting minutes, and steering committee presentations. During our two years retrospective data collection, the interviewees were selected by both judgment and snowball sampling method (Marshall 1996, Taherdoost 2016). The interviews were semi-structured, as they were guided by the research objectives and questions (Wright and Wright 2002, Kallio et al. 2016). Structured questions with prompts to guide the interviewee were used.

The next section shows our interpretive approach and its advantages here: 1) it is helpful to understand the dynamics between absorptive capacity and blockchain traceability system; 2) it is necessary to uncover the dynamics of ACs among the loose-connected actors; and 3) it is able to provide an integrated view about the influence of contextual changes on the interconnected ACs and the related working practices.

4   Data Interpretation

This section provides a narrative of the blockchain food traceability system deployment and upgrade. In September 2019, Alpha rolled out its ETS system to market. This ETS system adopted the blockchain technology and provided the traceability service for tracing the food from its origin, logistics, distribution, into retail store. At the end of 2019 Bate and Omega agreed with Alpha to access and share their data on ETS.

At end of 2019 Alpha was starting to connect Beta and Omega into the ETS. Although, Alpha had the experience to connect the vegetable, chicken, and online shop into the blockchain traceability system, but first time to connect the pig and supermarket data. Alpha reconfigured the chain for Beta uploading its pig data, such as the ID (bar code on ear tag), specs, days, weight, and location, into the blockchain. However, at that moment, Beta did not use any farming software and all these data have been recorded on Office Excel. Therefore, its staff had to manually copy and paste the data into ETS on the daily base. Compared with Beta Omega was better, as it has a small IT team and running an ERP system. It took Alpha three months to collaborate with the ERP system vendor to access the database and share certain the data on the blockchain. In June 2020 Alpha released its smart e-tag for pig. This smart e-tag is an innovative product, which can record the pig temperature and movement in 24 h for 6 months and help us to monitor and predict pig's health condition. It received great welcome from Beta, as the plague has become severe issue. Applying the e-tag allowed to add some new data into the chain. At the end of 2020, local government also provided the financial support for firm to adopt the blockchain traceability in the business. With this financial support, the ETS was further adopted by these three actors. From the project documentation, interview with key actors, and on-site observation, three project phases were identified. There three phases are not strictly sequential, but overlap in certain time of period as shown in Fig. 1.

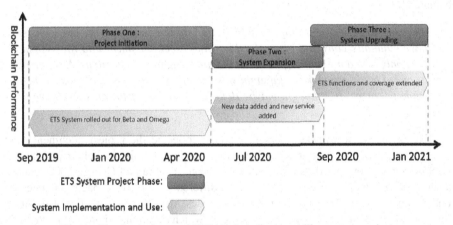

Fig. 1. The three phases of ETS blockchain traceability system project

In Fig. 1, the grey rectangle demonstrates the project phases, and the orange hexagon presents the ETS system practices. The system implementation and use are in sequence but can also overlap. For example, when Alpha developed e-tag applied at Beta and system expansion is not fully updated, the local government already provided the financial support for these three companies to upgrading their blockchain system. Hence, Phase Two and Phase Three overlap during certain time of period. A deeper analysis is conducted in the next section. We take another look at the three phases under the theoretical lenses of AC to discover the interactions between the blockchain nodes (actors) and their respondence on the contextual changes.

Phase One: Project Initiation

In May 2019, Alpha decided to extend its product line from the vegetable and fish farm into pig and cattle farm section. Based on the existing blockchain traceability system, it took Alpha three months to develop extend the system into pig and cattle farm. This new system was released on September 2019 as ETS, which acted as a trigger lead to a serial of following practices. Alpha's existing client, Beta, became the first user for ETS, as it agreed to connect the ETS into its existing system. Beta had its own ERP system for managing the supermarket. To connect the traceability system into the ERP system is not easy as well, which took Alpha and the ERP vendor three months. Alphas' agriculture blockchain is private and required a series of work to connect any new node into the chain, as Alpha Engineer Vincent explained:

> *"This blockchain based farm management system is not just a software system to actually implied it into the actual work, we need to set up the new business policy for managing the system, the right of data access for sharing and communicate with the other actors in the blockchain network".*

Rather than join the chain with itself, Beta also introduced its meat supplier Omega into the chain. Omega own a pig farm and most of its pig supply to Beta's supermarket. At that moment, Omega has low IT capacity. Therefore, this blockchain system did not really bring any benefit to it and only added extra working load. As its accountant June explained:

> *"My manager asked me to input the pig data into the system on the daily basis. I have manually copy and paste the data from excel document into the system, which only added my working load, but did not bring any benefit to us. Also, there was once I made a mistake as input the misdate into system, which did take us lots of time to correct it. I thought maybe Beta is our major customer, so we have to do it."*

Except interview with key person, we also collected the project documents and conduct the onsite observation for indeed understanding. In this blockchain project, the ETS system roll out acted as the Contextual trigger (Zahra and George 2002) caused a serial of practices. These practices leaded different absorptive capacity changes on both potential and realized aspects for various nodes. Moreover, the practice also caused different blockchain performance for each actor, which accumulated presenting the ETS performance. Table 1 offers synthesis of the ETS practice from these three actors through the AC perspective.

Based on the above discussion, we able to systematically analyze the dynamics between the absorptive capacities and blockchain adaptation. The blockchain traceability system the chain connected various actors into the network, and also impacted the actors differently. From AC perspective, each actor took a different role in the chain, their capacity for acquiring, assimilating (Potential AC), transforming, and exploiting (Realized AC) were different as well. Therefore, the performance and benefit of join the chain various significantly. In this case, Alpha and Beta benefit from join the chain, but Omega did not receive any benefit yet.

Phase Two: System Expansion

The re-emerging African swine fever in 2019 almost killed eight million pigs for about half of China's pig population (Mighell and Ward 2021). And it cause the neighbor town killed about 1,000,000 pigs. The prior study has indicated the accuracy of adopting the IoT technology, such as the accelerometer, temperature, GPS, for animal tags for recognizing pig health condition (Kamminga et al. 2018). By combining the Neural

Table 1. Phase one AC and practice analysis

Node (Actor)	Absorptive capacity		Blockchain related practice
	Potential absorptive capacity	Realized absorptive capacity	
Alpha	Alpha CEO realized the market of the blockchain system in pig and cattle industry	Added the blockchain knowledge into the new industry	The ETS was developed; Alpha started to market this blockchain system
Beta	Beta management team learn the benefit of join the blockchain network	It staffs learned the basic system knowledge from ETS	Beta agreed to join the blockchain and became one actor in the chain; The ETS started to provide data service for ETS customers
Omega	None	Only one staff in Omega learn to input data into the system	ETS added working load at Omega; Omega did not need to access the ETS

Network and online activity recognition systems, it will be the practical solution for monitoring the animal health condition, including the African swine fever, in the real-time (Kamminga et al. 2017, Tran et al. 2021). In order to solve the pig health issue, Alpha has extended its research focus from the blockchain traceability to the IoT based solution. In May 2020, Alpha released a new product, the electrical pig ear tag sensor with following measurement in Table 2:

Table 2. Ear tag measturement

Weight	Temperature accuracy	Working time	Communication standard	Waterproof
15 Gram	±0.2 °C	200 Days	Bluetooth and Lora	IP 67

Through this e-tag and ETS, the pig farmer was able to know their pig health condition in the real time. Also, each e-tag has a blockchain ID for the following supply chain activities. This e-tag caused great attention for Omega, as it could reduce their risk dramatically for the swine fever. For testing purpose, Omega tapping the e-tag for each sow for two weeks of time. Omega was satisfied about the test results and later put it on each its pig.

Beat's sale team noticed that this meaningful data could add its market competition strength. Beta collaborated with Alpha expanded the ETS system to share the pig health data, as the pig temperature and working steps, to the supermarket customers. Moreover, for certain pig cuts, the customer can know the pig health data by scan bar code on the meat box. It is helping Omega to build up their customer trust and develop its market competitive ability. Table 3 demonstrates synthesis of the ETS practice and the AC adaptation.

Table 3. Phase two AC and practice analysis

Node (Actor)	Absorptive capacity		Blockchain related practice
	Potential absorptive capacity	Realized absorptive capacity	
Alpha	Alpha noticed the blockchain traceability system was not enough for its development	The ear e-tag was developed for recording the pig and cattle temperature and movement	The blockchain data was extended as the pig and cattle health data added
Beta	Beta's marketing team noticed the value of the e-tag data	E-tag data was shared on the blockchain	The realtime pig health data was projecting on the screen in the supermarket; The pig health data was shared to the meat purchasing customers
Omega	Omega management team noticed the importance of IT technology in farming industry	Realized the value of monitoring the pig temperature and movement in the really time	Catching up the pig health data and share the data with the other actors in the blockchain

Table 3 summarized trigger (e-tag) caused the sequenced changes on these three nodes' AC and blockchain related practice. This e-tag first changed the blockchain practice on Alpha, as it added the function of recording health data into the ETS, then Omega applied the e-tag and uploaded the health data into the blockchain, later Beta shared these data with customer for improving its reputation. Their ACs are developed in sequence.

Phase Three: System Upgrading

In August 2020, the local government provided the fund for supporting organization's technology application in agriculture industry. Alpha, Beta and Omega all received the government technology fund with varied amount, because their technology investment and industry are different. Based on the interviews and company documents from these three actors, they have applied the fund differently as the followings: Alpha had applied this funding to develop the mobile app for the providing traceability service, named ETS APP. project document recorded that Alpha's ETS mobile app provides the services on three aspects: *1. pig's health situation for the customer who purchased the meat; 2. Traceability information 'from the farm to plate' for covering entire supply chain; 3. Services for the related auditing institutes.* Beta had used the fund to install more sensors in their supermarket, warehouse and delivery trucks to monitor the entire supply chain by IoT devices. Omega was applied the fund to payback for the e-tag installation and farming system implementation. Table 4 shows the AC and the three actors' practices.

Table 4. Phase three AC and practice analysis

Node (Actor)	Absorptive capacity		Blockchain related practice
	Potential absorptive capacity	Realized absorptive capacity	
Alpha	Absorbed the external knowledge for adding the supply chain data into the system	Updated the ETS system with more functions and wider accessible	The blockchain encompass more data and more service for more actors
Beta	Learn more blockchain and supply chain knowledge	Adding more supply chain data into the blockchain	The blockchain was able to access the supply chain data
Omega	None	None	None

In this phase, the government fund, act as the contextual trigger, lead and fund the Alpha and Beta to continually added more data and services into the blockchain. These new data and services were available for Beta's customer and extended the availability of the blockchain. Alphas absorbed the 'new' knowledge and realized the knowledge with mobile software. As the following, Beta also add the supply chain data into the blockchain for improving the customer service. Although, government funded Omega, but the fund has been applied for supporting the phase two activity, and this trigger did not lead to the AC change in Omega. Therefore, we can see that one trigger may lead to a serial of activity and AC changes, may not cause any activity and AC change for certain actors.

This longitudinal case study clearly illustrates the dynamics among the actors in the ETS developed blockchain network. The actor's AC and blockchain related practices are all co-constructed and co-evolved in a turbulent context The following section will discuss the dynamics in more detail.

5 Dicussion and Implications

The prior data interpretation summarizes the ETS system project development, implementation and use among Alpha, Beta and Omega. The interpretation based on Zahra's interpretation of absorptive capacity (2002) and adopt Marabelli's research method of applying the absorptive capacity on enterprise system study (2019, 2009). In this section, we further depict the dynamics among absorptive capacity and blockchain related changing working practices in the turbulent context. Based on the above tables and the analysis, Fig. 2 has reinterpreted these three actors' (organizations) PACAP, RACAP and blockchain related practice from the longitudinal perspective.

In Fig. 2, the ETS system project is divided into three phases. In each phase the pentagon presents the contextual trigger, which caused the following system related practices; the cloud shows the actual practices for responding to the triggers; the rectangle indicates the actor's potential absorptive capacity (PACAP) and realized absorptive capacity (RACAP); and the arrow underpins the conditioning and enabling relationship.

The above figure highlights the key roles of absorptive capacity in the blockchain based traceability supply chain project; it points out the co-constructed and co-evolved of the PACAP and RACAP in the turbulent context; and it underpins the role of the contextual change trigger in the ETS system project. Below has discussed each of these three perspectives in details.

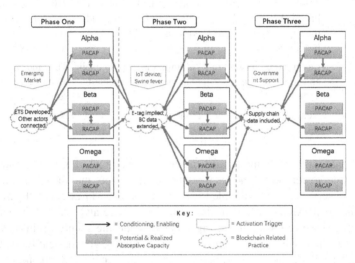

Fig. 2. Interactions among blockchain related practice and absorptive capacity at ETS system project

1. The role of AC in the blockchain traceability project – the above vignettes and analysis illustrate the key role of AC in blockchain traceability system adoption. Compared with the majority study of AC in a large single organization, or the group (Omidvar et al. 2017, Gao et al. 2017), The blockchain provides an unique environment for the AC, as a 'chain' connected environment and each node's AC interacted with the others. For example, in phase one, Alpha's RACAP heavily connected to Beta's RACAP on the system adaptation, and they worked together developed ETS. However, it did not contribute to RACAP at Omega, as Omega's accountant was still manually copying the data from Excel and pasting it into the system one figure by one figure. Also in phase two, Alpha developed pig E-Tag for monitoring the pig health condition, which developed the RACAP at Beta and Omega differently, as Beta demonstrate the data at its supermarket for the customer and applied the E-Tag at its farm. Various actors play different roles in the blockchain, their absorptive capacity condition and enabled their practices, meanwhile the practices also facilitate the absorptive capacity development.

2. The interaction of the blockchain connected ACs – Rather than linear linked from PACAP to RACAP, in this case, the PACAP development at one actor not only led to its RACAP development, but also causes the PACAP and RACAP development at the other actors. For example, Alpha for recognizing the market opportunity for adopting blockchain on food traceability, not only lead to its RACAP development for developing the ETS system, but also cause the PACAP and RACAP development at Beta to use this system; Alpha's e-tag, act as the contextual trigger, brought IT into Beta daily management. Beta staffs can monitor their pig health condition through the ETS, rather than visit the pig farm for onsite observation and personal judgement; and Beta added the pig health data into the blockchain, Omega's changes its potential AC, as adopted the data differently for improving its customers trust with the realized AC. We call this blockchain linked absorptive capacity as the loose-connected absorptive capacity.

3. The role of contextual trigger in blockchain traceability system – This figure demonstrates the contextual triggers initiate a series of practices, the triggers are either predictable or unpredictable, and the triggers could come from both internal or external; more over one actors internal trigger may other actor's external trigger; even the same trigger even the same trigger may play different roles for various actors. In this case, we noticed that the emerging blockchain technology and market demanding on traceability system triggered Alpha to develop the ETS system and explore the market. Through the implementation of the ETS at various actors, Omega also noticed the farm demanding and business opportunity for the E-tag. The re-emerging African swine fever in 2019 almost killed eight million pigs for about half of China's pig population (Mighell and Ward 2021), which caused the demanding for monitoring the pig health for 24 h. Alpha developed the e-tag for monitoring the pig's temperature and movement in real time. Omega showed the great interests for adopting this e-tag at their pigs, by the way it enabled it to adopt the ETS system on its farm management. This e-tag also created the 'new' business opportunity for Beta to demonstrate the pig health condition on their supermarket to build up the customer confidence. In 2020, the financial support from local government for the technology development and adaptation also acted as the trigger caused Alpha and Omega to further develop their technology development and adaptation. Therefore, the contextual trigger may come from quite wide background, and even the same trigger may play different roles for various actors. For example, the same government funding adopted by Alpha for developing the mobile app, by Beta to payback for the prior investment, and by Omega to develop the marketing software. Even the same trigger may play different roles for various actors. For example, the same government funding adopted by Alpha for developing the mobile app, by Beta to payback for the prior investment, and by Omega to develop the marketing software.

Drawing on the substantive model of the ETS blockchain traceability system project and the above findings, a generalized model is presented as below. The model adopts the social constructive perspective, which explains that the technology appropriation results from the constitution of human users, social histories and organizations (Orlikowski 2010, Gare and Melin 2013), which is compatible with the loose connected network like blockchain. Figure 3 shows the dynamics among the absorptive capacity, blockchain related practice and contextual triggers in the blockchain based supply chain system from the longitudinal perspective. In this figure, the pentagon presents the contextual trigger led to the practice change, the rectangle indicates each actor's absorptive capacity on both PACAP and RACAP perspectives, the cloud presents the blockchain supply chain system related practices from all the actors, and the arrow underpins the conditioning and enabling relationship.

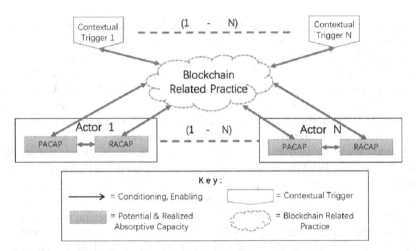

Fig. 3. Dynamics of blockchian related practice and absorptive capacity

Change is the nature of any business and one of the most threatening aspects in information technology implementation and use (Altamony et al. 2016, Lichtenthaler 2009). Absorptive capacity is context sensitive phenomenon responsive to change (Lichtenthaler 2009), and it will developed through the changing practices (Omidvar et al. 2017). For absorptive capacity, the contextual triggers have been identified and extended from various aspects, such as the internal prior knowledge, working practice and system structure (Marabelli and Newell 2019, Martinkenaite and Breunig 2016), and the external marketing, technology, and supply chain (Golgeci and Kuivalainen 2020, Omidvar et al. 2017, Saad et al. 2017). Therefore, to understand the dynamics among the AC and working practice in the blockchain, we cannot avoid the impact of contextual changes in our modelling. Through this study, these contextual triggers are further defined as activation triggers, which caused the changes in blockchain related practice. Compared with the prior AC studies majority in one organization or group, the blockchain connected actors come from quite different background, such as IT, farming, retail, government, and others. The activation trigger may come from wide range, internal and external of the blockchain, be predictable, unpredictable. Moreover, these triggers may interconnect or overlap to enable the change of practices, even the same trigger may play different roles for various actors.

The activation trigger leads blockchain related change of practice is conditioned by the actor's AC. However, the AC is not only a conditioning agent, but itself is also liable for change and transformation in the practice. The changing practice as new knowledge is acquired and assimilated into the adopting actor and the related practice too develops the AC. This has been identified as the endless process of revisions and enhancements (Markus et al. 2000) where each process encompasses different degrees of knowledge exploration and exploitation (Marabelli and Newell 2019). From the longitudinal perspective, in the blockchain based supply chain network, the related practice and the AC are overlappingly development. The information technologies can develop knowledge management and learning in organization (Iyengar et al. 2015), through implementing knowledge management systems (Kuo and Lee 2009, Wang et al. 2007, Lee et al. 2007) and enterprise system (Chadhar and Daneshgar 2018, Acar et al. 2017), but the blockchain creates an unique environment which is composed from organizational level to operational level (Agrawal et al. 2021), and from one to rack all the entire supply chain (Madhwal et al. 2021, Xu et al. 2021). This study has clearly shown that in the blockchain supply chain, the PACAP and RACAP are not linear connected, one actor's PACAP may not only impacts its RACAP, but also interact with other actor's PACAP and RACAP through the related practice. Therefore, we call this blockchain linked various actor's absorptive capacity as the 'loose-connected absorptive capacity'. Companying the blockchain related practices, the changing on one actor's absorptive capacity could impacts the other actors' absorptive capacity in the different way, and these absorptive capacities are co-construct and co-evolved.

The AC is a dynamic capability and gaining the advantage when its dimensions gain resources and competencies (Teece et al. 1997). This means that AC can change over time depending on factors. The ETS provides us a unique opportunity to uncover the role of AC in agriculture and blockchain supply chain system. In this blockchain network, the actor's absorptive capacity, the blockchain system implementation and system use are co-construct and co-evolving overtimes. Compared with the traditional enterprise system, the blockchain based supply chain system provides a loose-connected network, as only certain limited data and service are connected.

6 Conclusion and Limitation

Blockchain is an immutable digital ledger, which provides the unique strength for traceability (Demestichas et al. 2020), but, as a novel technology, applying the blockchain technology still has many mysteries waiting for unveil. Blockchain provides a quite different environment for the knowledge transferring and data sharing, as all nodes may come from quite different industry, such as the farm, manufacture, logistics and even retails; all the notes are loosely connected by the limited data access; the network may shift quick as the nodes (actors) are loosely connected for quickly change. The blockchain is emerging out for taking an important role on the supply chain and traceability system (Mann et al. 2018), but this loose connected network also creates a unique context waiting for the future study.

This research adopted the AC as the theoretical lens for understanding the knowledge absorption and development under the loose-connected network. Our research has explored the importance of knowledge processing capacity in blockchain supply chain system project. We have therefore suggested that adopt AC as the theoretical lens will enlighten the research on blockchain technology application. From this longitudinal perspective the benefit of blockchain based supply chain system emanates from the co-construction and co-evolution among the system implementation, system use and AC. In this co-construct/co-evolving process, the AC plays a mediator role, as it conditions the interaction between the system implementation and the related working practice. At the same time, the supply chain system implementation and the working practice also transform the AC itself. This transformation allows the AC to condition the interaction between the system practice and practice in a dynamic manner. Therefore, it is worth for us to take the blockchain through the AC perspective.

From this study we noticed that the node's (actors) AC determinates the blockchain performance. Also depending on the contextual trigger (contextual changes), the change on one AC will lead to the changes on the other AC in various ways and. Moreover, these blockchain connected nodes may come from various business. Therefore, they are sensible for different contextual change and responding the changes with various feedback. For example, one change may lead to various practices from different actors, and these practices may lead to the other practices from the linked actors, in which the responding practices can a chain of practices in the network form. Although previous study about AC uncovered its context sensitive characteristics (Volberda et al. 2010, Todorova and Durisin 2007). Our results further this finding and suggests that the blockchain system contextual change acts as the activation trigger leads to the change on both system implementation and system practice, which also limited by and contribute to various actor's absorptive capacity in the different way.

This study has some inherent limitations that also suggest future research possibilities. First, the data were gathered at only one blockchain food traceability system in early stage. A broader survey from various blockchains traceability may provide further insight into the role of AC, adding perhaps more details of the interactions among the actors. Second, the research focus is on the high-level constructs amongst the node's ACs and related blockchain working practice. More elaborate study into finer elements of those constructs is likely to add further value for applying this discovery in real word applications.

Acknowledgement. This study should say thanks to the support of the national Key R&D program (Grand No. 2017YFB1401800), and Harbin Technology Start Up Program (Grand No. 2019CYJBCG0006), The National Key Research and Development Program of China (2020YFB1006104).

References

Acar, M.F., Tarim, M., Zaim, H., Zaim, S., Delen, D.: Knowledge management and ERP: Complementary or contradictory? Int. J. Inf. Manage. **37**, 703–712 (2017)

Agramunt, L.F., Berbel-Pineda, J.M., Capobianco-Uriarte, M.M., Casado-Belmonte, M.P.: Review on the relationship of absorptive capacity with interorganizational networks and the internationalization process. Complexity **2020**, 20 (2020)

Agrawal, T.K., Kumar, V., Pal, R., Wang, L., Chen, Y.: Blockchain-based framework for supply chain traceability: a case example of textile and clothing industry. Comput. Ind. Eng. **154**, 107130 (2021)

Akkermans, H., Helden, K.V.: Vicious and virtuous cycles in ERP implementation: a case study of interrelations between critical success factors. Eur. J. Inf. Syst. **11**, 35 (2002)

Altamony, H., Al-Salti, Z., Gharaibeh, A., Elyas, T.: The relationship between change management strategy and successful enterprise resource planning (ERP) implementations: a theoretical perspective. Int. J. Bus. Manag. Econ. Res. **7**, 690–703 (2016)

Aung, M.M., Chang, Y.S.: Traceability in a food supply chain: safety and quality perspectives. Food Control **39**, 172–184 (2014)

Chadhar, M., Daneshgar, F.: Organizational learning and ERP post-implementation phase: a situated learning perspective. J. Inf. Technol. **19**, 138–156 (2018)

Cohen, W., Levinthal, D.: Absorptive capacity: a new perspective on learning and innovation. Adm. Sci. Q. **35**, 128–152 (1990)

Demestichas, K., Peppes, N., Alexakis, T., Adamopoulou, E.: Blockchain in agriculture traceability systems: a review. Appl. Sci. **10**, 4113 (2020)

Denicolai, S., Ramirez, M., Tidd, J.: Overcoming the false dichotomy between internal R&D and external knowledge acquisition: absorptive capacity dynamics over time. Technol. Forecast. Soc. Change **104**, 57–65 (2016)

Doolin, B., McLeod, L.: Sociomateriality and boundary objects in information systems development. Eur. J. Inf. Syst. **21**, 570–586 (2012)

Esmaeilian, B., Sarkis, J., Lewis, K. Behdad, S.: Blockchain for the future of sustainable supply chain management in Industry 4.0. Resour. Conserv. Recycl. **163**, 105064 (2020)

Ferreras-Méndez, J.L., Newell, S., Fernández-Mesa, A., Alegre, J.: Depth and breadth of external knowledge search and performance: the mediating role of absorptive capacity. Ind. Mark. Manage. **47**, 86–97 (2015)

Galvã£o, J.A., Margeirsson, S., Garate, C., viãarsson, J.R., Oetterer, M.: Traceability system in cod fishing. Food Control, **21**, 1360–1366 (2010)

Gao, S., Yeoh, W., Wong, S.F., Scheepers, R.: A literature analysis of the use of absorptive capacity construct in IS research. Int. J. Inf. Manage. **37**, 36–42 (2017)

Gare, K., Melin, U.: Sociomaterial actors in the assimilation gap: a case study of web service, management and IT-assimilation. IseB **11**(4), 481–506 (2013). https://doi.org/10.1007/s10257-012-0205-9

Golgeci, I., Kuivalainen, O.: Does social capital matter for supply chain resilience? The role of absorptive capacity and marketing-supply chain management alignment. Ind. Mark. Manage. **84**, 63–74 (2020)

Grandinetti, R.: Absorptive Capacity and Knowledge Management in Small and Medium Enterprises. Taylor & Francis, New York (2016)

Iyengar, K., Sweeney, J.R., Montealegre, R.: Information technology use as a learning mechanism: the impact of IT use on knowledge transfer effectiveness, absorptive capacity, and franchisee performance. MIS Q. **39**, 615–642 (2015)

Kallio, H., Pietilä, A.M., Johnson, M., Kangasniemi, M.: Systematic methodological review: developing a framework for a qualitative semi-structured interview guide. J. Adv. Nurs. **72**(2954), 2965 (2016)

Kamilaris, A., Fonts, A., Prenafeta-Boldú, F.X.: The rise of blockchain technology in agriculture and food supply chains. Trends Food Sci. Technol. **91**, 640–652 (2019)

Kamminga, J.W., Bisby, H.C., Le, D.V., Meratnia, N., Havinga, P.J.M.: Generic online animal activity recognition on collar tags. In: Proceedings of the 2017 ACM International Joint Conference on Pervasive and Ubiquitous Computing and Proceedings of the 2017 ACM International Symposium on Wearable Computers. Association for Computing Machinery, Maui, Hawaii (2017)

Kamminga, J.W., Le, D.V., Meijers, J.P., Bisby, H., Meratnia, N., Havinga, P.J.M.: Robust sensor-orientation-independent feature selection for animal activity recognition on collar tags. In: Proceeding of the ACM Interactive Mobile Wearable and Ubiquitous Technologies, vol. 2, Article 15 (2018)

Klein, H.K., Myers, M.D.: A set of principles for conducting and evaluating interpretive field studies in information systems. MIS Q. **23**, 67–93 (1999)

Kouhizadeh, M., Saberi, S., Sarkis, J.: Blockchain technology and the sustainable supply chain: Theoretically exploring adoption barriers. Int. J. Prod. Econ. **231**, 107831 (2021)

Kuo, R.Z., Lee, G.G.: KMS adoption: the effects of information quality. Manage. Decis. **47**, 1633–1651 (2009)

Lee, S.M., Lee, Z., Lee, J.: Knowledge transfer in work practice: adoption and use of integrated information systems. Ind. Manage. Data Syst. **107**, 501–518 (2007)

Lichtenthaler, U.: Absorptive capacity, environmental turbulence, and the complementarity of organizational of organizational learning processes. Acad. Manage. J. **52**(822), 846 (2009)

Lin, J., Shen, Z., Zhang, A., Chai, Y.: Blockchain and IoT based Food Traceability for Smart Agriculture (2018a)

Lin, J., Shen, Z., Zhang, A., Chai, Y.: Blockchain and IoT based Food Traceability for Smart Agriculture. In: Proceedings of the 3rd International Conference on Crowd Science and Engineering. Association for Computing Machinery, Singapore (2018b)

Liu, H., Ke, W., Wei, K.K., Hua, Z.: The impact of IT capabilities on firm performance: the mediating roles of absorptive capacity and supply chain agility. Decis. Support Syst. **54**, 1452–1462 (2013)

Luther, W.J.: Getting off the ground: the case of bitcoin. J. Inst. Econ. **15**(189), 205 (2019)

Madhwal, Y., Chistiakov, I., Yanovich, Y.: Logging multi-component supply chain production in blockchain. In: 2021 The 4th International Conference on Computers in Management and Business. Association for Computing Machinery (2021)

Mann, S., Potdar, V., Gajavilli, R.S., Chandan, A.: Blockchain technology for supply chain traceability, transparency and data provenance. In: Proceedings of the 2018 International Conference on Blockchain Technology and Application. Association for Computing Machinery, Xi'an, China (2018)

Manski, S.: Building the blockchain world: technological commonwealth or just more of the same? Strateg. Change **26**(511), 522 (2017)

Mao, D., Hao, Z., Wang, F., Li, H.: Novel automatic food trading system using consortium blockchain. Arab. J. Sci. Eng. **44**(4), 3439–3455 (2018). https://doi.org/10.1007/s13369-018-3537-z

Maouchi, M.E., Ersoy, O., Erkin, Z.: Decouples: a decentralized, unlinkable and privacy-preserving traceability system for the supply chain. In: Proceedings of the 34th ACM/SIGAPP Symposium on Applied Computing. Association for Computing Machinery, Limassol, Cyprus (2019)

Marabelli, M., Newell, S.: Organizational learning and absorptive capacity in managing ERP implementation projects. In: ICIS 2009 Proceedings, vol. 136 (2009)

Marabelli, M., Newell, S.: Absorptive capacity and enterprise systems implementation: the role of prior-related knowledge. ACM SIGMIS Database DATABASE Adv. Inf. Syst. **50**, 111–131 (2019)

Mariano, S., Walter, C.: The construct of absorptive capacity in knowledge management and intellectual capital research: content and text analyses. J. Knowl. Manag. **19**, 372–400 (2015)

Markus, M., Tanis, C., van Fenema, P.: Enterprise resource planning: multisite ERP implementations. Commun. ACM **43**, 42–46 (2000)

Marshall, M.N.: Sampling for qualitative research. Fam. Pract. **13**, 522 (1996)

Martinkenaite, I., Breunig, K.J.: The emergence of absorptive capacity through micro–macro level interactions. J. Bus. Res. **69**, 700–708 (2016)

Mighell, E., Ward, M.P.: African Swine Fever spread across Asia, 2018–2019. Transbound Emerg Dis. **68**(5), 2722–2732 (2021)

Neuman, W.L.: Social Research Methods: Quantitative and Qualitative Methods. Allyn & Bacon, Boston (2010)

Omidvar, O., Edler, J., Malik, K.: Development of absorptive capacity over time and across boundaries: the case of R&D consortia. Long Range Plan. **50**, 665–683 (2017)

Orlikowski, W.J.: The sociomateriality of organisational life: considering technology in management research. Camb. J. Econ. **34**(125), 141 (2010)

Patterson, W., Ambrosini, V.: Configuring absorptive capacity as a key process for research intensive firms. Technovation **36–37**, 77–89 (2015)

Ranjan, S., Jha, V.K., Pal, P.: Literature review on ERP implementation challenges. Int. J. Bus. Inf. Syst. **21**, 388–402 (2016)

Ringsberg, H.: Perspectives on food traceability: a systematic literature review. Supply Chain Manage. **19**(558), 576 (2014)

Ruoti, S., Kaiser, B., Yerukhimovich, A., Clark, J., Cunningham, R.: Blockchain technology: what is it good for? Commun. ACM **63**(46), 53 (2019)

Saad, M., Kumar, V., Bradford, J.: An investigation into the development of the absorptive capacity of manufacturing SMEs. Int. J. Prod. Res. **55**, 6916–6931 (2017)

Taherdoost, H.: Sampling methods in research methodology; How to choose a sampling technique for research. Int. J. Acad. Res. Manage. **5**(2), 18–27 (2016)

Teece, D.J., Pisano, G., Shuen, A.: Dynamic capabilities and strategic management. Strateg. Manage. J. **18**, 509–533 (1997)

Tian, F.: A Supply Chain Traceability System for Food Safety Based on HACCP, Blockchain and Internet of Things (2017)

Todorova, G., Durisin, B.: Absorptive capacity: valuing a reconceptualization. Acad. Manage. Rev. Arch. **32**, 774–786 (2007)

Tran, H.T.T., et al.: Genetic characterization of African swine fever viruses circulating in North Central region of Vietnam. Transbound Emerg Dis. **68**, 1697–1699 (2021)

Tse, D., Zhang, B., Yang, Y., Cheng, C., Mu, H.: Blockchain Application in Food Supply Information Security (2017)

Tzokas, N., Kim, Y.A., Akbar, H., Al-Dajani, H.: Absorptive capacity and performance: the role of customer relationship and technological capabilities in high-tech SMEs. Ind. Mark. Manage. **47**, 134–142 (2015)

van den Bosch, F.A., Volberda, H.W., de Boer, M.: Coevolution of firm absorptive capacity and knowledge environment: organizational forms and combinative capabilities. Organ. Sci. **10**, 551–568 (1999)

Vasconcelos, A.C., Martins, J.T., Ellis, D., Fontainha, E.: Absorptive capacity: a process and structure approach. J. Inf. Sci. **45**, 68–83 (2019)

Volberda, H.W., Foss, N.J., Lyles, M.A.: Absorbing the concept of absorptive capacity: how to realize its potential in the organization field. Organ. Sci. **21**, 931–951 (2010)

Walsham, G.: Interpreting Information Systems in Organizations. Wiley, New York (1993)

Walsham, G.: Doing interpretive research. Eur. J. Inf. Syst. **15**(320), 330 (2006)

Wang, Y.-S., Wang, H.-Y., Shee, D.Y.: Measuring e-learning systems success in an organizational context: scale development and validation. Comput. Hum. Behav. **23**, 1792–1808 (2007)

Wright, S., Wright, A.M.: Information system assurance for enterprise resource planning systems: unique risk considerations. J. Inf. Syst. **16**, 99–113 (2002)

Xu, X., Zhu, D., Yang, X., Wang, S., Qi, L., Dou, W.: Concurrent practical byzantine fault tolerance for integration of blockchain and supply chain. In: ACM Transactions on Internet Technology, vol. 21, Article 7 (2021)

Zahra, S.A., George, G.: Absorptive capacity: a review, reconceptualization, and extension. Acad. Manage. Rev. **27**, 185–203 (2002)

Zahra, S.A., Hayton, J.C.: The effect of international venturing on firm performance: the moderating influence of absorptive capacity. J. Bus. Ventur. **23**, 195–220 (2008)

Zou, B., Guo, F., Guo, J.: Absorptive capacity, technological innovation, and product life cycle: a system dynamics model. Springerplus **5**(1), 1–25 (2016). https://doi.org/10.1186/s40064-016-3328-5

Asycome: a JointCloud Data Asynchronous Collaboration Mechanism Based on Blockchain

Linhui Li, Peichang Shi[✉], Xiang Fu, Shengtian Zhang, Tao Zhong, and Ming Chen

National Key Laboratory of Parallel and Distributed Processing, College of Computer Science, National University of Defense Technology, Changsha 410073, China
{lilinhui,pcshi,fuxiang13,zst0023,zhongtao12,chenming20}@nudt.edu.cn

Abstract. In the *Internet of Everything (IoE)*, due to its issues of complexity and heterogeneity, message delay cannot be guaranteed, and it is not enough to leverage a centralized model for data collaboration. By leveraging the features of blockchain and asynchronous consensus algorithms, a new trust collaboration model can be established in an untrusted environment. Besides, the scalability issue of blockchain poses a challenge to data asynchronous collaboration. In this paper, we propose *Asycome*, a JointCloud data asynchronous collaboration mechanism based on *Directed Acyclic Graph (DAG)*. This mechanism introduces the new *Gossip about gossip* protocol, driven by message-transmitting events, to keep data synchronized in an asynchronous environment. Through two stages of voting and committing. Transactions on the same time series do not need to reach the final confirmed state before proceeding to the next transaction processing. Over time, all transactions are connected to the *DAG*, ensuring that the consensus is finally reached. We evaluated the performance of the mechanism with experiments on throughput and latency. And the feasibility of *Asycome* is analyzed from the liveness and security. The results show that higher throughput, lower latency, and *Asynchronous Byzantine Fault Tolerance (ABFT)* characteristics can meet the technical requirements of complex and asynchronous data collaboration of the *IoE* to some extent.

Keywords: JointCloud · Asynchronous · Blockchain · DAG · Hashgraph

1 Introduction

Data collaboration enables the original and single data from multi-source Data Service Providers (DSPs) to be integrated, value-added, and converted to meet the customization needs of Data Service Consumers (DSCs), make the data play its real value, and improve processing efficiency. Meanwhile, it can ensure integrity, privacy, and security. Asynchronous collaboration refers to the process

© Springer Nature Singapore Pte Ltd. 2021
H.-N. Dai et al. (Eds.): BlockSys 2021, CCIS 1490, pp. 530–544, 2021.
https://doi.org/10.1007/978-981-16-7993-3_41

of collaboration between collaborators in an asynchronous environment, where there is no reliable network and message latency is not guaranteed. This enables transactions in the same time series to proceed to the next transaction without reaching the final confirmed state. JointCloud [1] is a new generation of cloud computing model. Cloud services as the carrier of a large amount of data, Joint-Cloud computing can analyze information and bring the value of multiple types of data to full play.

The asynchronous model can better support the complex interaction of the *IoE*, but it is difficult to reach a consensus in the asynchronous environment. In *IoE*, the interaction among multiple centers will lead to complex data collaboration. Synchronization does not serve multi-domain data collaboration well. On the one hand, the large amount of data will consume too much system resources. On the other hand, it is difficult to reach a consensus on the distributed clock. There are also the effects of the device itself and the network environment. Asynchrony is based on the event-driven model [2,3]. Compared with synchronization, the event-driven model can significantly reduce the consumption of system resources with a good response time.

A mode that relies entirely on central management and control faces some challenges in terms of cost and efficiency. At present, most of the Internet of things (IoT) ecosystem still relies on a centralized model. Collecting data and information with a centralized platform like OneNet [4], Yeelink [5], all devices are connected by a centralized cloud service. In *IoE*, the collaborators are in different places and different fields. There is a lack of natural mutual trust and a centralized organization for cross-domain arbitration. There may be "Byzantine" nodes that hinder collaboration. Therefore, it is necessary to develop a mechanism to implement the trusted exchange of data in a distributed environment.

By its characteristics, blockchain [6] can establish new trust collaboration patterns. The blockchain is resistant to modification of its data. In the meantime, it can trace the original data. The nodes in the blockchain network can reach effective consensus for the new data, and propagate the information to the whole network. The above features can make up the deficiency of the existing data collaboration methods. However, the performance problems of blockchain have been criticized. Bitcoin is poor in scalability and does not have resistance to 51% attack [7]. Besides, mining for Bitcoin consumes a mass of energy. DAG is a distributed ledger technology different from the blockchain. The transaction can be executed concurrently, and the process of reaching consensus does not require mining. Hashgraph [8] is a consensus algorithm for DAG that is faster and more secure than conventional blockchains. In *IoE*, the dynamics and uncertainty of complex asynchronous interactions directly determine the difficulty of data collaboration. DAG technology is fairer and more efficient, which can solve the above challenges. The main contributions of this paper can be summarized as follows:

(1) We propose *Asycome*, a JointCloud data asynchronous collaboration mechanism based on DAG, to solve the problem of poor scalability due to blockchain-based data collaboration.

(2) We design an asynchronous collaboration mechanism. Moreover, the feasibility of this method is qualitatively analyzed from the aspects of liveness and security.

(3) We conduct experiments to evaluate throughput and latency on different scales. This shows that the mechanism can achieve more efficient consensus. To some extent, the need for asynchronous collaboration of data in *IoE* is solved.

2   Related Work

It is a feasible solution to adopt blockchain to solve asynchronous interactions in the *IoE*. The blockchain is still confronted with scalability issues. Therefore, it is necessary to study how to reach consensus in the asynchronous network and improve the scalability of the blockchain to establish a fairer, more efficient, and safer asynchronous collaboration mechanism.

2.1   Asynchronous Network Models

Blockchain includes not only the consensus protocol and its participants, but also the connections among participants, known as the network model.

The basic network models include the synchronous model [9], semisynchronous model [10], and asynchronous model [9]. The main feature of the asynchronous model is that participants have no upper limit of time when receiving, processing, and responding to messages, and the system has no global clock, which is similar to the Internet. However, in a fully asynchronous distributed system, in which at least one process may have a crash failure, it has been proven in the famous FLP impossibility [11] result that a deterministic algorithm for achieving consensus is impossible.

At present, there are mainly methods to reach asynchronous consensus, such as modifying determinism and adding time assumptions. Modifying determinism is to introduce the concept of randomization and design probabilistic or non-deterministic algorithms. The hashgraph [8] algorithm has been verified as an asynchronous and non-deterministic algorithm. Non-determinacy means that after r rounds (r may grow to infinity), the probability that a non-error process is still undetermined approaches zero [12]. We designed the mechanism in the same way.

2.2   Directed Acyclic Graph

There are already some solutions to the problem of blockchain performance, including lightning network [13], sidechain [14], sharding [15], and so on. Another way is DAG technology. In the blockchain, each block records multiple transactions of multiple users and cannot be executed concurrently. This creates efficiency issues. Bitcoin, for example, averages 7 transactions per second (tps), and Ethereum is about 20 tps [16]. The DAG unit is a TX (transaction), which records transactions of a single user, and can record transactions simultaneously or asynchronously. This naturally meets the needs of asynchronous collaboration.

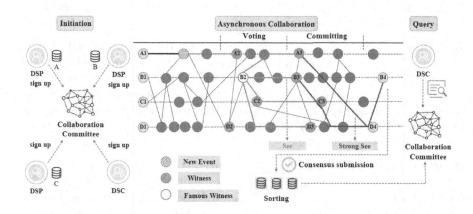

Fig. 1. *Asycome*, a JointCloud data asynchronous collaboration mechanism.

IOTA's [17] tangle is a distributed ledger structure based on DAG. The consensus is executed in parallel, so the network can expand as the number of transactions increases. However, IOTA has no handling fee, so there is no incentive for miners and may face denial of service attacks [18]. Byteball [19] introduces the concept of main chain and witness. However, due to the relationship between the main chain and the witness, Byteball's current expansion capabilities and speed are limited to a certain extent. Hashgraph uses the *Gossip about gossip* protocol [8] to synchronize data continuously. Over time, all nodes have the same hashgraph. With their local DAG, users can know what consensus is recognized by most people in the entire network. Compared with other consensus algorithms, the consensus of hashgraph [20] is carried out locally without additional communication overhead.

In summary, there are no conditions for achieving synchronous and deterministic consensus in the *IoE*, and DAG-based solutions still have performance limitations. We should adopt feasible and effective methods to establish safe and efficient asynchronous JointCloud data collaboration.

3   Asynchronous Data Collaboration Mechanism

In this section, we will introduce the design of the JointCloud data asynchronous collaboration mechanism and the detailed data collaboration process.

3.1   Data Asynchronous Collaboration Mechanism

We propose *Asycome*, an asynchronous collaboration mechanism for JointCloud data. As shown in Fig. 1, the mechanism consists of three modules, including **Initiation**, **Asynchronous Collaboration**, and **Query**. The DSPs share their data. Multiple DSPs can upload concurrently. The data is encapsulated as an event, including timestamp, transaction data, self-parent hash, and other-parent hash. This event will be propagated within a certain range. The detailed introduction of each module is as follows:

Initiation. We assume a collaboration committee consisting of three DSPs and one DSC. Everyone in the committee has a pair of public and private keys, which are generated by the key generation system ed25519 [21]. The public key can be shared with committee members. The private key is kept secret. Each DSP uses the public key to encrypt the data, and the DSC uses the private key to sign the data. Only the designated recipient can decrypt. Each member encapsulates its transaction data into the event.

Asynchronous Collaboration. The asynchronous collaboration period consists of two stages: the *voting* stage and the *committing* stage. Members will first communicate with each other randomly through the *Gossip about gossip* protocol before voting and committing. Each member needs to execute two main steps: 1) Constantly synchronize event with a random node; 2) Determine whether to attach data from another member to create a new event. In a gossip network, each member may know all other members, or may only know a few neighbors. They communicate with each other randomly. For example, Alice randomly selects a neighbor, Bob, to send all the information that she knows but that Bob does not. Bob generates a new event. Bob also randomly sends a message to Carol that he knows but Carol does not. After a messy communication process, the event is continuously synchronized. Eventually, all members have the same ledger, recording all transaction data and communications, and knowing who verified which transaction and when. The ledger is a DAG. This is the key to ensuring that the events can finally reach an agreement. Then the asynchronous collaboration process is through voting to reach a consensus on an event. But it is virtual voting, and members do not actually send voting information. The strongly seeing or seeing between events is used as the vote standard, which is based on the witness message and digital signature. After two stages of voting and committing, a consensus was finally reached. Submit the consensus. The consensus events are sorted according to the values of the round received. When the values of the round received are equal, they are sorted according to the consensus timestamp.

Query. By querying the same distributed ledger, the consensus result is returned if the consensus is confirmed. At the same time, the consensus timestamp and order will be obtained. Of course, only members of the collaboration committee have the right to query.

3.2   Collaboration Mechanism Details

After the initiation phase, the DSP uploads the data. In Fig. 1, the dots represent events one by one, and the four timelines A, B, C, and D represent four members respectively. All events sent by each member are arranged in their timelines in order from left to right. Each new event needs to contain the hash value of the previous event on the same timeline and is called the self-parent hash of the new event. The new event also contains another hash value, which is the hash value of an event on another timeline, called the other-parent hash. For example, if B sends some

---

Algorithm 1. *Asycome*, Data asynchronous collaboration process.

Input: Committee members [A, B, C] as DSPs, committee member D as a DSC, $TX[Data_i]=Data_A$, $Data_B$, $Data_C$.

Output: Reach a consensus.

Initialize: Each member encapsulates its transaction data into the event.

Event{timestamp, transactions, self-parent hash, other-parent hash}

1: **while** isNewEvent **do**
2:    B sends all known events to a random member.
3: **if** isNeighbor **then**
4:    A receives events from its neighbor, B.
5:    A creates a new event that contains the event sent to it by B and A's original event.
6: **else**
7:    continue
     /* Each node votes and confirms according to its local DAG; */
8: **while** True **do**
9:    boolean isWitness();
10: /* The first event created by each member in a round is called witness; */
11:    boolean isFamous();
12: /* If the witness of round r can be seen by a supermajority (more than 2/3 of the total) of the witnesses of round $r+1$, then it is a famous witness; */
13:    If an event can be seen by all the famous witnesses in the r round, then the event's round received is r, i.e., the event reached the confirmed state.
14:    getConsensusTimestamp();
15: /* Sort events based on round received and consensus timestamps; */
16: **return** consensus

---

information to neighbor A, A generates a new event containing the hash of A and B, respectively. Then continue to do this, gossiping event randomly to other members in an encrypted manner. Each member receives events sent by other members, saves them locally, and eventually forms a DAG based on the hash pointer. If an unspecified member does not have the key to decrypt the event after receiving the event, the event will be discarded. Otherwise, the witness information will be added and it will continue to spread to other members. These correspond to the steps in lines 1–7 of Algorithm 1. The following is a detailed description:

Voting. There are multiple rounds of collaboration. When a new event spreads to the next member, that member adds witness information. These witness messages are used to manage the round created and the round received. When the event is created, it is assigned to the round number. The round created of an event is r or $r+1$, where r is the maximum round of the parent of the event. The round created of the event is $r+1$ if and only if a supermajority of round r witnesses are strongly seeing for the event. Witnesses are a special type of event, that is, the first event created in a round. In Fig. 1, witnesses are highlighted in blue, such as A_2, A_3, etc. In a certain round, there may be no witnesses, because the member does not send events in this round. The new round of witnesses will vote to determine whether the previous round of witnesses is famous or not, and then the next round of witnesses will count the votes. Only witnesses send and receive votes. The round number of event x is round r. Whether it is a famous witness needs to be decided by later witnesses. The witnesses in round $r+1$ are members of the voting committee. If x is seen, cast YES, otherwise cast NO. (*See*: A node creates two events x and y. If event z has x as an ancestor but does not have y as an ancestor, then event z can see event x.)

Committing. The witnesses of round $r+2$ collect the votes in round $r+1$ if the witnesses of round $r+2$ can strongly see the witnesses of round $r+1$. (*Strongly see*: Event x can strongly see event y when it can find that all paths of event y pass through more than $2n/3$ nodes, where n is the number of nodes.) That is, if the number of votes exceeds $2/3$, the event is determined to be a famous witness. If not enough votes are collected, more rounds are continued until a decision is made. In Fig. 1, event B_2, highlighted in yellow, are famous witnesses. Deciding whether an event is a famous witness will not go on forever. When all or most of the famous witnesses see an event, the event reaches a final confirmation status. From the time dimension, the event needs to go through the two stages of voting and committing before it is possible to reach the final confirmation status. These correspond to the steps in lines 8–16 of Algorithm 1.

4   Experiments and Discussion

In this section, we describe the process of building an asynchronous collaboration prototype system and evaluate the performance of the proposed mechanism in several ways.

4.1   Implementation

We build an asynchronous data collaboration prototype system using the Hedera consensus service [22]. First, We introduce some words:

Client: A client that has a valid account ID, public and private key pair. The client sends the transaction to the network to reach a consensus.

Testnet node: A node that reaches consensus on transactions in the Hedera network.

Mirror node: A node that receives post consensus transactions from testnet.

Topic: A topic is used to identify related transactions, with a uniquely identified topicID.

Message: A string of data submitted to a specific topic.

A client sends a message to other clients, and the message reaches a consensus through the testnet nodes. The mirror node can view the consensus status through the topicID. To build a network of collaborative committees, some nodes need to be established. Configure keys on these nodes so that the nodes that own the keys can see each other. We also need to obtain the client's account ID and the public key and private key pair associated with it. This information is sent to the testnet as an account credential for signing.

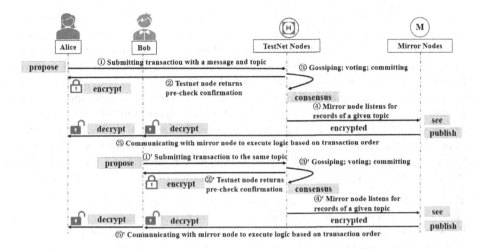

Fig. 2. The flow of asynchronous data collaboration between Alice and Bob.

As shown in Fig. 2, we describe asynchronous data collaboration between two clients. First, Alice creates a transaction that contains messages and a topic. The topicID is attached to the message and sent to the testnet. Topics will allow messages with the same topicID to be grouped. Alice can either delete a topic or specify a collaborating member to submit a message to that topic. The message includes details about the transaction. With topicID, the data sharing scope is set so that only members who know the topicID can see it. It improves the privacy and security of data. The testnet will verify whether the topicID is valid and return Alice a pre-checked confirmation result. If the message is valid, it is packaged as an event. The testnet will gossip about the event to other parts of the network. Otherwise, the message is discarded. Bob is the collaborator with Alice who submits his transactions to the same topicID. He can also submit to another topic. Let's assume that the topicID is the same. And it goes through two stages of voting and committing, and finally determines the consensus timestamp of the event. It needs to wait until an agreement is reached and then persists the message to the mirror node for a display to other nodes. Then a record will be generated which includes the message, topic, sequence, and consensus timestamp. The timestamp for reaching a consensus is 100% final, usually reached within a few seconds. The mirror node listens for records for a given topic. Since the mirror node receives all the information from the testnet, it knows the transaction and consensus order. It can also construct a proof of status to third parties. The mirror node sees the new message and publishes it to topic subscribers Alice and Bob. They can check whether a consensus has been reached by looking at a web browser (such as Kabuto or DragonGlass).

4.2   Verification

Through multiple tests, we found that there was no loss or error in the transmission of data, and the JointCloud data asynchronous collaboration could be achieved quickly. Throughput and latency are important indicators to evaluate the scalability of a blockchain. Throughput is defined as the number of transactions committed per second. Latency is defined as the time it takes for an event to reach a consensus. For further verification, we evaluated the performance of the *Asycome* mechanism and conducted several sets of experiments to compare the throughput and latency on different scales. We implemented the mechanism evaluation in Java and deployed it on a server, which has 8 cores and 32 GB memory. For the sake of simplicity, we assume that each node has the same computing power in the system, which means that performance differences between nodes are ignored. Also, assume that each transaction is the same size, 100 bytes. Specifically include the following 7 indicators:

Trans/sec: The number of transactions received per second.
cEvents/sec: The number of events created by the node per second.
Events/sec: The number of events received by the node per second.
secC2C: The time from creating an event to reaching a consensus.
secC2H: The time from a consensus being reached to being handled.
secR2C: The time from another member receiving the event to a new event being created.
secR2nR: The time from the first event received in one round to the first event received in the next round.

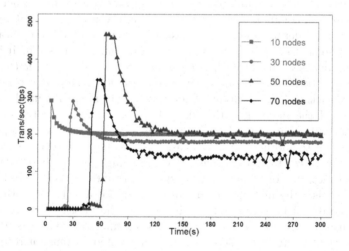

Fig. 3. The number of transactions received per second.

The Effect of the Different Number of Nodes on Throughput. We set the number of nodes from 10 to 70. Figure 3 shows the number of transactions received per second, in tps. We recorded five minutes of data. The average throughput is about 200 tps. According to the experimental data, the maximum can reach about 465 tps, and the number of nodes at this time is 50. When the number of nodes is less than 50, as the number of nodes increases, more transactions are created per second. As the scale of the system increases, nodes receive

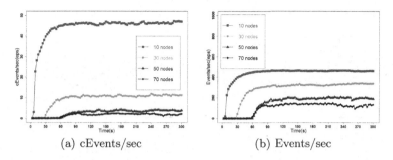

(a) cEvents/sec   (b) Events/sec

Fig. 4. cEvents/sec: The number of events created per second. Events/sec: The number of events received per second.

more and more synchronization information. It can be foreseen that the throughput of the system will decrease as the number of nodes increases. Also, when the number of nodes is between 10 and 30, it takes less time to start up than when the number of nodes is 50 and 70. Figure 4(a) and Fig. 4(b) respectively show the number of events created by the node per second and the number of events received by the node per second. In general, as the number of nodes in the network increases, fewer events are created per second, and fewer events are received per second. Of course, throughput is not a fixed value. If computing resources increase, throughput may be improved.

The Effect of the Different Number of Nodes on Latency. We also evaluated the latency at the different number of nodes, as shown in Fig. 5. They are all in seconds. With a fixed number of nodes, the time from creation to consensus of an event does not increase continuously. When increased to a certain extent, the time will gradually level off. At a fixed time, as the number of nodes increases, the time from event creation to consensus gets longer, which means the latency gets longer as well. Because over time, each node needs to synchronize more and more events. We calculated the average of the time required for an event to reach consensus. With the increase in the number of nodes, the average time for the event to reach consensus gradually increases. When the number of nodes is 70, the latency is about 22 s. The 70 nodes can be regarded as a part of *IoE*, and consensus can be reached in this part. When multiple similar consensuses are reached respectively and combined, the *IoE* global consensus is reached. As can be seen from Fig. 6, the latency of collaboration mainly comes from the consensus of the event. When the number of nodes is 10, the average secC2H can reach as low as 0.00104 s. The sorting time after the event reaches a consensus and the time it takes to create a new event after receiving the event are very short.

In the same environment, we conducted experiments to compare the scalability of IOTA and *Asycome*. Table 1 shows the result. Compared with IOTA, the performance of *Asycome* is obvious. It can be seen from the table that the throughput of *Asycome* is at least 10 times that of IOTA at the same scale. When the number of nodes is 10, it's even about 50 times. *Asycome* has high

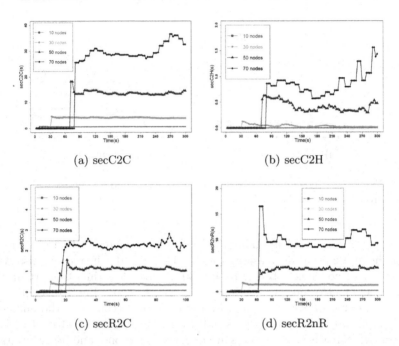

Fig. 5. The latency at the different number of nodes. (a) secC2C, the time from creating an event to reaching a consensus; (b) secC2H, the time from a consensus being reached to being handled; (c) secR2C, the time from another member receiving the event to a new event being created; (d) secR2nR, the time from the first event received in one round to the first event received in the next round.

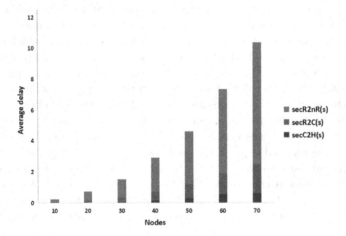

Fig. 6. Average latency under different nodes.

Table 1. Improvements of latency and throughput.

System Scale	Latency(s)		Throughput(tps)	
	IOTA	*Asycome*	IOTA	*Asycome*
n = 10	4.89	0.55	4	200.29
n = 30	19.83	3.77	9	182.36
n = 50	31.01	12.74	11	213.20
n = 70	55.96	25.08	15	161.57

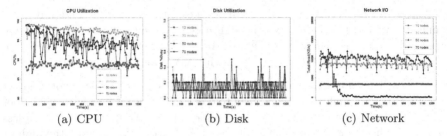

(a) CPU   (b) Disk   (c) Network

Fig. 7. When the number of nodes is 10, 30, 50, and 70, the corresponding CPU utilization, disk utilization, and network conditions.

throughput and low latency, which means it has better scalability so that is more applicable to larger systems.

In addition, we also evaluated some external indicators, such as CPU, disk, and network. We use "*nmon*", a tool for monitoring system resources. During the experiment, *nmon* captured the resource consumption of the server system. We select experimental data with the number of nodes 10, 30, 50, and 70, as shown in Fig. 7, the corresponding CPU utilization, disk, and network conditions under different nodes. CPU utilization refers to the overall CPU data at each monitoring point, including User% and Sys%. Disk-related data refers to the busy status of each *hdisk* at each monitoring point in time. The network status displays the read and write data transmission rate of each network adapter at each monitoring time point, in kilobytes/second. For each set of experiments, we recorded 20 min. As can be seen from the first figure, when the number of nodes increases, each CPU utilization is close to 100%. This can indicate to a certain extent that the resource utilization of the program is very high, and the resources of the CPU can be fully utilized. When the expansion is continued, performance can be further improved, and the problem of increasing scale can be dealt with, that is, scalability.

Of course, these data are constantly changing. This is related to the network environment and the configuration of the computer used. High throughput and low latency are still maintained under the influence of the network, which can also explain the good performance of the *Asycome* to a certain extent.

4.3 Analysis and Discussion

Liveness: If all correct entities initiated the protocol, then, eventually, all correct entities output some value. Simply put, it means that the valid events created by honest nodes will always reach a consensus. In a system with n nodes, reaching a consensus on a Yes/No problem requires at least $O(n^2)$ communication complexity, and some may even require $O(n^3)$. Virtual voting and the "Gossip about gossip" protocol reduce the communication overhead, because the consensus is reached locally. The *Asycome* adopts the Byzantine protocol, and its round-based structure has a delay time of $O(n\log n)$. The gossip algorithm is also called Anti-Entropy [23]. In a bounded network, each node randomly communicates with other nodes, and through messy communications, all nodes will eventually reach the same state. Due to the fast convergence of the gossip protocol, every new message can quickly reach every node in the network.

Security: The *Asycome* mechanism has ABFT characteristics. For double-spending attacks, malicious nodes need to create forks. It is impossible to tamper with data under the premise that the number of the "Byzantine" nodes is less than $n/3$, where n is the number of nodes. ABFT attributes provide the highest level of security, making *Asycome* obvious security. This enables the system to ensure that consensus is reached, even under the assumption of malicious nodes. At the same time, because there is no leader, all nodes are peer nodes, avoiding the risk of potential distributed denial-of-service (DDOS) attacks.

5 Conclusion and Future Works

This paper proposes *Asycome*, an asynchronous collaboration mechanism for JointCloud data based on DAG. It can be realized in an asynchronous environment, without affecting the collaboration process between multi-type and multi-source principals, thus transactions on the same time series do not need to reach the final confirmed state before proceeding to the next transaction processing. Over time, a consensus is reached. It significantly improves security and collaboration efficiency. Our performance evaluation shows that the *Asycome* is significantly better than the blockchain in terms of latency and throughput. To some extent, it supports the construction of DAG-based JointCloud data asynchronous collaboration in complex and asynchronous environments.

Acknowledgments. This work was supported in part by the National Natural Science Foundation of China under Grant 61772030, in part by Major Scientific Research Project of Zhejiang Lab (2021PE0AC01) and in part by GF Innovative Research Program.

References

1. Wang, H., Shi, P., Zhang, Y.: Jointcloud: a cross-cloud cooperation architecture for integrated internet service customization. In: 2017 IEEE 37th International Conference on Distributed Computing Systems (ICDCS), pp. 1846–1855. IEEE (2017)
2. Xiao, Y., Zhang, N., Li, J., Lou, W., Hou, Y.T.: Distributed Consensus Protocols and Algorithms. Blockchain for Distributed Systems Security 25 (2019)
3. Attiya, H., Welch, J.: Distributed Computing: Fundamentals, Simulations, and Advanced Topics, vol. 19. Wiley, Hoboken (2004)
4. Wang, B., Xiang, W., Ma, K., Mu, Y.Q., Wu, Z.: Design and implementation of intelligent walking stick based on onenet internet of things development platform. In: 2019 28th Wireless and Optical Communications Conference (WOCC), pp. 1–5. IEEE (2019)
5. Jiang, H., Li, Y., Li, D.: Indoor environment monitoring system based on linkit one and yeelink platform. In: 2016 2nd IEEE International Conference on Computer and Communications (ICCC), pp. 933–937. IEEE (2016)
6. Nakamoto, S.: Bitcoin: A peer-to-peer electronic cash system. Technical Report, Manubot (2019)
7. Reyna, A., Martín, C., Chen, J., Soler, E., Díaz, M.: On blockchain and its integration with IoT. challenges and opportunities. Future Gener. Comput. Syst. **88**, 173–190 (2018)
8. Baird, L.: Hashgraph consensus: fair, fast, byzantine fault tolerance. Swirlds Tech Report, Technical Report (2016)
9. Dwork, C., Lynch, N., Stockmeyer, L.: Consensus in the presence of partial synchrony. J. ACM (JACM) **35**(2), 288–323 (1988)
10. Attiya, H., Mavronicolas, M.: Efficiency of semisynchronous versus asynchronous networks. Math. Syst. Theor. **27**(6), 547–571 (1994)
11. Fischer, M.J., Lynch, N.A., Paterson, M.S.: Impossibility of distributed consensus with one faulty process. J. ACM (JACM) **32**(2), 374–382 (1985)
12. Bracha, G.: Asynchronous byzantine agreement protocols. Inf. Comput. **75**(2), 130–143 (1987)
13. Seres, I.A., Gulyás, L., Nagy, D.A., Burcsi, P.: Topological analysis of bitcoin's lightning network. In: Pardalos, P., Kotsireas, I., Guo, Y., Knottenbelt, W. (eds.) Mathematical Research for Blockchain Economy. SPBE, pp. 1–12. Springer, Cham (2020). https://doi.org/10.1007/978-3-030-37110-4_1
14. Singh, A., Click, K., Parizi, R.M., Zhang, Q., Dehghantanha, A., Choo, K.K.R.: Sidechain technologies in blockchain networks: an examination and state-of-the-art review. J. Netw. Comput. Appl. **149**, 102471 (2020)
15. Dang, H., Dinh, T.T.A., Loghin, D., Chang, E.C., Lin, Q., Ooi, B.C.: Towards scaling blockchain systems via sharding. In: Proceedings of the 2019 International Conference on Management of Data, pp. 123–140 (2019)
16. Li, C., Li, P., Zhou, D., Xu, W., Long, F., Yao, A.: Scaling nakamoto consensus to thousands of transactions per second. arXiv preprint arXiv:1805.03870 (2018)
17. Popov, S.: The tangle (2018). Available at: http://www.descryptions.com/Iota.pdf
18. Attias, V., Vigneri, L., Dimitrov, V.: Preventing denial of service attacks in IoT networks through verifiable delay functions. arXiv preprint arXiv:2006.01977 (2020)
19. Churyumov, A.: Byteball: A decentralized system for storage and transfer of value. https://byteball.org/Byteball.pdf (2016)

20. Baird, L., Luykx, A.: The hashgraph protocol: Efficient asynchronous bft for high-throughput distributed ledgers. In: 2020 International Conference on Omni-layer Intelligent Systems (COINS), pp. 1–7. IEEE (2020)
21. Brendel, J., Cremers, C., Jackson, D., Zhao, M.: The provable security of ed25519: theory and practice. IEEE Security & Privacy (2021)
22. James, J., Hawthorne, D., Duncan, K., St. Leger, A., Sagisi, J., Collins, M.: An experimental framework for investigating hashgraph algorithm transaction speed. In: Proceedings of the 2nd Workshop on Blockchain-enabled Networked Sensor, pp. 15–21 (2019)
23. Montresor, A.: Gossip and epidemic protocols. Wiley Encyclopedia of Electrical and Electronics Engineering, pp. 1–15 (1999)

Smart Tourism Identity Authentication Service Based on BlockChain and Decentralized Identifier

Jianing Li[2], Qian He[1,2(⊠)], Rengang Liang[2], and Bingcheng Jiang[1,2]

[1] State and Local Joint Engineering Research Center for Satellite Navigation and Location Service, Guilin University of Electronic Technology, Guilin 541004, China
heqian@guet.edu.cn
[2] Guangxi Key Laboratory of Cryptography and Information Security, Guilin University of Electronic Technology, Guilin 541004, China

Abstract. Smart tourism has carried the hope of the tourism industry from the very beginning, and has provided new solutions for the improvement of efficiency, humanization of services and scientific management. However, as the continuous development of smart tourism industry, various types of dishonest even illegal behavior have gradually emerged. Due to the absence of an effective identity authentication mechanism for the travel services provider, there are illegal travel agencies, unqualified part-time tour guides, etc., thereby harming the rights and interests of tourist. Considering the above problems, this paper proposes a smart tourism identity authentication service based on blockchain and Decentralized Identifier (DID). The service requester can verify the attributes of the DID, and then check the certificate. By exploiting the collaborative management of on-chain and off-chain data, the entire process of smart tourism service identity authentication is safe, reliable and traceable. In order to alleviate the storage pressure of blockchain, the InterPlanetary File System (IPFS) is introduced to store DID document and Verifiable Credential certificate. The simulation experiments demonstrated that the proposed identity authentication system is both available and effective. The purpose of this paper is to help customers improve their identification ability, and promote the comprehensive and sustainable development of smart tourism.

Keywords: Smart tourism · Blockchain · Identity authentication · DID · IPFS

1   Introduction

The concept of smart tourism in international can be traced back to 2000 when Gordon Phillips defined smart tourism as simply taking a holistic, long-term and sustainable approach to planning, developing, operating and marketing tourism products and businesses [1]. Leveraging the emerging technologies such as social

H.-N. Dai et al. (Eds.): BlockSys 2021, CCIS 1490, pp. 545–558, 2021.
https://doi.org/10.1007/978-981-16-7993-3_42

media and e-commerce, analysis of big data and online public opinion [2], internet of things and smart cities [3,4], blockchain and distributed edge computing, smart tourism can greatly improve the quality of tourism services to serve tourists and promote tourism marketing [5,6].

In China, internet companies cooperate with governments to create a global tourism industry pattern [7], which can provide tourists with a full-process smart experience and improve the convenience, fun and interactivity of smart tourism services through social media, real-time park entry, smart tour guides, virtual customer service and other functions. The smart tourism platform builds a big data exchange engine to integrate various data resources and provide data support for various application systems. After processing, it provides tourists with more real-time tourism information related to place of interest and personalized attractions recommendation considering user preferences [8]. However, the massive information contains a lot of fraudulent information such as false propaganda. Various vicious incidents of tourism consumption have been frequently exposed. Tour guides without certification and attractions which aim at forcing people to shopping have emerged one after another, result in rights of tourists have been seriously infringed. Therefore, it is necessary to construct an effective smart tourism authentication service mechanism to improve the identity authentication of practitioners in the tourism industry and help users identify industry practitioners such as tour guides and travel agency consultants.

At present, in the development of smart tourism, traditional identity authentication services in the edge environment have security problems such as scattered identity authentication information, poor authentication compatibility, lack of self-sovereignty of authentication certificates, and single point of failure. To solve the above problems, we introduce introduces Decentralized Identifier (DID) [9], a new type of identifier, which can be used for verifiable distributed digital identities. The main advantage is that it implementation is independent of any Centralized registration form, identity provider or certificate certification authority. Blockchain [10] as a decentralized, traceable, high-security technology can combined with DID to solve the problem of smart tourism in the edge environment [11] issues such as single point of failure, poor compatibility, low security, and inability to trace the source of certification process in distributed certification process. Based on the above two technical advantages, in this paper, we propose a smart tourism identity authentication service with blockchain and DID to bring service personnel engaged in the tourism industry into supervision. Our scheme provides legal DID documents and identity authentication certificates for regular travel agencies, tourist groups, intermediaries, and tour guides with national qualifications, while refuses to provide authentication services to illegal practitioners. The identity authentication system proposed in this paper has certain theoretical and practical significance for the standardization of identity authentication management in tourism industry and the development of smart tourism.

The main contributions of this paper include the following three aspects.

1) A DID-based identity authentication service system is developed to solve the problem of identity authentication in smart tourism scenarios. The system

generates a DID for the tourism service provider, and the service requester can verify the DID by certificate to ensure the security of identity authentication.

2) Taking advantage of the immutability, traceable, and decentralized characteristics of blockchain, a secure traceability method of identity authentication process based on blockchain is proposed. In order to address the problem of storage pressure in blockchain nodes, we introduce private cluster IPFS to store DID documents and VC certicates. The openness, transparency, security and traceability of identity authentication is realized by the collaborative management of on-chain and off-chain data.

3) Based on the Hyperledger fabric platform and DID, a tourism identity authentication system is designed and implemented. Theories and experiments demonstrated that the proposed identity authentication system is both available and effective, which solves the compatibility, security, and traceability of the authentication process in the construction of smart tourism.

2 Related Work

With the development of smart tourism, the identity of tourists and related practitioners in the tourism industry has another form of expression—a decentralized, self-sovereign digital identity. The wide application of blockchain in the construction of smart tourism [12] has given a new solution to the realization of self-sovereign identity. Using blockchain technology as framework, Alkhansaa et al. designed different smart contracts for indexing and retrieval to improve the automation, decentralization and security of smart tourism city services [13] by integrating the Internet of Things, intelligent transportation and big data platforms. Yunifa designed a smart tourism destination scoring system that combines the 6AsTD framework and blockchain. As a shared architecture system, tourists can connect to the blockchain network through smart mobile devices to obtain real-time tourism destination ranking data [14]. Trung-Viet proposed a blockchain-based evaluation framework to ensure the reliable evaluation of tourism services through a consensus mechanism and smart contracts. Users can track evaluation information in real time through smart devices [15].

Greg et al. proposed an identity management system based on Ethereum in response to the needs of specific services such as banking and email. The system binds all the user's identity certificates based on the unique UportD of each node, and builds a user-centric, user-self-sovereign identity management system.

For the mobile communication network application environment, BIDaaS cooperation has proposed a service management model based on a decentralized and immutable private chain and a new digital identity. BIDaaS directly obtains information from the blockchain to verify customer identities, without the need to create a new ID or Share security credentials with partners [10]. Zhu Xiaoyang et al. [16,17] applied the blockchain-based identity management architecture to IoT devices with unique identities, and realized hierarchical intelligent terminal identity management.

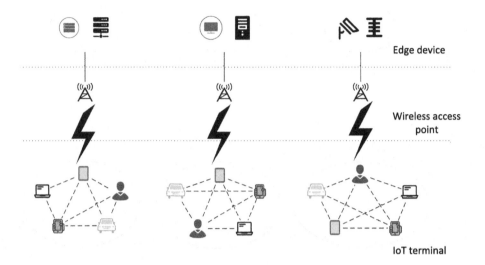

Fig. 1. Smart city terminal device interaction in the edge environment

Relevant research in the past year has shown that in the construction of smart cities at home and abroad (the terminal interaction diagram in the edge environment of smart cities is shown in Fig. 1) [18], researchers also use the integration of blockchain and Internet of Things (IoT) while other related technologies have improved the operational efficiency and service quality of smart cities. [19]

3   System Model

3.1   System Framework

Smart Tourism Identity Authentication Architecture. This paper constructs a smart tourism identity authentication system based on blockchain and DID to achieve a more secure and effective identity authentication service. The system architecture, which contains Authority Layer, Service Authentication Layer and Storage Layer, is shown in Fig. 2.

And the details of smart tourism service identity authentication is described as follows.

(1) Authority Layer: includes DID, verifiable DID certificate, as well as the issuing authority of the VC document, the private key of the certification service requester, and issuing authority of public key.

(2) Service Authentication Layer: The authentication data based on the Blockchain and Storage Layer provides identity authentication services for the authentication layer personnel. The service authentication layer is mainly composed of Authentication Service Requester (ASR), Authentication Service Provider (ASP), and corresponding DID identifier, DID document, VC certificate, and ASVP.

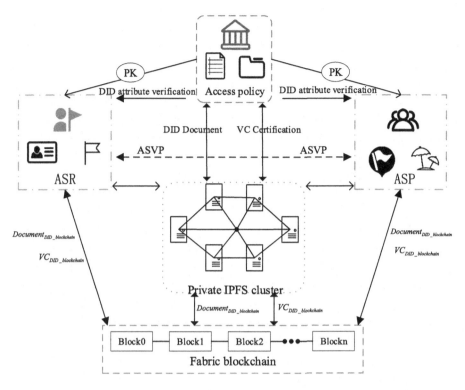

Fig. 2. Smart tourism service identity authentication architecture based on blockchain and DID

1) DID: A unique identifier formed by the concatenation of attribute strings, including identity attributes and representation attributes.

2) DID Document: DID documents are generated after parsing the unique identifier of service requester. The DID document includes attribute declaration information like DID unique identifier, public key information and identity verification protocol.

3) VC(Verifiable Credential): The credibility of the attributes of the person requesting authentication and the evidence-based trust of the authentication service entity is realized based on technologies such as digital signatures.

4) ASVP(Authenticate Service Verifiable presentation): ASVP is the data that is used by ASR to identify itself to ASP.

5) ASR(Authentication Service Requester): Industry practitioners entering tourist attractions or other areas served by this certification system need to apply for registration certification.

6) ASP(Authentication Service Provider): The edge devices, servers, and personnel who have completed the certification in the certification system.

(3) Storage Layer: The generated DID document and VC Certificate are stored on the private cluster IPFS through the smart contract, at the same time,

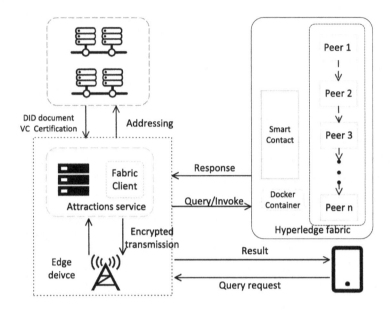

Fig. 3. Intelligent terminal query service

the relevant identification information of DID document and VC Certificate and key data such as the index location of file stored in the IPFS are stored on the blockchain. Each record in the ledger has a time constraint and a unique cryptographic signature, thereby achieving the traceability of the authentication service call.

Terminal Query Architecture. The process of smart terminal query in the smart travel service identity authentication is shown in Fig. 3. The main process of identity authentication is executed by server, and visitors can send ASVP identity authentication query requests to edge communication devices (edge base stations, wireless access points, etc.) through smart terminal devices. Edge server sends an instruction to query the chain code to the alliance chain through fabric-java-sdk. The previously deployed smart contract will return relevant identification information of DID document and VC certificate, and the index location of file stored in IPFS. Finally, the edge server will obtain and verify the corresponding DID document and VC certificate in IPFS through the specific location information that is queried, and return the result to the smart terminal through the edge communication device.

3.2   Interaction Protocol and Data Structure

DID. The DID of the authentication service requester, which is formed in accordance with w3c's distributed identifier specification, is shown in the following formula.

$$did : example : 0xbb96163789a4e16790f3d213319bd4cf2b517582$$

did: URL identifier. This item is fixed, indicating that the string is a did identification string.

Example: This item is DID method identifier, which indicates the method of defining and operating DID identifier. The user of this DID method can customize and register to the W3C website (https://w3c.github.io/did-spec-registries/did-methods).

0x+hash(Attributes): The identifier specified in the DID method. This item represents the unique identification string under the did method.

DID Document. The specific structure and components of the DID document are as follows.

$$\left\{ \begin{array}{l} @context, ID_{doc}, Authentication, PKlist_{doc}[id, type, controller], Service, \\ Time_{doc}, Sign\left[H\left(ID_{doc}||PKList_{doc}||Authentication||Service||Time_{doc}\right)\right] \end{array} \right\}$$

In order to alleviate the storage pressure of blockchain, the generated DID document is stored in private cluster IPFS, and just return the corresponding IPFS index address($Index_{Ipfs\_DocumentAddr}$), $Document_{DID\_blockchain}$ will be stored in the distributed ledger of blockchain. Its structure can be expressed likes.

$$\left\{ ID_{doc}, Index_{Ipfs\_DocumentAddr} \right\}$$

VC Certificate. VC(Verifiable Claims), The specific content of the VC certificate is as follows.

$$\left\{ \begin{array}{l} ID_{vc}, ExpirationTime, IssuanceTime, Issuer, Claim, \\ Sign\left[H\left(ID_{vc}||ExpirationTime||IssuanceTime||Issuer||Claim\right)\right] \end{array} \right\}$$

The authority generates VC Certificate while storing it in the private cluster IPFS, and returns the corresponding IPFS index address($Index_{Ipfs\_VCAddr}$), $VC_{DID\_blockchain}$ will be stored in the distributed ledger of the blockchain. Its structure can be expressed as follows.

$$\left\{ ID_{vc}, Index_{Ipfs\_VCAddr} \right\}$$

ASVP. ASVP(Authenticate Service Verifiable presentation), The composition of ASVP is: certificate ID, certificate holder's DID, ASVP signature value. ASVP is expressed in the following structure.

$$\left\{ ID_{vc}, ID_{doc}, Timestamp, Sign\left[H\left(ID_{vc}||ID_{doc}||Timestamp\right)\right] \right\}$$

4   Key Technology Realization

4.1   Identity Authentication Service Process

The Authentication Service requester must first register DID. DID authority can formulate a reasonable verification strategy to verify according to actual request information, so that it can truly control the management of the identity authentication system. The specific process of identity authentication service consists of three parts: DID distributed identifier registration, DID document and VC certificate data chaining and identity verification.

DID Registration. ASR applies for DID registration from authority, and authority verifies the identity request information of ASR according to relevant national departments and related regulations of the tourism industry. After the verification is passed, it generates ASR's DID identifier and DID document, VC certificate, ASR's private key and authority's public key according to W3C's decentralized identifier specification.

DID Document and Chaining of VC Certificate. The solution only stores the DID documents, $Index_{Ipfs\_DocumentAddr}$, $Index_{Ipfsv CAddr}$ and VC certificates on the chain, and synchronizes them to all nodes in blockchain network through the Gossip protocol in blockchain to realize the consistency of distributed ledger data among the nodes in the blockchain, which allows each node in blockchain to retrieve and access content such as DID documents and VC certificates when performing identity verification. The pseudo code about DID distributed identifier registration, DID document and the chaining of VC certificate data is as follows.

Algorithm 1. DID document and VC certificate data on-chain algorithm

---

Input: $ASR_{DID\_attribute}$
Output: $NULL$
1: DID ← generate DID distributed identifier
2: ID_{doc} ← generate DID document
3: ID_{vc} ← generate DID verification certificate
4: $Index_{Ipfs\_DocumentAddr}$ ← store DID document to IPFS
5: $Index_{Ipfs\_VCAddr}$ ← store Verification certificate to IPFS
6: $Contract executes$:
7: **if** $registration contract_{AuthCheck}(DID)$ **then**
8:     $TraceContract_{register\_DocIndes}(ID_{doc}, Index_{Ipfs\_DocumentAddr})$
9:     $TraceContract_{register\_VCIndes}(ID_{vc}, Index_{Ipfs\_VCAddr})$
10: **end if**
11: **return** $True$

Authentication. The authentication service requester ASR sends a service request with ASVP information to the identity authentication service provider ASP through the system, and the ASP authenticates the ASR based on the ASVP data provided by the ASR. Identity verification mainly includes three stages: DID attribute verification, ASVP verification and VC certificate verification.

DID attribute verification: ASP parses the ASVP data provided by ASR, obtains the distributed identifier DID of ASR, and performs attribute verification based on the DID. First, verify whether the DID method in the distributed identifier DID matches. If matches, verify the distributed identifier DID which have identity and label attributes, otherwise the ASR identity authentication fails. ASP decomposes the decentralized identifier DID, and performs hash calculation based on its own attribute requirements to obtain the corresponding hash value, and matches the decentralized identifier DID through with the hash value calculated. If match, the corresponding attribute is satisfied. Otherwise, the identity verification fails and the identity verification ends.

ASVP verification: ASP first obtains the DID decentralized identifier of ASR through the smart contract and queries the $Index_{Ipfs\_DocumentAddr}$ from the blockchain, which is used to obtain the DID document on IPFS, then obtains the ASR public key which is correspondent to the DID document. The signature value of the ASVP data is verified by the obtained ASR public key. If the signature value verification fails, the identity verification fails and the identity verification ends.

VC certificate verification: ASP queries the $Index_{Ipfs\_VCAddr}$ from blockchain through the smart contract and VC certificate ID value in ASVP data, and obtains the VC certificate on IPFS using $Index_{Ipfs\_VCAddr}$ for certificate verification. The verification process of the VC certificate is shown as follows.

Step 1: Verify the validity time of the VC certificate.

Step 2: Verify the issuer of the VC certificate.

Step 3: Verify the signature value of the VC certificate through the public key of the issuer.

4.2   Security Traceability of Identity Authentication Access Process

This paper is based on the point-to-point IPFS for off-chain storage of DID documents and VC certificates, and provides (DID documents and VC certificates) storage and retrieval services for nodes that join a private cluster, which improves the efficiency of authentication data transmission while relieves the storage pressure of blockchain.

When DID documents and VC certificates are stored in a distributed IPFS cluster, the hash index of the corresponding files will be returned. Among them, the relevant metadata and the corresponding hash index of DID document and VC certificate are stored in the Hyperledger in the IPFS.

Through the DID document and VC certificate generation and other related information and the user information called by the distributed digital identity verification interface, the user information is stored on the chain to realize the digital authentication from the registration of the DID symbol, the generation of the DID document and VC certificate to the distributed digital identity verification interface invocation.

5 Proof of Safety

This section will analyze the security of the solution in this paper from two aspects, namely the blockchain security and the system security, and perform performance analysis through experiments.

(1) Proof of Blockchain Security
    In this paper, Raft is used as the protocol algorithm of distributed storage and consensus mechanism to complete the consensus process of data blocks in the block chain. It has characteristics likes election security, leader completeness, and state machine security.
(2) Proof of System Security
    In order to ensure the function of interaction between verification services and meet the necessary security conditions required for data security, this paper evaluates the data consistency, robustness, and authenticity of the identity authentication model in the distributed application scenario.

1) Consistency and authenticity. Due to the one-way and anti-collision properties of hash function and the immutability and unforgeability characteristics of blockchain itself, the identity authentication scheme uses cryptographic algorithms to ensure the authenticity, reliability, and integrity of information transmission. The issuer of the DID documents needs to sign the hash value of the declared variable data in the certificate.
2) Robustness. In this solution, the user's DID document, VC certificate, and index address stored in IPFS initiate a transaction after consistent verification and are stored on the blockchain through a smart contract. The data consistency of distributed ledger is maintained by all nodes in the blockchain together.
3) Privacy. Through the W3C-based DID identification specification, the autonomous identity sovereignty between nodes is realized to ensure the privacy and security of edge services.

6 Experiment Analysis

6.1 Blockchain Performance Test

To solve the problem of data storage pressure, this paper designs a fabric1.4 network performance test experiment based on raft sorting, and introduces a lightweight testing tool Caliper to simulate the blockchain environment through four servers, and a total of four nodes are divided into two organizations. The parameter symbols and their meanings used in the test are shown in Fig. 4.

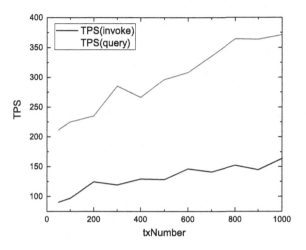

Fig. 4. Blockchain performance test

Using TPS (Throughout capacity) as performance indicator, Fig. 5 shows the result of block chain throughput test. A total of 11 experiments have been carried out. The horizontal axis indicates txNumber (number of concurrent queries). The vertical axis represents the system throughput obtained for each query. The red line and the black line represents the system throughput of the invoke method and the system throughput of the query method separately. According to the result of test, the average throughput of the query method is 269.618, while the average throughput of the invoke method is 130.573.

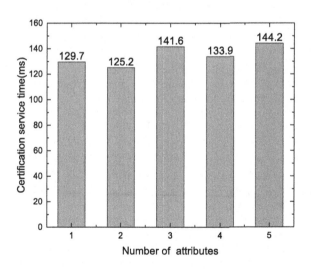

Fig. 5. Identity authentication performance test

6.2   Identity Authentication Performance Test

The smart tourism identity authentication service based on blockchain and DID includes three processes: DID identifier verification, ASVP verification, and VC certificate verification. Figure 5 shows the results of DID identity authentication performance test, which indicates the relation between the total time of authentication service and number of attributes.

7   Conclusion

To solve the problem of identity authentication in tourism market, we propose a smart tourism identity authentication service based on blockchain and DID. The system use blockchain and distributed identifier, and resolve the data storage pressure problem in blockchain with distributed private cluster IPFS to reduce the requirements for storage space of blockchain nodes. Safety, reliability, openness, transparency and traceability of the entire process of smart tourism identity authentication is realized through the collaborative management of on-chain and off-chain data. Experiments show that the identity authentication system has certain validity and practical value, it not only solves the problems of traditional identity authentication, such as scattered identity authentication information, poor authentication compatibility, security, and lack of self-sovereignty of authentication certificates, but also serves as an important supplement to smart tourism service, which provide solutions of the "last mile" problem of specific tourists and promote the healthy and sustainable development of smart tourism.

Acknowledgments. This work is supported in part by the National Natural Science Foundation of China (61661015,61967005), Guangxi Innovation-Driven Development Project (AA17202024), Guangxi Key Laboratory of cryptography and information security Found (GCIS201701), Guangxi Collaborative Innovation Center of Cloud Compu-ting and Big Data Found (YD1901), Innovation Project of GUET Graduate Education (2019YCXS046), CETC Key Laboratory of Aerospace Information Applications Found, Young and middle-aged backbone teacher of Guangxi colleges and universities Found and High Level of Innovation Team of Colleges and Universities in Guangxi Outstanding Scholars Program Funding.

References

1. Figueredo, M., et al.: From photos to travel itinerary: a tourism recommender system for smart tourism destination. In: 2018 IEEE Fourth International Conference on Big Data Computing Service and Applications (BigDataService), Bamberg, Germany, pp. 85–92 (2018)
2. Vecchio, P.D., Mele, G., Ndou, V., et al.: Creating value from social big data: implications for smart tourism destinations - Sciencedirect. Inf. Process. Manage. **54**(5), 847–860 (2018)
3. Hwoij, A., Khamaiseh, A.H., Ababneh, M.: SIEM architecture for the internet of things and smart city. In: International Conference on Data Science, E-learning and Information Systems 2021 (DATA 2021), pp. 147–152. Association for Computing Machinery, New York (2021)

4. Koo, J., Kim, Y.G.: In: Proceedings of the 36th Annual ACM Symposium on Applied Computing (SAC 2021), pp. 690–698. Association for Computing Machinery, New York (2021). https://doi.org/10.1145/3412841.3441948

5. Gretzel, Z., et al.: Mobile tourist guide supporting a smart city initiative: a Brazilian case study. Int. J. Tourism Cities **2**(2), 164–183 (2016)

6. Kontogianni, A., Efthymios, A.: Smart tourism: state of the art and literature review for the last six years. Array. **6**, 100020 (2020)https://doi.org/10.1016/j.array.2020.100020

7. Xu, C., Huang, X., Zhu, J., Zhang, K.: Research on the construction of Sanya smart tourism city based on internet and big data. In: 2018 International Conference on Intelligent Transportation, Big Data Smart City (ICITBS), Xiamen, China, pp. 125–128 (2018). https://doi.org/10.1109/ICITBS.2018.00040

8. Jorro-Aragoneses, J.L., Díaz Agudo, M.B., Recio García, J.A.: Madrid live: a context-aware recommender systems of leisure plans. In: 2017 IEEE 29th International Conference on Tools with Artificial Intelligence (ICTAI), Boston, MA, USA, pp. 796–801 (2017). https://doi.org/10.1109/ICTAI.2017.00125

9. W3C: Decentralized identifiers (DIDs). https://www.w3.org/TR/did-core/

10. Lee, J.: BIDaaS: blockchain based ID as a service. IEEE Access **6**, 2274–2278 (2018). https://doi.org/10.1109/ACCESS.2017.2782733

11. Shi, W., Sun, H., Cao, J., Zhang, Q., Liu, W.: Edge computing–an emerging computing model for the internet of everything era. J. Comput. Res. Dev. **54**(05), 907–924 (2017)

12. Srivastava, S.K.: An IAD type framework for Blockchain enabled smart tourism ecosystem. J. High Technol. Manage. Res. **32**(1), 100404 (2021)

13. Abuhashim, A., Tan, C.C.: Smart contract designs on blockchain applications. In: 2020 IEEE Symposium on Computers and Communications (ISCC), Rennes, France, pp. 1–4 (2020). https://doi.org/10.1109/ISCC50000.2020.9219622

14. Arif, Y.M., Nurhayati, H., Harini, S., Susiki Nugroho, S.M., Hariadi, M.: Decentralized tourism destinations rating system using 6AsTD framework and blockchain. In: 2020 International Conference on Smart Technology and Applications (ICoSTA), Surabaya, Indonesia, pp. 1–6 (2020). https://doi.org/10.1109/ICoSTA48221.2020.1570614662

15. Le, D.-T., Nguyen, T.-V., Lê, L.-S., Kurniawan, T.A.: reinforcing service level agreements in tourism sector the role of blockchain and mobile computing. In: 2020 International Conference on Advanced Computing and Applications (ACOMP), Quy Nhon, Vietnam, pp. 160–164 (2020). https://doi.org/10.1109/ACOMP50827.2020.00032

16. Zhu, X., Badr, Y.: Fog computing security architecture for the internet of things using blockchain-based social networks. In: 2018 IEEE International Conference on Internet of Things (iThings) and IEEE Green Computing and Communications (GreenCom) and IEEE Cyber, Physical and Social Computing (CPSCom) and IEEE Smart Data (SmartData), Halifax, NS, Canada, pp. 1361–1366 (2018). https://doi.org/10.1109/Cybermatics_2018.2018.00234

17. Zhu, X., Badr, Y., Pacheco, J., Hariri, S.: Autonomic Identity Framework for the Internet of Things. In: 2017 International Conference on Cloud and Autonomic Computing (ICCAC), Tucson, AZ, USA, pp. 69–79 (2017). https://doi.org/10.1109/ICCAC.2017.14

18. Hodson, E., Nader Sayún, M., Vainio, T.: Decoding the smart city. In: Proceedings of the 11th Nordic Conference on Human-Computer Interaction: Shaping Experiences, Shaping Society (NordiCHI 2020), New York, pp. 1–3, Article 124, Association for Computing Machinery (2020). https://doi.org/10.1145/3419249.3420076
19. Ale, L., Zhang, N., King, S.A., Guardiola, J.: Spatio-temporal bayesian learning for mobile edge computing resource planning in smart cities. ACM Trans. Internet Technol. **21**(3), 21 (2021). Article 72. https://doi.org/10.1145/3448613

ActAnyware - Blockchain-Based Software Licensing Scheme

Wei-Yang Chiu[1], Lu Zhou[2], Weizhi Meng[1(✉)], Zhe Liu[2], and Chunpeng Ge[2]

[1] DTU Compute, Technical University of Denmark, 2800 Kgs. Lyngby, Denmark
weme@dtu.dk
[2] College of Computer Science and Technology, Nanjing University of Aeronautics
and Astronautics, No. 29 Yudaojie, Nanjing, China

Abstract. Software validation is a long battle between software developers and software pirates. License validation is proposed as the protection of both developer's revenue and intellectual properties. However, as the license model becomes more complex alongside the constant changing of technology and the economic environment, a trusted and auditable software licensing validation method is required. In this paper, we briefly discuss the desirable characteristics of licensing validation method and how Blockchain can provide these desirable characteristics.

Keywords: Blockchain · Decentralized system · Software licensing · Trusted storage · IPFS

1 Introduction

Licensing is an action for competent authority granted permission to engage in a business or occupation or in an activity otherwise unlawful [1]. However, it is always a challenge to ensure that the licensee's usage is always under the End-Users License Agreement (a.k.a EULA) [2], which adequately protect both the user's right and the software companies revenue. Software Licensing Validation (SLV) is the mechanism dedicated to ensuring that the software is used under license agreement regulation [3]. The validation methods can be various, from easy and gritty to complex and nuanced. However, to avoid tightly binding the software to a specific platform or require a particular prerequisite, a software validation system should have the following requirements [4].

- The system must be inexpensive and easy to use
- The system must be compatible with other software
- The system must be easy to integrate into product or distribution

However, with the advancing information technology, standardization is inevitable. Specific hardware tricks, such as formatting disks in proprietary file systems and intercepting and redirecting low-level BIOS calls [5], are no longer preferable options. Multitasking, as Protected Mode introduced to microprocessors and the Hardware Abstract Layer introduced to the general-used operating system, forced the software validation to play on with fewer options.

© Springer Nature Singapore Pte Ltd. 2021
H.-N. Dai et al. (Eds.): BlockSys 2021, CCIS 1490, pp. 559–573, 2021.
https://doi.org/10.1007/978-981-16-7993-3_43

As most of the protection methods rely on software codes, it is unpreventable for software piraters to reverse-engineering the software in order to know the validation mechanism, so that bypass can be written, or that a keygen can be made. This is where code protection is dedicated to prevent. However, this is not enough to protect the software from distributing [6].

Moreover, with the rising complexity of the software itself and the constant-changing competing environment, the perpetual software license model is moving away from the companies' welcoming options. Software Licensing Models have become more complex and flexible, in which finding policies that satisfied both software developers' income and the shrewd customers' spending. These require software validation methods to be more difficult to implement. A successful software validation method should have the following characteristics [3]. 1) The license mechanism should be hard to duplicate; 2) Validation of the usage rights should be easy; 3) Others cannot generate software licenses repeatedly, and 4) The mechanism must be prevented from MiTM (man-in-the-middle) attacks.

In this work, we advocate that the use of Blockchain and smart contract is beneficial, and propose a solution called ActAnywhere, based on Blockchain and IPFS. Blockchain holds critical licensing information with smart contracts' enforceability, while IPFS holds the encrypted, protected software components for the software. It can provide the following benefits.

- `Integrity and Immutability`: Blockchain is an append-only datastore that requires all participants to validate and guard the existing records. Records are cryptographically sealed in connected blocks. All participants should keep a full or partial copy of the ledger as a reference to audit others.
- `Automation with Trust`: Smart contracts are small programs that utilize Blockchain as their storage for codes and states. Codes are immutable after being published. States are considered are transactions - hence, every change of the state is irreversible and traceable. The practice creates a transparent automation environment.
- `Ubiquitous`: No more "server is down". Run it locally, affect broadly.

Paper Organization. In Sect. 2, we will briefly discuss some standard software licensing models and their SLVs, some common ways of getting around with SLVs. Section 3 details the design of our system and Sect. 4 explores the system's performance and how the system can defeat the common ways of cheating-finally. Section 5 concludes the work.

2   Related Work

2.1   Software Licensing Model and Software Licensing Validation

There are various software licensing models to fit the need of different end-users. Different models require different implementations of software licensing validation to enforce the EULA. The followings are some models that are constantly mentioned.

Perpetual License. Being one of the first license models, Perpetual License is one of the most common types. Such a license is applied to software that is sold one-time. The purchaser can use the copy of the software forever. However, it usually does not come with software upgrades. Hence, it is dedicated to a specific version of the software [11].

However, though being the easiest mode, software developers are moving away to other models for better revenue. There are several ways of implementing validation (SLVs) of perpetual license. Here are some common methods.

- `Limited Installation Count`: This simple scheme can be seen in the early years of software licensing. The installer may keep records of installation count, whether cryptographically or plainly. Although this scheme effectively prevents software piracy from sharing genuine installation media, it can be easily defeated by either directly copying the installation media or, in some cases, making the installation media read-only. Such a scheme is rarely seen nowadays.
- `Product Key Verification`: Product key verification usually occurs during product installation or the first boot-up of the software. If the end-user cannot provide a valid product key, either the installer will refuse to complete the installation, or the software will refuse to startup [7]. Usually, either the software or installer itself has a calculation step to verify the product key's validity. However, the measure of ascertaining product keys should be carefully protected from the public. Otherwise, such a method is nothing more than a hassle step.
- `Online Activation (Registration)`: Requiring users to perform online software activation is roughly appeared around the early 2000s [12]. Most of them are considered as an extension step of product key verification. However, in this case, the product key is usually a mere step to check whether the software can be installed. Different from the product key verification model, the activation server holds the software usage permit. Hence, after the installation is completed, the software requires the user to activate in a period of time [10]. Otherwise, the software will refuse to start or continue with limited functionality. Although the scheme mending the disadvantage of the product key verification model that the software company cannot perform a double-check, it does not mean such method is unbreakable.
- `Account Control`: Account control can be considered as the latest model of perpetual software licensing. The software license is bounded with a personal account. The accounts and software licensing distribution are either managed by the software company itself or a digital publishing platform.

Floating License. A floating license is a term that describes a group of users sharing a limited number of allowances. It creates a mechanism that, once all allowances have been checked out, others have to wait until the license to be returned [10].

Since floating licensing requires constant monitoring of the number of software that runs concurrently, the software license validation works differently and usually more costly than a perpetual license validation model.

– `Network Licensing Server`: A network license server is a controller for a floating license scheme. It maintains the licensing pool and manages the license verification request from the software client. Usually, the licensing server is either hosted privately or managed by the software company (or a trusted third party). Software clients will send heartbeats toward the licensing server, in which the licensing server can keep the licensing pool up-to-date [10].

Subscription License. A subscription license is that the usage allowance should be periodically reviewed and renewed. Typically, such a license type does not have a precise termination date, it depends on the end-users' decision [11].

– `Online Activation (Registration)`: Although the schematic works no difference from a perpetual license verification will do, it adds the duration allowance. Each key is bounded with a time period. It requires the user to reactivate the product when a period ends. This scheme can be easily found in Antivirus software during the mid-2000s [13].
– `Account Control`: It works similarly to a perpetual license that bounded to an account. However, it adds the license duration as a factor.

To get around the SLVs, there are several methods as below.

Key Generators. Key generators (Keygen) is a small program that generates product keys that a software license verifier can accept. Suppose the step of verifying the product key can be easily revealed by reverse engineering, or the formation of a valid key can be simply done by observation [14]. In that case, it is no doubt that a keygen can be easily created. Without either an unreversible product key verification step (such as a hash step) or another pair of eyes to audit (e.g., online activation), it is not easy to prevent keygens.

Crack/Patch. A crack or patch is a tampered software that either has the verification steps removed or makes a fake allowance. The tampered software makes the verifier believe that it is used under license [14]. In some cases, for software that requires online activation, a crack or patch will deliberately trick the verifier to believe that no network connection is existed so that other keygen tamper-able activation methods can be triggered (e.g., Phone activation).

Activation Server. An activation server can be a genuine activation server that has been accessed unauthorized or a piece of software sending bogus heartbeat to trick the software verifier to believe that the software is used according to the license agreement [15].

2.2   Related Proposal

Blockchain ensures the integrity of records, and the addition of smart contract functionality provides additional automation, enabling the capability of such platform to be a software license verifier. However, there are only a few implementations of applying Blockchain technology for software license verification.

In early 2015, Jeff and Alan proposed a software license validation method upon Blockchain technology. It is inspired by the way cryptocurrency platforms exchanging tokens between wallets. In their method, each software license agreement is considered as a token. Purchasing software can be considered as an asset transfer between the two. Simultaneously, the underlying blockchain provides the auditability and transparency of the records and ensures the transaction integrity [3].

Later, in 2018, they demonstrated an upgraded version of their previously proposed - The ReSOLV. Unlike viewing the software licenses as a token, they change the data structure of Blockchain to keep licensing records. Rather than a regular blockchain structure that contains multiple transaction records, the proposed ReSOLV block data structure is shown as below [9]:

- **Token (T1):** A token that acts as a unique license validation identifier, managed by the ReSOLV platform maintainer.
- **License Key (K1):** The software license key that may identify the license type.
- **Software Hash (SH):** To ensure the software is not tampered.
- **Bootstrap:** The software's bootstrap code.
- **Signature from the Software Vendor:** Ensure the vendor to acknowledge the agreement.

Privacy is always an issue of Blockchain. Except that the Software Vendor's Signature requires the software vendor's public key to validate, others can only be decrypted or validated by the user's private key.

Recently, Federico et al. [8] demonstrated an efficient software license management scheme upon Blockchain. The model focuses on the pay-as-you-grow business model. Hence, the software licenses may have constant changes due to the demand. The topic focuses on a Business-to-Business model that involves two critical roles. The practice enables an always online and unified license pool for companies to combine ease-of-management and high availability for their endpoint software verifiers. Software companies can also benefit from smart contracts' automation for dynamically locating usage allowance when their customers require it.

3 Our Proposed System

Our system is targeted toward a Business to Client (B2C) model, hence that most of our customers here are assumed, home users. A Business to Business (B2B) model can be more flexible and complex than the retail market, in which we may not be our expertise in response. However, we leave flexibilities to let developers extend the validation process's customized routine for exceptional cases. Here, we want to start with a short recall and our responses to the discussed problem.

- **Difficulties of validation in a distributed environment:** To ensure that the software is always under the usage of EULA, a license verifier without the threat of being tampered is the fundamental requirement. As mutable storage requires an additional reference to ensure the integrity of the executables (e.g., Signatures), we cannot deny the possibility of both being altered. Blockchain and the smart contract can provide a trusted, undeniable, and traceable execution environment, which will raise the difficulties of cheating on another level.

- The integrity of software components: People argue that, as long as the software resides on mutable storage, we can find a way to alter and be able to fool the software to believe that it is licensed. Blockchain, again, provides a way for the software company to publish integrity software components integrity references with confidence (e.g., Hash Value).

- Inevitable distributing: We basically agree that distributing software is inevitable. However, it does not mean that we should start our arguing about how to prevent distributing rather than ensure that the licensed software is running under license condition. We applied IPFS for software companies to securely distributed software components that should be intellectually protected. These components are encrypted with the mix of both destinated user's key, the distribution-specific keys, and the target machine UUID. This practice allows the software to be continuously distributed without the confidence of being misused.

3.1 System Overview

The whole network consists of three critical parties: the software companies, the user, and the software. Companies publish and access software license profiles through the license gateway on their local premises. While the end-users and software can rely upon their device to join the network.

The network also contains two subsystems - The License Blockchain to enforce the software used on the license agreement, and the IPFS to both transfer the protected components securely to the destination and ensure that no others are able to access with its DHT locating design - without an address, you cannot access it. Participants must join both of the subsystems as a prerequisite for our proposed license verifier mechanism to work. We describe the system structure with a broadview in Fig. 1.

3.2 Critical Roles

Software Companies are mainly firms that responsible for software development. However, in our system, Software companies are companies that are responsible for distributing software licenses. Although in most cases, they are the software developer themselves.

Software companies are required to equip their license management system to connect and interact with Blockchain and IPFS. This piece of middleware or the management system itself is named license gateway in our proposed system.

End-Users are the software buyers or users that either obtain a new license or have an existing license. Users have their key pair respectively. The key pair enables the user to sign and protect their purchased assets from others.

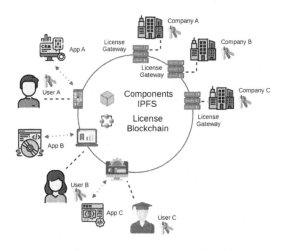

Fig. 1. System overview

Table 1. Blockchain storage consumption with different amount of smart contract.

Records on the chain				
Records	500	10,000	100,000	1,000,000
Full node	12 MB	48.1 MB	180.6 MB	1,792.4 MB

Software Packages are software that users can either obtain from retail or through online digital delivery. When users obtain the software, it is a piece of software either with limited functionality or does not come with a bootstrapped, depending on the software companies decision.

Users must activate the software and complete registering their licenses to obtain the other parts of the software component through IPFS.

3.3   Network Properties

IPFS can be a relatively simple file-sharing and observing-oriented peer-to-peer file system. However, Blockchain may be a more complicated problem toward our implementation. As there exist a lot of different types of Blockchain platforms, we will detailly describe the implementation of our network.

License Blockchain. Blockchain, according to its design, requires participants to obtain a whole chain or partial chain that, at least, able to represent the latest state of all records. However, this can run into a problem. We emulated the disk space consumption with amounts of our smart contract deployed to estimate the storage requirement in the future. When reaching one million of sold copies, the chain-size is generally unbearable in a limited computing platform, as shown in Table 1.

Table 2. Light node storage consumption with different amount of smart contract.

Records on the chain				
Records	500	10,000	100,000	1,000,000
Light node	1.3 KB	5.5 KB	20.7 KB	205.6 KB

Our chain only contains the licensing information rather than previous implementation that will contain a small amount of software bootstrapper code in the transaction. In our case, such storage requirement may be acceptable when sufficient IT infrastructure is implemented on the software company side, however, not on the customer premises. If we adopt the previous model to include a small amount of bootstrapper code, we cannot estimate the feasibility of the system because of the amount of data that every party is going to store.

If Blockchain needs to be applied, there must be some changes. We embedded our system upon Ethereum with few tweaks.

- **Enabling light node on customer's premesis**
  Light mode is a special mode for an Ethereum Client. Different from a regular full node or partial node, a light node only downloads and stores block headers of the chain. This practice shrinks the data that the client has to store significantly. In Table 2, we displayed that how light node can make the Blockchain desirable for clients, even for resource-limited devices. Light node provides a featherweight solution, however, it has some downside. The client relies on a partial or full node to complete the transaction request, either downloading or uploading.

- **Miners only mine when there are pending transactions**
  The property of immutability makes blockchain an append-only decentralized datastore. Constant mining may be profitable for a public blockchain, however, not for a dedicated one. Mining, even there are no pending transactions, raises the mining difficulties by adding blocks (data) into the storage - slowing down the later transaction speed and growing the chain size with no usefulness.

- **Separating by chainID and networkID**
  It is not fair for customers to hold much unrelated information. For example, an Adobe user may not be interested in holding registration data from Microsoft. Using chainID and networkID to separate the chain accordingly can also effectively shrink the storage requirement on the customer's premises.

IPFS Component. InterPlantary File System (IPFS) is a distributed file system designed to expand the lifespan of current Internet contents. It shares some similarities with the famous P2P file-sharing software BitTorrent [16].

All users are responsible to hold partial data of the whole network. However, people may be misunderstood the concept a little bit. Each IPFS client is equipped with a cache. When the user retrieves data through the IPFS network, it stays on the user's local cache - Hence, the user is interested in this piece of information. Garbage collection, in computer terminology, is an act of releasing unused resources, shortened as GC. IPFS may periodically trigger GC to remove uninteresting contents from the cache (e.g., users not accessing it frequently). Users can deliberately tell the IPFS to pin a particular resource so it will not be removed by GC. This enables the flexibility of IPFS, naturally fading out uninteresting contents. We use IPFS as our components network is because,

- **Friendly toward storage** The customer only has to hold her related software components. If the software is uninstalled or expired, the software component package, which is encrypted, will be naturally fade out.
- **Resource can be securely accessed** Without the address, there is no possible way other than brute force to find the file.

3.4 Actions and Steps

Actions and steps are the core of the system. Before we start our introduction toward the basic steps, we have to describe our smart contract design detailly. Figure 2 illustrates the smart contracts and their in-between relationship.

User Profile. The user profile contains the basic information of the user. However, as privacy is always an inevitable concern on the Blockchain platform, we simplified the user profile as below.

- `owner`: The user's wallet address.
- `userIdentifier`: The user identifier is a UUID to each user profile.
- `userPublicKey`: The user's public key encoded in Base64 format.

License Contract. The License contract is the key to our system - The main software verifier. When a user buys a license from the software company, the company will create this contract for the software to reference.

- `owner`: The user's profile address. This is required since some functions allow only the user to operate.
- `issuer`: The firm's profile address. This is required as the same reason of the owner.
- `totalLicenseCount`: The total allowance of running software concurrently on different machines.
- `usedLicenseCount`: Keeping records of used licenses.
- `expireDate`: The license expiration date.
- `license_pool`: The license pool contains the information of the registered machine and its related dispatch of software components. The machineID is encrypted with the firm's public key, while the ULA is encrypted with the user's public key.
- `softwareInfo`: This is the address to connect to the software profile.
- `license_type`: This describes what license type the user chooses.

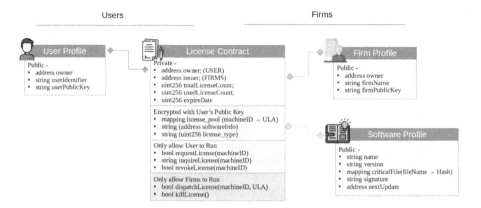

Fig. 2. Smart contract relationship overview

- `requestLicense`: When a user selects a new machine to obtain a license, this function will be called.
- `inquireLicense`: When an existed license requires validation.
- `revokeLicense`: When a user likes to deactivate software on a particular machine.
- `dispatchLicense`: When a user requests a license, this function will be triggered. It will check the usedLicenseCount and totalLicenseCount accordingly to dispatch the software's critical components through IPFS. If the components are successfully dispatched, it will update the mapping table with the new ULA that is encrypted with the user's public key.
- `killLicense`: Kill the contract.

Firm Profile. The firm profile contains the basic information of the firm. Firms can extend the contract to hold more information.

Software Profile. Although this is another profile that holds the basic information for a piece of software, however, the profile has a critical file hash table. This critical file hash table enables installed software to determine whether important files have been tampered with.

User Buys a Software License. When a user purchases a software license, the software company immediately issues a license contract with the address of the user and the address of the software company. The software company can preconfigure all variables except the license pool.

Software Activation. The license contract is created, but there is no machine has been registered. Activation requires the user to send the machine ID that is encrypted by the firm's public key to the `requestLicense()` function in the License smart contract.

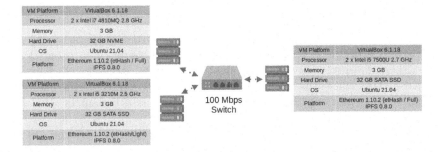

Fig. 3. Environmental configuration

`requestLicense` will check the license_pool mapping table to ensure that the machine did not double-registered. Then check both the `totalLicenseCount` and `usedLicenseCount` to decide whether to raise issue of requesting the firm to dispatch license.

The firms will run the `dispatchLicense` function, with the machine ID that is encrypted with the firm's public key, and the ULA that is encrypted with the user's public key as input. `dispatchLicense` will lookup the license_pool mapping table, then the `totalLicenseCount`, and the `usedLicenseCount` as reference.

When `dispatchLicense` occurred, the license gateway will prepare the critical software component encrypted twice with:

- 1. Proposed Machine ID as AES Key
- 2. User's Public Key

After the encryption process, the license gateway will dispatch the package onto the IPFS network.

Software Validation. The software first hashes its critical components as a reference to compare. Then using the user's private key to obtain the address of the softwareInfo. When the softwareInfo contract is reached, the software will perform two operations.

- 1. Validate the signature of the software profile contract
- 2. Obtain criticalFile mapping table to compare.

If either one of those criteria cannot be met, the software will be considered as being tampered with and refused to start.

4 Evaluation

The system is expected to be used over the Internet. Rather than running in a virtual machine, we put the experiment into a wired local area network. Figure 3 shows the configuration setup of the environment.

4.1   Performance

As one of the most mature smart contract platforms, it is no doubt that Ethereum is a desirable option. A permissioned Ethereum chain is our default case. Ethereum provides 2 consensus algorithms for its permissioned chain. The original etHash consensus algorithm and the new Clique consensus algorithm. etHash is the traditional PoW-based, while Clique is a variant of BFT algorithm [17].

Most of the BFT algorithms are expected to have better performance than PoW. However, most of the BFT algorithm requires a broadcast-like architecture, it may not be a preferable option in a large-scale network. Moreover, Ethereum currently allows only etHash-based chains to apply light chain mode. Hence, we have to put our focus more on etHash. If light chain mode is introduced in the later Ehtereum release, that will be our future work.

Table 3. The time consumption of the Ethereum-etHash when handling transactions simultaneously

Sym.	Records on the chain			
Trans.	500	10,000	100,000	1,000,000
1	1,906 ms	3,526 ms	4,066 ms	5,842 ms
10	2,238 ms	3,899 ms	5,549 ms	8,933 ms
100	3,830 ms	3,960 ms	5,821 ms	84,659 ms
1000	18,696 ms	25,803 ms	28,133 ms	353,607 ms

Table 4. The time consumption of the Ethereum-etHash (Light) when handling transactions simultaneously

Sym.	Records on the chain			
Trans.	500	10,000	100,000	1,000,000
1	2,564 ms	4,583 ms	5,285 ms	6,101 ms
10	5,064 ms	5,293 ms	7,213 ms	12,777 ms

Data Writing - etHash. Difficulties and chain length tend to slow down the transaction on the chain. Although it may not be favorable, PoW is the most proven consensus algorithm for large-scale networks.

In Table 3, we observed that when the chain becomes longer, it does take some service penalties on users. However, the time consumption is still bearable. When many concurrent transactions occurred, it can take a while for the system to complete. There is a need to apply strategies to separate into multiple small chains from a huge slumpy chain.

After testing the transaction speed on the full chain, it is time to move to the customer side. Since they use a light node that all transactions require a full node to finish, hence, taking up more network resources, we have to find out how much performance penalty that may cause.

Comparing with the data writing result from a full node, a light node did have some performance penalties. It took 10%–30% more time than a full node to complete a transaction (see Table 4). However, it is more acceptable than a huge amount of data. Furthermore, changing license status is not constantly happened in most of the customers' usage.

Data Reading - etHash. For a full or partial node, they can directly access the records in their drive, because they have a copy of the ledger. Accessing data should not be a problem. We can see that the reading speed is not related to the chain length (see Table 5).

IPFS. Since IPFS is more close to a BitTorrent with cache, it does not have the Blockchain characteristics. While users may feel performance bottleneck during the first time when the software just got a license. We tested the IPFS in our small network, performed as expected (see Table 6).

Table 5. The time consumption of the Ethereum reading on-chain data

Records on the chain			
1000	10,000	100,000	1,000,000
274 ms	268 ms	279 ms	273 ms

Table 6. Time consumption of IPFS when storing different sizes of data

1 MB	10 MB	100 MB	1 GB
30.2 ms	136.5 ms	882.1 ms	6,866.4 ms

4.2 Counterfeiting SLVs in Action

Keygens. Keygens are programs that are able to generate valid product keys to bypass or activate the software. However, in our design, software references license information on its related Blockchain smart contract. Keygens have to defeat the first difficult problem: Brute-force out a valid license among the Blockchain network. Second, if keygen can eventually search out a valid license, it cannot decrypt the access for a software component.

Patch. Since we encouraged software developers to keep either the critical functions or the bootstrappers on their side. Legally reachable software may not contain all function calls. Without obtaining a license, a patch cannot do much on an "already limited" software package. Secondly, if the software has been tampered with, software validation can quickly respond due to the difference with the reported hash value.

Activation Server. Blockchain can provide a trusted software verifier environment. Activation servers are those small decentralized smart contracts on the Blockchain, which use other's licenses to return to the problem of cracking other's keypair challenges.

5   Conclusion

In this paper, we investigated how the software licensing model changes due to environmental and economical changes. Then we discussed how software developers desired a software license validation method. Based on the analysis results, we figured out the dilemma of software license validation, and further discussed the license model and their related protection methods, including how software pirates get around the restriction. Having an overview of the picture, we proposed a system that aimed to solve the dilemma by leveraging Blockchain's decentralized and trusted storage environment and the IPFS's secure and flexible distribution system. During our implementation, we also discussed how to overcome the storage issue a blockchain-based technology might pose to the user.

Acknowledgments. This work (the authors from NUAA) is partially supported by the National Key R&D Program of China (Grant No. 2020YFB1005900), the National Natural Science Foundation of China (Grant No. 62032025, 62071222, U20A201092), the National Key R&D Program of Guangdong Province (Grant No. 2020B0101090002), the Natural Science Foundation of Jiangsu Province (Grant No. BK20200418).

References

1. License — Definition of License by Merriam-Webster. https://www.merriam-webster.com/dictionary/license
2. Desautels, E.: Software License Agreements: Ignore at Your Own Risk, US-CERT (2005). https://us-cert.cisa.gov/sites/default/files/publications/EULA.pdf
3. Herbert, J., Litchfield, A.: A novel method for decentralized peer-to-peer software license validation using cryptocurrency blockchain technology. In: Proceedings of ACSC, pp. 27–35 (2015)
4. Suhler, P.A., Malek, M., Bagherzadeh, N.: Software authorization systems. IEEE Softw. **3**(5), 34–41 (1986)
5. Morgan, M.J., Ruskell, D.J.: The software piracy - the problems. Ind. Manag. Data Syst. **87**(3/4), 8–12 (1987)
6. Bahaa-Eldin, A.M., Sobh, M.A.A.: A comprehensive software copy protection and digital rights management platform. Ain Shams Eng. J. **5**(3), 703–720 (2014)
7. Manoharan, S., Wu, J.: Software licensing: a classification and case study. In: Proceedings of ICDS, pp. 33–33 (2007)
8. Magananini, F., Ferretti, L., Colajanni, M.: Efficient license management based on smart contracts between software vendors and service providers. In: Proceedings of NCA, pp. 1–6 (2019)
9. Herbert, J., Litchfield, A.: ReSOLV: applying cryptocurrency blockchain methods to enable global cross-platform software license validation. Cryptography **2**(2), 10 (2018)

10. Ferrante, D.: Software licensing models: what's out there? IT Prof. **8**(6), 24–29 (2006)
11. Kwashnik, G.: Best Practice for Negotiating Cloud-Based Software Contracts. https://www.esi.mil/download.aspx?id=4783
12. Microsoft Extends Anti-Piracy Features in Office (2000). https://news.microsoft.com/1998/12/09/microsoft-extends-anti-piracy-features-in-office-2000/
13. Symantec Moves Against Piracy with Product Activation Requirements. https://www.technewsworld.com/story/31448.html
14. Honick, R.: Software Piracy Exposed (2005). ISBN: 978-1932266986
15. Why doesn't Microsoft ban KMS? https://www.programmersought.com/article/73915750159/
16. Benet, J.: IPFS - Content Addressed, Versioned, P2P File System. arXiv preprint arXiv:1407.3561
17. De Angelis, S., Aniello, L., Baldoni, R., Lombardi, F., Margheri, A., Sassone, V.: PBFT vs proof-of-authority: Applying the CAP theorem to permissioned blockchain (2018)

Towards an Aligned Blockchain Standard System: Challenges and Trends

Xiaodan Tang[✉]

China Electronics Standardization Institute, Beijing, China
tangxd@cesi.cn

Abstract. As a rapidly-developing emerging technology, blockchain met the challenges of standardization. In order to analyze the systematic degree of blockchain standards, 3 developing stages of both blockchain industry and standard system are comparatively studied. The current status of blockchain standardization in the aspect of participants including ISO, ITU-T, IEEE-SA and national level organizations are summarized. A total number of 167 blockchain standard projects have been collected and studied. Highlighted topics including foundational, security, privacy & identity, application, data, test & assessment are analyzed. Finally, a blockchain standard system composed of 10 categories of blockchain standards is given, based on which the challenges and trends of blockchain standardization are analyzed.

Keywords: Blockchain · Distributed leger technology · Standardization · Standard · Blockchain standard system

1 Introduction

Blockchain was burn in 2008 in a paper on design of Bitcoin written by Satoshi Nakamoto [1]. The wide application of blockchain in the following decade not only created great value, but also brought challenges. The lack of consensus on concepts and basic technologies of blockchain in various industries makes the development of the industry fragmented. The development of blockchain industry faces some practical problems, such as compatibility and interoperability of blockchain applications, and lack of evaluation methods of security, reliability and interoperability. Since 2016, standardization organizations such as International Organization for Standardization (ISO) and Telecommunication Standardization Sector of the International Telecommunications Union (ITU-T) have accelerated the proceeding of blockchain standardization, and have made good progress. A series of standard projects have been approved and some standards have been published. However, the blockchain standardization is not mature enough, and there is still a long way to go for a systematic standard system.

The key directions and standard system of blockchain standardization have been discussed and studied since the beginning of blockchain standardization. In the policy level, China and Australia [2] both released publications on blockchain standards in 2016–2017. Anjum A. et al. [3] analyzed the requirements of blockchain standards

© Springer Nature Singapore Pte Ltd. 2021
H.-N. Dai et al. (Eds.): BlockSys 2021, CCIS 1490, pp. 574–584, 2021.
https://doi.org/10.1007/978-981-16-7993-3_44

on compliance and trust. Gramoli V. et al. [4] studied the progress and challenges of blockchain standards. König L. et al. [5] compared the blockchain standards from different organizations. However, further researches on the latest progress of blockchain standard system have not been seen. Considering the progress that have been made, it's essential to investigate the existing standard projects and study the feasibility and roadmap for constructing an aligned blockchain standard system. In this paper, the stages of both blockchain industry and standards are studied. Based on this, the current status of blockchain standardization in the aspects of participants, standard projects and topics, is summarized. Finally, a blockchain standard system is given, based on which the challenges and trends of blockchain standardization are analyzed.

2 Stages of Blockchain Industry and Standardization

Based on the development of blockchain technology, application, standardization and industry ecology, the development of blockchain industry can be considered to have experienced 3 stages since the origin of first blockchain application, Bitcoin, in 2008, as is displayed in Fig. 1.

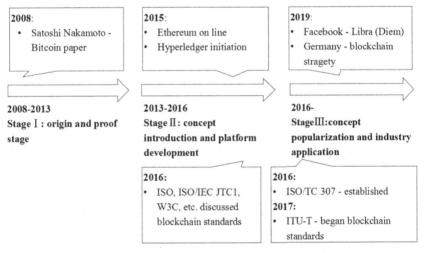

Fig. 1. Timeline of blockchain industry and standardization

2.1 Technology Origin and Proof Stage

The first stage is from 2008 to 2013, which is the origin and proof stage of blockchain technology. The main progress was that the blockchain technology was verified through the stable operation of Bitcoin. At this stage, the public blockchain technology achieved great development, the exploration of the applications of cryptocurrency had just begun, and a typical feature of the industry ecology was the gradual development of the ecology around cryptocurrency. The term "blockchain" did not appear until around 2012, and the standardization of blockchain was almost a blank then.

2.2 Concept Introduction and Platform Development Stage

The second stage, from 2013 to 2016, is the stage of blockchain concept introduction and platform development. At this stage, Ethereum, Hyperledger and many other platforms developed rapidly, and the applications of smart contract and other technologies promoted the explorations of the applications of blockchain in more fields.

At the same time, related standardization organizations began to discuss topics about blockchain standards. W3C convened its first workshop on blockchain in June 2016 and the question whether any aspects of blockchain were ripe for standardization was discussed. In August 2016, an advisory group of ISO/IEC JTC 1 (Joint technical committee for information technology) proposed to established a new blockchain sub-committee in ISO/IEC JTC 1.

2.3 Concept Popularization and Industry Application Promotion Stage

The third stage, from 2016 to present, is the stage of concept popularization and industry application promotion of blockchain. As the inter-chain, privacy protection technology, smart contract and other related technologies are developing rapidly, the explorations of applications of blockchain in the fields of supplychain finance, food traceability, judicial, public services, etc., are more and more extensive. Some active applications expand scale quickly, such as blockchain applications in food traceability and public services. The explorations of blockchain infrastructures are accelerated since around 2019. Facebook released Libra Whitepaper referring to the goal of constructing a global blockchain-based financial infrastructure. The European Commission promoted a multinational blockchain application service infrastructure.

The standardization of blockchain was pushed forward rapidly by related organizations at this stage since late 2016. ISO established a new technical committee named ISO/TC 307 in September 2016, and its scope is standardization of blockchain and distributed ledger technologies. ITU-T started its first blockchain standard project in early 2017. Both ISO and ITU-T gradually promoted the development of a series of blockchain standards in the following. Besides, IEEE SA (IEEE Standards Association) also began the blockchain standardization work in around 2018.

3 Status of Blockchain Standards

3.1 Participants of Blockchain Standards

Blockchain standardization has attracted much attention of worldwide standardization organizations, governments, and blockchain enterprises. ISO, ITU-T, W3C, IETF (The Internet Engineering Task Force), and IEEE-SA have shown interest on blockchain standards [4]. Some of the standardization organizations established new bodies to develop blockchain standards, such as ISO, ITU-T, IEEE-SA. There are also national level organizations plunging in developing domestic blockchain standards, such as China and Australia.

ISO. Besides ISO/TC 307, there are also other technical committees developing blockchain standards, such as ISO/TC 68 (Technical Committee for Financial Services), ISO/TC46 (Technical Committee for Information and documentation), and ISO/IEC JTC 1 (Technical Committee for Information Technology). As a technical committee focused on blockchain, ISO/TC 307 has 46 participating members and 14 observing members by April 2021, and has created several working groups, study groups and advisory groups to foster blockchain standards in security, smart contract, use case, interoperability, and other directions.

ITU-T. ITU-T established a focus group on blockchain, and started research on blockchain standard in terminology, use cases, architecture, evaluation, security, regulation, etc. ITU-T also set up special research groups in SG16 (study group on multimedia) and SG 17 (study group on security). SG 13 (study group on Future networks & cloud) and SG 20 (study group on IoT, smart cities & communities) have also started the standardization work related to blockchain.

IEEE-SA. Among the 39 societies in IEEE, there are by far 5 societies involved in developing blockchain standards, which are respectively IEEE Consumer Technology Society, IEEE Computer Society, IEEE Vehicular Technology Society, IEEE Power and Energy Society, IEEE Engineering in Medicine and Biology Society. IEEE Consumer Technology Society and IEEE Computer Society have respectively established a standard committee on blockchain.

National Level Organizations. In 2017, the Standards Australia (SA) released report named Roadmap for Blockchain Standards, in which several priority issues of blockchain standardization were given. In China, Standardization Administration of China (SAC) has established a national standardization technical committee on blockchain, and a bunch of blockchain standards, including national standards, industry standards and consortium standards, are under development or have been published.

3.2 Progress of Blockchain Standards Development

The blockchain standards in terminology and reference architecture started in around 2017, following by a series of projects initiated in the next 2–3 years. In this section, in order to analyze the hot topics of blockchain standards up to now, a total number of 167 blockchain standard projects from ISO, ITU-T, IEEE-SA, and local standards in China were collected, as shown in Table 1. According to public information, ISO has approved 16 blockchain standard projects, among which 4 standards have been published. ITU has started 38 blockchain standard projects. IEEE has started 58 blockchain standard projects, among which 6 standards have been published. 55 Chinese standards in blockchain are collected, among which over 40 standards have been published. It

Table 1. Distribution of blockchain standard projects number.

Categories	Number of blockchain standard projects
ISO standards	16
ITU standards	38
IEEE standards	58
Chinese standards	55

is noted that since most of the blockchain standards have not yet been published, the following analysis is based on all the standard projects including under developing ones.

The keywords of these projects were divided into 3 levels based on the frequency of the given keywords appearing in all the standard titles, as displayed in Fig. 2. The keywords of 1st level (frequency in all the projects n ≥ 20) are architecture/framework, data, application and security. The keywords of 2nd level (20 > n > 5) are test/assessment, traceability, cryptocurrency, smart contract, and identity. The keywords of 3rd level (n ≤ 5) are platform, cryptographic, enterprise, judicial, governance, interoperability, financial, privacy, vocabulary/terminology, talent, use case, taxonomy, supplychain, and regulation.

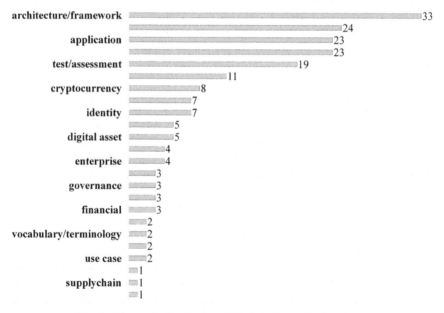

Fig. 2. Keywords distribution of blockchain standard projects.

3.3 Highlighted Topics of Blockchain Standardization

Foundational. Foundational standards represent the basic consensus of the industry. The categories of foundational standards include vocabulary/terminology standards which give the definitions of terms related to blockchain, reference architecture standards which specify the framework and characteristics of blockchain systems, taxonomy standards which identify the taxonomy related to blockchain technology. ISO/TC 307 established a foundational working group to develop foundational blockchain standards. 3 standard projects have been approved and the ISO 22739:2020 - vocabulary standard has been published. ISO and ITU have respectively started their reference architecture standard project, and both projects are under development now. There are also 3 reference architecture standard projects among Chinese standards. As for the taxonomy standard, there is only 1 standard under development by ISO.

Security, Privacy and Identity. Standards on security, privacy and identity provide essential guarantee for blockchain systems and applications. ISO has approved 1 security standard project, 1 privacy standard project and 2 identity standard projects on blockchain. ITU has started 11 security standard projects and 2 identity standard projects. IEEE has 2 security standard projects, 3 identity standard projects. There are 8 security standard projects, 1 privacy standard project among Chinese standards. It should be noted that many of the security standard projects focused on specific application scenes, such as voting, cryptocurrency, food traceablity, etc.

Application. The application blockchain standards include use case standards, application guide standards, framework standards of application systems, and standards on security of applications, etc. In ISO, there are 2 use case standard projects, 1 application guide standard project on electric record, and 1 standard project on security for blockchain applications in finance. In ITU, there are 15 application standard projects. In IEEE, there are over 30 blockchain application standard projects, which account for more than half of the total number of IEEE blockchain standard projects. There are 20 standard projects related to application of blockchain in China. The application scenes involved in all the standard projects are very extensive, including crytocurrency, payment, agriculture, e-commerce, omnidirectional pandemic, intelligent property management, etc. Compared to other organizations, IEEE is apparently more interested in application standards in blockchain, and there are 10 application standard projects in the field of omnidirectional pandemic alone.

Data. Data standards are standards related to data-centric activities and process. ISO has approved a standard project on data flow. ITU has 5 standard projects on data management, data exchange and other subjects. In IEEE, there have been 13 standard projects on data management, data format and data in blockchain applications, etc. There are also 5 data standard projects among the Chinese standards.

Test and Assessment. Test standards specify the test activities for blockchain systems on performance, functional, security and reliability, etc. Assessment standards are for the assessment or identification of blockchain related technologies, applications, enterprises and talents. There is by far no test & assessment standard in ISO. The number of test &

assessment standard projects of ITU, IEEE are respectively 1 and 3. As for Chinese standards, 13 test & assessment standard projects have been tracked.

4 A Blockchain Standard System and Issues Related

4.1 A Blockchain Standard System

A standard system is a system established based on the relationships between different standards or different categories of standards. Elements of a standard system can be theses or categories of standards. The main function of a standard system is guiding the selection of theses and development process of standards in a specific subfield.

A blockchain standard system is given based on the current development of blockchain standards, as is displayed in Fig. 3. It's not necessary to draw up an exhaustively detailed standard system for an emerging field full of uncertainty, and a simple system including one level of standard categories is enough for blockchain. There are 10 standardization subfields in the system. The basic subfield is foundational standards, and the subfield of application standards penetrates all the other 9 subfields. On both sides of application standards are interoperability standards, governance standards, data standards, security, smart contract standards, privacy & identity standards, test & assessment standards, and infrastructure & platform standards.

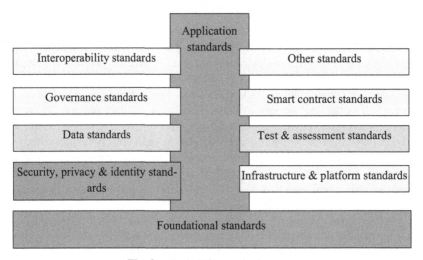

Fig. 3. Blockchain standard system

According to the analysis in Sect. 3.2 and Sect. 3.3, the subfields of foundational standards, security, privacy & identity standards, and application standards are relatively well-developed. The subfields of data standards and test & assessment standards have been developed actively but imbalanced. The subfields of interoperability, governance, smart contract, infrastructure & platform are to some extent just started.

Foundational Standards. The functions of foundational standards are unifying blockchain-related terminology, concepts and models; identifying categories of technologies, data, applications and systems for blockchain; and providing support for developing other blockchain standards. For instance, demarcation of blockchain and distributed ledger in ISO 22739:2020 and other related standards helps terminating ambiguous status and mixed use of the two terms. In the aspect of time sequencing, the developing of foundational standards should be prior.

Security, Privacy and Identity Standards. The function of security, privacy & identity standards is guiding the realization and assessment of privacy protect, information security and identity authentication related to blockchain. The development of security, privacy & identity standards should focus on clarifying the requirements, levels and key technologies that systems and applications should meet under the condition of blockchain technology and current regulatory environment.

Application Standards. The functions of application standards is normalizing and guiding the design, development, deployment, assessment, delivery and maintenance of blockchain applications in various industries. The key directions of application standards for blockchain include the combination of technical values and industry demands, process and requirements of blockchain application, blockchain application model in specific industry, and practice experience of blockchain use cases, etc.

Data Standards. To some extent, blockchain is a tool for collaborative handling of transaction data, and data standards are essential to blockchain. The data standards should address recommended data taxonomy, categories and characteristic of data flows, lifecycle of blockchain data, guidelines for data exchange and processing, as well as requirements of data structure and data format, etc. There are also other issues such as data governance, data security and data interoperability which are cross-cutting with other subfields of this blockchain standard system.

Test and Assessment Standards. Test or assessment activities for blockchain systems, applications, talents and enterprises, provide a path for guaranteeing the quality of blockchain products and reference for selecting employees and suppliers. The standards in this subfield help normalize these activities and increase the credibility of results output from these activities. Test & assessment standards should give categories, process, methods, requirements and index systems of related activities and stakeholders.

Governance Standards. Governance standards can provide supports for governance activities for blockchain systems, applications, data, infrastructures and platforms, etc. Issues for governance standards include but not limited to goals, principles, objects, contents and mechanism of governance, as well as roles and their responsibilities when governance is implemented. The difference of governance between public blockchain, consortium blockchain and private blockchain should also attach attention when developing governance standards for blockchain.

Smart Contract Standards. Smart contract standards for blockchain involve design, development, execution and interactions of smart contracts realized by blockchain technology. The identification of legally binding smart contracts, normalization of smart contract languages and formal verification methods for smart contract are also directions which requires standardization. Standardized smart contracts for different scenarios will also be beneficial to the extension of smart contracts.

Interoperability Standards. Interoperability standards for blockchain can support the coordination between different blockchain systems as well as between blockchain systems with other systems. The interoperability-related requirements, method, models for blockchain should be given in standards of this subfield. Standards on application programming interfaces and crosschain are also essential directions.

Infrastructure and Platform Standards. The function of infrastructure & platform standards is normalizing the design, construct, maintain and use of blockchain infrastructure & platforms. Standards related to requirements, frameworks and application of Blockchain as a Service (BaaS) and blockchain application infrastructure are also foundations for blockchain applications.

4.2 Challenges of Blockchain Standardization

It can be understood that blockchain standardization is still full of chaos because less than 5 years is not enough for the developing of a whole, complete blockchain standard system. There are several shortcomings in blockchain standardization, and the challenges are still existing.

Repeated Standards. It should be acknowledged that 167 is not a small number for standards for an emerging technology. However, over-development is very typical for blockchain standards. Among all the blockchain standard projects, there are a lot of projects share the same or similar titles. For instance, as two of the largest international standardization organizations, ISO and ITU are both developing reference architecture/framework standards and security standards on financial applications. Repeated standards mean the delusion of standardization resources, and may bring about separation of standardization. If more organizations considered, the problem can be more serious.

Alignments Between Standards. It's an obvious fact that tens of standard projects can be approved by different organizations, and the developing work is proceeded simultaneously. Under the circumstances, the alignments of different standards, especially standards from different organizations are quite difficult. Although variety of liaison relationships have been built between blockchain standardization organizations, the synchronization is still not enough to ensure the alignments. One example is the solution of discrimination of blockchain and distributed ledger (DLT) technologies: ISO/TC 307 uses blockchain and DLT, while ISO/TC 46 uses blockchain, and ITU-T uses DLT in their standard projects. Behind this are the different understandings of the two terms.

Uneven Development Among Different Directions. Generally speaking, the development of application standards and security & identity is relatively sufficiently, however, the progress of interoperability standards, governance standards and smart contract standards is much slower. In order to proceed interoperability standards, ISO/TC 307 established an interoperability working group, however, there are by far no standard projects in this subfield.

4.3   Trends of Blockchain Standard Development

An apparent advantage of blockchain standardization by now is the enthusiasm of the industry. There is reason to believe that the development of blockchain standards will be more well-organized, and the blockchain standards will be more systematic in the near future.

More Solid Standardization Work. Since most of the blockchain standards are under development, the standardization work has not unfolded yet and the facilitation to the industry is not obvious. When more standards are published, the application of more standards should improve consensus, interoperability, security and other aspects of the blockchain industry.

More Revision Projects. As blockchain industry is developing speedily, the related technologies are updated quickly, and the applications models frequently evolve, the revisions of some standards become necessary. For instance, ISO started a revision project soon after the publication of the vocabulary standard. Revision is also a good way to improve the quality of standards and reduce the inconsistency of different standards.

Standards on Emerging Subfields. Blockchain industry has several transitions since the beginning. The constantly innovations open an immense imagination space for the industry in the future. Two of the typical trends is development of blockchain infrastructure and hardware devices, which may trigger the development of related standards.

5   Conclusion

Although over 150 blockchain standard projects are ongoing or have led to the publishment of standards, the blockchain standardization is still in the early age. Firstly, the number of published standards especially international standards is very limited, and the large-scale applications of blockchain standards are unlikely at this stage. Secondly, the unbalanced development of different directions and inconsistence between existing standards may last for a longer time. Among the subfields in the blockchain standard system, the standardization in interoperability, governance, smart contract requires more attention, and the standardization of data, test & assessment requires more balance. Emerging subfields related to new technologies or novel models of blockchain such as infrastructure are also worthy of remark.

Acknowledgments. This work was supported by National Key R&D Program of China (2018YFC0830200).

References

1. Nakamoto, S.: Bitcoin: A Peer-to-Peer Electronic Cash System. https://bitcoin.org/bitcoin.pdf
2. Standards Australia: Roadmap for Blockchain Standards. https://www.standards.org.au/StandardAU/Media/SA-Archive/OurOrganisation/News/Documents/Roadmap_for_Blockchain_Standards_report.pdf
3. Gramoli, V., Staples, M.: Blockchain standard: can we reach consensus? IEEE Commun. Stand. Mag. **2**(3), 1–14 (2018)
4. Anjum, A., Sporny, M., Sill, A.: Blockchain standards for compliance and trust. IEEE Cloud Comput. **4**, 84–90 (2017)
5. König, L., et al.: Comparing blockchain standards and recommendations. Future Internet **12**(12), 222 (2020)

Legal Protection of Blockchain from the Perspective of the Cybersecurity Law: Legislation and Practice of China

Xuemei Bai[1(✉)] and Ling Zhong[2]

[1] School of Information Science, Guangdong University of Finance and Economics, Guangzhou 510320, China
[2] School of Law, Guangdong University of Finance and Economics, Guangzhou 510320, China

Abstract. Blockchain security has become a new cybersecurity legal issue. *Cybersecurity Law of the People's Republic of China* provides overall legal protection for blockchain security, and has begun to address the special legal issues of cybersecurity arising from blockchain through special legislation. Blockchain security is facing new challenges, and the legal protection of blockchain security should be further promoted through the coupling of technology, standards, and law.

Keywords: Blockchain · Cybersecurity · Information security · Cybersecurity Law · Legal protection

The Political Bureau of the CPC Central Committee conducted the 18th collective study on the development status and trends of blockchain technology on October 24, 2019. When presiding over the study, General Secretary Xi Jinping emphasized that the integrated application of blockchain technology plays an important role in new technological innovation and industrial transformation. It is necessary to take the blockchain as an important breakthrough in independent innovation of core technologies, clarify the main direction, increase investment in this sector, focus on several core key technologies and accelerate the development of blockchain technology and industrial innovation. Based on the current status of legal protection for the cybersecurity of blockchain in China, this article discusses the coupling of technology and the rule of law to ensure blockchain security.

1 The Cybersecurity Law Provides Overall Legal Protection for Blockchain Security

The blockchain itself has higher security than the Internet. Its distributed ledger can effectively guarantee the integrity and immutability of information, and it can adopt consensus-based specifications and protocols to enable all nodes in the entire system to automatically and securely exchange data in a trustless environment without any human intervention. It can prevent information disclosure and fraud, which is of great value

© Springer Nature Singapore Pte Ltd. 2021
H.-N. Dai et al. (Eds.): BlockSys 2021, CCIS 1490, pp. 585–592, 2021.
https://doi.org/10.1007/978-981-16-7993-3_45

to cybersecurity, especially network information security. Therefore, we should give full play to the unique advantages of blockchain and use legal means to promote the in-depth use of blockchain in various industries and fields. At the same time, we should also pay attention to the legal supervision of the blockchain with the characteristics of decentration and anonymity, to prevent the security problems and the social risks caused by it. The coupling of technology and the rule of law promotes the security of the blockchain and promotes the blockchain, the safe operation of the blockchain system, and the sustainable development of the blockchain industry. For example, the *Big Data Security Management Regulations of Guiyang City* prescribes, "Responsible units for safety are encouraged to use blockchain and other new technological means to optimize the common architecture of data aggregation, strengthen trust authentication and tamper-proof design, to improve the security protection level of big data".

Although blockchain security has its particularities, the legislation on cybersecurity applies to blockchain security, thus providing overall legal protection for cybersecurity. According to *Cybersecurity Law of the People's Republic of China* (adopted on November 7, 2016, and implemented on June 1, 2017, hereafter called the *Cybersecurity Law*), the network is defined as a system composed of computers or other information terminals and related equipment that collects, stores, transmits, exchanges and processes information following certain rules and procedures. Network security refers to the ability to keep the network in a stable and reliable operating state, at the same time ensure the integrity, confidentiality, and availability of network data by taking necessary measures to prevent the attack, intrusion, interference, destruction, and illegal use of the network as well as accidents. Therefore, the *Cybersecurity Law* and other cybersecurity legislation are applicable to blockchain and its industrial application, while the *Cybersecurity Law* is the "fundamental law" in the field of cybersecurity. The *Cybersecurity Law* provides for the support and promotion of cybersecurity, network operation security, network information security, monitoring, and early warning, as well as emergency response, etc., thereby establishes the basic legal compliance with cybersecurity. The legal liabilities stipulated in the *Cybersecurity Law* include civil liabilities, administrative liabilities, and criminal liabilities. Therefore, other relevant legislation also synergistically acts on the legal guarantee of cybersecurity.

Among the relevant legislation, *Cryptography Law of the People's Republic of China* (passed on October 26, 2019, and implemented on January 1, 2020, hereafter called the *Cryptography Law*) has a very high degree of connection with the blockchain, and its connection point is "cryptography". Article 2 of the *Cryptography Law* stipulates, "cryptography" means technologies, products, and services that affect encryption protection or security certification of information and the like by adopting the method for specific conversion. The law divides cryptography into core cryptography, ordinary cryptography, and commercial cryptography, and establishes the application and management system of the cryptography respectively, and scientific research, production, sales, service, import and export, testing, equipment, use and destruction, and other activities of cryptography have been taken in legal track. This can realize the legislative purposes of standardizing the application and management of passwords, promoting the development of cryptography, ensuring network information security, safeguarding the national security and social public interests, and protecting the legitimate rights and interests of citizens, legal persons, and other organizations. Since encryption technology is the key technology of blockchain, the *Cryptography Law* will directly act on the blockchain field, which is of great significance for the research, development, application, and standardized development of blockchain technology.

2 The Specific Legislation of Blockchain Provides Special Legal Safeguards for Blockchain Security

On January 10, 2019, the Cyberspace Administration of China issued the *Administrative Regulations on Blockchain Information Services* (implemented on February 15, 2019). The *Administrative Regulations on Blockchain Information Services* aim to clarify the management responsibility for information security of blockchain information service providers, standardize and promote the healthy development of blockchain technology and related services, avoid the security risks of blockchain information services, and provide an effective legal basis for the provision, use, and management of blockchain information services. The main contents are as follows.

First of all, according to its responsibilities, the Cyberspace Administration of China is responsible for the supervision, management, and law enforcement of blockchain information services nationwide. Cyberspace Administration of provinces, autonomous regions, and municipalities are responsible for the supervision, management, and law enforcement of blockchain information services in their respective administrative regions according to their duties.

Second, the main obligations of blockchain information service providers are as follows. They shall implement management responsibilities for information content security, establish and improve user registration, information review, emergency response, security protection, and other management systems. They shall have the technical conditions suitable for their services. For information content prohibited by laws and administrative regulations, they shall have the immediate and emergency handling ability to release, record, store, and disseminate it, and the technical solution shall conform to the relevant national standards and specifications. They shall formulate and publish management rules and platform conventions, sign service agreements with blockchain information service users, clarify the rights and obligations of both parties, and require them to commit to comply with legal regulations and platform conventions. They shall comply with the *Cybersecurity Law*, authenticate the users of the blockchain information service with their real identity information based on the organization code, ID card number or mobile phone number, etc. If a blockchain information service provider develops a new product, application, or function, it should report to the Cyberspace Administration of the state, province, autonomous region, or municipality directly under the Central Government for security assessment according to relevant regulations. Blockchain information service providers and users must not use blockchain information services to endanger national security, disrupt social order, or infringe on the legitimate rights and interests of others, etc. Blockchain information services shall not be used to produce, copy, publish or disseminate information prohibited by law and administrative regulation.

The third is the handling of information security issues. The main relevant regulations are as follows. Blockchain information service providers shall cooperate with the supervision and inspection carried out by Cyberspace Administration according to the law, and provide necessary technical support and assistance. Blockchain information service providers shall accept social supervision and set up convenient complaint report entrance, timely deal with complaints and reports from the general public. If the blockchain information service provided by the blockchain information service provider has hidden risks of information security, it shall be rectified and can not provide information services until it complies with relevant provisions of law, administrative regulations, and relevant national standard specifications. Blockchain information service providers should take disposal measures like warnings, functional restrictions, and accounts closing in accordance with laws and regulations against blockchain information service users who violate laws, administrative regulations, and service agreements. They should also take corresponding measures for illegal information content in time to prevent the spreading out of information, save relevant records, and report to competent authorities. Blockchain information service providers should record the content and logs released by users of blockchain information services. Record backups should be kept no less than six months and be provided when relevant law enforcement agencies make inquiries according to law.

In general, except for some provisions in normative documents and local regulations related to blockchain, the only special legislation on blockchain at present is the *Administrative Regulations on Blockchain Information Services*. According to the particularity of blockchain, the *Administrative Regulations on Blockchain Information Services* stipulates the main issues of information service management and legal liability, so that there are laws for regulatory and law enforcement activities to follow. However, the content of this regulation is also limited to information service management, and the content of legal protection related to blockchain security is also limited to information security, which is determined by the legislative purpose and scope of the regulation. In July 2017, the Cyberspace Administration of China and related departments drafted the *Regulations for the Security Protection of Critical Information Infrastructure (Exposure Draft)*, which has been included in the State Council's 2020 legislative work plan, which also includes the security protection of blockchain. Some local governments have also issued policies and normative documents to promote and guarantee the development of blockchain. For example, in May 2020, Guangzhou Municipal Industry and Information Technology Bureau issued the *Implementation Suggestions on Promoting Innovative Development of Blockchain Industry in Guangzhou (2020–2022)*. In May 2020, the People's Government of Guizhou Province issued the *Opinions on Applications and Industry Development of Blockchain Technology*. It can be predicted that policies and legislation of blockchain technology and industrial innovation and development will enter the "fast lane".

3   The Coupling of Technology, Standards, and Law Further Promote the Legal Protection of Blockchain Security

At the press conference of the *Administrative Regulations on Blockchain Information Services*, the responsible person from the Cyberspace Administration of China said that, as an emerging technology, blockchain has the characteristics of immutability and anonymity, which will bring opportunities to the development of the country and the society. While brings convenience, it also brings certain safety risks. Through the integration with the field of communication, it is used by some lawbreakers to spread illegal and harmful information, execute illegal and criminal activities on the Internet, and damage the legitimate rights and interests of citizens, legal persons, and other organizations. Some blockchain information service providers do not have a strong sense of security responsibility, and their management measures and technical support capabilities are unsound, which brings new challenges to Internet information security [1].

The industry is concerned about the security issues of the blockchain, mainly focusing on the use of the blockchain for illegal and criminal activities, privacy security, digital currency theft, software vulnerabilities, anarchism, and authoritarianism. For example, blockchain technology has also received widespread attention and rapid application at home and abroad, from digital currency to smart contracts, and gradually extended to many fields such as culture and entertainment, social management, and the Internet of Things. As the scope and depth of blockchain applications gradually expand, security issues such as theft of digital currencies, smart contracts, wallets, and mining software vulnerabilities will become more prominent [2]. Although the technological innovation of the blockchain system is indeed exciting, one must be cautious about "untrusted" technology platforms, which will enforce a contract-based relationship between individuals who evade society [3]. Blockchain is also known as "the technology most likely to change the business model in the next ten years", but it is also known as a haven for criminal activities, Ponzi schemes, anarchism, and authoritarianism [4]. Therefore, it is also necessary to pay attention to the new cybersecurity issues brought by the blockchain. Chen Chun, the academician of the Chinese Academy of Engineering and director of the Blockchain Research Center of Zhejiang University, believes that the public blockchain has become a new media communication medium because the public blockchain itself has the characteristics of decentralization, immutability, non-deletion, and low-cost. Therefore, without a specific basis for supervision, the cost of using public blockchain to spread harmful information, network rumors, and inflammatory and offensive information is very cheap [5]. For public blockchain, since anyone can write data in its database, the supervision of its information content has also become a problem. In this regard, China first issued special regulations on the provision of blockchain information services. The characteristics of the blockchain make it difficult for the data on the chain to be tampered with, and the blockchain may become a carrier for disseminating information that endangers public security, involves terrorism and bad information. With the development of supervision, any illegal and criminal activities related to the dissemination of Internet content using public blockchain technology must be investigated for legal liabilities in all countries.

Regarding the security issues of the blockchain, A distinction should be made between the security of the blockchain itself and the security of the blockchain application, although the formation, prevention, and sanctions of the two are often accompanied or merged. For cybersecurity issues in the application of blockchain, it can be dealt with or sanctioned in accordance with relevant laws and regulations such as the *Cybersecurity Law*, the *Civil Code*, and the *Criminal Law*. There is no essential difference, and they are all tools for delinquency. The possible difference is that when using the anonymity of the blockchain or using digital currencies such as Bitcoin to commit crimes such as money laundering, it will bring a greater difficulty to investigation or evidence collection. The security of the blockchain itself should be the emphasis of the legal protection of blockchain security. The first thing to note is that the security issues of the blockchain cannot be generalized. Instead, private blockchain, consortium blockchain, and public blockchain should be treated differently, combining their respective technical characteristics and application functions to analyze differences in their cybersecurity issues and provide corresponding legal protection. Secondly, some rules of the Cybersecurity Law in the Internet age no longer adapt to the cybersecurity problems caused by the unique technical mechanism of the blockchain. For example, how to determine the owner or controller of personal data and how to determine the sharing of responsibility in distributed accounting of blockchain? How to realize the right to be forgotten, the right to delete data, and the right to data portability? Issues such as these will be key and difficult issues in the legal protection of blockchain cybersecurity. Finally, the decentralized decision-making mechanism and resource allocation model of the blockchain has been fully understood, but its changes to the structure of social organizations and the possible legal issues about cybersecurity still need to be observed with the in-depth practical application of blockchain.

Regardless of blockchain security, or blockchain technology research, industrial applications, and technical standards are the top priority. If organizations continue to build new "island-style" solutions based on different standards, it will lead to countless complex, closed solutions based on different standards that have undergone major compromises. Only after establishing technical standards will companies become more operational with blockchain. Only when industry standards are established, can interoperation between organizations be realized [6]. In May 2017, China Electronics Standardization Institute issued the *Blockchain Reference Architecture* standard. In March 2018, the Ministry of Industry and Information Technology of the People's Republic of China issued the *Key Points for Informatization and Standardization of Software Service Industry 2018*, proposing to promote the establishment of the National Technical Committee of Integration of Informatization and Industrialization Management Standardization, and the National Technical Committee for Standardization of Blockchain and Distributed Accounting Technology. On November 7, 2019, at the blockchain standardization work symposium organized by the Information Technology Development Division in Beijing, the relevant person in charge of the Information Technology Development Division stated that they will work with relevant departments to strengthen the research on blockchain standardization, accelerate the development and application of critical and urgently needed standards. At the same time, they will actively connect with international standards organizations to enhance international discourse power and rule-making power [7]. On April 10, 2020, the Ministry of Industry and Information Technology issued the *Guidelines for the Development of a System of Network Data Security Standards (Draft for Comment)*, which proposed that by 2021, a preliminary network data security standard system should be established to effectively implement network data security, Promote the application of standards in key enterprises and key fields, and develop more than 20 standards for network data security industry. By 2023, it is necessary to improve the network data security standard system, significantly improve the standard technical level, application level, and internationalization level, vigorously promote the improvement of industry network data security protection capabilities, and develop more than 50 network data security industry standards. On February 5, 2020, the People's Bank of China officially issued the *Financial Distributed Ledger Technology Security Specification (JR/T 0184-2020)*, which is a financial industry standard. National standards such as *Information Technology-Blockchain and Distributed Accounting Technology Deposit-Application Guide, Information Technology-Blockchain and Distributed Accounting Technology-Smart Contract Implementation Specification*, and other national standards are being formulated. On April 13, 2020, the Ministry of Industry and Information Technology issued the *Announcement on the Establishment of the National Blockchain and Distributed Accounting Technology Standardization Technical Committee*, which will undertake the specific tasks of systematically advancing the development of blockchain standards.

In terms of law enforcement and supervision, China has brought blockchain into the vision of law enforcement and supervision. As of April 24, 2020, the Cyberspace Administration of China has announced three batches of blockchain information service registration numbers. Filing is different from accreditation, nor is it equal to the recognition of the subject of the record and its products and services. The record registration is a means of supervision, which marks the inclusion of blockchain information services into the standardized regulatory system. Blockchain information service enterprises should be self-disciplined, develop in compliance, and also accept the supervision of regulatory authorities according to law. What needs to be mentioned in particular is that on April 2, 2021, the National Radio and Television Administration issued the *Blockchain-based Content Approval Standard System (2021 version)*, which is based on the blockchain-based content approval standard system to promote media content with the goal of healthy and sustainable development, starting from the actual development of the content approval business, covering the blockchain-based content approval system, business processes, security, management, and other links, and promoting the standardized construction and standardized operation of the blockchain-based content approval system. The system standards mainly regulate the system architecture, data format, system interface, and other technical requirements based on blockchain content audit, including the overall technical specification of the system, media content classification and identification, media content storage and sharing, blockchain data format, system interface, cross-chain technology, and other standards. Business standards mainly regulate the business process of blockchain-based content review, including content review, content traceability, and rereview standards. Security standards are mainly based on the basic requirements of blockchain content audit security, including system security technical requirements, security management audit standards, and other standards. Management standards mainly regulate the regulatory requirements of blockchain-based content audit, including standards of supervision, system and node evaluation, content audit evaluation, and so on.

In recent years, regulators have been focusing on exploring the use of blockchain to solve issues such as information sharing and cybersecurity in government administration. In the practice of law enforcement and supervision, how to coordinate the relationship between cybersecurity and innovation development has always been a difficult problem in law enforcement and supervision. From the perspective of China's regulatory practice, the concept of inclusive and prudent law enforcement supervision has become the consensus of law enforcement and supervision. An integrated and penetrating law enforcement supervision system that is transparent, efficient, and information symmetry is steadily advancing. Blockchain-enabled e-government will further promote reform of the institutional system of law enforcement and supervision. The reform is more conducive to properly coordinating the relationship between cybersecurity and innovation and development in supervision, promoting autonomic controllable research and application of blockchain, and effectively guarantee the safe operation of the blockchain system.

4   Conclusion

How to ensure the security of the blockchain is a common problem faced by all countries. For example, in July 2019, the European Parliament's Panel for the Future of Science and Technology (STOA) issued the *Blockchain and the General Data Protection Regulation: Can distributed ledgers be squared with European data protection law?*. The research report analyzed the conflict between blockchain and GDPR, but did not propose specific and feasible countermeasures. China attaches great importance to the social application value of blockchain, and has been exploring the security guarantee of blockchain from the aspects of technology, laws, and standards, and has made positive progress. Blockchain security technology is constantly evolving, but blockchain security will continue to encounter new problems. It is necessary to integrate application technology, laws, standards, and other measures to deepen the security of the blockchain.

Acknowledgments. This paper is supported by the Major Program of the National Social Science Fund of China "Theoretical Model and Practical Approach of Integrating Socialist Core Values into the Construction of Rule of Law in Smart Society" (No.20VHJ009).

References

1. Cyberspace Administration of China Homepage. http://www.cac.gov.cn/201901/10/c_1123 971138.htm. Accessed 10 Jan 2019
2. Wang, X., Han, Z., Xu, J.: A review of China's internet cybersecurity situation in 2018. J. Secrecy Sci. Technol. **5**, 4–9 (2019)
3. Herian, R.: Regulating Blockchain: Critical Perspectives in Law and Technology. In: Translated by Wang, Y., Guo, M., 1st edn. Shanghai People's Publishing House, Shanghai (2019)
4. Werbach, K., Lin, S.: Trust, but verify: Why the blockchain needs the law. J. Orient. Law **4**, 83–115 (2018)
5. Hong, H., Jiang, Y.: Academician Chun Chen: there are four core technologies that need to be broken through in the development of blockchain in China. http://digitalpaper.stdaily.com/ http_www.kjrb.com/kjrb/html/2019-11/01/content_433956.htm?div=-1. Accessed 27 Apr 2021
6. Huang, X.: Building trust with blockchain—interview with Chen Chun, academician of Chinese academy of engineering. J. High Technol. Commercialization **7**, 30–33 (2017)
7. Ministry of Industry and Information Technology of the People's Republic of China Homepage. https://www.miit.gov.cn/xwdt/gxdt/sjdt/art/2020/art_f814b868b447429a8812ddca7d9 7e217.html. Accessed 27 Apr 2021

Evaluation Method of the Excellent Employee Based on Clustering Algorithm

Bin Wang[✉]

Beijing Institute of Space Mechanics and Electricity, Beijing, China

Abstract. Excellent employees bring considerable benefits to the company, but once they leave, they will also cause great losses to the company. Therefore, it is necessary to establish a credible evaluation system for the behavior of outstanding employees, evaluate their daily performance, and predict their probability of leaving. Based on data mining technology, this paper analyzes the resignation information of employees' data provided by kaggle. According to Price-Muller employee separation theory and analogy with customer life cycle theory, we further excavate and analyze the reasons why employees leave. Finally, we define and evaluate the excellent employees in the enterprise.

Keywords: Price-muller employee resignation model · Clustering · Employee resignation prediction · Excellent employees

1 Preface

The credible evaluation system of employee behavior helps to evaluate the daily performance of employees and classify their behavior. The credible evaluation system is of great significance for maintaining the stability of the company's employees and reducing employee turnover. Brain drain caused by poor employee stability is a prominent problem in company management [1]. It is very important for companies to reasonably assess the level of employees' belonging to the enterprise and to quantitatively analyze the resignation rate of employees. Employees with strong capabilities and great contributions to the company can create greater value for the company. Establishing models to identify these employees and prevent the loss of these employees can save cost for companies [2].

2 Analysis of Kaggle Employees Resignation Data Set

The data set used in this paper is collected from the sample data of 14999 employees'turnover situation provided by Kaggle platform, which contains 10 indicator variables. As shown in Table 1 below.

© Springer Nature Singapore Pte Ltd. 2021
H.-N. Dai et al. (Eds.): BlockSys 2021, CCIS 1490, pp. 593–600, 2021.
https://doi.org/10.1007/978-981-16-7993-3_46

Table 1. Variable description table.

Variable name	The meaning of variable	Variable type	Detail information	Value range	Remarks
Left	Whether you have already resigned	Component variable	Qualitative variables,2 levels	0 is not quit,1 is quit	
Satisfaction_level	Satisfaction with the company	Numerical variable		0 ~ 1	The average satisfaction is 0.6
last_evaluation	performance evaluation	Numerical variable		0 ~ 1	The average performance evaluation
number_project	Number of projects worked	Numerical variable	unit: pcs	2 ~ 7	The average number of projects is 4
average_monthly_hours	Average working hours per month	Numerical variable	unit: hours	96 ~ 310	
time_spend_company	years of working	Numerical variable	unit: years	2 ~ 10	
Work_accident	Have you ever missed work	Component variable	Qualitative variables,2 levels	0 is not happening, 1 is happening	The percentage of errors is 14.46%
sales	profession	Component variable	Qualitative variables,10 levels		
salary	salary	Component variable	Qualitative variables,3 levels	medium, low, high	High accounted for 8.2%, low accounted for 48.8%

3   Introduction of the Price-Muller Model

3.1   Hypothesis of the Price-Muller Model

Before conducting an empirical analysis of employee resignation, the Price-Muller model needs to satisfy a series of assumptions [3]. Firstly, it is assumed that employees come into the organization with certain expectations, they will be more satisfied with the company and have a tendency to stay in the organization if the organization meets their current expectations. Secondly, it is assumed that there is a fair "benefit exchange" relationship between employees and the organization. In other words, the employee's labor or service creates profits for the organization, and the organization rewards employees with a salary that corresponds to their work at the same time. Thirdly, it is assumed that employees always pursue the maximization of net income during their tenure in the organization. In other words, if there are more than one optional "cost-benefit" items for chosen, employees will balance their interests to maximize their net return.

3.2   Indicator and Variables of the Price-Muller Model

The Price-Muller model has four types of variables related to employee turnover, which are environmental variable, individual variable, structural variable, and intermediary variable [4]. The core theory of the Price-Muller model is that employees' willingness to leave and their tendency and behaviors to look for other jobs are directly affected by environmental variables. However, individual variables and structural variables indirectly affect employees' turnover tendency and behavior through the role of intermediary variables. Based on the Price-Muller model ,combined with the actual situation of employee turnover in Kaggle,this paper integrated and improved the original 9 dependent variables in the data set, and then formed 11 new indicator variables, so as to carry out empirical analysis better and improve the explanatory effect of the model for employees' turnover reasons.

Environment Variables

$$Opportunity = (promotion\_last\_5years) * (time\_spend\_company) \quad (1)$$

From the data analysis, it is known that whether to be promoted within five years is a "0–1" variable. If an employee has worked in the company for ten years but doesn't have a promotion prospect within five years, this employee won't be able to take advantage of external opportunities [5].

Individual Variables

$$Positive/NegativeSentiment = [(Satisfaction\_Level)^2 + (last\_evaluation)^2]^{1/2} \quad (2)$$

$$Workparticipation = performanceevaluation(last\_evaluation) \quad (3)$$

Structural Variables

$$Autonomy = time\_spend\_company \quad (4)$$

$$Distribution fairness : (salary)/(average\_monthly\_hours) \quad (5)$$

$$Promotionopportunity = promotion\_last\_5years \quad (6)$$

$$Salary = salary \quad (7)$$

$$Workpressure = [(number\_project)^2 + (average\_monthly\_hours)^2]^{1/2} \quad (8)$$

The higher value of "distributional fairness" represents greater inequity [6]. For example, if the salary level is low and working hours are 200 h, the value of "distributional fairness" is 1/200; However, if the salary level is high and working hours are 200 h,the value of "distributional fairness" is 3/200. In summary, employees with lower salary levels are in an unfair position under the same number of working hours.

Intervening Variables

$$Job - seekingbehavior = (time\_spend\_company)/(satisfaction\_level) \quad (9)$$

$$Resignation intention = [(satisfaction\_level)^2 + salary^2]^{1/2} \qquad (10)$$

$$Job satisfaction = satisfaction\_level \qquad (11)$$

The smaller value of "job-seeking behavior" represents a lower tendency for employees to look for other jobs [7]. For example, if the time_spend_company is 6 years and satisfaction_level is 0.5, the value of job-seeking behavior is 12; However, if the time_spend_company is 6 years and satisfaction_level is 0.6, the value of job-seeking behavior is 10. By comparision, when the working years are the same, if employees are more dissatisfied with the company, they will be more likely to leave and look for other job opportunities.

4   Introduction to Employee Life Cycle Theory

The employee life cycle theory is described as follows: According to a 6-month cycle, the value of a new employee in a certain position in an organization can be divided into 4 cycles, which are learning input stage, value formation stage, ability display stage and value promotion stage [8]. In the first stage, the employees are often unable to create obvious value for the company. On the contrary, the company still needs to invest some time and resources to cultivate them. In the second stage, employees start trying to create value for the company, and gradually have positive or negative emotions. In the third stage, employees are already creating value for the company. Therefore, this paper uses work-autonomy and work-participation to measure their working ability. The fourth stage is a continuation of the third stage. In this stage, what matter is whether employees have management potential and the ability to make progress. During this stage, some employees are promoted and obtain better resources, some employees have the intention to leave and further generates Job-seeking behavior. Therefore, this paper uses promotion opportunity, turnover intention, and job-hopping behavior to examine employees in this stage.

5   Excellent Employees Based on K-Means Clustering Algorithm Evaluation

5.1   Introduction to K-Means Clustering Algorithm

The k-means clustering algorithm, also known as the k-means distance algorithm, is a method of constructing k divided clusters $\{D_1, D_2...D_k\}$ from a data set D containing n data objects [9]. Each cluster contains at least one data object, and each data object must belong to one and only one cluster. At the same time, Data objects in the same cluster should be close to each other and data objects in different clusters should be estranged from each other. That is, minimizing the squared error E:

$$E = \sum_{i=1}^{k} \sum_{x \in D_i} \|x - \mu_i\|_2^2$$

Where μ_i is the mean vector of cluster D_i, also called centroid, and the expression is:

$$\mu_i = \frac{1}{|D_i|} \sum_{x \in D_i} x$$

The k-means algorithm flows as follows: First, according to the k categories to be classified, randomly select k data objects. Each data object represents an initial cluster center; For each remaining object, according to its similarity (distance) to each cluster center, assign it to the cluster that corresponds to its most "similar" cluster center; Recalculate the average of all objects in the cluster for each node added, and use it as a new cluster center. Repeat the above process until the criterion function becomes convergent, in another word, the centroids of all clusters do not change significantly.

5.2 Result Analysis of Employee Dimission Types Based on K-Means Algorithm

Based on the Price-Muller (2000) employee turnover model and employee life cycle theory, we have established six indicators, which are positive/negative emotions, resignation intention, job-seeking behavior, promotion opportunities, autonomy, and job participation. Also combining the k value obtained from the previous contour coefficient analysis [10] and the actual situation of Kaggle employees, this paper uses the K-means algorithm to cluster the employees, and the number of clusters k is 3 classes. The clustering results of all data objects in the Kaggle data set are shown in Fig. 1.

According to statistics, the number of various types of employees is shown in Fig. 2.

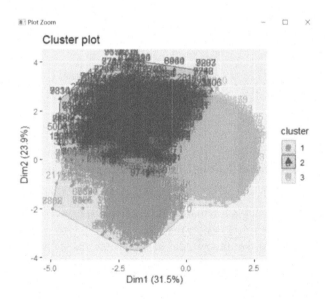

Fig. 1. K-means clustering results.

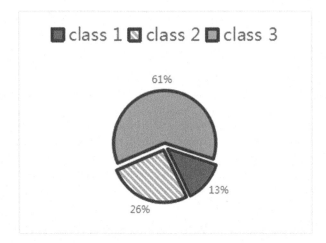

Fig. 2. Proportion chart of each employee category.

The radar chart distribution of different categories of employees under the six indicators of clustering is shown in Fig. 3. For programming convenience, we use abbreviations. In the clockwise direction, they are acne (positive/negative emotion), ou (intention to leave), fi (job-seeking behavior), ch (promotion opportunity), per (autonomy), and ac (work participation) in turn.

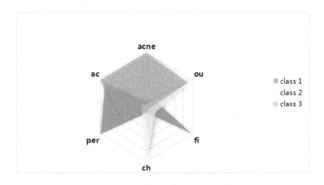

Fig. 3. Radar chart distribution results of each category.

The radar chart provide a concise and intuitive way to determine the characteristics of different employee categories. According to the characteristics, we make the following summary. Class1 are some excellent employees, they have higher ac (work participation/performance evaluation) and per (autonomy/working years), have a tendency to do job-seeking behaviors.At the same time, they have a low intention of ou (resignation), and they are the more reliable backbone of the enterprise. Class2 are some stable employees, they pay more attention to ch (promotion opportunity), but they are more likely to leave when they cannot get the promotion opportunity. Class3 are some silent employees, accounting for 51% of all employees. This type of employee have low ac (work participation/performance evaluation) and high acne (positive/negative emotion), which means that they have a permissive mood towards work and has no hope for job promotion.Because of their limited abilities, they prefer to stay in their current positions than job-hopping. Therefore, this type of employee can also be called xianyu employees.

5.3   Definition of Outstanding Employees

According to the above classification of excellent employees, stable employees, and silent employees, excellent employees own higher values in indicators like ac (work participation/performance evaluation) and per (autonomy/working years) and they have a tendency to do job-seeking behaviors. Therefore, the characteristics of "excellent employees" include: (1) work participation/last_evaluation $\geq$ 0.7; (2) autonomy/time_spend_company $\geq$ 0.4; (3) number_project$>$ 5; (4) acne (positive/negative emotion) $\geq$ 0.8; (5) job_seeking_behavior $\geq$ 25.

6   Conclusion

In this paper, we have classified the employees in the company by the method of clustering, and defined the excellent employees. Excellent employees can create greater value for the company, and their resignation will cause a considerable loss of company resources. The model proposed in this paper can identify excellent employees by a few simple indicators, and make prevention in advance to reduce the loss of the company's human resources.

References

1. Sun, C.J., Wu, J.X.: Employee stability and enterprise development. Contemp. Econ. **23**, 76–77 (2013)
2. He, Y.Y.: Analysis of Causes and Countermeasures of Core Employees. Wuhan University, Wuhan (2005)
3. Wu, K.: Review of the three major models of employee separation. Technology Information (31), 527+525 (2009)
4. Zhang, M., Zhang, D.: Empirical study on the regulation of value variables in price-mueller disession model. Manag. Rev. **09**, 46–5164 (2006)
5. Han, T.H.: Study on Employee Loss of G Bank S Branch Based on Price-Mueller Model. Hebei University of Economics and Trade, Hebei (2020)
6. Bai, X.D.: Compensation Equity, Employee Behavior, and Company Performance. Southwest University of Finance and Economics, El Paso (2014)
7. Ro, F.: Active Separation Risk of Insurance Employees Based on Price-Mueller (2000) Model. Tianjin University of Technology, Tianjin (2009)
8. Li, Y.S.: Research on knowledge-based employee incentive under leadership life ecycle theory. Contemp. Econ. (second half) **09**, 73–74 (2008)

9. Wang, Q., Wang, C., Feng, Z.Y., Ye, J.F.: Research review of k-means clustering algorithm. Electron. Des. Eng. **20**(07), 21–24 (2012)
10. Zhu, L.J., Ma, B.X., Zhao, X.Q.: Analysis of clustering effectiveness based on conile coefficient. Comput. Appl. **30**(S2), 139–141198 (2010)

A Study on the Challenges and Countermeasures of Blockchain Industry and Technology Development - Guangdong Province as an Example

Li Li[ID] and Taoye Wang[✉]

Guangdong Institute of Scientific and Technological Information Guangzhou, Guangzhou 510030, China

Abstract. Blockchain establishes a decentralized credit mechanism in the network, and gradually promotes and applies digital currency to more industries, becoming the focus and hot spot of research in the information field. However, there is a lack of overall research on its technological development. To ensure the rapid development of the blockchain industry and technology in China, by comparing and analyzing the development of blockchain industry technology at home and abroad, this paper takes the development status of the blockchain in Guangdong Province as the analysis object. The advantages and challenges of the development of blockchain industry technology in Guangdong Province were analyzed in detail from the four dimensions of blockchain basic platform, innovation carrier, market application, industrial ecology, and countermeasures were studied and discussed from the aspects of technology system construction, innovation platform improvement, tal-ent introduction, and standard deployment.

Keywords: Blockchain · Core technology · Industrial application · Countermeasures and suggestions

1 Introduction

Blockchain was first proposed by Nakamoto in 2008 and used to realize electronic currency bitcoin [1]. At present, bitcoin has become the most popular electronic currency in the world, with more than 13 million users and a total market value of US$400 billion. With the development of e-money, blockchain technology has gradually entered the public field of vision and become the focus of academic research in recent years. Blockchain establishes a tamper-proof distributed storage system through a P2P network and disperses the applications that can only be run through trusted intermediaries to unfamiliar nodes, to solve the problems of high trust, low efficiency, and unsafe data storage in the centralized system [2]. The 13th five-year national information plan issued by the State Council [3] points out that the Internet of things, blockchain, and other new technologies

© Springer Nature Singapore Pte Ltd. 2021
H.-N. Dai et al. (Eds.): BlockSys 2021, CCIS 1490, pp. 601–613, 2021.
https://doi.org/10.1007/978-981-16-7993-3_47

drive the evolution of cyberspace from the Internet of everyone to the Internet of everything, and digital, networked, and intelligent services will be everywhere. Blockchain and other related technologies are officially listed as strategic frontier technologies by the state. In 2018, Gartner, a famous consulting company, listed blockchain technology as one of the top ten strategic technologies that will have a significant impact on most enterprises.

With the wide application of blockchain in supply chain finance, electronic certificates, anti-counterfeiting traceability, government affairs, and people's livelihood, blockchain technology will enter the 3.0 era [4]. The change brought about by blockchain technology is sweeping the globe, and countries around the world have taken a series of strategic measures to deal with it [5]. The United States passed the Blockchain Promotion Method in July 2019 and released the National key technology and emerging technology strategy on October 15, 2020. In its "Germany Blockchain Strategy," Germany noted that blockchain technology was the cornerstone of the future Internet and that Germany would further consolidate its leadership in that area. The Political Bureau of the Central Committee of the Communist Party of China carried out the eighteenth collective learning on the status and trend of blockchain technology development on October 24, 2019. In presiding over the study, the general secretary of the CPC Central Committee stressed:' The integrated application of blockchain technology plays an important role in new technological innovation and industrial change. We should take blockchain as an important breakthrough in the independent innovation of core technologies, clarify the main direction, increase investment, focus on overcoming several key core technologies, and accelerate the development of blockchain technology and industrial innovation.

To promote the development of blockchain industrial technology, Guangdong Province has successively issued documents such as "Some Policy Measures on Further Promoting Scientific and Technological Innovation", "Guangdong Provincial Action Plan for Cultivating Blockchain and Quantum Information Strategic Emerging Industries Cluster (2021–2025)," and "Notice of the Shenzhen Municipal People's Government on the issuance of special fund support policies for strategic emerging industries," provide corresponding support for Guangdong Province to build an international highland of blockchain industrial technology from the aspects of blockchain technology research, industrial application, platform carrier and so on. However, the application of the blockchain industry in the province is still in its infancy, and there are the following problems: 1) The core technology autonomy of blockchain is not high. 2) Blockchain open innovation research system has not been established. 3) Industrial ecology such as evaluation and supervision is not perfect. In general, the blockchain industry in Guangdong Province is in the early stage of the outbreak, so it is of great significance to analyze and study its technology and application status.

The rest of the paper is organized as follows. Section 2 first summarizes and compare the related researches. Then, Sect. 3 introduces the principles and industrial technology advantages of blockchain. Section 4 presents the technological development of the blockchain industry in Guangdong Province. Section 5 summarizes the corresponding countermeasures and suggestions. Finally, the paper concludes in Sect. 6.

2 Related Work

At present, the global blockchain industry is in a stage of rapid development. Blockchain technology is widely used in digital currency, finance, the Internet of Things, medical security, energy, government affairs, artificial intelligence, big data, and other fields in China and abroad. Overall, blockchain technology is mainly used in the financial sector, and financial institutions around the world are committed to using blockchain technology to improve back-end process efficiency and reduce operating costs. Thus, the positive actions shown by various countries in the development of blockchain technology and applications will help further promote the development of the blockchain industry.

2.1 Application Status of Blockchain Technology in Foreign Countries

Blockchain is currently used in a wide range of applications, and foreign research on blockchain covers a wide range of aspects. In the field of supply chain finance, researchers have worked on improving transaction processing and performance [6], security and data privacy [7], automation of financial contracts [8], corporate finance [9], etc. IBM has set up a blockchain lab and the UK has issued an e-money license. R3CEV, a blockchain startup, has launched the R3 blockchain consortium, which has so far attracted 42 giant banks' participation. Blockchain can provide the trust mechanisms needed for IoT applications, ensuring the integrity of the data collected and related interactions, as well as transparency. Researchers have integrated blockchain into IoT decentralization [10], security [11], anonymity [12], and device management [13]. Samsung Ventures has been involved in IBM's ADEPT project, a decentralized IoT using Bitcoin and the Ethernet network, and the Filament project, which creates an IoT by using small and advanced hardware devices to put various electronic devices, especially appliances, on the blockchain. In the field of healthcare, blockchain has a wide range of applicability, with research results currently focused on the management of electronic medical records (EMRs) [14], biomedical research [15], etc. Tierion has announced the completion of its first project with Philips Healthcare to build a medical data storage and validation platform using blockchain records. In the energy sector, blockchain technologies based on energy and energy management are becoming mainstream, including directions such as electricity market control [16], energy trading [17], and energy grid security. In government work, current research is focused on e-government [18], e-voting [19], value registration and other areas. In artificial intelligence, a synergy between blockchain and AI can track the origin of training models [20], improve the efficiency of transportation systems [21], increase robot control [22], etc. In big data, blockchain can help establish a data-sharing platform for all participants to interact [23], improve data reliability between participants [24], increase data security, and provide timestamps. Foreign blockchain subjects are mostly open source-based, several typical blockchain technology applications Etherenum, Hyperledger Fabric, etc. are open source, so foreign blockchain development is well sustained.

2.2 Application Status of Blockchain Technology in China

Due to the huge financial risk of the digital currency, it is not suitable for China's unique economic environment, so it is still in its infancy, but in other fields, the application of blockchain technology is basically synchronized with the world. Zhejiang Province supports Zhejiang University to declare and prepare for the construction of the National Key Laboratory of Blockchain. Hangzhou Ant Group ranks first in the world in terms of the average patent strength index in the field of blockchain for three consecutive years. The domestic autonomous controllable blockchain infrastructure platform developed by fun chain science and technology has realized the application of multiple scenarios with its research and development of data collaboration, cross-chain, open services, and other platforms. The' Conflux tree blockchain public chain system' independently developed by Shanghai tree blockchain research institute is expected to take a place in public chain technical rules. China Ping An has successfully joined the R3 blockchain alliance. Wanxiang Group established a blockchain laboratory, China Internet Finance Association established a blockchain research working group, and the People's Bank of China deployed a special team to study blockchain technology. The China Blockchain Application (North America) Research Center was established. The Microfinance Industry Alliance of Blockchain was officially established in Beijing. The Lujiazui Blockchain Finance Development Alliance was established in Shanghai. The China Postal Savings Bank and IBM (China) Co., Ltd. launched an asset custody system based on blockchain. Beijing issued Beijing Blockchain Innovation and Development Action Plan (2020–2022) in the early stage, and recently released the first domestic autonomous controllable blockchain hardware and software technology system "Chang' a Chain" and established the Chang' a Chain Ecological Alliance. Shenzhen Weizhong Bank Joint Gold Chain Alliance.

2.3 Comparative Analysis

Blockchain, as one of the basic technology for reconstructing modern credit systems and supporting the high-quality development of the digital economy, has seen fierce competition at home and abroad, and hundreds of basic platform projects have been made public. The main blockchain platforms are shown in Table 1, and the competition will further intensify globally in the short term due to its importance [25]. In terms of development path, foreign countries focus on open-source blockchain original code, build developer communities, accelerate key technological innovation and form blockchain industrial ecology. Domestic blockchain research enterprises are mainly divided into two types of Internet majors represented by BATJ and startups represented by Wellcom, Bubi, Fun

Chain and Wisdom, which mainly focus on commercial packaging and technical optimization based on foreign open-source code. The main focus is on the commercial packaging and technical optimization based on foreign open-source code, to meet the requirements of independent control, and to explore its potential application value and business model.

Table 1. Major blockchain platforms at home and abroad.

Blockchain platform	Type	Representative application	R & D subject
Bitcoin	Public Blockchain	Cryptocurrency transfer	Open source community
Ethereum	Public Blockchain	Decentralized Finance	Open source community
Super ledger fabric	Consortium Blockchain	–	IBM > open source community
Quorum	Consortium Blockchain	–	JPMorgan Chase
COCO	Consortium Blockchain	–	Microsoft Research
Ant blockchain	Consortium Blockchain	Hangzhou judicial blockchain, etc.	Alibaba/Ant financial services
FISCO-BCOS	Consortium Blockchain	People's network copyright platform, etc.	Weizhong bank
Tencent blockchain	Consortium Blockchain	Shenzhen electronic invoice, etc.	Tencent
Ping An blockchain	Consortium Blockchain	Tianjin Port cross border trade platform	Ping An, China
Baidu super chain	Consortium Blockchain	Copyright certificate, etc.	Baidu

3 Blockchain Principles and Industrial Technology Advantages

3.1 Overview of Blockchain Principles

The blockchain is essentially a decentralized distributed database, where all interaction (transaction) records generated in the system are stored in the form of blocks linked into chains on each section in chronological order. Each transaction is guaranteed by cryptography and proof-of-work algorithms to be difficult to tamper with and difficult to forge, so that each node in the system can achieve peer-to-peer secure transactions.

3.2 Data Structure of Blockchain

In terms of the composition of blockchain, the literature [26] classifies it into the data layer, network layer, consensus layer, incentive layer, contract layer, and application layer. The literature [27] divides the blockchain architecture into three layers from the perspective of privacy protection: the network layer, the transaction layer, and the application layer. From the perspective of data analysis, literature [28] divides the blockchain into three horizontal and one vertical structure. As shown in Fig. 1, the data layer is the lowest level of technology and performs two main functions: authentication of accounts and transactions data storage.

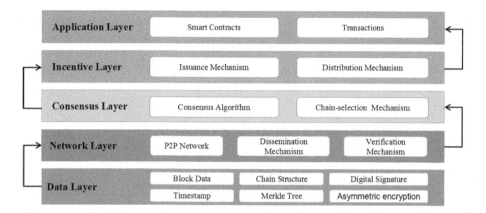

Fig. 1. The architecture of blockchain.

3.3   Industrial Technology Advantages of Blockchain

Advantages of blockchain technology: 1) Reduce costs. Blockchain does not require the establishment of a central server, avoiding expensive operation and maintenance costs. Blockchain's smart contracts can perform transaction operations under specific conditions, which can greatly save human resource costs and facilitate the maintenance of equipment. 2) Identity authentication. Blockchain's authentication and consensus mechanisms help avoid illegal or even malicious nodes from accessing the IoT. 3) Privacy protection. All transmitted data in the blockchain are strictly encrypted, and users' data and privacy will be more secure. 4) Cross-subject collaboration. Blockchain's distributed peer-to-peer structure and open and transparent algorithm can establish mutual trust at low cost, break the shackles of information silos, and promote horizontal information flow and multi-party collaboration. 5) Traceability and evidence. As long as the data is written into the blockchain by consensus, it is difficult to tamper with and can be traced back to its source by relying on the chain structure.

4   Blockchain Industry Technology Development in Guangdong Province

At present, Guangdong Province has initially formed a whole industrial chain of blockchain-based on industrial technology research, which integrates upstream chips, computing power, and other infrastructure, the underlying framework platform in the middle reaches, general technology, downstream applications, ecological services, and regulatory protection. The key links of the industrial chain and the distribution of main enterprises are shown in Table 2. The province's blockchain patent applications account for about one-third of the country. Blockchain services provide strong support for government affairs, people's livelihood, and finance. For example, blockchain electronic invoices have access to nearly ten thousand enterprises, cross-border transactions have reached ten million levels, and supply chain finance has reached a billion levels. It constructs an industrial pattern with Shenzhen and Guangzhou as the core to promote the coordinated development of Foshan, Zhuhai, and Dongguan. However, there are also insufficient technical integration support and weak interoperability.

Table 2. Distribution of blockchain industry chain in Guangdong Province.

Industrial chain	Key links
Upstream hardware and infrastructure	Chip, Foundation layer and platform layer provide and integrate the underlying computing power and hardware support for the blockchain
Core ecological tools and protocols	It provides the underlying architecture, development platform and ecological blockchain platform for various blockchain applications, making blockchain applications more convenient to deploy and be applied, as well as a common technology for developers and users
Downstream applications and ecological services	The blockchain is applied to various industries, scenarios and vertical applications serving end users
Support tools	Blockchain technology evaluation, standards, regulatory tools, etc.

4.1   Weak Blockchain Autonomy and Controllability

Guangdong Province has developed well in terms of blockchain underlying infrastructure platforms, and many distinctive blockchain underlying platforms have emerged. For example, BCOS, an enterprise-grade alliance chain underlying platform developed by Weizhong Bank, BaaS platform and FiMAX underlying framework for financial blockchain applications developed by Shenzhen One Account, Trust SQL underlying platform for enterprise-grade blockchain infrastructure developed by Tencent, and Xunlei blockchain open platform developed by Shenzhen Xunlei Network Technology Co. However, influenced by the technical path, domestic blockchain service platform technology mostly comes from the deep transformation of existing open-source technology from abroad, such as Micro bank FISCO BCOS initially originated from the C++ version of Ethernet and later carried out deep customization, refactoring, and optimization according to the financial scenario on security, functionality, performance and regulatory compliance requirements. The Xunlei blockchain open platform draws on foreign frameworks such as Ether and EOS on secondary research and development. Faced with the escalation of the Sino-US game, the challenges of network security, and the requirements of autonomous control, it is necessary to accelerate the research and development of autonomous and controllable blockchain technology to create a homemade secure and controllable blockchain infrastructure platform.

4.2   Blockchain Application Industry Lacks Cohesion

There are more than 220 enterprises for the record of blockchain information services in Guangdong Province, accounting for about 1/5 of the national record. The main distribution is shown in Fig. 2, covering all aspects of the blockchain industry chain and having many listed companies and individual champions such as Huawei, Tencent, MicroBank, Xunlei, Shunfeng, Fangxin Technology, Matrix Element, NetCore Technology. Sun Yat-sen University, Guangzhou University, and Shenzhen University have established blockchain research institutes (centers) respectively. However, most of the blockchain enterprises in Guangdong Province are small and relatively scattered. Some enterprises' main business is not blockchain services, and the profit model is not clear enough. Most of the research on blockchain in university research institutes originates from large information and electronic fields such as artificial intelligence and network security. Cross-disciplinary research is insufficient, while the overall scientific research strength and industrial cohesion of blockchain are relatively dispersed.

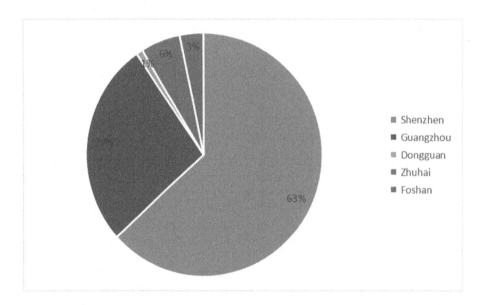

Fig. 2. Distribution of registered enterprises.

4.3   Serious Lack of Triggered Blockchain Applications

With the continuous breakthrough of blockchain technology, blockchain in Guangdong Province has been widely used in the fields of financial technology, supply chain management, and government and livelihood services [29]. In the field of financial technology, Fangxin Technology's "Tax Chain" has issued the country's first upgraded blockchain electronic invoice. In the supply chain management sector, One Account has built the first interconnected and shared blockchain network in the Greater Bay Area that connects ports, customs, logistics, enterprises, finance, and other trade processes, enhancing cross-border trade facilitation in the Greater Bay Area. In the area of government, Digital Guangdong has built a blockchain infrastructure platform for e-government, solving the problems of open sharing and system integration between heterogeneous chains. The blockchain traceability platform developed by the Institute of Software Application Technology of the Chinese Academy of Sciences in Guangzhou in the area of people's livelihood has been promoted and applied in the Pearl River Delta region. At present, the applications based on blockchain technology are blossoming, but the bottlenecks involved in blockchain technology such as distribution, scalability, and security have not yet been effectively solved [30]. In addition, the excessive concentration of applications in the financial field has led to the slow cultivation of some scenarios, unclear business model, and the 'detonating' application has not yet appeared, and the enduring power of 'blockchain +' towards maturity remains to be strengthened.

4.4   Blockchain Industry Lacks International Influence

Guangdong Province is at the forefront of blockchain base park construction in China. Guangzhou has been approved to create the first blockchain development demonstration zone in China; Shenzhen has Nanshan Science and Technology Park and Futian Financial CBD blockchain industry zone; Huangpu District has many industrial parks or incubation carriers such as Blockchain International Innovation Center and Ant-Mi Blockchain Crowd Space; Guangdong Financial High-tech Zone has gathered many innovative blockchain enterprises and leading financial technology enterprises to form "blockchain+" fintech industry cluster. In terms of the policy environment, at the provincial level, there is the Action Plan for Fostering Blockchain and Quantum Information Strategic Emerging Industry Clusters in Guangdong Province (2021–2025), and cities such as Guangzhou, Shenzhen, and Foshan have also formulated corresponding policies to support the development of blockchain industry according to their characteristics. However, Guangdong Province has insufficient reserves of high-value blockchain patents and papers, a blockchain measurement and evaluation system have not been fully established, insufficient investment in core technologies and basic algorithms, weak discourse in open source communities, and an overall lack of international influence.

5   Countermeasures and Suggestions

With the continuous breakthrough of blockchain technology, the blockchain industry is about to enter the outbreak period. Guangdong should take the initiative in the key technology research, platform construction, standard specification, evaluation system formulation, safety supervision, and intellectual education of blockchain, strengthen the planning of the province's blockchain industry innovation and development layout, and strive to build new advantages and new kinetic energy of high-quality economic development.

5.1   Improving Blockchain Technology Innovation System

Blockchain technology is a comprehensive technology, involving distributed storage, encryption, consensus mechanism, and other technologies. It is suggested that Guangdong Province should guide key enterprises, scientific research, universities, and user units to strengthen cooperation, study blockchain technology roadmap, formulate blockchain technology and industrial development planning at the provincial level, focus on the key core technologies of blockchain, and deeply explore the innovative application fields of blockchain. Given the current situation of blockchain technology development in the early stage, the basic theory research of blockchain is continuously carried out to promote the innovation of blockchain technology such as intelligent contracts, consensus algorithms, encryption algorithms, and distributed systems. The core technology research and development of rotary mechanism, hash locking, side chain, and distributed private key control is carried out to realize the breakthrough of core algorithms such as cross-chain transaction interoperability and cross-chain asset transfer [31], encourage relevant code to open source and improve the technological innovation system of blockchain.

5.2   Taking Advantage of Blockchain Ecology

Blockchains, whether they are federated or public, have the opportunity to become the business infrastructure of the future. However, at present, in this field, the public chain holds the leading position in Bitcoin and Ether, while the super ledger Fabric, which is in the absolute leading position in the coalition chain ecology, is led by IBM in research and development [32]. To prevent possible "necking" in the blockchain field, Guangdong Province needs to take the initiative to seize opportunities, develop blockchain service platforms with a focus on alliance chains, accelerate research on public chain technology, promote the development and application of domestic, independent, and controllable blockchain systems, benchmark advanced foreign blockchain systems, and promote the open-source and application of domestic blockchain in China to enrich the application ecology of domestic blockchain and establish ecological advantages.

5.3   Establishing a High-Level Innovation Platform for Blockchain

Centering on the breakthrough innovation and development needs of blockchain, guide universities and research institutes in the province, such as Sun Yat-sen University and Pengcheng Laboratory, to give full play to their advantages in basic research and application basic research, and deeply participate in the basic theory and key core technology research of blockchain. Support blockchain enterprises to build innovation platforms such as key laboratories, engineering technology research centers, testing service platforms, new research and development institutions, and industrial technology alliances with the United Nations' advantageous universities and institutes, to make joint efforts to overcome key common technologies, establish technical standards and form a perfect innovation platform system.

5.4   Introducing High-End Talents Abroad

To fully grasp the construction opportunities of Guangdong-Hong Kong-Macao Greater Bay Area, we should focus on the basic theory, core technology, and original algorithm of blockchain, increasing the introduction of talents and teams, coordinate the existing talent projects, encourage different innovation subjects to introduce talents by the diversification of market-oriented methods, and provide intellectual support for the layout of blockchain in Guangdong Province. Strengthening the construction of blockchain-related disciplines, promoting the cultivation of interdisciplinary, multi-level, comprehensive talents, and taking blockchain as the key direction of cryptography to speed up the solution of talent shortage.

5.5   Creating an Effective Ecosystem of Blockchain

Actively take the initiative to connect with national blockchain standard research institutions and take the lead or participate in the formulation of international and domestic blockchain technology and industry standards to enhance the discourse of the blockchain industry in Guangdong Province, accelerate the formulation of provincial blockchain standards and technical specifications, especially blockchain security supervision standards and systems, to regulate market operations, encourage scientific research and assessment institutions to join industry associations to deploy blockchain security assessment and performance assessment systems. To drive the high-quality development and risk control of the blockchain. At present, although the blockchain alliance chain has been applied in various industries, it is still a huge distance from replacing the original business model. The government can introduce relevant policies to support the establishment of industrial alliances from the government's perspective, promote the business model represented by the alliance blockchain to advance faster, take the lead in balancing the interests of all parties, and promote industrial reform. Blockchain technology and digital currency represent the direction of emerging technology development, and the emerging technology requires the regulator to bring in multiple forces to participate in the construction of the regulatory sandbox and crackdown on all kinds of scams cloaked in blockchain "garb", to create a fertile ecological environment.

5.6   Encouraging the Development of Blockchain Application Enterprises

To select many key blockchain enterprises, typical products, and services in the province with the orientation of technological innovation and industry leadership, give certain support, and open up some scenarios to achieve promotion and demonstration. Support leading enterprises in the industry, such as Huawei and Tencent, to strengthen the layout of blockchain underlying technology platforms and provide underlying support services for the blockchain industry in Guangdong Province, establish an information bank of specialized and special new enterprises in the blockchain field, closely track and serve several blockchains innovative enterprises, and carry out targeted tiered classification services.

6 Conclusion

Blockchain, as one of the disruptive technologies leading a new round of global technological and industrial change, is constantly penetrating all aspects of our lives and providing strong support for the high-quality development of the digital economy. However, in promoting the development of the blockchain industry and technological innovation, there will also be problems such as the core technology has not been broken through and the industrial ecology is not perfect. These need to be discussed jointly by enterprises, industries, and government departments, and promote the solution of the problem from multiple aspects of technology, industry, and supervision, to provide a good environment for the safe and orderly development of the blockchain industry.

References

1. Nakamoto, S.: Bitcoin : A peer-to-peer electronic cash system (2009)
2. Hai-wu, H., An, Y., Zehua, C.: Survey of smart contract technology and application based on blockchain. J. Comput. Res. Dev. **55**, 2452 (2018)
3. Shao, Q.F., Jin, C.Q., Zhang, Z., Qian, W.N., Zhou, A.Y.: Blockchain: architecture and research progress. Chin. J. Comput. **41**(5), 969–988 (2018)
4. Sun, W., Zhu, X., Zhou, T., Su, Y., Mo, B.: Application of blockchain and rfid in anti-counterfeiting traceability of liquor. In: 2019 IEEE 5th International Conference on Computer and Communications (ICCC) (2019)
5. Gradstein, H.L., Krause, S.K.: Distributed ledger technology (dlt) and blockchain (2017)
6. Tasca, P., Aste, T., Pelizzon, L., Perony, N.: [new economic windows] banking beyond banks and money, understanding modern banking ledgers through blockchain technologies: Future of transaction processing and smart contracts on the internet of money, vol. 2016, no. Chapter 13, pp. 239-278. https://doi.org/10. 1007/978-3-319-42448-4
7. Singh, S., Singh, N.: Blockchain: future of financial and cyber security. In: 2016 2nd International Conference on Contemporary Computing and Informatics (IC3I) (2017)
8. Karaivanov, A.: Blockchains, collateral and financial contracts, Discussion Papers (2021)
9. Momtaz, P.P., Rennertseder, K., Schröder, H.: Token offerings: a revolution in corporate finance? SSRN Electron. J. (2019)
10. Su, B., Wu, C., Bao, W., Guleng, S., Ji, Y.: Empowering blockchain in vehicular environments with decentralized edges. IEEE Access **8**, 202032–202041 (2020)
11. Khan, M.A., Salah, K.: IoT security: Review, blockchain solutions, and open challenges. Future Gener. Comput. Syst. **82**, 395–411 (2018)
12. Christidis, K., Devetsikiotis, M.: Blockchains and smart contracts for the internet of things. IEEE Access **4**, 2292–2303 (2016)

13. Wu, J., Dong, M., Ota, K., Li, J., Yang, W.: Application-aware consensus management for software-defined intelligent blockchain in IoT. IEEE Network **34**(1), 69–75 (2020)
14. Zhang, A., Lin, X.: Towards secure and privacy-preserving data sharing in e-health systems via consortium blockchain. J. Med. Syst. **42**(8), 140 (2018)
15. Benchoufi, M., Porcher, R., Ravaud, P.: Blockchain protocols in clinical trials: transparency and traceability of consent. F1000 Res. **6**, 66 (2017)
16. Lundqvist, T., Blanche, A.D., Andersson, H.: Thing-to-thing electricity micro payments using blockchain technology. In: Global Internet of Things Summit (2017)
17. Munsing, E., Mather, J., Moura, S.: Blockchains for decentralized optimization of energy resources in microgrid networks. In: IEEE Conference on Control Technology & Applications (2017)
18. Batubara, F.R., Ubacht, J., Janssen, M.: Challenges of blockchain technology adoption for e-government: a systematic literature review. In: the 19th Annual International Conference (2018)
19. Corradini, F., Paganelli, E., Polzonetti, A.: Smart card distribution for e-government digital identity promotion: problems and solutions. In: 28th International Conference on Information Technology Interfaces (2006)
20. Paik, H.Y., Xu, X., Bandara, H.D., Lee, S.U., Lo, S.K.: Analysis of data management in blockchain-based systems: from architecture to governance. IEEE Access **99**, 1 (2019)
21. Yuan, Y., Wang, F.Y.: Towards blockchain-based intelligent transportation systems. In: IEEE International Conference on Intelligent Transportation Systems (2016)
22. Lopes, V., Alexandre, L.A., Pereira, N.: Controlling robots using artificial intelligence and a consortium blockchain (2019)
23. Chen, J., Xue, Y.: Bootstrapping a blockchain based ecosystem for big data exchange. In: 2017 IEEE International Congress on Big Data (BigData Congress) (2017)
24. Abdullah, N., Hakansson, A., Moradian, E.: Blockchain based approach to enhance big data authentication in distributed environment. In: 2017 Ninth International Conference on Ubiquitous and Future Networks (ICUFN) (2017)
25. Yang, W., Aghasian, E., Garg, S., Herbert, D., Kang, B.: A survey on blockchain-based internet service architecture: Requirements, challenges, trends, and future. IEEE Access **99**, 1 (2019)
26. Han, Q., Ge, W.: A review of foreign research of blockchain technology. Sci. Technol. Prog. Policy **35**(1), 154–160 (2018)
27. Weili, A.C., Zhen, Z.: Blockchain data analysis: a review of status, trends and challenges (2019)
28. Sun, Y.L., Zhang, W.J., Wei, J., Wu, Q.J., Wang, L.: Application and research of blockchain technology in electric power industry (2018)
29. X. N. Agency, Guangdong tax bureau and fangxin technology "invoicing on the chain" blockchain electronic invoice platform upgrade. https://baijiahao.baidu.com/s?id=1619632583130663961&wfr=spider&for=pc
30. Ma, X., Li, W., Wu, J.: Research on the operation of e-commerce enterprises based on blockchain technology and bilateral platforms. Wirel. Commun. Mob. Comput. **2021**(1), 1–10 (2021)
31. Aitong, L.U., Zhao, K., Yang, J., Wang, F.: Research on cross-chain technology of blockchain. Netinfo Secur. **19**(8), 83–90 (2019)
32. He, B., Zhang, Y., Sude, Q.: Overview of blockchain technology (2019)

Trustworthy System Development

Key Agreement Protocol Under Multi-service Architecture

Yanli Wang, Bo Liu, Xueqing Sun, Xiao Li, and Fengyin Li[✉]

School of Computer Science, Qufu Normal University, Rizhao 276826, China

Abstract. With the widespread application of technologies such as big data, cloud computing, and mobile Internet, a large amount of personal information is uploaded to the Internet. In existing application scenarios, data is transmitted on public channels. The adversary can use the public channels to carry out impersonation attacks and pretend to be legitimate participants to communicate, causing the user's privacy disclosure. In order to ensure the confidentiality of data and the privacy of users, it is necessary to perform access control on users before communicating, and relevant parties need to establish a legal session key. The existing key agreement protocol under the multi-server architecture lacks user anonymity and untraceability, and cannot effectively protect the user's identity. In order to achieve confidential communication, this paper proposes a new key agreement protocol under the multi-server architecture based on Diffie-Hellman (D-H) key exchange technology. The key agreement protocol uses public key encryption to hide the user's identity, generates a session key to prepare for later encrypted communication between the user and the big data server. Performance analysis shows that the protocol achieves anonymity under the premise of ensuring security.

Keywords: Key agreement · Multi-service architecture · Anonymity · D-H · Privacy

1 Introduction

With the widespread application of technologies such as big data [11], cloud computing [16], and mobile Internet [7], a large amount of personal information is uploaded to the Internet. However, there are a large number of adversaries in the open network environment, and the adversaries carry out passive attacks [9] and active attacks [12] through public channels. In the passive attacks, the adversary can eavesdrop on the message transmitted in the channel, causing the user's privacy disclosure [1]. In the active attacks, the adversary can not only eavesdrop on the message transmitted in the channel, but can also modify the content of the message, or even pretend to be a participant in the communication. Therefore, the confidentiality of the data and the privacy of the user cannot be guaranteed. In order to achieve safe and reliable communication, the server needs to control the user's access before the communication [6], and the relevant parties need to establish a legal session key.

© Springer Nature Singapore Pte Ltd. 2021
H.-N. Dai et al. (Eds.): BlockSys 2021, CCIS 1490, pp. 617–623, 2021.
https://doi.org/10.1007/978-981-16-7993-3_48

Under the multi-server architecture, multiple servers are connected, and these servers share the same application and database computing tasks together, which can improve the response time of key large-scale applications [17]. In addition, each server also undertakes some fault tolerance tasks [13]. Once a server fails, the system can isolate this server from the system with the support of the system software, and complete the new load distribution through the load transfer mechanism of each server. The user only needs to complete one registration operation at the registration server, and can use the same set of identity and authentication factors to establish a session key with the big data server that provides different services in the system [4], thereby obtaining corresponding network services.

The existing key agreement exchange is mainly divided into Diffie-Hellman key exchange and public key infrastructure. Public key infrastructures have been proposed as a workaround for the problem of identity authentication, however certificate authority does not guaranteed for the security of any particular individual, unable to resist impersonation attacks. Diffie–Hellman key exchange is a method of securely exchanging cryptographic keys over a public channel. Traditionally, secure encrypted communication between two parties required that they first exchange keys, the Diffie–Hellman key exchange method allows two parties that have no prior knowledge of each other to jointly establish a shared secret key over an insecure channel. This key can then be used to encrypt subsequent communications. In order to ensure the confidentiality of data and the privacy of users, this paper proposes a key agreement protocol under multi-server architecture. The main contributions are as follows:

This paper designs a key agreement protocol based on D-H. Firstly, the key agreement protocol uses biometric keys to verify user identity for the purpose of ensuring the user's physical security. Secondly, it uses public key encryption to hide user identity for the purpose of achieving user anonymity and untraceability. The key agreement protocol completes the generation of the session key between the big data server and the user, and prepares for the later encrypted communication between the user and the big data server. On the basis of ensuring anonymity, the key agreement protocol simplifies the key agreement process, reduces the communication cost and calculation cost in the key agreement process. Finally, this paper uses security analysis and performance comparison to show that the protocol guarantees user anonymity while resisting multiple attacks and has high efficiency.

2   Preliminaries

2.1   Bilinear Map

G_1 is an additive cyclic group, G_2 is a multiplicative cyclic group, both of them have a large prime order q. Let $\hat{e} : G_1 \times G_1 \to G_2$ denote a bilinear map. Suppose P is the generator of G_1 and g is the generator of G_2, the bilinear map $\hat{e}$ has the following properties [2]:

(1) Bilinearity: $\forall P, Q \in G_1$ and $\forall a, b \in Z_q^*$, we have $\hat{e}(aP, bQ) = \hat{e}(P, Q)^{ab}$.

(2) Computability: $\forall P, Q \in G_1$, there is an algorithm that can compute $\hat{e}(P, Q)$ efficiently.

(3) Non-degeneracy: $\forall P, Q \in G_1$, such that $\hat{e}(P, Q) \neq 1$, where 1 is a generator of G_2.

2.2 Security Goals

The key agreement protocol under multi-server architecture is to provide a secure communication environment for the communicating parties. In addition to the basic functions, the protocol also needs to consider the following security goals:

User anonymity and untraceability [10]: The protocol needs to achieve user anonymity and untraceability, that is, the attacker cannot obtain the user's identity (ID), nor can it determine whether the two sessions are from the same user, and therefore cannot track the user's behavior.

Perfect forward secrecy [18]: When an attacker can obtain the long-term private key of one or more parties, it is necessary to ensure that the session key generated by the user and the big data server is still safe.

Session key agreement [3]: The session key should be agreed between the user and the big data server, and cannot be generated and distributed by one party.

3 The Key Agreement Protocol

This paper designs a key agreement protocol based on D-H, it anonymously generates a session key between the user and the big data server. Only after obtaining the session key, the two parties can communicate confidentially.

3.1 Entities

The entities of the entire protocol are described as follows:

(1) Registration server: Registration servers have the highest authority of the protocol. They are responsible for generating the system public key, system public parameters, and the private key of the users.

(2) User: Users use devices to upload and download data to the big data server to obtain the corresponding network services. We mark the user i as U_i (suppose there are I users in the protocol, $0 \leq i \leq I$).

(3) Big data server: Big data servers can communicate with users and provide services to users: upload user data, download user data, and retrieve corresponding data. We mark the big data server j as N_j (suppose there are J users in the protocol, $0 \leq j \leq J$).

3.2   Initialization

In the initialization phase, the registration server generates initialization parameters for the key agreement phase. The registration server runs the generation function $Gen(1^n)$ which takes a security parameter $n \in Z^+$, then output parameters as follows:

(1) Choose the bilinear map

The registration server chooses the bilinear map G_1 and G_2 with a prime order q, P is the generator of G_1 and $g = \widehat{e}(P, P) \in G_2$, $\hat{e} : G_1 \times G_1 \to G_2$ is a bilinear map.

(2) Generate system master key and system public key

The registration server chooses a random number $s(\forall s \in Z_q^*)$ as the system master key and computes the system public key $P_{pub} = sP \in G_1$.

(3) Choose cryptographic hash functions

The registration server chooses the cryptographic hash functions $H_1 : \{0,1\}^* \to Z_q^*$, $H_2 : G_2 \to Z_q^*$, $H_3 : \{0,1\}^* \to G_1$, $H_4 : \{0,1\}^* \to \{0,1\}^n$.

(4) User registration

The registration server computes the user U_i's private key $d_{U_i} = \frac{1}{s+H_1(ID_{U_i}\|e_{U_i})} \cdot P$, where $e_{U_i}(e_{U_i} \in \{0,1\}^n)$ is the expiration time of user U_i's private key. The registration server sends it to U_i through a secure channel.

(5) Big data server registration

The big data server N_j chooses random numbers r_{N_j} $(\forall r_{N_j} \in Z_q^*)$, computes $g_{N_j}^2 = g^{r_{N_j}}$. N_j sends his intermediate parameter $g_{N_j}^2$ to the registration server through a secure channel.

The registration server computes the big data server N_j's private key $d_{N_j} = \frac{1}{s+H_1(ID_{N_j})} \cdot P$ and sends it to N_j through a secure channel.

(6) Publish parameter list in the system

The registration server publishes the parameters as follows:

$$\left\{ G_1, G_2, q, \widehat{e}, P, P_{pub}, g, H_1, H_2, H_3, H_4, g_{N_j}^2 \right\}$$

3.3   The Key Agreement Protocol Based on D-H

In this section, we design a key agreement protocol based on D-H, which implements key agreement between users and big data servers under a multi-service architecture. The specific process is as follows:

(1) The user U_i computes the session key $sk_{U_i-N_j}$

The user U_i chooses the random number r_{U_i} $(\forall r_{U_i} \in Z_q^*)$ to compute $sk_{U_i-N_j} = H_2\left(\left(g_{N_j}^2 \right)^{r_{U_i}} \right)$.

(2) The user U_i sends a request to the big data server N_j

The user U_i uses the system public key P_{pub} to compute the identity ciphertext of the big data server N_j: $C_{U_i-N_j} = r_{U_i} \cdot (H_1(ID_{N_j}) \cdot P + P_{pub})$, and compute an intermediate parameter $F_{U_i} = (ID_{U_i}\|e_{U_i}) \oplus H_2(g_{U_i}^1)$. The user uses the $C_{U_i-N_j}$ and F_{U_i} to send a key agreement request, and send them to the big data server through a public channel.

(3) The big data server N_j computes the session key $sk_{U_i-N_j}$

After receiving $\{C_{U_i-N_j}, F_{U_i}\}$, the big data server N_j uses its private key d_{N_j} to compute equation $g_{U_i}^1 = g^{rv_i} = \widehat{e}\left(C_{U_i-N_j}, d_{N_j}\right)$ to obtain $g_{U_i}^1$. The big data server N_j computes $F_{U_i} \oplus H_2\left(g_{U_i}^1\right)$ to obtain the user's identity ID_{U_i}.

The big data server N_j uses the random number r_{N_j} to compute the session key $sk_{U_i-N_j} = H_2\left(\left(g_{U_i}^1\right)^{r_{N_j}}\right)$, where r_{N_j} is generated in the big data server registration phase.

Through the above processes, the two parties in communication have obtained the session key $sk_{U_i-N_j}$.

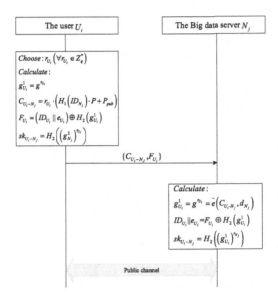

Fig. 1. The key agreement protocol

4   Performance Analysis

We analyze the security of the key agreement protocol under multi-server architecture as follows:

User anonymity and untraceability: According to our proposed protocol, the user's identity ID_{U_i} only exists in ciphertext $F_{U_i} = (ID_{U_i} \| e_{U_i}) \oplus H_2\left(g_{U_i}^1\right)$. In order to obtain ID_{U_i}, the adversary needs to compute $g_{U_i}^1 = g^{rv_i} = \widehat{e}\left(C_{U_i-N_j}, d_{N_j}\right)$. This requires an adversary to solve the difficult problem of discrete logarithm. As we all know, it is difficult to solve the discrete logarithm problem, thus our protocol can guarantee the anonymity and untraceability of users.

Perfect forward secrecy: It is assumed that the adversary obtains the private key of the user and the big data server. Using the private key of the big data server, the adversary can calculate $g_{U_i}^1 = g^{r_{U_i}} = \widehat{e}\left(C_{U_i-N_j}, d_{N_j}\right)$. In order to obtain the session key, the adversary must calculate $\left(g_{U_i}^1\right)^{r_{N_j}} = \left(g_{N_j}^2\right)^{r_{U_i}} = (g^{r_{N_j}})^{r_{U_i}}$. Therefore, the adversary must solve the CDH problem. We know that it is difficult to solve the CDH problem, so our protocol is perfect forward secrecy.

Session key agreement: The session key generated by the user and the big data sever need to be negotiated by both parties, $sk_{U_i-N_j} = \left(g_{U_i}^1\right)^{r_{N_j}} = \left(g_{N_j}^2\right)^{r_{U_i}} = (g^{r_{N_j}})^{r_{U_i}}$. Both parties have equal contributions to the generation of the session key.

In order to show the advantages of our proposed protocol, we compare our proposed protocol with four recently proposed key agreement protocols. We focus on the realization of user anonymity, the ability to resist replay attacks, smart card loss attacks, man-in-the-middle attacks and counterfeiting attacks. From Table 1, we can see that our protocol can safely respond to all security threats and implement various features. We notice that the past protocols, including Kumari [8], Feng [5], Sood [15] and Shen [14], etc., do not implement all the basic security features, and our protocol can implement all at the same time. The protocol proposed by Kumari et al. cannot resist the smart card loss attack. Feng et al.'s protocol cannot be resisted by smart card loss attacks and man-in-the-middle attacks. The protocol proposed by Sood et al. cannot prevent impersonation attacks. The protocol of Shen et al. cannot satisfy user anonymity.

Table 1. Security performance comparison.

Security performance	Kumari	Feng	Sood	Shen	Protocol proposed in this paper
User anonymity	√	√	√	×	√
Resist replay attacks	×	×	√	√	√
Resist smart card loss attacks	√	√	√	√	√
Resist man-in-the-middle attacks	√	×	√	√	√
Resist impersonation attacks	√	√	×	√	√

5 Conclusion

In this paper, we propose a key agreement protocol based on D-H under multi-server architecture. The protocol uses public key encryption to hide the user's identity, generates a session key to prepare for later encrypted communication among users and big data servers. We have simplified the key agreement process and reduced the communication cost and calculation cost in the key agreement process. Performance analysis shows that the protocol achieves user anonymity and untraceability. In the future, we will continue to optimize our protocol and continue to improve the efficiency of the protocol on the basis of ensuring security.

References

1. Aghasian, E., Garg, S., Gao, L., Yu, S., Montgomery, J.: Scoring users' privacy disclosure across multiple online social networks. IEEE Access **5**, 13118–13130 (2017)
2. Cohen, A., Moshkovitz, G.: Structure vs. randomness for bilinear maps. arXiv preprint arXiv:2102.04657 (2021)
3. Cui, J., Wang, Y., Zhang, J., Xu, Y., Zhong, H.: Full session key agreement scheme based on chaotic map in vehicular Ad Hoc networks. IEEE Trans. Veh. Technol. **69**(8), 8914–8924 (2020)
4. Dey, S., Hossain, A.: Session-key establishment and authentication in a smart home network using public key cryptography. IEEE Sens. Lett. **3**(4), 1–4 (2019)
5. Feng, Q., He, D., Zeadally, S., Wang, H.: Anonymous biometrics-based authentication scheme with key distribution for mobile multi-server environment. Futur. Gener. Comput. Syst. **84**, 239–251 (2018)
6. Hu, C., Li, W., Cheng, X., Yu, J., Wang, S., Bie, R.: A secure and verifiable access control scheme for big data storage in clouds. IEEE Trans. Big Data **4**(3), 341–355 (2017)
7. Iosifidis, G., Gao, L., Huang, J., Tassiulas, L.: Efficient and fair collaborative mobile internet access. IEEE/ACM Trans. Netw. **25**(3), 1386–1400 (2017)
8. Kumari, S., et al.: A provably secure biometrics-based authenticated key agreement scheme for multi-server environments. Multimedia Tools Appl. **77**(2), 2359–2389 (2018)
9. Nasr, M., Shokri, R., Houmansadr, A.: Comprehensive privacy analysis of deep learning: passive and active white-box inference attacks against centralized and federated learning. In: 2019 IEEE symposium on security and privacy (SP), pp. 739–753. IEEE (2019)
10. Olaleye, S.B., Ojha, S.: Improved advanced encryption using four square cipher for user anonymity and untraceability in mobile cloud computing. Int. J. Innov. Sci. Eng. Technol. **4**(2), 113–121 (2017)
11. Oussous, A., Benjelloun, F.Z., Lahcen, A.A., Belfkih, S.: Big data technologies: a survey. J. King Saud Univ. Comput. Inf. Sci. **30**(4), 431–448 (2018)
12. Shahzad, F., Pasha, M., Ahmad, A.: A survey of active attacks on wireless sensor networks and their countermeasures. arXiv preprint arXiv:1702.07136 (2017)
13. Sharma, G., Yadav, A., et al.: Fault tolerance in real time distributed system. Rev. Comput. Eng. Res. **5**(2), 20–24 (2018)
14. Shen, H., Gao, C., He, D., Wu, L.: New biometrics-based authentication scheme for multi-server environment in critical systems. J. Ambient. Intell. Humaniz. Comput. **6**(6), 825–834 (2015)
15. Sood, S.K., Sarje, A.K., Singh, K.: A secure dynamic identity based authentication protocol for multi-server architecture. J. Netw. Comput. Appl. **34**(2), 609–618 (2011)
16. Varghese, B., Buyya, R.: Next generation cloud computing: new trends and research directions. Futur. Gener. Comput. Syst. **79**, 849–861 (2018)
17. Wu, T.Y., Lee, Z., Obaidat, M.S., Kumari, S., Kumar, S., Chen, C.M.: An authenticated key exchange protocol for multi-server architecture in 5G networks. IEEE Access **8**, 28096–28108 (2020)
18. Xiong, L., Peng, D., Peng, T., Liang, H., Liu, Z.: A lightweight anonymous authentication protocol with perfect forward secrecy for wireless sensor networks. Sensors **17**(11), 2681 (2017)

The Intellectual Property of Factor-Oriented Trial Intelligent Judicial System Based on Knowledge Graph

Jing Bian[1,2(✉)], Danyun Deng[3], Yinmu Sun[4], Yehao Yan[5], and Jinhao Hu[6(✉)]

[1] School of Computer Science and Engineering, Sun Yat-Sen University, Guangzhou 510006, Guangdong, China
[2] Science and Technology on Parallel and Distributed Processing Laboratory (PDL), Changsha 410073, Hunan, China
[3] Guangzhou Court of Internet, Guangzhou 510335, Guangdong, China
[4] Gongdao Network Technology Co., Ltd., Hangzhou 311100, Zhejiang, China
[5] Guangzhou No.113 Middle School, Guangzhou 510000, Guangdong, China
[6] Guangdong University of Finance and Economics, Guangzhou 510320, Guangdong, China

Abstract. The combination of technology innovation and justice can not only fully highlight the judicial value of efficiency and equity, but also boost the speed in hearing a volume of cases. With the application of knowledge graph and other AI technologies, Guangzhou Court of Internet has designed a factor-oriented trial intelligent judicial system. This system establishes a new intelligent judicial paradigm that is available for one step solution of intellectual property right (IPR) cases including prosecution, filing cases, giving proof, delivering litigation documents as well as judging and so on. The system is of great significance for intellectual property cases to realize the separation of complex and simple flow, optimize the allocation of trial resources and improve the quality and efficiency of litigation.

Keywords: Artificial intelligence · Knowledge graph · Intellectual property · Factor-oriented judicial system

1 Introduction

When it comes to the new era, the latest demand of judicial trial is to improve the statue of legalization of intellectual property protection. In addition, it is essential to promote the quality and efficiency of intellectual property trials [1]. In April 2017, the Supreme People's Court (SPC) issued the document of *Outline for the Judicial Protection of Intellectual Property Rights in China*, which clarified the trial procedures for IPR cases, so as to make sure the speedy trial of simple cases and refined trial of complex cases. In January 2019, SPC issued *the Pilot Program of the Reform of Separation between Complicated Cases and Simple Ones in Civil Procedure*, which was a new step to carry out the separation of judicial procedure into simple cases and complicated ones, trivial

© Springer Nature Singapore Pte Ltd. 2021
H.-N. Dai et al. (Eds.): BlockSys 2021, CCIS 1490, pp. 624–633, 2021.
https://doi.org/10.1007/978-981-16-7993-3_49

cases and major ones, and summary trial cases and ordinary ones. The reform will improve the efficiency of trial, and meet the diversified litigation demands of people.

With the equitable adjustment of the social and economic structure in our country, an increasing number of innovative activities have been produced, which not only highlights the value of intellectual property rights (IPR), but also rises the awareness of the IPR protection among enterprises and individuals. Meanwhile, the application of the Internet has also lowered the threshold of intellectual creation and accelerated the speed of dissemination, which resulted in causing the explosion of IPR litigation and the pressure of judicial resources. Such cases have some common characteristics: ① The number of cases is climbing year by year. Zhou Qiang, President of the Supreme People's Court, pointed out in the work report of the Two Sessions, in 2020, the people's courts concluded 466,000 first-instance intellectual property cases with an increasing index of 11.7% year-on-year [2]. ② IPR cases are usually seemed as long cycle of litigation, high degree of difficulty, and wide range of involved cases, which is a huge challenge for the judge's trial ability. ③ Facts of most case are simple so that the attributes of infringement can be clarified through the automated process, which is in accordance with the Factor-oriented Trial. ④ Inherent volatility. With the help of internet and information processing technology, the cost of infringement of IPR is reduced. The same product may be infringed by many times, compelling the same plaintiff to file a lawsuit against different defendants, causing fluctuations in the number of judicial cases as well as shortage of resources for judicial trial.

Nowadays, each people's court in China is facing with two difficulties of judicial trial. The first one is how to deal with the increasing cases under the burden of limited trial period. The second one is how to fully meet the demands of solving cases in a speedy and effective way. With the development of national informational construction and artificial intelligence (AI) technology, the application of AI in the judicial field is also advancing further. The combination with AI and justice is the crucial way to make big data to work for people and alleviate the pressure of judicial resources [3]. As AI is embedded into judicial system, it will greatly enhance the capability of judgment, and accelerate the construction of smart courts, which has been highly recommended at domestic and abroad. The American Daniel Katz with his team applies machine learning methods and historical data to predict the verdicts of the U.S. Supreme Court during 1816 to 2015, with an accuracy rate higher than 70% [4]. In China, the "Chinese Digital Network Service Platform of Legal Application (Faxin)", "Smart Court Navigation System", and "Smart Case Retrieval System " have been successively established and put into use.

As the knowledge brain of AI, knowledge graph plays an irreplaceable role in the factor-oriented intelligent judicial system, which is also the promising technique for the further development of AI in the judicial field. Technically speaking, Knowledge graph is composed of entities, concepts, attributes, relationships and other elements, making it a large-scale semantic network that reveals the relationships of entities. Meanwhile, knowledge graph is able to analyze problems from the perspective of "similarity" through knowledge extraction, knowledge fusion, knowledge reasoning. This process mainly contains two steps. Firstly, it needs to update and upgrade the data system, mapping human's cognition of the objective world to the computer world. Secondly, it should be described with the entities, attributes and relationships of the objective world based on machine language. Moreover, knowledge graph has the advantages of objectivity, efficiency, accuracy and impartiality, which is very suitable for the factor-oriented cases trial.

In terms of the feature of IPR litigation such as huge volume, factor-orientation, high similarity and batch processing, the Guangzhou Internet Court is establishing a AI judicial system based on knowledge graph. In addition, the system aims at strengthening the protection of network copyright through the deep integration of internet, blockchain, AI and 5G, etc. Fundamentally, the system use factors disintegration method to establish a new intelligent judicial paradigm that support the one step solution for filing cases, giving proof, delivering litigation documents as well as judging and so on, which can improves the efficiency of filing and trial. The system makes full use of latest technology to strengthen the protection of IPR, and solves the problems about tough proofing, long period, high cost, and low compensation of IPR litigation. Therefore, the system is not only a significant achievement to safeguard the development of network culture industry, but also a beneficial exploration for the court's digitalization.

2   Intellectual Property Factor-Oriented Intelligent Judicial System Based on Knowledge Graph

Factor-oriented trial is a judicial method that is based on summarizing the commonalities of typified cases, sorting out the factual basis, extracting the legal factors, inferring the relationship logically, simplifying the trial procedures for non-controversial factors so as to focus on the controversial factors [5]. This trial mechanism can optimize the litigation process and overcome the applicable difficulties of judicial data in intelligent system. The factor-oriented trial can process judicial data with systematically optimization and scientific classification. On the one hand, the AI trial system is valuable for common extraction and machine learning of factor-oriented legal documents. On the other hand, the system is highly compatible for knowledge graph to apply natural language processing to extract and integrate judicial data.

Knowledge Graph is a large-scale semantic network that was officially established by Google in 2012. Knowledge Graph is consisted of entity, node, node value and edge [6], which can be mainly divided into data layer and model layer. The data layer is presented in the triple form of "entity, relationship, entity" or "entity, attribute, value". The model layer works for data extraction, processing and integration based on the data layer in order to build the normative connection between entities, attributes and relationships. By doing so, it can provide decision-making information for knowledge reasoning. For instance, if the data layer runs as "Zhang San-plagiarized works-Li Si", what is mapped to the model layer would be "infringer -civil infringement relationship-the infringed". HP Labs has developed the Jena Knowledge Graph Management System [7], which can build up semantic web and connect with data applications, is run by Apache now. The technical framework of the knowledge graph is mainly made up of knowledge extraction, knowledge fusion and knowledge reasoning. Knowledge graph can not only deeply analyze the basic information of works involved in the lawsuit, but also assist judges in decision-making. Meanwhile, knowledge graph can continuously extract the core data from IPR cases with updating learning, promoting the evolution of judicial knowledge maps, which is of much significance of the intelligent trial system.

The factor-oriented intelligent trial system, created by the Guangzhou Internet Court, is focus on the feature of IPR cases. The construction way of the intelligent trial system can be divided into three parts. The first part is to deconstruct similar cases and reconstruct the knowledge graph of cases. The second part is to extract the suing elements of the right holder and the defending elements of the infringer. The last part is to use intelligent approach to self-define "metadata" model. Based on the above process, the structure of system is composed of case element module, page collection module, storage module, calculation processing module and element display module, which is under the repeatedly iterating to form a complete chain. As long as litigants initiates a factor-oriented prosecution, the judge will take over the factor-oriented intelligent trial system, thus making it complete the factor-oriented judicial trial.

The system builds a platform to support legal modelers to import prepared legal knowledge, reasoning rules and key elements of cases based on the former instructions. Meanwhile, the system requires for the online drawing of knowledge graph and algorithm collaboration. It covers a number of 375 different content node, among which is including 78 different types of computing nodes, 168 element nodes and 129 other logical nodes. Figure 1 shows a schematic diagram of the intelligent judicial system based on knowledge graph factory. The operational principle of the system runs on the following way. First, storing and transforming the judge's professional legal knowledge into code logic that is understandable for machine. Second, performing logical inferences and calculations on various factor of inputted evidence. Eventually, generating the judicial verdict by the AI system. The reasoning ability mentioned here is a universal logical reasoning ability, and it can be reused in any scenario where the result is derived from inputted data.

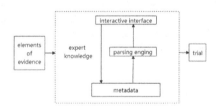

Fig. 1. Schematic diagram of the intelligent judicial system

The data of knowledge graph are mainly based on crawler technology and originated from the judicial field such as the national database of legislation, the national judgment document, legal instruments that are stored in the interior of court, including evidence material, answer brief and case information [8]. Graph Factory is mainly composed of metadata, interactive interface and analytical inference engine components. The metadata layer provides different definitions of data model and storage capabilities, including data types, data structures, and inheritance and reference relationships among data models. On the application area, under the cooperating with the front-end controls, it allows the page to be automatically adapted and rendered by following the data structure. The interactive interface is mainly composed of nodes and lines. Operator nodes can define different types of calculation logic units, while the result nodes are used to store the calculation results of each step. Figure 2 shows the use of metadata, analytical inference engine, and operators to complete the process of intelligent judgment inference.

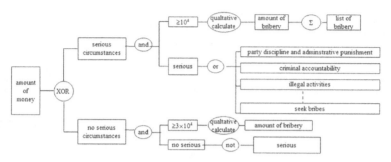

Fig. 2. Schematic diagram of smart trial calculation

The process of case trial includes: ① Factor modeling is carried out based at the preset factor table in order to obtain various case types. The preset factor table includes not only multiple case factors that are corresponding to each case type, but also the attributes and rules that are corresponding to each case factor. ② Build the page of factor value collection due to the model that is corresponding to each case type. ③ Collect the factor value which is inputted by the parties in the cases on the page of factor value collection. ④ Receive the mapping relation of object and storage mode of legal factors corresponding to each collected factor value, storing each factor value in the database according to the object mapping relation and storage mode. ⑤ Obtain the factor values corresponding to the case information from the database according to the case information that needs be trialed, and generate the factor display page and output the factor values. By implementing the above procedures, the intelligent judicial system which is constrained with the rational of trial process, case factors, related laws and regulations of IPR cases, etc., can extract the core concepts and related attributes of IPR, so as to construct an intellectual property map with strong hierarchical structure and less redundancy. As shown in Fig. 3, the pattern layer of intellectual property map consists of three core factors: right object, right attribution and infringement fact. In addition, the relationships and attributes of these factors are included here.

The construction of data layer includes three parts: knowledge extraction, knowledge integration and knowledge update. Knowledge factors such as entities, relationships and attributes can be extracted from semi-structured and unstructured data by knowledge extraction. Intellectual trial system extracts knowledge from previous cases of IPR. As for semi-structured data that has been standardized and recorded in the system, it can be extracted only by simple transformation. In terms of cases with missing records or unstructured data such as paper documents, it is necessary to write specific rules to complete knowledge extraction. Due to standardized records, knowledge extraction can be done efficiently and accurately on the data in cases. With the help of knowledge fusion, the ambiguity between reference items such as entities, relations and attributes and factual objects can be eliminated, making a high-quality knowledge base be formed.

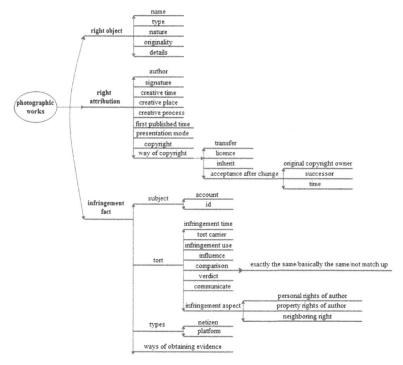

Fig. 3. Intellectual property knowledge graph

Sometimes there is discrepancy in descriptions of the same entity in IPR case records. In order to solve this problem, the intelligent trial system uses natural language processing technique to calculate the similarity of text, complement the missing descriptions of the full text and Integration and refer to the same entity, while the knowledge that cannot be automatically merged is manually processed. Through knowledge updating, we can detect the timeliness and correct the knowledge in the application process of knowledge graph, ensuring the quality of knowledge in the knowledge base. With the on-going numbers and updating types of IPR cases, the regulated system such as laws, policies and trial are quired to be enhanced, which enforces the intellectual property map to update itself to ensure the knowledge is newest. New cases may also have concepts that have not been defined in the current model layer, which are necessary to be updated with the model layer. In doing so, it can update the knowledge structure for new factors of cases and new regulations, such as text types, entity types, relationship types, etc. When the schema layer is updated, the data layer needs to be updated accordingly. The new cases are added to the original graph after knowledge extraction and knowledge fusion by incremental updating [9]. In addition, the update process of data layer also includes testing the quality, validity and timeliness of knowledge, deleting the wrong and invalid knowledge in time, which is done by computer-aided professionals.

Figure 4 shows the module diagram of IPR factor-oriented intelligent trial system. The system is based on knowledge graph technique, metadata model-driven development, blockchain, matching algorithm of deep text similarity, Query understanding and robot NLU, electronic evidence intelligent comparison technology and so on. These techniques allow the system to realize the value of both efficiency and intelligence of IPR trial procedure. With the application of intelligent component technology, the basic function of litigation risk assessment, class case release, law release, evidence classification, picture comparison, document error correction, etc. are available in the system. In conclusion, intelligent trial system creates a new collaborative paradigm in which intellectual property cases were generated by filing, accepting, giving evidence, delivering documents to judges for trial and judging documents, thus improves the filing speed and trial efficiency of IPR cases.

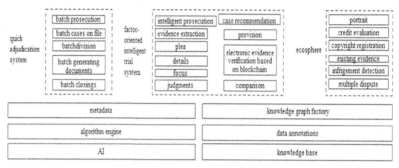

Fig. 4. Application architecture diagram of the intellectual property factor-oriented intelligent trial system

Guangzhou Internet Court organized a team of judges and technical teams to logically sort out the main types, ownership of works, infringement facts, claims for compensation and other factors of Internet-related intellectual property cases, in order to establish a trial knowledge map model with more than 1,500 factors [10]. The map model combines the judge's trial experience of online copyright cases and relevant legislation, concludes the mind map with those trial factors, and converts it into a knowledge graph that can be recognized by the machine, thus establishing a knowledge system of cyber copyright trial. Figures 5, 6 and 7 respectively show the dispute focus page, the article comparison analysis page and the one-click generation of judgment document page. On the calculation result page, it shows that articles are used to compare the statistical fields such as repeated words, repeated paragraphs, repeated sentences and similar fragment distribution. In the content, the repeated part will be marked in red so as to remind the judge. The bottom of the article counts the basic information of the article, such as the total number of words, sentences, paragraphs, etc. After analyzing the disputes and comparison results, the intelligent judicial system will draw a conclusion automatically and generate an initial judgment document, which can helpfully simplify the work of judge.

Through introducing the intelligent comparison technology of text, image and video, the intelligent trial system realizes the function of automatic judgment in simple infringement and the automatic calculation in infringement degree, assisting judges to judge infringement facts with the intuitive scores. In addition, it brings online technical officers to assist judges in ascertaining infringement facts through online inspection. Under

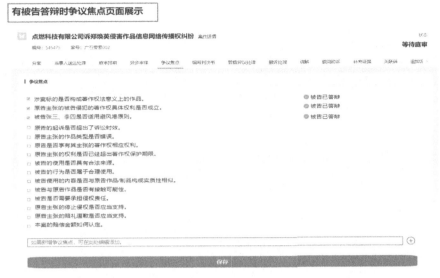

Fig. 5. The page of dispute core

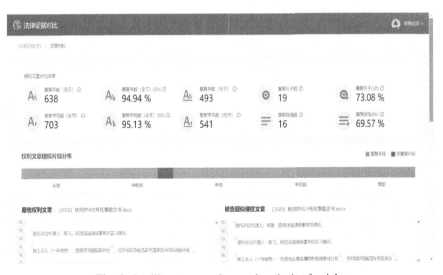

Fig. 6. Intelligent comparison and analysis of articles

the use of NLP natural language processing technique and knowledge graph, personalized documents are generated due to learning the previous judgment documents. Besides, The relevant information from knowledge base can smartly screen and analyze the complexity of cases, so as to generate factor-based judgment documents in batches for simple cases. When handling with new complex cases, system will make analysis of case factors in-depth, compare the big data of similar cases, and realize the automatic generation of

Fig. 7. Autonomic generation of judgment document

judgment with the accuracy of 95%. Undoubtedly, the system will greatly improves the trial efficiency compared with traditional trials.

3   Conclusion

The combination of technological innovation and justice highlights the value of the technological effect in empowering justice. Driven by the reform of the judicial trial system and the construction of the people's courts, the factor-oriented intelligent trial system which has the advantages of diverting complex and simple cases and improving the judicial efficiency, becomes a masterpiece in "AI & factor-oriented trial". As the knowledge brain of AI, knowledge graph plays an irreplaceable role in the factor-orient intelligence trial system, which is also the core element for the future development of AI in the judicial field. Under the use of knowledge graphs and other AI processing technologies, the Guangzhou Internet Court has designed a set of intellectual property element-based intelligent trial system. The system establishes an one-click generation function of intellectual property cases by filing, accepting, providing evidence, delivering judgment documents, etc. Facing the judicial situation where new types of cases such as IPR are emerging rapidly and the number of lawsuits is rising sharply, people's court should explore new models of intelligent justice, strengthen the innovation of information, technology, and institution, thus effectively promote the judicial modernization of network system and capability.

Acknowledgments. This work is supported by Key-Area Research and Development Program of Guangdong Province (No.2020B0101090005), the National Natural Science Foundation of China and Guangdong Provincial Joint Fund (No. U1911202).

References

1. Xinhua News Agency: Xi Jinping emphasized comprehensively strengthening intellectual property protection in the twenty-fifth collective study of the Political Bureau of the Central Committee, stimulating innovation vitality and promoting the construction of a new development pattern. http://www.xinhuanet.com/politics/2020-12/01/c_1126808128.htm. Accessed 10 Apr 2021
2. Zhou, R.: The promotion in high-quality trial service innovation. In: Journal of The People's Court Report, 24 March 2021
3. Li, X.: Research on the application of artificial intelligence in court trial. In: Journal of Chongqing University of Posts and Telecommunications, 21 June 2020
4. Xiao, F., Zeng, X.: Mode Selection and Realization Path of Intelligent Judgment Generation. J. People's Court Daily 4–5 (2019)
5. Huang, Z.: Essential trial: the reform path and mode choice of trial mode of typed cases. J. Appl. Law **9**, 3–12 (2020)
6. Nie, B., Sun, S.: Knowledge graph embedding via reasoning over entities, relations, and text. J. Future Gener. Comput. Syst. 426–433 (2019)
7. Han, H., Li, Y.: Research and application of custom rule construction method in Jena intelligent reasoning query. J. Softw. Guide **7**, 13–15 (2014)
8. Chen, J., Huang, Y., Cao, G.: Research and implementation of visualization of judicial cases based on knowledge map. J. Hubei Univ. Technol. **5**, 72–77 (2019)
9. Li, X., Jie, Z., Feng, J.: Learning with rethinking: recurrently improving convolutional neural networks through feedback. J. Pattern Recogn. **1**, 183–194 (2018)
10. Pei, R., Wu, X., Li, Y.: The electronic way of intellectual property multiple dispute resolution mechanism in the era of "Internet Court". In: Journal of Research on the Comprehensive Reform of Judicial System and Criminal Trial, The 30th National Court Symposium, pp. 698–706 (2019)

Performance Evaluation of Price-Muller Model Based on Classification Algorithm

Bin Wang[✉]

Beijing Institute of Space Mechanics & Electricity, Beijing, China

Abstract. In today's society, frequent transfers of personnel and work have led to a lack of stability in the company's business. In order to avoid employee resignation, it is urgent to propose a credible framework to analyze the behavior of employees and provide a valuable reference for whether they are willing to resign. Based on the data mining technology and machine learning algorithm, this paper analyzes the resignation information of Kaggle employees. By comparing the original features of the data set, new features can be calculated using Price-Muller's employee resignation theory, and the new features will be input into a BP neural network and classified, so as to predict whether employees have a tendency to leave.

Keywords: Price-muller employee resignation model · Neural network · Employee resignation prediction

1 Introduction

Employee resignation and brain drain have become a problem that every company has to face. The resignation of outstanding talents will have a great negative impact on the operation of the company. Therefore, it is necessary to analyze the behavior of departing employees and use predictive models to perform credible classification and evaluation of their behavior. If they have abnormal behaviors, early warning is needed to reduce the company's losses. On the other hand, companies hope to analyze the reasons why some excellent employees choose to resign through a scientific method, and they also want to predict in advance which excellent employees have the tendency to leave by establishing a forecasting model with the collected employee data. The Price-Muller model is an important resignation research model which has great theoretical value. It is practically significant to study employee resignation issues through this mainstream model and provide effective feedback to the company management [1,2].

2 Analysis of the Kaggle Employee Resignation Data Sets

The data set used in this paper is collected from the sample data of 14999 employees' turnover related situation provided by Kaggle platform, which contains 10 indicators.

© Springer Nature Singapore Pte Ltd. 2021
H.-N. Dai et al. (Eds.): BlockSys 2021, CCIS 1490, pp. 634–647, 2021.
https://doi.org/10.1007/978-981-16-7993-3_50

2.1 Correlation Analysis of Employees' Resignation Reasons

For the factors of employees' resignation is various, and the working department(sales) are character data which is hard to quantify, so these two indicators are not included in the induction of correlation. Therefore, through the correlation analysis of the eight dependent variables and independent variables in the employee resignation data set, we can get the correlation data among the variables as shown in Fig. 1. Among them, the data marked red are those with a correlation of more than 0.3.

	satisfic ation	evalua tion	project	montly hour	service year	accide nt	left	promo tion	SG
satisfic ation	1	0.11	-0.14	-0.02	-0.1	0.06	-0.39	0.03	0.06
evaluat ion	0.11	1	0.35	0.34	0.13	-0.01	0.01	-0.01	-0.01
project	-0.14	0.36	1	0.42	0.2	0	0.02	-0.01	0
monthl y-hour	-0.02	0.34	0.42	1	0.13	-0.01	0.07	0	0
service year	-0.1	0.13	0.2	0.13	1	0	0.14	0.07	0.05
accide nt	0.06	-0.01	0	-0.01	0	1	-0.15	0.04	0.01
left	-0.39	0.01	0.02	0.07	0.14	-0.15	1	-0.06	-0.16
promo tion	0.03	-0.01	-0.01	0	0.07	-0.06	-0.06	1	0.1
SG	0.05	-0.01	0	0	0.05	-0.16	-0.16	0.1	1

Fig. 1. Correlation data chart of employee turnover variables. (Color figure online)

2.2 Descriptive Analysis of Employee Turnover Reasons

Through the statistics of the data set, we can get the descriptive data statistics, including the maximum value, the upper quartile, the median, the lower quartile and the minimum value of each index variable. The statistical results are shown in Fig. 2.

According to the correlation chart of the above variables, this paper explores the relationship between the satisfaction of employees to company (satisfaction _level), the performance evaluation (last_evaluation), the average working hours

	satisfaction	evaluation	project	monthly -hour	service year	accident	left	promotion
max	1.00	1.00	7.00	310.00	10.00	1.00	1.00	1.00
Q1	0.82	0.87	5.00	245.00	4.00	0	0	0
mean	0.61	0.72	3.80	201.05	3.50	0.14	0.24	0.02
Q3	0.44	0.58	3.00	156.00	3.00	0	0	0
min	0.09	0.36	2.00	96.00	2.00	0	0	0

Fig. 2. Descriptive statistical chart.

per month (average_month_hours), the number of working years (time spend company) and the employee resignation (left) by drawing box line chart [3]. And we can find some connections between the four independent variables and the dependent variables:

Firstly, the scores of the departed employees are obviously low, and their satisfaction with the company fluctuated greatly, most of them are around 0.4, and some of them even lower than 0.2.

Secondly, the level of performance evaluation is relatively high and the index of resigned employees is relatively concentrated, and the values are all above 0.8.

Thirdly, the median of the average monthly working hours of the resigned employees is relatively high, with more than half of them exceeding the average value (200 h). At the same time, on the whole, the average working hours of resigned employees fluctuate greatly, the highest is higher than working staff, and the lowest is lower than them.

Fourthly, the index values of the number of working years of the resigned employees are all about 4 years, indicating that most of the resigned employees can not meet their expectations in the mid and long term and make the decision to leave (Fig. 3).

In addition, we can draw a stacked bar chart [4] to explore the relationship between the relationship between employee occupation (sales), number of project (number_project), work accident (work_accident) and employee resignation (left). The horizontal axis is the value of the dependent variable, the brown part represents the non departing employee and the blue part represents the leaving employee.

Firstly, among all positions, the number of sales personnel is the largest, and the number of management personnel is the least. Meanwhile, the resignation rate of HR is the highest, and the resignation rate of management is the lowest; Secondly, the higher the number of projects, the higher the resignation rate(except for the sample with item 2). In other words, the higher the intensity and density of work, the higher the resignation rate; Thirdly, the number of accidents in enterprises is relatively small, and the resignation rate in the number of accidents is also relatively low (Fig. 4).

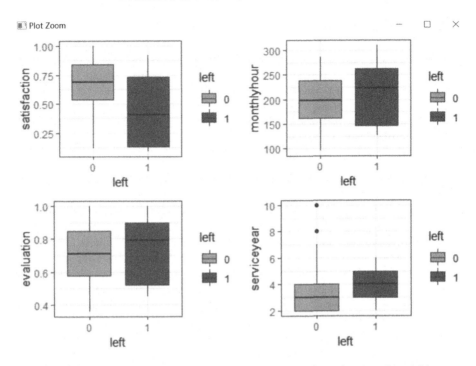

Fig. 3. Box diagram of relationship between resigned employee and variables.

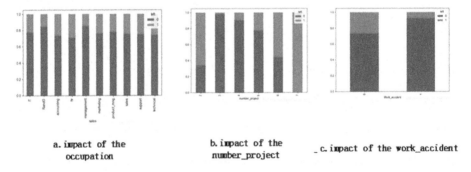

| a. impact of the occupation | b. impact of the number_project | _ c. impact of the work_accident |

Fig. 4. Stacked bar chart of relationship between employee turnover and variables. (Color figure online)

3 Related Theories

3.1 The Establishment of Price-Muller Model

Presupposition of Price-Muller Model. Before conducting an empirical analysis of employee resignation, the Price-Muller model needs to satisfy a series of assumptions [5]. Firstly, it is assumed that employees come into the organization with certain expectations, they will be more satisfied with the company and have a tendency to stay in the organization if the organization meets their current expectations. Secondly, it is assumed that there is a fair "benefit exchange" relationship between employees and the organization. In other words, the employee's labor or service creates profits for the organization, and the organization rewards employees with a salary that corresponds to their work at the same time. Thirdly, it is assumed that employees always pursue the maximization of net income during their tenure in the organization. In other words, if there are more than one optional "cost-benefit" items for chosen, employees will balance their interests to maximize their net return.

Index Variables of Price-Muller Model. There are four kinds of variables related to employee resignation in Price-Muller model, which are environmental variables, individual variables, structural variables and intervening variables. Among them, structural variables are often represented as the working conditions that employees expect and these are some fixed indicators, while the environmental variables are often the external environment conditions that employees expect. The core theory of the Price-Muller model is that employees' willingness to leave and their tendency and behaviors to look for other jobs are directly affected by environmental variables. However, individual variables and structural variables indirectly affect employees' resignation tendency and behavior through the role of intermediary variables. Based on the Price-Muller model, combined with the actual situation of employee turnover in Kaggle, this paper integrated and improved the original 9 dependent variables in the data set, and then formed 11 new indicator variables, so as to carry out empirical analysis better and improve the explanatory effect of the model for employees' resignation reasons.

Environmental Variables

$$Opportunity = (promotion\_last\_5years) * (time\_spend\_company) \qquad (1)$$

The Price-muller model also presents "relative responsibility" [6] as an environmental variable. However due to the lack of relevant features in the original data set, it is difficult to analyze from other features. Therefore, this paper only takes "opportunity" into the environmental variables [7]. From the data analysis, it is known that whether to be promoted within five years is a "0–1" variable. If an employee has worked in the company for ten years but doesn't have a promotion prospect within five years, this employee won't be able to take advantage of external opportunities.

Individual Variables

$$Positive/NegativeSentiment = [(Satisfaction\_Level)^2 + (last\_evaluation)^2]^{1/2} \qquad (2)$$

$$Workparticipation = performanceevaluation(last\_evaluation) \qquad (3)$$

Since the evaluation of the company; s satisfaction and performance in the original data are positive numbers, the positive/negative emotion is also evaluated by a positive number. The larger the value, the more positive the employee's attitude towards work, and if the value is small, it means that the employee has a negative attitude.

Structural Variables

$$Autonomy = time\_spend\_company \tag{4}$$

$$Distribution fairness : (salary)/(average\_monthly\_hours) \tag{5}$$

$$Promotion opportunity = promotion\_last\_5years \tag{6}$$

$$Salary = salary \tag{7}$$

$$Workpressure = [(number\_project)^2 + (average\_monthly\_hours)^2]^{1/2} \tag{8}$$

The larger the value of "distribution fairness" in the above structural variables, the more unfair it is [8]. For example, if the salary level is low and working hours are 200 h, the value of "distributional fairness" is 1/200; However, if the salary level is high and working hours are 200 h, the value of "distributional fairness" is 3/200. In summary, employees with lower salary levels are in an unfair position under the same number of working hours.

Intervening Variables

$$Job - seeking behavior = (time\_spend\_company)/(satisfaction\_level) \tag{9}$$

$$Resignation intention = [(satisfaction\_level)^2 + salary^2]^{1/2} \tag{10}$$

$$Jobsatisfaction = satisfaction\_level \tag{11}$$

In the above intermediate variable, the smaller the value of "job seeking behavior" [9], the less tendency for employees to look for other jobs. For example, if the time spend in company is 6 years and satisfaction level is 0.5, the value of job-seeking behavior is 12; However, if the time spend in company is 6 years and satisfaction level is 0.6, the value of job-seeking behavior is 10. By comparision, when the working years are the same, if employees are more dissatisfied with the company, they will be more likely to leave and look for other job opportunities.

3.2   The Introduction of BP Network

BP neural network is a kind of feed-forward neural network, including input layer, hidden layer and output layer [10]. The basic principle of the network for classification and prediction as follows: The input signal acts on the input node and generates output signal through non-linear transformation of hidden layer. Each original sample of the network training includes the input vector X and the expected output quantity t. However, there is a deviation between the network output value Y and the expected output value t. At this time, the connection weight W_{ij} between the input nodes and the hidden layer nodes, the connection weights T_{jk} between the hidden layer nodes and the output nodes and the threshold θ are adjusted by means of back propagation, so that the error decreases along the gradient direction. After repeated learning and training, the network parameters (weights and thresholds) corresponding to the minimum errors can be determined, and the training stops [11]. At this time, the trained neural network can process the input information of similar samples and output a number by itself. By judging whether it is close to 0 or close to 1 to give a category prediction, so as to achieve a two-class classification of the test sample. The BP neural network structure in this paper is shown in Fig. 5.

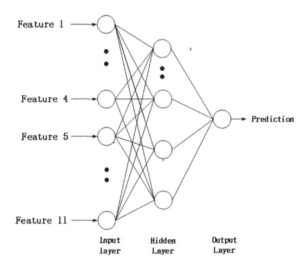

Fig. 5. BP neural network structure.

4 Prediction Model of Employee Turnover Based on Neural Network Classification Algorithm

4.1 Summary of Model

Based on the above analysis, this paper aims to classify the 11 dependent variables of the Price-Muller model as input features, and classify left as the output category, and compare the performance with the classification results of the original features of the data set. Since each piece of data in the Kaggle data set has a complete input and output, we use a supervised BP neural network for classification. As the amount of data is far greater than the number of features, and the number of features is small. So this paper uses a neural network with only one hidden layer for prediction Among them, the number of hidden layer nodes is set to 6 [12], and the maximum number of feedback iterations maxit is set to 1000 times. At the same time, in order to prevent the phenomenon of over-fitting, the input weight modification positive parameter decay is set to 10^{-4} in the neural network [13], which indicates the decreasing feedback of the weight. The algorithm flow of the BP neural network is shown in Fig. 6.

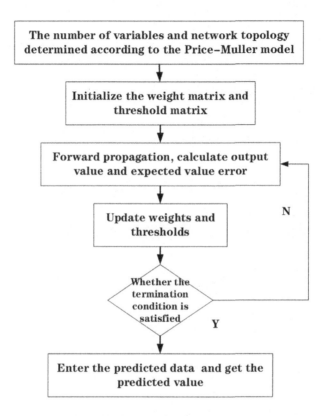

Fig. 6. The flow chart of BP neural network algorithm.

4.2 Data Sets and Experimental Settings

Cross Validation. This paper uses the method of 5-fold cross validation [14], which means the original data set D is divided into 5 disjoint subsets, and the number of samples in each subset is the same. The corresponding subset is called $\{D1, D2, D3, D4, D5\}$. During each training, one group is taken from the divided subset as the test set, and the other 4 groups are used as the training set. After the training of sets, the classifier is applied to the test set to obtain the evaluation indexes such as classification accuracy. Finally, based on the classification accuracy obtained from 5 sessions training, take the mean value of the result or use other combination methods to get a single evaluation as the real classification accuracy of this classification method. The method of cross-validation is to select the most suitable parameters for the model, so that the model performance and generalization ability become stronger. Cross-validation also can simultaneously and repeatedly use randomly generated sub-sample data sets for training and verification, so as to make the model more consistent with the data.

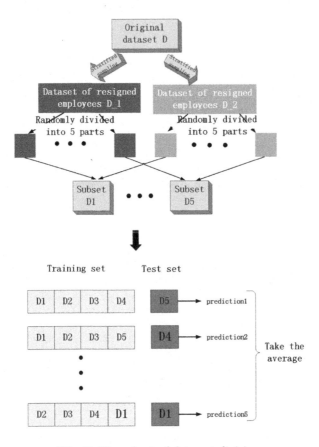

Fig. 7. Flow chart of data set division.

Stratified Sampling. In this paper, Kaggle employee resignation data is concentrated, the resigned employees accounted for 23.81%, which is far less than non-resigned employees. In order to avoid the accuracy reduction of the model caused by the uneven proportion of the two training sets, and ensure the accuracy of the operation after sampling, the random stratified sampling method is use in the cross validation. This can make the training set and test set have the same data feature distribution as the original data set, reducing the error caused by uneven data distribution. The data set division process is shown in Fig. 7.

4.3   The Index of Experimental Evaluation

After each training, since it is known whether the employees in the test set have resigned or not, the recall and precision of the round prediction can be calculated according to the confusion matrix [15]. The confusion matrix in this article is a 2×2 matrix, in which each column represents the model's category prediction for the data sample, and each row represents the true category of the sample. This is a visual way to compare the model classification results with the actual predictions. The calculation chart is shown in Table 1.

Table 1. Confusion matrix

	Actual value	
Predicted value	Counter-example	Positive example
Counter-example	True counter-examples	False counterexample
Positive example	False positive example	True positive example

In the confusion matrix, the true counter example in the first row is regarded as the model of counter-example, and the prediction is regarded as the counter-example, which means the prediction is true. However, false counter-example represents that the model predicts positive examples as counter-example, which means the prediction is false. In the second row, the true positive examples represents that the model predicts the positive examples as the positive examples, which means that the prediction is true; while the false positive example represents that the model predicts the counter examples as the positive examples, which means that the prediction is failed. The confusion matrix can be used to calculate the recall rate of the predicted result, that is the proportion of true positive examples in actual positive examples. The formula is as follows.

$$recall\ level = \frac{True\ positive\ example}{True\ positive\ example + False\ counter\ example}$$

In the same way, we can also calculate the precision ratio of the prediction results, that is the proportion of true positive examples to predicted positive examples. The formula is as follows.

$$precision\ level = \frac{True\ positive\ example}{True\ positive\ example + False\ positive\ example}$$

4.4   Comparative Analysis of the Forecast Results and Original Model Forecast Results Based on Price Muller Model

Prediction of Original Parameters by BP Neural Network. There are 8 dependent variables in the original data as input characteristics, so the number of input nodes of the neural network is 8; The independent variable in the original data (whether the employee has resigned) is used as the output category, so the number of output nodes is 1, in which the resignation is 1 and the non-resignation is 0; The number of hidden nodes is 6, and attenuation parameter of the weight is 0.0005. The confusion matrix of the output prediction results is shown in Fig. 8.

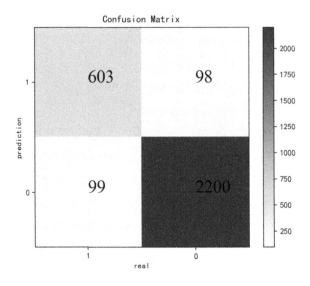

Fig. 8. Confusion matrix of BP neural network.

According to the confusion matrix, by using the original data set as a parameter to predict, it can be concluded that the accuracy and recall of the predicted results were 94.1%, 86.02% and 84.6% respectively.

Prediction of Price-Muller Model Optimization Parameters Based on BP Neural Network. In this paper, 11 new dependent variables are proposed based on the Price-Muller model, so the number of input nodes of the neural network is 11. The output category is still whether the employee leaves or not, so the output node is 1, where leaving is 1 and not leaving is 0. The attention parameters of hidden nodes and weights are unchanged. The confusion matrix for output prediction results is shown in Fig. 9.

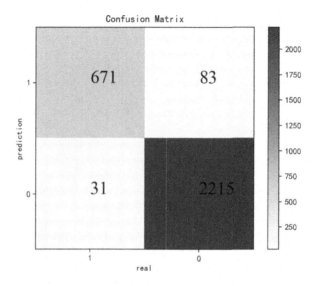

Fig. 9. Confusion matrix of BP neural network.

According to the confusion matrix, by using the parameters of the Price-Muller model optimization to predict, it can be concluded that the accuracy and recall of the predicted results were 96.2%, 89.01% and 89.1% respectively.

Evaluation of Model Prediction Results. From the prediction results of accuracy, recall and precision evaluation training set above, we can conclude that the results of the model based on Price-Muller perform better on all three indicators. In order to achieve a better comparison to their learning performance, this paper will use ROC [16] curve to evaluate the results of two different parameters. If the ROC curve of one model is closer to the upper left corner, or can completely cover the ROC curve of the other model, it means that the learning performance of the former is better than the latter; If the ROC curves of the two models cross, it is difficult to judge whether the learning performance of the two models is better or worse. At this time, a more reasonable basis for judgment is to compare the area under the ROC curve, that is, to compare the AUC value.

The ROC curve of BP neural network prediction under two different parameters can be obtained through experiments as shown in Fig. 10 and Fig. 11.

Comparing the drawn ROC curve graphs, it can be found that the ROC curve predicted using the original data set parameters has an AUC value of 92%, and the ROC curve predicted using the parameters optimized by the Price-Mueller employee turnover model has an AUC value of 97% and it shows that in this prediction, the neural network using the Price-Mueller employee turnover model to optimize the parameters has better classification performance than the neural network using the parameters of the original data set.

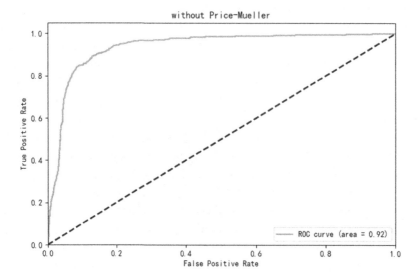

Fig. 10. The comparison of neural network ROC curves of original parameters and optimized parameters.

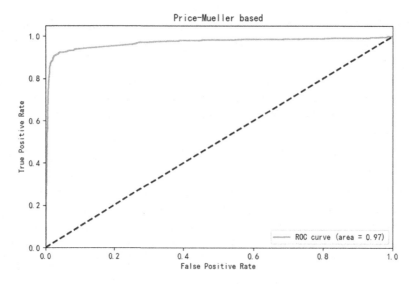

Fig. 11. The comparison of neural network ROC curves of original parameters and optimized parameters.

5   Conclusion

This paper use the original data set as parameters and the BP neural network with the Price-Mueller (2000) employee turnover model as the parameters to perform two-class prediction, and evaluates the precision level, recall level and AUC values of the two prediction results. In the analysis based on Kaggle employee turnover data set, the classification based on the Price-Mueller employee turnover model has better performance and higher accuracy.

References

1. Zhang, M., Zhang, D.: Empirical study on the regulation of value variables in price-mueller disession model. Manage. Rev. **2006**(09), 46–51 + 64 (2006)
2. Luo, F.: Active Separation Risk of Insurance Employees Based on Price-Mueller (2000) Model. Tianjin University of Technology (2009)
3. Dong, Y.W., She, J.Y., Chen, D.Y., She, Y.C., Deng, B.C.: Study on ecological landscape stability of Dongfang City, Hainan Province based on box map. J. Central South Univ. Forestry Sci. Technol. **36**(08), 104–108 + 120 (2016)
4. Hu, Y.M., A.L. Application of different types of data visualization methods in educational research. Educ. Meas. Eval. **2016**(08), 10–23 (2016)
5. Wu, K.: Review of the three major models of employee separation. Technol. Inf. **2009**(31), 527+525 (2009)
6. Zhao, J.X., Wang, M.X., Zhao, D.L.: Study on the impact factors of internet company employees based on price-mueller model. J. Hebei Univ. Econ. Trade **39**(05), 93–101 (2018)
7. Han, T.H.: Study on Employee Loss of G Bank S Branch Based on Price-Mueller Model. Hebei University of Economics and Trade (2020)
8. X.D.Bai., Compensation Equity, Employee Behavior, and Company Performance. Southwest University of Finance and Economics (2014)
9. Ro, F.: Active Separation Risk of Insurance Employees Based on Price-Mueller (2000) Model. Tianjin University of Technology (2009)
10. Wu, C.Y.: The Research and Application of the Neural Network. Northeastern Agricultural University (2007)
11. Bai, Y.J., Zhang, J., Wu, J., Wang, X.Q.: Evaluation and Strategic Research on the Sustainable Supply of Important Mineral Resources. Economic Daily Press (2015)
12. Wang, R., Xu, H.Y., Li, B., Feng, Y.: Study on the determination of BP neural network. Comput. Technol. Dev. **28**(04), 31–35 (2018)
13. Jin, L., Kuang, X.Y., Huang, H.H., Qin, Z.X., Wang, Y.H.: Overfit study of the artificial neural network prediction model. Meteorology **01**, 62–70 (2004)
14. Shi, J.Y., Zhou, L.W., Qian, Y.: Study on tourist flow forecast in Beijing - Comparison of different prediction models based on 50% off cross validation method. Econ. Stat. (quarterly) **02**, 73–85 (2017)
15. Zhao, C.X.: Comparison of the classifier performance evaluation indicators based on the confounding matrix. Electron. Technol. Softw. Eng. **13**, 146–147 (2020)
16. Zou, H.X., Qin, F., Cheng, Z.K., Wang, X.Y.: The ROC curve generation algorithm for the class II classifier. Comput. Technol. Dev. **19**(06), 109–112 (2009)

Author Index

Printed in the United States
by Baker & Taylor Publisher Services